ANTARCTIC RESEARCH SERIES

American Geophysical Union

ANTARCTIC
RESEARCH
SERIES

American Geophysical Union

Volume 1
BIOLOGY OF THE ANTARCTIC SEAS
Milton O. Lee, *Editor*

Volume 2
ANTARCTIC SNOW AND ICE STUDIES
Malcom Mellor, *Editor*

Volume 3
POLYCHAETA ERRANTIA OF ANTARCTICA
Olga Hartman

Volume 4
GEOMAGNETISM AND AERONOMY
A. H. Waynick, *Editor*

Volume 5
BIOLOGY OF THE ANTARCTIC SEAS II
George A. Llano, *Editor*

Volume 6
GEOLOGY AND PALEONTOLOGY OF THE ANTARCTIC
Jarvis B. Hadley, *Editor*

Volume 7
POLYCHAETA MYZOSTOMIDAE AND SEDENTARIA OF ANTARCTICA
Olga Hartman

Volume 8
ANTARCTIC SOILS AND SOIL FORMING PROCESSES
J. C. F. Tedrow, *Editor*

Volume 9
STUDIES IN ANTARCTIC METEOROLOGY
Morton J. Rubin, *Editor*

Volume 10
ENTOMOLOGY OF ANTARCTICA
J. Linsley Gressitt, *Editor*

Volume 11
BIOLOGY OF THE ANTARCTIC SEAS III
Waldo L. Schmitt and George A. Llano, *Editors*

Volume 12
ANTARCTIC BIRD STUDIES
Oliver L. Austin, Jr., *Editor*

Volume 13
ANTARCTIC ASCIDIACEA
Patricia Kott

Volume 14
ANTARCTIC CIRRIPEDIA
William A. Newman and Arnold Ross

Volume 15
ANTARCTIC OCEANOLOGY
Joseph L. Reid, *Editor*

Volume 15 ANTARCTIC RESEARCH SERIES

Antarctic Oceanology I

Joseph L. Reid, *Editor*

Published with the aid of a grant from the National Science Foundation

PUBLISHER

AMERICAN GEOPHYSICAL UNION

OF THE

National Academy of Sciences—National Research Council

1971

Volume 15 | ANTARCTIC RESEARCH SERIES

ANTARCTIC OCEANOLOGY

JOSEPH L. REID, *Editor*

Suite 435, 2100 Pennsylvania Avenue, N.W.
Washington, D. C. 20037

Library of Congress Catalogue Card No. 78-151300
International Standard Book No. 0-87590-115-8

List Price, $22.00

Printed by
THE HORN-SHAFER COMPANY
DIVISION OF
Geo. W. King Printing Co.
Baltimore, Maryland

THE ANTARCTIC RESEARCH SERIES

The Antarctic Research Series is designed to provide a medium for presenting authoritative reports on the extensive and detailed scientific research work being carried out in Antarctica. The series has been successful in eliciting contributions from leading research scientists engaged in antarctic investigations; it seeks to maintain high scientific and publication standards. The scientific editor for each volume is chosen from among recognized authorities in the discipline or theme it represents, as are the reviewers on whom the editor relies for advice.

Beginning with the scientific investigations carried out during the International Geophysical Year, reports of research results appearing in this series represent original contributions too lengthy or otherwise inappropriate for publication in the standard journals. In some cases an entire volume is devoted to a monograph. The material published is directed not only to specialists actively engaged in the work but to graduate students, to scientists in closely related fields, and to interested laymen versed in the biological and the physical sciences. Many of the earlier volumes are cohesive collections of papers grouped around a central theme. Future volumes may concern themselves with regional as well as disciplinary aspects, or with a comparison of antarctic phenomena with those of other regions of the globe. But the central theme of Antarctica will dominate.

In a sense, the series continues the tradition dating from the earliest days of geographic exploration and scientific expeditions—the tradition of the expeditionary volumes which set forth in detail everything that was seen and studied. This tradition is not necessarily outmoded, but in much of the present scientific work one expedition blends into the next, and it is no longer scientifically meaningful to separate them arbitrarily. Antarctic research has a large degree of coherence; it deserves the modern counterpart of the expeditionary volumes of past decades and centuries which the Antarctic Research Series provides.

With the aid of a grant from the National Science Foundation in 1962, the American Geophysical Union initiated the Antarctic Research Series and appointed a Board of Associate Editors to implement it. A supplemental grant received in 1966, the income from the sale of volumes in the series, and income from reprints and other sources have enabled the AGU to continue this series. The response of the scientific community and the favorable comments of reviewers cause the Board to look forward with optimism to the continued success of this endeavor.

To represent the broad scientific nature of the series, the members of the Board were chosen from all fields of antarctic research. At the present time they include: Eugene L. Boudette, representing geology and solid Earth geophysics; A. P. Crary, seismology and glaciology; George A. Llano, botany and zoology; Martin A. Pomerantz, aeronomy and geomagnetism; Morton J. Rubin, meteorology; Waldo L. Schmitt, marine biology and oceanography; and Laurence M. Gould, honorary chairman. Fred G. Alberts, secretary to the U. S. Advisory Committee on Antarctic Names, gives valuable assistance in verifying place names, locations, and maps. AGU staff members responsible for the series are: Judith S. McCombs, managing editor, and Jane Bruce, style editor.

Morton J. Rubin
Chairman, Board of Associate Editors
Antarctic Research Series

PREFACE

THE ANTARCTIC WATERS PROVIDE one of the extreme sets of characteristics for the world's oceans. Its waters are cold, low in salinity, dense, and high in dissolved oxygen, and, although comparable values may be found in the Norwegian Sea, it is the out-flow from the Antarctic that fills most of the deep ocean basins of the world. The interaction of these high-latitude waters with those having the characteristics of tropical or North Atlantic waters has long been one of the major studies of oceanology, yet only in the last few decades have we been able to begin to collect the appropriate data.

Recent developments, such as the acceptance of the concept of continental drift and sea floor spreading, have made the antarctic regions as important to geologists and geophysicists as to physical oceanographers and biologists.

The thirteen papers in this volume of the *Antarctic Research Series* constitute the first volume of *Antarctic Oceanology* and cover a fairly wide range of studies. The work ashore has been carried out at the University of Southern California, Florida State University, Lamont-Doherty Geological Observatory, Yale University, and the University of Alaska.

The work has been largely supported by the United States Antarctic Research Program of the National Science Foundation, though some of the investigators have received additional support from other agencies, which they acknowledge separately.

Much of the work at sea has been carried out on the extensive expeditions of the USNS *Eltanin* into the Antarctic and other regions, though several of the studies have incorporated observations of other expeditions carried out earlier or concurrently.

In this volume are included studies of the topography, magnetics, and seismicity of the sea floor, the characteristics and circulation of the water masses, and the sediments and their constituents and chemistry.

Bandy, Casey, and Wright have considered planktonic zonation, magnetic reversals, and radiometric dates over a region encompassing both the antarctic and tropic waters and attempted to establish a coherent historical pattern from the various sets of evidence.

Goodell, Meylan, and Grant have examined ferromanganese deposits of the South Pacific Ocean, Drake Passage, and Scotia Sea, using data from cores, dredge hauls and photographs, and have considered the distribution and the chemical and mineralogical character of these deposits against the background of depth, water characteristics, and circulation.

Echols has dealt with the foraminifera in the sediments of the Scotia Sea and considered them in relation to the bottom topography, the characteristics of the water columns in the upper layers and in the various deep basins, and the terrigenous materials.

Gordon's two studies of the southwest Atlantic and Pacific sectors of the antarctic waters and the antarctic polar front zone include a review of antarctic oceanography that is extremely useful to the understanding of the other papers in this volume.

Hayes and Ewing have investigated the existence of an important oceanic ridge by examining bathymetric and magnetic data in the context of sea floor spreading.

Herron has examined topographic, magnetic, and seismic data from the Albatross Cordillera and Chile Rise in the light of sea floor spreading.

Farther west, the Macquarie Ridge has been examined on the basis of profiler data by Houtz, Ewing, and Embley, who discuss whether the ridge originated as a shear zone or an island arc.

Nayudu has studied the upper parts of core samples from the central part of the subantarctic region of the Pacific in terms of their lithology and chemistry and attempted to relate the distribution of a number of elements to the sediment lithology.

Paster has examined the chemical characteristics of submarine basalts with the view of determining which specimens are most representative of the basalt pillows' original chemical composition.

Theyer has examined the morphology of *Cyclammina cancellata* Brady in the environment of the Peru-Chile Trench and suggests the paleoecological implications of the observed distributions.

Turekian, Bower, and Woodburn have presented the results of alkalinity measurements along east-west sections at 28°S and 43°S extending from Australia to Chile and discussed them in terms of the deep and abyssal circulation.

Watkins and Self have classified rocks dredged from the Scotia Sea by the *Eltanin* and discussed them in terms of the geology of the adjacent land areas and the possibilities of ice-rafting or in situ formation.

JOSEPH L. REID

CONTENTS

LATE NEOGENE PLANKTONIC ZONATION, MAGNETIC REVERSALS, AND RADIOMETRIC DATES, ANTARCTIC TO THE TROPICS

ORVILLE L. BANDY

University of Southern California, Los Angeles, California 90007

RICHARD E. CASEY

San Fernando Valley State College, Northridge, California 91324

RAMIL C. WRIGHT

Beloit College, Beloit, Wisconsin 53512

Abstract. Five new radiolarian zones are proposed in antarctic biostratigraphy, one in the upper Brunhes normal magnetic epoch based upon a paleoclimatic change, and four in the Gauss-Gilbert magnetic epochs involving extinction datum planes for mostly Miocene species of polycystines, including orosphaerids. None of the extinction datum planes, marking new zonal boundaries, is obviously correlative with magnetic reversals. Four major cold cycles are recorded in the Brunhes, with temperature minima at or below 0°C; these are based upon the ratio of antarctic to subantarctic radiolarians, and they may represent the classic Günz-Mindel-Riss-Würm glaciations. Antarctic cooler cycles of the Matuyama, Gauss, and upper Gilbert magnetic epochs have minima at about 5°C, perhaps less; maxima are between 10°C and 15°C. One of the most pronounced warmer cycles spans the Gilsa event. These warmer cycles are based upon variations in the abundances of temperate species of radiolarians. Evidence for the warmest interval encountered in antarctic cores is the presence of tropical collosphaerids below the approximate level of Gilbert *c*. Glacial deposits are known to occur in antarctic cores down to about the upper limit of the collosphaerids. Four important horizons in antarctic cores are: (1) a temperature reduction at or near the Brunhes-Matuyama boundary; (2) the *Eucyrtidium calvertense* extinction datum plane near the base of the Gilsa event; (3) a *Prunopyle titan* extinction datum plane in the Gauss normal magnetic epoch; and (4) the presence of tropical collosphaerids below the level of Gilbert *c*.

In warm temperate and tropical regions, the *Sphaeroidinella dehiscens* datum plane occurs in the Gauss at approximately the same position as the *Prunopyle titan* datum plane of the Antarctic, representing the approximate position of the Miocene-Pliocene boundary. Extinction datum planes for *Sphaeroidinellopsis subdehiscens* and *Globoquadrina altispira* are near the points of origin of *Sphaeroidinella dehiscens*, *Pulleniatina obliquiloculata*, and *Globigerinoides trilobus fistulosus*; this zone of overlap has been clearly identified in deep-sea cores in the Gauss normal magnetic interval, and it is also characteristic of Neogene zone 19.

The appearance of *Globorotalia truncatulinoides*, from its ancestor *G. tosaensis*, represents the Pliocene-Pleistocene boundary at or near the base of the Gilsa event, which correlates with the extinction level of discoasters and in the Antarctic with the extinction level for *Eucyrtidium calvertense*.

In temperate and tropical regions there are three major cold cycles defined paleontologically. One of these is in the upper Miocene in Neogene 17, which is represented in the tropics by the presence of a temperate *Globigerina bulloides* fauna. In temperate regions it is represented by a *Globorotalia (Turborotalia) pachyderma* left-coiling population, and in the Antarctic it is the level at which the first glacial deposits appear, at or above Gilbert *c*. This upper Miocene cold cycle appears to occur between Gilbert *a* and *c*. An upper Pliocene cold cycle occurs in Neogene 21, in the lower Matuyama, also represented by the presence of cooler climatic indices than normal in tropical and temperate areas. The third major cooling is that associated with the Brunhes, a series of much colder cycles in the Antarctic. In temperate areas this event is represented by a marked influx of left-coiling populations of *Globorotalia (Turborotalia) pachyderma*, and in the tropics it is represented by a significant decline in the abundance of the tropical index *Sphaeroidinella dehiscens* and at the same time an increase in the numbers of temperate species. A revised paleoclimatic model is developed, plotted against the current Neogene planktonic zones. It supports the hypothesis that there was a long preglacial Pleistocene interval before the Günz glaciation.

Planktonic datum planes of the later Neogene, now correlated with the magnetic scale and its radiometric dates, indicate that the potassium-argon dating of marine ash and glauconites in the later Neogene of California is providing ages that are often from 3 to 5 times too old.

INTRODUCTION

Remarkable advances have been made recently in developing antarctic radiolarian zonation for the later Cenozoic based upon studies of deep-sea cores [*Hays*, 1965; *Hays and Opdyke*, 1967] and in relating this zonation to magnetic stratigraphy and the radiometric scale. In those reports and in our subsequent studies, a number of radiolarian species diagnostic of the Tertiary have been discovered in the lower sections of a number of cores. It is the purpose of this study to present additional antarctic radiolarian data and to correlate the major later Neogene planktonic datum planes of the Antarctic with those of temperate and tropical regions, using data from deep-sea cores of critical regions and relating these to classic land sections where pertinent.

For some years critical disparities have existed in concepts about the implied stratigraphic positions of many planktonic indices of deep-sea cores and the stratigraphic implications of these same species in sections from land areas as exemplified in the works of *Ericson et al.* [1963, 1964] and *Ericson and Wollin* [1968], *Bandy* [1963, 1964, 1967*a*], *Parker* [1967], *Hays et al.* [1969], *Berggren* [1969], *Lamb* [1969], and in other studies. With the development of a greater understanding of planktonic zonation of the tropics and temperate areas over the past decade or two [*Bolli*, 1957; *Blow*, 1959, 1969; *Bandy*, 1964; *Banner and Blow*, 1965; *Hay et al.*, 1967; *Bandy and Ingle*, 1970], it is clear that there are striking similarities in the zonations of deep-sea cores and land-based sections. It is equally clear that if it is assumed that the planktonic zonation is a dependable method of correlation, there is a major defect in either radiometric dates or in the paleomagnetic scale [*Bandy and Casey*, 1969].

ANTARCTIC PLANKTONIC DATUM PLANES, MAGNETIC SCALE, AND PALEOCLIMATOLOGY

General

The antarctic radiolarian zonation of Hays consists of six zones (Table 1) in which the upper limits of occurrence in the cores are employed [*Hays*, 1965, 1967; *Hays and Opdyke*, 1967]. Three of the antarctic cores studied by Hays and Opdyke were restudied for additional information about radiolarian zonation (Figures 1–4). One core, E14-8, was taken from the western flank of the Albatross Cordillera in the South Pacific Ocean and two cores, E13-3 and E13-17, were taken from the Southeast Pacific Basin (Table 2). As noted by Hays and Opdyke, there is an upper layer of diatom ooze in E13-17 (0–1020 cm) and in E14-8 (0–1710 cm), and a radiolarian clay in E13-3 (0–1000 cm). Underlying this upper siliceous ooze in the cores is a tan clay that is barren in E13-3 (1000–1603 cm) and E14-8 (1710–1830 cm), but which contains interbedded layers of radiolarian and diatomaceous clays in E13-17. The magnetic stratigraphy shown is that of Hays and Opdyke.

It was noted earlier [*Bandy*, 1967*a*] that the widespread occurrence of *Prunopyle titan* in the lower portions of many antarctic cores might be taken as the upper limit of the Miocene in view of the restriction of this species to upper Miocene beds previously [*Campbell and Clark*, 1944; *Ingle*, 1967]. The apparent extinction point for this species in antarctic cores

TABLE 1. Radiolarian zones combining those of *Hays* [1965], *Hays and Opdyke* [1967], and those of this study. Upper limits of occurrence used in each case as a boundary unless noted otherwise. Letter subdivisions of Hays' zones are new subdivisions proposed in this study.

Ω (Omega) Zone	*a.*	Modern *Spongoplegma antarcticum* complex with warm water forms such as *Theoconus zancleus* and *Saturnulus planetes*
	b.	Modern *Spongoplegma antarcticum* complex without a warmer water influence
Ψ (Psi) Zone		*Acanthosphaera* sp. group (middle Brunhes)
X (Chi) Zone		*Saturnulus planetes* and *Pterocanium trilobum* (upper Matuyama boundary
Φ (Phi) Zone		*Eucyrtidium calvertense* (Gilsa event)
Υ (Upsilon) Zone	*a.*	*Desmospyris spongiosa* and *Helotholus vema* (lower Matuyama)
	b.	*Prunopyle titan* and *Lychnocanium grande* (upper Gauss)
	c.	*Oroscena* (digitate) and *Oroscena carolae* (upper Gilbert)
	d.	*Cyrtocapsella tetrapera* and *Theocyrtis redondoensis* (upper Gilbert)
T (Tau) Zone	*a.*	*Triceraspyris* sp. (Gilbert *b*)
	b.	*Ommatocampe hughesi* and *Cannartiscus marylandicus* (Gilbert *c*)

Note: The Omega/Psi boundary has been dated radiometrically as about 400,000 years [*Hays*, 1967]. A complete listing of radiolarians and planktonic foraminifera with authors is given in Table 3. See Plates 1–3 for illustrations of the most important radiolarians.

TABLE 2. Core Locations

Core	Latitude	Longitude	Water Depth, m	Length, cm
E13-3	57°00'S	89°29'W	5090	1603
E13-17	65°41'S	124°06'W	4720	2642
E14-8	59°40'S	160°17'W	3875	1830
V12-5	21°12'N	45°21'W	3000	735

seems to be consistently within the upper part of the Gauss magnetic epoch (Figures 2–4). To develop additional biostratigraphic data for paleoceanography and correlation, three groups of radiolarians were investigated in the three cores: warm water polycystines that are still living today, a group of Miocene polycystines that with one exception have been reported almost exclusively from Miocene strata, and several orosphaerids that include some very important Miocene index species.

Antarctic Radiolarian Zonation and Magnetic Stratigraphy

The radiolarian zonation of *Hays* [1965, 1967] and *Hays and Opdyke* [1967] is combined with the additional zones of this study (Table 1). The zonation of Hays is indicated in each core study (Figures 2–4); supplementary radiolarian ranges are indicated only for the members of the three groupings studied for this report (warm water indices, Miocene polycystines, and orosphaerids). The magnetic stratigraphy used is that of *Cox* [1969].

Omega a. This zone is characterized by the modern *Spongoplegma antarcticum* complex, which includes some temperate species as shown in core E14-8 (Figure 2).

Omega b. Modern *Spongoplegma antarcticum* complex lacking the temperate influences.

Psi zone. This is the zone with an upper limit marked by the disappearance of the *Acanthosphaera* sp. group. The Psi/Omega boundary has been dated as 400,000 years [*Hays*, 1967].

Chi zone. The upper limit of this zone is defined by the upper limits of occurrence of *Saturnulus planetes* and *Pterocanium trilobum*, two temperate species that disappeared at this level because of cooler temperatures. Their displacement toward northern temperate areas marks one of the prominent features of cooling in the later Quaternary. Their displacement at this level coincides approximately with the Brunhes-Matuyama boundary at about 700,000 years.

Phi zone. The upper limit of this zone is marked by the approximate upper limit of *Eucyrtidium calvertense*, which occurs at or near the Gilsa event (Olduvai event of *Hays and Opdyke* [1967]) within the Matuyama magnetic epoch. This approximates the Pliocene-Pleistocene boundary if the Calabrian cor-

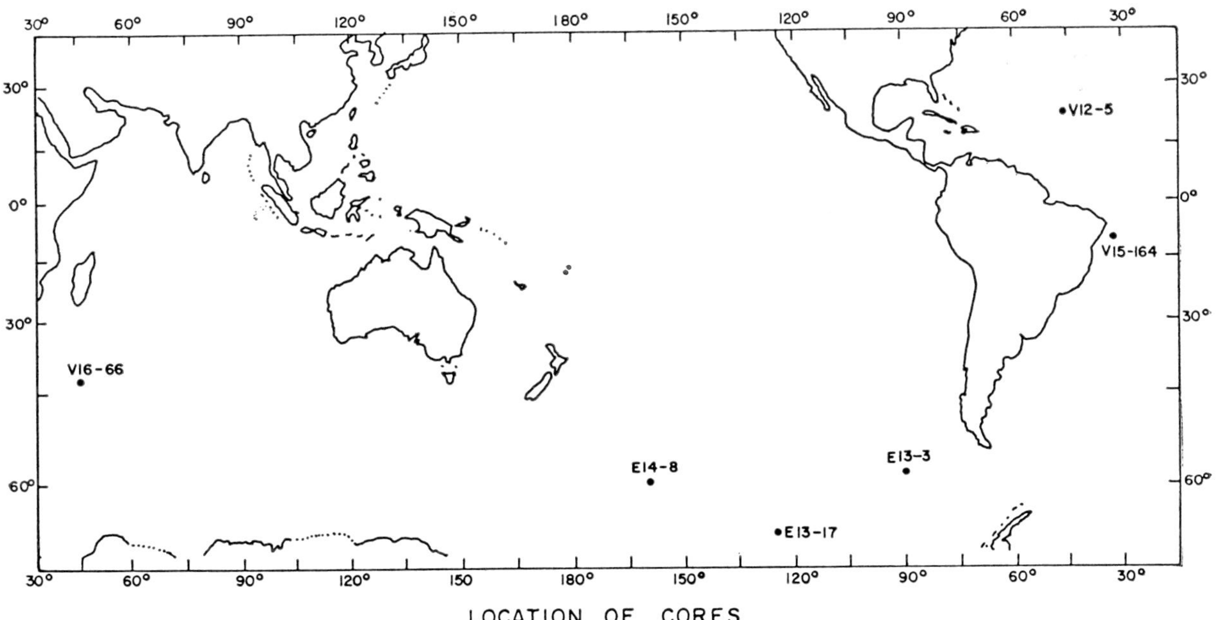

Fig. 1. Location of *Eltanin* and *Vema* cores.

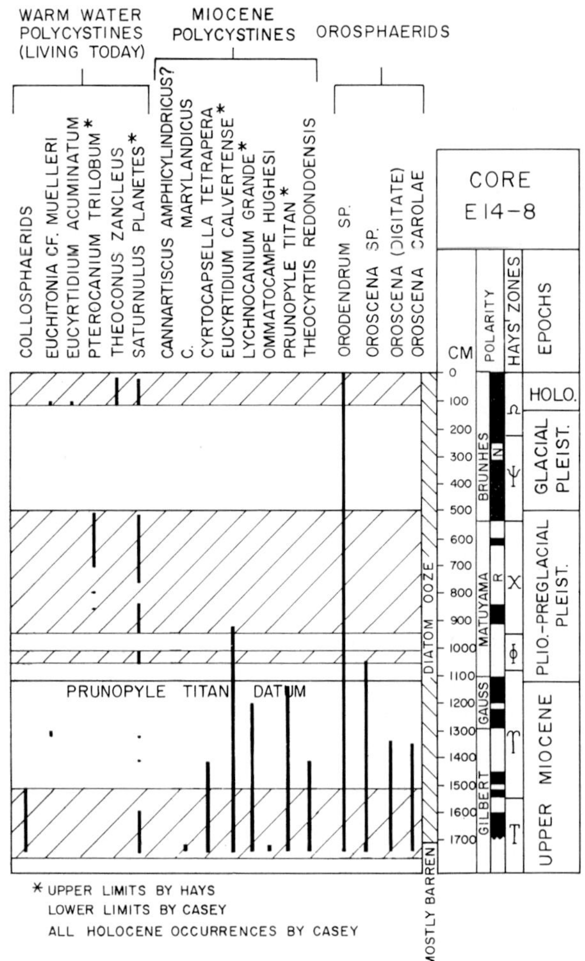

Fig. 2. Distribution of polycystine and orosphaerid radiolarians in core E14-8. Cross-hatching indicates principal occurrences of temperate or warmer water radiolarian groups. The collosphaerids are the warmest water indices. See Table 1 for zones of *Hays* [1965].

relates in part with this event [*Phillips et al.*, 1968], and this should be about 1.79 million years ago [*Cox*, 1969].

Upsilon a. The upper limit of this zone is marked by the upper limits of *Desmospyris spongiosa* and *Helotholus vema* within the lowermost part of the Matuyama reversed magnetic epoch [*Hays and Opdyke*, 1967].

Upsilon b. The upper limit of this zone is defined by the upper limits of occurrence of *Prunopyle titan* and *Lychnocanium grande* within the Gauss normal magnetic epoch (Table 1, Figures 2–4). These species are upper Miocene indices (Figure 5) and suggest that the Miocene-Pliocene boundary is within the Gauss epoch.

Upsilon c. The upper boundary of this zone is defined by the upper limits of *Oroscena* (digitate) and *Oroscena carolae*, two important Miocene orosphaerids (Figures 2, 4, 5). This boundary occurs within the upper part of the Gilbert reversed magnetic epoch.

Upsilon d. The upper boundary of this unit is marked by the upper limits of *Cyrtocapsella tetrapera* and *Theocyrtis redondoensis*, two important Miocene polycystine radiolarians (Figures 2, 4, 5). This boundary occurs just below that of Upsilon *c* within the upper Gilbert.

Tau a. The upper limit of this unit is that of the upper limit of *Triceraspyris* sp. of *Hays and Opdyke* [1967], which appears to coincide with Gilbert *b* rather than Gilbert *a* as suggested by them.

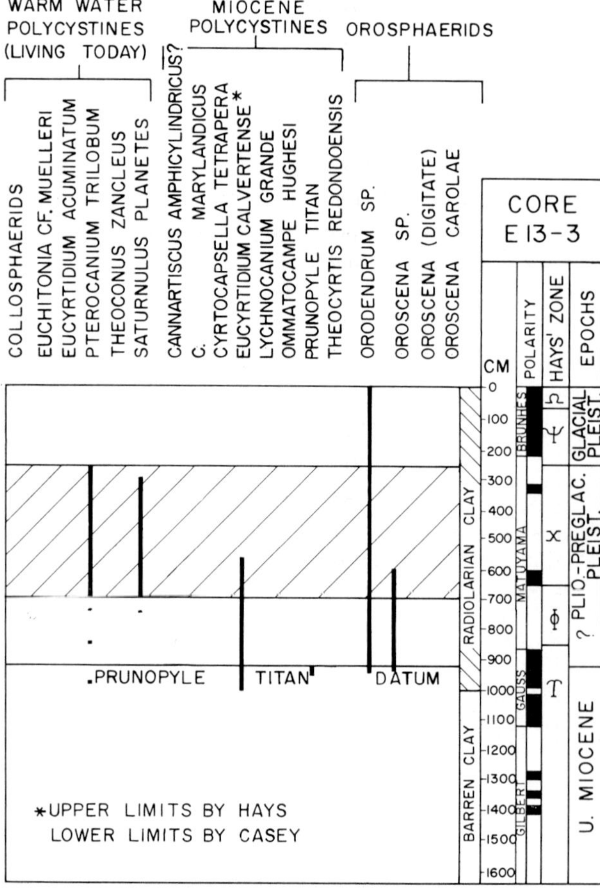

Fig. 3. Distribution of polycystine and orosphaerid radiolarians in core E13-3. Cross-hatching indicates principal occurrence of temperate radiolarians. See Table 1 for zones of *Hays* [1965].

Tau b. This unit has an upper boundary defined by the upper limits of *Ommatocampe hughesi* and *Cannartiscus marylandicus* (Figures 2, 4, Table 1), two important Miocene polycystines (Figure 5). The upper boundary of this zone coincides approximately with Gilbert *c*.

It appears that there is great consistency to the upper limits of the various radiolarian species of the studies by Hays when compared to magnetic stratigraphy. One of these to be highlighted is that which represents the Pliocene-Pleistocene boundary, the upper limit of *Eucyrtidium calvertense* (the Phi zone) that coincides roughly with the base of the Gilsa event as used in this study (Olduvai event of *Hays and Opdyke* [1967]). This level, the *Eucyrtidium calvertense* extinction datum plane, may be related to the base of the Gilsa event in cores from other parts of the ocean basins and to land-based sections. A second important level to be emphasized here is that representing the upper limits of the *Prunopyle titan* group within the Gauss normal magnetic epoch, the *Prunopyle titan* extinction datum plane. Here also is an association with an independent event, the Gauss magnetic epoch, that makes it possible to relate this level to the magnetic stratigraphy of cores from other parts of the world's oceans. It represents the upper limits of Miocene radiolarian species of this study; it may represent the Miocene-Pliocene boundary.

Antarctic Paleoclimatic Cycles

In order to construct temperature curves for cores E14-8, E13-3, and E13-17 (Figures 6–8), it was necessary to examine Holocene samples from locations under the critical water masses, from the tropics to the Antarctic. These samples, obtained from Scripps Institution of Oceanography, are from the following locations in the Pacific Basin:

MSN 135	4°26′S	149°24′W
MSN 114	37°02′S	163°14′W
MSN 111	40°37′S	164°08′W
MSN 99	52°37′S	178°57′W
MSN 85	57°43′S	169°12′E
MSN 88	60°58′S	170°16′E
MSN 91	64°11′S	165°56′W

In the above samples, collosphaerids were common only in those sediments underlying water masses in which the average summer surface temperatures are in excess of 20°C. Temperate conditions are related to the assemblage of *Eucyrtidium acuminatum*, *Lamprocyclas maritalis*, and *Saturnulus planetes*, which become fairly common components in waters that have temperatures of 10°C or somewhat greater. Still cooler temperatures are evaluated by determining the ratio of the antarctic species *Spongotrochus glacialis* and *Lithelius nautiloides* to the subantarctic species *Lithamphora furcaspiculata* and *Theocalyptra bicornis;* when this ratio is near 1:1 the surface temperature is about 5°C, whereas when the ratio is about 9 ant-

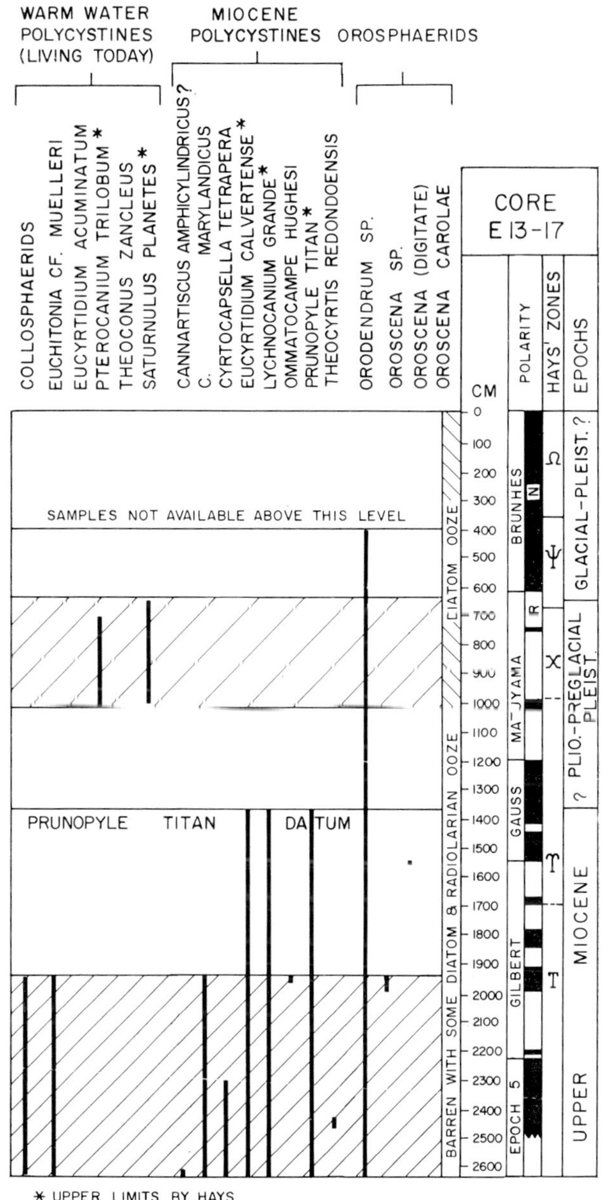

Fig. 4. Distribution of polycystine and orosphaerid radiolarians in core E13-17. Cross-hatched areas indicate main occurrences of temperature or warmer water radiolarians. The collosphaerids are the warmest water indices. See Table 1 for zones of *Hays* [1965].

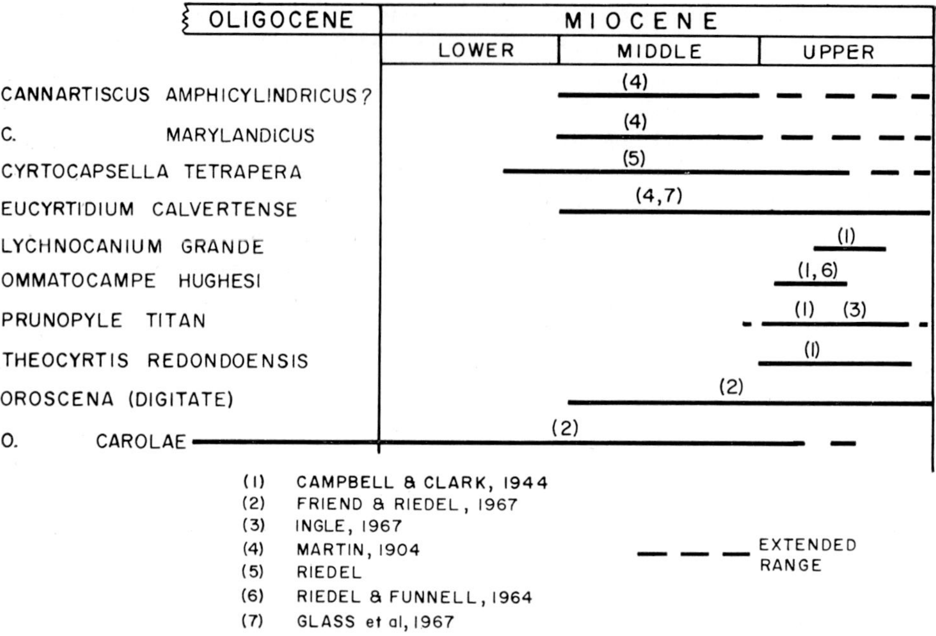

Fig. 5. Known stratigraphic ranges of Miocene index radiolarians occurring in Antarctic cores. *Eucyrtidium calvertense* is known to range up through the Pliocene as well. Reference to Riedel (5) is personal communication.

arctic species to 1 subantarctic species the temperature is less than 0°C.

Core E14-8 (Figure 6) gives the best record in that it is represented by good recovery, the section is not barren, and samples were available from the entire core. The Brunhes normal magnetic epoch is represented from 0 to slightly over 500 cm, and it is in this section that three, perhaps four, major cold cycles are recorded. Core E13-3 (Figure 7) shows four distinct cold cycles within the Brunhes, labeled the Pleistocene and Holocene.

It is interesting to point out that *Selli* [1967] and *Selli and Tongiorgi* [1967] consider that the glacial Pleistocene, commencing with the Donau glaciation, was about 800,000 years ago and that the Günz commenced about 600,000 years ago. This age for the Günz is preferred by *Richmond* [1969]. The base of the Pleistocene is placed at about 1.8 million years in both reports, providing a very long preglacial Pleistocene. Thus, the classic Günz-Mindel-Riss-Würm glaciations are thought to have occurred during the past 600,000 years; perhaps the four major cold cycles outlined in the Bruhnes are representative of these.

A distinct temperate influence is recorded throughout much of the Pliocene and preglacial Pleistocene which embraces the Matuyama and that part of the Gauss down to the *Prunopyle titan* datum plane (Figures 2–4, 6–8). The presence of greater numbers of temperate species such as *Eucyrtidium acuminatum, Lamprocyclas maritalis,* and *Saturnulus planetes* suggests temperature fluctuations between 5° and 15°C, as opposed to the dominance of much colder index radiolarians in the Brunhes. In each core the most prominent warmer interval is that spanning the Gilsa event of the Matuyama reversed magnetic epoch. Between three and five cold or cooler cycles are recorded in this part of cores E14-8 and E13-3 (Figures 6 and 7); rather poor preservation and sparse samples in this section of the third core (E13-17) make it of little value in defining paleoclimatic values. It is clear that there are cool or cold intervals both above and below the Gilsa event.

Referring to the sections of cores below the Gilsa event and above the lower major warm interval, there is a much reduced temperate influence as noted by the absence there of marked warmer cycles (Figures 6–8). This is the basis for indicating a cold interval in the core studies (Figures 2–4) in this part of the section. The major warm period in the Antarctic is that which occurs below Gilbert *a* (Figure 2) or near Gilbert *c* (Figure 4) with surface water temperatures approaching 20°C if the abundance of collosphaerids there is a dependable criterion (Figures 6, 8).

In analyzing paleoclimatic variations in the Ant-

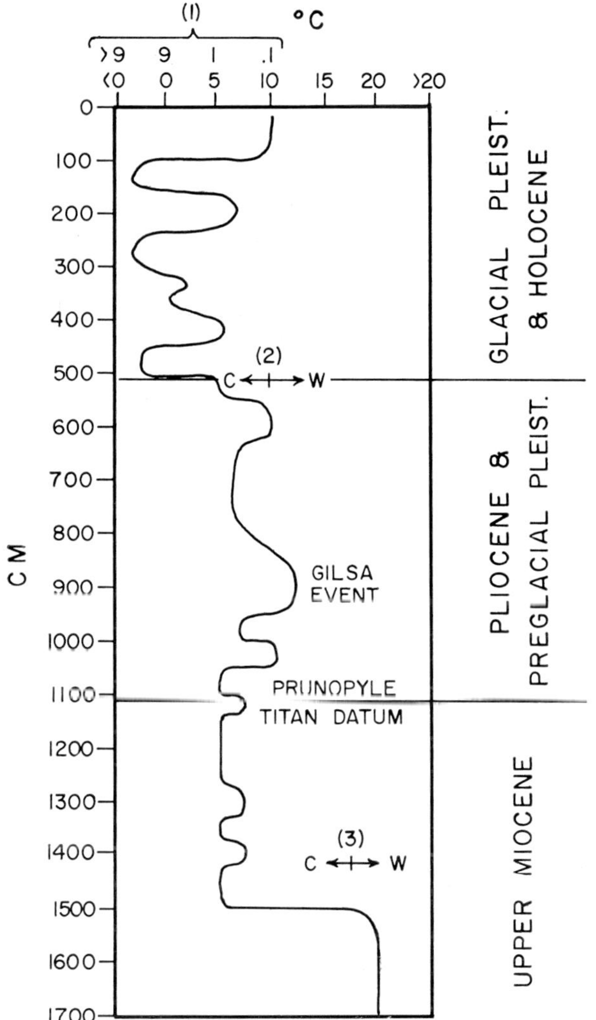

Fig. 6. Paleotemperature variations, core E14-8. There are three levels of temperature-related groups. (1) The first represents temperatures of less than 5°C and is based upon the ratio of the antarctic *Spongotrochus glacialis* and *Lithelius nautiloides* to the subantarctic *Lithamphora furcaspiculata* and *Theocalyptra bicornis*. When the ratio of the antarctic to the subantarctic group is about 9:1 or more, the surface temperature is 0° or less than 0°C. When the ratio is about 1:1, the surface water temperature is about 5°C. (2) Added to the criteria used in (1) are fluctuations in the abundance of temperate radiolarians *Eucyrtidium acuminatum*, *Lamprocyclas maritalis*, and *Saturnulus planetes;* these temperate species suggest variations in surface water temperatures of from about 5°C to about 15°C. Where they are very common the temperature approaches 15°C; where they are rare the temperatures are considered to be about 10°C; and where this group is very rare the temperatures are thought to be near the lower limit of about 5°C. (3) Subtropical temperatures of about 20°C are represented by the influx of the collosphaerid radiolarian group.

arctic, it should be noted that those of this study are in contrast to those of *Kennett* [1969], *Ericson and Wollin* [1968], and others in one important way; they are similar in another. The similarity is expressed in the continuous cyclic variations represented, with perhaps four cold cycles in the curve by Kennett within the Brunhes. The contrast is in the much colder cycles in the Brunhes and the more temperate character of the cycles below the Brunhes in our study as contrasted to the reverse by others.

Comparing our data with the conclusions of *Hays and Opdyke* [1967] reveals a general correspondence. We have defined more precisely the cyclic variations and there are some critical differences. First, we find no major disparity among the cores as to the major cool and warm events, whereas Hays and Opdyke point to a major change occurring 2 million years earlier in E13-17 than in the other two cores. A second contrast is that we find no evidence of warmer water indices in E13-3 below 860 cm, whereas they report evidences of these. The major points of similarity between the results of Hays and Opdyke and ours are in the major shift toward cooler conditions from the upper Matuyama into the Brunhes and in the detection of warmer water indices below a depth of about 2000 cm in core E13-17. The cooler conditions in the Brunhes, approximately the Omega and Psi zones of Hays, are supported by the study of diatoms [*Donahue*, 1967].

TEMPERATE AND TROPICAL PLANKTONIC DATUM PLANES, MAGNETIC STRATIGRAPHY, AND PALEOCLIMATOLOGY

General

Studies of Cenozoic planktonic foraminiferal zonation have been made by many investigators, including *Bolli* [1957, 1964, 1966], *Blow* [1959, 1969], *Bandy* [1964], *Banner and Blow* [1965], *Asano and Takayanagi* [1965], *Parker* [1967], *Jenkins* [1967], *Dondi and Papetti* [1968], and by many others. Many investigators are employing the numerical zonation (Figure 9) of *Banner and Blow* [1965] as further elaborated by *Blow* [1969].

Paleoceanographic variations, as they affect zonation, have been highlighted in a number of reports, including those by *Ericson et al.* [1954], *Ericson and Wollin* [1956*a*, 1956*b*], *Ericson* [1959], *Bandy* [1959, 1960*a*, 1960*b*, 1964, 1967*a*, 1967*b*, 1968*a*, 1968*b*, 1969], *Ingle* [1967], *Kennett* [1968*a*, 1968*b*, 1968*c*, 1969], *Asano et al.* [1969], and others.

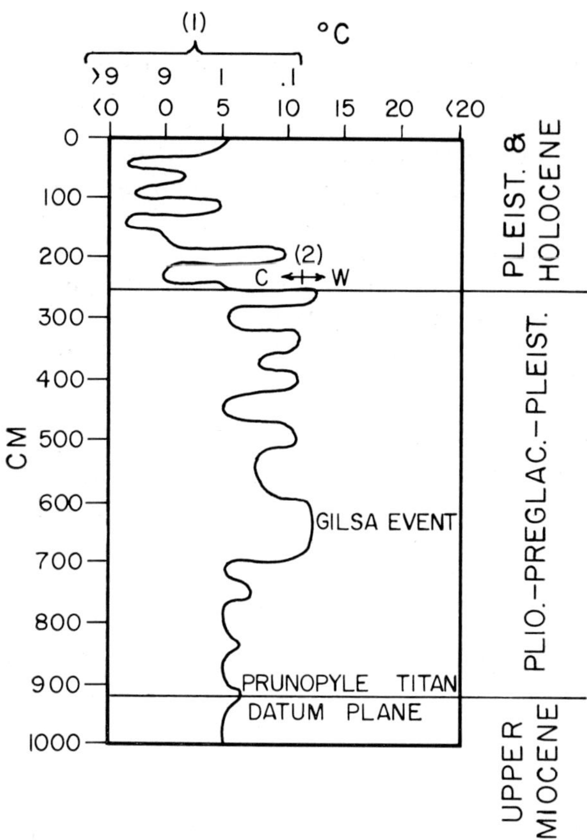

Fig. 7. Paleotemperature variations, core E13-3. See Figure 6 for explanation of criteria employed.

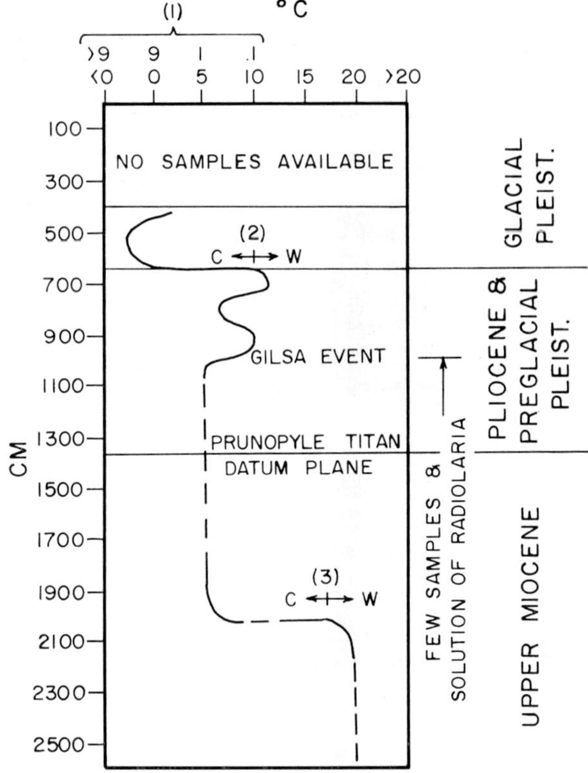

Fig. 8. Paleotemperature variations, core E13-17. See Figure 6 for explanation of criteria employed.

Magnetic stratigraphy, related to later Cenozoic planktonic zones, has been worked out for deep-sea cores by *Opdyke et al.* [1966], *Glass et al.* [1967], *Hays and Opdyke* [1967], *Berggren et al.* [1967], *Phillips et al.* [1967], *Berggren* [1968, 1969], *Kennett* [1969], *Beard* [1969], *Lamb* [1969], *Hays et al.* [1969], and others.

The Miocene-Pliocene Boundary and the Magnetic Scale

In discussing the Miocene-Pliocene boundary it is important to refer to the Messinian stratotype (neostratotype) of the upper Miocene of Italy [*Selli,* 1964], which *Blow* [1969, Figure 19] correlates with Neogene zones 16 (middle) up to the top of N-18 (Figure 10). The Trubi beds, as a Pliocene stratotype, on the other hand, are shown to correlate with the sequence from the middle of N-18 to the top of N-19. Thus, in the classic sense, one is faced with the possibility of placing this boundary at the base of the Trubi beds, in the middle of N-18, or at the top of the Messinian neostratotype, which is the boundary between N-18 and N-19, according to Blow. This latter boundary is the datum plane that separates *Sphaeroidinellopsis subdehiscens* (below) from *Sphaeroidinella dehiscens* (above) with only questionable forms of the former

Plate 1

1. *Eucyrtidium calvertense* Martin ×500. Core E14-8, 1750–1752 cm. Hypotype U.S.C. No. 1289.
2. *Lychnocanium grande* Campbell and Clark ×200. Core E14-8, 1750–1752 cm. Hypotype U.S.C. No. 1290.
3. *Ommatocampe hughesi* Campbell and Clark ×400. Core E14-8, 1750–1752 cm. Hypotype U.S.C. No. 1291.
4. *Theocyrtis redondoensis* Campbell and Clark × 480. Core E14-8, 1728–1730 cm. Hypotype U.S.C. No. 1292.
5. *Cannartiscus marylandicus?* Martin ×400. Core E14-8, 1750–1752 cm. Hypotype U.S.C. No. 1293.
6. *Prunopyle titan* Campbell and Clark ×400. Mohole, EM8-15, 242–245 cm. Hypotype U.S.C. No. 1294.
7. *Prunopyle titan* Campbell and Clark ×200. Core E14-8, 1728–1730 cm. Hypotype U.S.C. No. 1295.
8. *Prunopyle titan* Campbell and Clark ×200. Core E14-8, 1728–1730 cm. Hypotype U.S.C. No. 1296.
9. *Prunopyle titan* Campbell and Clark ×200. Core E14-8, 1429–1431 cm. Hypotype U.S.C. No. 1297.
10. *Prunopyle titan* Campbell and Clark ×100. Mohole, EM8-9, 8–11 cm. USC Spl. 21, Sinistral *Globorotalia (Turborotalia) pachyderma* zone. Hypotype U.S.C. No. 1298.

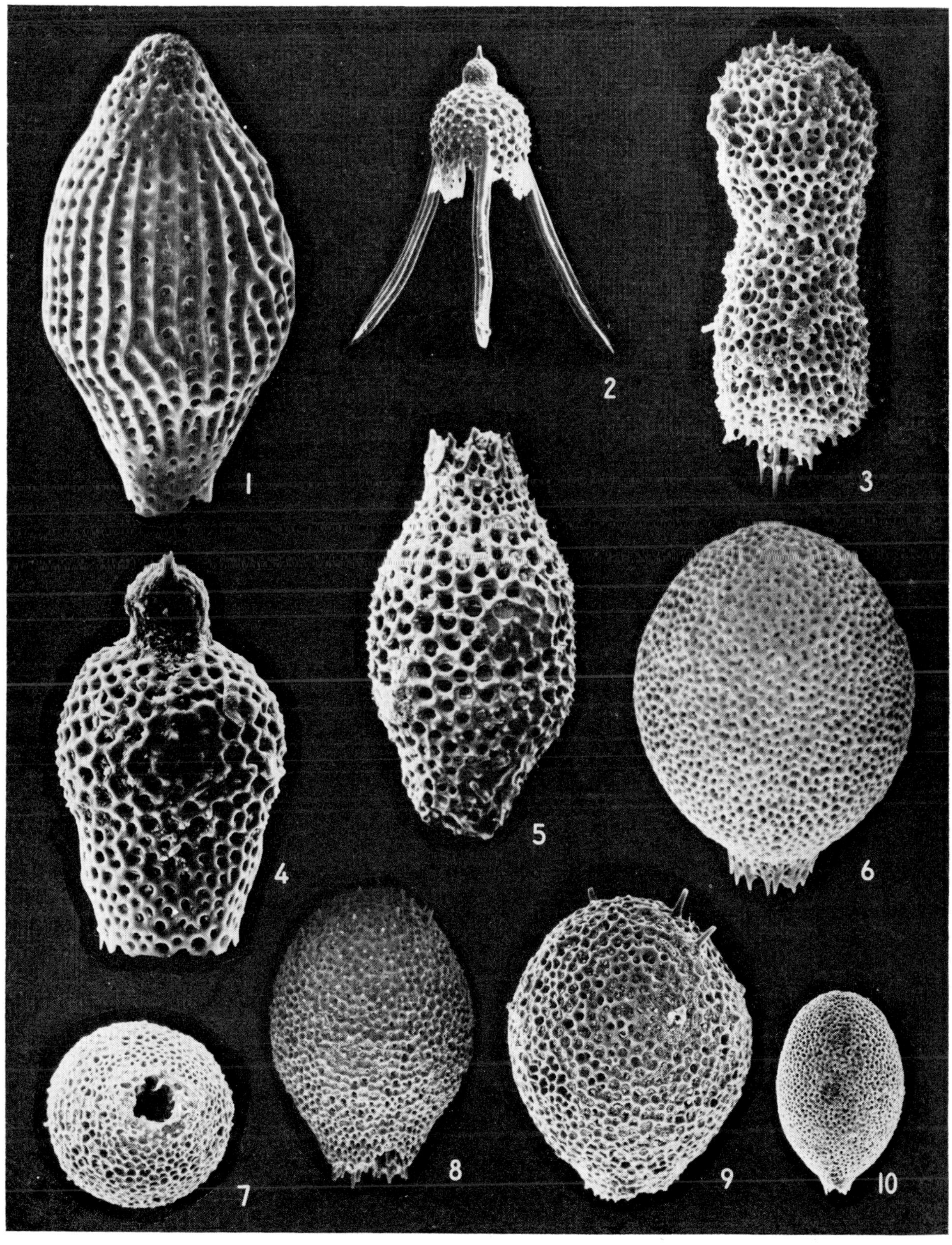
1
2
3
4
5
6
7
8
9
10

overlapping the lower range of the latter (Figures 9, 10). The latter choice seems preferable in that the boundary of the two zones defines the boundary of the two epochs; we prefer this definition.

Use of the genera *Sphaeroidinellopsis* and *Sphaeroidinella* is made here as paleontological form genera; these forms have been found to be growth forms of species of *Globigerinoides* that develop in deeper water by the addition of a crust and cortex [*Bé*, 1965; *Bandy et al.*, 1967]. *Blow* [1969] rightly points out that *Globigerinoides conglobatus*, a more recent species, could not give rise to *S. subdehiscens*, an upper Miocene form. On the other hand, there are now a number of growth series showing the complete transition from both *G. conglobatus* and *G. trilobus sacculifer* into forms of *S. dehiscens* (in preparation).

The upper significant limit of *Sphaeroidinellopsis subdehiscens* has now been clearly established in the Gauss normal magnetic epoch (Figure 11) just above the Mammoth event [*Glass et al.*, 1967; *Hays et al.*, 1969]. A major point of this correlation is its consistency in so many different deep-sea cores, where it defines the boundary between N-18 and N-19 according to *Blow* [1969] and *Berggren* [1969]; this faunal level was defined by *Parker* [1967] in tropical Pacific cores (Figure 11). Blow suggests that the forms representing the uppermost part of the range of *S. subdehiscens* in N-18 and questionably in N-19 are possibly the juvenile forms of *S. subdehiscens paenedehiscens.*

Additional faunal relationships (Figure 11) that assist in the recognition of the upper limit of *S. subdehiscens* include six points that corroborate the correlation of this level in the cores of *Hays et al.* [1969] with those studied by *Parker* [1967]:

1. First, *Sphaeroidinella dehiscens* is thought to have arisen from *S. subdehiscens* at the upper limit of occurrence of the latter with very little overlapping of the ranges of the two. The rare occurrences [*Hays et al.*, 1969] of *S. dehiscens* below the upper limit of *S. subdehiscens* are likely rare contaminants in the piston cores in the same manner as rare occurrences far down section of *G. truncatulinoides* that we have noted in other cores. If the zone of overlap is actual, then part of N-19 spans 1.5 million years or more, extending from the middle Gauss all the way down to below Gilbert *c*, a relationship that is highly unlikely.

2. Second, *Globigerinoides trilobus fistulosus* commences near the upper limit of *S. subdehiscens*, and its range is largely in the lower part of the range of *S. dehiscens*, extending from within N-18 up to the upper part of N-21. *Blow* [1969] considers this species, or subspecies, to be Pliocene with only its lowermost range extending down into the uppermost Miocene.

3. Third, *Pulleniatina primalis* appears first in N-17 according to *Blow* [1969] and it ranges up to the lower part of N-20 (Figure 9). In deep-sea cores its upper limit overlaps most of the range of *Globigerinoides trilobus fistulosus* (Figure 11) in some cores and not in others. One explanation of this variation is the existence of hiatuses in cores, which could effectively eliminate a zone, thus resulting in N-21's resting directly upon N-19, as is suggested in some of the cores studied by *Parker* [1967].

4. Fourth, *Pulleniatina obliquiloculata* originated from *P. primalis* in the lower part of N-19 (Figure 9) and the two species continue together upward into N-20, perhaps higher. In deep-sea cores (Figure 11), the point of origin of *P. obliquiloculata* is consistently in the middle or upper part of the Gauss just above the extinction level of *Sphaeroidinellopsis subdehiscens.*

5. Fifth, the upper range of *Globoquadrina altispira* that extends up through N-19 and only very questionably above this (Figure 9) overlaps the lower part of the range of *G. fistulosus* in the study of *Hays et al.* [1969], whereas it appears to range somewhat higher in the study by *Parker* [1967]. Its extinction level appears to be within the upper Gauss as shown also in the report by *Lamb* [1969]. *G. altispira* also overlaps the lower range of *Pulleniatina obliquiloculata* primarily in N-19 (Figure 9); this range of overlap in

Plate 2

1. *Cyrtocapsella tetrapera* Haeckel ×500. Core E14-8, 1750–1752 cm. Hypotype U.S.C. No. 1299.
2 and 3. *Oroscena* sp. with digitate spines ×100. Core E14-8, 1750–1752 cm. Hypotype U.S.C. No. 1300. Only the spines are figured here.
4. *Oroscena carolae* Friend and Riedel ×200. Core E14-8, 1725–1727 cm. Hypotype U.S.C. No. 1301. Only the spine is figured.
5. *Eucyrtidium acuminatum* (Ehrenberg) ×500. Core E14-8, 107–109 cm. Hypotype U.S.C. No. 1302.
6. *Lamprocyclas maritalis* Haeckel ×400. Santa Barbara Basin, California. Holocene. Hypotype U.S.C. No. 1304.
7. *Pterocanium trilobum* (Haeckel) ×500. Core E14-8, 653–655 cm. Hypotype U.S.C. No. 1304.
8. Collosphaerid ×200. Core E14-8, 1662–1664 cm. U.S.C. No. 1305.
9. Collosphaerid ×200. Core E14-8, 1640–1642 cm. U.S.C. No. 1306.
10. *Euchitonia* cf. *E. muelleri* Haeckel ×200. Core E14-8, 107–109 cm. Hypotype U.S.C. No. 1307.

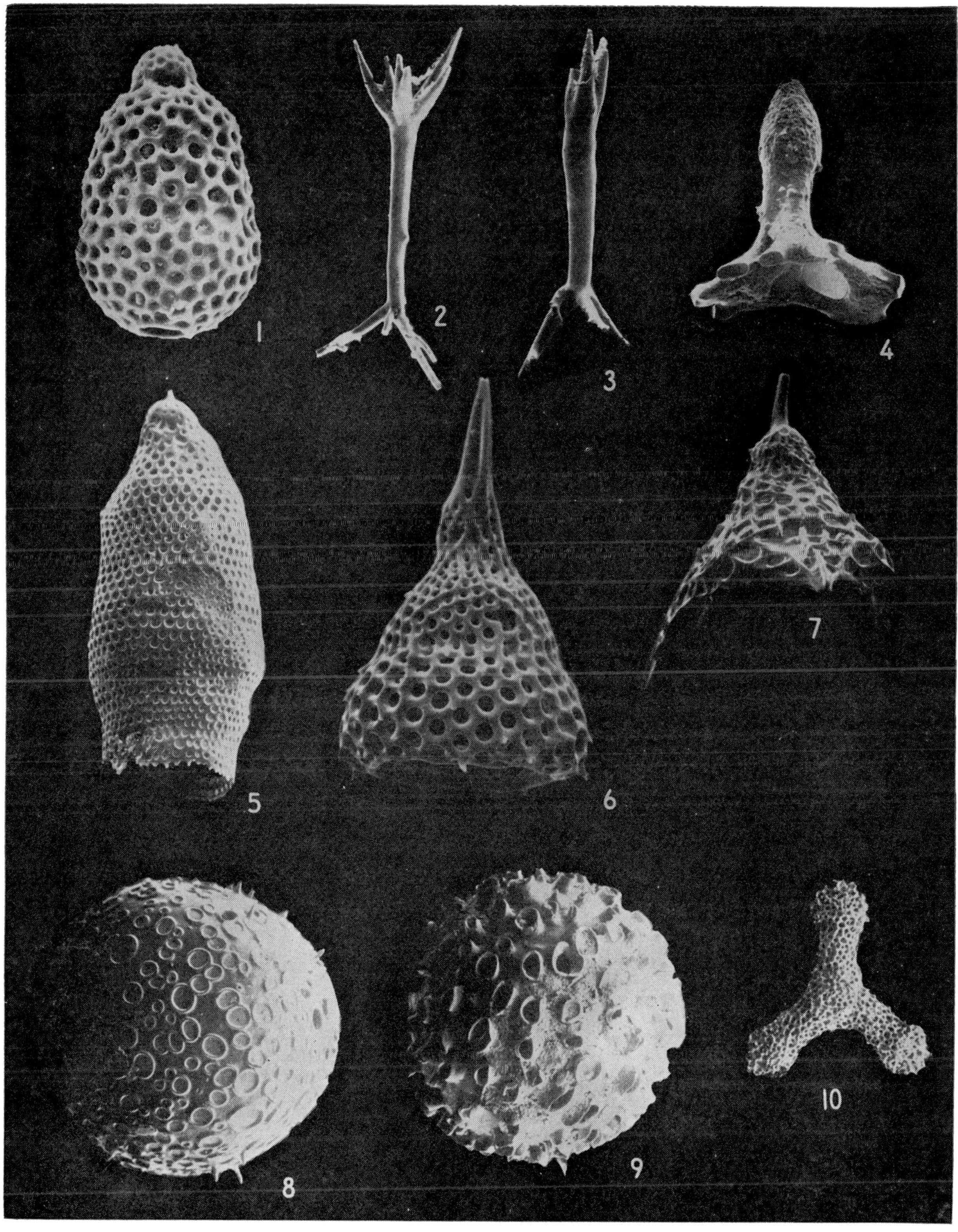
1
2
3
4
5
6
7
8
9
10

deep-sea cores is in the middle Gauss (Figure 11) as noted by *Hays et al.* [1969] and *Lamb* [1969].

6. Sixth, the extinction level for the Miocene radiolarians *Prunopyle titan* and *Lychnocanium grande* is within the upper Gauss in the Antarctic (Table 1, Figures 2–4). *P. titan* also disappears approximately with *Sphaeroidinellopsis subdehiscens* in California near the upper boundary of the Miocene as recognized there [*Ingle*, 1967; *Bandy and Ingle*, 1970].

One species presenting a problem as to its position in the Neogene scale as compared with its ranges in deep-sea cores is *Globigerina nepenthes.* It is considered to be a solution-susceptible species by *Hays et al.* [1969]; it is known to have quite variable upper limits according to the records of its occurrence in the literature as noted by *Blow* [1969]. For example, in the Pozon Formation *Blow* [1959] gave a very restricted range for the species, as have many other authors, well down within the Miocene. *Hays et al.* [1969] show its upper limit well below the level of extinction of *Sphaeroidinellopsis subdehiscens,* as did Blow in his study of the section in Venezuela, and they conclude that its level of extinction is about Gilbert *a* (Figure 11). *Parker* [1967], on the other hand, shows *G. nepenthes* extending as high as and even higher than the range of *S. subdehiscens* in the tropical Pacific (Figure 11). Perhaps this species was more temperature sensitive than other tropical forms; in this way it would disappear below the upper Miocene cool cycle that centers in N-17 (Figure 10) in those marginal tropical areas that were affected by somewhat cooler water masses. Certainly, where its full range is recorded, it is known to have an extinction point near the point of origin of *Pulleniatina obliquiloculata,* and it is known to overlap the lower part of the range of *Globigerinoides trilobus fistulosus.* Its upper limits differ in the two cores of *Hays et al.* [1969]; there is a major variation between these and its upper limits in the work of *Parker* [1967], supporting the concept that paleoceanographic changes played a most important role in determining the range of this species.

A second species about which there is a major difference of opinion is *Globorotalia hirsuta margaritae.* This is likely a temperate species in view of its close relationship to *G. hirsuta,* which is a modern temperate form. *G. hirsuta margaritae* is considered to be a lower Pliocene index by Italian workers [*Dondi and Papetti,* 1968]. *Blow* [1969] has re-examined the evidence and reaffirms that this form ranges from the middle of N-16 to the middle of N-19 (Figure 9). Blow described a new subspecies, *G. hirsuta praehirsuta,* that ranges from N-18 to N-22; the two forms are essentially identical, as shown by the illustrations of the sinistrally coiled holotype figures. It would be very easy to confuse the two subspecies, if they are actually separable, and thus contribute to different concepts about the total range of either. *Parker* [1967] shows *G. hirsuta margaritae* ranging well above the limit of *Sphaeroidinellopsis subdehiscens* where it is associated partly with the lower ranges of *Pulleniatina obliquiloculata* and *Globigerinoides trilobus fistulosus* (Figure 11). *Hays et al.* [1969] show its extinction well below the upper limits of *S. subdehiscens,* which is below Gilbert *a* on the magnetic scale. In view of the great consistency in the upper limits of *S. subdehiscens* in the Gauss normal magnetic epoch [*Glass et al.*, 1967; *Hays et al.*, 1969], Parker's data (Figure 11) would seem to show an entirely different and younger occurrence or range for *G. hirsuta margaritae* in that it ranges above the approximate range of the Gauss. It is considered to be solution-susceptible, which may explain some of the variation in its range by various authors. On the other hand, as a probable temperate species, its most typical and complete range would be in temperate areas, whereas its range in tropical areas would be most abbreviated and restricted to the upper Miocene cool cycle that centered in N-17 (Figure 10). This same cool interval centering in N-17 marked the invasion of temperate *Globigerina bulloides* faunas into some tropical areas and the very cold sinistral *Globorotalia (Turborotalia) pachyderma* faunas into temperate areas [*Bandy*, 1969].

If one assumes that the boundary between Neogene zones N-20 and N-21 occurs in the middle of the Gauss as indicated by *Phillips et al.* [1968], *Hays et al.*

Plate 3

1. *Lithelius nautiloides* Popofsky ×400. Core E14-8, 42–44 cm. Hypotype U.S.C. No. 1308.
2. *Spongotrochus glacialis* Popofsky ×370. Core E14-8, 42–44 cm. Hypotype U.S.C. No. 1309.
3. *Theocalyptra bicornis* (Popofsky) ×500. Core E14-8, 516–518 cm. Hypotype U.S.C. No. 1310.
4. *Clathrocyclas bicornis* Hays ×400. Core E14-8, 930–932 cm. Hypotype U.S.C. No. 1311. This form is combined with *Theocalyptra bicornis* in the paleotemperature analysis. They may be variants of the same species.
5. *Lithamphora furcaspiculata* Popofsky ×500. Core E14-8, 23–25 cm. Hypotype U.S.C. No. 1312.
6. *Saturnulus planetes* Haeckel ×400. Core E14-8, 107–109 cm. Hypotype U.S.C. No. 1313.
7. *Theoconus zancleus* Haeckel ×500. Santa Barbara Basin, California. Holocene. Hypotype U.S.C. No. 1314.

1
2
3
4
5
6
7

[1969], and *Berggren* [1969], the pertinent Neogene zones of *Banner and Blow* [1965, 1967] and *Blow* [1969] are invalid. For example, the extinction point of *Sphaeroidinellopsis subdehiscens,* which is so uniform in its location in deep-sea cores near the upper limit of the Mammoth event, would then be above the base of N-21 in contrast to its extinction level near the upper limit of N-18 [*Berggren,* 1969] in the standard classification (Figure 9). The range of *Globigerinoides trilobus fistulosus* would be from upper N-20 through N-21 only, in contrast to its range from N-18 to N-21 in the Neogene classification (Figure 9). The extinction level for *Pulleniatina primalis,* which is in the lower part of N-20 in the Neogene classification of *Blow* [1969], would occur instead in the uppermost part of N-21, since it is shown to range above the Gauss into the lower Matuyama reversed magnetic epoch by *Hays et al.* [1969, Figure 6] and *Phillips et al.* [1968]. The origin of *Pulleniatina obliquiloculata* that occurs in the middle of N-19 in the Neogene classification [*Blow,* 1969] would arise instead in N-21. *Globoquadrina altispira,* which probably has an extinction level at the top of N-19, would instead have an extinction level within N-21 or near the upper limit of the Pliocene (Figures 9, 11).

It is very apparent that there are many hiatuses or missing sections in deep-sea cores, and it is also clear that many piston cores have disturbed sections. Note the missing sections in the cores studied by *Parker* [1967]: in one case the Quaternary rests directly on N-16; in two cores N-21 rests on N-19. Similarly, in V20-163 of *Hays et al.* [1969] *Globorotalia tosaensis* overlaps the upper range of *Sphaeroidinellopsis subdehiscens,* which suggests a missing section in this core with some reworking. Its location on the eastern scarp of the Ninety East Ridge in the Indian Ocean makes it suspect.

The Pliocene-Pleistocene Boundary and the Magnetic Scale

The origin of *Globorotalia truncatulinoides* from its ancestor *Globorotalia tosaensis* marks the base of the Quaternary, making this a most important planktonic datum plane. It has been shown to correlate with the base of the Gilsa event (given as Olduvai), according to the extensive core study by *Glass et al.* [1967]. *Banner and Blow* [1965] defined the origin of *G. truncatulinoides* in the Calabrian of Italy, the stratotype for the lower Pleistocene. Most investigators are now following this usage in studies of deep-sea cores, placing the base of the Pleistocene at the base of the Gilsa event [*Cox,* 1969]. *Kennett* [1969] has reported now that in the zone of overlap of these two species, which would be approximately N-22, there is an alternation of keeled and nonkeeled populations. He reports that the keeled forms are associated with subtropical planktonic species, and the nonkeeled forms are associated with temperate or transitional species such as *Globorotalia inflata.*

Additional planktonic criteria for the recognition of the Pliocene-Pleistocene boundary are the extinction datum planes for discoasters and for *Globigerinoides trilobus fistulosus,* and the first appearance of *Globorotalia hirsuta hirsuta* and *Pulleniatina obliquiloculata finalis* (Figure 9). There is general consistency in the way these indicator species occur and are employed in the various reports.

In earlier studies of the Philippine section [*Bandy,* 1963; *Bandy and Wade,* 1967], *Globorotalia tosaensis* was referred to as *G. truncatulinoides,* which would make much of the Pliocene section there middle and upper Pliocene (N-20–N-21). It would appear that the lower range of *G. tosaensis,* a cooler water species [*Kennett,* 1969], may indeed vary considerably, being

Plate 4

1. *Globorotalia (Truncorotalia) tosaensis* Takayanagi and Saito ×200. Sample 3-1442, Pliocene, Philippines. Hypotype U.S.C. No. 1315. Ventral view. The edge is rounded with no evidence of a keel.
2. *Globorotalia (Truncorotalia) truncatulinoides* (d'Orbigny) ×200. Ventral view of specimen from Timms Point Silt, California. Hypotype U.S.C. No. 1316. There is a well-developed keel on the edge.
3. *Globorotalia (Truncorotalia) truncatulinoides* (d'Orbigny) ×200. Ventral view of specimen from sample 36, Santa Maria di Catanzaro, Italy. Hypotype U.S.C. No. 1317. There is a well-developed keel on the edge.
4. *Sphaeroidinellopsis subdehiscens* (Blow) subspecies *subdehiscens* (Blow) ×200. Ventral view of ideotype. Hypotype U.S.C. No. 1318. Specimen from W. H. Blow, from the *Globorotalia menardii* zone of Trinidad, Neogene zone 15, upper Miocene.
5. *Sphaeriodinellopsis subdehiscens* (Blow) subspecies *subdehiscens* (Blow) ×200. Ventral view of ideotype. Hypotype U.S.C. No. 1319. Specimen from W. H. Blow, from the *Globorotalia menardii* zone of Trinidad, Neogene zone 15, upper Miocene.
6. *Sphaeroidinellopsis sphaeroides* Lamb ×200. A. Ventral view. B. Dorsal view. Specimen from Lower Pliocene Repetto Formation, Malaga Cove, California. Hypotype U.S.C. No. 1320.
7. *Sphaeroidinella dehiscens* (Parker and Jones) ×100. Dorsal view of specimen from the Atlantic core, V 12-5, at a depth of 5 cm. Hypotype U.S.C. No. 1321. This specimen has developed from *Globigerinoides conglobatus* (Brady).
8. *Sphaeroidinella dehiscens* (Parker and Jones) ×100. Oblique view of specimen showing multiple apertures. Same sample as specimen figured in 7. Hypotype U.S.C. No. 1322.

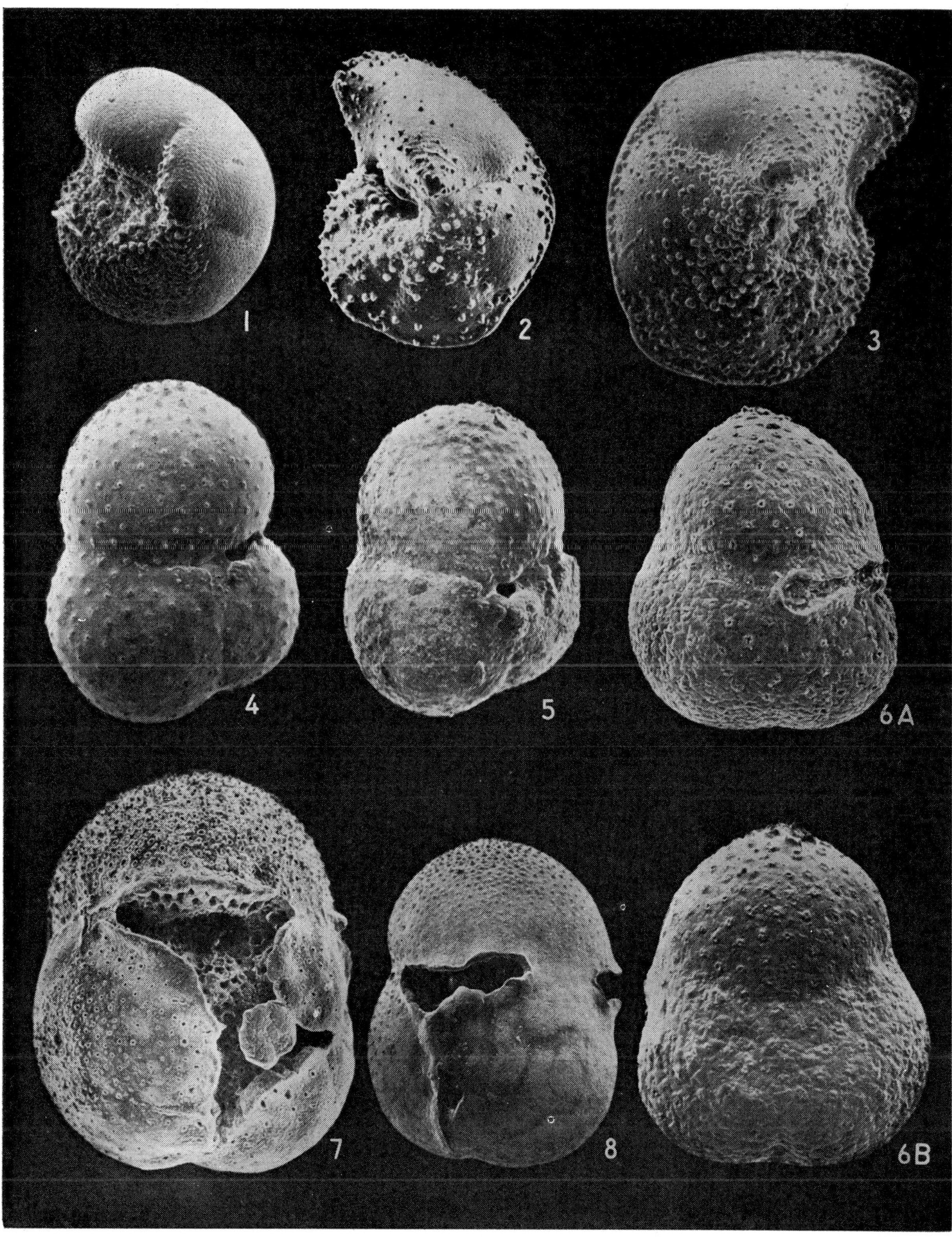
1
2
3
4
5
6A
7
8
6B

TABLE 3. Listing of Species with Authors

See *Martin* [1904], *Campbell and Clark* [1944], *Hays* [1965], and *Friend and Riedel* [1967] for taxonomy of radiolarians. See *Bolli* [1957], *Blow* [1959] *Banner and Blow* [1967], and *Blow* [1969] for taxonomy of planktonic foraminiferal species.

RADIOLARIANS

Acanthosphaera sp.
Cannartiscus amphicylindricus Haeckel
Cannartiscus marylandicus Martin
Clathrocyclas bicornis Hays
Collosphaerids
Cyrtocapsella tetrapera Haeckel
Desmospyris spongiosa Hays
Euchitonia cf. *E. muelleri* Haeckel
Eucyrtidium acuminatum (Ehrenberg)
Eucyrtidium calvertense Martin
Helotholus vema Hays
Lamprocyclas maritalis Haeckel
Lithamphora furcaspiculata Popofsky
Lithelius nautiloides Popofsky
Lychnocanium grande Campbell and Clark
Ommatocampe hughesi Campbell and Clark
Orodendrum sp.
Oroscena (digitate)
Oroscena carolae Friend and Riedel
Oroscena sp.
Prunopyle titan Campbell and Clark
Pterocanium trilobum Haeckel
Saturnulus planetes Haeckel
Spongoplegma antarcticum Haeckel
Spongotrochus glacialis Popofsky
Theocalyptra bicornis (Popofsky)
Theoconus zancleus Haeckel
Theocyrtis redondoensis Campbell and Clark
Triceraspyris sp.

PLANKTONIC FORAMINIFERA

Globigerina bulloides d'Orbigny
Globigerina nepenthes Todd
Globigerinoides conglobatus (Brady)
Globigerinoides trilobus fistulosus (Schubert)
Globigerinoides trilobus sacculifer (Brady)
Globoquadrina altispira (Cushman and Jarvis) *altispira* (Cushman and Jarvis)
Globoquadrina dehiscens (Chapman, Parr, and Collins) *dehiscens* (Chapman, Parr, and Collins)
Globorotalia hirsuta (d'Orbigny) *hirsuta* (d'Orbigny)
Globorotalia hirsuta (d'Orbigny) *margaritae* Bolli and Bermudez
Globorotalia hirsuta (d'Orbigny) *praehirsuta* Blow
Globorotalia menardii (d'Orbigny) *limbata* (Fornasini)
Globorotalia menardii (d'Orbigny) *menardii* (d'Orbigny)
Globorotalia merotumida Blow and Banner
Globorotalia multicamerata Cushman and Jarvis
Globorotalia tumida (Brady) *plesiotumida* Blow and Banner
Globorotalia tumida (Brady) *tumida* (Brady)
Globorotalia ungulata Bermudez
Globorotalia (Truncorotalia) crassaformis (Galloway and Wissler)
Globorotalia (Truncorotalia) tosaensis Takayanagi and Saito

TABLE 3. *Continued*

Globorotalia (Truncorotalia) truncatulinoides (d'Orbigny)
Globorotalia (Turborotalia) acostaensis Blow
Globorotalia (Turborotalia) continuosa Blow
Globorotalia (Turborotalia) inflata (d'Orbigny)
Globorotalia (Turborotalia) pachyderma (Ehrenberg)
Globorotalia (Turborotalia) puncticulata (Deshayes) *padana* Dondi and Papetti
Globorotalia (Turborotalia) puncticulata (Deshayes) *puncticulata* (Deshayes)
Neogloboquadrina dutertrei (d'Orbigny) *dutertrei* (d'Orbigny)
Neogloboquadrina dutertrei (d'Orbigny) *subcretacea* (Lomnicki)
Pulleniatina obliquiloculata (Parker and Jones) *finalis* Banner and Blow
Pulleniatina obliquiloculata (Parker and Jones) *obliquiloculata* (Parker and Jones)
Pulleniatina primalis Banner and Blow
Pulleniatina spectabilis Parker
Sphaeroidinella dehiscens (Parker and Jones) *dehiscens* (Parker and Jones)
Sphaeroidinella dehiscens (Parker and Jones) *excavata* Banner and Blow
Sphaeroidinellops kochi (Caudri)
Sphaeroidinellopsis seminulina (Schwager) *seminulina* (Schwager)
Sphaeroidinellopsis sphaeroides Lamb
Sphaeroidinellopsis subdehiscens (Blow) *paenedehiscens* Blow
Sphaeroidinellopsis subdehiscens (Blow) *subdehiscens* (Blow)

more complete in temperate areas than in tropical regions [*Ingle*, 1967; *Parker*, 1967]. Perhaps its range in tropical areas is restricted to N-21 and the lower part of N-22 in view of the cooler cycle centering there (Figure 10); in temperate areas its first appearance is in N-19, the lower Pliocene.

LATER NEOGENE PALEOCLIMATIC CYCLES, TEMPERATE AND TROPICAL REGIONS

As noted by many authors, it is important to take into consideration the effect of paleoceanographic changes when evaluating planktonic zones and variations of indicator species in this framework. In tropical areas, it is predictable that temperate species will appear in the sections rather briefly during cooler cycles, such as those centered in zones N-17 of the upper Miocene, N-21 of the upper Pliocene, and those of the glacial Pleistocene. Conversely, it is to be expected that tropical species will be carried farther into temperate areas briefly during warmer cycles such as that represented by N-18 to N-20 inclusive (Figure 10).

A paleoclimatological model was suggested [*Bandy*, 1967*a*, 1968*a*, 1968*b*, 1969] for the upper Neogene, based upon cyclic variations or expansions and con-

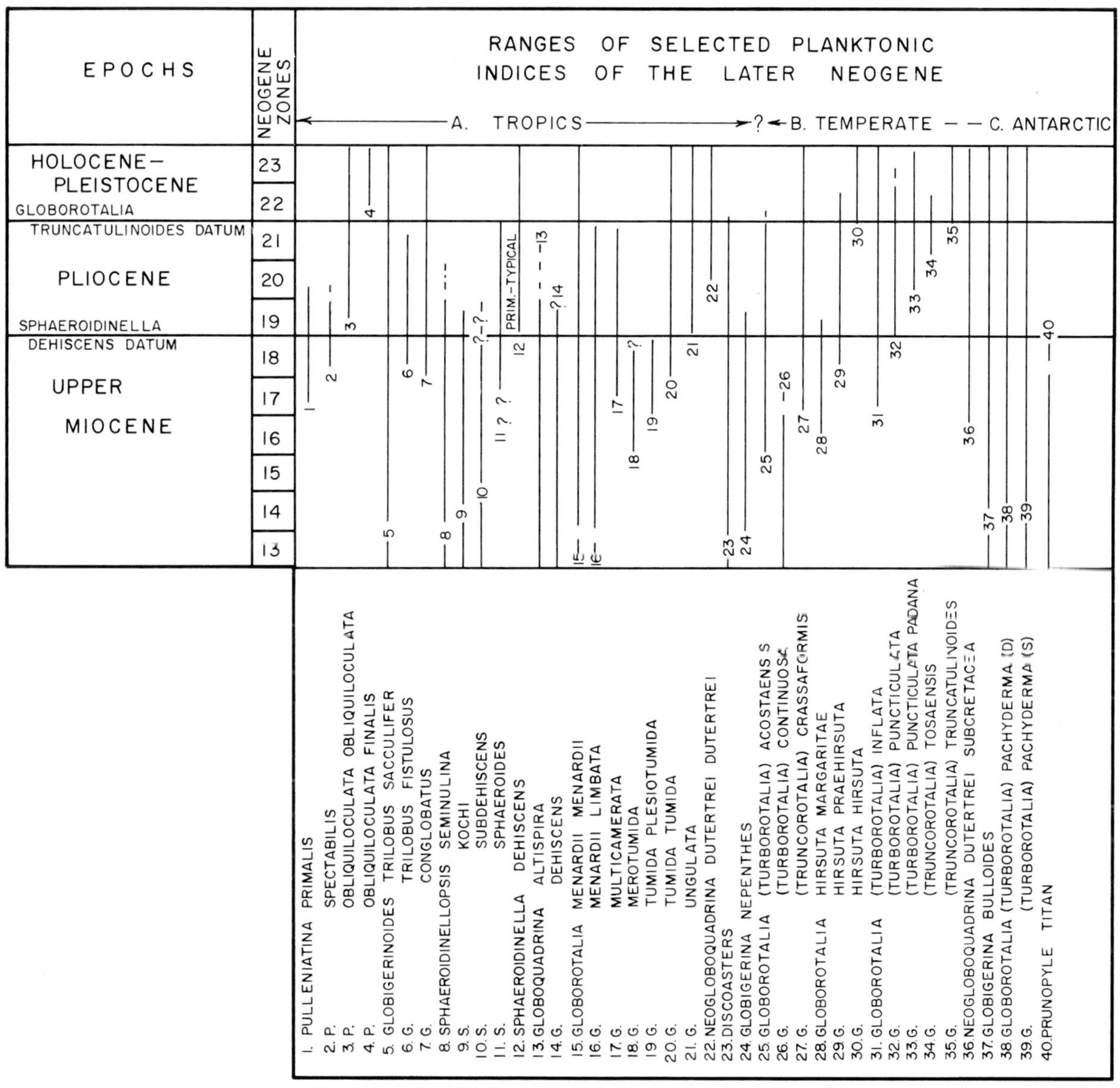

Fig. 9. Ranges of selected later Cenozoic planktonic indices grouped generally into (*A*) tropical forms, (*B*) temperate forms, and (*C*) cold water or antarctic forms. The basic zonation of *Banner and Blow* [1965] and *Blow* [1969] is used here with only some slight modifications. These modifications consist of adding *Sphaeroidinellopsis sphaeroides* Lamb [*Lamb*, 1969], the elimination of the uppermost part of the range of *Globorotalia (Turborotalia) puncticulata* (Deshayes), the addition of *Globorotalia (Turborotalia) puncticulata padana* Dondi and Papetti, use of *Neogloboquadrina dutertrei subcretacea* (Lomnicki) for the *subcretaceaeggeri* complex, and the addition of ranges for *Globorotalia (Turborotalia) pachyderma* (Ehrenberg) and a radiolarian and discoasters. Most of the critical species were selected that are employed in defining the uppermost Miocene, Pliocene, and Pliocene-Pleistocene boundary. A complete listing of planktonic foraminiferas referred to is given in Table 3. A few critical species are illustrated on Plate 4.

tractions of polar planktonic faunas in the stratigraphic sections of the circum-Pacific. Radiometric dates associated with that model suggested that the Miocene-Pliocene boundary should be placed at about 9 million years and the Pleistocene base should be placed at about 3 million years. These dates appear now to be too old by a factor of about 3. The Pleistocene in this case was defined on the basis of the major influx of polar planktonic populations, the *Globorotalia (Turborotalia) pachyderma* sinistrally coiled forms, into temperate areas such as California and New Zealand.

From existing data reviewed by *Bandy* [1969],

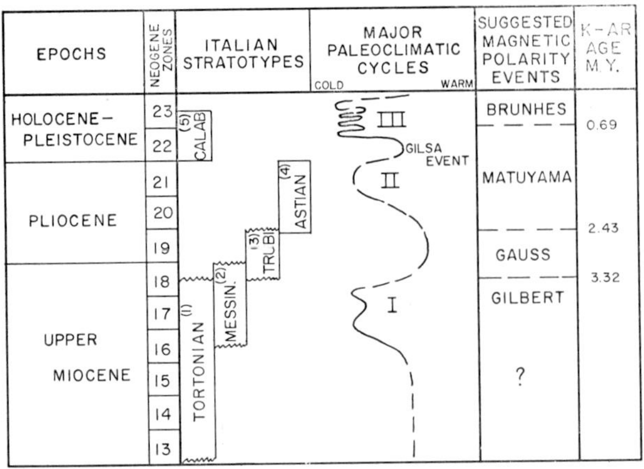

Fig. 10. Correlation of planktonic Neogene zones [*Blow*, 1969], Italian stratotypes, and the paleoclimatic cycles and magnetic events suggested in this paper.

especially that of *Bé* [1969], it is clear that the coiling ratios of *pachyderma* populations reflect a significant variation in temperature, offering in this way a powerful paleoclimatic tool (Figure 12). Populations of this species, which are more than 90% sinistral, are predominant in temperatures of less than about 5° or 6°C, and they are most abundant in waters that are less than 2°C. Conversely, dextral populations are most characteristic of waters with a temperature range of from 9° to about 15°C and are the predominant group near the warmer end of this range. The dextral population is associated with other transitional species such as *Globorotalia (Turborotalia) inflata* and *Globigerina bulloides*. Tropical indices (Figure 9) include the *Globorotalia menardii* group, and especially *Sphaeroidinella dehiscens*. The latter is most characteristic of temperatures in excess of about 23.5°C.

Referring to the established planktonic datum planes as they are represented now, the paleoclimatic model suggested earlier can be related to the Neogene zones of *Banner and Blow* [1965], offering an auxiliary method of making interregional correlations (Figure 13). The first major cold cycle of the later Neogene is that of the upper Miocene, centering in N-17, which resulted in the expansion of sinistral *pachyderma* populations far into temperate areas; in turn the temperate group with *Globigerina bulloides* expanded far into many tropical areas. Colder climates in the later Miocene are now reflected in many kinds of reports. For example, *Jenkins* [1967] noted sinistral populations of *Globorotalia (Turborotalia) pachyderma* in the Messinian of Italy (Figure 10). *Berto-*

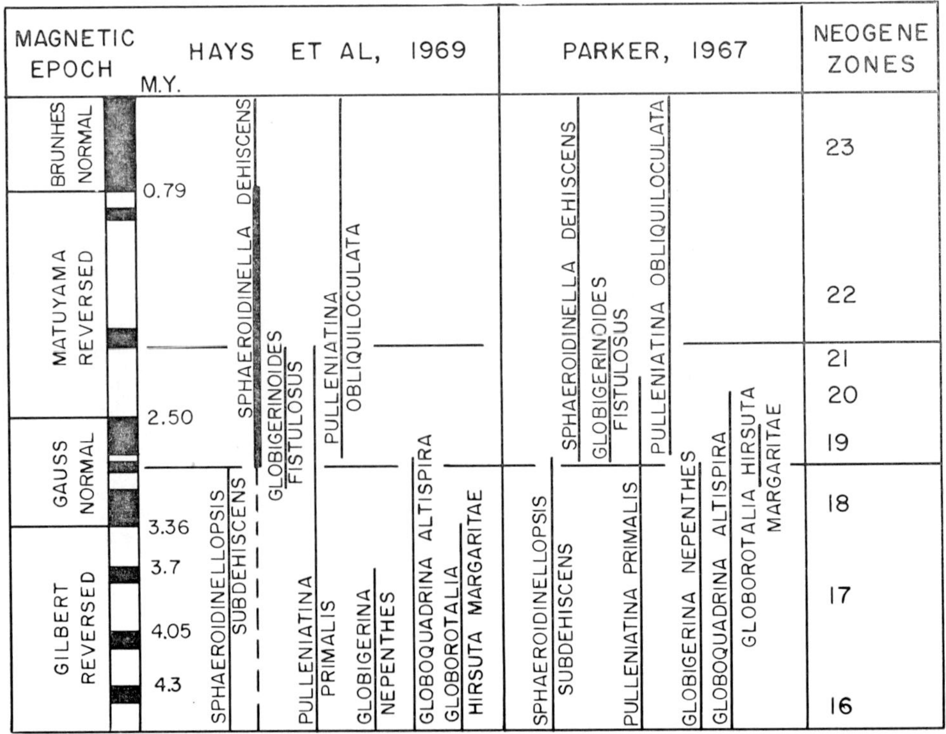

Fig. 11. Comparison of faunal boundaries of *Hays et al.* [1969], *Parker* [1967], and Neogene zones.

lani Marchetti [1968] reported colder climates in the Messinian of Italy on the basis of vegetation and pollen characteristics. *Rutford et al.* [1965] have dated antarctic glaciation as late Miocene, using radiometric dates. Upper Miocene marine glacial deposits of the lower Yakataga Formation of Alaska appear with the association of sinistral *pachyderma* faunas there [*Bandy et al.*, 1969]. *Wolfe and Hopkins* [1967] have recorded a cool temperate cycle in the later Miocene of the northwestern United States. *Denton and Armstrong* [1969] have dated continental glaciation in Alaska as older than about 10 million years, using radiometric dates. It is clear that an upper Miocene cool cycle was bipolar in its effects, that glaciation occurred in high latitudes at that time, that there was reduced circulation between the open sea and the Mediterranean resulting in evaporites, and that tropical planktonic species were eliminated from or reduced in temperate areas.

Neogene zones 18, 19, and 20 appear to be associated with a warmer cycle (Figure 12). Dextral *pachyderma* populations replaced the sinistral populations in temperate areas such as New Zealand, California, the Mohole section off Baja California, and apparently in Italy as well. Dr. M. A. Chierici has indicated (personal communication) that the coiling patterns of the *pachyderma* populations of Italy are rather similar to those of the California section. Tropical species expanded again into temperate areas, a marine transgression affected many areas such as Italy [*Iaccarino and Papani,* 1967], and there was improved circulation between the open sea and basins such as the Mediterranean.

A major late Pliocene cold cycle is recorded in a manner similar to that of the later Miocene, centering in N-21 (Figure 13). *Glass et al.* [1967] report a cold zone below the Pliocene-Pleistocene boundary in deep-sea cores, and *Berggren* [1968] summarizes the data for deep-sea core V16-66 in the southwestern Indian Ocean, which shows glacial evidences in the lower Matuyama below the Pliocene-Pleistocene boundary. *Ikebe* [1969] refers to a cool phase in the Otadai Formation of Japan, suggesting that it may correlate with the Arquatian cool phase of Italy (Astian equivalent) which was discovered by *Lona* [1962]. *Beard* [1969], working on sections in the area of the Gulf of Mexico, shows a prominent cold phase in the basal Matuyama which he refers to as Nebraskan; however, it is not clear that this cool phase is correlative with the Nebraskan of continental stratigraphy. In California [*Bandy and Casey,* 1969] the Pliocene cold interval,

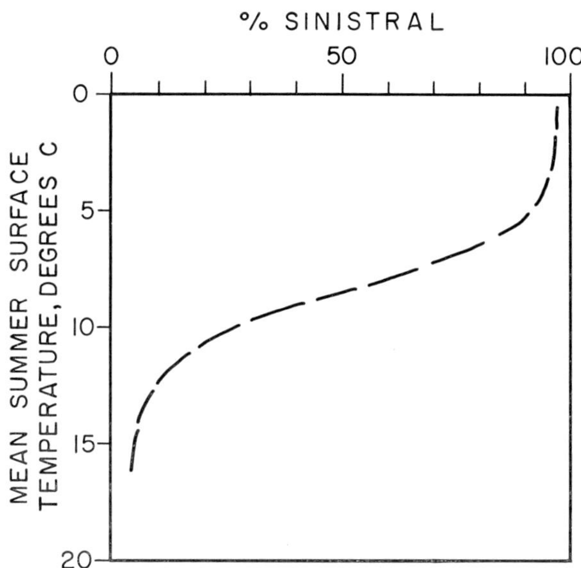

Fig. 12. Temperature and coiling relationships for *Globoro talia (Turborotalia) pachyderma.* The suggested curve is based largely upon the live planktonic data of *Bé* [1969].

defined by the prominent influx of sinistral *pachyderma* populations [*Bandy,* 1960*b*, 1964, 1967*a*, 1967*b*], occurs just beneath the *Globorotalia truncatulinoides* datum plane.

The Committee on Mediterranean Neogene Stratigraphy (CMNS) has recently reviewed planktonic foraminiferal research in the Neogene of the Mediterranean region [*Cati et al.*, 1968]. The first appearance in the stratigraphic column of cool water immigrants was accepted as evidence for recognizing the transition from a warm Pliocene to cool Pleistocene. However, the faunal criteria mentioned were the cool index species *Hyalinea baltica, Arctica islandica,* and sinistrally coiled populations of *Globorotalia (Turborotalia) pachyderma.* It is interesting and important to note that the two benthic cool water indices appear in the Calabrian section at Santa Maria di Catanzaro; however, in samples collected by O. L. Bandy and Piero Ascoli, the *pachyderma* populations are more than 90% dextral, as are most of the populations in the Le Castella section of Italy (paper in preparation). The planktonic populations in the Calabrian have an abundance of dextrally coiled *pachyderma* populations and *Globigerina bulloides.* Chierici (in *Dondi and Papetti* [1968, pp. 84–85]) discovered the influx of sinistral *pachyderma* populations near the Pliocene-Pleistocene boundary in Italy; however, this occurs well above the Calabrian. Thus, the Calabrian has a

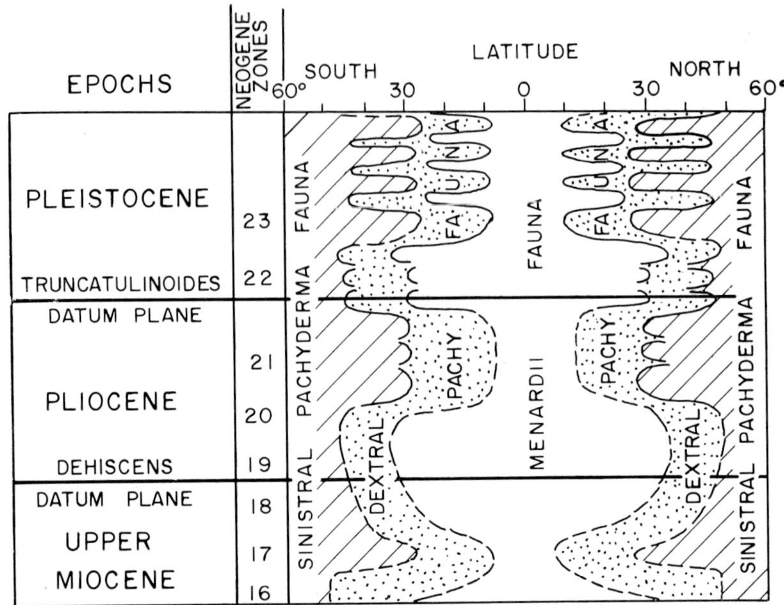

Fig. 13. Later Cenozoic paleoclimatic cycles correlated with Neogene zones [*Banner and Blow*, 1965] and major planktonic datum planes. The sinistral *Globorotalia (Turborotalia) pachyderma* group suggests surface water temperatures less than 8°C; the dextral populations of this species, together with *Globigerina bulloides* and other temperate species, suggest a temperature of from 9°C to about 15°C or more. The tropical *Globorotalia menardii* population suggests temperatures greater than 18.5°C, especially in the range of 23°C to 27°C. These temperature ranges are mostly from the live planktonic data of *Bé* [1960, 1969].

temperate or transitional planktonic fauna, and it is replaced by a colder water fauna upsection.

Selli [1967] pointed out that a long preglacial Pleistocene (Calabrian) was followed by a glacial Pleistocene; we suggest that the glacial Pleistocene in this case can be identified by the influx of sinistral *pachyderma* populations. A cool or cold cycle in the Astian, a temperate or warmer interval for the Calabrian, and a cold cycle beginning in the post-Calabrian may correlate with a reduced sea level in the Astian, raised sea level in the Calabrian, and reduced sea level in the post-Calabrian. In this way improved migration conditions may have permitted the influx of *Arctica islandica* and *Hyalinea baltica* during the temperate cycle recorded by the Calabrian.

Referring to isotope analyses of *Emiliani et al.* [1961], it was found that no major temperature change occurred across the base of the Calabrian. Surface temperatures are reported to range from 21°C to more than 30°C in the late Pliocene, from 16°C to more than 30°C in the late Pliocene-early Pleistocene, and from 12°C to 28°C in the late Pleistocene. Thus, the isotope data are consistent with the long preglacial Pleistocene concept of *Selli* [1967] and with the suggested change from temperate conditions in the Calabrian to colder conditions in the post-Calabrian, indicated by the changes in planktonic faunas. Sinistral *pachyderma* faunas would suggest water temperatures below 8°C.

The colder glacial Pleistocene is likely equivalent to the Brunhes, perhaps including the uppermost Matuyama (Jaramillo event and above) reversed magnetic epoch. As in the Antarctic, a planktonic faunal change is recorded in temperate regions with the influx there of sinistral *pachyderma* faunas, and in tropical areas there is a major decrease in the *Sphaeroidinella* faunas. Selecting *Sphaeroidinella dehiscens* (tropical index in waters warmer than 23.5°C) and the *Globorotalia puncticulata padana* group (temperate index related to *Globorotalia inflata* and referred to as *Globorotalia* sp. 1 by [*Ericson et al.*, 1964], it is clear that there is a pronounced decrease in the relative percentage of *S. dehiscens* in this complex near the Brunhes-Matuyama boundary (Figure 14). *Glass et al.* [1967] refer

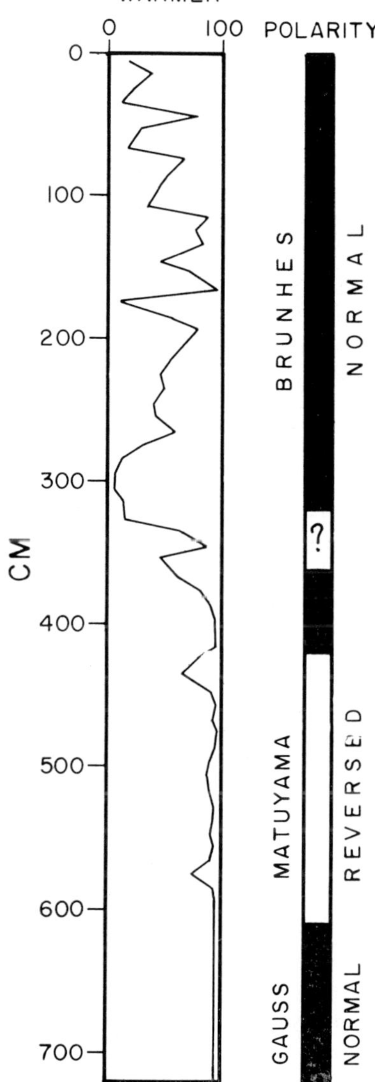

Fig. 14. Abundance (in per cent) of *Sphaeroidinella dehiscens* in the combined *S. dehiscens-Globorotalia puncticulata padana* complex. The latter is similar to *Globorotalia inflata* in some respects, differing in the flat dorsal side, curved and tangential radial sutures on the dorsal side, and smaller size. It was described by *Dondi and Papetti* [1968] from the Pliocene of the Italian section. It is also the form referred to as *Globorotalia* sp. 1 by *Ericson et al.* [1964].

most of the upper part of this core (V12-5) to the Brunhes and Matuyama, whereas *Ericson et al.* [1964] placed the entire core in the lower Pleistocene. *Blow* [1969] correlates most of this core above about 600 cm with the Quaternary or with N-22 and N-23. Although *S. dehiscens* is relatively rare in the Brunhes, there do not seem to be four well-defined cooler cycles in the tropical regions using this method. On the other hand, *Beard* [1969, cf. figs. 2 and 3] shows four colder cycles within the Brunhes section. *Selli* [1967], *Richmond* [1969], *Ikebe* [1969], and others favor the correlation of the main glacials, Günz-Mindel-Riss-Würm sequence, to the Brunhes in contrast to usage on the Gulf of Mexico coast [*Beard*, 1969; *Lamb*, 1969].

LATE NEOGENE PLANKTONIC DATUM PLANES AND RADIOMETRIC DATES

The *Sphaeroidinella dehiscens* Datum Plane

The *Sphaeroidinella dehiscens* datum plane (Figure 15) in this study is essentially correlative with the *Sphaeroidinellopsis subdehiscens* extinction datum plane (Figures 9, 11), and it is only slightly below the level that could be referred to as the *Pulleniatina obliquiloculata* datum plane in the tropics. In temperate areas the *Globorotalia puncticulata* datum plane, or the *Prunopyle titan* extinction datum plane, are approximately correlative with the *S. dehiscens* datum plane. In the Antarctic the *Prunopyle titan* extinction datum plane, or the *Lychnocanium grande* extinction datum plane, would represent approximately the same horizon as the *S. dehiscens* datum plane.

The *S. dehiscens* datum plane and its equivalent datum planes in temperate and antarctic cores are correlative with a level in the upper Gauss normal magnetic epoch above the Mammoth event, perhaps above the Kaena event. *Cox* [1969] and others assign a K-Ar age of less than 3 million years to this level. On the other hand, the paleontological events that define this level in the California section [*Ingle*, 1967; *Bandy and Ingle*, 1970] fit a radiometric framework that suggests an age of about 9 million years, perhaps less. The California dates from the upper Miocene [*Bandy*, 1967*a*; *Ingle*, 1967; *Turner*, 1968] are glass dates, and it would appear that they are too old by a factor of about 3 [*Bandy and Casey*, 1969]; if not, then the radiometric dates associated with the magnetic scale are too young.

The *Globorotalia (Truncorotalia) truncatulinoides* Datum Plane

The *Globorotalia truncatulinoides* datum plane of this

study is that of many other investigators, correlating approximately with the extinction limit of discoasters, where the species arose from its ancestor *Globorotalia tosaensis* (Figures 9, 15). This level has been correlated with the lower boundary of the Calabrian of Italy [*Banner and Blow*, 1965; *Blow*, 1969], and it has been defined in deep-sea cores as being at the base of the Gilsa event (Olduvai of some authors) by *Glass et al.* [1967] and many other investigators. In the Antarctic the *Eucyrtidium calvertense* extinction datum plane is approximately equivalent to the base of the Gilsa event; it is thus the cold water equivalent of the *G. truncatulinoides* datum plane and the discoaster extinction datum plane.

In deep-sea cores the *G. truncatulinoides* datum plane seems to be consistently near the base of the Gilsa event, which has a radiometric age of about 1.79 million years; in California [*Bandy and Casey*, 1969] this level is near the base of the Wheelerian Stage, which has previously been referred to the upper Pliocene there. In Balcom Canyon, California, there is an ash bed, the Bailey ash, that has been dated about 1 million years [*Yeats*, 1965] on glass shards (K-Ar), 5.1 ± 0.5 million years [*Bandy and Ingle*, 1970] on feldspar, and within the range of 8.4 and 9.7 million years on the basis of K-Ar dates of sanidine and biotite [*Yeats et al.*, 1967]. In view of the highly discordant radiometric dates obtained from this ash, and in view of its position in the zone where *G. tosaensis* gives rise to *G. truncatulinoides*, we assume that it should have an age of about 1.8 million years, and that it should be correlative with the base of the Gilsa event in magnetic stratigraphy and the base of the Calabrian in the Italian section (Figure 15). Further, in work in progress, J. A. Wilcoxon has noted the extinction of discoasters in the zone which is in the lower Wheelerian Stage of Balcom Canyon. Thus, it would seem that K-Ar glass dates for the Bailey ash are too young, feldspar dates are about 3 times too old, and K-Ar dates of other minerals are perhaps 5 times too old, assuming that the radiometric scale associated with the magnetic scale is valid.

The Günz Datum Plane

The Günz Datum Plane is proposed for the base of the pronounced cooler paleoclimatic cycles associated with the Brunhes normal magnetic interval. A most pronounced colder series of paleoclimatic fluctuations is recorded in the Brunhes normal magnetic intervals in the Antarctic (Figures 6–8), where the ratio of subantarctic and antarctic radiolarians defines variations of water temperature between about 5°C and less than 0°C in contrast to somewhat warmer cycles in the Matuyama. In temperate areas such as Italy, California, New Zealand, and elsewhere, there is a major influx of sinistrally coiled populations of *Globorotalia (Turborotalia) pachyderma* at a level much above the *G. truncatulinoides* datum plane, indicating a major cooling event that we suggest correlates with the prominent cooling noted near the Brunhes-Matuyama boundary in the Antarctic (Figure 15). In tropical regions, the Brunhes interval shows a marked reduction in the abundance of the tropical index *Sphaeroidinella dehiscens* and a corresponding increase in the numbers of temperate or transitional planktonic species (Figure 14). The classic glacial Pleistocene, beginning with the Günz, is considered to be associated with the Brunhes normal magnetic epoch, and it is this interval that may represent N-23.

DISCUSSION

Unresolved problems exist in relating radiometric dates of the California marine Pleistocene section with the planktonic events there [*Bandy and Ingle*, 1970]. The Pliocene-Pleistocene boundary of the Los Angeles Basin has been defined as the stratigraphic level at which there is a major influx of cold water sinistral populations of *Globorotalia (Turborotalia) pachyderma* (given as *Globigerina pachyderma*) replacing the temperate dextral populations of the 'upper Pliocene' [*Bandy*, 1960*b*, 1964, 1967*a*, 1967*b*, etc.]. This level is now known to be stratigraphically well above the *G. truncatulinoides* datum plane or the Pliocene-Pleistocene boundary that is coincident with the base of the Gilsa event (Figure 15). Yet the event marked by this influx of polar planktonic populations is recorded in the base of the Lomita Marl which has been dated radiometrically (K-Ar dates on glauconite) by *Obradovich* [1965, 1968] as 3.04 ± 0.09 million years. He reports a Rb/Sr age of 3.1 ± 2.6 million years for the Lomita. Thus, the Lomita Marl dates must be about 3 times too old if the planktonic events are properly related to the magnetic scale and its K-Ar ages (Figure 15). Since the radiometric dates related to the magnetic scale are obtained upon nonmarine basalts and eruptive rocks, it is suggested that the marine ash beds and glauconites are giving highly erroneous radiometric dates by use of the potassium-argon method.

If one prefers to use the available radiometric dates from the California section as a means of correlating it with the magnetic scale [*Berggren*, 1969] and its

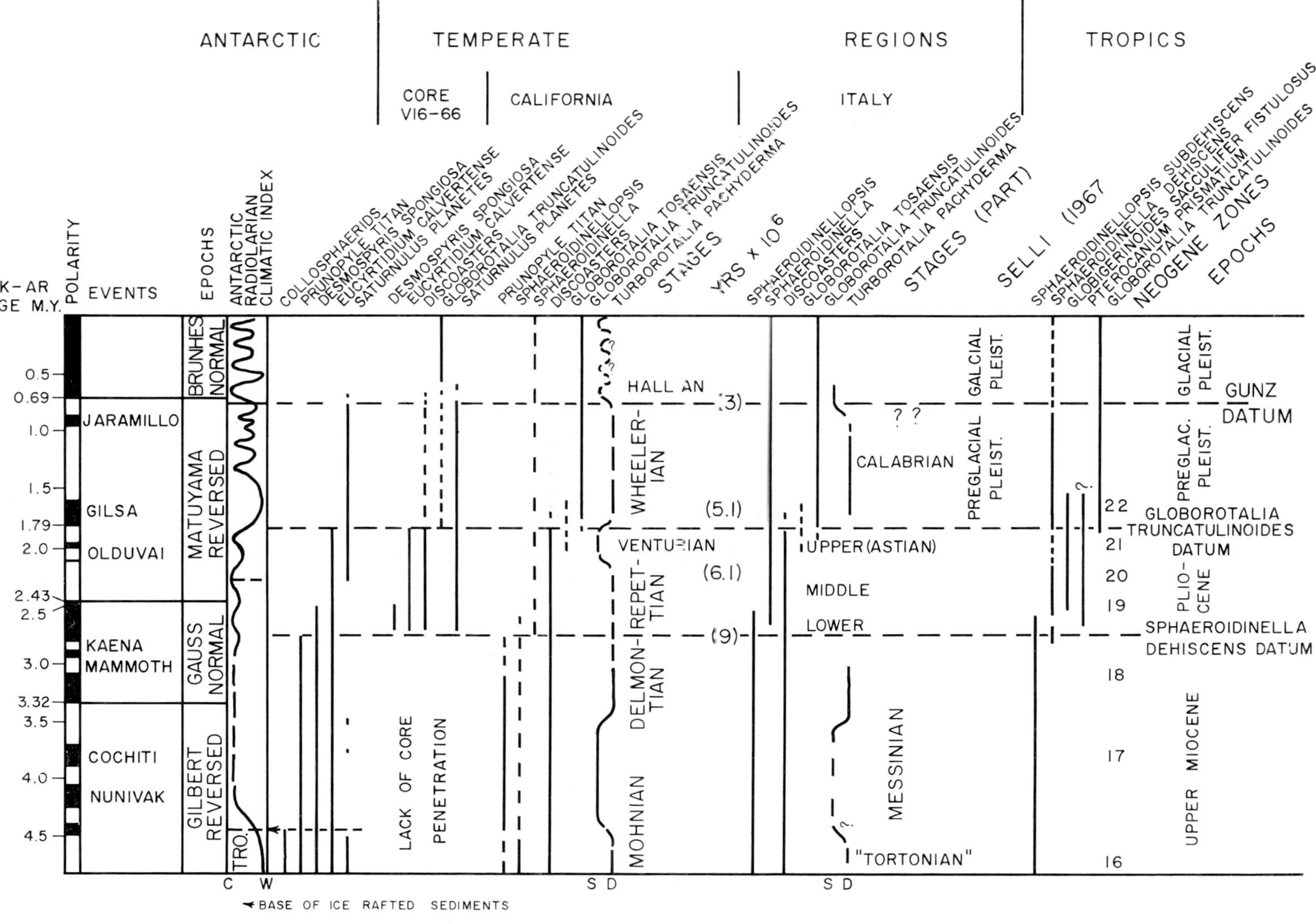

Fig. 15. Correlation of major Neogene planktonic events, from the Antarctic to the tropics. In the temperate area, data for core V16-66 are from *Glass et al.* [1967], that for California is from *Bandy and Ingle* [1970], and in Italy the usage of *Selli* [1967] is employed for preglacial Pleistocene and glacial Pleistocene. The antarctic and tropical zonation is that of *Cox* [1969]. S = sinistrally coiled, D = dextrally coiled. This summary correlation chart is modified from *Bandy and Casey* [1969]. Radiometric dates for the California section are from *Bandy and Ingle* [1970]: the 3 million year date is by *Obradovich* [1965, 1968], the 5.1 million year date is by Geochron on the Bailey ash of Balcom Canyon [*Ingle*, 1967], the 6.1 million year date is on the upper Repetto Formation of Malaga Cove, California, by *Obradovich* [1968], and the 9 million year figure is an extrapolated age for the *S. dehiscens* datum plane of California in view of a glass date by Geochron of about 10 million years just below this datum [*Bandy*, 1967*a*; *Ingle*, 1967].

dates, the *Globorotalia truncatulinoides* datum plane of California is about 8 or 9 million years before the present, which would place it well below the upper Miocene boundary. The contradictory nature of potassium-argon dates, especially those of minerals from marine strata, suggests that the planktonic sequences provide a more reasonable means of correlation. Additional kinds of radiometric dating are needed from marine strata for clarification of the inconsistencies of potassium-argon ratios. This problem is pointed out in the recent study of *Dymond* [1969].

With the close correlation of magnetic and planktonic events [*Hays and Opdyke*, 1967; *Glass et al.*, 1967; *Hays et al.*, 1969; etc.], it is clear that mutual corroboration of these two correlation methods exists. Studies of the magnetic scale of marine sections exposed on land are yet to be made in large part. Recently, *Nakagawa et al.* [1969] worked out the late Cenozoic geomagnetic chronology of the Bōsō-hantō (peninsula) in Japan. Their study is of considerable interest in that it presents seven magnetic epochs. The Kurotaki Formation, considered to be basal Pliocene in previous studies [*Asano*, 1962; *Aoki*, 1963; *Asano and Takayanagi*, 1965; *Matoba*, 1967], is located at the base of their magnetic epoch 6, and it is this horizon in which *Pulleniatina obliquiloculata* (perhaps *P. primalis*), *Globorotalia truncatulinoides* (perhaps *G. tosaensis*), and *Sphaeroidinella dehiscens* occur initially [*Aoki*, 1963, fig. 5]. It is to be expected that magnetic studies of a very thick section such as that of the Bōsō-hantō will reveal many more magnetic events than those recognized in the short compact sections of deep-sea cores.

Assuming that *Globorotalia tosaensis* is the form reported in the Kurotaki Formation and if the *Pulleniatina* is *P. obliquiloculata*, then these should be no older than the Gauss and lower Matuyama magnetic epochs. It would seem that magnetic epoch 3 of *Nakagawa et al.* [1969], as the Gauss, is correctly identified, number 4 is the Kaena event, number 5 is middle Gauss, number 6 is the Mammoth event, and number 7 is the basal Gauss. This would correlate the Miocene-Pliocene boundary with the base of the Mammoth event, which is also the base of the Kurotaki Formation. This would, if correct, bring the magnetic scale and the planktonic zonation into proper focus in terms of deep-sea stratigraphy. It is to be expected that events such as the Kaena and Mammoth, which are greatly abbreviated in deep-sea cores, will be much better developed and expanded in the very thick sections on land. Even in some deep-sea cores these events occasionally are much expanded [*Hays et al.*, 1969, Figure 9] relative to the normal parts of the Gauss. Thus, there is not necessarily any major contradiction between magnetic stratigraphy and planktonic events as yet.

Acknowledgments. Support for this study was provided by the National Science Foundation under grants GA-10204 and GB-8628. We are grateful to Mr. William Riedel of the Scripps Institution of Oceanography for discussions about the radiolarians and for making available sediment samples from the Pacific Ocean. We thank the National Science Foundation for assistance and for help in making available cores from the *Eltanin* program in the Antarctic. Core samples of V12-5 were provided by the Lamont-Doherty Geological Observatory. Foraminiferal and radiolarian illustrations were made by Ramil C. Wright in the Central Electron Microscope Laboratory of the University of Illinois. The instrument used, the Cambridge Stereoscan Mark II, was purchased by funds from NSF (NSF GA-1239), PHS (PH FR-07030), and the Illinois University Research Board. We thank Dr. B. V. Hall, Director of the CEM Laboratory, and Dr. W. W. Hay, L. Dryer, R. Harmer, and Mrs. O. Stayton for aid and assistance.

This is contribution 218 of the Department of Geological Sciences, University of Southern California, Los Angeles, California.

REFERENCES

Aoki, N., Pliocene and Pleistocene foraminifera from along the Yoro River, Boso Peninsula, *Sci. Repts. Tokyo Kyoiku Daigaku, Sect. C., 8*(78), 203–227, 1963.

Asano, K., Faunal change of planktonic foraminifera through the Neogene of Japan, *Koninkl. Nederl. Akad. Wetensch. Amsterdam, Proc., Ser. B, 65*(1), 1–16, 1962.

Asano, K., and Y. Takayanagi, Stratigraphic significance of the planktonic foraminifera from Japan, *Sci. Repts. Tohoku Univ., Ser. 2* (Geology), *37*(1), 1–14, 1965.

Asano, K., J. C. Ingle, Jr., and Y. Takayanagi, Neogene planktonic foraminiferal sequence in northeastern Japan, *Proceedings First International Conference on Planktonic Microfossils, Geneva*, vol. 1, edited by P. Bronnimann and H. H. Renz, pp. 14–25, E. J. Brill, Leiden, 1969.

Bandy, O. L., The geologic significance of coiling ratios in the foraminifer *Globigerina pachyderma* (Ehrenberg), *Geol. Soc. Am. Bull., 70*(12-2), 1708, 1959.

Bandy, O. L., Planktonic foraminiferal criteria for paleoclimatic zonation, *Sci. Repts. Tohoku Univ., Ser. 2* (Geology), Spec. Vol. 4, 1–8, 1960*a*.

Bandy, O. L., The geologic significance of coiling ratios in the foraminifer *Globigerina pachyderma* (Ehrenberg), *J. Paleontol., 34*(4), 671–681, 1960*b*.

Bandy, O. L., Miocene-Pliocene boundary in the Philippines as related to late Tertiary stratigraphy of deep-sea sediments, *Science, 142*(3597), 1290–1292, 1963.

Bandy, O. L., Cenozoic planktonic foraminiferal zonation, *Micropaleontology, 10*(1), 1–17, 1964.

Bandy, O. L., Problems of Tertiary foraminiferal and radiolarian zonation, circum-Pacific area, *Eleventh Pacific Science Congress, Tokyo, Japan, August, 1966, Symposium 25, Tertiary Correlations and Climatic Changes in the Pacific*, pp. 95–102, Sasaki, Sendai, Japan, 1967*a*.

Bandy, O. L., Foraminiferal definition of the boundaries of the Pleistocene in Southern California, U.S.A., *Progress in Oceanography*, vol. 4, edited by M. Sears, pp. 27–49, Pergamon, New York, 1967*b*.

Bandy, O. L., Paleoclimatology and Neogene planktonic foraminiferal zonation, *Giorn. Geol., Ser. 2, 35*(2), 277–290, 1968*a*.

Bandy, O. L., Cycles in Neogene paleoceanography and eustatic changes, *Palaeogeog., Palaeoclimatol., Palaeoecol., 5*, 63–75, 1968*b*.

Bandy, O. L., Relationships of Neogene planktonic foraminifera to paleoceanography and correlation, *Proceedings First International Conference on Planktonic Microfossils, Geneva*, vol. 1, edited by P. Bronnimann and H. H. Renz, pp. 46–57, E. J. Brill, Leiden, 1969.

Bandy, O. L., E. A. Butler, and R. C. Wright, Alaskan upper Miocene marine glacial deposits and the *Turborotalia pachyderma* datum plane, *Science, 166*(3905), 607–609, 1969.

Bandy, O. L., and R. E. Casey, Major late Cenozoic planktonic datum planes, Antarctica to the Tropics, *Antarctic J. U. S., 4*(5), 170–171, 1969.

Bandy, O. L., and J. C. Ingle, Jr., Neogene planktonic events and radiometric scale, California, in Radiometric dating and paleontological correlation, edited by O. L. Bandy, *Geol. Soc. Am. Spec. Paper 124*, 133–174, 1970.

Bandy, O. L., J. C. Ingle, Jr., and W. E. Frerichs, Isomorphism in *Sphaeroidinella and Sphaeroidinellopsis, Micropaleontology, 13*(4), 483–488, 1967.

Bandy, O. L., and M. E. Wade, Miocene-Pliocene-Pleistocene boundaries in deep-water environments, *Progress in Oceanography*, vol. 4, edited by M. Sears, pp. 51–66, Pergamon, New York, 1967.

Banner, F. T., and W. H. Blow, Progress in the planktonic foraminiferal biostratigraphy of the Neogene, *Nature, 208* (5016), 1164–1166, 1965.

Banner, F. T., and W. H. Blow, The origin, evolution and taxonomy of the foraminiferal genus *Pulleniatina* Cushman, 1927, *Micropaleontology, 13*(2), 133–162, 1967.

Bé, A. W. H., Ecology of Recent planktonic foraminifera, part 2, Bathymetric and seasonal distributions in the Sargasso Sea off Bermuda, *Micropaleontology, 6*, 373–392, 1960.

Bé, A. W. H., The influence of depth on shell growth in *Globigerinoides sacculifer* (Brady), *Micropaleontology, 11* (1), 81–97, 1965.

Bé, A. W. H., Planktonic foraminifera, *Antarctic Map Folio Series, Folio 11*, pp. 9–12, American Geographical Society, New York, 1969.

Beard, J. H., Pleistocene paleotemperature record based on planktonic foraminifers, Gulf of Mexico, *Trans. Gulf Coast Assoc. Geol. Soc., 19*, 535–553, 1969.

Berggren, W. A., Micropaleontology and the Pliocene/Pleistocene boundary in a deep-sea core from the south-central north Atlantic, *Giorn. Geol., Ser. 2, 35*(2), 291–312, 1968.

Berggren, W. A., Rates of evolution in some Cenozoic planktonic foraminifera, *Micropaleontology, 15*(3), 351–365, 1969.

Berggren, W. A., J. D. Phillips, A. Bertels, and D. Wall, Late Pliocene-Pleistocene stratigraphy in deep-sea cores from south-central North Atlantic, *Nature, 216*, 253–254, 1967.

Bertolani Marchetti, D., Vegetational features in sediments of Messinian 'Formazione gessoso-solfifera' in Emilia and Sicily (Italy) and paleoclimatic problems, *Intern. Geol. Congr., 23rd, Czechoslovakia, Abstr.*, 271, 1968.

Blow, W. H., Age, correlation, and biostratigraphy of the upper Tocuyo (San Lorenzo) and Pozon formations, eastern Falcon, Venezuela, *Bull. Am. Paleontol., 39*(178), 67–251, 1959.

Blow, W. H., Late middle Eocene to Recent planktonic foraminiferal biostratigraphy, *Proceedings First International Conference on Planktonic Microfossils, Geneva*, vol. 1, edited by P. Bronnimann and H. H. Renz, pp. 199–421, E. J. Brill, Leiden, 1969.

Bolli, H. M., Planktonic foraminifera from the Oligocene-Miocene Cipero and Lengua formations of Trinidad, B. W. I., *U. S. Natl. Museum Bull., 215*, 97–123, 1957.

Bolli, H. M., Observations on the stratigraphic distribution of some warm water planktonic foraminifera in the young Miocene to Recent, *Eclogae Geol. Helvet., 57*(2), 541–552, 1964.

Bolli, H. M., Zonation of Cretaceous to Pliocene marine sediments based on planktonic foraminifera, *Venez. Geol. Min. Petrol., Bol. Inf., 9*(1), 3–32, 1966.

Campbell, A. S., and R. L. Clark, Miocene radiolarian faunas from southern California, 76 pp., *Geol. Soc. Am. Spec. Paper 51*, 1944.

Cati, F., M. L. Colalongo, U. Crescenti, S. D'Onofrio, U. Follador, C. Pirini Raddrizzani, A. Pomesano Cherchi, G. Salvatorini, S. Sartoni, I. Premoli Silva, F. C. Wezel, V. Bertolino, G. Bizon, H. M. Bolli, A. M. Borsetti Cati, L. Dondi, H. Feinberg, D. G. Jenkins, E. Perconig, M. Sampo, R. Sprovieri, Biostratigrafia del Neogene mediterraneo basata sui foraminiferi planctonici, *Boll. Soc. Geol. Ital., 87*, 491–503, 1968.

Cox, A., Geomagnetic reversals, *Science, 163*(3864), 237–245, 1969.

Denton, G. H., and R. L. Armstrong, Miocene-Pliocene glaciations in southern Alaska, *Am. J. Sci., 267*, 1121–1142, 1969.

Donahue, J. G., Diatoms as indicators of Pleistocene climatic fluctuations in the Pacific sector of the southern ocean, in *Progress in Oceanography*, vol. 4, edited by M. Sears, pp. 133–140, Pergamon, New York, 1967.

Dondi, L., and I. Papetti, Biostratigraphical zones of Po Valley Pliocene, *Giorn. Geol., Ser. 2, 35*(3), 63–98, 1968.

Dymond, J., Age determinations of deep-sea sediments: A comparison of three methods, *Earth Planet. Sci. Lett., 6*, 9–14, 1969.

Emiliani, C., T. Mayeda, and R. Selli, Paleotemperature analysis of the Plio-Pleistocene section at Le Castella, Calabria, southern Italy, *Geol. Soc. Am. Bull., 72*, 679–688, 1961.

Ericson, D. B., Coiling direction of *Globigerina pachyderma* as a climatic index, *Science, 130*(3369), 219–220, 1959.

Ericson, D. B., M. Ewing, and G. Wollin, Pliocene-Pleistocene boundary in deep-sea sediments, *Science, 139*(3556), 727–737, 1963.

Ericson, D. B., M. Ewing, and G. Wollin, The Pleistocene epoch in deep-sea sediments, *Science, 146*, 723–732, 1964.

Ericson, D. B., and G. Wollin, Correlation of six cores from the equatorial Atlantic and the Caribbean, *Deep-Sea Res., 3*, 104–125, 1956*a*.

Ericson, D. B., and G. Wollin, Micropaleontological and isotopic determinations of Pleistocene climates, *Micropaleontology, 2*(3), 257–270, 1956*b*.

Ericson, D. B., and G. Wollin, Pleistocene climates and chronology in deep-sea sediments, *Science, 162*, 1227–1234, 1968.

Ericson, D. B., G. Wollin, and J. Wollin, Coiling direction of *Globorotalia truncatulinoides* in deep-sea cores, *Deep-Sea Res., 2*(2), 152–158, 1954.

Friend, J. K., and W. R. Riedel, Cenozoic orosphaerid radiolarians from tropical Pacific sediments, *Micropaleontology, 13*(2), 217–232, 1967.

Glass, B., D. B. Ericson, B. C. Heezen, N. D. Opdyke, and J. A. Glass, Geomagnetic reversals and Pleistocene chronology, *Nature, 216*, 437–442, 1967.

Hay, W. W., H. P. Mohler, P. H. Roth, R. R. Schmidt, and J. E. Boudreaux, Calcareous nannoplankton zonation of the Cenozoic of the Gulf Coast and Caribbean-Antillean area and transoceanic correlation, *Trans. Gulf Coast Assoc. Geol. Soc., 17*, 428–480, 1967.

Hays, J. D., Radiolaria and late Tertiary and Quaternary history of Antarctic seas, *Biology of Antarctic Seas II, Antarctic Res. Ser. 5*, edited by George Llano, pp. 125–184, American Geophysical Union, Washington, D. C., 1965.

Hays, J. D., Quaternary sediments of the Antarctic Ocean, in *Progress in Oceanography*, vol. 4, edited by M. Sears, pp. 117–131, Pergamon, New York, 1967.

Hays, J. D., and N. D. Opdyke, Antarctic radiolaria, magnetic reversals, and climatic change, *Science, 158*(3804), 1001–1011, 1967.

Hays, J. D., T. Saito, N. D. Opdyke, and L. H. Burckle, Pliocene-Pleistocene sediments of the equatorial Pacific: their paleomagnetic, biostratigraphic, and climatic record, *Geol. Soc. Am. Bull., 80*, 1481–1514, 1969.

Iaccarino, S., and G. Papani, La trasgressione del Pliocene inferiore ('Tabianiano') sul Tortoniano del Colle di Vigoleno (Piacenza), *Riv. Ital. Paleontol., 73*(2), 679–700, 1967.

Ikebe, N., A synoptical table on the Quaternary stratigraphy of Japan, *J. Geosciences, Osaka City Univ., 12*(4), 45–51, 1969.

Ingle, J. C., Jr., Foraminiferal biofacies variation and the Miocene-Pliocene boundary in southern California, *Bull. Am. Paleontol., 52*(236), 217–394, 1967.

Jenkins, D. G., Recent distribution, origin, and coiling ratio changes in *Globorotalia pachyderma* (Ehrenberg), *Micro-Paleontol., 52*(236), 217–394, 1967.

Kennett, J. P., *Globorotalia truncatulinoides* as a paleo-oceanographic index, *Science, 159*, 1461–1463, 1968*a*.

Kennett, J. P., Latitudinal variation in *Globigerina pachyderma* (Ehrenberg) in surface sediments of the southwest Pacific Ocean, *Micropaleontology, 14*(3), 305–318, 1968*b*.

Kennett, J. P., Paleo-oceanographic aspects of the foraminiferal zonation in the upper Miocene-lower Pliocene of New Zealand, *Giorn. Geol., Ser. 2, 35*(3), 143–156, 1968*c*.

Kennett, J. P., Foraminiferal studies of southern ocean deep-sea cores, *Antarctic J. U. S., 4*(5), 178–179, 1969.

Lamb, J. L., Planktonic foraminiferal datums and late Neogene epoch boundaries in the Mediterranean, Caribbean, and Gulf of Mexico, *Trans. Gulf Coast Assoc. Geol. Soc., 19*, 559–578, 1969.

Lona, F., Prime analisi pollinologiche sui depositi Terziari-Quarternari di Castell'Arquato, *Boll. Soc. Geol. Ital., 81*, 89–91, 1962.

Martin, G. C., *Radiolaria*, Maryland Geologic Survey, Miocene, pp. 447–459, 1904.

Matoba, Y., Younger Cenozoic foraminiferal assemblages from the Choshi District, Chiba Prefecture, *Sci. Repts. Tohoku Univ., Ser. 2, 38*(2), 221–263, 1967.

Nakagawa, H., N. Niitsuma, and I. Hayasaka, Late Cenozoic geomagnetic chronology of the Boso Peninsula, *J. Geol. Soc. Japan, 75*(5), 267–280, 1969.

Obradovich, J. D., Age of the marine Pleistocene of California, *Bull. Am. Assoc. Petrol. Geol., 49*(7), 1087, 1965.

Obradovich, J. D., The potential use of glauconite for late-Cenozoic geochronology, in *Means of Correlation of Quaternary Successions*, vol. 8, edited by R. M. Morrison and H. E. Wright, Jr., pp. 267–279, University of Utah Press, 1968.

Opdyke, N. D., B. Glass, J. D. Hays, and J. Foster, Paleomagnetic study of Antarctic deep-sea cores, *Science, 154*, 349–357, 1966.

Parker, F. L., Late Tertiary biostratigraphy (planktonic foraminifera) of tropical Indo-Pacific deep-sea cores, *Bull. Am. Paleontol., 52*(235), 115–203, 1967.

Phillips, J. D., W. A. Berggren, A. Bertels, and D. Wall, Paleomagnetic stratigraphy and micropaleontology of three deep-sea cores from the south-central North Atlantic, *Earth Planet. Sci. Lett., 4*(2), 118–130, 1968.

Richmond, G. M., Comparison of the Quaternary stratigraphy of the Alps and Rocky Mountains, 17 pp., presidential address at the 8th INQUA Congress, Paris, August 30-September 5, 1969.

Riedel, W. R., and B. M. Funnell, Tertiary sediment cores and microfossils from the Pacific Ocean floor, *Geol. Soc. London, Quart. J., 120*(3), 305–368, 1964.

Rutford, R. H., C. Craddock, and T. W. Bastien, Possible late Tertiary glaciation, Jones Mountains, Antarctica (abstract), *Program 1965 Ann. Meeting, Geol. Soc. Am.*, 142, 1965.

Selli, R., The Mayer-Eymar Messinian 1867 proposal for a neostratotype, *Intern. Geol. Congr., 21st, Norden, 1960*, part 28, 311–333, 1964.

Selli, R., The Pliocene-Pleistocene boundary in Italian marine sections and its relationship to continental stratigraphies, in *Progress in Oceanography*, vol. 4, edited by M. Sears, pp. 67–86, Pergamon, New York, 1967.

Selli, R., and E. Tongiorgi, Working Group: Absolute age, *Committee on Mediterranean Neogene Stratigraphy, 4th Congress, Bologna*, September 19–30, pp. 1–6, 1967.

Turner, D. L., Potassium-argon dates concerning the Tertiary foraminiferal time scale and San Andreas fault displacement, 99 pp., Ph.D. dissertation, University of California, Berkeley, 1968.

Wolfe, J. A., and D. M. Hopkins, Climatic changes recorded by Tertiary land floras in northwestern North America, *Eleventh Pacific Science Congress, Tokyo, Japan, August, 1966, Symposium 25, Tertiary Correlations and Climatic Changes in the Pacific*, pp. 67–76, Sasaki, Sendai, Japan, 1967.

Yeats, R. S., Pliocene seaknoll at South Mountain, Ventura basin, California, *Am. Assoc. Petrol. Geol. Bull., 49*(5), 526–546, 1965.

Yeats, R. S., W. A. McLaughlin, and G. Edwards, K-Ar mineral age of ash bed in Pico formation, Ventura basin, California, *Am. Assoc. Petrol. Geol. Bull., 51*(3), 486, 1967.

FERROMANGANESE DEPOSITS OF THE SOUTH PACIFIC OCEAN, DRAKE PASSAGE, AND SCOTIA SEA

H. G. GOODELL, M. A. MEYLAN, AND B. GRANT

Florida State University, Tallahassee, Florida 32306

Abstract. Bottom photography, dredging, and coring by the *Eltanin* have established the distribution, nature, and chemical and mineralogical character of fields of ferromanganese concretions in the South Pacific Ocean, Drake Passage, and the Scotia Sea (Southern Ocean). A continuous belt of ferromanganese concretions lies beneath the Antarctic Convergence at 60°S latitude on all types of sediment and in all depths of water. This field, and others north and south of it, is associated with volcanics and evidence of bottom currents. Concretion morphology is dependent on the number and arrangement of nucleation sites, proximity to element sources, and currents. The principal Mn mineral is todorokite with minor birnessite; Fe occurs in large part as amorphous or cryptocrystalline hydrated ferric oxide with minor goethite and maghemite. Concretion-incorporated detrital minerals that increase in importance toward Antarctica consist principally of quartz, feldspar, ferromagnesian, and clay minerals. A Mn-(chalcophile) related suite of elements consisting of Ni, Mo, Cu, Co, and Sn delineates a geochemical province in the Southwest Pacific Basin. An Fe-(lithophile) related suite of elements that consists of Ti, V, Zn, Co, Ba, and Sr dominates the Albatross Cordillera (Pacific-Antarctic Ridge). Both suites are found along the Albatross Cordillera and Chile Rise. Except for Zr, which is clearly derived from the Antarctic Continent, the elements comprising the concretions are derived principally from volcanic sources and moved by bottom currents, coprecipitating en route. Their formation probably exceeds 60 mm per 1000 yr.

INTRODUCTION

The first twenty-seven cruises of the *Eltanin* have produced 552 piston cores, 380 dredge hauls, and almost 7000 bottom photographs at 526 stations from 27°W to 154°E longitude and from 33°S to 78°S latitude. Ferromanganese concretions of a size suitable for analysis were recovered in 83 (15%) of the cores and 122 (32%) of the dredge hauls and observed at about 20% of the camera stations. 'Ferromanganese concretion' is used as a general term covering a wide variety of morphological forms containing as major constituents hydrated oxides of Fe and Mn. Other authors have used equivalent terms: manganese nodules, manganese-iron concretions, manganous-iron-oxide nodules, and the like. This paper reports on the occurrence, distribution, morphology, mineralogy, and geochemistry of the ferromanganese deposits from the South Pacific Ocean, the Drake Passage, and the Scotia Sea.

PREVIOUS WORK

The voyage of the *Challenger* (1873–1876) produced the first deep-sea ferromanganese concretions [*Thomson*, 1874; *Murray*, 1876]. *Murray and Renard* [1891] pointed out that, based on their chemical analyses, these nodules should be classed as 'wad or bog manganese ore' and, therefore, were related to psilomelane. They summarized the current opinions of nodule genesis as: (1) inorganic precipitation of elements derived from submarine volcanics; (2) reduction of metal sulfates in sea water by organic matter with subsequent oxidation and precipitation; (3) precipitation from submarine spring emanations; and (4) precipitation of metal oxides derived from dissolved metal bicarbonates in sea water. With only slight modification to include the sediment-water system and hydrothermal activity, there is today a growing consensus that these mechanisms are not necessarily alternatives or mutually exclusive. However, for any one particular deposit in a specific geographic area or environment of deposition, one of the mechanisms probably dominates [*Goldberg*, 1954; *Graham and Cooper*, 1959; *Pettersson*, 1959; *Niino*, 1959; *Arrhenius*, 1963; *Arrhenius and Bonatti*, 1965; *Arrhenius et al.*, 1964; *Bonatti and Nayudu*, 1965; *Lynn and Bonatti*, 1965; *Goodell*, 1965, 1967*b*; *Manheim*,

TABLE 1. Manganese Minerals Reported from Ferromanganese Concretions

Mineral	Formula
10 Å Manganite	$3MnO_2 \cdot Mn(OH)_2 \cdot 3H_2O$
Todorokite	$(Mn^2, R, R^2, R^3)_2\ Mn_5{}^4O_{12} \cdot 3H_2O$
7 Å Manganite	$4MnO_2 \cdot Mn(OH)_2 \cdot 2H_2O_4$
Birnessite	$(Mn^2, R, R^2, R^3)_2\ Mn_7{}^4O_{16} \cdot 2H_2O$
δ-MnO_2-Birnessite Cryptocrystalline	$(Na, Ca)\ Mn_7O_{14}\ 2 \cdot 8H_2O$
γ-MnO_2-Nsutite	$Mn_{1-x}Mn_xO_{2-2x}(OH)_{2x}$
β-MnO_2-Pyrolusite	MnO_2
Ramsdellite	MnO_2
Psilomelane	$(Ba, R_9)O_{18} \cdot 2H_2O(Mn^2Mn^4)$
Rancieite	$(CaMn^2)Mn_4{}^4O_9 \cdot 3H_2O$

Sources: *Buser and Grütter* [1956]; *Hewett and Fleischer* [1960]; *Frondel et al.* [1960]; *Bricker* [1965].

1965; *Boström and Peterson,* 1966; *Bonatti and Joensuu,* 1966; *Price,* 1967].

Most of the chemical and mineralogical data from which this consensus is emerging have been accumulated only in the last twenty years, although occurrences of ferromanganese deposits have continued to be reported since the *Challenger* voyage with a regularity that seems to be a function of the number of oceanographic ships at sea.

The Pacific deposits are the best known, as a result of the voyages of the *Albatross* [*Agassiz,* 1901, 1906; *Murray and Lee,* 1909]; the Mid-Pacific Expedition [*Dietz,* 1955; *Hamilton,* 1956]; the Downwind Expedition [*Menard and Shipek,* 1958]; the cruises of the *Vitiaz* [*Skornyakova,* 1960]; the Wahine Expedition [*Moore and Heath,* 1966]; and the continuing voyages of the *Eltanin* [*Goodell,* 1964, 1965, 1967*b*]. The Pacific occurrences, summarized by *Menard* [1964] and *Mero* [1965], are unique in that concretions cover large areas of the sea floor, often with high density, estimated at 20–30% in the southwestern Pacific [*Menard and Shipek,* 1958], 10% in the northeastern Pacific [*Skornyakova,* 1960; *Mero,* 1960], and up to 100% across the South Pacific beneath the Antarctic Convergence [*Goodell,* 1967*b*]. Although occurrences outside the Pacific basin are more rare, ferromanganese deposits appear ubiquitous in almost all marine and many nonmarine environments [*Mero,* 1965; *Manheim,* 1965; *Beals,* 1966; *Price,* 1967; *Rossman and Callender,* 1968].

Ferromanganese concretions consist of an intimate admixture of authigenic and detrital mineral components in varying proportions. The authigenic mineralogy is dominated by both amorphous and crystalline hydrated oxides of Mn and Fe in varying oxidation states. *Feitknecht and Marti* [1945] and *Buser et al.* [1954] synthesized Mn oxides in the laboratory. A comparison of these synthetic phases with ferromanganese oxides found in Mn nodules permitted a mineralogic model to be constructed [*Buser and Grütter,* 1956; *Grütter and Buser,* 1957; and *Buser,* 1959]. Three basic crystalline phases were recognized: δ-MnO_2, 7-Å manganite, and 10-Å manganite. δ-MnO_2 consists of disordered sheets of Mn(IV) dioxide in units as small as 50–100 Å. The manganites are double-layer structures; one of the layers is an ordered Mn(IV) dioxide unit, and the alternate layer is comprised of disordered Fe or Mn hydroxide in which calcium, sodium, and other ions partially substitute for Fe and Mn. When Fe hydroxide predominates in the disordered manganite layer, the layer is called a ferric manganite; when Mn hydroxide predominates, a manganous manganite results. A difference in thickness of the disordered manganite sheet produces different basal spacings. A 10-Å manganite contains two discrete OH and/or H_2O layers, whereas 7-Å Mn contains only one (OH or H_2O) such layer. *Buser* [1959] considered δ-MnO_2 to be the most oxidized, followed by 7-Å manganite, with 10-Å manganite, which is the most hydrated, being the least oxidized. *Glemser et al.* [1961] recognized three varieties of 7-Å manganites based on degree of crystallinity (X-ray peak broadening) and considered these, as well as those having no basal 7-Å X-ray reflections, as δ-MnO_2. More recent work by *Bricker* [1965] casts some doubt on the concepts of disordered manganites and oxidation-sensitive structures. *Bricker* [1965] and *Manheim* [1965] consider δ-MnO_2 and some 7-Å manganites to be identical with birnessite [*Jones and Milne,* 1956]. On the other hand, the Mn-oxide mineral todorokite has been given structural formulas similar to 10-Å manganites [*Frondel et al.,* 1960] (Table 1). This study recognizes a threefold division of Mn mineral phases based on X-ray diffraction patterns: (1) 10-Å manganite, probably equivalent to todorokite; (2) 7-Å manganite, probably equivalent to birnessite; and (3) δ-MnO_2, probably a 7-Å manganite, which is so very fine grained as to preclude basal X-ray spacings.

Ferromanganese concretion mineralogy was first reported by *Buser and Grütter* [1956], *Grütter and Buser* [1957], and *Buser* [1959], as consisting of δ-MnO_2, 7-Å manganite, and 10-Å manganite. *Burns and Fuerstenau* [1966] and *Barnes* [1967] also recognized these phases. *Barnes* [1967] suggested that the minerals were depth-dependent, δ-MnO_2 being the low-pressure (shallow) variety. However, these mineralogic relationships are at odds with reported O/Mn ratios that increase with depth [*Riley and Sinhaseni*, 1958; *Manheim*, 1965; *Price*, 1967] and therefore should indicate a predominance of δ-MnO_2 in deeper water.

Some workers favor use of recognized mineral names for the Mn minerals of concretions. Todorokite has been reported most commonly as a deep-sea Mn mineral [*Hewett et al.*, 1963; *Manheim*, 1965; *Sorem*, 1967; *Meylan and Goodell*, 1967; *Meylan*, 1968]. The latter four references also report birnessite in concretions.

Other Mn oxides detected include psilomelane [*Murata and Erd*, 1964]; a form of ramsdellite [*Manheim*, 1965], which is now believed to be nsutite (Manheim, written communication, 1968); rancieite [*Sorem*, 1967], and nsutite [*Gattow and Glemser*, 1961].

The crystalline Fe phases have usually been reported as goethite [*Buser*, 1959] with minor maghemite [*Meylan and Goodell*, 1967; *Meylan*, 1968], although X-ray amorphous hydrated Fe oxides seem to dominate [*Grütter and Buser*, 1957; *Arrhenius and Korkisch*, 1959; *Arrhenius*, 1963; *Meylan and Goodell*, 1967; *Meylan*, 1968]. *Burns and Fuerstenau* [1966] indicated that Fe-hydroxide-δ-MnO_2 sheets alternate. *Goldberg and Arrhenius* [1958] hypothesized that such an alternation of layers might have genetic significance, with Fe hydroxides serving as a catalytic surface for precipitation of Mn oxides. Both Fe- and Mn-hydrated oxide phases are extremely fine-grained with surface areas of from 6 to 190 m^2/g [*Buser and Grütter*, 1956].

Authigenic minerals other than Mn and Fe oxides that have been reported include clay minerals, zeolites, barite, celestite, apatite, aragonite, calcite, opal, rutile, anatase, and possibly feldspar and quartz [*Murray and Renard*, 1891; *Riley and Sinhaseni*, 1958; *Goldberg and Arrhenius*, 1958; *Arrhenius*, 1963; *Mero*, 1965; *Manheim*, 1965; *Meylan and Goodell*, 1967; *Grant*, 1967; *Meylan*, 1968].

The Fe- and Mn- hydrated oxides are usually precipitated on a macronucleus such as ice-rafted erratics, volcanic fragments, animal hard parts, and even brass shell fragments; micronodules (1 mm and less) are nucleated on protozoan tests or silt and sand-sized clasts of terrestrial or submarine volcanic origin [*Murray and Renard*, 1891; *Goldberg and Arrhenius*, 1958; *Mero*, 1965].

The size of Mn concretions varies greatly. Micronodules less than 1 mm in diameter are very abundant in pelagic red clay [*Mero*, 1965]. Slabs many meters in extent can be seen in bottom photographs [*Menard and Shipek*, 1958; *Goodell*, 1964, 1965]. According to *Mero* [1965], concretions seen in bottom photographs generally average between 2 and 4 cm in diameter, and most of the concretions recovered by dredging do not exceed about 8 cm in diameter. *Menard* [1964] reported that spherical nodules range upward in size to about 20 cm, but that larger nodules assume flattened forms.

The over-all morphology of the concretion is generally set by the shape of the macronucleus. *Murray and Renard* [1891] divided ferromanganese concretions into three morphological groups: (1) more or less pyramidal or irregularly shaped; (2) spheroidal or ellipsoidal; and (3) flattened, mammillated, and irregular. *Grant* [1967] classified South Atlantic and South Pacific Ocean (Southern Ocean) concretions (based on nucleus size and shape, number of nuclei present, and on the external expression of these internal characteristics) into four morphological categories: nodules, botryoidals, agglomerates, and crusts. *Manheim* [1965] notes that shallow water concretions are often flattened and/or skirted, characteristics he attributes to precipitation of Mn at the sediment-water interface by Mn-rich waters from below.

In most ferromanganese concretions the internal structure is one of concentric shells, combined with radial dendrites, around a central nucleus or nuclei. Each shell is often varve like in that it consists of a dark high metal oxide layer and a lighter clayey, foraminiferal, or diatom/radiolarian layer, along which parting usually takes place [*Murray and Renard*, 1891; *Riley and Sinhaseni*, 1958; *Mero*, 1965]. In concretions where detrital minerals or other nonhydrous ferromanganese oxides are rare, internal structures show a 'fibrio-radiate disposition' [*Murray and Renard*, 1891]. These are sometimes septarian with the fractures filled with secondary mineralization and the like [*Menard*, 1964; *Manheim*, 1965].

Many authors have characterized the color of concretions as ranging from blue-black through reddish-brown to yellow-brown, with the darker colors having higher Mn concretions.

Detrital mineralogy, which may vary from less than 1% to more than 50%, has been reported as rock fragments, quartz, feldspars, ferromagnesian and other heavy minerals, clay minerals, volcanic shards, animal remains, and assorted artifacts [*Murray and*

Renard, 1891; *Riley and Sinhaseni*, 1958; *Goldberg and Arrhenius*, 1958; *Arrhenius*, 1963; *Mero*, 1965; *Manheim*, 1965; *Bonatti and Nayudu*, 1965; *Meylan and Goodell*, 1967; *Grant*, 1967; *Meylan*, 1968].

Hundreds of chemical analyses now exist for Fe, Mn, Ni, Co, and Cu concentrations in ferromanganese concretions that supplement the *Challenger* analyses of *Murray and Renard* [1891]. These analyses have permitted empirical element relationships to be noted via scatter diagrams or computed statistically: direct relationships of Mn-Ni, Mn-Cu, and Fe-Co [*Goldberg*, 1954; *Riley and Sinhaseni*, 1958; *Goodell*, 1967*b*], direct relationships of Fe-Ti [*Goldberg*, 1954], Cu-Ni [*Willis and Ahrens*, 1962; *Goodell*, 1967*b*], Mn-Mo [*Goldberg*, 1954], Fe-V [*Goldberg*, 1954], Mn-Pb [*Chow and Patterson*, 1962], and Mn-Th [*Goldberg and Picciotto*, 1955]. There has been little work attempted that would clarify the nature, role, and occurrence of trace elements within the mineralogic framework of the concretions. *Riley and Sinhaseni* [1958] concluded that Ba, Ti, and Zr occurred in barite, rutile, and zircon, the first two probably being authigenic [*Arrhenius*, 1963] and the third detrital. *Arrhenius* [1963] separated three phases on the basis of wet chemistry: (1) soluble and reducible by 1 *N* hydroxylamine (MnO_2); (2) HCl soluble; and (3) insoluble. The first was enriched in Cu; the first and second in Ni; the second in Co, Pb, Cr, and the rare earths; and Ti in the third. *Riley and Sinhaseni* [1958] found Zn, Cu, Ni, and Pb enriched in the soluble (in HCl) part of nodules, and *Burns* [1965] showed the affinity of Co with $FeO(OH) \cdot nH_2O$ in concretions. *Burns and Fuerstenau* [1966], using the electron probe, found Co enriched in δ-MnO_2 phases; Ti and Ca enriched in δ-MnO_2-FeOOH layers and Ni, Cu, Zn, Mg, Ba, Na, and K replacing Mn^{+2} in 10-Å manganite. *Barnes* [1967] found Co and Pb enriched in δ-MnO_2; Ni and Co in both 7-Å and 10-Å manganites, but rare earth concentrations independent of mineralogy. *A. M. Ehrlich* [1968] concluded that the rare earths were associated with the detrital mineral components. *Harriss et al.* [1968] attribute the noble element content of ferromanganese concretions to meteoritic sources.

There has been considerable speculation as to the nature and origin of the organic matter found in ferromanganese concretions. Most analyses reported the organic matter as carbon only; a few concretions have nitrogen in addition. *Thomas and Blumer* [1964] identified pyrene and fluoranthene in nodules from the Blake Plateau but noted that these are the two most abundant polynuclear hydrocarbons in sea water and could have been adsorbed during formation of the concretions. However, there is a possibility that the organic matter in concretions is the result of organisms living in or on the nodules. *Graham* [1959] and *Graham and Cooper* [1959], noting an affiliation of ferromanganese with organic matter in foraminiferal tests, argued that concretions originate through biochemical processes. *Price* [1967] summarized the available data and concluded that the organic matter in concretions was a function of the amount of organic matter in the environment in which the nodule was found.

Ehrlich [1963*a*, *b*, 1964], in a series of experiments, noted that bacteria that grow in the presence of a peptone might promote oxidation of Mn^2 in solution to MnO_2, which might adsorb Mn^2, which could, in turn, be oxidized. However, peptone concentrations are critical. *Trimble and Ehrlich* [1968] succeeded in culturing bacteria on crushed ferromanganese concretions, which reduce MnO_2 to $Mn(OH)_2$ when a suitable electron donor such as glucose is available. *H. L. Ehrlich* [1968] demonstrated the acceleration of Mn accretion to Mn oxides by an enzymatic step but found that oxygen and an absorbent such as Mn-Fe oxide are essential to such a reaction. He states that the cause of oxidation has not been directly determined.

In spite of the possible relevance of these experiments to the origin of ferromanganese concretions, the importance of bacterial intercession remains speculative and inconclusive.

The kinetics of concretion growth in the sea appear to vary a millionfold, based on U-Th disequilibrium and K-Ar methods: faster rates (10^4–10^6 mm/10^6 yr) are associated with shallow marine deposits [*Goldberg and Arrhenius*, 1958; *Manheim*, 1965] with pelagic rates clustering between 1–10 mm/10^6 yr [*Bender et al.*, 1966; *Goldberg*, 1961; *Ku and Broecker*, 1967; *Barnes and Dymond*, 1967]. The apparent extremely low depositional rates of deep water concretions are 10^3 to 10^4 times slower than rates of pelagic sedimentation [*Arrhenius*, 1963]. No feasible theory so far has been proposed to account for the fact that these sedimentation rates would preclude concretion formation, although there has been considerable speculation as to a role that benthic organisms or bottom currents might play in keeping concretions at the sediment-water interface [*Arrhenius*, 1963; *Mero*, 1965; *Goodell*, 1965; *Manheim*, 1965].

Sackett [1966] states that differential precipitation of TH^{230} and P^{231}, and postdepositional migration of U^{234}, Ra^{226}, and possibly TH^{230} in concretions, may render them useless for age determinations. These migrations had already been postulated in marine sediments [*Kroll*, 1954; *Koczy*, 1954; *Sackett*, 1964*a*, *b*; *Ku*, 1965]. Samples dated by K-Ar have utilized volcanic debris from concretion centers that may have excess argon [*Noble and Naughton*, 1968] but, in any event, these dates are only for the core alone and do not necessarily establish a rate of growth. There is considerable physical evidence, based on the internal colloform structures of most concretions, that suggests that deposition is sporadic [*Murray and Renard*, 1891; *Sorem*, 1967].

There are now sufficient data to support the fact that there are bathymetric and geographic differences in ferromanganese concretion geochemistry. Nearshore shallow water deposits appear to be enriched in Fe relative to Mn and markedly impoverished in most of the other metals relative to pelagic deposits [*Manheim*, 1965; *Price*, 1967]. These bathymetric relationships could be the result of differences in: (1) source (continental versus submarine volcanism) proximity; (2) the kinetics of oxidation and precipitation of Fe and Mn; (3) the apparent depositional rates between neritic and pelagic deposits; and (4) such other environmental parameters as amount and type of organic matter and biological metabolic processes.

Geographic parameters related to geochemical provinces control the metal content of ferromanganese concretions. *Mero* [1962], *Arrhenius* [1963], *Arrhenius et al.* [1964], *Arrhenius and Bonatti* [1965], and *Mero* [1965] showed areal differences both in Fe/Mn and in minor metal concentration that permitted elemental zonation of the Pacific basin: higher relative concentrations of Co, Cu, and Ni occur toward the center of the Pacific basin, high Mn and Fe zones being peripheral. *Goodell* [1968*a*] concluded that areas of high elemental concentration in the South Pacific were related to geochemical provinces and that changes in element ratios away from their primary sources were due to dispersion by currents and their dilution by continental detritus.

The arguments that remain over the origin of ferromanganese concretions revolve about (1) the relative importance of different elemental sources, i.e., continental versus submarine volcanic; (2) the mechanisms for dispersal of elements from source areas, including colloidal capacities and stabilities; (3) the coprecipitation of elements into a variety of mineral phases via precipitation from sea water, from the underlying sediment-water system, or through organic metabolism; (4) the role of minor elements in the host phases; and (5) the kinetics of precipitation, whether sporadic and episodic or constant.

BATHYMETRY AND CIRCULATION

Bathymetry

The sampled area includes all types of the major bathymetric elements of the ocean basins: a ridge-trench system, the Scotia Ridge and South Sandwich Trench; basins with moderately high relief; the East and West Scotia basins; an ill-defined rise in the Drake Passage; an abyssal plain with little relief, the Southeast Pacific Basin (Pacific-Antarctic Basin); the Albatross Cordillera (Pacific-Antarctic Ridge); another deep abyssal plain, the Southwest Pacific Basin, and a series of rises and basins between Australia-New Zealand and the Antarctic Continent, the Campbell Plateau (New Zealand Plateau), Campbell Spur (Campbell Rise), Hjort Basin, and Macquarie Ridge (Macquarie Rise) (Figure 1). This relief and structure, primarily the result of tectonism and volcanic activity, have been smoothed in the abyssal basins adjacent to the Antarctic Continent by sedimentation, although volcanic seamounts abound in the Southwest Pacific Basin, in parts of the Southeast Pacific Basin and in the Drake Passage and Scotia basins [*Zhivago*, 1962, 1967].

The mid-ocean ridge-rise system in the central South Pacific is a broad uplift, the Albatross Cordillera, that lacks a central rift comparable to that of the Mid-Atlantic Ridge, although its flanks are characterized by persistent ridge-and-trough topography probably produced by normal faulting [*Menard*, 1964]. It is offset by a number of transverse faults, the most prominent of which is centered at approximately 135°W longitude, 55°S latitude [*Pitman et al.*, 1968]. An apparent extension of this offset, known provisionally as the Eltanin Fracture Zone, crosses the Southeast Pacific Basin toward the Drake Passage [*Goodell*, 1965]. It is characterized in the center of that basin by a steep (7½°) scarp facing the Antarctic Continent [*Meylan*, 1966]. Another transverse feature, the Chile Rise, extends northwest-southeast from the Albatross Cordillera toward southern Chile. To the southwest, the Albatross Cordillera is seismically active and faulted into narrow asymmetrical ridges and troughs [*Ewing and Heezen*, 1956; *Menard*, 1964].

Circulation

The circulation of the South Atlantic, Pacific, and Indian oceans is dominated by the Antarctic Conver-

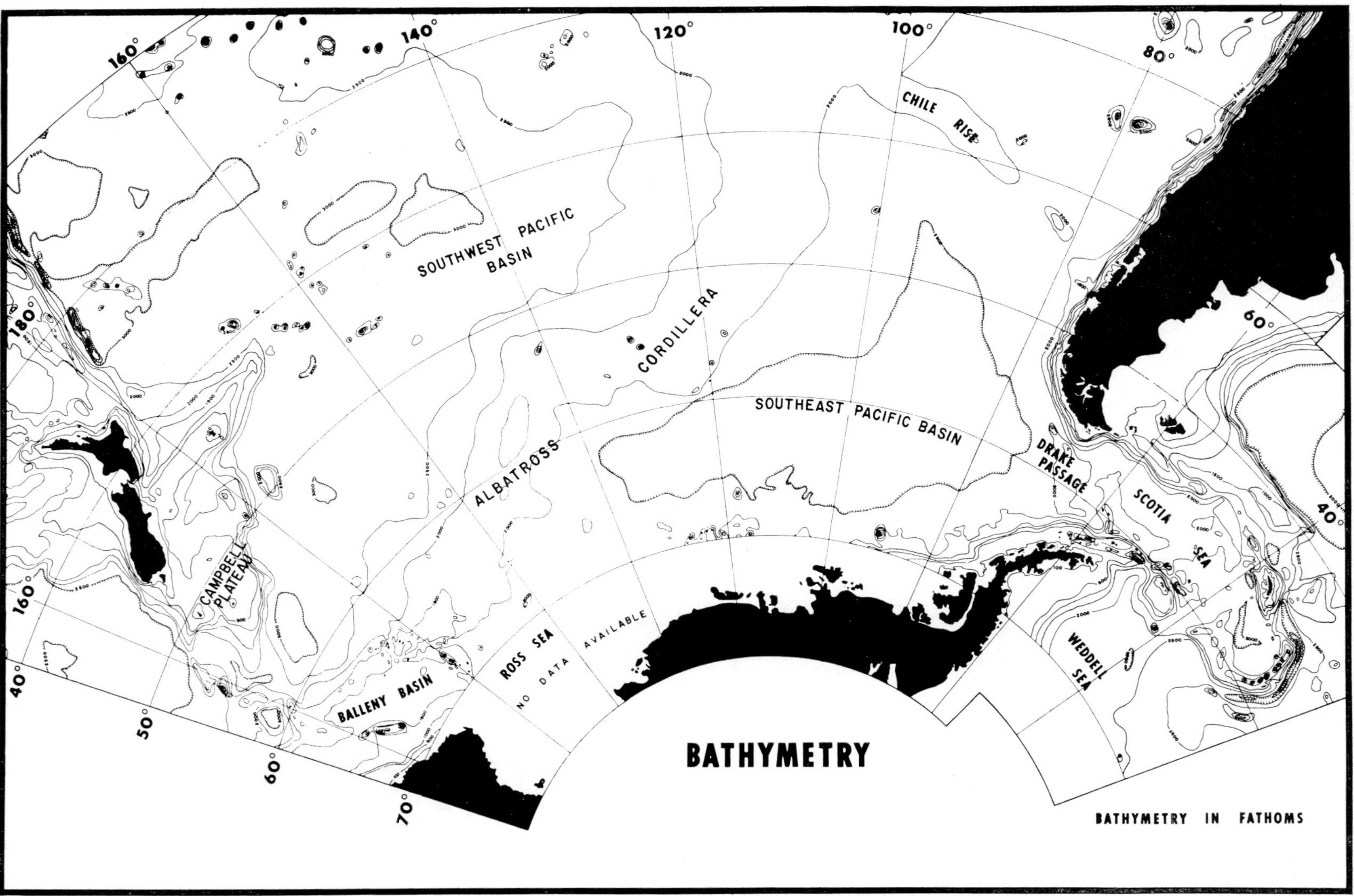

Fig. 1. Bathymetric elements of the South Pacific and South Atlantic oceans.

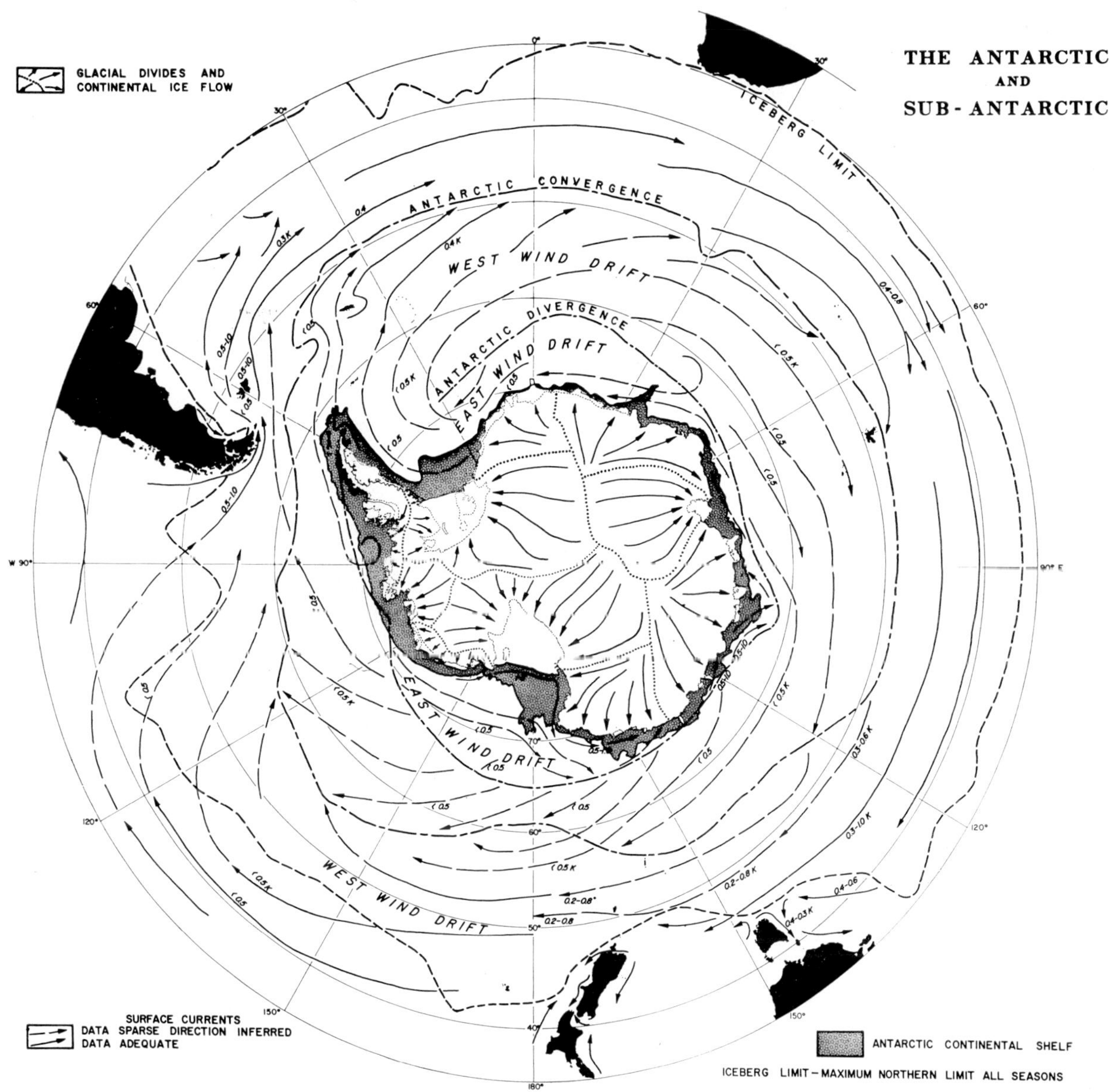

Fig. 2. Antarctic and subantarctic surface hydrography compiled after *U. S. Navy* [1957].

gence and the Antarctic Circumpolar Current [*Deacon*, 1937; 1963; *Gordon*, 1966, 1967]. Cold, low salinity waters generated in the Weddell and Ross seas by freezing sea ice flow downslope northward as antarctic bottom water. Associated north-flowing cold surface waters, caught in the eastward Antarctic Circumpolar Current, encounter the warmer, more saline subantarctic water mass to define the Antarctic Convergence. The surface waters sink and continue north, becoming the antarctic intermediate water, whereas the warm subantarctic water mass flows toward the continent beneath the antarctic surface water south of the convergence. Beneath the south-flowing subantarctic water, but above the Antarctic bottom water, is south-moving Atlantic, Pacific, and Indian deep water. *Gordon* [1967] states that the Antarctic Convergence covers a zone of 2°–4° of latitude and that a secondary polar front exists south of it between 104°–108°W longitude, probably controlled by bottom topography.

Around the Antarctic Continent the infinite fetch of the prevailing westerlies, restricted south of 50°S latitude only by the South American Continent at the Drake Passage, provides the driving force for the

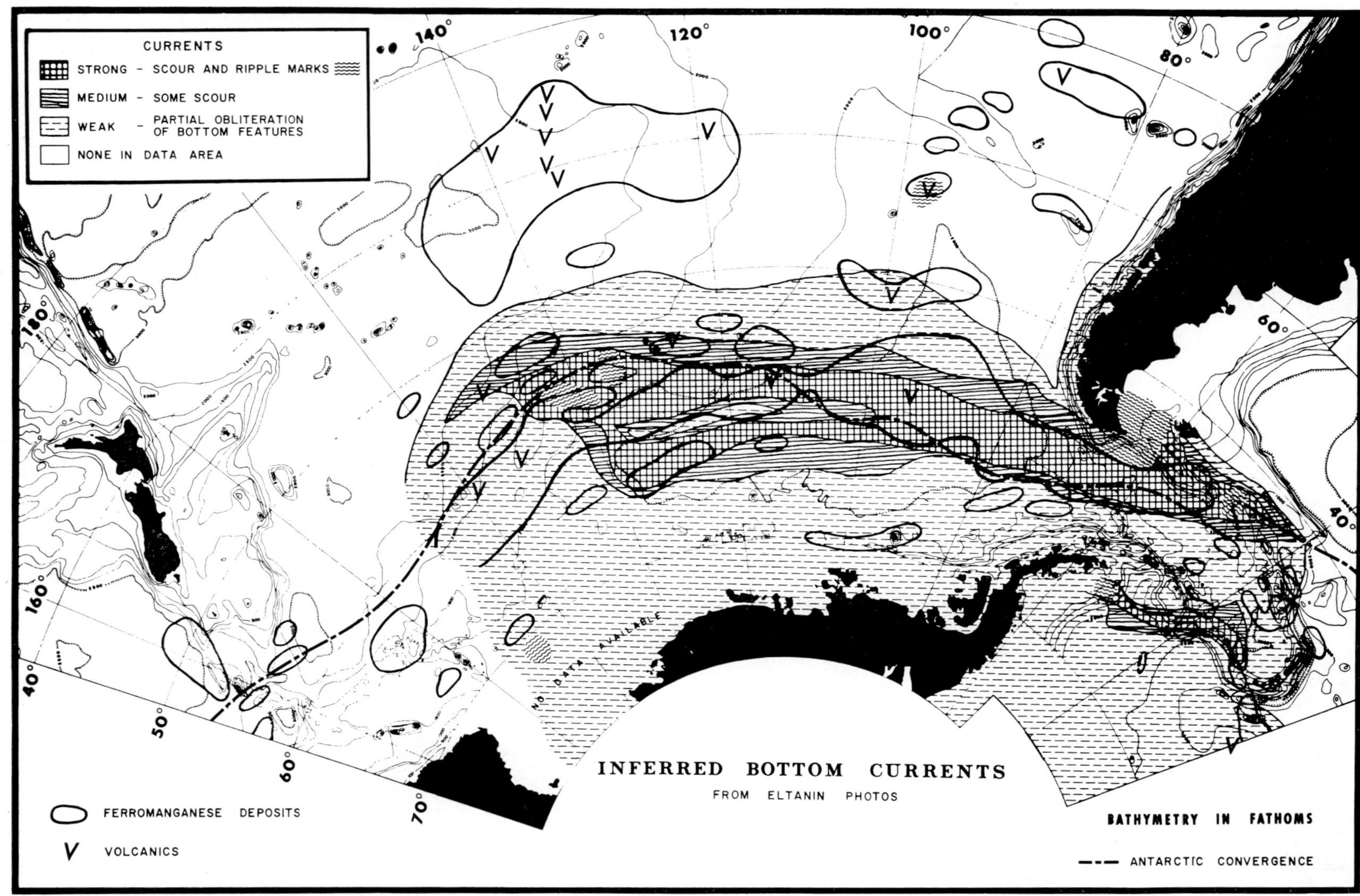

Fig. 3. Bottom currents in the South Atlantic and South Pacific oceans inferred from *Eltanin* deep sea bottom photography, cruises 1–27 (after *Goodell* [1968*b*]).

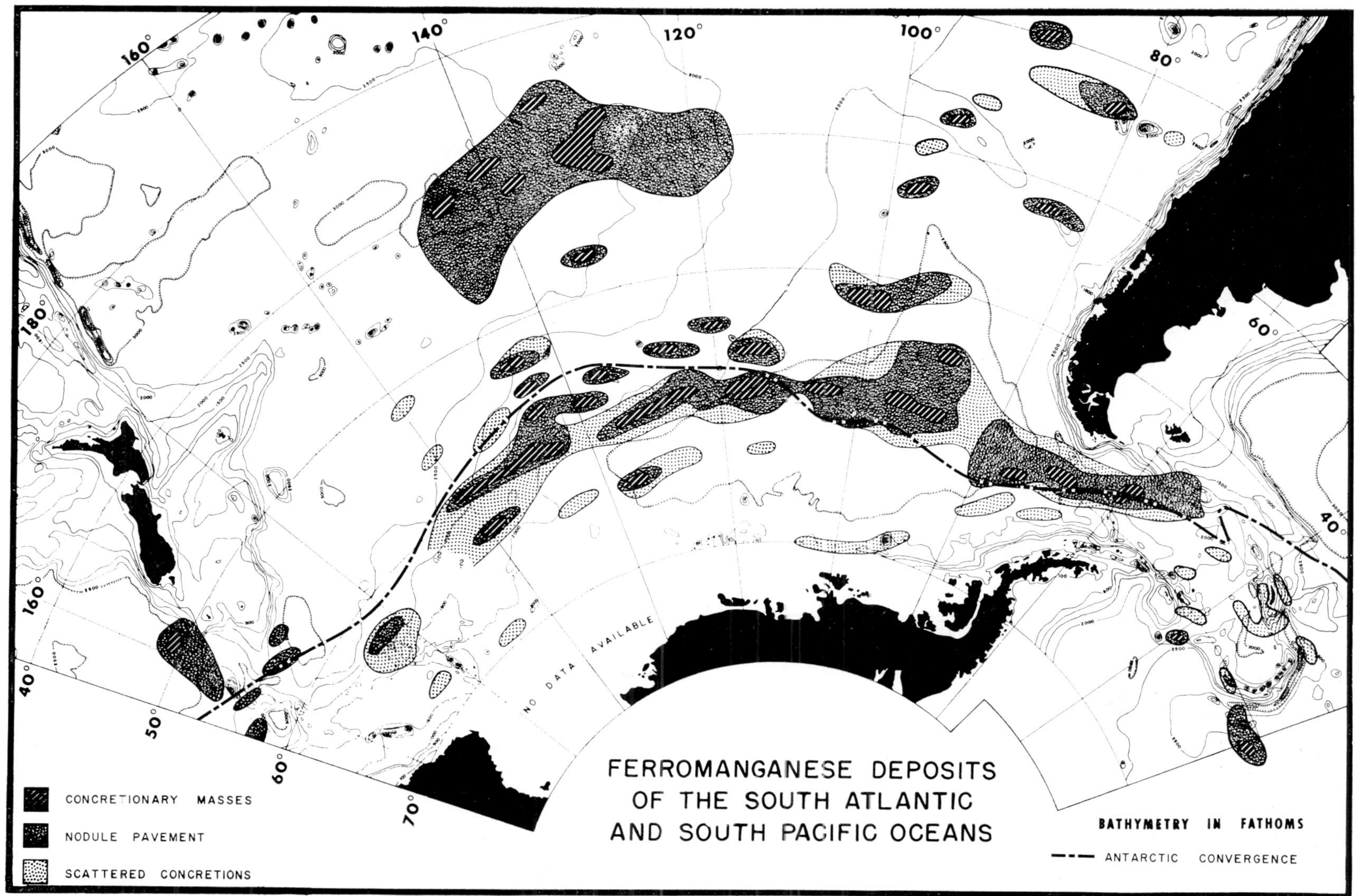

Fig. 4. Occurrence of ferromanganese deposits in the South Atlantic and South Pacific oceans from photography, dredge hauls, and cores (after *Goodell* [1968*b*]).

Fig. 5. Concretionary masses of ferromanganese draped on submarine basalts in the center of the Drake Passage (location 59°14′S, 68°49′W; water depth 1963 fm; camera station 5–11). The bottom sediment is a yellowish (5Y7/2) carbonate ooze ($CaCO_3$ = 77.9%).

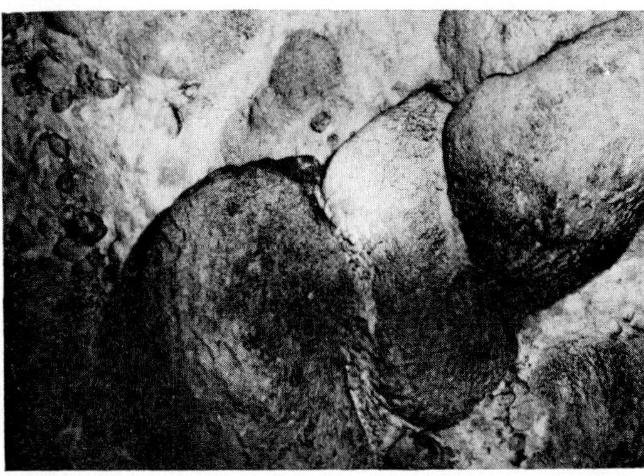

Fig. 6. A pavement of ferromanganese concretions 5–8 cm in diameter covers the sea floor in the eastern Southwest Pacific Basin (location 42°31′S, 145°06′W; water depth 2874 fm; camera station 24–5). The sediment is a moderate brown (5YR4/4) foraminiferal silty clay.

Antarctic Circumpolar Current (Figure 2). *Maksimov* [1962] states that the surface current direction and the current direction at a depth of 3000 meters are identical, and that the velocity at this depth averages 75% of the surface velocity. Surface velocities in the area of the Antarctic Convergence in the South Pacific probably average less than 0.5 knot [*U.S. Navy*, 1957], but bottom currents in the Drake Passage may reach velocities of 50 cm/sec, or slightly in excess of one knot [*Heezen and Hollister*, 1964]. The observance of ripple marks, scour, and cut and fill structures in *Eltanin* bottom photos has permitted mapping of relative bottom current velocities across the Albatross Cordillera and Southeast Pacific Basin, through the Drake Passage, across the Burdwood Bank, and around the Scotia Ridge (Figure 3). The correspondence between the highest velocities and the position of the convergence is striking. The bifurcation in the polar front documented by *Gordon* [1967] to the east of the offset in the Albatross Cordillera is also clearly evidenced by the low velocity thread between higher velocities (Figure 3).

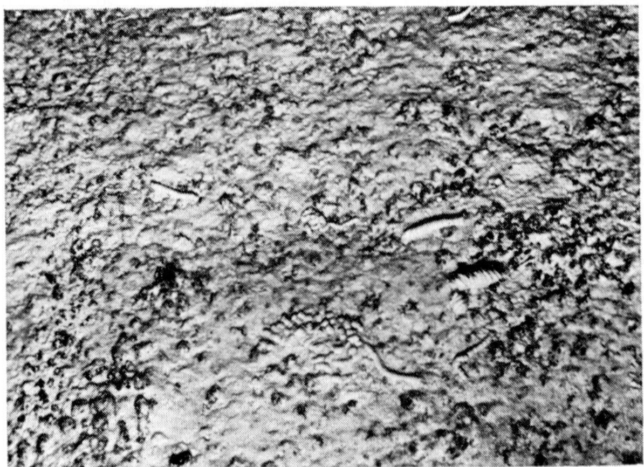

Fig. 7. Scattered ferromanganese concretions partially buried by yellowish-brown (10YR4/2) siliceous ooze on the southeast flank of the Albatross Cordillera near the western margin of the Southeast Pacific Basin. Holothurian fecal casts are numerous.

Fig. 8. Bottom sediments from the crest of the Albatross Cordillera (location 55°59′S, 134°27′W; water depth 1740 fm; camera station 15–18). See figure legends 9 and 10 for further information.

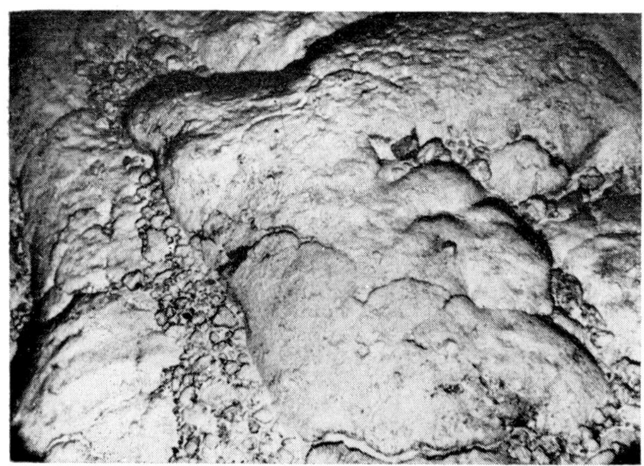

Fig. 9

Fig. 10

Bottom sediments from the crest of the Albatross Cordillera (location 55°59′S, 134°27′W; water depth 1740 fm; camera station 15–18). The bottom sediments are a light olive gray (5Y6/2) calcareous ooze. Ripple marks, huge concretionary masses of ferromanganese deposits, pavements of manganese nodules (not shown), and angular jointed and brecciated basalt flows are all seen at this camera station, an association which is common at many other camera stations.

CONCRETION DISTRIBUTION, OCCURRENCE, AND RELATED SEDIMENTS

The data on the occurrence and distribution of ferromanganese deposits in the South Atlantic and Pacific oceans come primarily from the bottom photography, secondarily from the dredge hauls, and last from the piston and gravity cores. Photo-station coverage between 50° and 70°S is excellent, especially between 20° and 160°W. Above 50°S coverage is more sporadic, although good coverage exists over the eastern Southwest Pacific Basin, off Victoria Land in the Ross Sea, and south of New Zealand. Since most ship stations included in addition to photography a piston and gravity core, as well as a dredge haul, three sources of information are often available at the same location.

An almost continuous belt of ferromanganese deposits up to 300 miles wide lies roughly beneath the Antarctic Convergence between 170° and 50°W longitude (Figure 4) and corresponds for the most part with the zone of high velocity bottom currents (Figure 3). The deposits grade from extensive concretionary masses of ferromanganese draped across volcanics and sediments (Figure 5), through pavements of more familiar nodules of various shapes (Figure 6), to scattered and sporadic occurrences of small-sized ferromanganese gravel with only occasional nodules (Figure 7). North and south of this belt are smaller isolated deposits that may cover tens to several thousands of square miles and whose exact shape is conjectural; they are portrayed elliptically for convenience. The largest of these, on the eastern margin of the Southwest Pacific Basin and western flank of the Albatross Cordillera, covers more than 100,000 square miles (Figure 4). The most striking similarity with all of these deposits is the association of submarine volcanics and current marks (Figures 8, 9, and 10). The deposits are found in water depths of more than 5,500 meters in the Southwest Pacific Basin to less than 1000 meters in the Drake Passage. They lie indiscriminately on all sediment types from creamy white calcareous and siliceous oozes to brown pelagic clays, to dark olive gray clayey silts (Figure 11).

CONCRETION PHYSICAL CHARACTERISTICS AND MORPHOLOGICAL DISTRIBUTIONS IN THE SOUTH ATLANTIC AND PACIFIC OCEANS

Sample Population

A completely representative sampling of ferromanganese concretions is not possible in the South Atlantic and Pacific oceans, inasmuch as most of the deposits occur draped on volcanic flows that are not readily sampled, or in the form of slabs too large to be picked up by conventional bottom dredges. Our samples are limited to fragments that were occasionally broken off these large accumulations, together with the multitude of smaller concretions that cover the sediment surface (Figure 12). The smallest concretions generally are not recovered by dredging, although piston and gravity cores collect even the most minute ferromanganese micronodules. However, these

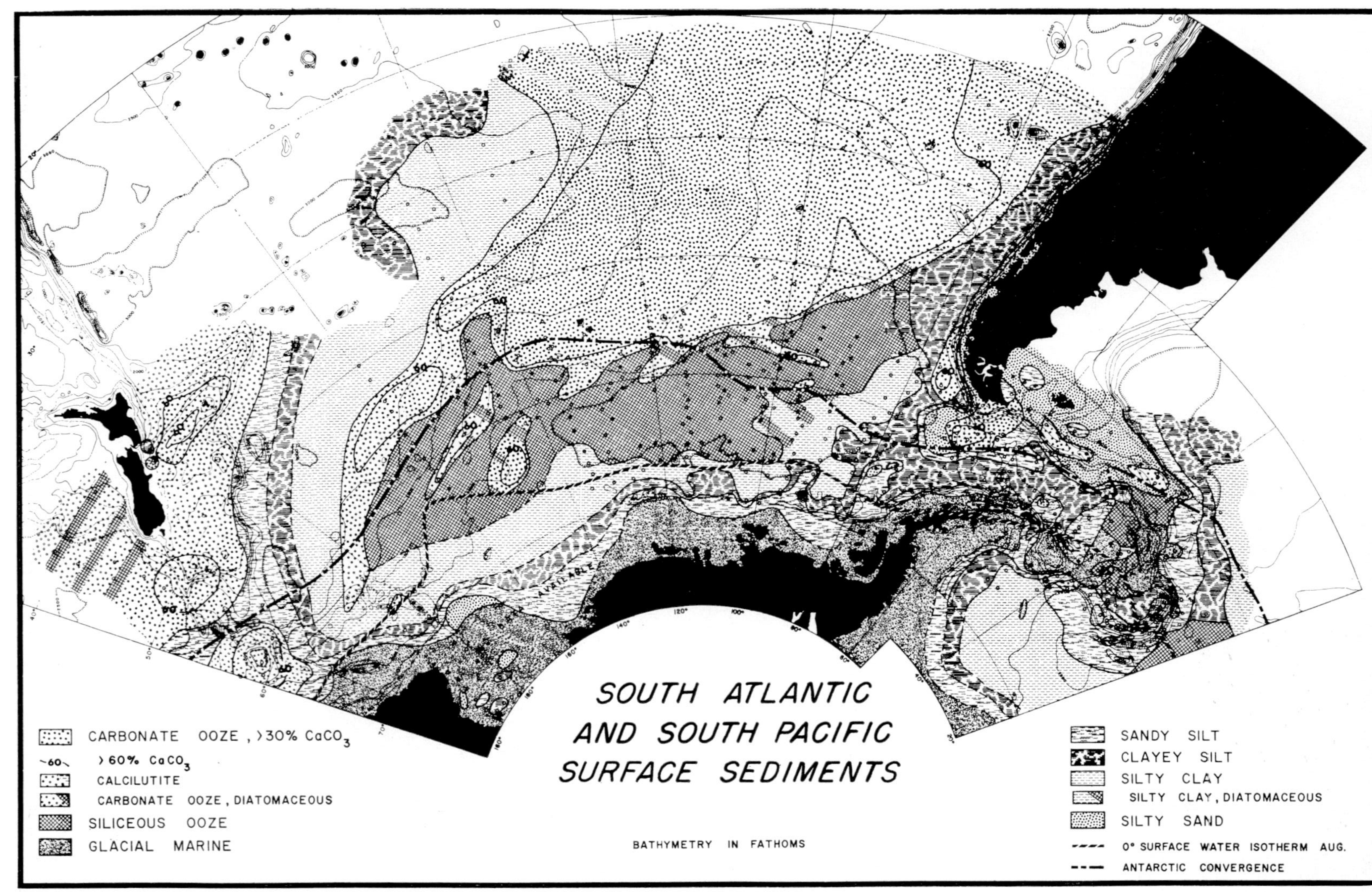

Fig. 11. South Atlantic and South Pacific surface sediment types (after *Goodell* [1968*b*]).

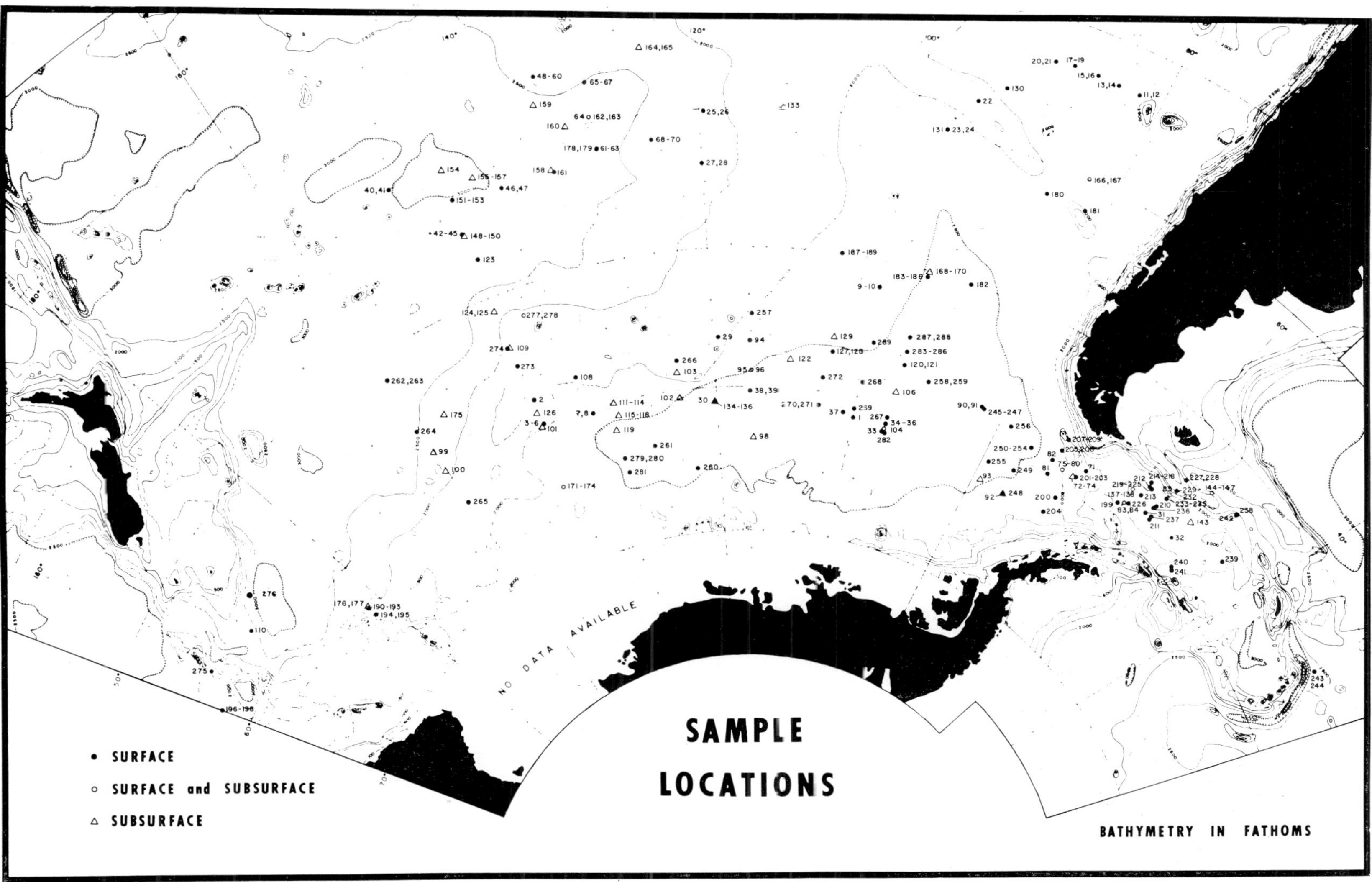

Fig. 12. Location of ferromanganese samples analyzed mineralogically and/or chemically.

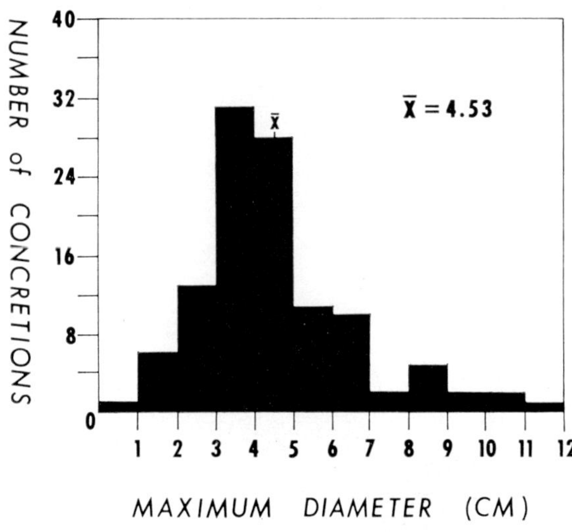

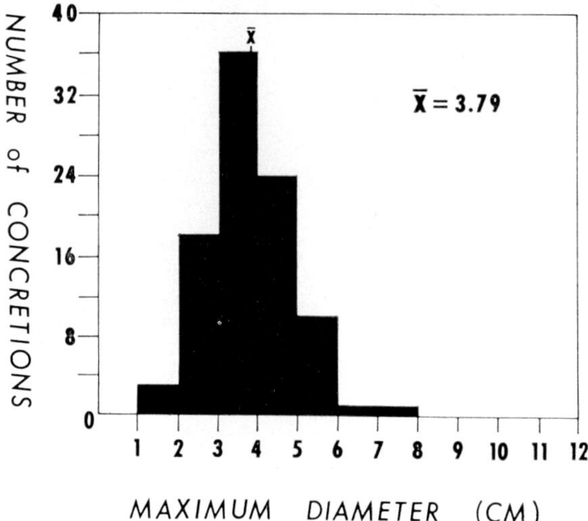

Fig. 13. Frequency distributions of ferromanganese concretion maximum diameters from *Eltanin* dredges (*left*) and cores (*right*) used for mineralogical and chemical analysis. Only whole concretions were tabulated.

coring devices are limited in that they cannot collect concretions with a horizontal diameter greater than 5.6 centimeters and 3.5 centimeters, respectively.

All dredge samples and sediment cores collected during *Eltanin* cruises 4–27 were examined for macroscopic ferromanganese accumulations. On all of these the following was accomplished: (1) measurement of the maximum, intermediate, and minimum concretion diameters; (2) examination of concretion shape and surficial features; (3) differentiation, when possible, of the internal structure into ferromanganese oxide crust, subcrust, and nucleus; and (4) measurement of the minimum and maximum thickness of the oxide crust or undifferentiated oxide crust-subcrust. Only samples with sufficient ferromanganese oxide material to measure and describe were selected for analysis; 207 of these were from dredges and 143 from piston cores. Concretions collected by the smaller phleger cores were generally disregarded because they did not have sufficient material for convenient X-ray diffraction and chemical analyses, and because they usually duplicated the nodules recovered by other devices at the same station.

Each of the samples selected for mineralogical and chemical analysis represents a single concretion population. A population is here defined as a group of concretions, all of which are characterized by similar nuclei and ferromanganese oxide accumulation geometry collected in a single dredge haul or at a sediment core horizon. Multiple populations can occur in an area sampled by a single dredge haul, or even in the same core interval. The physical characteristics that were used to separate concretions into populations are (1) a visibly different nucleus type; (2) single versus multiple nuclei; and (3) a markedly different oxide crust thickness. A single concretion field, which may be isolated or merged with adjoining fields, may consist of one or more populations over the space of a few tens of meters, depending upon the degree of variability.

Size

The *Eltanin* concretions closely resemble in size those found in areas exclusive of the South Pacific Ocean, Drake Passage, and the Scotia Sea (Figure 13). The size gap between about 1 and 5 mm reported by *Menard* [1964] apparently also exists over wide areas of the South Atlantic, Pacific, and Indian oceans and is probably related to the lack of suitable size nucleating material. When accumulations of 1–5 mm do occur, they are generally accreted as part of a larger multiple-nucleus concretion. The largest nodule recovered to date aboard the *Eltanin* is a slab 56 × 55 × 14 cm that was dredged from the floor of the Southwestern Pacific Basin (Figure 14).

The histograms show that most concretions from the South Atlantic and Pacific oceans have a maximum diameter of between 3 and 5 centimeters. A second mode would appear in the micronodule (< 1 mm) range if these concretions had been included. The mean maximum diameter of the core concretions is smaller, because the distribution is truncated by the core cutter diameter.

Bottom photographs generally show that nodules

Fig. 14. Ferromanganese slabs consisting of an oxide crust 1–3 cm thick on altered volcanics from the Southwest Pacific Basin (location 42°01′S, 130°02′W; water depth 2640 fm).

from a very restricted area tend to have very nearly the same sizes and shapes, except in the vicinity of submarine lava flows, where large concretionary masses are present. Even though dredge hauls generally cover a larger area than is viewed in a suite of bottom photographs from a single photo station, similarities in size and shape between concretions from a single dredge haul are usually apparent. In order to determine the distribution of concretion sizes in typical bottom collections, two hauls were chosen at random and the maximum diameter of each nodule in both hauls measured (Figure 15). Both histograms are leptokurtic, the peakedness of the distribution of RS 27-51 concretion sizes being quite pronounced.

Surface Features

One of the most distinguishing features of ferromanganese concretions is the mammillary surface, composed of closely spaced and/or coalescing mammillae or hemispherical protrusions (Figures 14 and 16). The

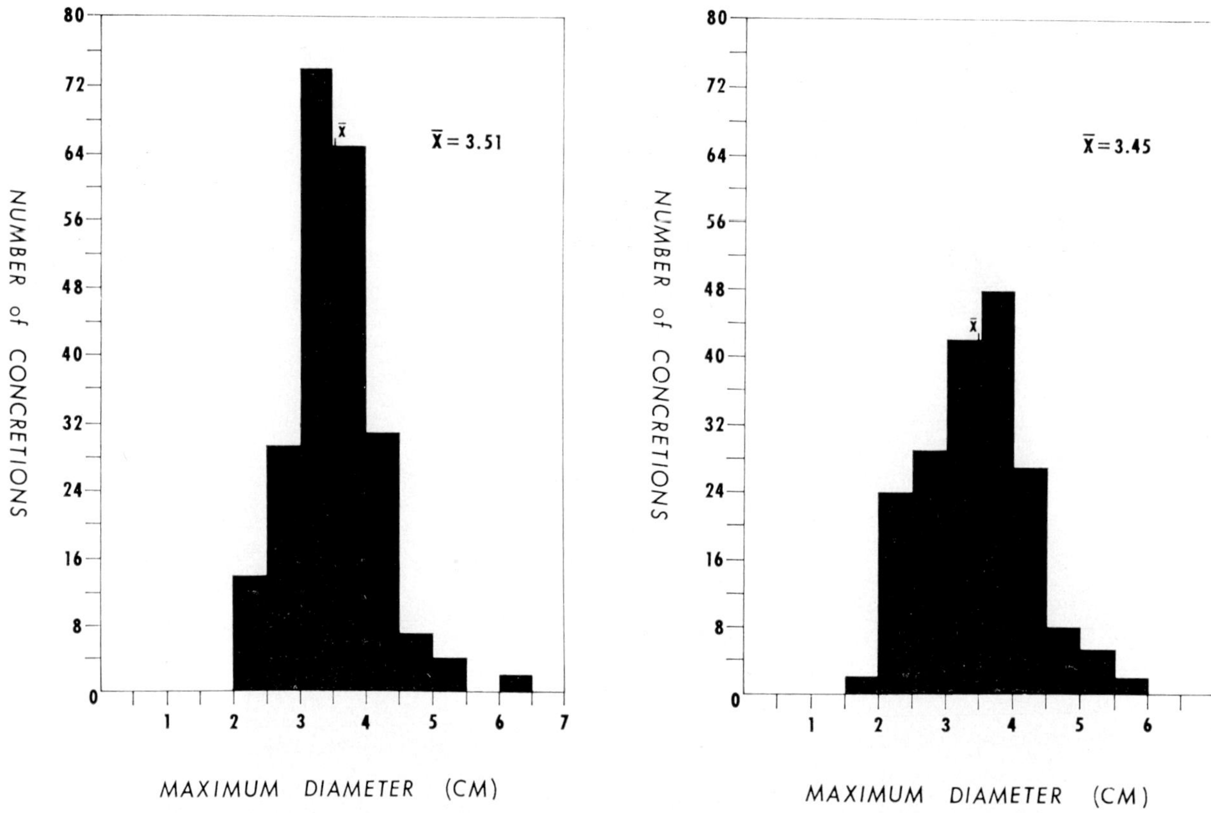

Fig. 15. Frequency distributions of ferromanganese concretion maximum diameters from *Eltanin* hauls 27-28 (*left*, location 57°55'S, 153°57.5'E; water depth 1894 fm) and 20-5 (*right*, location 60°20'S, 137°46'W; water depth 2320 fm).

size of the mammillae relative to nodule size varies greatly, as does the 'relief' of the mammillae, i.e., the prominence above the general nodule surface. Usually at least two generations of mammillae development are present on a single nodule, with tiny mammillae superimposed on larger ones. The mammilla shape is the result both of the habit of precipitation of hydrated Fe and Mn oxides and of the irregularities introduced by the coating of detrital granules settling onto an accumulating ferromanganese oxide deposit. The latter protrusions often initially deviate from a hemispherical form.

Murray and Renard [1891] first noted that the mammillarity of a concretion was not always uniform on every side. They dredged a concretion having half of its surface mammillated, the other half smooth and bearing attached organisms, and postulated that the smooth surface was the upper one. Differences in mammillarity of many South Atlantic, Pacific, and Indian Ocean ferromanganese concretions are usually related to asymmetrical thicknesses of ferromanganese oxides, the surface having the thicker oxide accumulations having mammillae of higher relief and larger size. It seems reasonable that the surface exposed to sea water for the greatest length of time develops more prominent mammillae, whereas the mammillarity of the surface buried in sediment tends to be depressed. In addition, thin sections cut normal to precipitation surfaces show that heightened mammillarity is favored by low percentages of admixed fine detritus; large

Fig. 16. Ferromanganese concretion types. Some have been sectioned to show internal structures. *Nodules:* 17-4, location 60°03'S, 135°00'W; water depth 2370 fm. 6-7, location 58°06'S, 59°24'W; water depth 2383 fm. 6-10, location 55°06'S, 55°50'W; water depth 1570 fm. 24-2, location 38°58'S, 150°02'W; water depth 2770 fm. 15-7, location 57°51'S, 108°42'W; water depth 2560 fm. *Agglomerates:* 10-10, location 62°00.2'S, 75°10.3'W; water depth 2400 fm. 5-6, location 61°14'S, 67°43'W; water depth 2080 fm. *Botryoidals:* 21-4, location 33°03'S, 82°03'W; water depth 2120 fm. 21-6, location 33°02.5'S, 83°56.5'W; water depth 2002 fm. *Crusts:* 6-2, location 53°09.5'S, 59°36'W; water depth 321 fm. 21-11, location 39°51'S, 96°52'W; water depth 1990 fm.

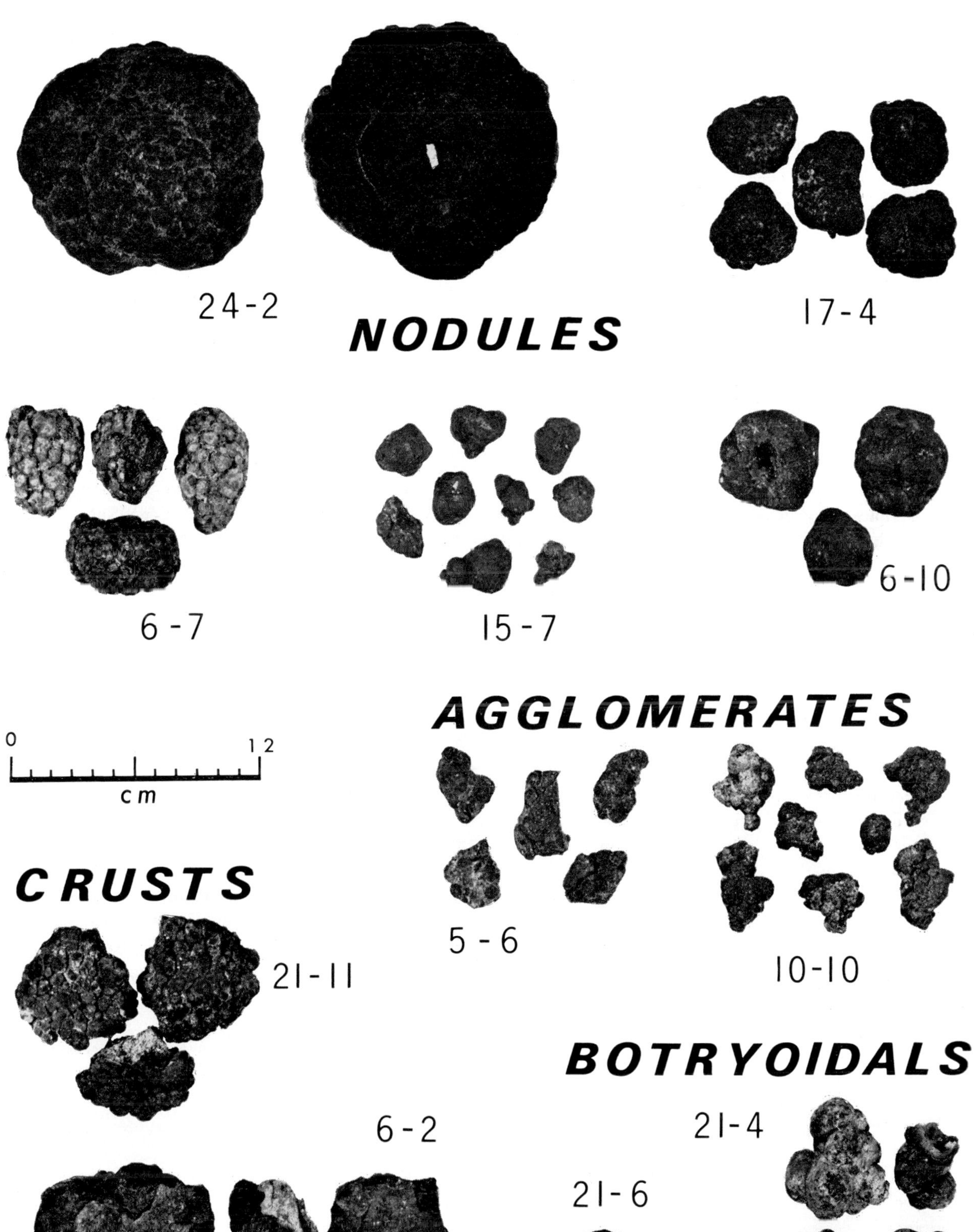
24-2
NODULES
17-4
6-7
15-7
6-10
AGGLOMERATES
0
12
cm
CRUSTS
5-6
10-10
21-11
BOTRYOIDALS
6-2
21-4
21-6

TABLE 2. *Eltanin* Ferromanganese Deposits, Sample Populations

Morphogenetic Categories	Dredges			At Core Tops			Buried in Cores			Total Population
	Populations Observed	X-ray Data	Chemical Data	Populations Observed	X-ray Data	Chemical Data	Populations Observed	X-ray Data	Chemical Data	
Nodules	47	29	35	12	11	8	40	26	11	99
Crusts	103	66	65	14	10	3	29	15	2	146
Botryoidals	30	17	22	3	3	1	15	14	3	48
Agglomerates	27	20	14	6	1	0	24	12	0	57
Agglutinations	4	0	0	2	0	0	47	0	0	53
Stained rocks	62	0	0	12	0	0	98	0	0	172
Crustal material	0	0	0	3	2	0	4	2	0	7

percentages of admixed coarse detritus depress mammillarity.

Morphology

The samples were categorized into the four morphogenetic classes of *Grant* [1967]: (1) nodules—roughly spherical concretions of any size usually containing a single micro- or macro-nucleus where the nucleus is much less than one-half of the nodule radius (Figure 16); (2) botryoidals—somewhat oval or flattened with several nuclei, some of which often appear to have been added periodically, which causes a grape-like cluster (Figure 16); (3) crusts—the center non-ferromanganiferous mass composes more than one-half of the sample with ferromanganese crust ranging from millimeters to tens of centimeters and with the entire deposit usually larger in two dimensions than in the third; these are the most common morphological types, although they are rare in cores (Figures 14 and 16); (4) agglomerates—multiple nonferromanganese nuclei represent about one-half of the nodule volume with the over-all shape a flattened irregular form composed of a great many uniform pebbles or granules cemented or encrusted together by a thin ferromanganese deposit (Figure 16). Three other categories representing ferromanganese oxide accumulations that cannot be termed concretions were designated: (1) agglutination—a group of granules and/or pebbles united by a thin film of ferromanganese oxide material; (2) stain—a thin film of ferromanganese oxides on some solid object; (3) crustal material—a group of sand-sized and finer particles that are coated and loosely cemented by ferromanganese oxides but not in any concretionary form.

A tabulation of the number of populations of each morphologic type found in dredge hauls, at the surface of sediment cores, and buried in sediment cores reveals that nodules are about as common as botryoidals plus agglomerates (Table 2). If the dredge haul data are representative, then crusts are as abundant as the other three concretionary varieties combined. A higher percentage of nodules and botryoidals were selected for analysis because of their greater relative ferromanganese crust thicknesses.

Another approach to a morphological classification of concretions is to use their geometric shape. On this basis, the general shapes of ferromanganese concretions are (1) spherical, (2) ellipsoidal, (3) tabular-discoidal, (4) polygonal, and (5) tubercular. Spherical and ellipsoidal shapes are characteristic of the nodule morphological class. Many crusts, frequently somewhat flattened, display an ellipsoidal shape, although tabular discoidal and polygonal shapes are also typical. Discoidal concretions usually have a nucleus of volcanic debris, whereas the polygonal form is often inherited from a dreikanter glacial erratic or a shark's tooth, both of which have a number of flat surfaces. Botryoidals and agglomerates most often have a shape that resembles tubercular plant roots having two or more coalescing lobes (Table 3).

TABLE 3. Comparison of Concretion Morphology with Geometric Types

Geometric Shape	Morphologic Type			
	Nodules	Crusts	Botryoidals	Agglomerates
Spheroidal	14	2	4	0
Ellipsoidal	30	25	10	8
Tabular Discoidal	2	11	2	3
Polygonal	3	4	1	1
Tubercular	4	6	16	21

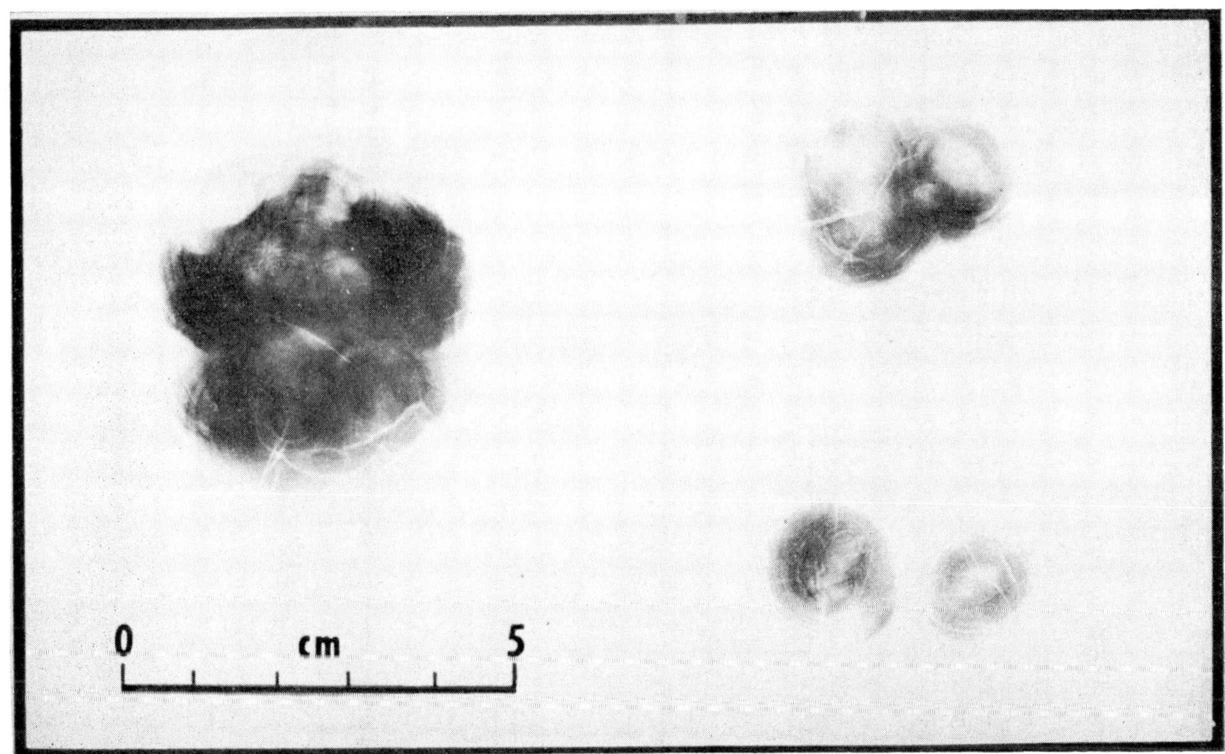

Fig. 17. X-ray radiographs of concretion internal structures. (*Left*) Nodule from *Eltanin* 24-8 (location 43°00'S, 139°56'W; water depth 2811 fm). (*Right*) Botryoidal from 24-17 (location 42°01'S, 130°05'W; water depth 2640 fm).

Structure and Morphologic Types

The structural components of ferromanganese concretions are defined as the oxide crust, the subcrust, and the nucleus. The relative thickness of each component varies, and one or two of the components may be absent in a particular concretion. In addition, a complete gradation between crust, subcrust, and nucleus exists in many concretions.

The oxide crust consists of hydrated oxides of Fe and Mn which have been precipitated in concentric shells and which have incorporated a minor amount of detrital crystallites. The subcrust usually consists of a zone of volcanic material that has been partially or wholly replaced by ferromanganese oxides; it often grades into the oxide crust and seldom displays the concentric laminations characteristic of the crust. In many instances the subcrust is slightly vesicular and, in cases of nearly complete alteration, ghost vesicles are seen. When the nucleus also consists of volcanic material, subcrust and nucleus usually grade into one another. The nucleus may be composed of any solid material.

Textural zones within ferromanganese concretions have been noted previously [*Murray and Renard*, 1891]. *Skornyakova et al.* [1962] described a sequence of Fe-Mn hydroxide bands, the thinnest characterizing the initial stages of alteration and replacement of hydropyroclastics. Such banding may lend a laminated appearance to subcrusts composed of fine volcanics not uncommonly deposited on a volcanic bomb or in the South Atlantic, Pacific, and Indian oceans, on a glacial erratic nucleus. *Sorem* [1967], studying polished thin sections, described a nodule with distinct inner and outer zones and suggested that these textural differences might be due to differential growth rates.

Concentric shells are easily split off most concretions, and fractures approximately perpendicular to the colloform layering are almost always present. *Menard* [1964] noted that above a certain size concretions tend to crack into eight equal sections, which may be recemented by septaria. South Atlantic, Pacific, and Indian Ocean nodules are not so constituted. The fracture patterns are randomly oriented, branching, and are frequently avenues of influx for clays from the surrounding ocean floor (Figure 17). The fractures are probably the result of the hydration and expansion or dehydration and contraction of any one of a number of mineral phases.

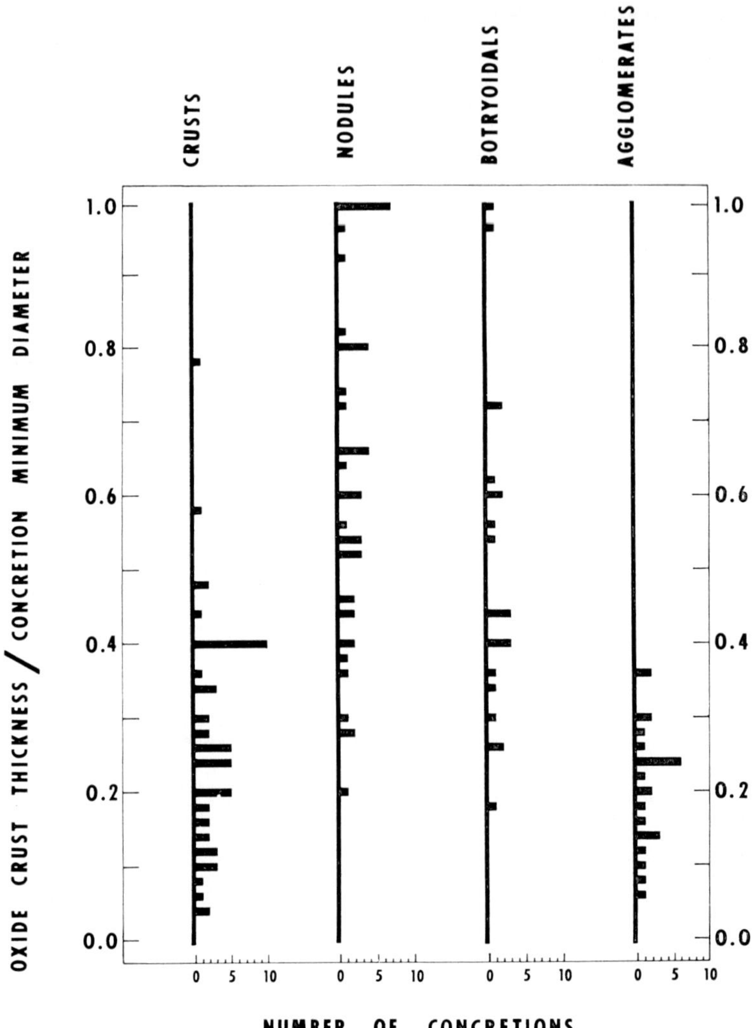

Fig. 18. Ratio of oxide crust thickness to concretion minimum diameter for morphologic types.

The ratio of oxide crust thickness to concretion minimum diameter for each of the four morphologic classes shows that most of the concretions designated as crusts and agglomerates have a relative thickness of ferromanganese oxide of less than 0.4 (Figure 18), whereas for most nodules and botryoidals it is greater than 0.4. These plots are somewhat subjective, because although the number of nuclei can be determined objectively, the measurement of the thickness of the oxide crust or subcrust is objective only when the components are well differentiated.

Morphologic Species Distribution in the South Atlantic and Pacific Oceans

Only crusts and nodules have been found on the Chile Rise and its flanks, and between the rise and Islas Juan Fernández (Robinson Crusoe Islands) (Figure 19). Crusts, nodules, and botryoidals are found in the Southwest Pacific Basin. Crusts are predominant on the Albatross Cordillera. All four types have been dredged from the Southeast Pacific Basin, Drake Passage, and Scotia Sea, although there is generally a greater diversity of types at localities in the Drake Passage-Scotia Sea than to the west. The most significant regional trend is the concentration of agglomerates, which almost always have glacial erratic nuclei, within 3°–4° of 60°S. No agglomerates are found north of 50°S. This suggests that concretions of this type are dependent on granule- and small pebble-sized ice-rafted clasts for nucleation centers, with some

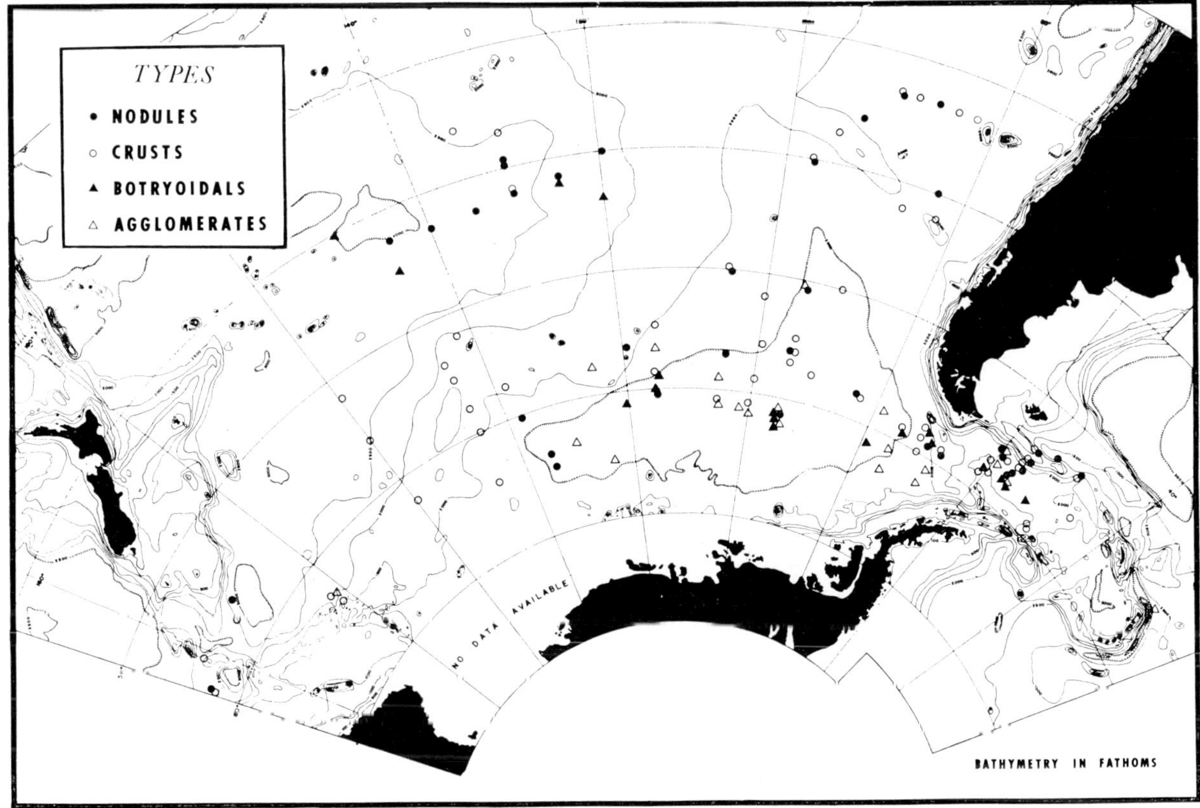

Fig. 19. Distribution of concretion types in the South Atlantic and South Pacific oceans.

agent such as bottom currents assisting to coalesce adjacent nuclei.

Although nodules and botryoidals display a wide variety of nucleus types, most common nuclei are volcanics in varying stages of alteration (Table 4). In the concretions with both volcanic and glacial erratic nucleation centers, the volcanic material is usually the initial nucleus, with ice-rafted granules and small pebbles added to the growing concretion (Figure 20). Nodules and botryoidals show a large number of indiscernible nuclei, in many cases because the original nucleus has been replaced by ferromanganese oxides. In a few instances the nucleus appears to be a fragment of the oxide crust of a previously existing concretion, a phenomenon first noticed by *Murray and Renard* [1891].

TABLE 4. Concretion Nucleus Types

Morphologic Type	Glacial Erratic Nuclei	Erratic and Volcanic Nuclei	Volcanic Nuclei	Biologic or Indiscernible Nuclei
Crusts	20	12	64	16
Nodules	13	6	34	23
Botryoidals	9	10	13	6
Agglomerates	35	17	2	1

Note: The nature of the nuclei was determined by visual inspection; in the case of fine-grained nuclei, the determination was often supported by X-ray diffraction analysis. Plutonic igneous, metamorphic, and sedimentary rock centers were all assumed to be ice rafted. Altered feldspathic material, palagonite, glass, angular basalt, zeolites, and montmorillonite were assumed to be derived from submarine volcanism.

The areal distribution of nucleus types follows a

TABLE 5. Comparison of Water Depth with Frequency of Concretion Occurrence

Depth, fm	Crusts, %	Nodules, %	Botryoidals, %	Agglomerates, %	Populations
0–1699	75	14	0	11	28
1700–1899	59	30	0	11	27
1900–2099	46	31	11	11	35
2100–2299	45	25	20	10	49
2300–2499	38	28	19	16	32
2500–2699	50	20	12	18	50
2700–2899	25	21	29	17	22

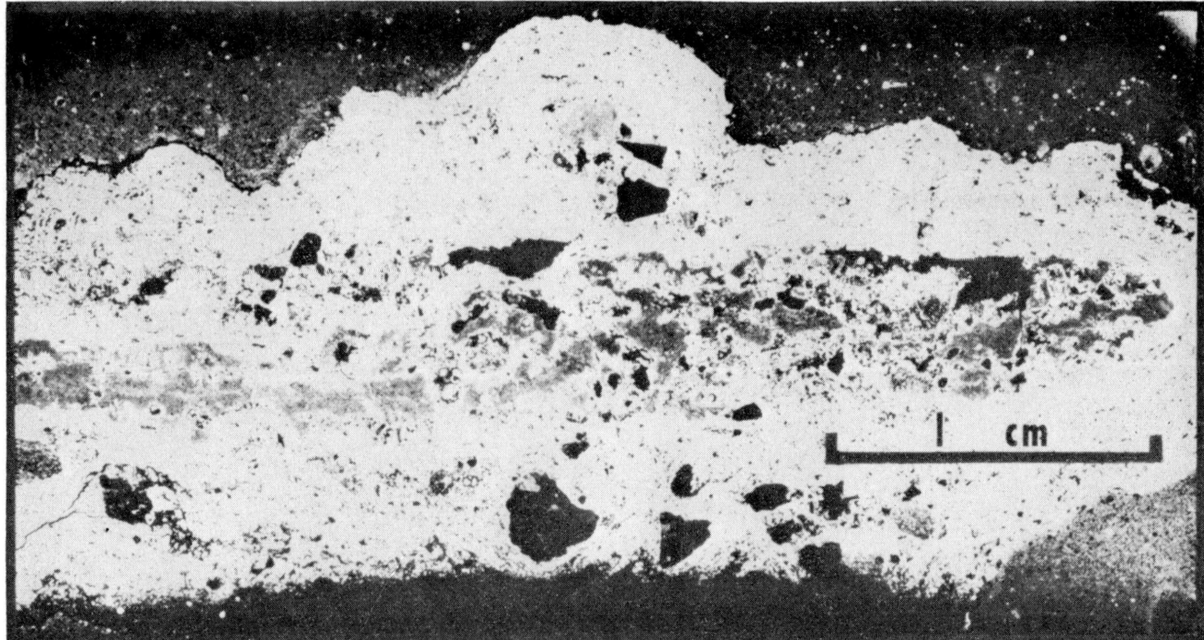

Fig. 20. Thin section of ferromanganese crust (*Eltanin* 5-4, location 59°02'S, 67°18'W; water depth 1900 fm) on a core of phillipsite, montmorillonite, palagonite, and other volcanic debris. Ice-rafted sand grains and small pebbles are incorporated in the crust.

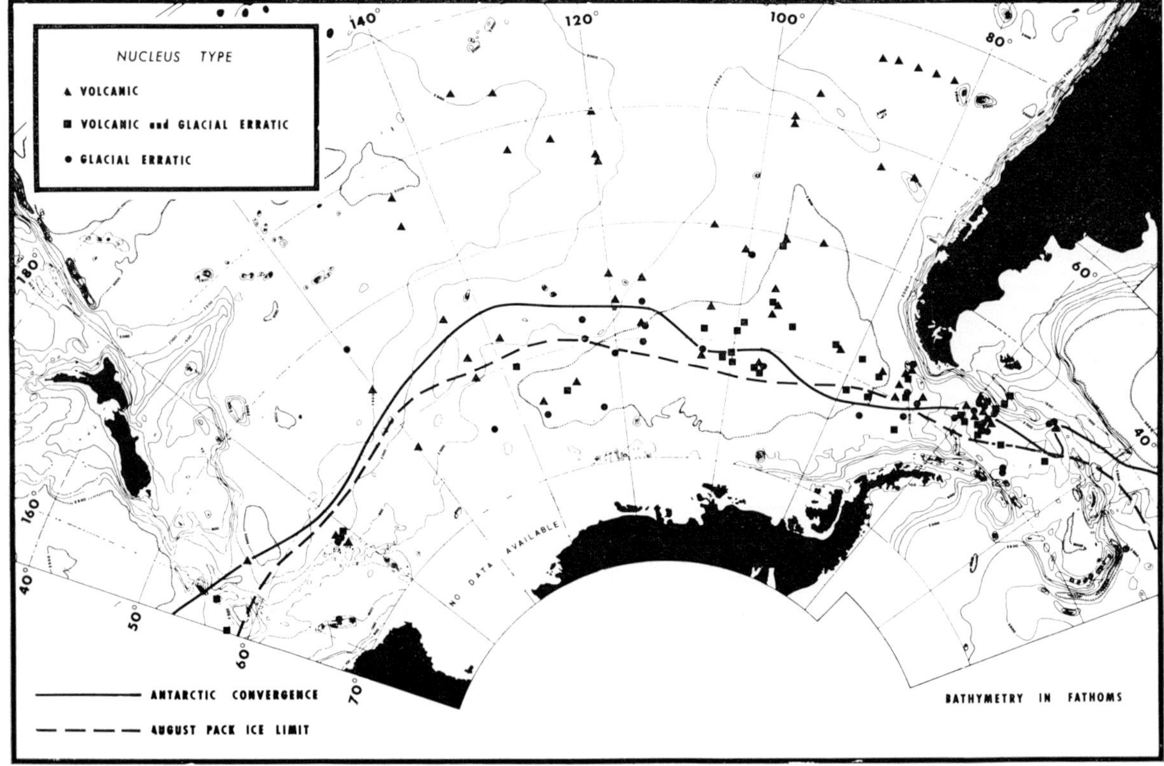

Fig. 21. The distribution of concretion nuclei types in the South Atlantic and South Pacific oceans.

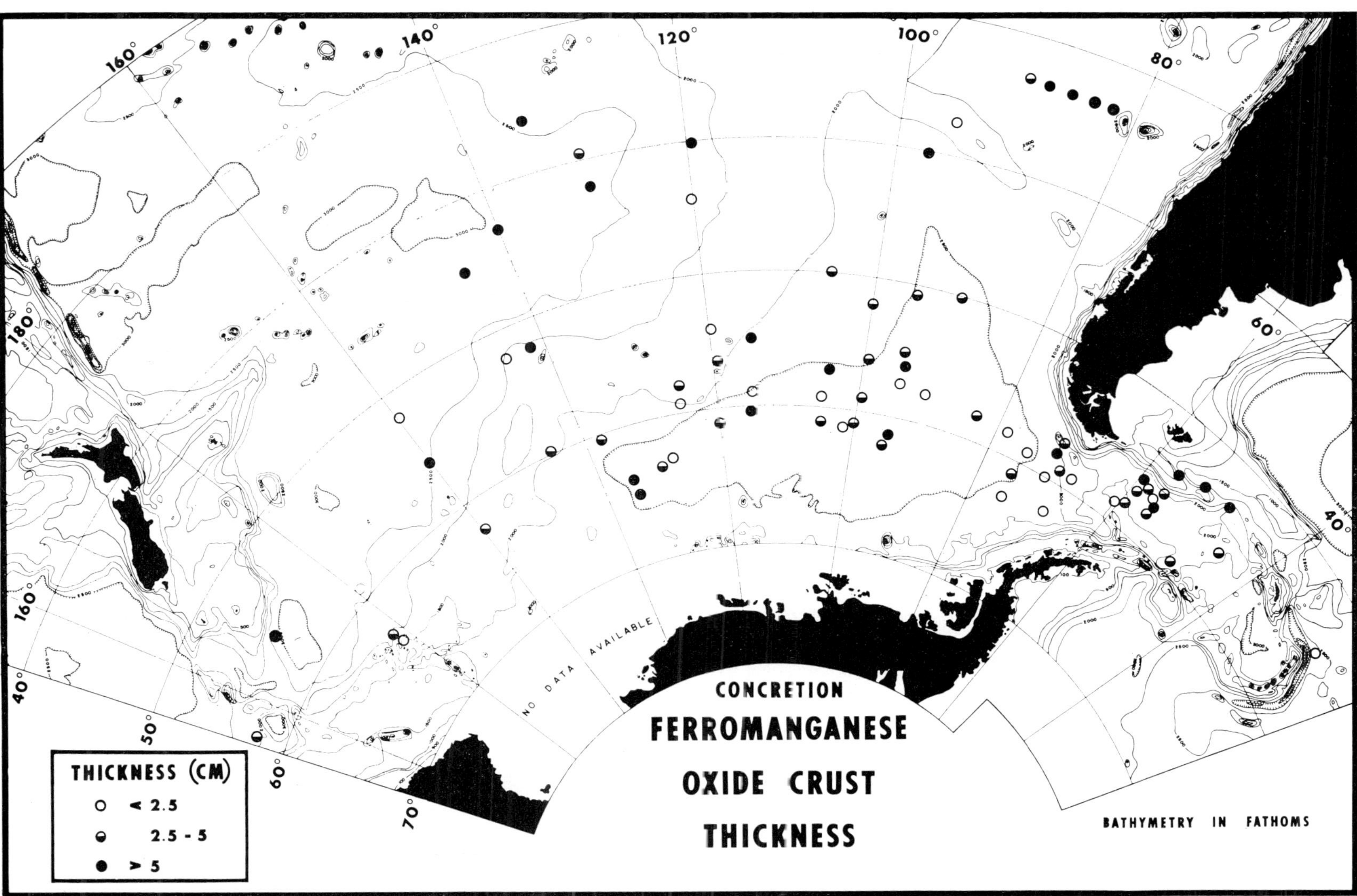

Fig. 22. The distribution of ferromanganese oxide crust thickness. The values are an average of minimum and maximum crustal thicknesses.

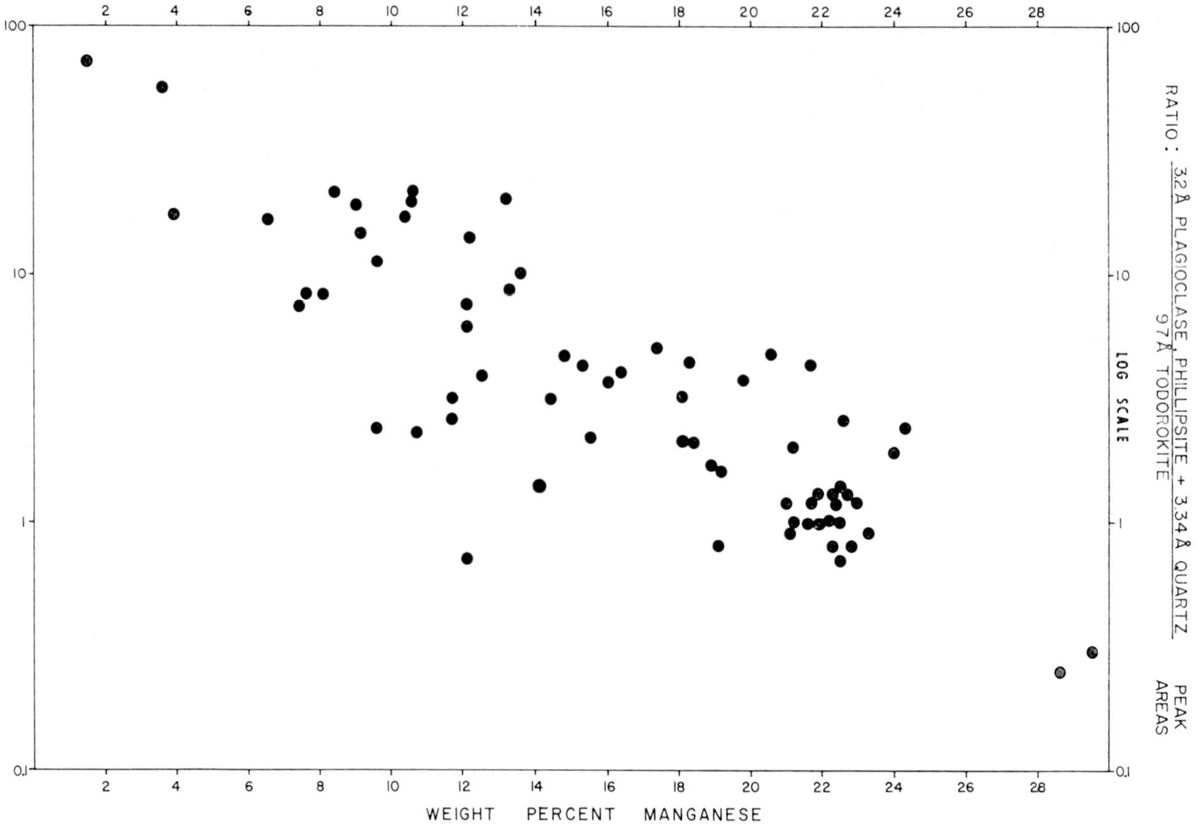

Fig. 23. Weight percent manganese in concretions versus peak areas of 3.43-Å quartz + 3.2-Å plagioclase-phillipsite/9.7-Å todorokite.

predictable pattern (Figure 21). Volcanic nuclei (angular aphanitic basalt, sideromelane, palagonite, and zeolites) are found throughout the area, which is not surprising in an area with extensive volcanism. Glacial erratic nuceli are found in concretions from stations within the range of berg ice drifting north and east from the Antarctic Continent. No coarse sand or glacial erratics are found in concretions north of about 51°S, even in those nodules buried in sediments that were deposited during times when the antarctic glaciation was more extensive than it is now.

The northern limit of glacial erratic nuclei occurrence is roughly related to the maximum limit of berg ice (Figure 2). In the west the limit is uncertain because of wide sample spacing; to the east the divergence of the limit of glacial erratic nuclei and the convergence across the Southeast Pacific is due to bergs being carried unusually far north by the Peru (Humboldt) Current.

Some relationship exists between morphologic type and depth (Table 5). Crusts show a general decrease with depth; the increase between 2500 and 2699 fathoms is due to their abundance in the Southwest Pacific Basin and to encrusted glacial erratics in the Southeast Pacific Basin. Both basins are characterized by abyssal hills and plains with depths of about 2500 to 2700 fathoms. The increase in botryoidals and agglomerates with depth reflects their concentration near the convergence in the position of the bottom currents across the depths of the Southeast Pacific Basin (Figures 3 and 19).

The thickest ferromanganese oxide encrustations (> 5 cm) occur in the Southwest Pacific Basin, northeast of the Chile Rise, in parts of the Southeast Pacific Basin, and in the northern half of the Drake Passage and Scotia Sea (Figure 22). Intermediate thicknesses (2½–5 cm) are found primarily on the Albatross Cordillera and its flanks, and in the center of the Scotia Sea. Thin deposits (< 2½ cm) are characteristic of areas adjacent to continents, and across the Southeast Pacific Basin just north of the zone of maximum current.

MINERALOGY

Authigenic and Detrital Concretion Mineralogy

X-ray diffraction studies of ferromanganese accumulations from the Scotia Sea, Drake Passage, and South Pacific Ocean reveal that todorokite, goethite, quartz, feldspar, phillipsite, and montmorillonite are almost invariably present, although the relative proportions of these constituents vary considerably. Minor amounts of birnessite, clinoptilolite, and maghemite are often present, whereas several other detrital and authigenic minerals are occasionally detected. Because a high Fe content without a significant crystalline Fe mineral fraction is generally the rule, the presence of an amorphous Fe hydroxide is inferred in most of the concretions. The basis of the mineralogic determinations is given in the appendix.

Todorokite diffraction peaks are readily identifiable in 224 of 228 diffractograms of South Atlantic and Pacific ferromanganese oxides. A log-linear relationship exists between the relative proportion of todorokite in a sample (3.34-Å quartz + 3.2-Å plagioclase-phillipsite/9.7-Å todorokite peak areas) and the weight percent Mn (Figure 23).

Birnessite is not a major hydrated Mn oxide phase in any of the South Atlantic and Pacific Ocean concretions. It only occasionally exceeds trace amounts; when present in minute quantities it may be obscured by phillipsite or chlorite. In 36 samples, mainly from the central South Pacific Ocean, birnessite is present in moderate amounts. A fragile fracture filling in one nodule was found to be composed of nearly pure birnessite. Ultracryptocrystalline birnessite (δ-MnO_2), lacking basal X-ray reflections, may be common in Mn nodules, but only occasionally does an exaggerated 2.4-Å diffraction peak present itself as evidence for the presence of δ-MnO_2. Several recurring peaks between 5 Å and 8 Å suggest hydrated oxides of Mn and Fe, such as psilomelane and β-FeOOH.

Goethite is probably present in all of the South Atlantic and Pacific Ocean nodules, but owing to its cryptocrystalline nature and Fe- and Mn-produced fluorescence, it was definitely identified in only a few samples.

Maghemite, γ-Fe_2O_3, has not been previously identified in ferromanganese concretions. However, *Machek* [1965] and *Mather* [1966] have found maghemite in sediment samples from antarctic waters. *Harrison and Peterson* [1965] described an authigenic mineral intermediate between magnetite and maghemite from the Indian Ocean. Maghemite may be produced artificially by dehydration of lepidocrocite (γ-FeOOH) or by the low temperature oxidation of magnetite [Hagg, 1935, cited in *Deer et al.*, 1962]. Since magnetite is common in the volcanic sediments of the area, oxidation of magnetite incorporated into concretions could produce maghemite. Maghemite is tentatively identified in many South Atlantic and Pacific Ocean nodules, but only in a few samples is its presence well established.

Griffin and Goldberg [1963] found montmorillonite to be the most abundant clay mineral in the South Pacific and observed no variation in the montmorillonite/illite ratio with either latitude or longitude. *Arrhenius* [1963] concluded that Fe-rich montmorillonite nontronite is abundant around centers of volcanic activity. Montmorillonite is not uncommon in sediments of the South Atlantic, Pacific, and Indian oceans adjacent to submarine volcanism [*Goodell and Scott*, 1968]. *Griffin et al.* [1968] found montmorillonite to comprise more than 50% of the > 2 micron fraction over most of the Albatross Cordillera and Chile Rise. However, adjacent to the Atlantic Continent (except near the Ross Sea) montmorillonite is the least important clay mineral [*Goodell*, 1965].

Montmorillonite is an almost invariable constituent of ferromanganese concretions of the South Atlantic, Pacific, and Indian oceans although its cation content and relative crystallinity vary considerably. It seldom comprises a large part of the silicate fraction in concretions, except in nuclei, and is assumed to have formed in situ by the alteration of volcanic glass.

Other than montmorillonite halos around areas of volcanism, illite and chlorite are the most common phyllosilicates in the South Atlantic, Pacific, and Indian oceans; both of them are considered to be mostly land-derived [*Goodell*, 1965; *Goodell and Scott*, 1968; *Griffin et al.*, 1968]. *Goodell* [1965] believes that some of the illite may be hydrothermally produced by sea water on extruded basalt. A small percentage of illite seems to be incorporated in Scotia Sea-Drake Passage manganese nodules, but chlorite is rarely identifiable, because its principal diffraction peak coincides with that of phillipsite.

Zeolites of the phillipsite-harmotome series have been reported many times in Pacific pelagic sediments and concretions. *Bonatti* [1963] discussed the Pacific distribution of phillipsite and its associated minerals and suggested that phillipsite is formed by the gradual alteration of palagonite. *Arrhenius and Bonatti* [1965] stated that the formation of harmotome appears to be limited to the earlier stages of glass-sea water interaction, with phillipsite engulfing harmotome nuclei and apparently replacing montmorillonite. *Morgenstein* [1967] reported the Ba-rich variety harmotome from near the Society Islands, but this identification is not supported by chemical analysis. *Rex* [1967] found that phillipsite is metastable in sea water, since long-term exposure produces etching of the crystal faces.

Phillipsite was found in 73 of 91 samples consisting partly or wholly of nuclei in varying stages of differentiation from the crust and subcrust; montmorillonite in 88 of 91. Inasmuch as Zemmels (verbal communication) could not detect Ba in a nearly pure phillipsite sample, it is concluded that harmotome is relatively unimportant. In addition, barite and celestobarite do not occur in detectable quantities, although their presence was noted by *Arrhenius* [1963, 1967]. Possibly the available Ba is incorporated into the todorokite structure.

Clinoptilolite was reported in pelagic sediments by *Biscaye* [1965] and *Goodell* [1965]. *Goodell* [1965] depicted patchy clinoptilolite distribution throughout the Scotia Sea, Drake Passage, and Southeast Pacific Basin in the clay-sized sediment fraction. He postulated that it is the stable zeolite from which silica could be provided by soluble opaline diatom and radiolarian frustules. Clinoptilolite appears to be a common trace constituent in ferromanganese concretions of the South Atlantic, Pacific, and Indian oceans. It is not abundant in a single sample, but it is tentatively identified in many concretions, and definitely in several others.

Quartz and feldspar are the most important silicates found in the vast majority of the marine ferromanganese deposits. They probably represent current, wind, and ice-rafted detritus, but submarine volcanism could supply a sizable proportion of feldspar. *Rex and Goldberg* [1958] noted the latitudinal dependence in the eastern Pacific of quartz (1–20 microns) in pelagic sediments and concluded that it was supplied by aeolian transport from continental deserts. They found the South Pacific to be essentially devoid of quartz with abundances decreasing from continents toward midocean, where rarely more than 6% quartz was found. However, *Peterson and Goldberg* [1962] found an abundance of volcanic quartz over the crest

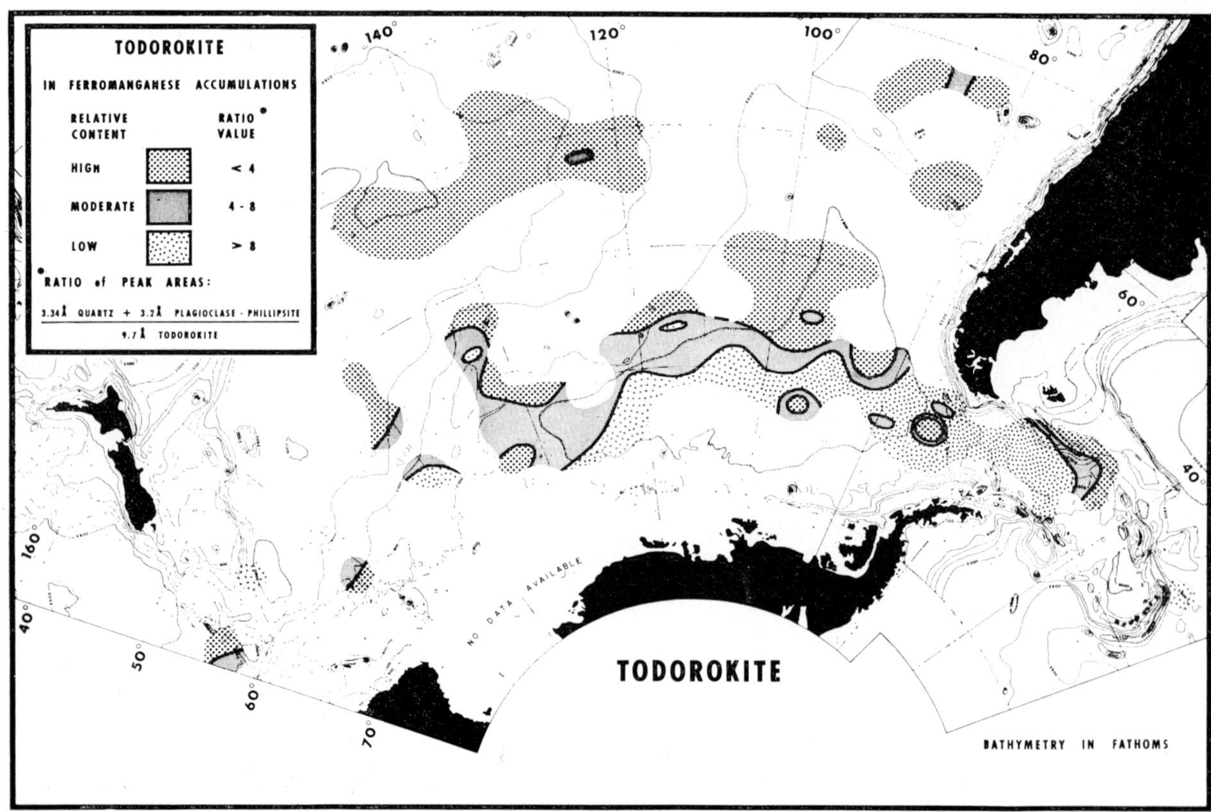

Fig. 24. The distribution of todorokite in ferromanganese concentrations in the South Atlantic and South Pacific oceans.

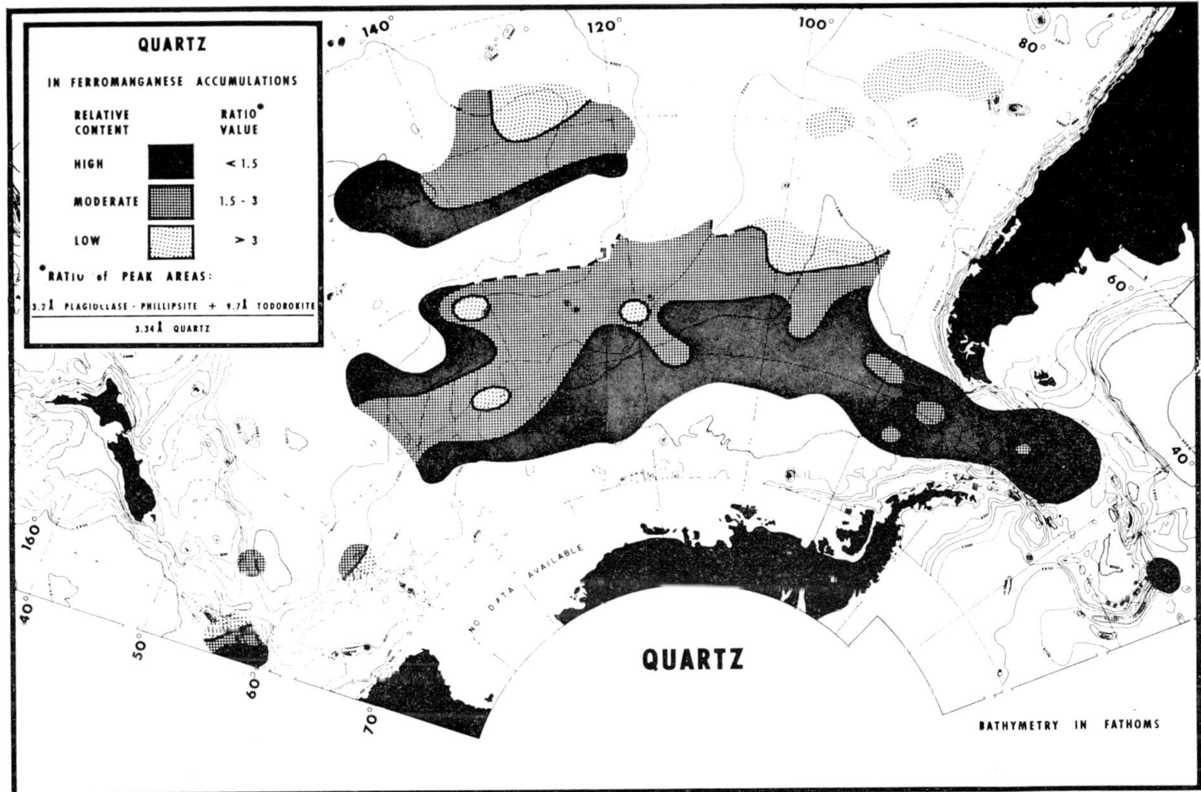

Fig. 25. The distribution of quartz in ferromanganese concretions in the South Atlantic and South Pacific oceans.

of the Albatross Cordillera. *Goodell* [1965] reported an increase in terrigenous material, much of it quartz, toward the Antarctic Continent. Quartz is intermixed with 223 of the 228 ferromanganese oxide accumulations studied, occurring in greatest abundance in the Scotia Sea, Drake Passage, and central Southeast Pacific Basin. It is present in all concretions from areas where ice-rafted detritus is found.

Peterson and Goldberg [1962] found abundant anorthoclase and lesser amounts of sanidine in the > 32-micron size fraction on the crest of the Albatross Cordillera and plagioclase (oligoclase-labradorite) on its flanks. In the 4–8 micron fraction anorthoclase and plagioclase were found both on the crest and on the flanks. They postulated a province of acidic volcanism associated with the Albatross Cordillera and concluded that most feldspars in the pelagic sediments of the southeastern Pacific have been derived from within the basin.

Plagioclase and possible trace amounts of sanidine are the only feldspars detected thus far in ferromanganese concretions in the South Atlantic, Pacific, and Indian oceans. Plagioclase is definitely present in 226 of 228 of the samples. Based on diffractograms, most of the plagioclase is in the oligoclase-anorthite range.

Amphibole is a common constituent of sediments from antarctic waters. *Goodell* [1965] mapped the distribution of amphibole in the less-than-2-micron size fraction and, finding it mostly restricted to the deeper portions of the Scotia Sea and South Pacific Ocean, concluded that most of it could have been derived from submarine basalts or by authigenesis. *Edwards and Goodell* [1969] found abundant sand-sized amphibole in sediments adjacent to the Antarctic (Palmer) Peninsula. Amphibole was only occasionally identified in South Pacific Ocean Mn nodules, but was usually found in nodules from the Drake Passage-Scotia Sea area.

A number of other minerals were found sporadically. Pyroxene, olivine, magnetite, and ilmenite(?) probably represent volcanic derivatives. The same is true of glass, which may be fairly ubiquitous, but is impossible to detect except when present in large quantities. Prehnite and analcime(?) probably formed during the latter stages of cooling of submarine lava flows. Apatite and calcite can be attributed to incorporated bones and foraminiferal tests, respectively. Talc/pyrophyllite and serpentine(?) may be contributed either by submarine volcanic processes or by transportation from continental metamorphic terranes.

Areal Distribution of Concretion Minerals

Inasmuch as concretions are formed by the precipitation of hydrated oxides of Fe and Mn that incorporate all available detritus, some of which is glass that may be converted to more stable phases with time, the proportions of minerals within the ferromanganese encrustations should reflect the available elements, the rate of precipitation, the associated sediment mineralogy, the surrounding sea water chemistry, and time. Regional trends dictated by associated sediment mineralogy are the easiest to evaluate, since the relative proportion of todorokite in a ferromanganese encrustation can be measured by its dilution by detrital minerals. Dilution by the amorphous Fe hydroxide phase does not alter peak area ratios, so that its effect can be ignored and the relative amount of todorokite is given by the ratio of peak areas 3.34-Å quartz + 3.2-Å plagioclase (plus phillipsite) versus 9.7-Å todorokite, the major crystalline constituents.

The highest concentrations of todorokite generally occur north of 60°S, several hundred miles from the nearest continent, in the Southwest Pacific Basin, the Albatross Cordillera, the Chile Rise-Islas Juan Fernández vicinity, the area between the Chile Rise and the Eltanin Fracture Zone, and the north-central segment of the Scotia Ridge (Figure 24). The lowest proportions of todorokite are found in concretions from the southern and eastern portions of the Southeast Pacific Basin, the Drake Passage and the West Scotia Basin, adjacent to the South Sandwich Trench, and on some parts of the Albatross Cordillera and its flanks.

The higher proportions of both quartz and feldspar in southerly latitudes reflect the influx of ice-rafted detritus from the Antarctic Continent (Figures 25 and 26). North of the influence of ice-rafted detritus, quartz and feldspar lose their latitudinal dependence. In the Southwest Pacific Basin concretion deposit, relative quartz content decreases from southwest to northeast and is also low on the Chile Rise (Figure

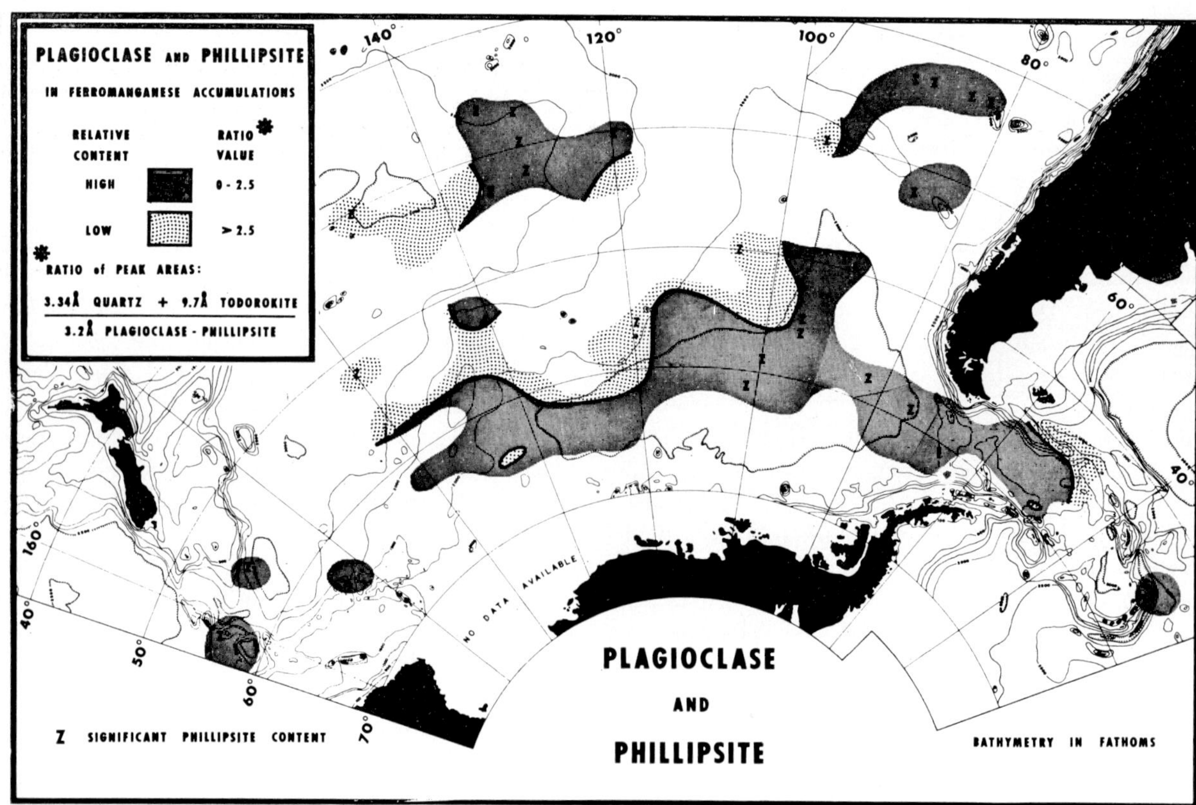

Fig. 26. The distribution of plagioclase feldspar-phillipsite in ferromanganese concretions in the South Atlantic and South Pacific oceans.

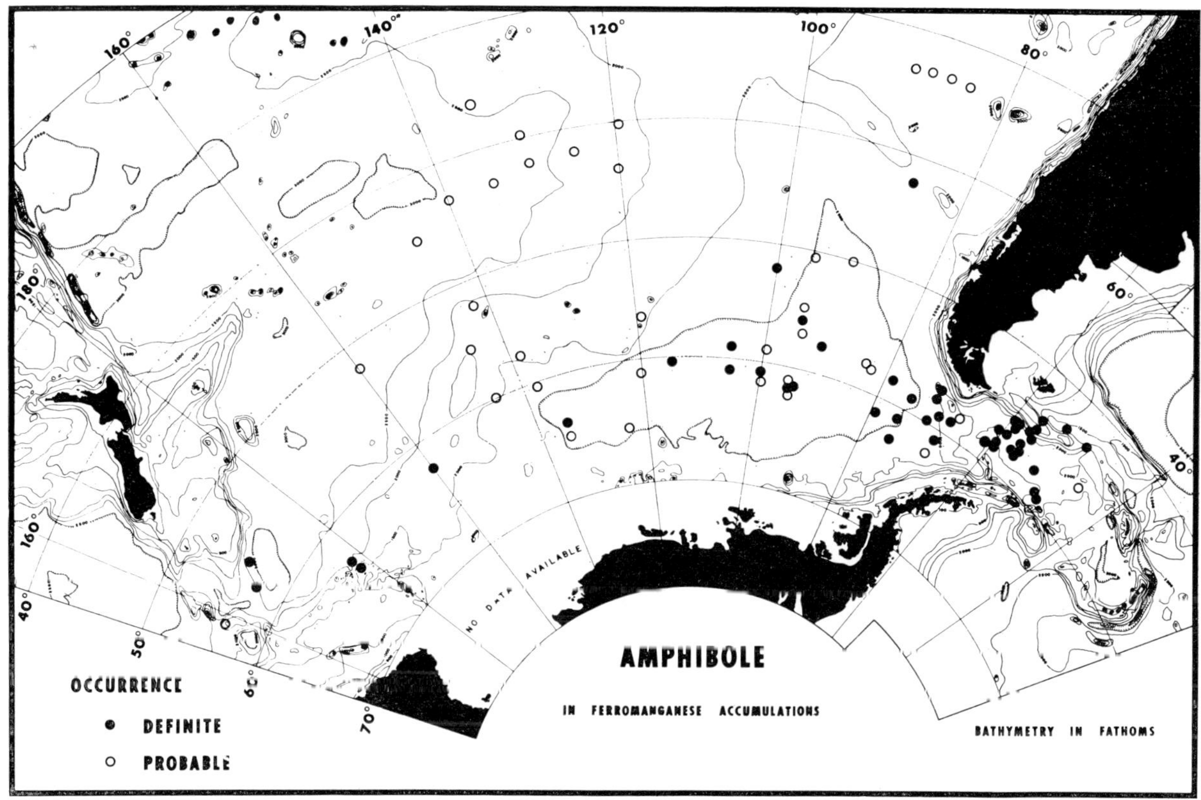

Fig. 27. The occurrence of amphibole in ferromanganese concretions in the South Atlantic and South Pacific oceans.

25). This distribution probably reflects aeolian quartz with sources in Australia-New Zealand [*Griffin et al.*, 1968].

Feldspar is the most constant of the three major crystalline constituents of ferromanganese accumulations, the extreme values for the 3.34-Å quartz + 9.7-Å todorokite/3.2-Å plagioclase-phillipsite ratio differing by 20 times (todorokite ratios differ by 225; quartz by 40). Concretions from the Albatross Cordillera, from the center of the Southwest Pacific Basin, and from the north-central Scotia Ridge show the lowest relative feldspar content (Figure 26). The importance of detrital feldspar appears to outweigh volcanic contributions, since areas of the Albatross Cordillera that might be expected to produce significant feldspar seem to contribute little.

Amphiboles, mainly hornblende, also show a distribution that is consistent with ice rafting (Figure 27). In the West Scotia Basin and Drake Passage, 30 of 34 stations have concretions with an appreciable amphibole content, whereas 3 of the other 4 stations have concretions that probably contain amphibole. Although several concretions from the Southeast Pacific Basin contain identifiable amphibole, only two samples north of the limit of glacial erratics definitely contain amphibole, one being from south of the Campbell Plateau and the other from the Chile Rise. Additional support for a detrital origin is the fact that in almost every case amphibole is contained in the oxide crust of the concretion, and not the nucleus.

The distribution of birnessite shows no definite pattern, although it is more prevalent in the center of the Southeast Pacific Basin and northeast of the Chile Rise. Montmorillonite, chlorite, maghemite, goethite, pyroxene, clinoptilolite, and analcime(?) show no discernible regional concentrations, being present in small amounts in concretions from every part of the area. The few definite illite occurrences are in nodules closest to the Antarctic.

From the distribution patterns of todorokite, quartz, feldspar, amphibole, and illite, it appears that ferromanganese deposits incorporate detritus settling from suspension in sea water or, in the case of nodules that may have rolled, from the sediment surface, in proportion to the relative rate of supply of the detrital constituents to a particular area rather than in pro-

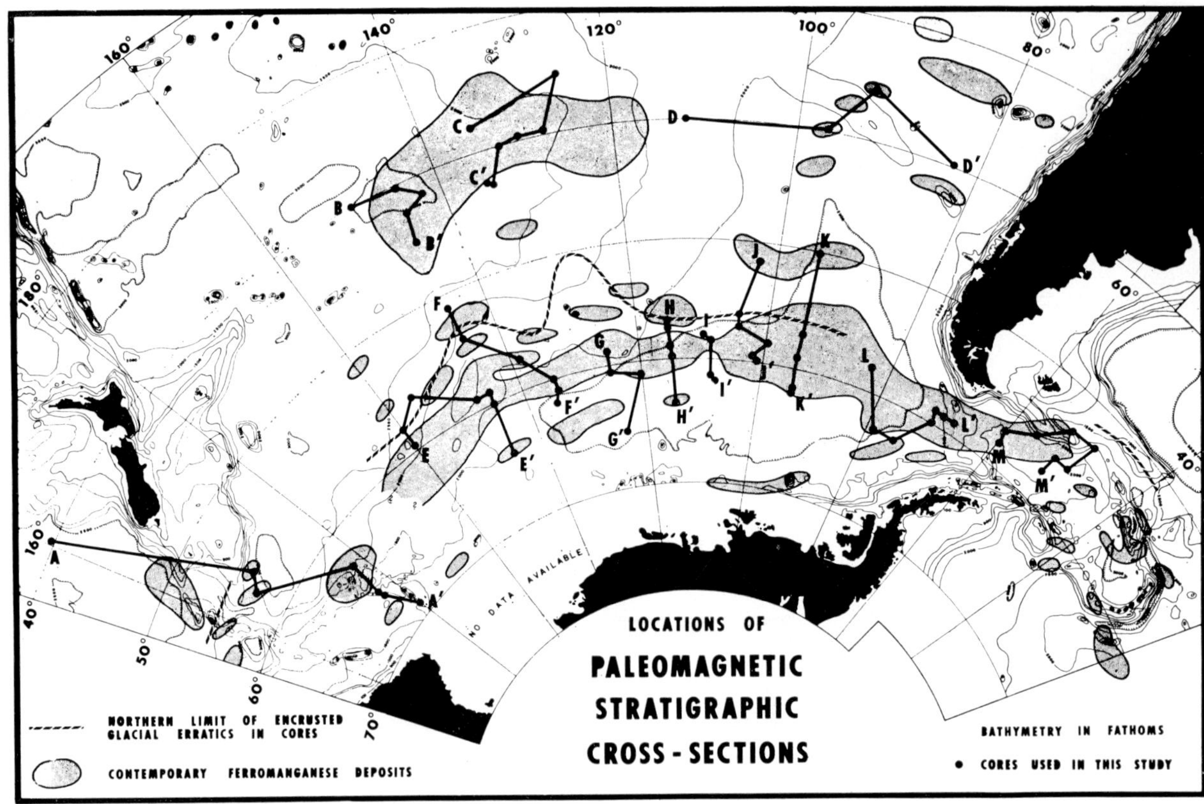

Fig. 28. Locations of paleomagnetic stratigraphic cross sections (Figs. 29, 30, and 31).

portion to the rate of accumulation of the Mn- and Fe-hydrated oxides.

BURIED CONCRETIONS

A large number of Southern Atlantic and Pacific Ocean piston and gravity cores contain fragmented or whole ferromanganese concretions: 14 contain concretions at the top only; 48 contain concretions at the top and at one or more intervals at depth; 15 contain nodules at depth only.

The oldest concretions recovered are in a core taken on the Albatross Cordillera (*Eltanin* 14-8, at sediment depths of 1600 and 1700 cm) and dated by the core's paleomagnetic stratigraphy as more than 3.4 million years. However, most concretions are found in the first meter of core (Table 6). This parallels findings of *Cronan and Tooms* [1967]. It is remarkable that as many concretions have been recovered by coring as have been, for a successful recovery requires a concretion to pass smoothly into a 5.3-cm-diameter core barrel and to continue upward without impediment. The probabilities of coring concretions at several intervals, smoothly and with continued core penetration, must be very small, yet a number of cores have been recovered successfully.

The cores are correlated (Figures 28, 29, 30, and 31) according to the geomagnetic polarity as inter-

TABLE 6. Distribution of Concretions in Cores from the South Atlantic and Pacific Oceans

Depth	Top	0–1	1–2	2–3	3–4	4–5	5–6	6–7	7–8	8–9	16–27
Conc.	14	47	11	8	3	3	2	2	1	1	2

Depth given in meters.

TABLE 7. Comparison of Sediment Core Length per Paleomagnetic Epoch with Number of Concretion Intervals per Paleomagnetic Epoch

	Nodule Horizons	Cores Terminated by Nodules	Total Length of Sediments, cm	Sediment per Nodule Horizon, cm
Brunhes	96	15	28,560	297
Matuyama	29	2	13,580	468
Gauss	4	0	4,305	1,076
Gilbert	2	0	825	412

preted by *Goodell and Watkins* [1968] and Watkins (personal communication). A majority of the cores do not reach the Brunhes-Matuyama boundary (Table 7). This constitutes some support for a model of ferromanganese concretion formation with increasing frequency in the past few hundred thousand years, since concretion horizons occur more frequently per given length of sediment core in the Brunhes than in older sediments (Table 7). This is true even when we eliminate all of the cores that consisted only of a large nodule or nodule fragments at the surface that prevented penetration of the core into underlying sediment. If sediment compaction with depth is taken into account, the importance of the Brunhes paleomagnetic epoch as a time of ferromanganese deposition is magnified. To date, no massive ferromanganese deposits comparable to those accumulated around sea floor lava flows have been struck beneath more than a few centimeters of sediment.

Buried ferromanganese concretions resemble those

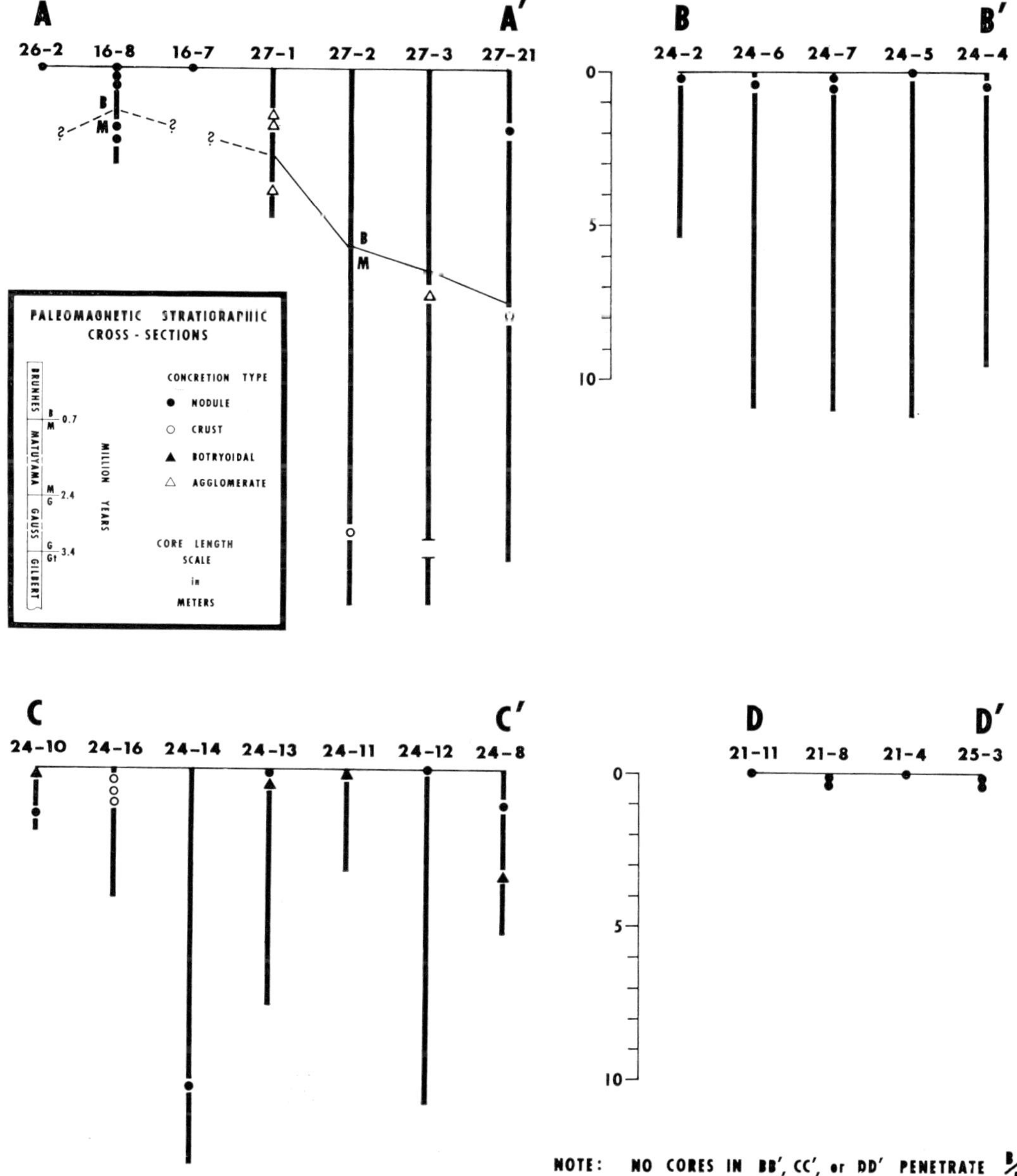

Fig. 29. The occurrence of ferromanganese concretions at depth in stratigraphic cross sections south of New Zealand (A–A′), in the Southwest Pacific Basin (B–B′ and C–C′), and across the Chile Rise (D–D′).

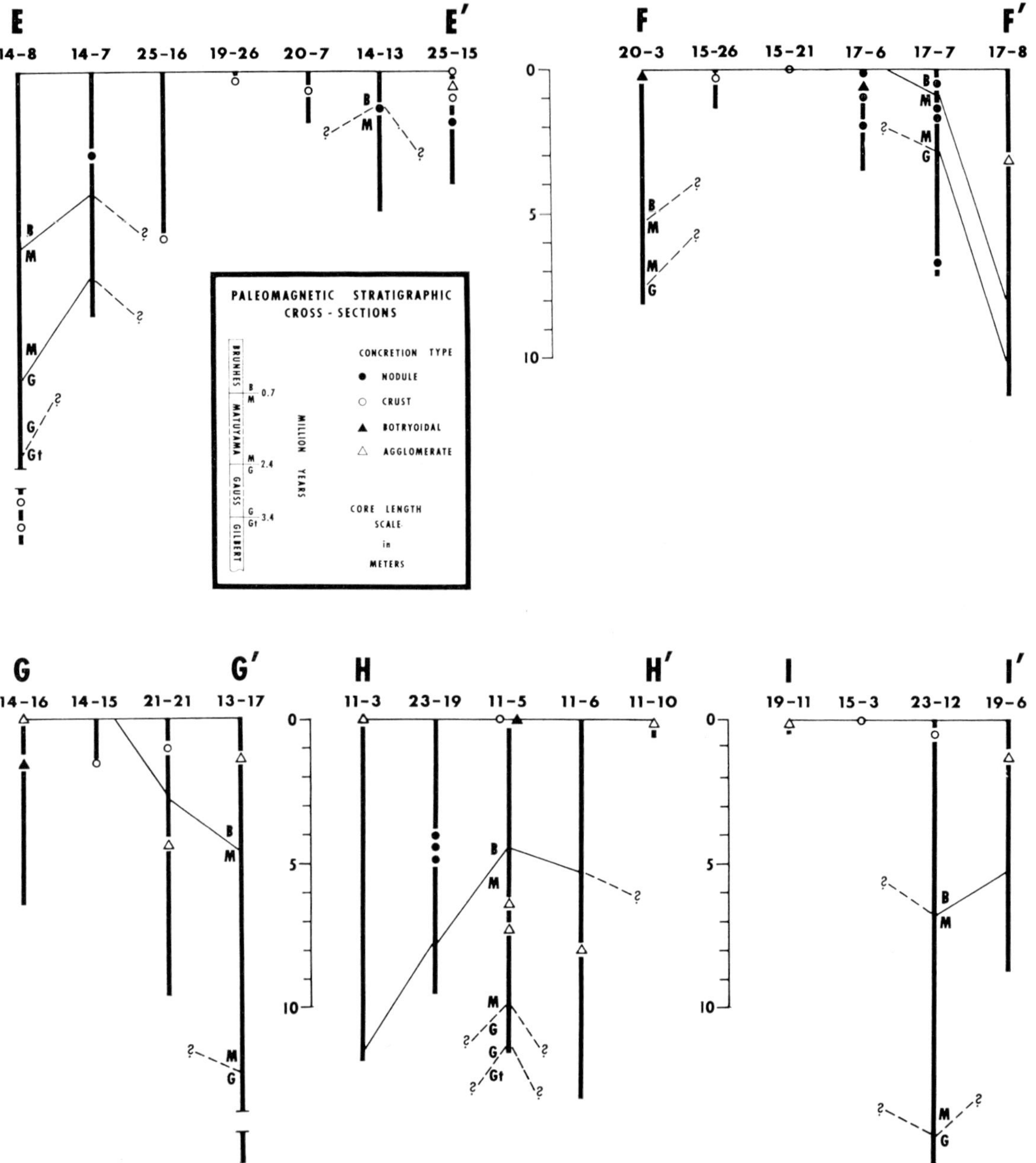

Fig. 30. The occurrence of ferromanganese concretions at depth in stratigraphic cross sections across the western Southeast Pacific Basin.

now found at the surface in distribution, structure, mineralogy, and chemistry. The areal extent of the surficial deposits and the buried concretions do not differ appreciably; exceptions are found near the Chile Rise-Albatross Cordillera and west of New Zealand (Figure 28), where samples are widely distributed.

Although the relative proportions of todorokite, quartz, and feldspar fluctuate in concretions from any one core, these fluctuations are usually minor, suggesting that over the past few hundred thousand years the relative rates of detrital deposition versus todorokite growth have not varied significantly at any one location. In addition, in most places the northern limit of glacial erratics incorporated into subsurface concretions is slightly south of the present limit, al-

TABLE 8. South Atlantic and Pacific Ferromanganese Concretions, Element Weight Percentages, Water Free

	Arithmetic		After Transgeneration*		Pacific Ocean†		
Element	Mean, %	Standard Deviation	Mean, %	Standard Deviation	Maximum	Minimum	Mean
Iron	15.78	± 4.90	15.52	20.89–11.18	26.6	2.4	14.0
Manganese	11.69	± 7.73	11.06	20.05– 3.20	50.1	8.2	24.2
Titanium	.64	± .27	.574	.92– .360	1.7	0.11	0.67
Nickel	.45	± .38	.31	1.01– .078	2.0	0.16	0.99
Cobalt	.24	± .17	.20	.46– .10	2.3	0.014	0.35
Copper	.21	± .15	.17	.32– .091	1.6	0.028	0.53
Barium	.10	± .08	.095	.19– .035	0.64	0.08	0.18
Strontium	.08	± .03	.077	.13– .047	0.16	0.024	0.081
Zirconium	.07	± .05	.050	.13– .020	0.12	0.009	0.063
Vanadium	.06	± .03	.046	.099– .025	0.11	0.021	0.054
Zinc	.06	± .03	.052	.088– .031	0.08	0.04	0.047
Molybdenum	.04	± .02	.036	.060– .021	0.15	0.01	0.052
Water	14.60	± 5.80	14.03	20.89– 8.55	39.0	15.5	25.8

*Fe, Mn, H_2O — x_i = arc sin $\sqrt{x_i}$; remainder — $x_i = \log_{10} x_i$.
†After *Arrhenius* [1963].

though the subsurface boundary takes into account all nodules deposited before the last several thousand years (Figures 21 and 28).

GEOCHEMISTRY

Ferromanganese Concretion Data

Chemical analyses on 168 of the concretion crusts and on 7 of the concretion nuclei were performed by the Materials Laboratory of the Newport News Shipbuilding and Drydock Company: Fe, Mn, Cu, Co, and Ni by X-ray fluorescence and Ba, Sr, Zr, Ti, Mo, Sn, V, Cr, Ag, W, Hg, and Sc by atomic absorption. The last five of these proved to be so consistently below the detection threshold of the method of the laboratory in the ferromanganese matrix (Cr < 0.03; Ag < 0.02%; W < 0.05%; Hg < 0.02%, and Sc < 0.10%) that no further discussion of these is warranted. Details of sample preparation are given in the appendix. Element weight percentages are reported on a dry weight basis (Table 8). The three major components of concretions are Fe, Mn, and H_2O. Titanium

TABLE 9. South Atlantic and Pacific Manganese Concretions, Element Correlation Matrix

Fe	Mn	Ni	Co	Cu	Ba	Sr	Zr	Ti	Mo	Sn	V	Zn	H_2O	
	—.371	—.341		—.372			.376		—.361	—.307			—.373	Lat
	.529	.413	.292	.329	.227	.405		.352	.396				.443	Long
—.354				.463							—.401			Depth
		—.403	.426	—.591	.320	.333	.376	.561	.241		.459	—.279	.398	Fe
		.742	.499	.471	.577	.622	—.216		.673		.214	.369	.708	Mn
				.705	.358	.339	—.236		.429			.514	.408	Ni
				—.236	.539	.694		.542	.473	—.289	.329		.548	Co
							—.425	—.301	.225	.283	—.289	.397		Cu
						.676		.243	.514	—.277	.247		.496	Ba
								.357	.550				.580	Sr
								.303		—.461				Zr
											.234	—.263	.313	Ti
											.389		.640	Mo
														Sn
													.389	V
														Zn
														H_2O

$N = 168$; $r_{.995} = 0.214$; Fe, Mn, H_2O — x_i = arc sin $\sqrt{x_i}$; remainder of elements — $x_i = \log_{10} x_i$.

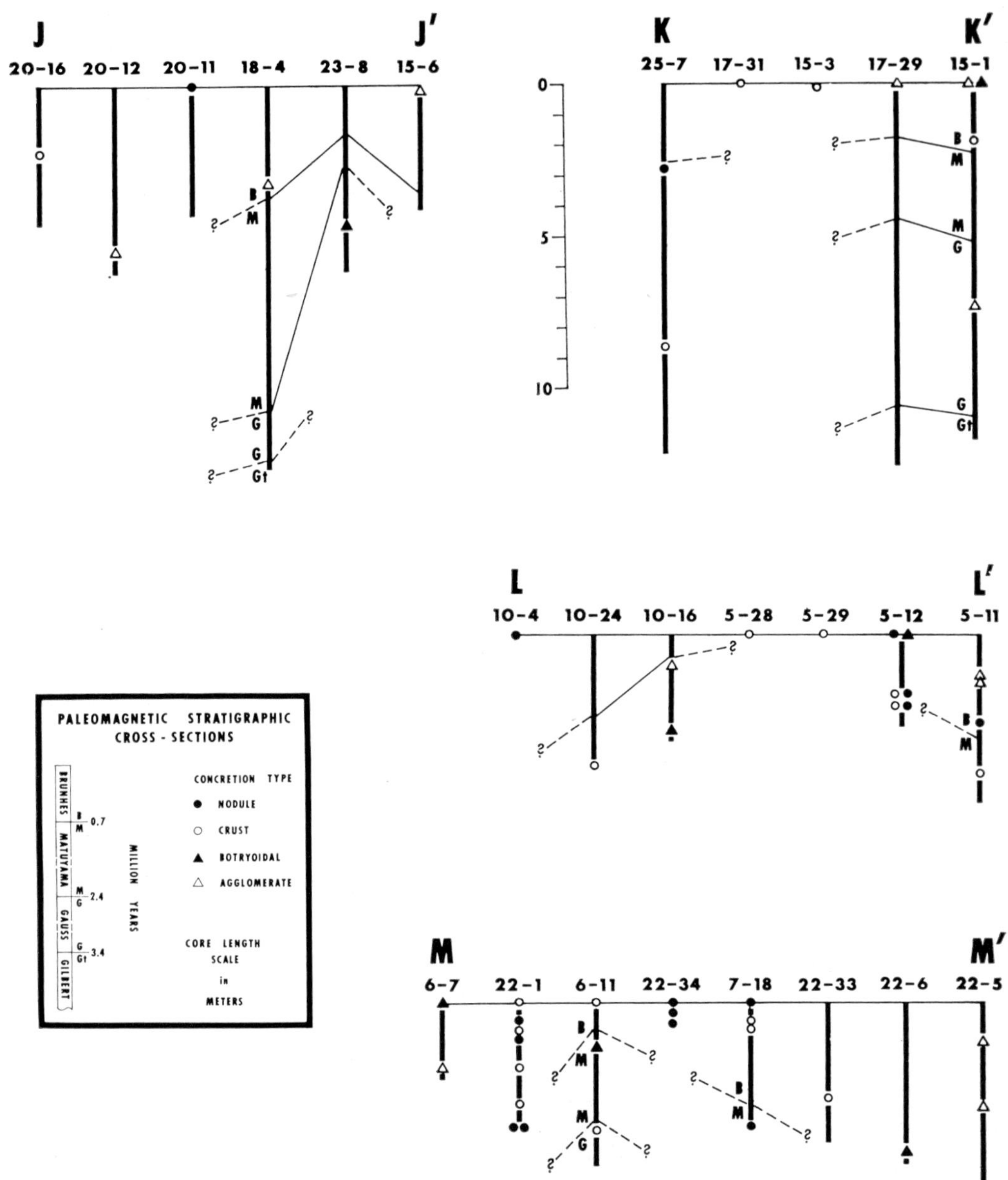

Fig. 31. The occurrence of ferromanganese concretions across the eastern Southeast Pacific Basin (J–J′ and K–K′), Drake Passage (L–L′), and Scotia Sea (M–M′).

and Ni often exceed 1.0%, whereas Co, Cu, and Ba are usually between 0.1 and 1.0%, and the remaining elements are generally less than 0.1%.

The distributions of all of the concretion elements, with the exception of Fe, Mn, and H_2O, are skewed (Figure 32). This is in part the result of the large regional differences in element concentration and in part due to the log-normal distributions of trace elements [*Ahrens*, 1954*a*, *b*, 1957].

Statistical analyses were performed on the element

TABLE 10. All Oceans Correlation Matrix: Ferromanganese Concretion Elemental Analysis

Fe	Ni	Co	Cu	
−0.542	0.451		0.391	Mn
	−0.406	.434	−0.436	Fe
			.849	Ni

$n = 156$; $r_{0.995} = .226$; data from *Mero* [1965].

data as follows: correlation, regression, stepwise multiple regression, and multiple regression. The 95% confidence level was used for rejection throughout except in correlation ($r = 0.995$). All calculations were made by digital computer (CDC 6400) at the Florida State University Computing Center.

Correlation. Latitude, longitude, and water depth were added as variables to the 13 elements analyzed (Table 9). East longitudes were converted to west longitudes greater than 180°W. The transgeneration $x_i = \log_{10} x_i$ was performed on the minor element percentages and $x_i = \arcsin \sqrt{x_i}$ on Fe, Mn, and H_2O percentages before calculation to symmetrize the distributions and stabilize the variances. Data from analyses of worldwide concretion collections were compiled from *Mero* [1965], and correlations were calculated for Fe, Mn, Ni, Co, and Cu for comparison (Table 10).

Whereas Fe and Mn show an inverse worldwide correlation, no relationship at all exists in the South Atlantic, Pacific, and Indian oceans (Tables 9 and 10). Water is correlated directly with Fe and Mn, although the latter relationship is much stronger. The positive relationships between the elements given in Table 9 are sorted out between the major components, Fe, Mn, H_2O, Ni, and Ti, in order to establish sequences of highly correlated elements (Table 11).

Tin is the only minor metal analyzed that does not positively correlate with one of the five major components; its only association is with Cu.

One or more of the geographic parameters of latitude, longitude, and water depth are related to all of the elements except Zn (Table 9). The relatively low numerical value of some of the correlation coefficients is attributed to nonindependence, large variability, and nonlinearity.

Regression. In order to test nonlinearity, polynomial regression was performed using the model $x = (a_0 + a_1 y)^n$ and an analysis of variance with an $f_{0.95}$ test for rejection. Two criteria had to be met for nonrejection: (1) the regression (n) had to reduce the over-all variability significantly; and (2) the regression ($n + 1$) was a significant reduction over (n). In an attempt to reduce the variability, only data from south of 50°S latitude were used, but no transgenerations of the data were performed.

TABLE 11. Elements Correlated with Major Components Listed in Decreasing Order of Importance

Fe	Mn	H_2O	Ti	Ni
Ti	Ni	Mn	Fe	Mn
V	H_2O	Mo	Co	Cu
Co	Mo	Sr	Sr	Zn
H_2O	Sr	Co	H_2O	H_2O
Zr	Ba	Ba	Zr	Mo
Sr	Co	V	Ba	Ba
Ba	Cu	Fe	V	Sr
Mo	Zn	Ni		
	V	Ti		

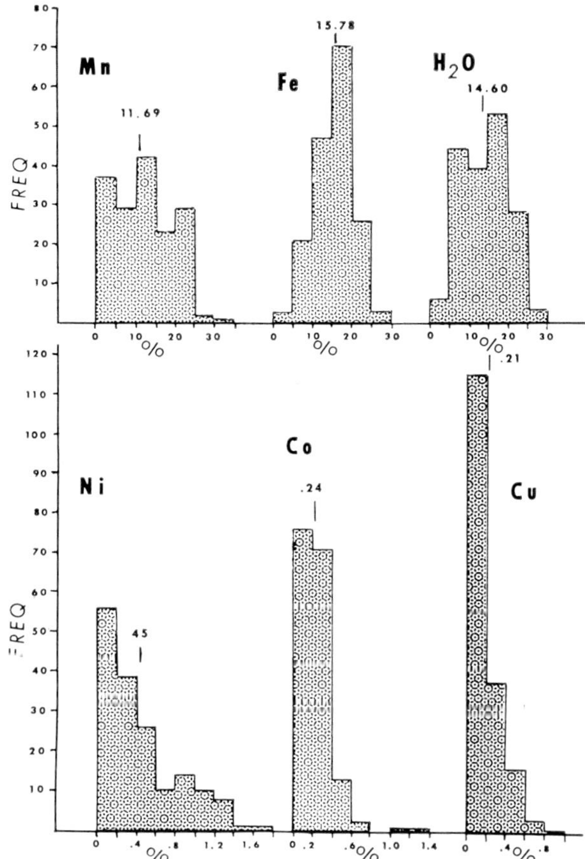

Fig. 32. Element distributions in South Atlantic and South Pacific ferromanganese concretions. The arithmetic mean is noted for each. The population consists of 168 analyses.

Both Fe and Mn as a function of each other show quadratic relationships (Figure 33), although neither accounts for a very large percentage of the other's variability, the lowest Mn percentage occurring at about 10% Fe and the highest Fe percentage at about 17% Mn. Nickel has no significant regression with Fe but is quadratic as a function of Mn, which accounts for 61% of its variability (Figure 34). Copper exhibits a cubic relationship with Ni but a negative linear one with Co (Figure 35). Cobalt is only linearly related to both Fe and Mn, although the former is

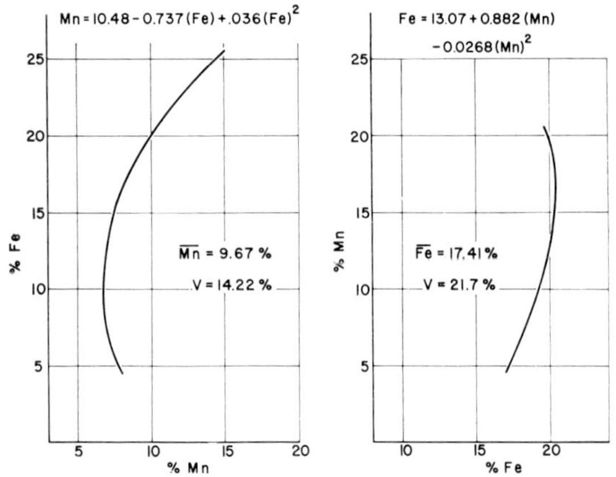

Fig. 33. The regression of Fe on Mn and Mn on Fe for samples south of 50°S latitude. Average values for iron ($\overline{Fe}$) and manganese ($\overline{Mn}$) are noted as well as the variability (V) accounted for by regression.

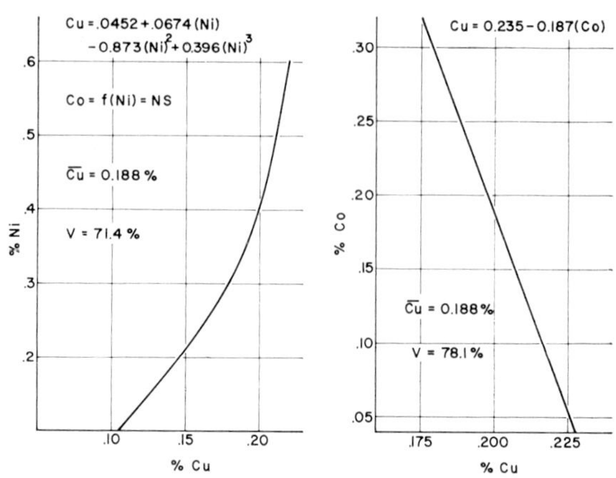

Fig. 35. The regression of Cu on Ni and Co for samples south of 50°S latitude. Copper averages 0.188%. Cu = f(Ni) is quadratic; Cu = f(Co) is negative linear.

stronger (Figure 36). Copper shows a linear negative relationship with Fe but a cubic relationship with Mn, which is almost symmetrical about Cu = 0.20% (Figure 36). It is therefore not surprising that the linear relationship presumed in correlation of Cu with Mn is not significant (Table 9).

Inasmuch as the quadratic relationships between Mn and Fe are extremely steep (Figure 33), the non-correlation of these elements when data from the entire South Atlantic, Pacific, and Indian oceans are used is not surprising (Table 9). The linearity of the relationship of Cu versus Co, the relative unimportance (10^{-4}) of the quadratic coefficient in Ni versus Mn, and the reversal in curvature in the cubic Cu versus Ni all argue for linearity as a good approximation to the element relationships.

Stepwise multiple regression. In an effort to sort out more quantitatively the relationships among the elements and between the elements and the geographic parameters, stepwise multiple linear regression was employed. The data were transformed using arc sin $\sqrt{x_i}$ and $\log_{10} x_i$ as before. The model consists of a linear equation of the form:

$$y = a_0 + a_1x_1 + a_2x_2 \cdots a_nx_n + E$$

The principal independent variable x_i is initially chosen by virtue of its having the highest correlation coefficient with y. The remainder are added one at a time as the analysis proceeds, using as selection criterion that variable having the largest partial correla-

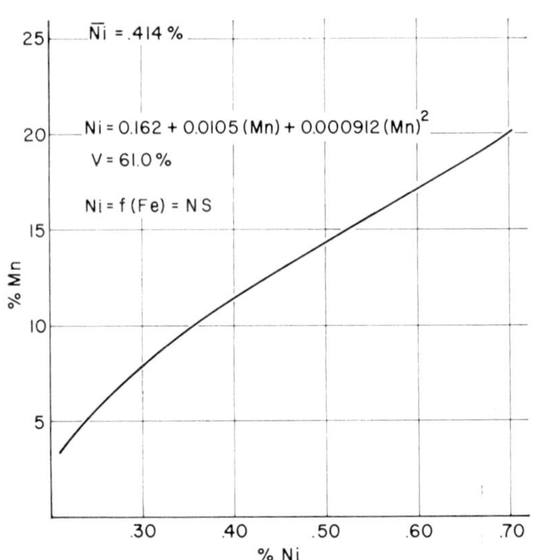

Fig. 34. The regression of Ni on Mn for samples south of 50°S latitude. Nickel averages 0.414%, and 61% of the variability of nickel is accounted for by regression. Both regressions are quadratic.

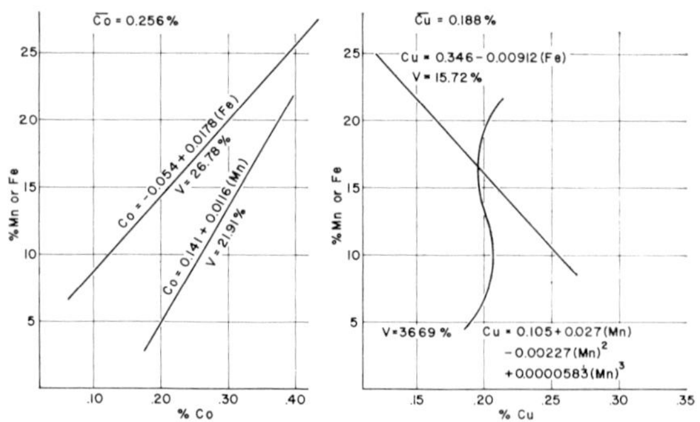

Fig. 36. The regression of Co and Cu on Mn and Fe. Co averages 0.256% and is linear with both Fe and Mn. Cu is negatively linear with Fe but cubic with Mn.

tion coefficient with the residuals *E* with an analysis of variance for nonrejection. Variables already selected are tested after each addition of a new variable to the regression to determine whether or not the sums of squares attributed to their regression remain above a critical *f*-level. The critical *f*-level for inclusion or deletion was selected as 1.00.

The analysis continues until all variables that have significant partial correlation coefficients have been added and all variables have been deleted whose significance has eroded. The result is a predicting equation for the dependent variable. Variability unaccounted for is attributed to independent variables not measured, interdependence of variables, nonlinearity of variables, and true random variation.

To maximize positive element associations, a second stepwise regression was accomplished in which all of the variables that had significant negative partial correlation coefficients were systematically restricted from consideration (Table 12).

Nickel. Using all of the variables, Mn and Cu account for 71.28% of the variability in Ni with seven other significant parameters comprising the remainder of the 79.44% variability accounted for. When negative partial correlation coefficients are restricted, Mn, Cu, Zn, and Co alone are significant (Table 12).

Titanium. With unrestricted entry permitted, Fe and longitude account for 46.84% of Ti variation with seven others significant in lesser amounts for a total of 64.33%. With restricted entry, only Fe, longitude, depth, Co, and Zr are significant and account for 57.69% of Ti variability (Table 12).

Cobalt. Unrestricted regression allows 11 variables, which account for 76.35% of Co variability, of which Sr and Ti contribute 58.16%. When positive coefficients are forced, only Sr, Ti, V, Mn, and latitude are significant and account for 63.63% of variability.

Copper. Ten variables account for 79.08% of the variability of Cu, of which Ni and Co comprise 65.20%. When negative associations are restricted, Ni, depth, Sn, and Zn account for 79.47% of Cu variation, one of two instances where restriction leads to an improvement of the predicting equation (Table 12).

Vanadium. Nine variables account for 47.86% of V variability with Fe, Mo, and depth having 36.67%. When only positive correlations are allowed, Fe and Mo alone are significant (29.26%).

Molybdenum. Only Mn makes a large contribution (45.33%) to the total variability of Mo accounted for by nine variables. Restriction reduces the original variables by three but adds two new ones (Cu, Co). Both Mn and V are now important, and the predicting equation accounts for a larger percentage of Mo variability (60.13%) than before (54.26%).

Barium. Strontium accounts for 45.69% of total variability of Ba (63.96%). Restricting regression does not materially alter the relationships, although four variables are dropped and Ni and V added, and the total variability accounted for drops to 59.27% (Table 12).

Strontium. Cobalt and Ba constitute 61.06% of the variability of Sr with nine other variables, making small additional contributions for a total of 71.85%. Restricting regression does not greatly alter the relationships, although depth is added as a factor and the total variability drops from 71.85% to 67.83% (Table 12).

Zinc. Ten variables account for 46.57% of the variability of Zn, of which Ni alone contributes 26.42%. With regression restricted to positive correlations, Ni, V, Cu, and latitude are the only significant parameters and account for 29.68% of Zn variation.

Tin. Thirteen variables account for 44.91% of the variability of Sn, of which Zr accounts for 21.22%. Tin and Zr are anomalous in that the regression coefficient for each in terms of the other is negative and large. When negative coefficients are restricted, Cu is the only significant variable, but it accounts for only 8.69% of the variability.

Zirconium. Ten elements account for 44.74% of the variation in Zr, of which Sn constitutes 21.22%. When negatively correlated factors are eliminated, only latitude, Fe, and Ti are significant and account for 27.94% of Zr variation. This is the only element that has a geographic variable as a major parameter.

TABLE 13. Element Associations with Water in Southern Atlantic and Pacific Concretions

Water	No Water
Mn	Co
Fe	Cu
Mo	Ba
V	Sr
Zr	Ni
	Zn*
	Sn*
	Ti*

* Negative regression coefficients.

TABLE 12. Elemental Relationships by Stepwise Multiple Regression

Nickel			Titanium			Cobalt		
	Coeff.	% Var.		Coeff.	% Var.		Coeff.	% Var.
a_0	.811		a_0	— .995		a_0	.447	
Mn	1.121	55.09	Fe	1.651	31.43	Sr	.438	48.22
Cu	.686	16.19	Long	.002	15.41	Ti	.451	9.94
Sn	— .108	2.88	Depth	.0001	4.62	Sn	— .089	2.75
Fe	—1.202	1.94	Co	.357	5.38	Zn	— .276	1.66
Zn	.323	1.10	H_2O	— .558	4.95	Mn	.555	3.28
Co	.375	1.53	Sr	— .162	1.56	Cu	— .384	3.03
Lat	.004	.87	Zr	.047	.43	Ni	.167	2.46
Ti	.152	.23	Ni	— .043	.25	Depth	— .0001	.55
Zr	.068	.21	Lat	— .002	.30	Fe	—.527	.30
		79.44			64.33	Mo	.119	3.90
						Long	— .001	.21
								76.35
a_0	.599		a_0	—1.040		a_0	.003	
Mn	.986	55.10	Fe	1.507	31.43	Sr	.590	49.22
Cu	.848	16.18	Long	.001	15.41	Ti	.416	9.94
Zn	.434	2.39	Depth	.0001	4.62	V*	.181	3.68
Co	.333	1.81	Co	.198	5.38	Mn	.346	.94
		75.48	Zr	.052	.85	Lat*	.003	.85
					57.69			63.63

Copper			Vanadium			Molybdenum		
	Coeff.	% Var.		Coeff.	% Var.		Coeff.	% Var.
a_0	— .616		a_0	—1.751		a_0	—1.037	
Ni	.280	49.65	Fe	1.012	21.03	Mn	.262	45.33
Co	— .307	15.55	Mo	.346	8.23	Zr	— .085	2.55
Depth	.0001	6.37	Depth	—1.012	7.41	V	.190	1.87
Sn	.095	3.47	Sr	— .552	3.41	Sr	.190	2.06
Mn	.279	1.15	Mn	.359	3.07	H_2O	.554	.77
Fe	— .622	1.07	Cu	.221	2.35	Sn	.073	.51
Ba	.106	.57	Zn	.167	.86	Ba	.116	.63
Lat	— .003	.73	Co	.148	.82	Lat	— .002	.28
V	— .074	.35	H_2O	.461	.68	Long	.0004	.26
Zr	.106	.17			47.86			54.26
		79.08						
a_0	— .358		a_0	—1.425		a_0	— .901	
Ni	.339	49.65	Fe	1.496	21.03	Mn	.324	45.33
Depth	.0002	10.35	Mo	.352	8.23	V	.199	8.88
Sn	.196	7.44			29.26	Sn	.117	3.42
Zn*	.209	12.03				Sr	.130	1.08
		79.47				H_2O	.613	— .07
						Ba	.085	.85
						Cu*	.101	.32
						Co*	.081	.32
								60.13

Table 12 (Continued)

Barium	Coeff.	% Var.	Strontium	Coeff.	% Var.	Zinc	Coeff.	% Var.
a_0	—1.388		a_0	—1.089		a_0	—1.260	
Sr	.584	45.69	Co	.312	48.22	Ni	.223	26.42
Mn	1.053	4.02	Ba	.168	12.84	Co	— .400	5.95
Sn	— .681	4.74	Mn	.334	3.38	Depth	— .0001	7.07
Fe	—1.709	2.45	V	— .192	2.59	Sn	— .097	1.90
Lat	.008	2.16	Fe	.605	2.51	Mn	.564	2.76
Cu	.314	1.83	Long	.001	.74	Long	.001	.87
Long	— .001	1.43	Mo	.098	.43	V	.094	.67
Mo	.255	.94	Zr	.056	.31	H_2O	— .429	.48
H_2O	— .681	.70	Sn	.050	.48	Zr	.054	.45
		63.96	Ti	— .094	.35			46.57
					71.85			
a_0	—1.401		a_0	— .835		a_0	—1.029	
Sr	.640	45.69	Co	.289	48.22	Ni	.213	26.43
Mn	.622	4.02	Ba	.192	12.83	V	.144	1.07
Lat	.011	3.80	Mn	.320	3.39	Cu*	.162	.92
Fe	1.477	4.83	Long	.001	1.12	Lat*	.003	1.26
Ni*	.132	1.44	Sn	.065	.76			29.68
Cu	.181	.75	Zr	.049	.87			
V*	.131	.18	Fe	.276	.29			
		59.27	Depth*	.00003	.35			
					67.83			

Tin	Coeff.	% Var.	Zirconium	Coeff.	% Var.
a_0	—2.369		a_0	—2.731	
Zr	— .234	21.22	Sn	— .280	21.22
Ba	— .339	4.34	Fe	1.362	9.89
Lat	— .007	2.23	Lat	.009	5.98
H_2O	—2.001	1.51	Mo	— .397	2.70
Mo	.318	2.58	Sr	.381	1.35
Zn	— .283	1.48	Mn	—1.054	.81
Co	— .356	2.37	Ti	.257	.84
Sr	.307	3.03	Ni	.118	.87
Mn	.854	1.08	H_2O	.756	.64
Fe	1.753	1.46	Zn	.146	.44
Cu	.465	1.81			44.74
Ni	— .193	1.10			
Long	.001	.70			
		44.91			
a_0	1.880		a_0	—2.812	
Cu	.410	8.69	Lat	.017	14.14
		8.69	Fe	1.660	12.82
			Ti	.234	.98
					27.94

* Variables not appearing in unrestricted multiple regression above.

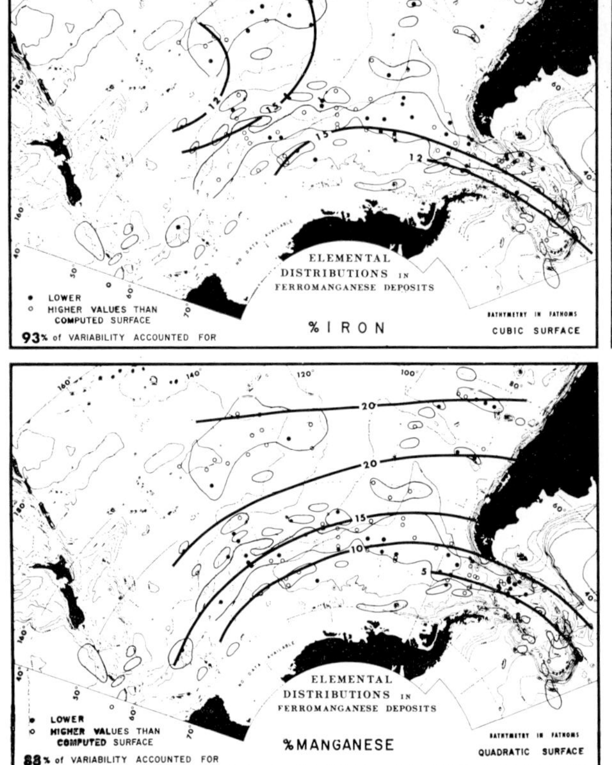

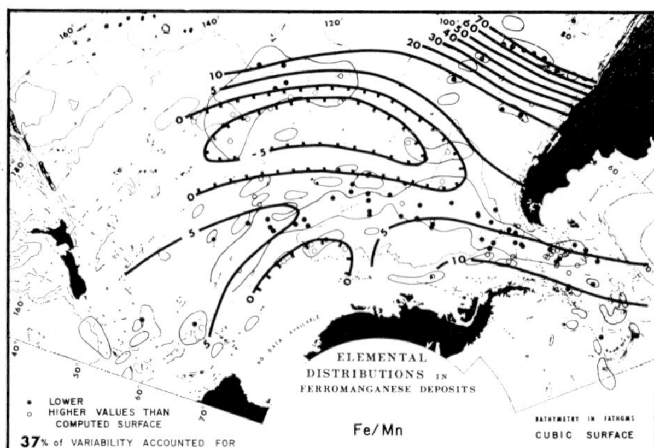

Figs. 37–39. Elemental distributions in ferromanganese deposits in the South Atlantic and South Pacific oceans.

Water. Only 5 of the 13 elements are associated with H_2O in stepwise regression. Two of these, Fe and Mn, are strongly related; the other three are related only as a secondary parameter (Table 13). Eight of the elements are not associated with water; three of these elements actually have negative regression coefficients.

Multiple regression. Inasmuch as the geographic parameters used in correlation were significant for all but one of the elements, and in order to smooth the data, the element percentages and certain element ratios were subjected to multiple regression. The element (or ratio) was considered a function of its location as: $z_i = (a_0 + a_1x + a_2y)^n$. The geographic coordinates (x and y) were raised to successively higher polynomials until by analysis of variance the regression polynomial ($n + 1$) added no significant reduction to the variability accounted for by polynomial (n). In addition, polynomial (n) must represent a significant reduction in the total variability. An $f_{0.95}$ test was used as the basis of nonrejection for both criteria, and no data transgenerations were used. Further discussion of the method is given in *Goodell* [1967*a*].

Since the x and y coordinates used were latitude and longitude to hundredths of a degree, they represent an arithmetic grid. However, a polyconic projection was used in the data portrayal, so that the element surfaces represented by the polynomials are warped, a plane, for example, becoming a polyconic. The polynomial element surfaces represent the broad regional relationships in the data; anomalies above and below the surface are data components not accounted for by the least-squares fitting and may be considered as local effects [*Krumbein and Graybill*, 1965].

The regional distribution of Fe is given by a cubic surface with its highest values along the southeastern flank of the Albatross Cordillera, the 15% isopleth following the trend of the ferromanganese belt beneath the circumpolar current (Figure 37). Values decrease toward the Antarctic Continent and into the Southwest Pacific Basin. The best fit surface for Mn is quadratic with its crest of more than 20% Mn

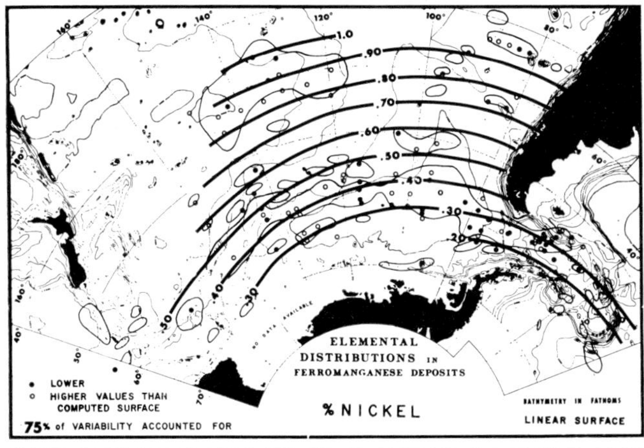

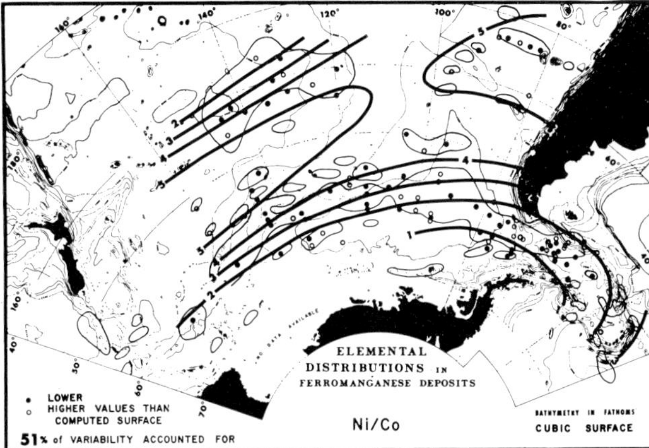

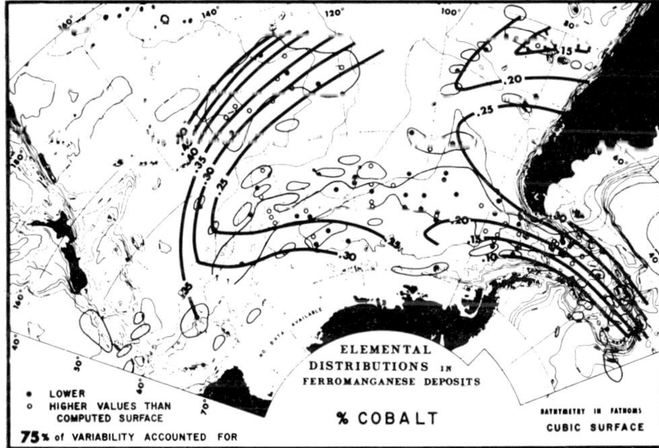

Figs. 40–42. Elemental distributions in ferromanganese deposits in the South Atlantic and South Pacific oceans.

lying across the Albatross Cordillera to include the Chile Rise and the Southwest Pacific Basin (Figure 38). Inasmuch as many of the minor elements correlate with Fe and Mn, the regional distribution of the Fe/Mn ratio was calculated (Figure 39). The extremely low values that lie across the Albatross Cordillera reflect small fractional values of Fe/Mn as contrasted to ratios over 10 in the Scotia Sea. Fractional ratios are again found in the southwestern quadrant of the Southeast Pacific Basin toward the Ross Sea.

Nickel values increase linearly northward almost paralleling latitude, the 1.0% Ni value crossing the Pacific-Atlantic Ocean at about 43°S (Figure 40). Cobalt values are represented by a cubic surface with values decreasing southwestward across the Albatross Cordillera and eastward into the Scotia Sea (Figure 41). Inasmuch as Ni and Mn are strongly related, the areal distributions of the Ni/Co ratio should show inverse lobes with the distribution of the Fe/Mn ratio. Both ratios are cubic (Figures 39 and 42). The highest Ni/Co values parallel the northwest flank of the Albatross Cordillera and cross the cordillera and the Chile Rise. This high roughly corresponds to the depression in the Fe/Ni surface, although the 'structures' are slightly canted to one another.

The highest Cu values are found in the Southwest Pacific Basin; the lowest values in the Drake Passage (Figure 43). The elements of the surface parallel the topography. The quadratic surface of Zn has its highest values on the Chile Rise and down the trend of the northwest flank of the Albatross Cordillera (Figure 44). Values decrease toward the continent and northward into the Southwest Pacific Basin. A direct correlation exists between Cu and Zn (Tables 9 and 12). However, the areal distribution of the ratio shows regional variations that decrease toward the Antarctic Continent (Figure 45). Ratios of 3 and 4 bracket the ferromanganese belt at 60°S.

There is a strong inverse relationship between Fe and Cu; a positive one between Fe and Co (Table 9). The high Cu values in the Southwest Pacific Basin create a zone of low Fe/Cu ratios that increase north, southeast, and southwest (Figure 46). The

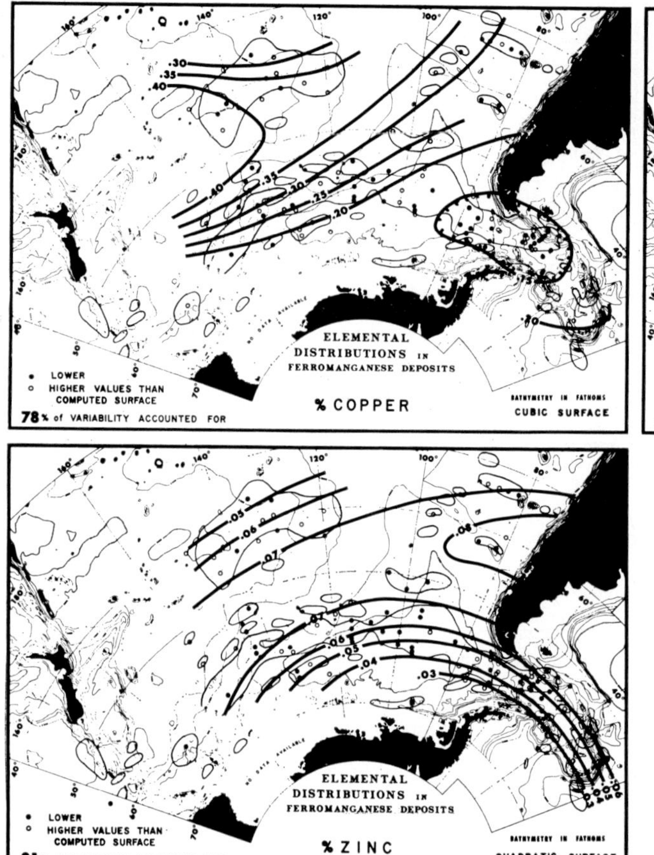

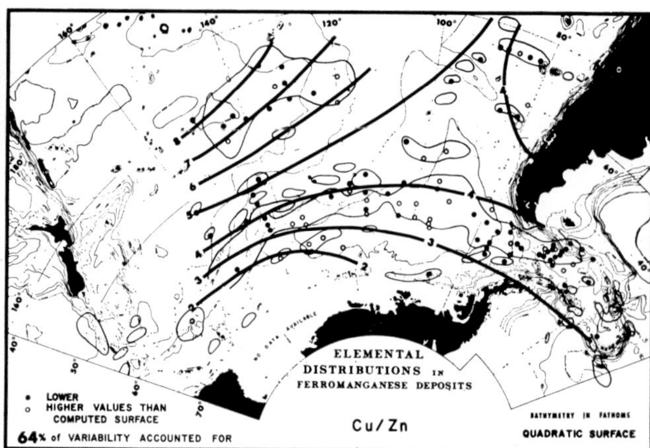

Figs. 43–45. Elemental distributions in ferromanganese deposits in the South Atlantic and South Pacific oceans.

distribution of the Fe/Co ratio is simpler, with the lowest ratios in the Southwest Pacific Basin increasing north and eastward with the isoplethal syncline axis following the trend of the 60°S ferromanganese belt (Figure 47).

The positive correlation between Mn and Ni is the strongest elemental relationship calculated. The geographic distribution of the ratio appears dominated by the latitude; the ratio decreases northward at about 4/10° (Ni increases 0.3%/10°) and cuts across all apparent topographic and hydrologic controls (Figure 48).

The distribution of Zr is latitudinally dependent, except that, unlike Ni, Zr values increase toward the continent (Figure 49). The distribution of Ti is also geometrically simple, decreasing linearly from about 180° to the South Sandwich Trench, with isopleths that cut all major topographic features at nearly right angles (Figure 50). Titanium is directly correlated with Fe, and the distribution of the Fe/Ti ratio reflects this interdependence, with larger ratios along the Albatross Cordillera, the Chile Rise, and the Drake Passage-Scotia Sea (Figures 37 and 51). The depressions in the Fe/Ti surface reflect the decrease in Fe toward the continent, coupled with general Ti increases and low Fe values in the Southwest Pacific Basin.

Highest values of V are found along the trend of the north flank of the Albatross Cordillera across the Cordillera and on the Chile Rise (Figure 52) with lower values toward the continent and to the north. The direct relationship of Fe/V falls between Fe-Ti and Fe-Co in strength (Tables 9 and 11). The distribution of Fe/V is strikingly similar in geometry to that of Fe/Co (Figures 47 and 53). In both instances the highest ratio values occur in the Southwest Pacific Basin and increase east and northeast with the isoplethal syncline axis following the trend of the 60°S ferromanganese belt. The correlation between Fe and Zn is negative. High values of both Zn and Fe are found in the central Pacific, although their highest concentrations are offset one from the other (Figures 37 and 44). The distribution of the Fe/Zn ratio shows a linear increase west to east (Figure 54). Al-

TABLE 14. South Atlantic and Pacific Basalt Elemental Analyses, Weight Per Cent

	5-4(G)	5-5(G)	15-5(V)	15-15(V)	21-8(G)	21-10(V)	24-15(V)	25-5(G)	Average Ocean Tholeiitic Basalt*	Average Alkali Basalt
Si	22.54	22.07	23.29	23.47	23.15	23.57	22.54	23.19	23.07	22.17
Al	7.31	7.62	7.84	7.84	7.25	8.37	7.25	7.94	9.02	9.54
Fe	9.89	8.58	7.22	7.33	10.11	6.83	9.29	7.51	6.69	7.43
Mg	3.49	4.20	4.52	4.49	4.40	4.67	3.59	4.17	4.34	2.89
Ca	6.59	6.83	8.14	9.46	7.27	8.44	6.63	7.36	8.38	8.65
Na	2.00	2.57	2.04	2.09	2.07	2.02	1.89	2.07	2.03	3.99
K	.67	1.16	.19	.11	.31	.08	.50	.40	.14	1.40
P	.074	.226	.061	.061	.078	.056	.069	.065	.069	.40
Ti	1.27	1.63	.86	.85	1.26	.80	1.31	1.01	.89	1.72
Mn	.111	.284	.118	.103	.142	.095	.142	.111	.134	.13
Co[5]	.0100	.0070	.0076	.0086	.0110	.0090	.0300	.0065	.0032	.0025
Cr	.013	.082	.045	.044	.017	.059	.031	.037	.0297	.0067
Cu	.0090	.0045	.0072	.0064	.0210	.0061	.0240	.0120	.0077	.0036
Ni	.0084	.0120	.0097	.0110	.0170	.0100	.0240	.0097	.0097	.0051
Sr	.012	.015	.017	.014	.013	.012	.012	.021	.013	.0815
V	.017	.013	.013	.018	.017	.016	.004	.013	.0292	.0252
Zr	.0130	.0021	.0110	.0089	.0180	.0098	.0280	.0130	.0095	.0333
Fe/Mn × 10†	8.9	3.0	6.1	7.1	7.1	7.2	6.5	6.8	5.0	5.0
Mn/Ni	13	24	12	9	8	10	6	11	14	26
Ni/Co	.8	1.7	1.3	1.3	1.6	1.1	.8	1.5	3.0	3.0
Fe/Cu × 10†	110	190	100	115	48	112	39	63	87	206
Fe/Co × 10†	99	123	95	85	92	76	31	116	209	297
Fe/Ti × 10†	.96	.81	.84	.86	.99	.85	.71	.74	.75	.75
Fe/V × 10†	58	66	56	41	60	43	232	58	23	27

G, glass; V, varioletic.

Wt % of first 10 elements from *Paster* [1968]; wt % of last 14 elements determined spectographically.

* *Engel et al.* [1965].

† Denominators multiplied by 10 to bring ratios down to same order of magnitude as in South Atlantic and Pacific concretions.

though Ti shows a similar eastward decrease (Figure 50), the orientations of the Fe/Zn isopleths are almost at right angles to those of Ti, and Zn and Ti are actually negatively correlated.

The areal distributions of Sn and Mo are roughly opposite (Figures 55 and 56). Tin increases southward and toward the Chile Rise but decreases both to the west into the Southwest Pacific Basin and eastward into the Scotia Sea. On the other hand, high values of Mo are found in the west in the central Southwest Pacific Basin eastward across the Albatross Cordillera and onto the Chile Rise, but they decrease to the north and south.

The H_2O content in the concretions varies from less than 5% to more than 25%. Lowest regional values are found toward the Antarctic Continent; the highest values occur south of New Zealand on the Albatross Cordillera and over the Cordillera and the Chile Rise (Figure 57).

Although Sr and Ba are strongly correlated, there are only gross similarities in their regional surfaces; they decrease eastward (Figures 58 and 59). The Sr plane is oriented approximately parallel to the mid-ocean ridge, reaching its highest values over its crest, decreasing into the Scotia Sea. The Ba surface maximum curving along the southeast margin of the mid-ocean ridge, and onto the Chile Rise to the northeast, decreases to the north and to the southeast. The Ba/Sr ratio roughly parallels latitude decreasing northward (Figure 60).

The variability accounted for by each of the element regression surfaces is excellent and ranges from a low of 68% (Sn and Ba) to a high of 94% (Sr). All but three are 73% or greater. The element ratio surfaces are much worse, ranging from 36% (Fe/Ti) to 74% (Fe/Cu).

Basalt Analyses

Eight samples of basalt that appear to be unquestion-

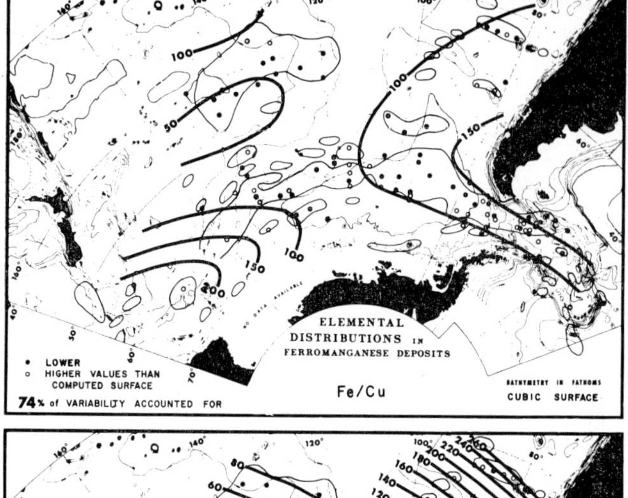

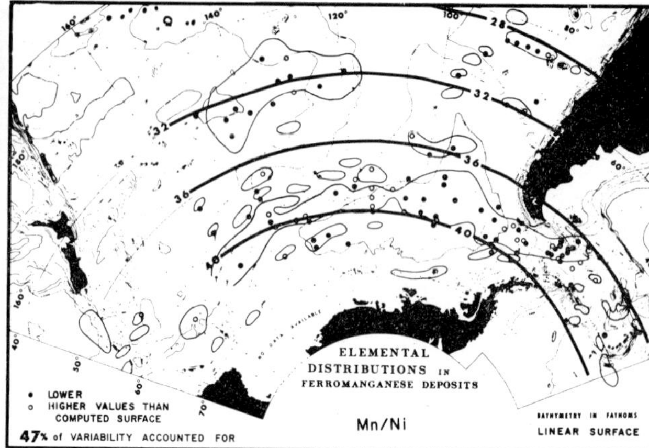

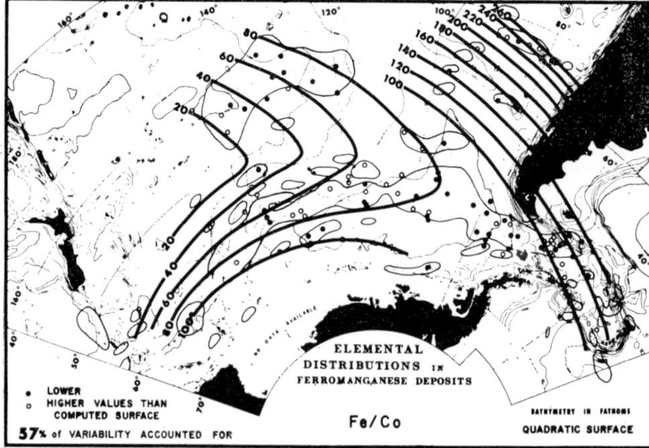

Figs. 46–48. Elemental distributions in ferromanganese deposits in the South Atlantic and South Pacific oceans.

ably of submarine origin have been recovered from *Eltanin* dredges (Figure 61). These give a fair geographic sampling of volcanic emanations over the entire area, although their number is too small for rigid statistical analyses (Table 14). Where possible the analyses of the unhydrated glass zone were chosen as most representative of original magma; as second choice the variolitic zone was selected [*Paster*, 1968]. Basalt 5-5 is an alkaline basalt dredged from a seamount in the Drake Passage; the remainder are oceanic tholeiites. The alkaline basalt (5-5) is 2–3× higher in Mn; highest in Ti; lowest in Cu, Co, Zr; and about the same in Fe, V, Ni, and Sr as the South Atlantic, Pacific, and Indian Ocean tholeiites. Except for Fe, which is depleted 10–100×, these elements are roughly in the same relative proportions as in ferromanganese concretions. There are striking regional differences in the tholeiite compositions.

The Fe/Mn ratio is lowest in the Southwest Pacific Basin (24-15) and highest in the Drake Passage (5-4), corresponding to regional trends in the ferromanganese concretions (Figure 39).

There is the same positive correlation of Mn and Ni values in the tholeiites as in the concretions. The highest Ni values are found in the more northerly basalts (24-15 and 21-8) with lower values to the south (5-4 and 15-5). This parallels the regional distributions of Ni and the Mn/Ni ratio in the concretions (Figures 40 and 48).

The highest Cu values in the basalts are found in the Southwest Pacific Basin (24-15); the lowest values are in the south (5-4, 15-5, 15-15). These follow the regional distribution of Cu in the concretions (Figure 43). The values of the Fe/Cu ratio in the basalts in general correspond to the topography of the Fe/Cu surface or anomalies to it (Figure 46).

The highest Co values in the basalts are from the Southwest Pacific Basin (24-15) with intermediate values along the Albatross Cordillera (15-15), the Southeast Pacific Basin (15-5, 25-5), and the Chile Rise (21-10). These trends parallel the distribution of Co in the concretions (Figure 41).

The regional variation in Ti in the basalts is opposite to Ti values in the concretions; in the basalts

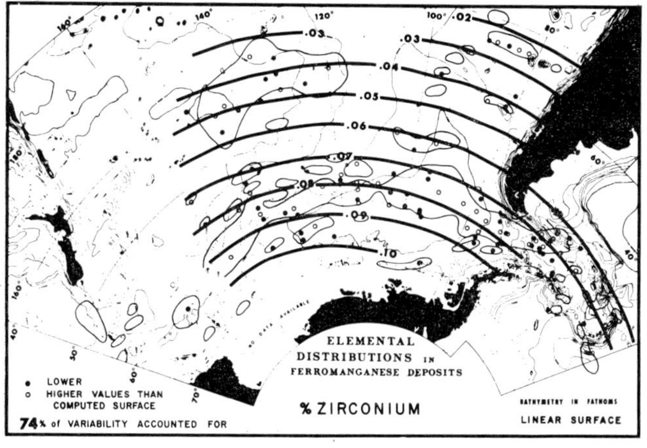

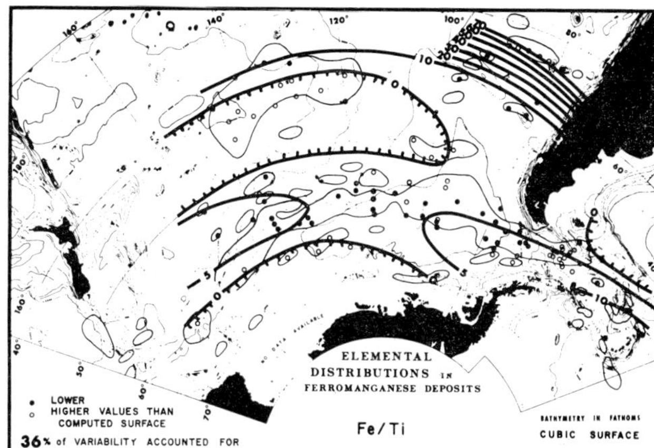

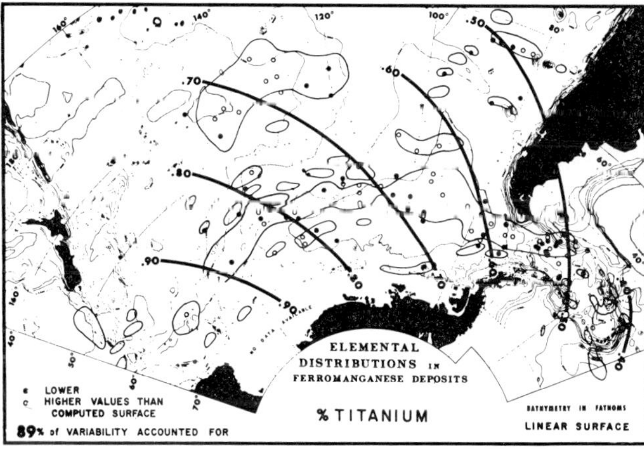

Figs. 49–51. Elemental distributions in ferromanganese deposits in the South Atlantic and South Pacific oceans.

they are high northeast and low southwest (Figure 50). The V distributions match only a little better. The lowest value in the basalts is in the Southwest Pacific Basin (24-15), which is also low in V in the concretions. However, the general tendency for V to decrease to the south (Figure 52) is not matched by basalts from the Drake Passage (5-4).

Radioelements

The laminated colloform internal structure of many concretions suggests that each layer could be a depositional unit. Three concretions from the Drake Passage, found within a 60-mile radius, were selected that showed colloform laminations about 5 mm thick. The outer two laminae were removed for radioisotope analysis (Table 15). A concretion from the Southeast Pacific Basin showing no laminations was peeled into 5-mm increments and the outer two peels were isotopically analyzed. Core 16-6, taken south of New Zealand, contained nine layers of ferromanganese deposits. The outer two 5-mm laminae of concretions from the upper three horizons and concretion fragments from the lower six were also analyzed (Appendix).

In the *Adams et al.* [1959] summary of Th and U geochemistry, the range of U in sea water is cited as from 0.001 to 0.006 ppm, with a Th/U ratio of about 10^{-2}. The Th^{232} values of these nodules range from 12 to 236 ppm, a concentration factor of $>10^6$; U^{238} values range from 4 to 20 ppm, a concentration factor of $> 10^4$. These ranges are of the same order of magnitude as those found for U and Th in other concentrations [*Picciotto and Wilgain*, 1954; *Tatsumoto and Goldberg*, 1959; *Arrhenius et al.*, 1964; *Sackett*, 1966].

The U^{232}/U^{238} values compared with the Mn/Fe ratios, although not conclusive for lack of sufficient data, show a tendency for Th to be associated more strongly with Mn, U with Fe, although both elements are strongly sorbed on either Mn or Fe.

Buried Nodule Geochemistry

The sample of analyzed buried nodules is not sufficiently large to say definitely whether or not significant changes have occurred in concretion geochemistry

TABLE 15. Radioelement Analyses in South Atlantic and Pacific Concretions

Sample	Location	Concretion Interval, mm	U^{238}, ppm	Th^{232}, ppm	Th^{232}/U^{238}	Mn	Fe	Mn/Fe
6-11*	55°58.5′S, 56°05′W	0–5	11	80	7.22	2.3	20.1	.114
		5–10	12	100	8.33			
6-5*	56°15′S, 58°20′W	0–5	6	65	10.82	1.1	18.2	.06
		5–10	9	60	6.68			
6-10*	55°06′S, 55°50′W	0–5	8	33	4.12	1.1	18.5	.06
		5–10	8	42	5.25			
11-3*	57°44′S, 114°58′W	0–5	21	75	3.57	16.0	25.5	.63
		5–10	20	40	2.00			
16-6†	59°03′S, 161°52′E							
at 12 cm		0–5	6	12	2.00			
		5–10	4	59	14.25			
at 27 cm		0–5	4	29	7.26			
		5–10	7	236	34.70			
at 45 cm		0–5	7	18	2.57			
		5–10	11	133	12.10			
at 91 cm		All	12	150	12.50			
at 160 cm		All	6	18	3.00			
at 200 cm		All	7	52	7.44			
at 225 cm		All	10	39	3.90			
at 300 cm		All	8	70	8.75			

* Surface bottom dredge samples.
† Piston core; subsample numbers indicate depth of concretion core.

with time (Table 16). However, it is obvious that areal distinctions in relative element concentrations are larger than temporal element changes within the cores. The opposite appears to be true of the radioelements.

The Matuyama/Gauss boundary at 2.43 m.y. lies beyond 5.7 meters in core 16-6 [*Goodell and Watkins*, 1968] with the first two concretion horizons lying within Brunhes age sediments (Table 15). Both U^{238} and Th^{232} concentrations are more variable between individual concretion laminae in the core than between laminae in the surface concretions. In addition, a considerable variation exists between concretion horizons within the core. The data suggest that large temporal radioelement fluctuations occur in any one area and that significant geographic variations exist between areas.

DISCUSSION

Element Associations

Correlation and regression provide the basis for dividing the analyzed elements into two groups: those related directly or indirectly to Fe and those related directly or indirectly to Mn (Table 17).

Two elements, Ti and V, are closely and strongly associated with Fe (Tables 9 and 12). Five others, Zn, Zr, Mo, Co, and Ba, are associated with Fe but only through their primary association with Ti or V. One element, Sr, is ferrophile only because of an association with Co and Ba.

Two elements, Ni and Mo, are closely and strongly associated with Mn (Tables 9 and 12). Five others, Zn, V, Cu, Co, and Ba, are manganophile because of associations with either Ni or Mo. Two, Sn and Sr, are related to Mn through associations with Cu and Ba.

Although Zn, Co, Ba, and Sr are found in both suites, their associations with the Mn suite are stronger, based on the sums of squares accounted for by stepwise multiple regression and by the magnitude of their correlation coefficients with Fe and Mn. The Mn suite has a strong chalcophile character; the Fe suite is lithophile.

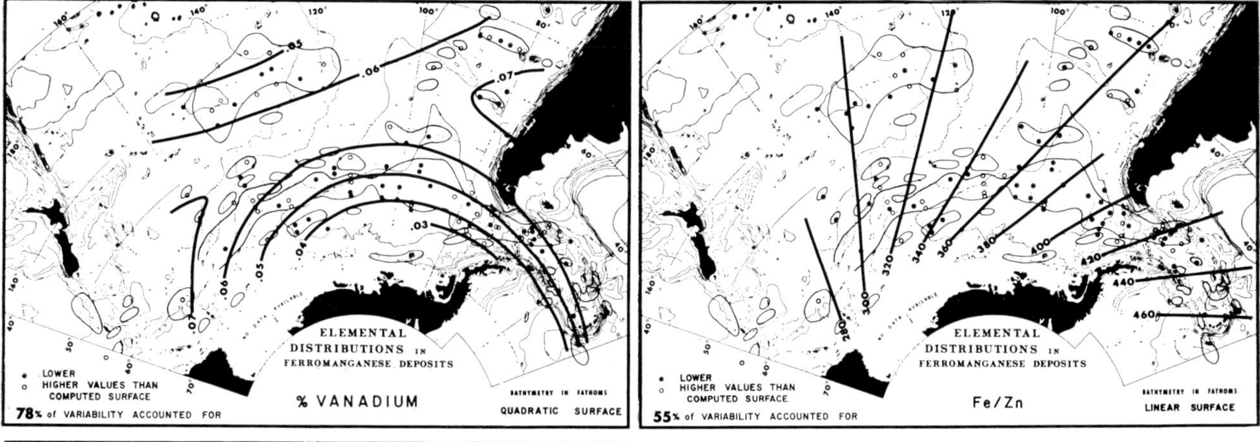

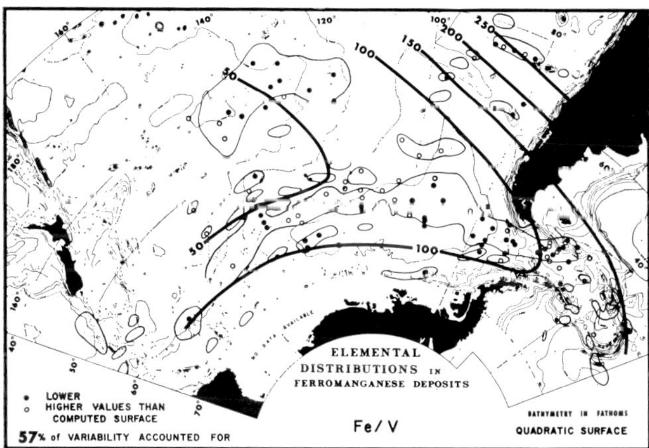

Figs. 52–54. Elemental distributions in ferromanganese deposits in the South Atlantic and South Pacific oceans.

These associations exist in the South Atlantic and South Pacific oceans because of common source, coherent distributive mechanisms, and parallel geochemical behavior.

Element Sources

The regional distributions of the elements analyzed in South Pacific Ocean ferromanganese concretions and in the submarine basalts delineate three major geochemical provinces (Table 18). The Mn suite of elements dominates the Southwest Pacific Basin; the Fe suite dominates the Albatross Cordillera, centered at about 60°S, 160°W; both suites occur in the third province, the Chile Rise-Albatross Cordillera between 40°–50°S. The existence of these provinces is attributed primarily to differences in crustal volcanic sources, and it is noteworthy that the lithophile (Fe) suite is primarily associated with the ridge-rise system and the chalcophile (Mn) suite with the abyssal basin. The Mn suite constitutes the same elements that *Wedephol* [1960] found enriched in pelagic sediments over nearshore clays. There is a common association of volcanics and ferromanganese deposits in many *Eltanin* photo stations from the Southwest Pacific Basin, on the entire ridge-rise system, and across the Southeast Pacific Basin and Drake Passage along the Eltanin Fracture Zone (Figure 3). This volcanism is spread throughout the time represented by *Eltanin* cores, although it appears to have increased its periodicity in the last 700,000 years, based on the concretion distribution in the cores.

The observed association of deep-sea ferromanganese concretions with basic volcanics goes back to the *Challenger* reports [*Murray and Renard,* 1891]. Submarine volcanism has been often reiterated as the principal source of elements in deep-sea concretions by many observers [*Pettersson,* 1959; *Skornyakova,* 1964; *Arrhenius and Bonatti,* 1965; *Moore,* 1965, 1966; *Nayudu,* 1964, 1965; *Bonatti and Nayudu,* 1965; *Bonatti and Joensuu,* 1966].

In the South Atlantic and South Pacific oceans volcanic nuclei are found in 56% of 281 concretion populations sampled (Table 4), and the largest volume of concretionary deposits lies largely unsampled on

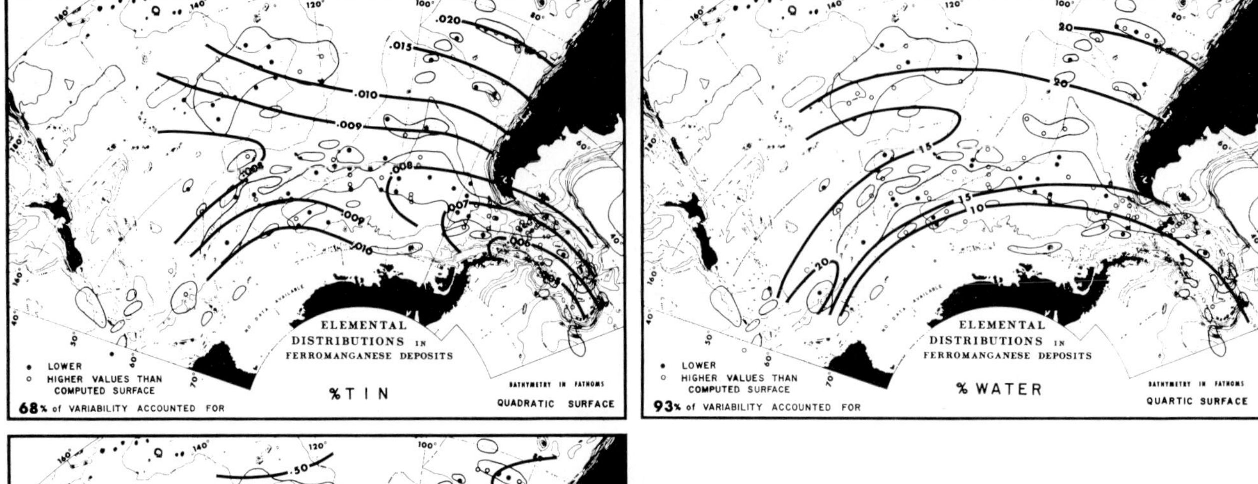

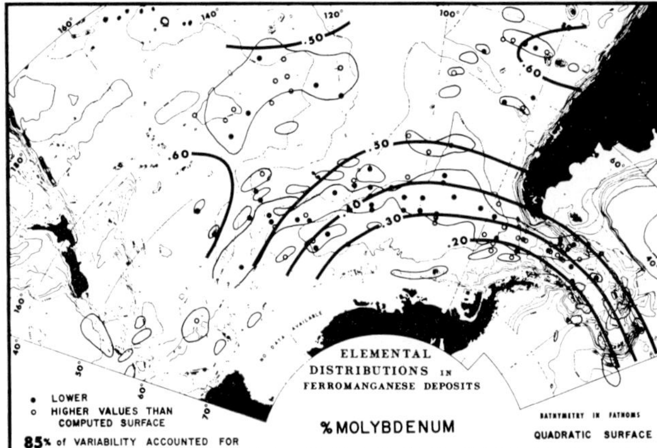

Figs. 55–57. Elemental distributions in ferromanganese deposits in the South Atlantic and South Pacific oceans.

the ocean floor, draped on the submarine flows observed in bottom photography (Figures 5 and 9). *Paster* [1968] has noted that the alteration of tholeiite lavas releases large quantities of Fe and Mn through hydration (palagonitization) of glass, serpentinization of olivine, and chloritization. He estimates that an altered flow 30 cm in diameter has released a minimum of 130 grams of Fe. *Boström and Peterson* [1966, 1969] attributed Fe- and Mn-rich sediments along the Albatross Cordillera to volcanic (hydrothermal) emanations. *Arrhenius and Bonatti* [1965] and *Arrhenius et al.* [1964] suggested that Mn/Co ratios below 300 were indicative of volcanic sources; South Atlantic and South Pacific Ocean concretions average 49.

There is no question that there are also terrigenous elemental contributions to South Atlantic and South Pacific Ocean concretions. The fact that quartz and feldspar both increase to the south (Figure 62) is ample evidence for continental sources of lithophile elements. The strong latitudinal dependence of Zr with values that increase toward Antarctica suggests the presence of detrital zircon (Figure 49). Both Ti and Sn increase slightly to the south toward East Antarctica, although both are in low concentration around the Antarctic Peninsula and in the Drake Passage-Scotia Sea (Figures 50 and 55). Titanium probably occurs as detrital ilmenite or spinel; Sn, which is associated with siliceous rocks, in cassiterite or sphene.

Biological elemental contributions are unquestionably present but appear relatively unimportant, except for perhaps Sr, whose distribution seems anomalous (Figure 58). It decreases eastward linearly from the Albatross Cordillera. Foraminiferal oozes dominate this portion of the South Pacific Ocean (Figure 11), and both Sr and Ba are concentrated somewhat in their calcite tests [*Arrhenius,* 1963]. However, tests seldom comprise as much as 1% of concretions even above the depth of $CaCO_2$ compensation, so that Ba and Sr concentrations should be far below their observed values. Barium is a biophile element, being concentrated especially in radiolarians [*Goldberg and Arrhenius,* 1958; *Chow and Goldberg,* 1960; *Arrhenius,* 1963; *Turekian and Tausch,* 1964; *Turekian and*

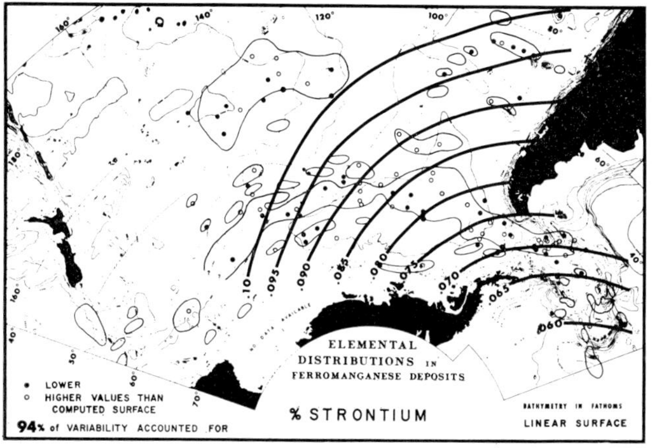

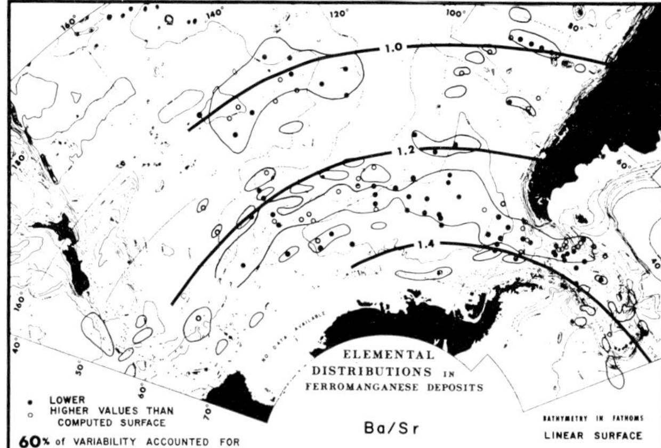

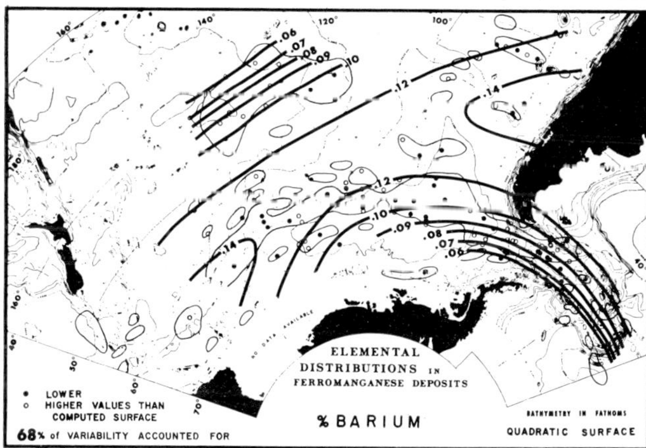

Figs. 58–60. Elemental distributions in ferromanganese deposits in the South Atlantic and South Pacific oceans.

Johnson, 1966; *Turekian*, 1968], yet Ba actually decreases regionally across the zone of siliceous oozes south of 60°S; anomalies to the regression surface over this area are about evenly distributed above and below it (Figure 59). Vanadium and Mo and Cu are also biophile elements enriched in organic shales, yet their distribution shows little relationship to the organic oozes (Figures 11 and 52).

There are undoubtedly minor elemental contributions from sea water. *Turekian* [1968] concluded that Ba, Co, and Ag concentrations in sediments on the South Atlantic mid-ocean ridge could be accounted for solely by continental fluvial contributions to the oceans. *Kuenen* [1950] and *Goldberg and Arrhenius* [1958] calculated a mass balance for Mn and concluded that fluvial sources more than accounted for its concentration in sea water, sediments, and nodules. *Schutz and Turekian* [1965] noted a tendency for increased concentrations of Co and Ni in South Pacific waters. However, the effect of sea water element contributions to South Atlantic and South Pacific Ocean concretions should be evened out by the rapid mixing inherent with the circumpolar current.

The sediments on which concretions lie have been postulated as major sources of elements. *Anikovchine* [1967] proposed a theoretical basis for element diffusion out of the sediment-water system. *Lynn and Bonatti* [1965] showed that there is a considerable upward mobility of Mn where a reducing clay underlies oxidized sediments. *Manheim* [1965] offers solid chemical and physical evidence for sediment-water sources of the Fe and Mn in shallow water concretions. *Price* [1967] strengthens these conclusions and suggests the importance of sediment organic matter in the chelation of minor elements.

However, in South Atlantic and South Pacific Ocean ferromanganese concretions, probably the smallest elemental contribution is made by connatal solutions from the sediment-water system. There are no observed Fe or Mn gradients in the cores, no halos of high concentration of Fe or Mn around buried nodules, and no noticeable decreases in ferromanganese micronodules with depth in cores. Most cores are uniformly oxidized throughout. There are a few that show alternate layers 1–5 cm thick of white, yellow, brown, green, and purple siliceous ooze. The

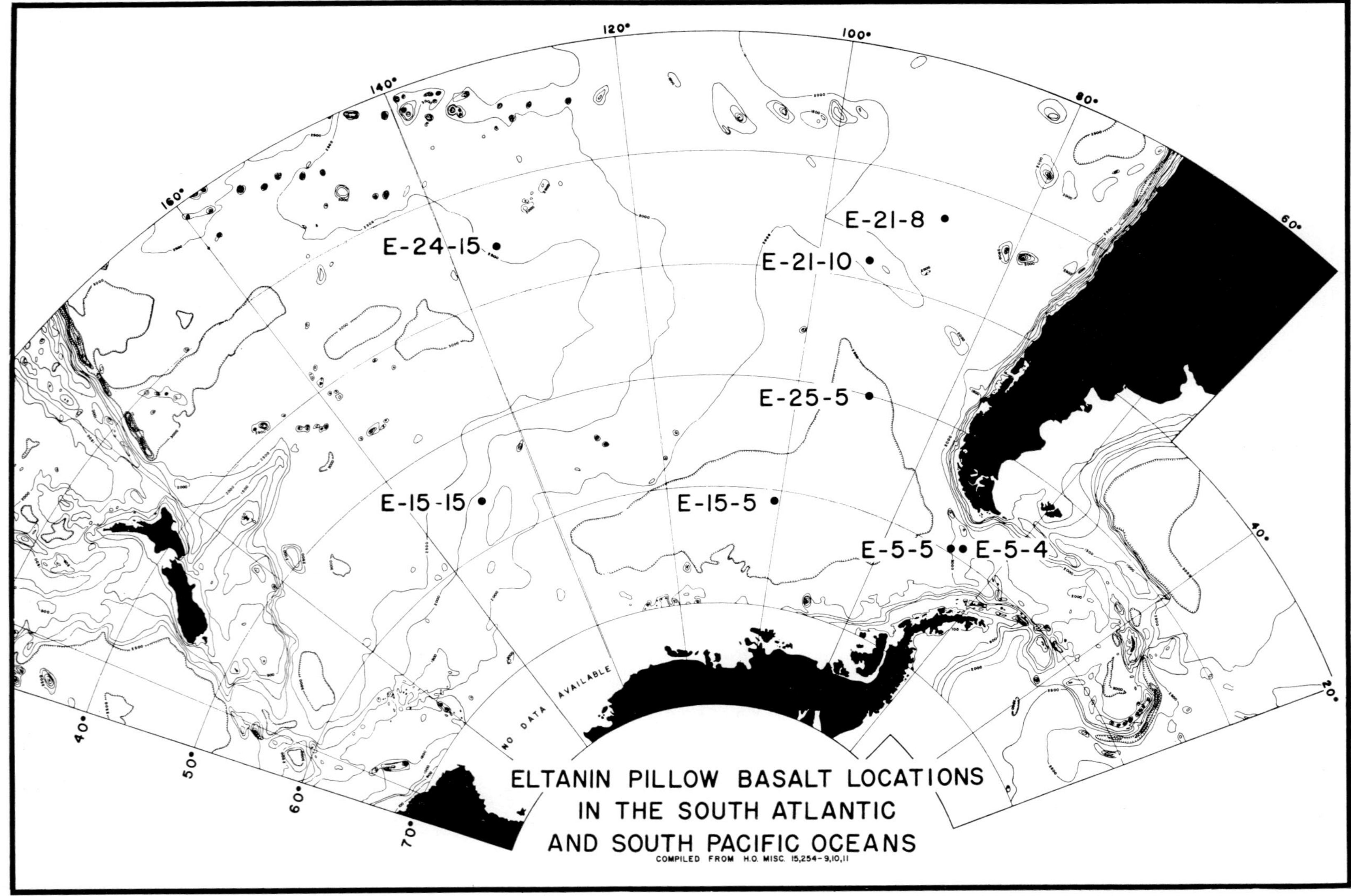

Fig. 61. The locations of dredged submarine basalts from the South Atlantic and South Pacific oceans.

TABLE 16. Element Ratios in Concretions from Cores

Eltanin Core No.	Location	General Area	Depth Interval, cm	Fe/Mn	Mn/Co	Mn/Ni	Ni/Cu
5-12	59°19'S, 69°17'W	Drake Passage	Top	1.82	37.1	65.0	1.3
			206–211	2.17	37.5	60.0	1.5
24-7	41°33'S, 142°20'W	Southwest Pacific Basin	5–8	.62	50.2	25.4	2.4
			11–15	.61	51.2	25.6	2.5
25-3	39°57'S, 82°57'W	Chile Rise	1–3	.49	179.2	19.3	2.6
			14–17	.54	185.8	22.1	2.2
17-6	60°03'S, 134°55'W	Western Southeast Pacific Basin	83–87	2.04	41.8	90.0	0.6
			193–198	1.89	45.0	105.0	0.7
22-1	57°03'S, 60°01'W	Drake Passage	0–11	3.03	34.5	58.5	1.0
			54–57	2.22	60.0	73.8	1.1
			69–72	2.63	49.4	120.0	0.6
22-34	55°23'S, 52°54'W	Drake Passage	Top	1.54	48.4	26.3	3.5
			18 22	1.70	55.8	32.1	1.4
			18–22	2.63	47.6	40.5	1.1
7-18	53°00.5'S, 48°53'W	West Scotia Basin	Top	4.17	13.8	110.0	0.1
			60	1.56	21.8	12.3	0.7

contacts between these layers are sharp, and no obvious lithologic differences exist, except that Mn micronodules are more numerous in the darker layers, although no diffusion is apparent. Similar data have been noted by *Arrhenius* [1952], *Revelle et al.* [1955], *Pettersson* [1959], and *Landergren* [1964].

Finally, glacial erratics recovered by *Eltanin* dredges show fresh uncoated rock surfaces on their undersides but are coated with ferromanganese stain and have attached organisms on their upper surfaces.

TABLE 17. Element Suites in South Atlantic and Pacific Ferromanganese Concretions

Iron	Manganese
Primary	
Ti	Ni
V	Mo
Secondary	
Zn(V)	Zn* (Ni, Cu)
Zr(Ti)	V(Mo)
Mo(V)	Cu(Ni, Sn, Zn)
Co(Sr, Ti, V)	Co* (Mn, Ni)
Ba(Sr, V)	Ba* (Mn, Ni, Cu)
Tertiary	
Sr(Co, Ba)	Sn(Cu)
	Sr* (Mn, Sn, Ba)

*More strongly associated with Mn suite than Fe suite; elements in parentheses give primary links to Fe or Mn.

They do not have the skirted rims often apparent on shallow water boulders described by *Manheim* [1965]. *Presley et al.* [1967] demonstrated that differences in interstitial water chemistry exist between different types of pelagic sediments, with red clays being significantly enriched in Mn and Ni. But the fact that the South Atlantic and South Pacific Ocean concretions are superimposed on all sediment lithologies supports the insignificance of the sediment-water system as an element source.

The radioelement data do not refute volcanism as a principal source of the concretion elements. *Pettersson*'s [1937] theory that Ra^{226} in deep-sea sediments originates from the decay of Th^{230} coprecipitated with Fe sought to explain the high radium content discovered by *Joly* [1908] in *Challenger* red clay samples.

TABLE 18. Geochemical Provinces

Albatross Cordillera 60°S, 160°W	Chile Rise-Albatross Cordillera 40°–50°S	Southwest Pacific Basin
Fe	Fe Mn	Mn
Ti	Ni	Ni
V	V Mo	Mo
Sr	Sr Cu	Cu
Co	Ba	Co
Ba	Sn	Sn
Zn	Zn	

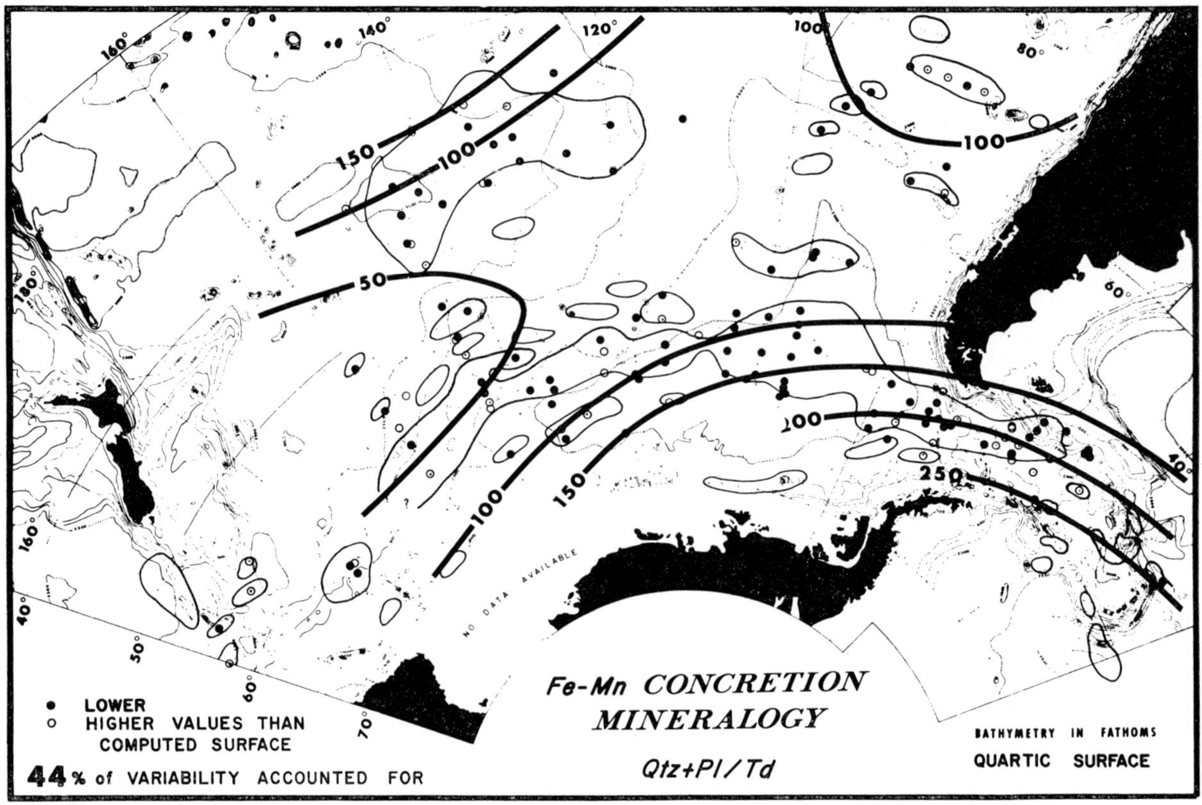

Fig. 62. South Atlantic and South Pacific Ocean ferromanganese concretion mineralogy. Isopleths are ratio of peak intensities of 3.2-Å plagioclase-phillipsite + 3.34-Å quartz/9.7-Å todorokite.

Piggot and Urey [1942] confirmed this theory and observed that different sediment types ought to have different Ra^{226}/Th^{230} ratios. The isotopes were presumed to be absorbed on the surface of particulate matter.

Based on the hydrolyzate character of Th, it has been postulated that Th/U values should decrease away from continental fluvial sources [*Goldberg and Koide*, 1962]. Although there have been no systematic investigations into areal differences in radioelements in deep-sea sediments, scattered analyses show a considerable variation in concentrations and ratios of U and Th isotopes. [*Goldberg and Picciotto*, 1955; *Arrhenius et al.*, 1964; *Goldberg et al.*, 1964; *Tatsumoto and Goldberg*, 1959; *Sackett*, 1966; *Ku*, 1965; *Somayajulu and Goldberg*, 1966; *Goldberg and Koide*, 1962, 1963].

The Drake Passage concretions are associated with light-colored foraminiferal oozes; dredge 11-3 in the mid-Pacific with brown diatomaceous oozes; whereas core 16-6 south of New Zealand is brown diatomaceous ooze throughout [*Goodell*, 1964, 1965, 1968*b*]. In addition, *Goldberg and Koide* [1963], *Goldberg et al.* [1964], and *Holmes* [1965] show that foraminifera concentrate Th. Yet the mid-Pacific concretion has as high a Th content as the near continent concretions associated with foraminiferal oozes in the Drake Passage (Table 15).

Holmes [1965] found that U concentrations average only 0.13 ppm in light-colored deep-sea carbonate (foraminiferal) oozes, compared with 1–8 ppm in pelagic clays [*Picciotto*, 1961; *Baranov and Kuzmina*, 1958]. The range in pelagic clay is undoubtedly due to the range in sorbed hydrated Fe and Mn oxides on the particulate matter. The mid-Pacific nodule, associated with brown siliceous oozes, has the highest U values (Table 15). There are often large Th^{232} variations between the outer and the next inner 5 mm laminae in the concretions; U^{238} concentrations are less variable (Table 15).

These regional and temporal fluctuations are somewhat surprising if one accepts the high rate of mixing in the South Atlantic and South Pacific oceans and the solubility of the $[(UO_2)(CO_3)_3]^{4-}$ anion with

TABLE 19. Percentage Removal of Cations by Colloids through Adsorption [after *Krauskopf*, 1955]

Cation	Hydrated Fe_2O_3, %	Hydrated MnO_2, %	Montmorillonite, %	Plankton, %
Cu	96	96	94	54
Ni	33	99	10	8
Co	35	93	18	8
Zn	95		99	40
Mo	25	50	35	15
V^4	>96		27	16
Pb	86		>96	

its 5.0×10^5 year residence time [*Goldberg*, 1965], unless periodic volcanism followed by rapid sorption and coprecipitation is an important source of U and Th in the deep sea.

If volcanism is to be considered as the principal source of the elements in South Atlantic and South Pacific Ocean ferromanganese concretions, the Pb isotope data of *Chow and Patterson* [1962] must be reconciled. Their area *D* in the far South Pacific ($Pb^{206}/Pb^{207} = 1.1966$) encompasses a portion of the area of this study. They found that the large majority of Pb in pelagic sediments and ferromanganese concretions occurs in authigenic mineral phases associated with Mn. Because of this association, they concluded that the Pb was precipitated from sea water, having been derived from continental sources. The addition of Pb to the manganophile group of elements is not surprising in view of its usual chalcophile character.

The strong covariance of Mn and Pb detailed by *Chow and Patterson* [1962] favors a common source. The residence time in the sea is about 10^3 years for both elements [*Goldberg*, 1965]. In view of the high mixing rates in the South Atlantic and South Pacific oceans, both elements should be spread evenly across pelagic sediments. Obviously Mn is not, inasmuch as it is concentrated in distinct fields of concretions on all sediment types with widely varying Mn concentrations. If the principal source of Mn in the South Atlantic and South Pacific oceans is submarine volcanism, then a similar source is highly probable for Pb.

It is pertinent to the argument that *Chow and Patterson* [1962] state that when large isotopic changes occur in cores they do so abruptly with no apparent textural or compositional changes. Such would be the mode of record of a period of submarine volcanism.

If the source of Pb in deep-sea concretions is volcanism, then Pb isotope ratios in South Atlantic and South Pacific Ocean concretions might reflect oceanic crustal ages and should be re-examined.

Distributive Mechanisms

The elements are moved from their volcanic sources by deep-sea currents, coprecipitating en route. There is almost a universal association of such current indications as scour, cut and fill structures, and ripple marks with ferromanganese concretions (Figures 3, 8, 9, and 10). Where the currents are strong and relatively constant, and have been in existence for some time, continuous overlapping fields of concretions occur between volcanic centers. Such a field lies beneath the circumpolar current at 60°S (Figure 4). The probable antiquity of the circumpolar current was suggested by *Goodell and Watkins* [1968], who noted the thinness of Brunhes age sediments beneath it (Figure 62). The belt of ferromanganese deposits coincides with the zone of minimum Brunhes sediment thicknesses at 60°S. Where currents are sporadic, concretions show a dusting of particulate matter, and where current systems are no longer operational a concretion field becomes buried. There are numerous examples of the latter from photo stations north and south of the 60°S concretion belt, suggesting some recent latitudinal shift of the circumpolar current.

Goldberg [1954] and *Krauskopf* [1955, 1956, 1957*a, b*] offer the most persuasive mechanisms for element transport. *Goldberg* [1954] proposed that hydrated Fe and Mn oxides scavenge more soluble metals by adsorption. Ferric hydroxide sols are generally positive; Mn sols are negative [*Rankama and Sahama*, 1950]. All of the elements under consideration except Sr and Ba and perhaps V are hydrolyzates. Vanadium may also be present as vanadate, in which case $FeVO_4$ is insoluble [*Goldschmidt*, 1954].

Krauskopf [1956] showed that Cu, Ni, Co, and Mo had a preference for hydrated MnO_2 over hydrated Fe_2O_3 (Table 19). However, his experiments were carried out with adsorbate concentrations of 0.6 to 2.5 ppm; Cu, Ni, and Co concentrations in concretions are 10 to 100× that. The elemental associations suggest that Ni- and Ti-hydrated oxide sols exist as separate transportative phases (Table 17). Both have positive correlation coefficients with H_2O (Tables 9 and 11), although neither shows a significant partial correlation coefficient with H_2O in stepwise regression (Tables 12 and 17).

The stability of metal hydrosols in sea water is unknown. The fact that Fe is impoverished in concre-

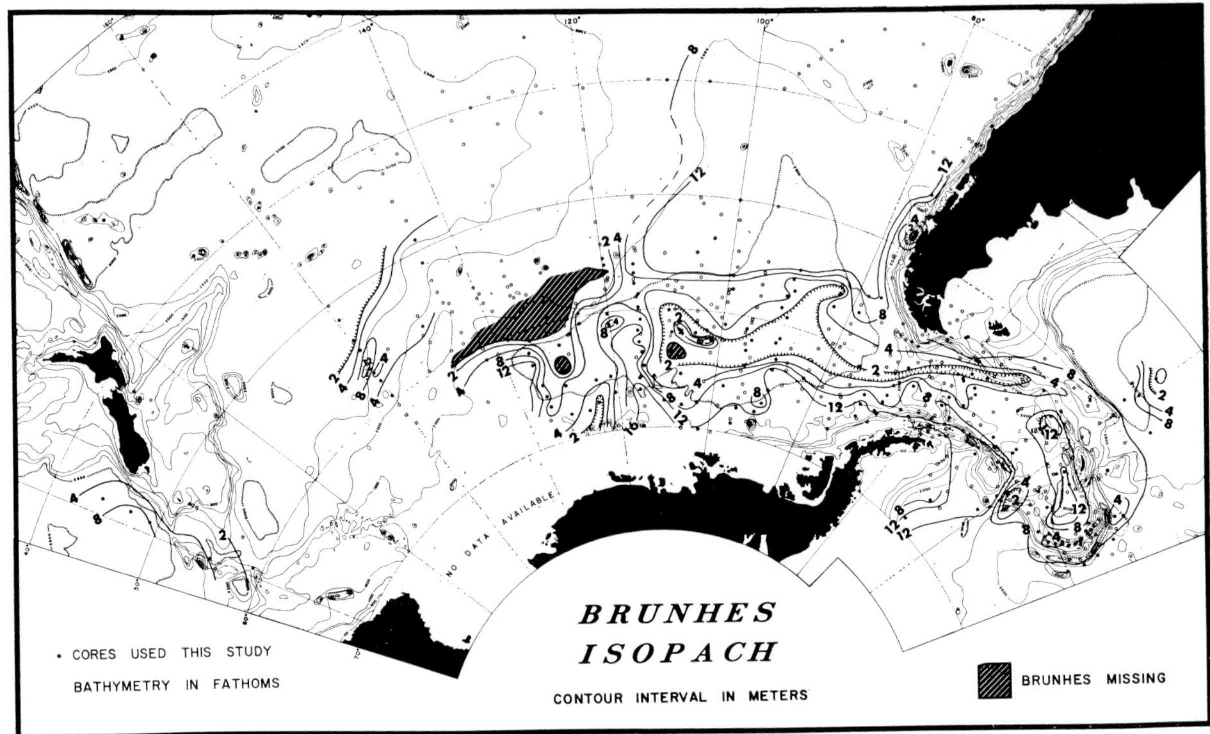

Fig. 63. Thickness of Brunhes-age sediments in the South Atlantic and South Pacific oceans (after *Goodell and Watkins* [1968]).

tions relative to other elements (as compared to tholeiites) points to the fact that 90–95% of the Fe is removed from immediate element sources, probably as a precipitate on particulate matter. Ratios of highly correlated elements that might be associated through adsorption might decrease down-current from element sources. The circumpolar current sweeps the Albatross Cordillera across the Fe-suite geochemical province and continues east through the Drake Passage. The Fe/Mn ratio increases eastward into the Scotia Sea (Figure 37). The ratios of Fe/V, Fe/Co, and Fe/Zn decrease in a striking fashion along this current zone (Figures 47, 53, and 54), yet there is no corresponding drop in Mn/Ni and only an ill-defined one in Ni/Co. However, the Southwest Pacific Basin where the Mn suite is enriched is well north of the circumpolar current and is blocked from the east by the Albatross Cordillera.

Mineralogy and Geochemistry

The distribution of elements between mineral phases in South Atlantic and South Pacific Ocean ferromanganese concretions seems to be primarily a function of colloid and solution chemistry and only secondarily of the atomic crystallographic parameters that normally govern diadochy.

The principal nondetrital crystalline Mn phase in the deposits is todorokite, whose distribution appears to be a function not only of the degree of dilution by other minerals (Figure 24), but perhaps also the Fe/Mn ratio (Figure 39). The highest todorokite concentrations are found on the northern flank of the Albatross Cordillera between the Fe and Mn geochemical provinces, where ice-rafted detritus is minimal and the Fe/Mn ratio is at a minimum. Possibly the availability of other metal ions influences the lattice parameters of todorokite, and hence also the X-ray diffraction expression of these parameters. But other cations are not essential to the formation of δ-MnO_2/birnessite, although its layer-like structure allows considerable substitution [*Bricker*, 1965]. The distribution of birnessite in Southern Ocean concretions does not appear to be related to any known factor. There is no apparent depth (pressure) dependency of either todorokite or birnessite, as has been proposed by *Barnes* [1967]. Instead, Eh-*p*H, precipitation kinetics, hydration, and other cations seem to be the most likely overriding parameters.

The majority of the Fe is either amorphous or, like δ-MnO_2, cryptocrystalline. Goethite (δ-FeO · OH) was definitely present in 56 of the samples but was tentatively identified in 144 others. The occurrence of maghemite (γ-Fe_2O_3) in five samples and its probable presence in all but 61 of the remainder is interesting, for it may indicate that a majority of the Fe is cryptocrystalline lepidocrocite (γ-FeO · OH).

The presence of maghemite suggests the possibility that other complex oxides might be present: perovskites ($SrTiO_3$, $SrSnO_3$, $SrZrO_3$, and their Ba equivalents), which would account for the distribution of alkaline earth elements in the absence of appreciable sulfate; and spinels ($CoFe_2O_4$, Co_2TiO_4, Ni_2MnO_4, or even $FeCo_2O_3$), which would partially account for the element associations encountered.

The close association and perhaps dependency of Cu and Co on Ni may be a reflection of the identity of their cubic close-packed structures, although Zn, which is similarly related, is hexagonally closest packed and would require a change in oxygen coordination for extensive diadochy in NiO · nH_2O.

Finally, the close association of Fe, Ba, Sr, Zn, and Mo with V suggests the possibility of (Fe, Ba, Sr, Zn) (Mo,V)O_4 vanadates.

Rates of Deposition

The wide discrepancies between the data on the rates of deposition of ferromanganese concretions and the data on depositional rates of pelagic sediments seem unreconcilable. Only in the center of the scour zone beneath the circumpolar current are sediment depositional rates as low as 1000 mm/10^6 yr, based on paleomagnetic stratigraphy (Figure 63). Lying on this scour zone is the South Atlantic and South Pacific Ocean belt of ferromanganese concretions. However, immediately north and south of this belt are fields of concretions that lie on top of sediments that were deposited at the rate of more than 10,000 mm/10^6 yr.

It might be argued that the concretions that comprise the belt at 60°S are of widely varying ages and were concentrated as a lag deposit by the scour of the circumpolar current. However, if this were the case, one might expect a wide range in sizes, with the older nodules much bigger from repeated episodes of deposition. But bottom photos reveal a monotonous uniformity of size and morphology at any one camera station and a rather homogeneous population from the area as a whole (Figures 13 and 15). The data suggest that the nodules within any one field are consanguineous and contemporaneous.

The continuity of the belt at 60°S is due in large part to closely spaced volcanic centers with frequent volcanic events, mostly fissure eruption. The absence of any reasonable mechanism for moving a solid object upward through an overlying sediment column suggests that all of these concretions must be younger than 700,000 years. The net growth rate of a scour zone nodule 2 cm in radius must considerably exceed 30 mm/10^6 yr. However, north and south of the scour zone concretions cannot be more than 10^3 or so years old, or they would have become buried. In the Southwest Pacific Basin several hundred thousand square miles at sea floor are covered with nodules up to 60 mm in radius (Figure 16, 24-2) lying on top of more than 10 meters of Brunhes age sediments (Figures 28 and 29). With sediment depositional rates in excess of 10,000 mm/10^6 yr, these nodules also cannot be much older than 10^3 years. The one illustrated in Figure 16 has a central core consisting of flat tabular volcanic fragment and 8± colloform layers 30, 8, 2, 7, 5, 4, 5, and 2 mm in thickness (inner to outer). Layer distinction, admittedly arbitrary, is made on the basis that the included sediments between layers represent hiatuses. These layers could represent a volcanic event every ± 10^2 years. Concretion crusts and large volcanic fragments dredged from the area often show only a single ferromanganese layer 10 to 30 mm thick, perhaps the layer associated with their extrusion (Figures 14 and 64). The conclusion seems inescapable that when volcanism is the source of concretion elements, a majority of a single colloform layer is perhaps deposited over the period of a single volcanic event, perhaps in as short a time as a few weeks. The thickness of the layer would be a function of the rate of supply of hydrated oxide.

The several horizons of concretions that occur buried beneath the present surface concretion fields (Figures 28, 29, 30, and 31) attest both to the periodicity of times of volcanic activity and to the burial of a concretion field when it is no longer actively accreting.

These conclusions are at variance with almost all of the literature data on rates of pelagic concretion growth and indeed with our own disequilibrium data. All of the 5–10 mm peels (Table 15) from the Drake Passage and mid-Pacific were in equilibrium, based on Th^{230}-U^{234}/Th^{232}. However, it is hard to conceive of concretions as a closed system, inasmuch as they often lose 10–15% of their weight in a few weeks of air drying and therefore must have considerable permeability and porosity. In addition, there are demonstrated wide variations in U^{238} and Th^{232} within a concretion. Both of these factors coupled with the suspected mobility of U^{234} and Th^{230} may cause isotope homogenization in a short period of time.

The effective density of most of the nodules, botryoidals, and agglomerates in water is about 0.5 g/cc. The very round nodules are almost always associated with current indications in bottom photographs.

Fig. 64. Pahoehoe tholeiite toe (24-15) from the Southwest Pacific Basin with a ferromanganese crust from 10 to 14 mm thick. Location 35°58′S, 134°50′W; water depth 2560 fm.

Threshold drag velocities (U_{*t}) might be as low as 20 cm/sec for round nodules 12 cm in diameter and only 1 to 2 cm/sec for grains of ferromanganese 1 cm in diameter (extrapolation from *Inman* [1963]). The current indicators present in bottom photography show velocities perhaps as great as 40–60 cm/sec.

The possibility that nodules form by rolling under the drag shear of bottom currents is quite likely in the South Atlantic and South Pacific oceans. Indeed, it even rationalizes the fact that nodule fields are usually only 1 nodule thick.

SUMMARY AND CONCLUSIONS

Bottom photography, dredging, and coring have established the distribution, nature, and chemical and mineralogical character of fields of ferromanganese concretions in the South Pacific, Drake Passage, and Scotia Sea as follows:

1. A continuous belt of concretions up to 300 miles wide lies beneath the circumpolar current at about 60°S latitude. Less continuous fields lie north and south of the belt, the largest of which covers more than 100,000 square miles in the Southwest Pacific Basin.

2. These fields are almost invariably associated with current indications and volcanics. Where no current indications are present, as in the fields a short distance north and south of the 60°S belt, they are partially buried with sediments.

3. The fields lie on top of all types of sediments, from calcareous oozes to siliceous oozes and pelagic clays of a wide range in color. They occur in water depths of less than 500 to more than 2500 fathoms.

4. The concretions are classified into four morphological varieties on the basis of their nuclei, relative thickness of hydrated oxide deposit, and external shape. Agglomerates are largely restricted to the southerly concretion fields and are dependent on abundant ice-rafted clasts for their morphology. Nodules are nearly always related to current indications. Crusts, the largest variety, are the least sampled, inasmuch as they occur draped on the sea floor on sediments and volcanics. The most common type of concretion nuclei is volcanic fragments, which are more or less altered. Concretions range in size from micronodules < 1 mm in diameter to slabs of ferromanganese crust many meters across. Within any one field the size and the shape of the concretions are uniform. Most of the concretions show an internal colloform structure with sediment particles concentrated between oxide layers.

5. The principal Mn mineral is todorokite, with smaller amounts of birnessite. There is no mineralogic depth dependency observed, and the highest concentrations of todorokite occur on the northwest flank of the Albatross Cordillera. Iron occurs principally as amorphous or cryptocrystalline hydrated ferric oxide and secondarily as goethite and maghemite. Other identified authigenic minerals are zeolites, clay minerals, and feldspars(?). Not identified but probably present are hydrated oxides of Ti, Ni, and perhaps spinels, vanadates, and molybdates. The principal incorporated detrital minerals are quartz, feldspar, ferromagnesian, and clay minerals, which increase proportionately toward the Antarctic Continent and are transported by ice rafting. The increase in quartz content in the Southwest Pacific Basin is attributed to aeolian transport from Australia and New Zealand.

6. Two element suites are delineated on the basis of statistical analysis: a Mn-(chalcophile) related suite consisting of Ni, Mo, Zn, V, Cu, Co, Ba, Sn, and Sr, and an Fe(lithophile) related suite consisting of Ti, V, Zn, Zr, Mo, Co, Ba, and Sr.

7. Three geochemical provinces are delineated where these element suites are enriched in concretions: the Albatross Cordillera (60°S, 160°W), the Fe suite; the Southwest Pacific Basin, the Mn suite; and the Chile Rise-Albatross Cordillera (40°–50°S), both suites. The chalcophile (Mn) suite is associated with an abyssal basin; the lithophile (Fe) suite with a mid-ocean ridge-rise system.

8. The elements that comprise the concretions are derived principally from volcanism, which is manifested by fissure eruptions, seamounts, and associated hydrothermal activity on the floor of the Southwest Pacific Basin, along the flanks and crest of the mid-ocean ridge-rise system, and along the Eltanin Fracture Zone across the Southeast Pacific Basin. A secondary source of lithophile elements is the Antarctic Continent, but biological and sea water contributions are negligible.

9. Elements are transported down current from volcanic sources, coprecipitating en route. The circumpolar bottom current has high enough velocities to move round nodules up to 12 cm in diameter under drag shear and is undoubtedly responsible for their morphology. The formation of concretions is considered to be extremely rapid, perhaps as fast as 60 mm/1000 yr.

APPENDIX

A representative sample was chosen from each concretion population for chemical and X-ray diffraction analysis. These samples were scrubbed with a plastic-bristled brush, rinsed in distilled water to remove clinging sediment, and broken open. The Fe-Mn oxide crust-subcrust portions were separated by hand from nucleus sections, lightly ground in a mortar and pestle, and then screened through silk brocade cloth of approximately 100 mesh. Zeolite and clay nuclei were similarly ground to a powder suitable for X-ray diffraction and chemical analysis.

Sample powders were shipped in glass containers to the Materials Laboratory of Newport News Shipbuilding and Drydock Company, Newport News, Virginia. X-ray fluorescence techniques were used to determine water-free weight per cents of Mn, Fe, Ni, Cu, and Co. Atomic adsorption was used to determine Ti, V, Zn, Sr, Mo, Sn, Zr, and Ba. Duplicate samples showed ± 5% replication for Fe and Mn and ± 10% for the remainder of the elements.

X-RAY DIFFRACTION

Most of the X-ray diffractograms were made with a Norelco diffractometer utilizing a gas-proportional detector and pulse-height analysis. Powders packed into an aluminum planchet were scanned at $1°2\theta$ per minute. Nickel-filtered Cu-$K\alpha$ radiation was used, and scale factors were varied as appropriate. Quartz, which was present in all samples, was used as an internal standard, and peak areas were calculated by multiplying the base width and peak half-height.

Some of the diffractograms were obtained using a monochromator instead of a proportional counter and pulse-height analyzer in order to eliminate Fe and Mn fluorescence so as to check peak area ratios and mineral identifications. Additional checks on the reliability of peak area ratios were made by both multiple runs on one powder and by scans of repacked powders.

Three problems hindered mineral identification in diffractogram peaks: (1) the Fe and Mn fluorescence, which increased background; (2) the frequent masking of certain peaks because of the larger number (usually 5–10) of minerals found in the ferromanganese deposits; and (3) the difficulty in distinguishing the presence of minerals that are present in only trace amounts. The first problem, that of fluorescence, was greatly reduced by pulse-height analysis. The other two problems are basically related and involve visual interpretation of the diffractograms. The criteria used in identification of the mineral phases are summarized in Table 20.

Todorokite and birnessite. Two coexisting Mn-oxide phases are probably present in most ferromanganese concretions in antarctic waters. However, X-ray diffractograms seldom reveal the presence of any phase other than todorokite. *Frondel et al.* [1960] listed X-ray diffraction data for todorokite from a number of terrestrial Mn deposits. *Manheim* [1965] compared diffraction data for continental and pelagic todorokites. Some students of Mn nodule mineralogy have called todorokite a 10-Å manganite on the basis of its most intense X-ray reflection.

Jones and Milne [1956] are the original source for X-ray data on naturally occurring birnessite. The most intense X-ray reflection of very fine-grained δ-MnO_2, which lacks a basal 7-Å reflection, coincides with todorokite and birnessite peaks at about 2.4 Å. The best evidence for the presence of δ-MnO_2 is a marked increase in intensity of the broad peak at 2.4 Å relative to basal todorokite and birnessite reflections (Table 21).

Goethite. Aside from the amorphous $FeOOH \cdot nH_2O$ phase, goethite is the most important Fe-bearing material in South Atlantic and South Pacific Ocean concretions. Only in a minority of samples was goethite important enough to display distinct diffraction peaks, however. The major peak at 4.18 Å usually appeared as a shoulder on the 4.26-Å quartz peak. Peaks at 2.69, 2.49, and 2.19 Å often were distinguishable.

Maghemite. Gamma-Fe_2O_3 may be a trace constituent in many Mn nodules from the study area. Only in a few samples are the major diffraction peaks at 2.52 and 2.95 Å unobscured by feldspar. A tentative identification in most samples is based on the presence of minor peaks at 5.90 and 2.09 Å.

Quartz. Quartz was detected in virtually every sample. This permitted the use of quartz as an internal standard without introducing still another mineral to the already complex mineral mixtures. The 1000 peak (4.26 Å) frequently obscured the major goethite peak. The most intense quartz peak ($10\bar{1}0$ at 3.34 Å) usually obscured the plagioclase 112 peak. The 1101 quartz peak at 2.46 Å was usually superimposed on the broad todorokite-birnessite peak in this region.

Feldspar. Like quartz, feldspars were present in nearly every sample. Unlike quartz, the *d*-spacings and relative peak intensities were quite variable, depending upon the composition and structure of the particular feldspar or range of feldspars present. Since plagioclase feldspars, especially intermediate and calcic varieties, were predominant, subtle distinctions between the X-ray diffraction patterns of the various plagioclases were utilized to approximate the composition following *Peterson and Goldberg* [1962].

TABLE 20. Sources of X-ray Diffraction Data

Mineral	Reference(s)	Comments
Todorokite	*Frondel et al.* [1960]	Charco Redondo, Cuba
Birnessite	*Jones and Milne* [1956]	Scotland, gravel pan
δ-MnO_2	*Buser et al.* [1954]	Synthetic
Goethite	*Rooksby* [1961]	α-FeOOH
Maghemite	*Rooksby* [1961]	See also *Harrison and Peterson* [1965]
	Machek [1965]	
Quartz	ASTM 5-0490	Internal standard
Plagioclase	ASTM 9-466	Albite
	ASTM 9-457	Oligoclase
	ASTM 10-359	Andesine
	ASTM 9-465	Labradorite
	ASTM 9-467	Bytownite
	ASTM 12-301	Anorthite
	ASTM 10-379	Anorthite
Alkali Feldspars	ASTM 13-456	Sanidine
	ASTM 9-478	Anorthoclase
	ASTM 10-479	Microcline
	ASTM 9-462	Orthoclase
Smectite	ASTM 3-0009	Montmorillonite
	ASTM 2-0008	Nontronite
	This study	Montmorillonite?
Phillipsite	*Lippman* [1958]	Sample impure?
	Morgenstein [1967]	Harmotome?
	This study	Sample nearly pure
Clinoptilolite	*Hathaway and Sachs* [1965]	Mid-Atlantic Ridge
	Mumpton [1960]	Heulandite differentiated
Analcime	ASTM 7-363	Zeolite, probably present
	ASTM 7-340	
Amphibole	ASTM 9-434	Hornblende
Pyroxene	ASTM 3-0623	Augite
	ASTM 7-216	Enstatite
	ASTM 2-5020	Hypersthene
Olivine	ASTM 7-75	Forsterite
	ASTM 7-156	Chryolite
Magnetite	ASTM 11-614	Primary volcanic
Prehnite	ASTM 7-333	Secondary volcanic
Illite/muscovite	ASTM 9-334	Illite
	ASTM 7-42	Muscovite
Chlorite	*Griffin and Goldberg* [1963]	
Talc/pyrophyllite	*Biscaye* [1965]	Pyrophyllite
	ASTM 3-0881	Talc
Apatite	*McConnell* [1938]	
Calcite	ASTM 5-0586	

TABLE 21. Comparison of X-ray Diffraction Data on Concretion Materials and Manganese Minerals

Albatross Cordillera Nodule [This Study]		Baltic Sea Nodule [*Manheim*, 1965]		Pacific Ocean Nodule [*Manheim*, 1965]		Todorokite [*Frondel et al.*, 1960]		Birnessite [*Jones and Milne*, 1956]		δ-MnO_2 [*Buser et al.*, 1954]	
d, Å	*I*	*d*, Å	*I*	*d*, Å	*I*	*d*, Å	*I*	*d*, Å	*I*	*d*, Å	*I*
9.7	10	9.7	100	9.7	10b	9.6	10				
7.2	2b	7.2	60b			7.15	¼d	7.27	s		
4.85	5	4.85	24b	4.87	15b	4.80	8				
		4.56	6b			4.45	1d				
								3.60	w		
		3.58	6b			3.40	½d				
						3.20	1				
						3.10	1				
2.45		2.45		2.46	100b	2.46	3.	2.44	m	2.43	s
through	4b	through	96b	2.39	10b	2.40	5				
2.38		2.34		2.34	20b	2.34	4				
		2.23	3b	2.24	10b	2.23	3				
						2.13	½d				
		2.06	5b								
		2.00	7			1.98	2				
						1.92	½				
1.50	½					1.78	1				
						1.74	1				
1.42	3b	1.42	21b	1.41	40b	1.53	1	1.412	m	1.42	s
		through				1.49	3				
1.375	½	1.39		1.385	10b	1.42	2				
						1.39	1				

Alkali feldspars, probably present in most of the ferromanganese oxide-silicate mixtures, constituted such minute quantities that X-ray identification was impossible in all but a few instances. Differentiation between alkali and plagioclase feldspars was relatively easy; the most intense reflection(s) of the alkali feldspars usually results from a 3.21–3.26 Å *d*-spacing(s), whereas plagioclases are characterized by at least one intense reflection in the 3.16–3.21 Å *d*-spacing range. The $20\bar{1}$ reflection of the alkali feldspars also differs from that of the plagioclases, and it can be used to identify the particular alkali feldspar present.

Montmorillonite. Montmorillonite is another nearly invariable constituent of Mn encrustations. The identification of this mineral was based primarily on the presence of a diffraction peak at about 4.45 Å, although one or more ill-defined peaks in the 12–15 Å regions were usually present. In addition, two peaks between 2.55 Å and 2.63 Å were often present, which, coupled with the 4.45-Å peak, confirmed the presence of montmorillonite. In nucleus materials comprised predominantly of montmorillonite, the twin 2.55–2.63 Å peaks were often not resolved at a scan speed of $1°2\theta$ per minute.

The precise composition of the montmorillonite, or more properly, montmorillonoid, was not determined. According to the criteria of *Warshaw and Roy* [1961], the mineral is a dioctahedral smectite. Most workers (including *Arrhenius* [1963] and *Bonatti* [1963] have attributed a nontronite composition to the montmorillonite formed by alteration of submarine basalts, however. The diffraction peaks displayed by the montmorillonite of this study do not agree well with published nontronite X-ray data.

Table 22 lists the spacings and intensities of peaks possessed by the montmorillonite found in South Atlantic and South Pacific Ocean Mn nodules, as well as data on nontronite and continental montmorillonite.

Phillipsite. Phillipsite was detected in a majority of the Mn nodules studied. The basic criterion used for identification was a relatively sharp peak at 7.1 Å, with additional peaks at 8.2, 5.36, 2.74, and 2.68 Å. Since chlorite also possesses a 7.1-Å peak, the other peaks are necessary for an unambiguous identification. Table 23 lists the X-ray diffraction data for a nearly pure sample of phillipsite separated from the palagonite rim of a submarine basaltic volcanic bomb, which had an outer encrustation of ferromanganese oxides.

Identical *d*-spacings and relative peak intensities were shown by a number of phillipsite nuclei scattered throughout the study area. Phillipsite that was incorporated into or formed within accumulating ferromanganese oxides usually displayed only the most intense peaks. Of course, in most of the powder samples the most intense peak at about 3.2 Å was coincident with the major plagioclase peak, so that an estimate of the relative importance of phillipsite in the sample depended on comparison of the 7.1-Å peak with secondary plagioclase peak areas.

The peaks displayed by marine phillipsite differ noticeably from values given for continental phillipsite [*Wyart and Chatelain*, 1938; *Hay*, 1964]. The only known set of diffraction data (Table 23) on marine phillipsite was published by *Lippman* [1958]; his sample was apparently somewhat impure. *Morgenstein* [1967] obtained data (Table 23) on a marine zeolite in scoriaceous pelagic sediments west of the Society Ridge, South Pacific, which he calls harmotome. However, the identification of the Ba analog of phillipsite is not supported by chemical analyses. *Arrhenius* [1963], among other workers, states that members of the harmotome-phillipsite series are common in pelagic sediments. However, no reference diffraction data are available.

X-ray fluorescence analysis of the nearly pure phillipsite mentioned above (Zemmels, verbal communication, 1967) demonstrated a lack of Ba and the presence of little Ca in the phillipsite. This zeolite is probably similar to the K-Na phillipsite studied by *Rex* [1967].

Clinoptilolite. Hathaway and Sachs [1965] have published diffraction data on an authigenic marine clinoptilolite. Their data agree well with those of *Mumpton* [1960], among other workers. Clinoptilolite appears to be a trace constituent in many of the South Atlantic and South Pacific Ocean samples studied, but because of the limited quantities present, many of the peaks were often obscured. For this reason, no single peak served as the basis for identification. Only when peaks appeared at several spacings not possessed by any other minerals was the presence of clinoptilolite deemed even probable. The most reliable peaks belong to the set 9.1–8.9, 8.0–7.9, 6.8–6.7, and 3.99–3.96 Å. The presence of several relatively intense peaks at low 2θ angles served to differentiate clinoptilolite from heulandite [*Mumpton*, 1960].

Analcime. This zeolite has not been definitely reported from South Pacific pelagic sediments. Its presence in Mn nodules of the study area is strongly suspected on the basis of many diffractograms displaying peaks at 6.9 Å and 5.6 Å. It should also be noted that other

TABLE 22. Montmorillonite Diffraction Data

Montmorillonite This Study		Montmorillonite ASTM 3-0009		Nontronite ASTM 2-0008	
d(Å)	I/I_0	d(Å)	I/I_0	d(Å)	I/I_0
15.2	10	15.3	10	13.9	10
5.12	1	5.15	8	7.1	2b
4.45	6	4.50	10	4.44	8
3.09	1	3.07	10	3.54	5
2.61	1?	2.61	10	2.79	1
2.56	4	2.55	10	2.59	2–5
2.40	1	2.41	4	2.51	2b
		2.24	2	2.27	1b
2.15	1	2.16	2		

TABLE 23. Phillipsite Diffraction Data

This Study		*Lippman* [1958]		*Morgenstein* [1967]	
d, Å	I/I_0	d, Å	I/I_0	d, Å	I/I_0
8.20	8	8.19	w		
7.12	57	7.14	w	7.08	80
6.38	6			6.23	60
5.36	13	5.34	w	5.30	50
5.03, 5.00	25	5.01	w	4.97	50
4.29	5				
4.11	3	4.13, 4.04 b	w	4.08	90
3.94, 3.93	1			3.91	20
3.76	< 1			3.65	20
3.245	28	3.26	m	3.25	50
3.185	100	3.18	s	3.21	50
3.09	< 1			3.15	100
2.95	13	2.94	w	3.12	20
2.90	< 1			2.97	30
2.84, 2.83	1				
2.745	13			2.73	45
2.685	24	2.67	w	2.71	10
2.56, 2.55	4			2.67	50
				2.65	10
2.52	1			2.54	20
2.46	< 1				
2.395	2				
2.33	2				
2.25	1				
2.225	< 1				
2.165	1				
2.075	< 1				
etc.					

zeolites (mordenite, erionite, and epistilbite) may be present, but the evidence is even less conclusive than that for analcime.

Amphibole. Amphibole minerals occur in nearly every Drake Passage-Scotia Sea concretion, and in several South Pacific samples. The basis for identification was a distinct peak at 8:45 Å. Published diffraction data show this peak to be less intense than peaks at 3.38, 3.09, and 2.70 Å (hornblende), but work by Edwards (verbal communication, 1967) shows hornblendes with relative peak intensities corresponding to those of hornblendes in Mn nodules. Besides the 8.45-Å peak, only peaks at 3.10–3.05 and 2.82–2.80 Å were occasionally defined. Other amphiboles displaying peaks from 8.25 to 8.65 Å were found in several samples.

Pyroxene, olivine, magnetite, and ilmenite. These four minerals were occasionally detected. The frequent small-to-medium 2.89–2.88 Å peaks probably belong to a pyroxene; none of the samples studied contained appreciable pyroxene. A single olivine-glass nucleus gave an excellent diffraction pattern, and many other samples showed peaks centered at 2.77 Å, which were attributed to olivine. A few samples displayed 2.98, 2.52 Å, and other peaks characteristic of magnetite. In feldspar-rich samples, exaggerated 2.52-Å peaks may have been due to the presence of magnetite. Well-defined, small peaks at 2.75 Å and 2.55 Å were interpreted as probable indicators of ilmenite.

Prehnite. Several nucleus samples and a few oxide crusts contained prehnite; observed *d*-spacings and relative intensities matched published data very well. In a few instances, the presence of a 3.28-Å peak shouldering on the 3.2-Å plagioclase peak may have been caused by prehnite.

Minor phyllosilicates. Illite/muscovite, chlorite, and talc/pyrophyllite were incorporated into a number of the ferromanganese oxide deposits. A sharp 10-Å peak was assigned to illite-muscovite; often this peak appeared as a shoulder on the more broad, adjacent todorokite peak. Diffraction maxima at 14 and 7 Å, where evidence for phillipsite was lacking, were used as evidence for chlorite. Talc/pyrophyllite displayed 9.4–9.2 Å peaks; no attempt was made to differentiate these two related minerals.

Other contaminant minerals. Bone apatites found within Mn nodules were characterized by three peaks in the 2.82–2.70 Å region, indicating a probable fluorapatite composition. A large 3.03-Å peak was assigned to calcite.

The X-ray diffraction data are semiquantitative. They have been used only to show broad regional trends. Duplicate values for peak area ratios were almost always well within ± 20%. The fluctuations caused by machine performance, differing grain sizes, and variable packing can in no way have significantly affected these trends.

Where more than one peak area ratio was obtained for a single station, the values were averaged. This was done at 17 stations of 111. For the maps showing the regional variation of the todorokite proportion (Figures 24 and 62), only two of the stations with multiple values had a single value significantly different from the average value for the station. At seven stations the individual values for feldspar are not representative of the average value. This may indicate that the regional feldspar trends have little meaning, since differences within a single dredge haul can be as great as the differences used to delineate distributional trends. Multiple quartz values are more constant, and therefore probably more reliable. Only three stations show disparate quartz proportions. It must be concluded that averaging has almost no effect on regional todorokite or quartz trends.

Radiochemistry

An outer segment of approximately 1 cm was taken from all samples and separated into 0.5-cm outer and inner intervals. These samples were fragmented but were not powdered so as to prevent possible inclusion of Th or U from nonmanganiferous substances. Duplicate three-gram portions from each sample were measured into acid-cleaned and distilled water-rinsed glass beakers, and sufficient dilute HCl was added to leach the samples. Measured amounts of Th^{234} and U^{232} were added to determine the efficiency of the analysis. The samples were allowed to come to equilibrium over a period of several days. Analyses were done in duplicate, and a spiked blank was included with each pair.

The assay closely followed the techniques discussed by *Holmes* [1965], which involve radioelement separation through columns containing anion exchange resins. Fractionated samples were extracted organically to improve the yield and the radioelements were electrolytically plated on stainless-steel planchets. Amounts of the radioelements present in each sample were determined by alpha pulse-height analysis and total beta activities corrected for final yields relative to the amounts of Th^{234} and U^{232} spikes recovered. In two instances, samples 6-11 and 11-3, the results of the initial analyses showed poor agreement between duplicate samples and they were reanalyzed by the same techniques. Subsequent results of these additional assays were compared with the original data and a best value was selected to represent the individual sample. The majority of the samples analyzed were in good agreement, including blanks.

Acknowledgments. This research was supported by the Office of Antarctic Studies of the National Science Foundation (GA 40, 523, 1066, 4001). Mr. Dennis Cassidy provided invaluable photographic assistance in the preparation of the illustrations. June Aloi labored many hours over the manuscript.

REFERENCES

Adams, J. A. S., J. K. Osmond, and J. W. Rogers, The geochemistry of thorium and uranium, in *Physics and Chemistry of the Earth*, vol. 3, edited by L. H. Ahrens, F. Press, K. Rankama, and S. K. Runcorn, pp. 298–348, Pergamon, London, 1959.

Agassiz, A., Albatross Expedition preliminary report, *Mem. Museum Comp. Zool., Harvard College, Cambridge, 26*, 1–111, 1901.

Agassiz, A., Albatross Expedition reports, *Mem. Museum Comp. Zool., Harvard College, Cambridge, 33*, 1–50, 1906.

Ahrens, L., The lognormal distribution of the elements, 1, *Geochim. Cosmochim. Acta, 5*, 49–53, 1954*a*.

Ahrens, L., The lognormal distribution of the elements, 2, *Geochim. Cosmochim. Acta, 6*, 121–131, 1954*b*.

Ahrens, L., The lognormal distribution of the elements, 3, *Geochim. Cosmochim. Acta, 11;* 205–212, 1957.

Anikouchine, W. A., Dissolved chemical substances in compacting marine sediments, *J. Geophys. Res., 72*, 505–509, 1967.

Arrhenius, G. O. S., Sediment cores from the East Pacific, *Reports of the Swedish Deep-Sea Expedition 1947–1948*, vol. 5, part 2, fasc. 2, pp. 95–186, 1952.

Arrhenius, G. O. S., Pelagic sediments, in *The Sea: Ideas and Observations on Progress in the Study of the Seas*, vol. 3, edited by M. N. Hill, E. D. Goldberg, C. O'D. Iselin, and W. H. Munk, pp. 655–727, Interscience, New York, 1963.

Arrhenius, G. O. S., Deep-sea sedimentation: A critical review of U. S. work, *Trans. Am. Geophys. Union, 48*, 604–631, 1967.

Arrhenius, G. O. S., and E. Bonatti, Neptunism and vulcanism in the ocean, in *Progress in Oceanography*, vol. 3, edited by M. Sears, pp. 7–22, Pergamon, London, 1965.

Arrhenius, G. O. S., and H. Korkisch, Uranium and thorium in marine minerals, *Intern. Oceanog. Congr. Preprints*, edited by M. Sears, p. 497, American Association for the Advancement of Science, Washington, D. C., 1959.

Arrhenius, G. O. S., J. Mero, and J. Korkisch, Origin of oceanic manganese minerals, *Science, 144*, 170–173, 1964.

Baranov, V. I., and L. A. Kuzmina, Radiochemical analysis of deep-sea sediments in connection with determination of the rate of sediment accumulation, in *Radioisotopes in Scientific Research*, vol. 2, edited by R. C. Extermann, pp. 619–633, Pergamon, London, 1958.

Barnes, S. S., Minor element composition of ferromanganese nodules, *Science, 157*, 63–65, 1967.

Barnes, S. S., and J. R. Dymond, Rates of accumulation of ferromanganese nodules, *Nature, 213*, 1218–1219, 1967.

Beals, H. L., Manganese-iron concretions in Nova Scotia lakes, *Maritime Sediments, 2*, 70–72, 1966.

Bender, M. L., Teh-Lung Ku, and W. S. Broecker, Manganese nodules: Their evolution, *Science, 151*(3708), 325–328, 1966.

Biscaye, P. E., Mineralogy and sedimentation of recent deep-sea clay in the Atlantic Ocean and adjacent seas and oceans, *Geol. Soc. Am. Bull., 76*, 803–832, 1965.

Bonatti, E., Zeolites in Pacific pelagic sediments, *Trans. N. Y. Acad. Sci., 25*, 938–948, 1963.

Bonatti, E., and O. Joensuu, Deep-sea iron deposit from the South Pacific, *Science, 154*, 643–644, 1966.

Bonatti, E., and Y. R. Nayudu, The origin of manganese nodules on the ocean floor, *Am. J. Sci., 263*, 17–39, 1965.

Boström, K., and M. N. A. Peterson, Precipitates from hydrothermal exhalations on the East Pacific Rise, *Econ. Geol., 61*, 1258–1265, 1966.

Boström, K., and M. N. A. Peterson, The origin of aluminum-poor sediments in areas of high heat flow on the East Pacific Rise (preprint), submitted to *Geochim. Cosmochim. Acta*, 1969.

Bricker, O., Some stability relations in the system $Mn\text{-}O_2\text{-}H_2O$ at 25° and one atmosphere total pressure, *Am. Mineralogist, 50*, 1296–1354, 1965.

Burns, R. G., Formation of cobalt(III) in the amorphous $FeOOH \cdot nH_2O$ phase of manganese nodules, *Nature, 205*, 999, 1965.

Burns, R. G., and D. W. Fuerstenau, Electron-probe determination of inter-element relationships in manganese nodules, *Am. Mineralogist, 51*, 895–902, 1966.

Buser, W., The nature of the iron and manganese compounds in manganese nodules, *Intern. Oceanog. Congr. Preprints*, edited by M. Sears, pp. 962–963, American Association for the Advancement of Science, Washington, D. C., 1959.

Buser, W., P. Graf, and W. Feitknecht, Beitrag zur Kenntnis der mangan (II)—manganite und des δ-MnO_2, *Helv. Chim. Acta, 37*, 2322–2333, 1954.

Buser, W., and A. Grütter, Über die Natur der Manganknollen, *Schweiz. Mineral. Petrogr. Mitt., 36*, 49–62, 1956.

Chow, T. J., and E. D. Goldberg, On the marine geochemistry of barium, *Geochim. Cosmochim. Acta, 20*, 192–198, 1960.

Chow, T. J., and C. C. Patterson, The occurrence and significance of lead isotopes in pelagic sediments, *Geochim. Cosmochim. Acta, 26*, 263–308, 1962.

Cronan, D. S., and J. S. Tooms, Sub-surface concentrations of manganese nodules in Pacific sediments, *Deep-Sea Res., 14*, 117–119, 1967.

Deacon, G. E. R., The hydrology of the Southern Ocean, *Discovery Rept., 15*, 1–124, 1937.

Deacon, G. E. R., The Southern Ocean, in *The Sea: Ideas and Observations on Progress in the Study of the Seas*, vol. 2, edited by M. N. Hill, pp. 281–296, Interscience, New York, 1963.

Deer, W. A., R. A. Howie, and J. Zussman, *Rockforming minerals*, vol. 5, *Non-silicates*, 371 pp., John Wiley, New York, 1962.

Dietz, R. S. Manganese deposits on the northeast Pacific sea floor, *Calif. J. Mines Geol., 51*(3), 209–220, 1955.

Edwards, D. S., and H. G. Goodell, The detrital mineralogy of ocean floor surface sediments adjacent to the Antarctic Peninsula, Antarctica, *Marine Geol.*, in press, 1969.

Ehrlich, A. M., Rare earth abundances in manganese nodules, A dissertation, 225 pp., Department of Chemistry, Massachusetts Institute of Technology, Cambridge, 1968.

Ehrlich, H. L., Bacteriology of manganese nodules, *Applied Microbiol., 11,* 15–19, 1963*a*.

Ehrlich, H. L., Further studies on manganese nodules, *Bacteriol. Proc. Abstr., RT 7,* 161, 1963*b*.

Ehrlich, H. L., Bacterial release from manganese nodules, *Bacteriol. Proc. Abstr., G156,* 1964.

Ehrlich, H. L., Bacteriology of manganese nodules 2, manganese oxidation by cell-free extract from a manganese nodule bacterium, *Applied Microbiol., 16,* 197–202, 1968.

Engel, A. E. J., C. G. Engel, and R. C. Havens, Chemical characteristics of oceanic basalts and the upper mantle, *Geol. Soc. Am. Bull., 76,* 719–734, 1965.

Ewing, M., and B. C. Heezen, Some problems of Antarctic submarine geology, in *Antarctica in the Geophysical Year, Geophys. Monograph 1,* edited by A. P. Crary, pp. 75–81, American Geophysical Union, Washington, D.C., 1956.

Feitknecht, W., and W. Marti, Manganite and artificial manganese dioxide, *Helv. Chim. Acta, 28,* 149–156, 1945.

Frondel, C., U. B. Marvin, and J. Ito, New occurrences of todorokite, *Am. Mineralogist, 45,* 1167–1173, 1960.

Gattow, Von G., and O. Glemser, Darstellung und Eigenschaften von Braunsteinen, 3 (Die ε-, β- und α-Gruppe der Braunsteine, über Ramsdellit und über die Umwandlungen der Braunsteine) *Z. Anorg. Allegem. Chem., 309,* (3–4), 121–150, 1961.

Glemser, Von O., G. Gattow, and H. Meisiek, Darstellung und Eigenschaften von Braunsteinen, 1 (Die δ-Gruppe der Braunsteine): *Z. Anorg. Allegem. Chem. 309,* (1–2), 1–19, 1961.

Goldberg, E. D., Marine geochemistry, 1, Chemical scavengers of the sea, *J. Geol., 62,* 249–265, 1954.

Goldberg, E. D., Chemistry in the oceans, in *Oceanography,* edited by M. Sears, pp. 583–597, American Association for the Advancement of Science, Washington, D.C., 1961.

Goldberg, E. D., Minor elements in sea water, in *Chemical Oceanography,* vol. 1, edited by J. P. Riley and G. Skirrow, chap. 5, pp. 163–196, Academic, London, 1965.

Goldberg, E. D., and G. O. S. Arrhenius, Chemistry of Pacific pelagic sediments, *Geochim. Cosmochim. Acta, 13,* 153–212, 1958.

Goldberg, E. D., and M. Koide, Geochronological studies of deep-sea sediments by the ionium-thorium method, *Geochim. Cosmochim. Acta, 26,* 417–443, 1962.

Goldberg, E. D., and M. Koide, Rates of sediment accumulation in the Indian Ocean, in *Earth Science and Meteoritics,* edited by J. Geiss and E. D. Goldberg, chap. 5, pp. 90–102, North-Holland, Amsterdam, 1963.

Goldberg, E. D., M. Koide, J. J. Griffin, and M. N. A. Peterson, A geochronological and sedimentary profile across the North Atlantic Ocean, in *Isotopic and Cosmic Chemistry,* edited by H. Craig, S. L. Miller, and G. J. Wasserburg, pp. 211–232, North-Holland, Amsterdam, 1964.

Goldberg, E. D., and E. Picciotto, Thorium determinations in manganese nodules, *Science, 121,* 613–614, 1955.

Goldschmidt, V. M., *Geochemistry,* 730 pp., edited by Alex Muir, Oxford University Press, London, 1954.

Goodell, H. G., The marine geology of the Drake Passage, Scotia Sea, and South Sandwich Trench: USNS *Eltanin* Marine Geology 1–8 (mimeographed), 263 pp., *Contrib. 7,* Sedimentology Research Laboratory, Department of Geology, Florida State University, Tallahassee, 1964.

Goodell, H. G., The marine geology of the Southern Ocean USNS *Eltanin* Marine Geology Cruises 9–15 (offset), 196 pp., *Contrib. 11,* Sedimentology Research Laboratory, Department of Geology, Florida State University, Tallahassee, 1965.

Goodell, H. G., The sediments and sedimentary geochemistry of the Southeastern Atlantic Shelf, *J. Geol., 75*(6), 665–692, 1967*a*.

Goodell, H. G., Ferromanganese deposits of the Southern Ocean (abstract), *Southeastern Sect., Geol. Soc. Am. Program,* 29–30, 1967*b*.

Goodell, H. G., Elemental distributions in ferromanganese concretions of the Southern Ocean, *Trans. Am. Geophys. Union, 49,* 223, 1968*a*.

Goodell, H. G., The marine geology of the Southern Ocean, USNS *Eltanin* Cruises 16–27, 245 pp., *Contrib. 25,* Sedimentology Research Laboratory, Department of Geology, Florida State University, Tallahassee, 1968*b*.

Goodell, H. G., and M. Scott, The clay mineralogy of Southern Ocean surface sediments (abstract), *Trans. Am. Geophys. Union, 49,* 223, 1968.

Goodell, H. G., and N. D. Watkins, The paleomagnetic stratigraphy of the Southern Ocean: 20° west to 160° east longitude, *Deep-Sea Res., 15,* 89–112, 1968.

Gordon, A. L., Potential temperature, oxygen and circulation of bottom water in the Southern Ocean, *Deep-Sea Res., 13,* 1125–1138, 1966.

Gordon, A. L., Structure of antarctic waters between 20° W and 170° W, *Antarctic Map Folio Series, Folio 6,* American Geographical Society, New York, 1967.

Graham, J. W., Metabolically induced precipitation of trace elements from sea water, *Science, 129,* 1428–1429, 1959.

Graham, J. W., and S. C. Cooper, Biological origin of manganese-rich deposits of the sea floor, *Nature, 183,* 1050–1051, 1959.

Grant, J. B., Environmental controls underlying the morphology and composition of ferromanganese concretions of the Southern Ocean (abstract), *Geol. Soc. Am. Program. 80,* 1967.

Griffin, J. J., and E. D. Goldberg, Clay-mineral distributions in the Pacific Ocean, in *The Sea,* vol. 3, edited by M. N. Hill, pp. 728–741, Interscience, New York, 1963.

Griffin, J. J., H. Windam, and E. D. Goldberg, The distribution of clay minerals in the world ocean, *Deep-Sea Res., 15,* 433–459, 1968.

Grütter, A., and W. Buser, Untersuchungen an Mangansedimenten, *Chimia (Aarau), 11,* 132–133, 1957.

Hamilton, E. L., Sunken islands of the mid-Pacific Mountains, 97 pp., *Geol. Soc. Am., Mem. 64,* 1956.

Harrison, C. G. A., and M. N. A. Peterson, A magnetic mineral from the Indian Ocean, *Am. Mineralogist, 50,* 704–712, 1965.

Harriss, R. C., J. H. Crocket, and M. Stainton, Palladium, iridium and gold in deep-sea manganese nodules, *Geochim. Cosmochim. Acta, 32,* 1049–1056, 1968.

Hathaway, G. C., and P. L. Sachs, Sepiolite and clinoptilolite from the mid-Atlantic Ridge, *Am. Mineralogist, 50,* 852–867, 1965.

Hay, R. L., Phillipsite of saline lakes and soils, *Am. Mineralogist, 49,* 1366–1387, 1964.

Heezen, B. C., and C. Hollister, Deep-sea current evidence from abyssal sediments, *Marine Geol., 1,* 141–174, 1964.

Hewett, D. F., and M. Fleischer, Deposits of the manganese oxides, *Econ. Geol., 55*(1), 1–55, 1960.

Hewett, D. F., M. Fleischer, and N. Conklin, Deposits of the manganese oxides, *Econ. Geol., Suppl. 58,* 1–51, 1963.

Holmes, C. W., Rates of sedimentation in the Drake Passage, 101 pp., Ph.D. dissertation, Florida State University, Tallahassee, 1965.

Inman, D. L., Sediments: Physical properties and mechanics of sedimentation, in *Submarine Geology,* 2nd ed., 577 pp., edited by F. P. Shepard, Harper and Row, New York, 1963.

Joly, J., On the radium content of deep-sea sediments, *Phil. Mag., 6,* 190, 1908.

Jones, L. H. P., and A. A. Milne, Birnessite, a new manganese oxide mineral from Aberdeenshire, Scotland, *Mineral. Mag., 31,* 283–288, 1956.

Koczy, F. F., Geochemical balance in the hydrosphere, in *Nuclear Geology,* edited by H. Faul, pp. 342–348, John Wiley, New York, 1954.

Krauskopf, K. B., Sedimentary deposits of rare metals, *Econ. Geol. 50th Anniver. Vol. 1905–1955,* part 1, edited by A. E. Bateman, pp. 411–463, 1955.

Krauskopf, K. B., Factors controlling the concentrations of thirteen rare metals in sea water, *Geochim. Cosmochim. Acta, 9,* 1–32, 1956.

Krauskopf, K. B., Separation of manganese from iron in sedimentary processes, *Geochim. Cosmochim. Acta, 12,* 61–84, 1957*a*.

Krauskopf, K. B., Separation of manganese from iron in the formation of manganese deposits in volcanic associations, *Symposium on Manganese, 9th International Geological Congress, Mexico,* pp. 119–131, 1957*b*.

Kroll, V., On the age determination in deep sea sediments by radium measurements, *Deep-Sea Res., 1,* 211–215, 1954.

Krumbein, W. C., and F. A. Graybill, *An Introduction to Statistical Models in Geology,* 475 pp., McGraw-Hill, New York, 1965.

Ku, Teh-Lung, An evaluation of the U^{234}/U^{238} method as a tool for dating pelagic sediments, *J. Geophys. Res., 70,* 3457–3474, 1965.

Ku, Teh-Lung, and W. S. Broecker, Uranium, thorium, and protactinium in a manganese nodule, *Earth Planet. Sci. Lett., 2,* 317–320, 1967.

Kuenen, P. H., *Marine Geology,* 568 pp., John Wiley, New York, 1950.

Landergren, S., On the geochemistry of deep-sea sediments, *Reports of the Swedish Deep-Sea Expedition, 10, Spec. Invest. 5,* 61–154, 1964.

Lippman, F., X-ray determination of phillipsite in a sediment core from the central Equatorial Pacific, *Reports of the Swedish Deep-Sea Expedition, 10, Spec. Invest. 3,* 41–42, 1958.

Lynn, D. C., and E. Bonatti, Mobility of manganese in diagenesis of deep-sea sediments, *Marine Geol., 3,* 457–474, 1965.

McConnell, D., A structural investigation of the isomorphism of the apatite group, *Am. Mineralogist, 23,* 1–19, 1938.

Machek, A., Identification of unknown mineral from antarctic core samples, 10 pp., Department of Geology, Florida State University, Tallahassee, 1965.

Maksimov, I. V., The nature of the Great East Drift, *Soviet Antarctic Exped. Inform. Bull., 4,* 33–35, 1962.

Manheim, F. T., Manganese-iron accumulations in the shallow marine environment, Proceedings of the Symposium on Marine Geochemistry, University of Rhode Island, October 29 and 30, 1964, *Narragansett Marine Lab. Occasional Pub., 3,* 217–276, 1965.

Mather, T. T., The deep-sea sediments of the Drake Passage and the Scotia Sea, 100 pp., Master's thesis, Florida State University, Tallahassee, 1966.

Menard, H. W., *Marine Geology of the Pacific,* 271 pp., McGraw-Hill, New York, 1964.

Menard, H. W., and C. J. Shipek, Surface concentrations of manganese nodules, *Nature, 182,* 1156–1158, 1958.

Mero, J. L., Mineral resources on the ocean floor, *Mining Congr. J., 46,* 48–53, 1960.

Mero, J. L., Ocean-floor manganese nodules, *Econ. Geol., 57,* 747–767, 1962.

Mero, J. L., *Mineral Resources of the Sea,* 312 pp., Elsevier, Amsterdam, 1965.

Meylan, M. A., Report of the Florida State University Marine Geology Program, USNS *Eltanin* Cruise 21, 5 pp., *Sedimentol. Res. Lab. Rept.,* Department of Geology, Florida State University, Tallahassee, 1966.

Meylan, M. A., Factors governing the mineralogy of Antarctic Ocean ferromanganese concretions (abstract), *Trans. Am. Geophys. Union, 49*(1), 223, 1968.

Meylan, M., and H. G. Goodell, Mineralogy of manganese nodules from the Southern Ocean (abstract), *Geol. Soc. Am. Program,* 149, 1967.

Moore, J. G., Petrology of deep sea basalts near Hawaii, *Am. J. Sci., 263,* 40–52, 1965.

Moore, J. G., Rate of palagonization of submarine basalt adjacent to Hawaii, Geological Survey of Research, 1966, *U. S. Geol. Surv. Prof. Paper 550-D,* D163–D171, 1966.

Moore, T. C., and G. R. Heath, Manganese nodules, topography and thickness of Quaternary sediments in the Central Pacific, *Nature, 212,* 983–985, 1966.

Morgenstein, M., Authigenic cementation of scoriaceous deep-sea sediments west of the Society Ridge, South Pacific, *Sedimentology, 9,* 105–118, 1967.

Mumpton, F. A., Clinoptilolite redefined, *Am. Mineralogist, 45,* 351–369, 1960.

Murata, K. J., and R. C. Erd, Composition of sediments from the experimental Mohole Project (Guadalupe site), *J. Sediment. Petrol., 34,* 633–655, 1964.

Murray, J., Preliminary report on specimens of the sea bottom, *Proc. Roy. Soc. (London), Ser. A., 24,* 471–532, 1876.

Murray, J., and G. V. Lee, The depth and marine deposits of the Pacific, *Mem. Museum Comp. Zool., Harvard College, Cambridge, 38,* 7–171, 1909.

Murray, J., and A. F. Renard, Deep sea deposits, in *Report on the Scientific Results of the Voyage of HMS Challenger,* edited by C. W. Thomson and J. Murray, vol. 5, 525 pp., H. M. Stationer's Office, London, 1891.

Nayudu, Y. R., Palagonite tuffs (hyaloclastites) and the products of post-eruptive processes, *Bull. Volcanol.,* 27, 1–20, 1964.

Nayudu, Y. R., Petrology of submarine volcanics and the sediments in the vicinity of the Mendocino fracture zone, in *Progress in Oceanography,* vol. 3, edited by M. Sears, pp. 207–220, Pergamon, Oxford, 1965.

Niino, H., Manganese nodules from shallow waters off Japan, *Intern. Oceanog. Congr. Preprints,* edited by M. Sears, pp. 646–647, American Association for the Advancement of Science, Washington, D. C., 1959.

Noble, C. S., and J. J. Naughton, Deep-ocean basalts: Inert

gas content and uncertainties in age dating, *Science, 162,* 265–267, 1968.

Paster, T. P., Petrologic variations within submarine basalt pillows of the South Pacific-Antarctic Ocean, 108 pp., Ph.D. dissertation, Florida State University, Tallahassee, 1968.

Peterson, M. N. A., and E. D. Goldberg, Feldspar distributions in South Pacific pelagic sediments, *J. Geophys. Res., 67,* 3477–3492, 1962.

Pettersson, H., Manganese and nickel on the ocean floor, *Geochim. Cosmochim. Acta, 17,* 209–213, 1959.

Pettersson, H., The proportion of thorium to uranium in rocks and in the sea, *Anz. Akad. Wiss. Wein, Math. Naturwiss, Kl.,* 127–128, 1937.

Picciotto, E. E., Geochemistry of radioactive elements in the ocean and the chronology of deep-sea sediments, in *Oceanography,* edited by M. Sears, pp. 367–390, American Association for the Advancement of Science, Washington, D. C., 1961.

Picciotto, E. E., and S. Wilgain, Thorium determination in deep-sea sediments, *Nature, 173,* 632–633, 1954.

Piggot, C. S., and W. D. Urey, Time relationship in ocean sediments, *Geol. Soc. Am. Bull., 40,* 1187–1210, 1942.

Pitman, W. C., III, E. M. Herron, and J. R. Heirtzler, Magnetic anomalies in the Pacific and sea floor spreading, *J. Geophys. Res., 73,* 2060–2085, 1968.

Presley, B. J., R. R. Brooks, and I. R. Kaplan, Manganese and related elements in the interstitial waters of marine sediments, *Science, 158,* 906–910, 1967.

Price, N. B., Some geochemical observations on manganese-iron oxide nodules from different depth environments, *Marine Geol., 5,* 511–538, 1967.

Rankama, K., and T. G. Sahama, *Geochemistry,* 912 pp., University of Chicago Press, Chicago, 1950.

Revelle, R., M. Bramlette, G. O. S. Arrhenius, and E. D. Goldberg, Pelagic sediments of the Pacific, *Geol. Soc. Am. Spec. Paper 62,* 221–236, 1955.

Rex, R. W., Authigenic silicates formed from basaltic glass by more than 60 million years' contact with sea water, Sylvania Guyot, Marshall Islands, *Proceedings, 15th Conference on Clay and Clay Minerals,* edited by S. W. Bailey, pp. 195–203, Pergamon, New York, 1961.

Rex, R. W., and E. D. Goldberg, Quartz contents of pelagic sediments of the Pacific Ocean, *Tellus, 10,* 153–159, 1958.

Riley J. P., and P. Sinhaseni, Chemical composition of three manganese nodules from the Pacific Ocean, *J. Marine Res., 17,* 466–482, 1958.

Rooksby, H. P., Oxides and hydroxides of aluminum and iron, in *The X-ray Identification and Crystal Structures of Clay Minerals,* edited by G. Brown, pp. 354–392, Mineralological Society, London, 1961.

Rossman, R., and E. Callender, Manganese nodules in Lake Michigan, *Science, 162,* 1123–1124, 1968.

Sackett, W. M., Measured deposition rates of marine sediments and implications for accumulation rates of extraterrestrial dust, *Ann. N. Y. Acad. Sci., 119,* 339–346, 1964*a.*

Sackett, W. M., Deposition rates by the protactinium method (preprint), 12 pp., paper presented at the 3rd Annual Symposium on Marine Geochemistry, University of Rhode Island, Kingston, 1964*b.*

Sackett, W. M., Manganese nodules: Thorium-230: Protactinium-231 ratios, *Science, 154,* 646–647, 1966.

Schutz, D. F., and K. K. Turekian, The distribution of cobalt, nickel, and silver in ocean water profiles around Pacific Antarctica, *J. Geophys. Res., 70,* 5519–5528, 1965.

Skornyakova, N. S., Manganese concretions in sediments of the northeastern Pacific Ocean, *Dokl. Akad. Nauk SSSR, 130,* 653–656, 1960.

Skornyakova, N. S., Dispersed iron and manganese in Pacific Ocean sediments, *Intern. Geol. Rev.,* 7(12), 2161–2176, 1964.

Skornyakova, N. S., P. F. Andruschenko, and L. S. Fomina, Chemical composition of the Pacific Ocean's iron-manganese concretions, *Okeanologiya, 2,* 264–277. (English Transl. in *Deep-Sea Res., 11,* 93–104, 1962.)

Somayajulu, B. L. B., and E. D. Goldberg, Thorium and uranium isotopes in seawater and sediments, *Earth Planet. Sci. Lett., 1,* 102–106, 1966.

Sorem, R. K., Manganese nodules: Nature and significance of internal structure, *Econ. Geol., 62,* 141–147, 1967.

Tatsumoto, M., and E. D. Goldberg, Some aspects of the marine geochemistry of uranium, *Geochim. Cosmochim. Acta, 17,* 201–208, 1959.

Thomas, D. W., and M. Blumer, Pyrene and fluoranthene in manganese nodules, *Science, 143,* 39, 1964.

Thomson C. W., Preliminary notes on the nature of the sea bottom procured by the soundings of HMS *Challenger, Proc. Roy. Soc. (London), Ser. A., 23,* 32–49, 1874.

Trimble, R. B., and H. L. Ehrlich, Bacteriology of manganese nodules, 3, Reduction of MnO_2 by two strains of nodule bacteria, *Applied Microbiol., 16*(5), 695–702, 1968.

Turekian, K. K., Deep-sea deposition of barium, cobalt, and silver, *Geochim. Cosmochim. Acta, 32,* 603–612, 1968.

Turekian, K. K., and D. G. Johnson, The barium distribution in sea water, *Geochim. Cosmochim. Acta, 30,* 1153–1174, 1966.

Turekian, K. K., and E. H. Tausch, Barium in deep-sea sediments of the Atlantic Ocean, *Nature, 201,* 696–697, 1964.

U. S. Navy, Oceanographic atlas of the Polar Seas, part 1, Antarctic, *Hydrograph. Off. Publ. 705,* 1957.

Warshaw, C. M., and R. Roy, Classification and a scheme for the identification of layer silicates, *Geol. Soc. Am. Bull., 72,* 1455–1492, 1961.

Wedepohl, K. H., Spurenanalytische Untersuchungen an Tiefseetonen aus dem Atlantik, Ein Beitrag zur Deutung der geochemischen Sonderstallung von pelagischen Tonen, *Geochim. Cosmochim. Acta, 18,* 200–231, 1960.

Willis, J. P., and L. H. Ahrens, Some investigations on the composition of manganese nodules with particular reference to certain trace elements, *Geochim. Cosmochim. Acta, 26,* 751–764, 1962.

Wyart, J., and P. Chatelain, Etude cristallographique de la christianite, *Bull. Soc. Franc. Min., 61,* 121, 1938.

Zhivago, A. V., Outlines of Southern Ocean geomorphology, in *Antarctic Research, Geophys. Monograph 7,* edited by H. Wexler, M. J. Rubin, and J. E. Caskey, Jr., pp. 74–80, American Geophysical Union, Washington, D. C., 1962.

Zhivago, A. V., Bathymetric and geomorphological maps, in *Atlas Antarktiki,* vol. 1, edited by E. I. Tolstikov, G.U.C.K., Moscow, 1966. (English Transl. in *Soviet Geography: Rev. Transl., 8,* American Geographical Society, New York, 1967.

DISTRIBUTION OF FORAMINIFERA IN SEDIMENTS OF THE SCOTIA SEA AREA, ANTARCTIC WATERS

Ronald James Echols

Allan Hancock Foundation and University of Southern California, Los Angeles, California

Abstract. There are two contrasting kinds of foraminiferal populations in the Scotia and northern Weddell seas. One is composed largely of planktonics and calcareous benthonics, and the other is composed largely of noncalcareous agglutinated benthonics. Calcareous populations, which are typical of areas north of the Antarctic Convergence at depths above 4000 meters, are largely restricted to areas of the Scotia Sea just south of the Antarctic Convergence. Thus, on the northern Scotia Ridge, at depths between 360 meters and about 3400 meters, 60 to 99 per cent of the benthonics are calcareous; but at similar depths on the southern and eastern Scotia Ridge, only 0 to 53 per cent of the benthonics are calcareous. Furthermore, deep-sea populations are predominantly noncalcareous, except for probable relict calcareous populations in five samples from 2000 to 3780 meters in the northern Weddell Sea.

A significant factor limiting the distribution of calcareous foraminifera is the rate of solution of calcium carbonate. The rate of solution has been qualitatively estimated from the ratio of living to total calcareous specimens, using the same ratio for noncalcareous specimens as a standard. Very high ratios for calcareous specimens indicate rapid destruction of empty calcareous skeletons. Solution of calcareous tests, evidenced by severely corroded specimens, occurs throughout the area, but the rate is apparently much higher in areas of noncalcareous populations than in areas of calcareous populations. Distribution of calcareous tests and of evidence of solution of calcareous tests may be explained by a compensation depth rising southward from greater than 3000 meters on the northern Scotia Ridge to less than 500 meters on the southern and eastern Scotia Ridge.

Depth distributions of calcareous and noncalcareous foraminifera were studied separately. A distinctive upper bathyal (330 to 750 meters) calcareous fauna on the northern Scotia Ridge is associated with the temperature maximum stratum of the Warm Deep Layer. At similar depths on the southern and eastern Scotia Ridge, temperatures are 1.6°C colder and the rate of carbonate solution is very high; here, calcareous species are dominantly eurybathyal. Noncalcareous foraminiferal depth boundaries were recognized at 1200 to 1300 meters and 2100 to 2300 meters.

Five foraminiferal biofacies associated with characteristic environments pattern the abyssal floors. The East Scotia Basin Biofacies is associated with diatomaceous sediments and moderate depths (2490 to 3470 meters). Volcanic sediments in the Trench Rim Biofacies are also diatomaceous, but depths are greater (3980 to 4650 meters). The Peripheral Weddell Sea Biofacies and the Central Weddell Sea Biofacies are associated with nondiatomaceous clays and silty clays. The Trench Biofacies is located below 5500 meters in the South Sandwich Trench.

One new genus, *Portatrochammina*, and five new species of Foraminiferida are described. The new species are: *Ammoflintina argentea*, *Conotrochammina kennetti*, *Gyroidina subplanulata*, *Portatrochammina eltaninae*, and *Trochammina quadricamerata*. The genus *Cystammina* Newmayr is emended and transferred from the Trochamminidae to the Rzehakinidae.

INTRODUCTION

General

The purpose of this study is to determine the distributions of foraminifera in sediments of the Scotia Sea area and to relate them to properties of water and substrate. The investigated area lies in the southwestern Atlantic Ocean and is bounded approximately by latitudes 48°S and 67°S and longitudes 21°W and 51°W (Figure 1). It includes the western part of the Scotia Sea; the U-shaped Scotia Ridge which bounds the Scotia Sea on the north, east, and south; and the contiguous parts of the seas beyond the Scotia Ridge, including the South Sandwich Trench to the east and the Weddell Sea to as far south as the Antarctic Circle.

The 90 samples on which this study is based were collected by staff members of the University of Southern California Marine Biology Program. Sampling was conducted from the U. S. Antarctic Research

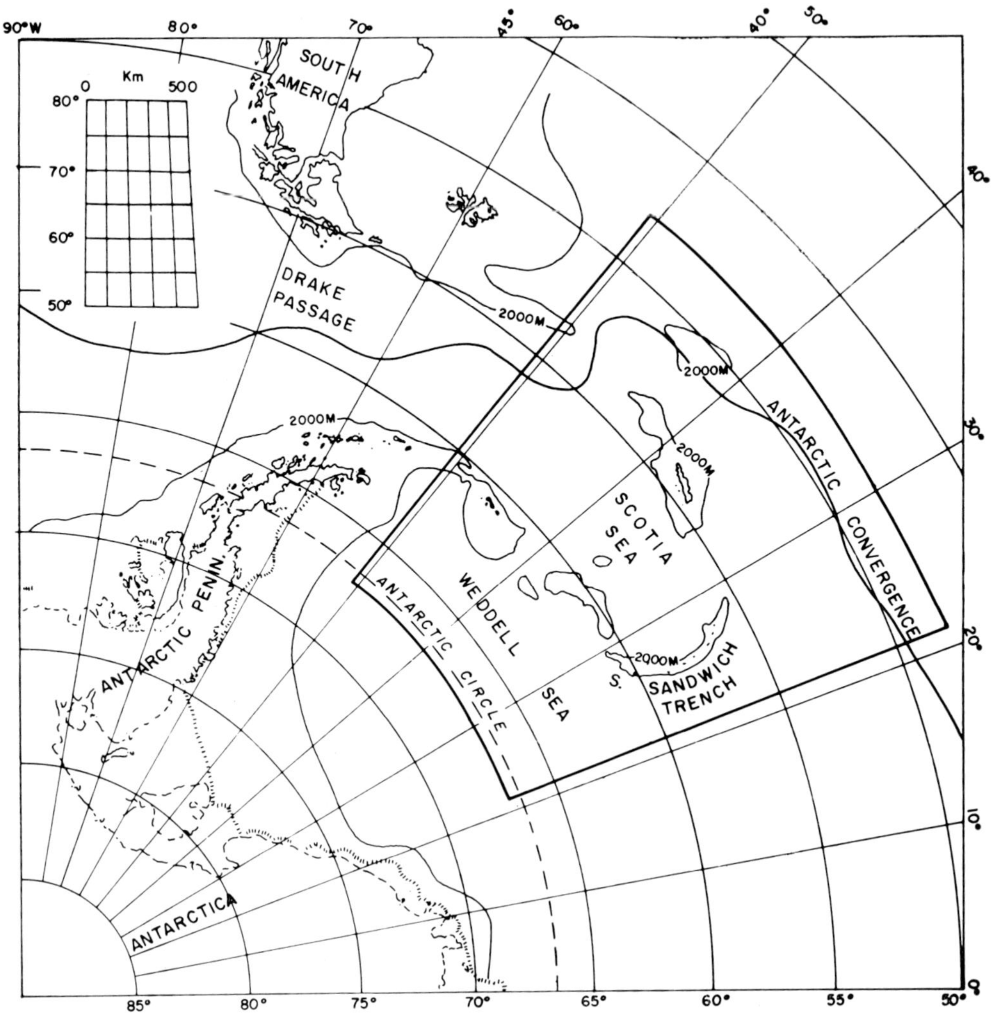

Fig. 1. Index map of the Scotia Sea area.

Ship USNS *Eltanin,* on cruises 7, 8, and 9 in 1963 and cruise 12 in 1964. In general, routine samples were taken about 1° of latitude apart along various north-south traverses, although a more complex sampling pattern was used in the area of the South Sandwich Trench (Figure 2). These basic sampling patterns were supplemented by three slope traverses located on the northern, southern, and eastern limbs of the Scotia Ridge. Depths of between 200 and 7700 meters were sampled.

Throughout this report the term bathyal refers to those benthonic environments from the edges of the insular shelves to 2000 meters, and abyssal to those from 2000 meters to somewhat more than 5000 meters, excluding the environments below sill depth in the South Sandwich Trench.

Previous Work

Foraminifera from the Scotia and Weddell seas collected by the Scottish National Antarctic Expedition and the Discovery Expedition were studied by Earland [1933, 1934, 1936]. His descriptions of samples, lists of species occurrences, and qualitative notes on abundance of species contain much useful information. An earlier report on the foraminifera of the Scottish National Antarctic Expedition was published by *Pearcey* [1914]. *Shishkevish* [1964] studied a few cores from the northern Scotia Sea.

Systematic descriptions of foraminifera from other parts of the South Atlantic, Pacific, and Indian oceans resulted from the Challenger Expedition [*Brady,* 1884], the British Antarctic Expedition [*Chapman,* 1916*a,* 1916*b*], the Terra Nova Expedition [*Heron-*

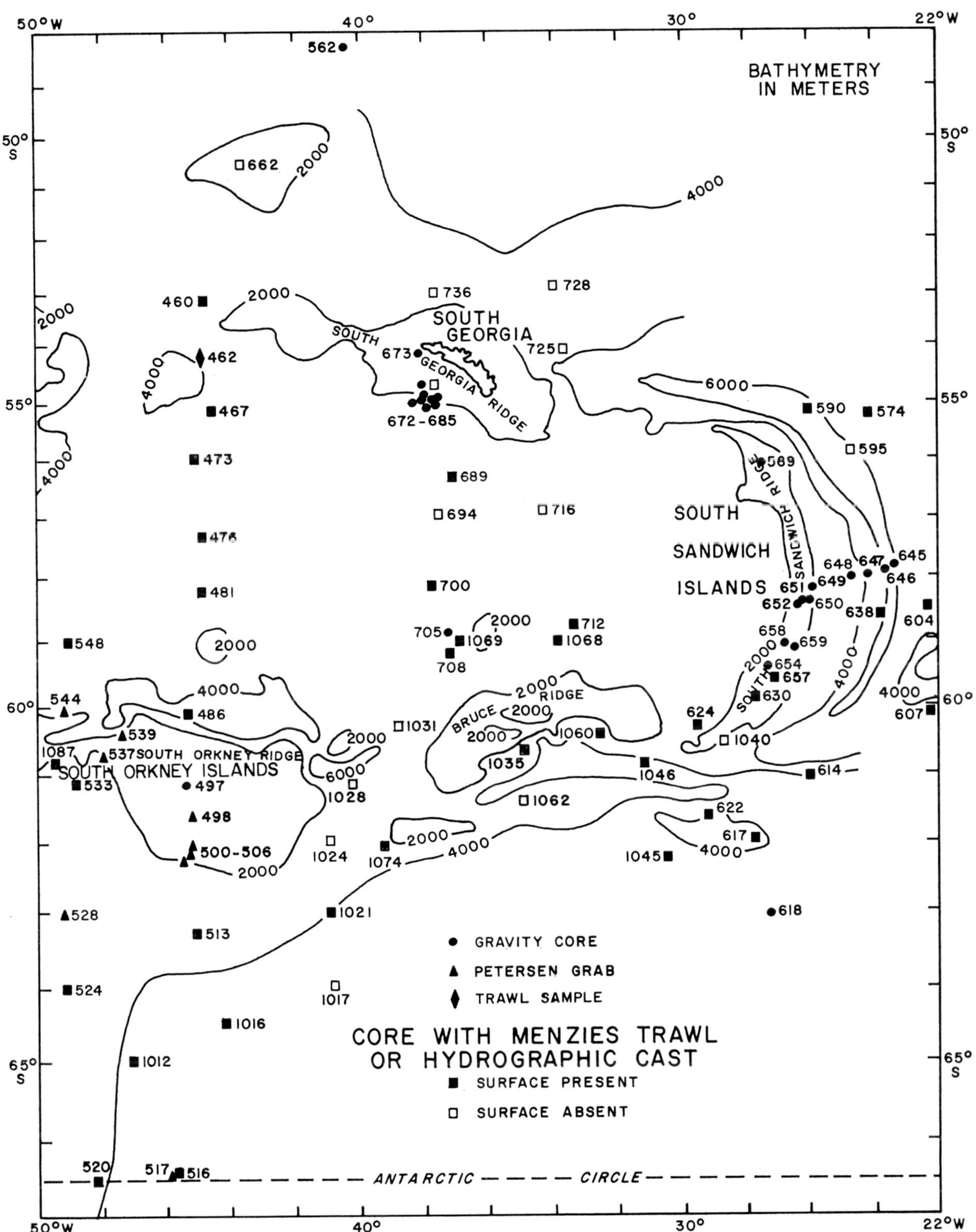

Fig. 2. Station locations. Bathymetry, in part, is after *Herdman* [1932] and Holmes [*Goodell*, 1964]. Echo soundings of the USNS *Eltanin* from *Heezen and Johnson* [1965] and from the hourly data sheets of the USNS *Eltanin* were also used.

Allen and Earland, 1922], the German South Polar Expedition [*Wiesner*, 1931], the Australasian Antarctic Expedition [*Chapman and Parr*, 1937], and the BANZARE Expedition [*Parr*, 1950]. Shorter reports were published by *Warthin* [1934] and *Cushman* [1945].

Uchio [1960*b*] published the first quantitative study of antarctic foraminifera based on 11 samples from Lutzow-Holm Bay. *McKnight* [1962] studied the ecology of foraminifera in the Ross Sea, and *Pflum* [1966] reported on four profiles distributed from the Ross Sea to the Bellingshausen Sea. *Blanc-Vernet* [1965] studied the foraminifera in some shallow-water samples from off Adélie Coast. *Kennett* [1966, 1968] studied 48 samples from the Ross Sea and, using evidence from the distribution of foraminifera, recognized a depth of effective carbonate solution of only 500 meters. Russian workers [*Saidova*, 1961; *Shchedrina*, 1964] studied the distribution of foraminifera in the South Pacific and Indian Ocean sectors. *Bandy and Echols* [1964] re-examined previous quantitative studies and compared the depth distributions of cosmopolitan species in the antarctic waters with their depth distributions in temperate oceans.

The distribution of planktonic foraminifera in bottom sediments on both sides of the Antarctic Convergence was studied by *Blair* [1965]. Living planktonic foraminifera from antarctic waters were studied by *Chen and Bé* [1965], *Chen* [1966], *Bé* [1969], and *Boltovskoy* [1966*a*].

Methods

A total of 76 gravity cores, 12 Peterson grabs, and 2 mud samples fortuitously retained in trawls were analyzed; supplementary information on large foraminiferal species (> 0.5 mm) was provided by Menzies trawl samples.

In addition to the usual method, gravity cores were taken by suspending the corers from the bridle of a Menzies trawl or at the end of the line during hydrographic casts. Because corers utilized in the latter two methods remained near the bottom until a primary sampling objective was completed, they usually made multiple penetration of the sediment. In 12 of these cores the surface sediment at the top was pushed beyond the core liners and lost. Although of questionable value, the upper segments of these 12 cores have been used for foraminiferal analysis to supplement the already meager coverage based on surface sediment.

The surface 2 cm or 5 cm of sediment in gravity cores and approximately the upper 2 cm of sediment in Petersen grabs were taken for foraminiferal analysis. The samples were weighed dry and then washed through a sieve with a 62-micron mesh. Foraminifera were concentrated by flotation on perchlorethylene until the procedure yielded few additional specimens. A representative split of 200 to 400 specimens taken with a modified Otto microsplitter were counted and identified. The material that did not float was split to an aliquot equal to that to which the concentrate was split and then sieved on a 125-micron mesh. Counting the foraminifera retained on the 125-micron mesh recovered most species that systematically resist concentration by flotation.

Rose bengal stain was added to samples that had been preserved in alcohol or a 10 per cent buffered formalin solution, so that foraminiferal tests containing protoplasm could be distinguished [*Walton*, 1952]. Stained specimens (the living population) were counted in 34 samples after completion of the study of total populations. Since most agglutinated specimens are opaque when dry, most were dampened individually or placed in a small drop of water on the counting tray to determine whether they contained stained protoplasm. This makes the test more transparent, causes slight expansion of the dried protoplasm, and brightens the stain. It was still often necessary to break agglutinated tests to verify the nature of the contents.

Sediment grain size analysis was carried out by screening the coarse fraction (> 62 microns) on 3-inch-diameter nesting Tyler sieves. The pipette method was used to analyze the fine fraction. Sediment textures are discussed using the nomenclature based on sand-silt-clay ratios introduced by *Shepard* [1954].

DESCRIPTION OF THE ENVIRONMENT

Bottom Topography

Within the Scotia Sea area, the Scotia Ridge is divided into four segments by gaps through which water depths are greater than 2000 meters. The northern segment bearing the island of South Georgia is the South Georgia Ridge. There are two southern segments: the western of these bears the South Orkney Islands and is designated the South Orkney Ridge while the eastern is named Bruce Ridge. The far eastern segment crowned by the South Sandwich Islands is the South Sandwich Ridge (Figure 2). South Georgia and the South Orkney Islands are composed of sediments, metasediments, and intrusive igneous rocks [*Anderson*, 1965]. They are surrounded by extensive insular shelves which, throughout most of

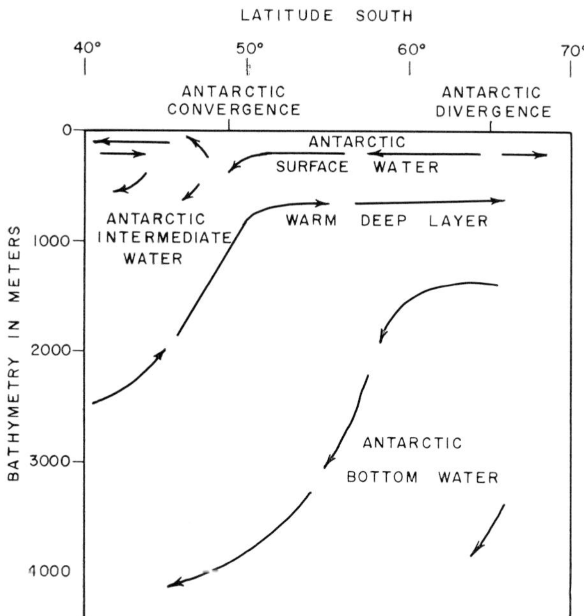

Fig. 3. Generalized vertical and meridional circulation of antarctic water masses in a vertical section from 40°S to 70°S (modified from *Deacon* [1963]).

their widths, lie at depths of from 200 to 450 meters and thus are considerably deeper than the world average for similar physiographic features. The eleven South Sandwich Islands form an arc of Late Tertiary and Recent volcanoes convex toward the east and bounded on its convex side by the South Sandwich Trench, which has been described in detail by *Heezen and Johnson* [1965]. The greatest known depth in the South Atlantic Ocean (8264 meters) occurs in the northeastern part of the trench.

Most of the floor of the Scotia Sea is rugged, especially the southeastern part, where ridges trending in a submeridional direction rise 1500 to 3000 meters over adjacent areas of level bottom [*Heezen and Tharp*, 1958; *Avilov and Gershanovich*, 1966]. By contrast the floor of the central area of the Weddell Sea is a smooth abyssal plain, lying below 4000 meters.

Oceanography

As the Antarctic Convergence is located along its northern boundary, the Scotia Sea area is within the antarctic zone of the South Atlantic Ocean. *Deacon* [1933, 1937, 1963] has made the most extensive study of the oceanography of this area.

South of the Antarctic Convergence there are three stratified water masses: Antarctic Surface Water, the Warm Deep Layer, and Antarctic Bottom Water. These water masses and their generalized vertical and meridional circulation are shown in Figure 3. In the Atlantic sector, all three water masses move in two basic circulation patterns. One of these is the east-setting Circumpolar Current, which enters the Scotia Sea from the Pacific sector through Drake Passage. The other is the clockwise Weddell Sea gyral, which transports westward near Antarctica, northward parallel to the Antarctic Peninsula in the western Weddell Sea, and eastward parallel to the flow of the Circumpolar Current in the northern Weddell Sea. Thus water in the Scotia Sea arrives from two directions: the Weddell Sea in the south and the Pacific Ocean in the west. Each water mass in the Weddell Sea gyral is colder than its counterpart from the Pacific Ocean. The circulation of the Warm Deep Layer is shown in Figure 4.

Antarctic Surface Water is a cold and dilute superficial stratum bounded below by a discontinuity layer at a depth of 150 to 250 meters in which temperature and salinity increase with depth.

The Warm Deep Layer, occupying an intermediate stratum, is identified by a temperature maximum in its upper levels and a salinity maximum in its deeper levels. From the Antarctic Convergence to well south of South Georgia its maximum temperature is greater than 2°C, and its maximum salinity approaches 34.8‰ in some areas. In the Weddell Sea it is cooled to little more than 0.5°C and diluted to 34.7‰ by mixing with surface and bottom water. The Warm Deep Layer along the southern and eastern Scotia Ridge is of the latter type (Figure 5). Oxygen concentrations are minimum in the upper part of the Warm Deep Layer, but they are always high when compared with the concentration in deep waters of other areas, never falling below 4 ml/l.

Antarctic Bottom Water is 1° to 2°C colder, but only slightly less saline than the Warm Deep Layer. It is formed primarily in the southwestern Weddell Sea and is therefore colder in the Weddell Sea than elsewhere in the bounding oceans. Antarctic Bottom Water from the 3200-meter level in the Weddell Sea crosses into the Scotia Sea through the deep gap between the South Orkney Ridge and Bruce Ridge at 39°W in the southern Scotia Ridge [*Gordon*, 1966]. From deeper levels in the Weddell Sea it spreads northward around the eastern side of the Scotia Ridge.

The western Weddell Sea is under perennial ice cover, but during the summer months a tongue free from ice extends westward along the Antarctic Circle to 40°W in the eastern Weddell Sea [*U. S. Navy*, 1957]. On the average, the southeastern Scotia Sea is covered

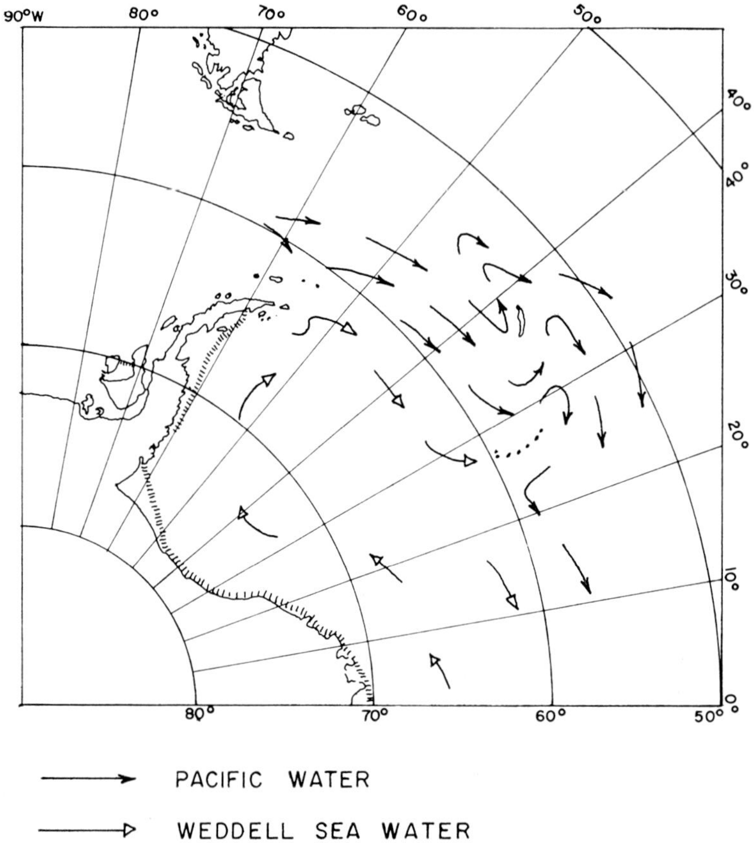

Fig. 4. Currents in the Warm Deep Layer (modified from *Sverdrup* [1941] and *Klepikov* [1960]).

by ice half the year, the maximum average extent of sea ice reaching almost to South Georgia.

Sediments

Sediments collected from the USNS *Eltanin* in the Scotia Sea area have been described by *Goodell* [1965]. Grain size analysis of the same samples used for foraminiferal analysis was carried out, however, because the samples studied by Goodell from the same ship station were often collected several kilometers away. In areas of considerable bottom relief these sediments may have significantly different properties.

The percentage of sand and gravel in sediments of 90 samples is shown in Figure 6, and the ratio of silt to clay for 73 samples is shown in Figure 7. Throughout most of the area, the coarse fraction is dominated by terrigenously derived mineral grains and rock fragments. Around the South Sandwich Islands, however, the coarse fraction is almost totally volcanic debris; this is also true of all samples in the South Sandwich Trench and east of the trench, reflecting sediment transport in the direction of prevailing winds and surface currents. The sample with abundant coarse material on the 'Falkland Ridge' in the northwestern corner of the study area is *Globigerina* ooze. Tests of planktonic foraminifera also account for much of the coarse fraction in isolated samples across the northern Weddell Sea, but these samples contain much sand and gravel as well. Diatoms, which are quantitatively important in most abyssal sediments except in the Weddell Sea, probably appear in textural analyses as silt.

The finest sediment in the area occurs in the interior of the Weddell Sea, with both silt and sand increasing toward the Antarctic Peninsula and the Scotia Ridge. High proportions of clay in the southern and southeastern Scotia Sea probably reflect transport of clay from the Weddell Sea as suggested by *Goodell* [1965]. North of the South Orkney Islands sedimentation rates are slow in the center of the Scotia Sea and increase both north and south [*Mather*, 1966]; thus the large proportion of coarse material in the center of the Scotia Sea may be due to lack of dilution by finer material. *Goodell* [1965] commented on the large

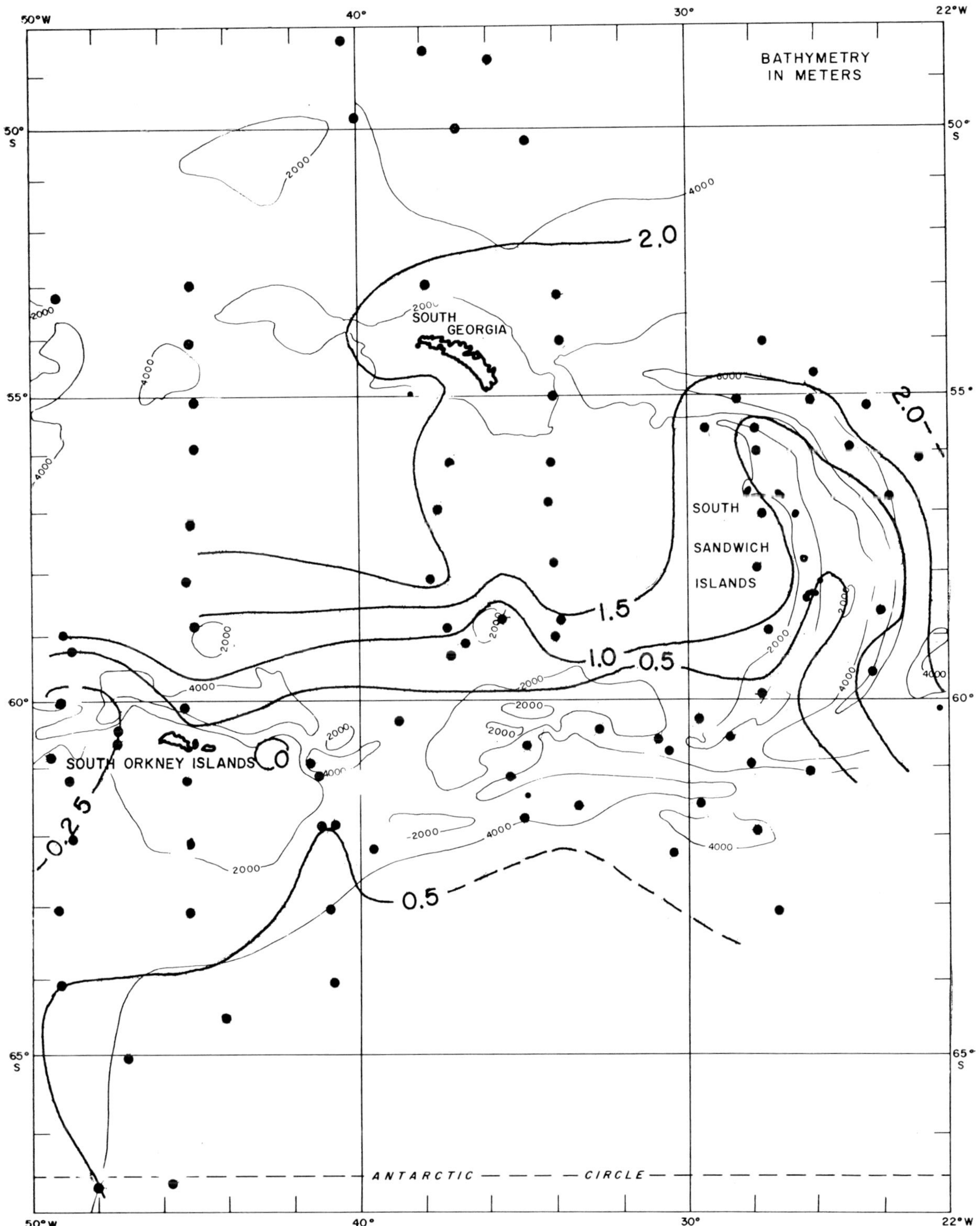

Fig. 5. Distribution of temperature at the level of maximum temperature in the Warm Deep Layer (data from *Jacobs* [1965]).

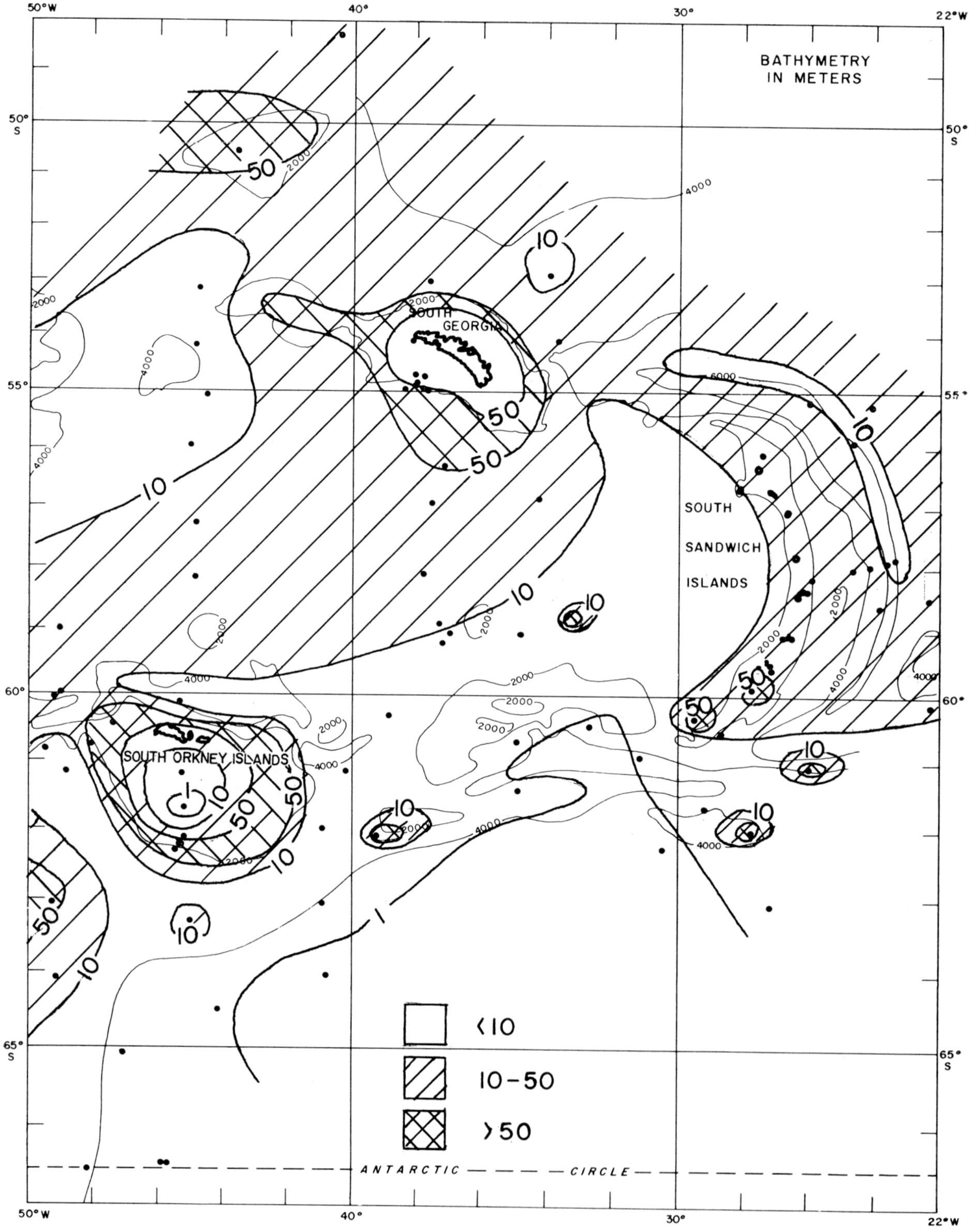

Fig. 6. Percentage of sand and gravel in bottom sediments.

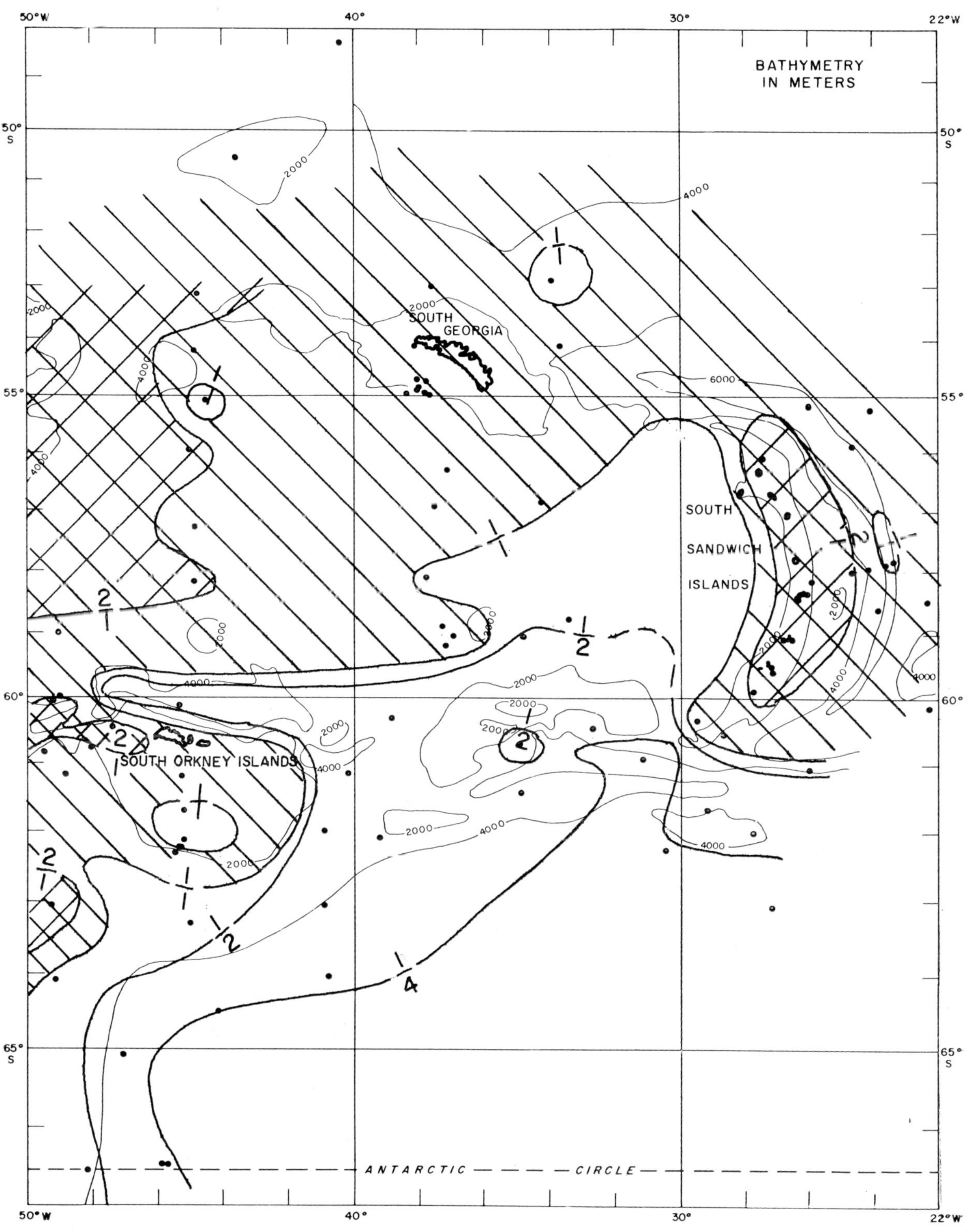

Fig. 7. Silt-clay ratio.

breadth of the halos of coarse material around the South Orkney Islands and South Georgia, compared with the present small size of these islands. Around the South Orkney Islands these coarse sediments appear to be restricted to the slopes, much finer sediments being typical of the shelf. Volcanic sediments near the South Sandwich Islands are predominantly silt.

Throughout much of the Scotia Sea area diatom frustules are quantitatively the most important biogenic component of bottom sediments. The contribution of diatom frustules to the sediment volume was estimated during routine sample description and ranked according to the following scale: ooze (> 30%), abundant (10–29%), common (0.5–9%), and rare or absent. The resulting distribution map (Figure 8) is believed to represent accurately trends in the abundance of diatoms within the area, although the percentage limits of each of the above classes may be quite inaccurate.

Within the Scotia Sea and to the north and east of it diatoms are a very conspicuous part of all bottom sediments; they are somewhat less abundant in the vicinity of islands than elsewhere, possibly because enough sediment is supplied locally by the islands to dilute the contribution of diatoms. Weddell Sea sediments, in contrast, contain virtually no diatoms. In these sediments, most of which are clays or silty clays, it is unusual to find a single frustule in the small amount of sediment retained on a 62-micron mesh or in water smears of the total sediments. The boundary between diatomaceous sediments and sediments that are almost diatom-free occurs just south of the Scotia Ridge in the northern Weddell Sea. Previous investigators who commented on the paucity of diatoms in the Weddell Sea have considered it an enigma [*Earland*, 1936] or have relied upon currents [*Pirie*, 1913] or dissolution of silica [*Clowes*, 1938] to remove the frustules produced by the diatom populations assumed to flourish there. Evidence has been presented elsewhere [*Echols*, 1967] that suggests that lower diatom production in the Weddell Sea than in the Scotia Sea is primarily responsible for differences in the frustule content of sediment from these two areas.

DISTRIBUTION OF PLANKTONIC FORAMINIFERA

From concentrations greater than 1000 tests per gram of dry sediment in the northwestern Scotia Sea the abundance of planktonic foraminifera falls off rapidly toward the south and east to concentrations generally less than 2 tests per gram (Figure 9). This trend is a manifestation of the marked fall-off toward the south in the percentage of biogeneous carbonate in deep-sea sediments that occurs beneath the Antarctic Convergence or somewhat south of it all around the Antarctic Continent [*Goodell*, 1965; *Lisitzin*, 1960]. Still farther south, along the northern margin of the Weddell Sea, there are scattered localities where sediments containing abundant planktonic foraminifera occur, but these are possibly not modern sediments.

The dominant planktonic foraminifer is the left-coiling form of *Globigerina pachyderma*. It occurs at 54 stations, more often than any other species, and it is the only planktonic species to occur in concentrations greater than 100 tests per gram of sediment. The only other commonly occurring planktonic species is *Globigerinita uvula*. It was found at 30 stations, but in concentrations greater than 1 per gram only on the northern Scotia Ridge and in the east-central Scotia Sea. On the northern Scotia Ridge it does not exceed 4 per cent of the planktonic foraminiferal population, but in the east-central Scotia Sea it is greater than 33 per cent because concentrations of *G. pachyderma* are low in this area. Seven other species that occur as rare specimens in a few samples are:

Globigerina bulloides	8 samples
Globorotalia inflata	7 samples
Globigerina quinqueloba	3 samples
Globigerinita glutinata	3 samples
Globorotalia truncatulinoides	1 sample
Globorotalia scitula	1 sample

Planktonic foraminiferal populations from the South Georgia Ridge are typical of those found in bottom sediments just south of the position of the Antarctic Convergence [*Blair*, 1965; *Kennett*, 1969]. *Bé* [1969] and *Kennett* [1969] have compared populations from bottom sediments near the position of the convergence with living populations in the overlying waters and have noted marked discrepancies that indicate a southward shift in ranges of subantarctic species and the right-coiling form of *G. pachyderma* subsequent to deposition of the surface 2 or 3 centimeters of deep-sea sediments. These authors conclude that at the time the surface deep-sea sediments were deposited the surface waters were appreciably colder than they are now.

The sediments with abundant planktonic foraminifera scattered across the northern Weddell Sea are possibly considerably older than those occurring on the South Georgia Ridge. They may be outcrops of older strata similar to one encountered in core USC 516, where over 1000 planktonic foraminiferal tests per gram occur in sediments from below 8.5 cm

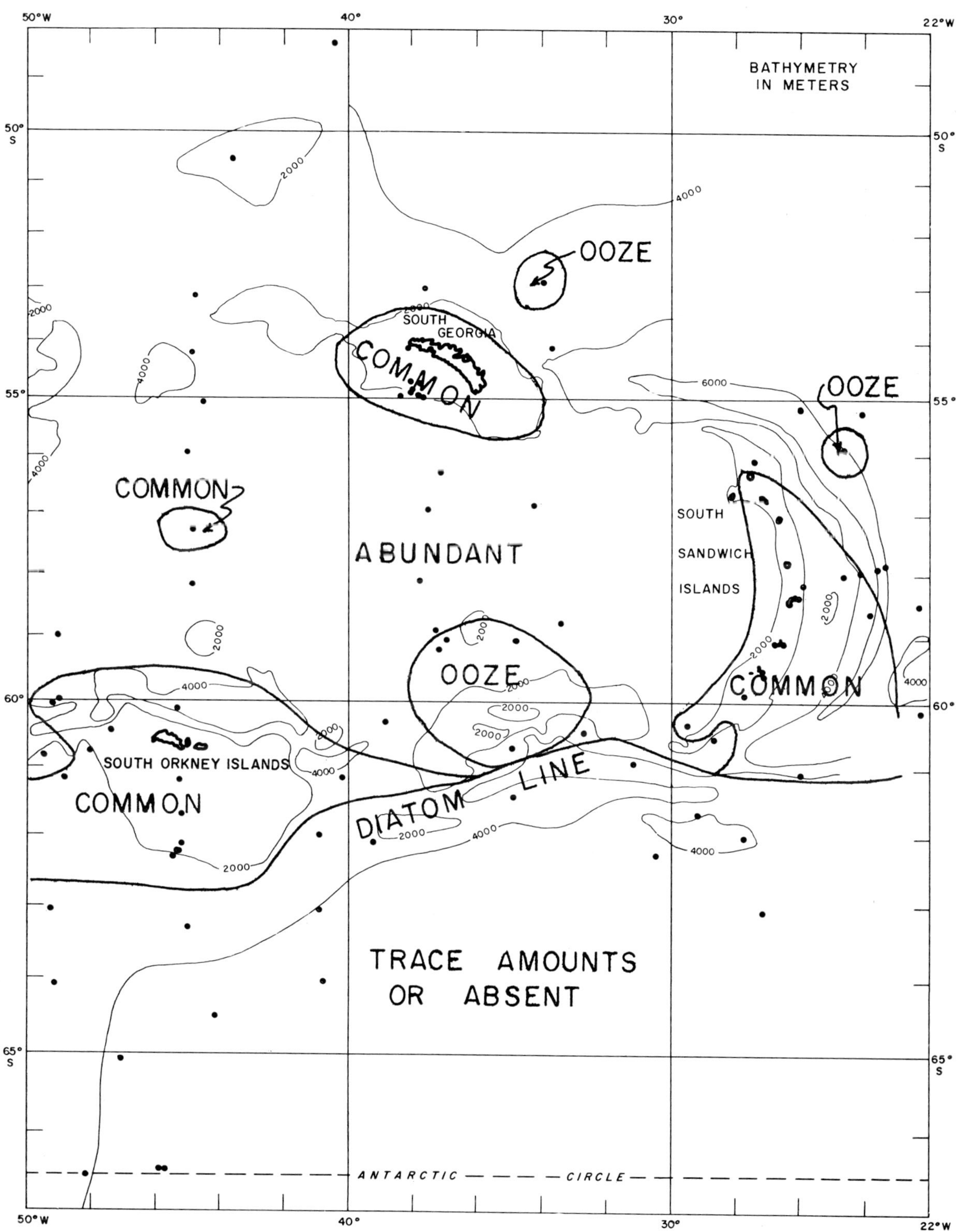

Fig. 8. Abundance of diatoms in bottom sediments.

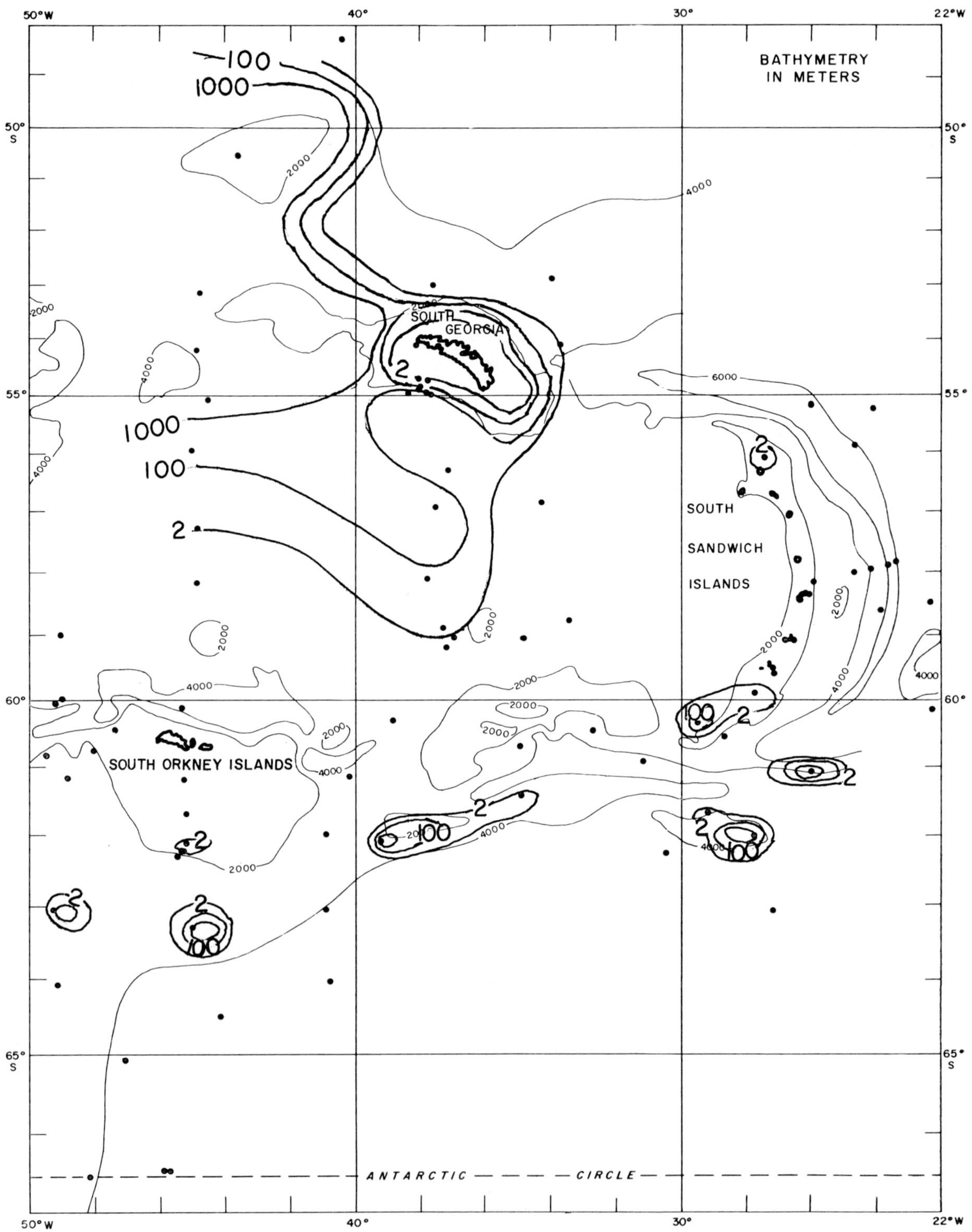

Fig. 9. Planktonic foraminifera; number per gram of dry sediment.

in the core, although the surface sediment layer contains only one planktonic test per gram. Furthermore, these possibly relict planktonic foraminiferal assemblages have a combination of characteristics that distinguishes them from other previously described populations in surface sediments of antarctic waters (Figure 10). Based on counts of 500 or more specimens, the sinistral coiling form is only 96 to 98 per cent of populations of *G. pachyderma,* a percentage typical of populations in surface sediments north of the Antarctic Convergence [*Blair,* 1965], yet the subantarctic species which are well represented north of the convergence are virtually absent in the Weddell Sea samples. Another distinguishing feature of the Weddell Sea populations is the high frequency of large individuals of *G. pachyderma;* 15 to 53 per cent are too large to pass through a 250-micron sieve. They share this unusual combination of characteristics with the fossil population below 8.5 cm in core USC 516, suggesting that the surface occurrences are also fossil and that sub-Recent occurrences of abundant planktonic foraminifera in this area, therefore, are restricted to the South Georgia Ridge.

DISTRIBUTION OF BENTHONIC FORAMINIFERA

Calcareous and Noncalcareous Populations

The eastward and southward fall-off in planktonic tests away from the northeastern Scotia Sea is matched by equally marked changes in calcareous benthonic tests (Figure 11). Like the planktonics, they are common on the South Georgia Ridge. They are very rare or absent in most of the southern and eastern parts of the Scotia Sea area but reappear in abundance in the same areas in the northern Weddell Sea that have abundant planktonic tests of inferred relict origin. They are relatively abundant where planktonic tests are rare only in sediments from water depths of a few hundred meters. However, where these marked horizontal changes are occurring in the abundance of calcareous benthonic and planktonic tests, the benthonic foraminifera with noncalcareous tests are relatively evenly distributed, and their highest concentrations occur where calcareous tests are infrequent (Figure 12). Throughout much of the Scotia Sea area noncalcareous tests vary only from 10 to 50 tests per gram of sediment, whereas they are more abundant than 50 tests per gram along parts of the South Orkney, Bruce, and South Sandwich ridges, the central Scotia Sea, and the southern Argentine Basin. All foraminiferal tests are rare in sediments of the central Weddell Sea.

From comparison of the horizontal distributions of concentrations of calcareous and noncalcareous benthonic tests, respectively, in Figures 11 and 12, it is evident that the total populations change from ones dominated by calcareous tests on the South Georgia Ridge and in the northwestern Scotia Sea to ones dominated by noncalcareous tests in the southern and eastern parts of the Scotia Sea area. Superimposed upon this horizontal trend there appear to be vertical trends, such that the higher percentages of calcareous tests in benthonic populations become restricted to shallower water depths toward the east and south away from the South Georgia Ridge and the northwestern Scotia Sea (Figure 13). Thus, on the South Georgia Ridge south of South Georgia calcareous tests dominate total benthonic populations, excepting the shallowest one at 200 meters, to a depth between 3000 and 3700 meters, in contrast to the South Orkney, Bruce, and South Sandwich ridges, where relative frequencies of calcareous tests greater than 5 per cent are almost restricted to depths less than 1600 meters, and the maximum frequency of calcareous test is only 53 per cent. Furthermore, geographically between the southern and northern Scotia Ridge in the southern Scotia Sea, submarine hills that reach water depths as shallow as 2500 meters are also populated by predominantly noncalcareous benthonic populations.

The percentage of calcareous tests in total populations, however, may be much lower than the percentage of individuals with calcareous tests in living populations (Figure 14). On the South Georgia Ridge south of South Georgia where calcareous tests are dominant in total populations there is little difference between the percentage of calcareous forms in total and living populations, but on the South Orkney, Bruce, and South Sandwich ridges above 1600 meters, where calcareous tests are 53 per cent or less of total assemblages, calcareous individuals are dominant in some living populations ranging from 48 to 73 per cent in 10 samples. In the deep sea away from the South Georgia Ridge and deeper than 1600 meters on the South Orkney, Bruce, and South Sandwich ridges, calcareous forms often have higher frequencies in living than total populations, but they do not dominate living assemblages, excluding some of the northern Weddell Sea assemblages with high concentrations of inferred relict planktonic tests.

The higher percentages of calcareous individuals in live than in total populations is related to very high live-total ratios within the calcareous populations (Figure 15). Expressed as a per cent (live: total × 100)

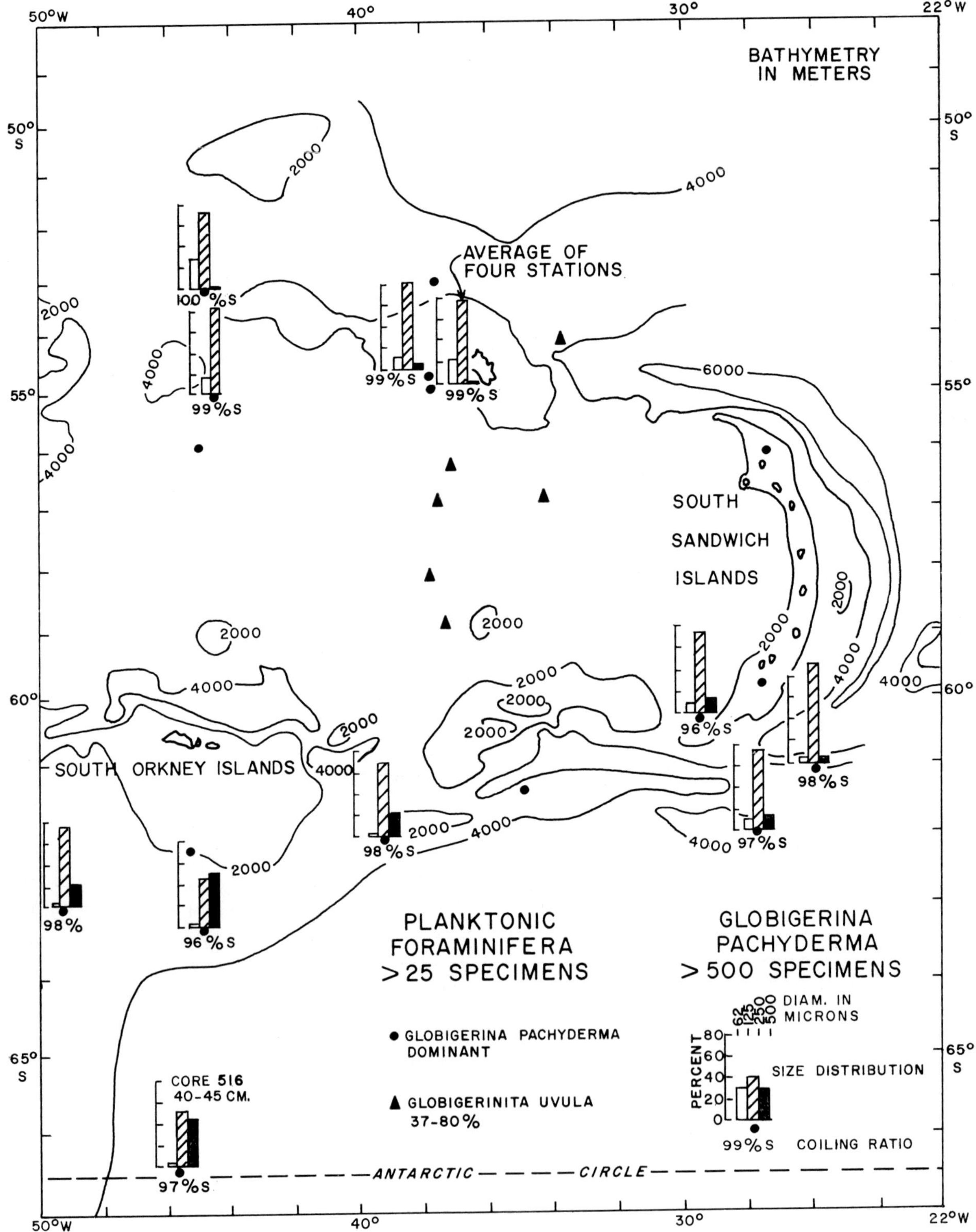

Fig. 10. Size and coiling ratios of *Globigerina pachyderma* and location of planktonic assemblages with high relative frequencies of *Globigerinita uvula*. The Weddell Sea planktonic populations are probably relict.

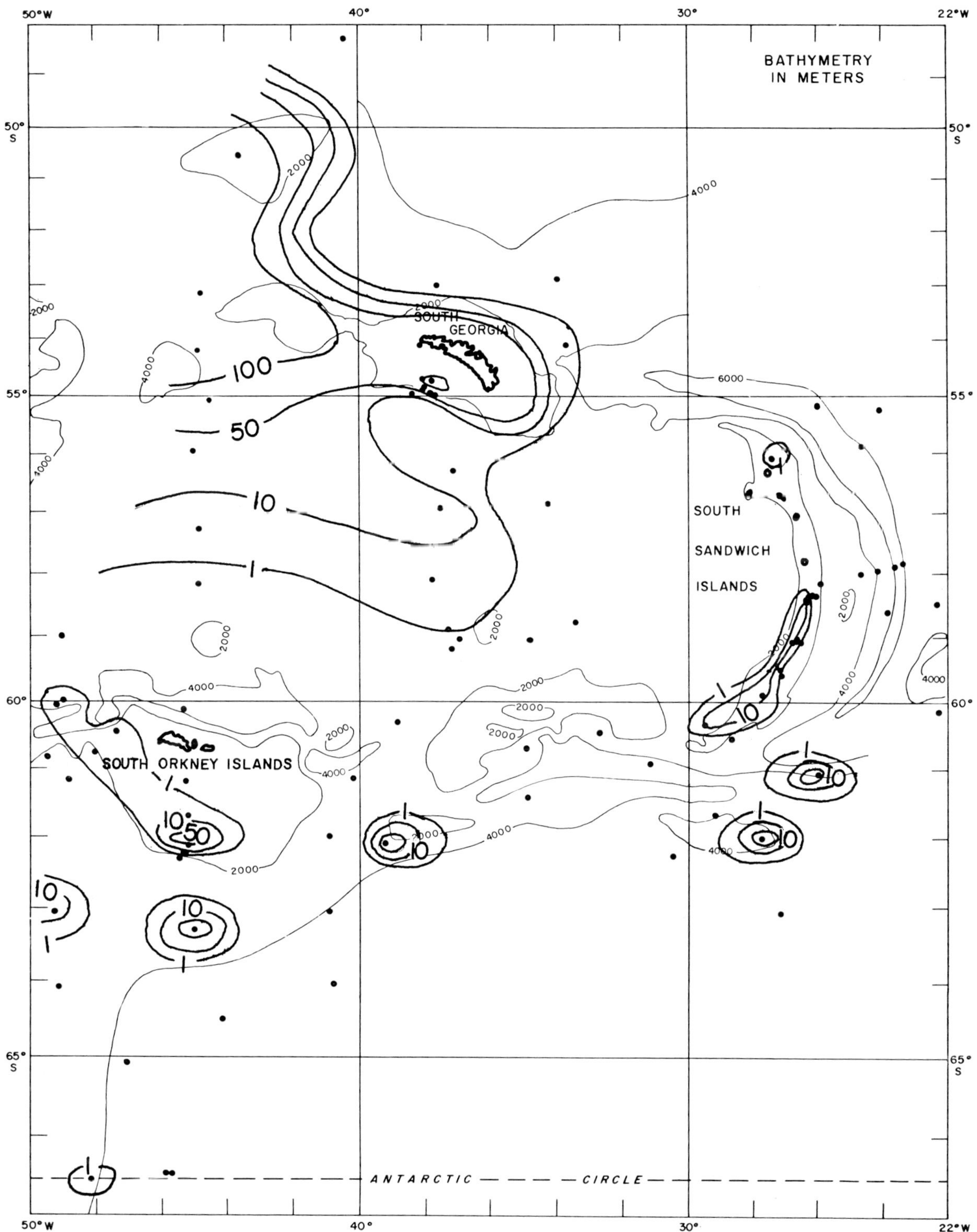

Fig. 11. Calcareous benthonic foraminifera; number per gram of dry sediment.

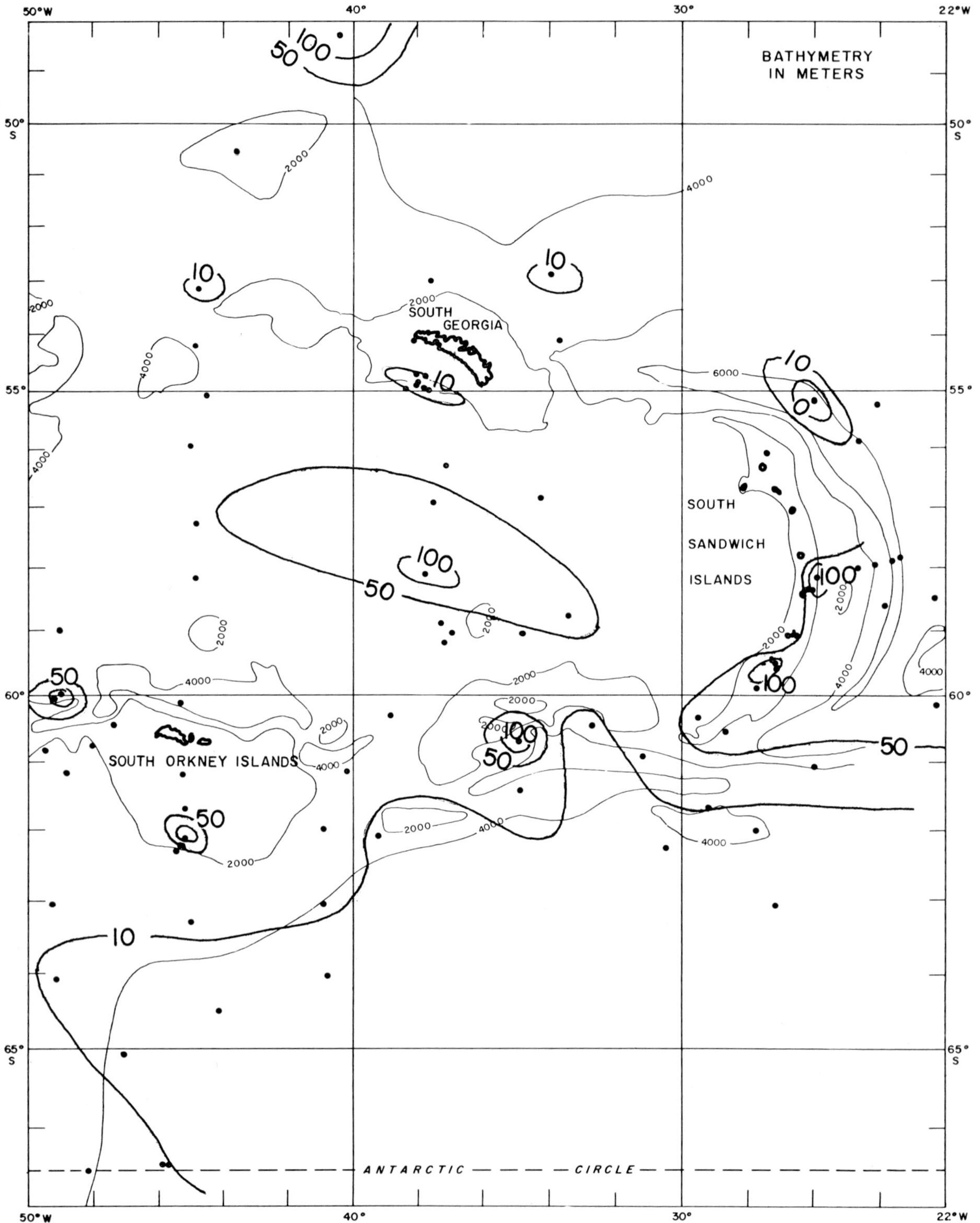

Fig. 12. Noncalcareous benthonic foraminifera; number per gram of dry sediment.

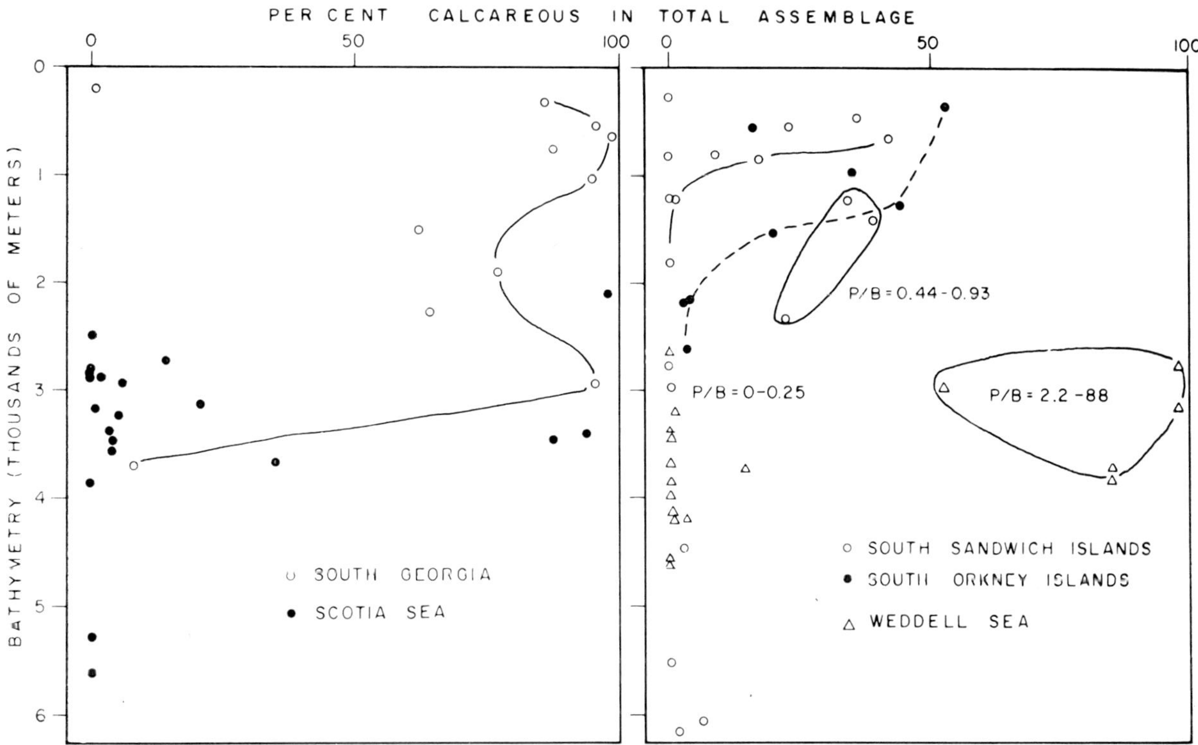

Fig. 13. Depth distribution of the percentages of calcareous specimens in total (live plus dead) benthonic assemblages. P/B = planktonic-benthonic ratio.

the live-total ratios are 33 to 96 per cent for 11 calcareous populations from the South Orkney, Bruce, and South Sandwich ridges, whereas for all noncalcareous populations studied they are less than 20 per cent and usually less than 10 per cent. A similar live-total ratio not distinguishing between calcareous and noncalcareous individuals has been widely reported in studies of other areas and used as an estimate of relative sedimentation rates, following the suggestion of *Phleger* [1951]. In other studies live-total ratios as high as those for calcareous populations from the South Orkney, Bruce, and South Sandwich ridges have been infrequently reported and then usually from areas of very high sedimentation such as the Mississippi Delta [*Phleger*, 1951] or for individual species with fragile arenaceous tests that are apparently easily destroyed [*Buzas*, 1965].

A significant factor causing high live-total ratios for calcareous populations may be destruction of empty calcareous tests by solution. Partial solution is demonstrated by intensely corroded calcareous tests which are found in most calcareous populations, and complete solution is demonstrated by internal organic linings free of their calcareous test found in some populations. Although it is possible that some test solution has been caused by the formalin preservative which, even though well buffered, may turn acid with time, corroded calcareous tests and internal linings also occur in samples preserved in alcohol, which is not known to dissolve calcium carbonate. Most of the internal linings are of the species *Eponides tumidulus*, which appears almost unique among the calcareous species present in the area in having a lining strong enough to survive alone in sediments (Table 1). Because *E. tumidulus* is usually far less abundant than other calcareous species, it seems likely that complete solution of other calcareous species is occurring also, even though internal linings are not numerous. The author is unaware of previous reports of internal linings from the deep sea, but they are apparently widespread in some marginal marine environments where the solution of the calcareous tests has usually been considered to occur after burial within strongly reducing sediments [*Parker and Athearn*, 1959; *Bartlett*, 1964; *Jarke*, 1961]. Although the black color and smell of hydrogen sulfide typical of highly reducing sediments were present in none of the samples of this study, the possibility that the solvent for the calcareous tests is interstitial rather than free bottom water cannot be ruled out.

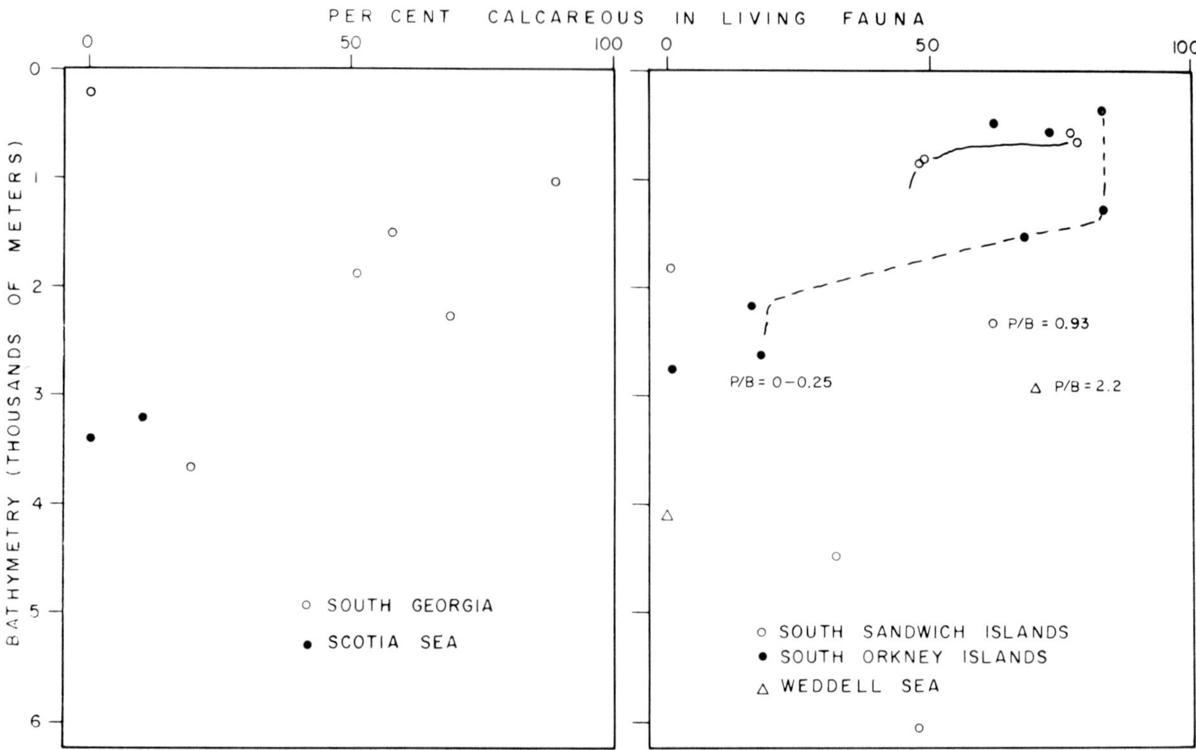

Fig. 14. Depth distribution of the percentages of calcareous benthonics in living foraminiferal assemblages. P/B = planktonic-benthonic ratio.

An alternative hypothesis that could explain much higher live-total ratios for calcareous than noncalcareous populations is a very recent environmental change to which the foraminifera have responded by an increase in calcareous species relative to noncalcareous species in the live populations. Since the calcareous test solution can be demonstrated, however, it seems the more likely cause.

Those total benthonic populations of samples from the northern Weddell Sea having a large proportion of inferred relic planktonic tests are identified in Figure 13 as those with a planktonic-benthonic ratio of 2.2 to 88. They contrast markedly with other Weddell Sea samples in being dominated by calcareous tests. Two of these contained a living foraminiferal population also dominated by calcareous species, but only one of these appears in Figure 14, because only five living specimens, too few to compute a percentage, were counted in the other. At least some benthonics in these samples, therefore, are not relict, but others may be, as the live-total ratios were lower for these two samples than for others in the area (Figure 15), and two others of the samples lacked living foraminifera. The fifth sample was not stained with rose bengal.

TABLE 1. Numbers of Internal Organic Linings of Calcareous Foraminifera Found at 13 Stations

Depths and percentages of calcareous foraminifera in the benthonic assemblages are given for each station.

Station number	473	476	504	537	539	544	604	624	647	649	672	673	716
Depth, meters	3680	3380	1540	2190	560	2620	4640	2350	4490	1840	3700	200	3170
Percentages of calcareous foraminifera	35	4	20	3	16	3	0	22	3	X	8	1	1
Eponides tumidulus													
Linings	1	3	1	2		1	3	1	4		3		
Whole tests	0	0	0	2		0	0	1	0		5		
Unidentified linings					1	4				1	1	6	1

X = less than 1 per cent.

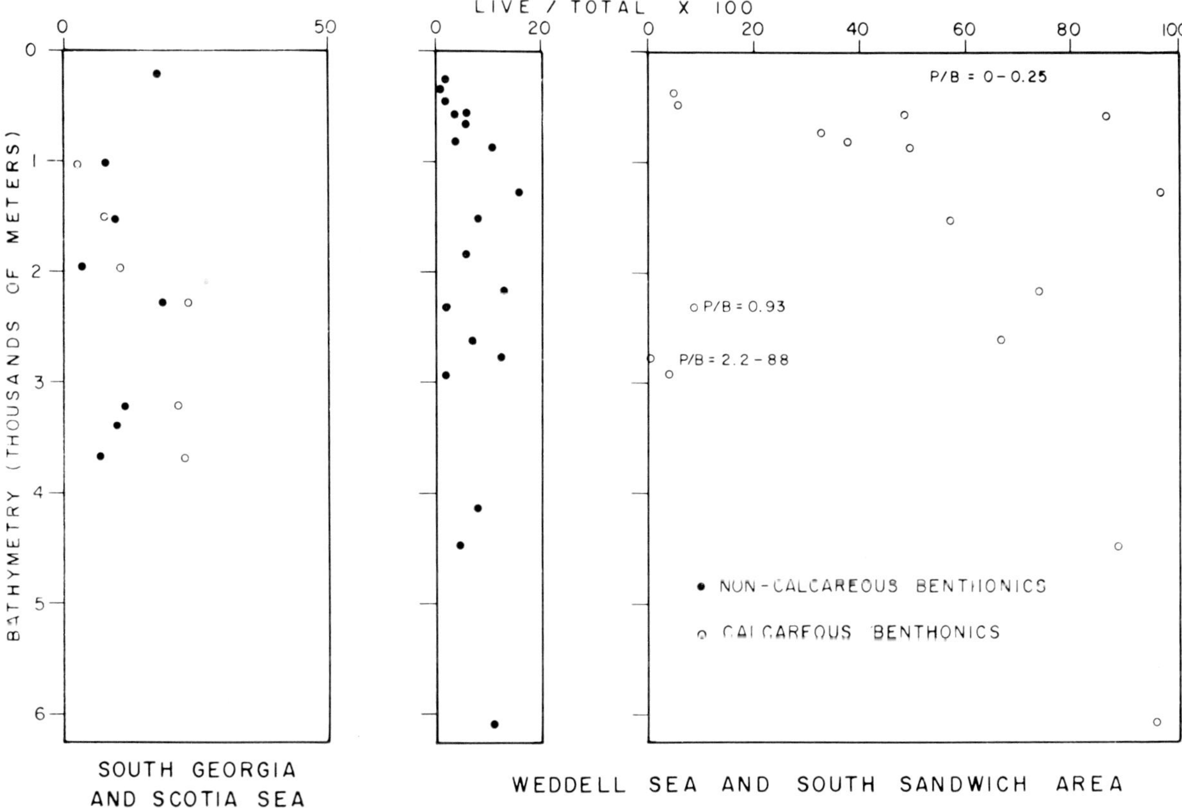

Fig. 15. Depth distribution of live-total ratios of calcareous and noncalcareous specimens. P/B = planktonic-benthonic ratio.

Calcareous and Possibly Siliceous Agglutinated Foraminifera

The distinction between calcareous and noncalcareous tests is primarily also a taxonomic one, because all species of the suborders Miliolina and Rotaliina have calcareous tests, and most species of the suborder Textulariina have noncalcareous tests. However, a few species of the Textulariina, which in the Scotia Sea area are all of the family Ataxophragmiidae, have agglutinated tests cemented by a calcareous material. *Wood* [1949] found the calcareous cement of some species of the Ataxopragmiidae to be calcite; he believed that this substance was secreted by the organism.

Calcareous agglutinated species never form more than a small per cent of the total benthonic populations in cores and grabs. One or more, usually two, of these species were found at a total of 16 stations (a Menzies trawl with attached core is here considered one station) (Figure 16). In 15 of these 16 stations, calcareous benthonics form more than 30 per cent of the total benthonic populations. Furthermore, in all but one of the samples of this study from below 1500 meters in which calcareous foraminifera were abundant, calcareous agglutinated forms were present. The very similar distributional patterns of benthonic calcareous tests of these different suborders, as well as planktonic tests in bottom sediments, suggest that either the function of forming and maintaining a calcareous wall or the post-mortem dissolution of calcareous tests, or both, is important in controlling these distributional patterns.

In addition to the tectinous cement that is prevalent in agglutinated foraminifera [*Hedley*, 1963] and a calcareous cement, a siliceous cement may be used by some agglutinated species. *Earland* [1933, 1934] regarded the cement of the species *Miliammina arenacea*, *M. lata*, and *Spirolocammina tenuis* as siliceous, because it withstood exposure to concentrated nitric acid, a treatment that destroys most agglutinated tests. The tests of these three species of the family Rzehakinidae are composed of tightly packed mineral grains firmly cemented by a colorless material forming relatively smoothly finished wall surfaces on both the interior and exterior. The white to light gray color of these tests distinguishes them, as most agglutinated tests are brown. Their tests are very similar to those

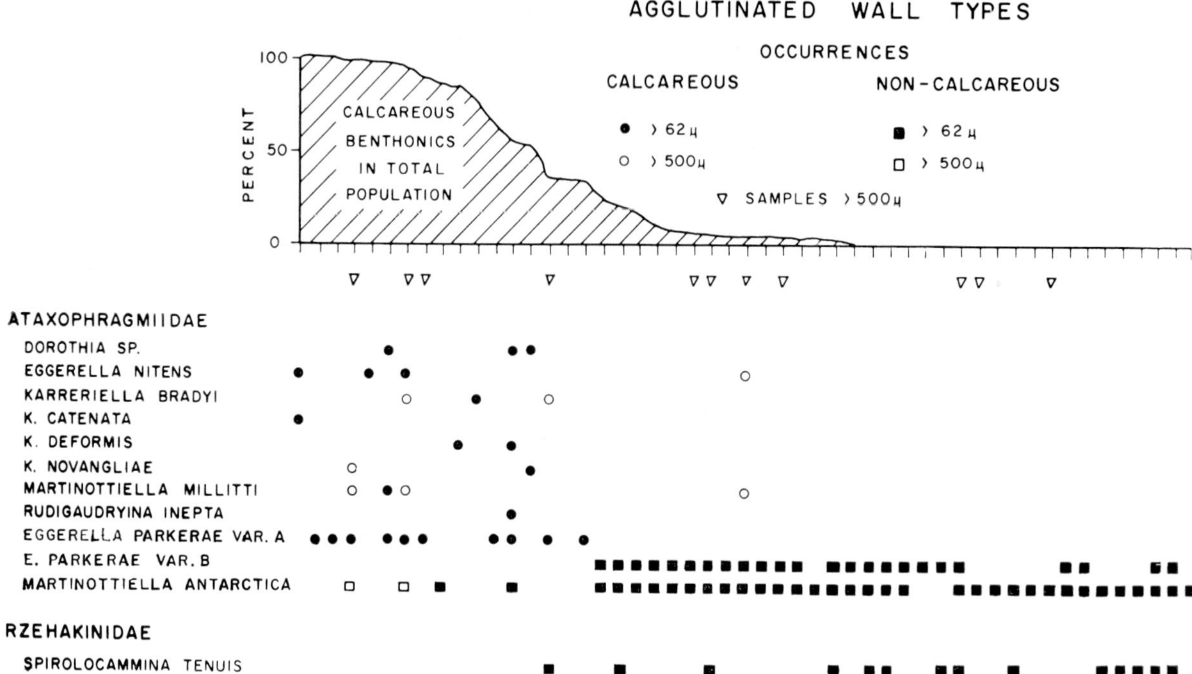

Fig. 16. Occurrences of those agglutinated foraminifera which have calcareous cement and those which have possibly siliceous cement compared with the percentages of calcareous foraminifera in total assemblages.

of the species *Martinottiella antarctica* and one form of the species *Eggerella parkerae* of the family Ataxophragmiidae. Evidence for a siliceous cement in the walls of any of these species is highly speculative and is mentioned here because these species have distinctive distributions, described later, that may be related to the availability of dissolved silica in interstitial waters if the cement is indeed silica.

Eggerella parkerae occurs as a calcareous form, distinguished as var. A, and a noncalcareous form, distinguished as var. B (Figure 16). *Eggerella parkerae* var. A occurs with calcareous populations and *E. parkerae* var. B occurs with noncalcareous populations, and the two varieties do not occur together, nor have they been observed to intergrade. *Martinottiella antarctica,* which has a test similar to *E. parkerae* var. B, however, occurs in both calcareous and noncalcareous populations, retaining a completely noncalcareous test in both kinds of populations.

Standing Crops

Standing crops are given as the number of individuals living on 10 cm^2 of sea bottom, which equals the area sampled by the gravity cores (Table 3). The upper 2 cm was studied in 20 core samples and the upper 5 cm or more in six core samples. Since foraminifera have been reported deeper than 2 cm in sediments [*Boltovskoy,* 1966*b*], this difference in core length could be significant. Standing crops could not be computed for the Petersen grab samples because the area sampled was uncertain. There are no previous studies of standing crops of benthonic foraminifera in the Antarctic, although two studies have reported living specimens [*Uchio,* 1960*b*; *Blanc-Vernet,* 1965].

It is difficult to generalize on so few samples spread over such a vast area. There is a suggestion, however, that along the South Sandwich Ridge standing crops are higher above 1000 meters (144 to 180 specimens per 10 cm^2) than deeper, and that below 1000 meters they are somewhat greater here (56 to 180 specimens per 10 cm^2) than on the slope south of South Georgia (36 to 66 specimens per 10 cm^2). Although standing crops are generally lower on basin floors than on slopes, the highest one measured (400 specimens per 10 cm^2) is from the center of the Scotia Basin. Four samples from the Weddell Sea have very small living populations (1 to 9 specimens per 10 cm^2).

Analysis of only the upper centimeter of cores as in previous studies may reveal slightly lower standing crops than study of the upper 2 cm or more, if foraminifera live at deeper levels in the sediment. As a first approximation, however, standing crops below 2000 meters in this area are similar to, and sometimes higher than, those below 1000 fathoms (1830 meters) in the Gulf of California (2–62 specimens/sample) studied by *Phleger* [1964]. None of the populations at lesser depths along the Scotia Ridge are as high as some of those from similar depths in the Gulf of California and off San Diego [*Uchio*, 1960*a*].

Diversity

In the discussion of benthonic depth zones and biofacies that follows, diversity is measured using the reciprocal of the diversity index suggested by *Simpson* [1949]

$$\frac{N\ (N-1)}{\sum_{i=1}^{k} n_i\ (n_i-1)}$$

where N is the total number of specimens counted, n_i is the abundance of the ith species, and k is the number of species in the population. The index was calculated only if the population count exceeded 50 individuals to avoid misleading results from small populations. It was found to range from 1.54 to 26.3 for total populations (Table 2) and from 2.34 to 21.8 (Table 3) for 14 living populations. A low number indicates that most individuals of a population are of a very few species, whereas a high number indicates that the individuals are distributed among a larger number of species, none of which occurs at a high relative frequency. *Gibson* [1966] used Simpson's index to study diversity of foraminiferal populations in Mississippi Sound.

Maximum diversity, including all values greater than 20, is encountered at depths greater than 2000 meters, although a large range is typical of all depths. In the deep sea the diversity of populations tends to be high in diatomaceous sediments from the Scotia Sea and east of the South Sandwich Islands, except in those from below sill depth in the South Sandwich Trench, where it is very low (3.13–4.81). It is low in sediments with few diatoms in the Weddell Sea (2.36–12.48). Populations of low diversity appear typical of environments to which few species are successfully adapted, although those few may occur in great abundance. *Gibson* [1966] attributed low diversity in populations of Mississippi Sound to the variability of the near-shore environment. In the Weddell Sea it may be caused by a general low level of food supply, as indicated by the lack of remains of primary producers, the diatoms, in bottom sediments. In the South Sandwich Trench, the position of the populations of low diversity below sill level appears significant, but associated environmental factors differing from those above sill level are undetermined. Low diversity in total populations is suspect when the dominant species has a robust noncalcareous test, as its high relative frequencies may be caused by destruction of the more delicate noncalcareous tests and dissolution of calcareous tests. Dominant species with tests believed to be especially resistant to destruction are *Miliamina arenacea, M. fusca, Martinottiella antarctica,* and *Cyclammina pusilla.* None of these species occurs where diversity is low in the South Sandwich Trench or the central part of the Weddell Sea, but *C. pusilla* is dominant in the marginal parts of the Weddell Sea.

Depth Zonation

Because in total populations calcareous foraminifera are relatively more abundant on the South Georgia Ridge and noncalcareous on the South Orkney, Bruce, and South Sandwich ridges, the depth distributions of these two groups of species have been studied separately to facilitate better comparison of the species distributions within each group on parts of the Scotia Ridge where it is dominant to other parts where it is subordinate. By concentrating on changes within each group this approach ignores the depth related changes in the relative abundance of the calcareous and noncalcareous groups that were described previously.

Because more total than live populations were studied, and because live populations were often small, the depth zonations are based on total populations. Comparison of live with total populations indicates no large-scale faunal mixing of the kind believed possible in polar areas as a result of ice rafting [*Phleger*, 1952; *McKnight*, 1962; *Bandy and Echols*, 1964]. Undoubtedly, downslope displacement of tests occurs in the Scotia Sea area as it does elsewhere, but clear evidence of this is also lacking.

Calcareous Depth Zonations

Slope South of South Georgia

Nine samples in the traverse across the southern slope of South Georgia ranging in depth from 330 to 2930 meters are dominated by calcareous foraminifera. The shallowest station of the traverse (200 meters) and the deepest (3700 meters) are dominated by noncalcareous foraminifera. An upper slope faunal zone from <330 meters to >750 meters is characterized by these five species, which cumulatively totaled more than 70 per cent of the foraminiferal assemblages (Figure 17):

Angulogerina earlandi
Astrononion echolsi
Bulimina aculeata
Cassidulinoides parkerianus
Fursenkoina fusiformis

TABLE 2. Relative Abundances of Foraminifera in Total Populations of the Scotia Sea Area

Frequencies calculated separately for planktonic and benthonic populations. $X = > 0.6\%$; $P =$ present (total population < 40 specimens); $T =$ 0–5 cm core segment; $B =$ 40–45 cm core segment.

SLOPES — S. GEORGIA

STATION NUMBER	673	675	674	685	676	679	680	681	686	682	672
DEPTH IN METERS	201	329	531	636	750	1032	1500	1900	2288	2924	3697
PLANKTONIC-BENTHONIC RATIO	0	.017	.17	2.6	.013	3.3	1.2	1.5	4.0	8.4	.20
SIMPSON'S DIVERSITY INDEX	3.12	6.90	6.11	5.61	7.05	11.32	15.68	15.61	25.32	8.11	24.90
PERCENTAGE CALCAREOUS FORAMINIFERA	1	86	96	99	88	95	61	73	64	96	8
PLANKTONIC SPECIES											
GLOBIGERINA BULLOIDES				X					X	X	
G. PACHYDERMA		P	100	97	P	100	98	100	98	99	96
G. QUINQUELOBA									X		
GLOBIGERINITA GLUTINATA									X		
G. UVULA		P		2			2	X	1	1	4
GLOBOROTALIA INFLATA				X					X		
G. SCITULA									y		
G. TRUNCATULINOIDES										X	
IMMATURE FORMS (MOSTLY G. PACHYDERMA)											
BENTHONIC SPECIES											
CALCAREOUS											
HYALINE											
ANGULOGERINA EARLANDI	X	24	11	17	17	9	5	6	3	3	
EPISTOMINELLA EXIGUA	1	X	1	2		3	1	3	1	7	
ASTRONONION ECHOLSI		13	10	7	10	9		4	2	2	
BOLIVINA PSEUDOPUNCTATA		1	X					1	X	X	
BULIMINA ACULEATA		1	17	33	27	14	2	2	2	X	
CASSIDULINOIDES CRASSA		6									
C. PARKERIANUS		22	38	15	14	3	1		1	X	
FISSURINA MARGINATA		4	2	2						X	
F. SEMIMARGINATA		X		X		X					
FURSENKOINA EARLANDI		1	3	2	6	12	1	1	1	X	
F. FUSIFORMIS		12	9		10	12	X	3		2	
FLORILUS JAPONICA		1	1			X					
LAGENA DISTOMA		X	X			X	X				
L. ELONGATA		1	1	X		X					
OOLINA APICULATA		X	X								
PULLENIA SUBCARINATA		X		X	1						
BUCCELLA TENERRIMA			1	X	X						
EPONIDES SP. A			X	X					1		
LAGENA QUADRALATA			X	X		1					
GLANDULINA ANTARCTICUM			X	X		X	X				

SLOPES — S. ORKNEY

STATION NUMBER	497	498	500	539	503	502	504	506	537	544	1087	1035	533	1060
DEPTH IN METERS	256	366	490	560	993	1279	1589	2159	2189	2627	2644	2790	2753	3642
PLANKTONIC-BENTHONIC RATIO	0	.029	.050	.014	.035	.037	.009	.087	.001	.005	.007	0	0	0
SIMPSON'S DIVERSITY INDEX	1.54	4.94	19.15	15.13	18.05	7.35	9.35	19.99	5.78	19.32	8.64	20.64	6.69	
PERCENTAGE CALCAREOUS FORAMINIFERA	0	53	36	16	35	44	20	4	3	3	0	X	0	
PLANKTONIC SPECIES														
G. PACHYDERMA		P	100	P	P	P	P	100		P	P			
G. UVULA				P					P					
BENTHONIC SPECIES														
ANGULOGERINA EARLANDI				X	5		1	1						
EPISTOMINELLA EXIGUA		27	4	X	1	X	3							
ASTRONONION ECHOLSI		2	4	1	1		1	1		X				
BULIMINA ACULEATA			2		X									
FISSURINA MARGINATA			X											
FURSENKOINA EARLANDI		X	2	11	X	15								
F. FUSIFORMIS		2												
LAGENA DISTOMA					X									
OOLINA APICULATA					X									
PULLENIA SUBCARINATA			X	X										

SLOPES — S. SANDWICH

STATION NUMBER	652	658	657	651	569	654	657	630	650	649	624	648	1040	647
DEPTH IN METERS	558	659	805	851	1043	1058	1199	1244	1244	1841	2345	2976	3206	4493
PLANKTONIC-BENTHONIC RATIO	0	.041	.013	.014	.59	.009	.024	.44	0	.002	.93	.003	.009	.007
SIMPSON'S DIVERSITY INDEX	7.53	12.44	9.31	7.37	8.05	10.10	2.54	15.10	10.82	13.67	21.08	18.68	9.97	20.60
PERCENTAGE CALCAREOUS FORAMINIFERA	23	42	0	17	39	9	1	34	1	X	22	1	1	3
PLANKTONIC SPECIES														
GLOBIGERINA BULLOIDES					8									
G. PACHYDERMA		P	P	P	86	P	P	100			100			P
GLOBIGERINITA GLUTINATA			P											
G. UVULA					1	P				P			P	P
GLOBOROTALIA INFLATA		P	P		5									
IMMATURE FORMS (MOSTLY G. PACHYDERMA)			P				P							
BENTHONIC SPECIES														
ANGULOGERINA EARLANDI	2	2		X	8			8						
EPISTOMINELLA EXIGUA	1	16		1				X			2		X	
ASTRONONION ECHOLSI	X	1				2		X						
BOLIVINA PSEUDOPUNCTATA	X	5												
BULIMINA ACULEATA		X			4	X		X			X			
C. PARKERIANUS	X	X												
F. SEMIMARGINATA								X						
FURSENKOINA EARLANDI	14	12		6	21	2		1	1					
LAGENA DISTOMA				X										
PULLENIA SUBCARINATA	1	X		X										
EPONIDES SP. A								4						
GLANDULINA ANTARCTICUM					X									

SLOPES — TRENCH and RIM

	TRENCH			RIM		
STATION NUMBER	638	646	645	574	604	607
DEPTH IN METERS	5545	6076	6167	3993	4644	4130
PLANKTONIC-BENTHONIC RATIO	.002	0	0	0	0	0
SIMPSON'S DIVERSITY INDEX	3.96	3.13	4.91	11.70	13.37	14.49
PERCENTAGE CALCAREOUS FORAMINIFERA	0	6	1	0	X	0
G. UVULA	P					

BASINS — SCOTIA SEA

STATION NUMBER	460	467	473	476	481	548	689	693	700	705	708	1067	1068	712	716	725	728	736	1031	1028	486	562
DEPTH IN METERS	2105	3472	3678	3382	2800	3854	3468	3138	3212	2937	2823	2485	3400	3157	3171	2722	2864	3084	3508	3880	5289	5587
PLANKTONIC-BENTHONIC RATIO	5.3	2.0	2.2	.040	.020	.011	.29	2.1	.46	.13	.017	0	0	0	.031	.18	.006	.039	0	0	.012	0
SIMPSON'S DIVERSITY INDEX	4.88	6.50	20.55	23.85	7.56	15.79	17.00	23.90	17.18	9.22	9.33	12.98	16.93	26.32	16.23	14.54	8.82	10.43			9.05	6.06
PERCENTAGE CALCAREOUS FORAMINIFERA	98	88	35	4	0	0	4	21	5	6	X	0	0	0	1	14	2	4			0	0
PLANKTONIC SPECIES																						
GLOBIGERINA BULLOIDES	X								2													
G. PACHYDERMA	93	100	100	P	P	P			43	33	P				P	63		P				
G. QUINQUELOBA	3																					
GLOBIGERINITA GLUTINATA	X																					
G. UVULA	4					P	80	53	46	67					P	37	P	P			P	
GLOBOROTALIA INFLATA	X								2													
IMMATURE FORMS (MOSTLY G. PACHYDERMA)							20	47	7							8		P				
BENTHONIC SPECIES																						
ANGULOGERINA EARLANDI	1								X									1				
EPISTOMINELLA EXIGUA	4	3	X				1	4		X					X	2						
ASTRONONION ECHOLSI	3								1									2				
BOLIVINA PSEUDOPUNCTATA								1														
BULIMINA ACULEATA							2	5	3	2	X					X	2					
FISSURINA MARGINATA	X																					
FURSENKOINA EARLANDI	2																					
F. FUSIFORMIS																		1				
OOLINA APICULATA			X																			
LAGENA QUADRALATA				X																		

BASINS — WEDDELL SEA

STATION NUMBER	618	622	1045	1017	1016	1046	1062	1024	1021	1012	524	520	517	516T	516B	614	617	1074	513	528
DEPTH IN METERS	4558	3737	4787	4542	4513	3806	3644	3484	4110	4182	3422	3722	4196	4196		3770	3199	2798	3784	2968
PLANKTONIC-BENTHONIC RATIO	0	.31	0	0	.051	.010	.25	.13	0	0	.019	.017	.013	.10	.36	8.8	75	88	24	2.2
SIMPSON'S DIVERSITY INDEX	3.36	8.65			3.76	12.48	2.71			7.53		2.36	6.55	4.28	6.49		7.23	8.21	2.85	15.32
PERCENTAGE CALCAREOUS FORAMINIFERA	0	3			5	0	2			0		15	1	3	100	85	98	97	85	53
PLANKTONIC SPECIES																				
GLOBIGERINA BULLOIDES																				X
G. PACHYDERMA		100			P	P	100	P			P	P			100	100	99	100	100	100
G. QUINQUELOBA																				X
G. UVULA											P		P							X
GLOBOROTALIA INFLATA																				X
IMMATURE FORMS (MOSTLY G. PACHYDERMA)																	1			
BENTHONIC SPECIES																				
ANGULOGERINA EARLANDI		2																		2
EPISTOMINELLA EXIGUA										P		X	X		5	14	21	27	X	15
BOLIVINA PSEUDOPUNCTATA																	X			X
FISSURINA MARGINATA																		:		
F. FUSIFORMIS															X					
PULLENIA SUBCARINATA																		X		
EPONIDES SP. A																	1	X		

TABLE 2. (continued)

SLOPES — S. GEORGIA

STATION NUMBER	673	675	674	685	676	679	680	681	686	682	672
DEPTH IN METERS	201	329	531	636	750	1032	1500	1900	2288	2924	3697
PLANKTONIC-BENTHONIC RATIO	0	.017	.17	2.6	.013	3.3	1.2	1.5	4.0	8.4	.20
SIMPSON'S DIVERSITY INDEX	3.12	6.90	6.11	5.61	7.05	11.32	15.68	15.61	25.32	8.11	24.90
PERCENTAGE CALCAREOUS FORAMINIFERA	1	86	96	99	88	95	61	73	64	96	8
PULLENIA SUBSPHAERICA	X	X	1	1	3	3	1	1			
BULIMINA ROSTRATA		X		X	2	3	X	X			
CASSIDULINA LAEVIGATA		X		X		X					
C. LENS		1			X						
C. SUBGLOBOSA		4	1	2	3	2	X	3	X		
CIBICIDES LOBATULUS IRREG.		X						1			
EHRENBERGINA GLABRA		X									
EILOHEDRA WEDDELLENSIS		2			9	17	12	23	3		
EPISTOMINELLA ARCTICA		X		4					12		
FISSURINA FIMBRIATA		X	X		X			X	X		
GYROIDINA SOLDANII		X			1	1	1	1			
G. SUBPLANULATA		X		6	9	5	1	1	X		
ISLANDIELLA QUADRATA		X	X								
LAGENA MERIDIONALIS		X		X		X	X				
LINGULINA TRANSLUCIDA		X		X							
NONIONELLA IRIDEA		12		13	16	13	2	2	3		
PARAFISSURINA LATERALIS		X		X			1	X	X		
VALVULINERIA LAEVIGATA			1	2	1						
BOLIVINA DECUSSATA				X		3	X	1			
LAGENA NEBULOSA				X							
ORIDORSALIS SIDEBOTTOMSI				1	4	1					
PARAFISSURINA CURTA				X	X		1				
P. FUSULINIFORMIS				X			2				
PULLENIA SIMPLEX				X		1	1	X			
UVIGERINA CF. U. ATTENTUATA				X		X					
DENTALINA ITTAI					X						
EPONIDES TUMIDULUS					X	X	3	3		2	
OOLINA MELO					X	X			X		
ASTRONONION ANTARCTICUM						X					
CIBICIDES GROSSEPUNCTATUS							1	1	X		

SLOPES — S. ORKNEY

STATION NUMBER	497	498	500	539	503	502	504	506	537	544	1087	1035	533	1060
DEPTH IN METERS	256	366	490	560	993	1279	1589	2159	2189	2627	2644	2790	2753	3642
PLANKTONIC-BENTHONIC RATIO	0	.029	.050	.014	.035	.037	.009	.087	.001	.005	.007	0	0	0
SIMPSON'S DIVERSITY INDEX	1.54	4.94	19.15	15.13	18.05	7.35	9.35	19.99	5.78	19.32	8.64	20.64	6.69	
PERCENTAGE CALCAREOUS FORAMINIFERA	0	53	36	16	35	44	20	4	3	3	0	X	0	
PULLENIA SUBSPHAERICA			3		6	8	1		X					
C. SUBGLOBOSA		12	6	X	1			1	X					
CIBICIDES LOBATULUS IRREG.					8	X		X	X					
EILOHEDRA WEDDELLENSIS			6	1	4	X	10	X	1	1		X		
GYROIDINA SOLDANII					X									
G. SUBPLANULATA			4	1	2	5	X							
NONIONELLA IRIDEA		2	X											
PARAFISSURINA LATERALIS				X										
LAGENA NEBULOSA			X							X				
P. FUSULINIFORMIS			X	X										
PULLENIA SIMPLEX			X	X	2	12				X				
DENTALINA ITTAI										X				
EPONIDES TUMIDULUS							X							
CIBICIDES GROSSEPUNCTATUS			1	X	3	2	1		X					

SLOPES — S. SANDWICH

STATION NUMBER	652	658	657	651	569	654	657	630	650	649	624	648	1040	647
DEPTH IN METERS	558	659	805	851	1043	1058	1199	1244	1244	1841	2345	2976	3206	4493
PLANKTONIC-BENTHONIC RATIO	0	.041	.013	.014	.59	.009	.024	.44	0	.002	.93	.003	.009	.007
SIMPSON'S DIVERSITY INDEX	7.53	12.44	9.31	7.37	8.05	10.10	2.54	15.10	10.82	13.67	21.08	18.68	9.97	20.60
PERCENTAGE CALCAREOUS FORAMINIFERA	23	42	0	17	39	9	1	34	1	X	22	1	1	3
PULLENIA SUBSPHAERICA	X	X		X	1	1		1						
CASSIDULINA LAEVIGATA					1			1						
C. LENS								X						
C. SUBGLOBOSA		1		X		X		X			X			1
CIBICIDES LOBATULUS IRREG.								X				X		
EILOHEDRA WEDDELLENSIS	X	X		6		3	1	13			12			1
GYROIDINA SOLDANII								X			X			
G. SUBPLANULATA								1			1			
LAGENA MERIDIONALIS								X						
NONIONELLA IRIDEA	5	1		1										
ORIDORSALIS SIDEBOTTOMSI						1					2			X
EPONIDES TUMIDULUS								X			3			
CIBICIDES GROSSEPUNCTATUS								1			1			

TRENCH and RIM

	TRENCH			RIM		
STATION NUMBER	638	646	616	574	604	607
DEPTH IN METERS	5545	6076	6167	3993	4644	4130
PLANKTONIC-BENTHONIC RATIO	.002	0	0	0	0	0
SIMPSON'S DIVERSITY INDEX	3.96	3.13	4.91	11.70	13.37	14.49
PERCENTAGE CALCAREOUS FORAMINIFERA	0	6	1	0	X	0

BASINS — SCOTIA SEA

STATION NUMBER	460	467	473	476	481	548	689	693	700	705	708	1067	1068	712	716	725	728	736	1031	1028	486	562
DEPTH IN METERS	2105	3472	3678	3382	2800	3854	3468	3138	3212	2937	2823	2485	3400	3157	3171	2722	2864	3084	3508	3880	5289	5587
PLANKTONIC-BENTHONIC RATIO	5.3	2.0	2.2	.040	.020	.011	.29	2.1	.46	.13	.017	0	0	0	.031	.18	.006	.039	0	0	.012	0
SIMPSON'S DIVERSITY INDEX	4.88	6.50	20.55	23.85	7.56	15.79	17.00	23.90	17.18	9.22	9.33	12.98	16.93	26.32	16.23	14.54	8.82	10.43			9.05	6.06
PERCENTAGE CALCAREOUS FORAMINIFERA	98	88	35	4	0	0	4	21	5	6	X	0	0	0	1	14	2	4			0	0
PULLENIA SUBSPHAERICA	2	X																				
BULIMINA ROSTRATA	X																					
CASSIDULINA LAEVIGATA										X												
C. SUBGLOBOSA	2	4	4				X	3	X	X												
EILOHEDRA WEDDELLENSIS	18	35	7					5	X							9						
EPISTOMINELLA ARCTICA	4																					
GYROIDINA SOLDANII		X																				
G. SUBPLANULATA	4	3								1						X						
NONIONELLA IRIDEA	39		X					X														
ORIDORSALIS SIDEBOTTOMSI		9																				
DENTALINA ITTAI		X																				
EPONIDES TUMIDULUS		3	X	2																		

BASINS — WEDDELL SEA

STATION NUMBER	618	622	1045	1017	1016	1046	1062	1024	1021	1012	524	520	517	516T	516B	614	617	1074	513	528
DEPTH IN METERS	4558	3737	4787	4542	4513	3806	3644	3484	4110	4182	3422	3722	4196	4196		3770	3199	2796	3784	2968
PLANKTONIC-BENTHONIC RATIO	0	.31	0	0	.051	.010	.25	.13	0	0	.019	.017	.013	.10	.36	8.8	75	88	24	2.2
SIMPSON'S DIVERSITY INDEX	3.36	8.65			3.76	12.48	2.71			7.53		2.36	6.55	4.28	6.49		7.23	8.21	2.85	15.32
PERCENTAGE CALCAREOUS FORAMINIFERA	0	3			5	0	2			0		15	1	3	100	85	98	97	85	53
PULLENIA SUBSPHAERICA		2												X		1	X	1		
CASSIDULINA LAEVIGATA																	X			
C. SUBGLOBOSA					1							X	X	X	6	11		2		1
CIBICIDES LOBATULUS IRREG.					1												X	3	2	
EILOHEDRA WEDDELLENSIS							X					X		X	4	14	29	11	1	13
EPISTOMINELLA ARCTICA																		X		
GYROIDINA SOLDANII																	2		1	
G. SUBPLANULATA															3	X	3	1		X
ISLANDIELLA QUADRATA																	2	11	11	
LAGENA MERIDIONALIS																				X
NONIONELLA IRIDEA														X			1	X		X
PARAFISSURINA LATERALIS																				X
LAGENA NEBULOSA												X			X			X		X
ORIDORSALIS SIDEBOTTOMSI												X				3				
P. FUSULINIFORMIS																				X
PULLENIA SIMPLEX															1	1			1	
EPONIDES TUMIDULUS															6	1	1	X		X
OOLINA MELO																				X
CIBICIDES GROSSEPUNCTATUS																	X	1	1	

TABLE 2. (continued)

SLOPES — S. GEORGIA

STATION NUMBER	673	675	674	685	676	679	680	681	686	682	672
DEPTH IN METERS	201	329	531	636	750	1032	1500	1900	2288	2924	3697
PLANKTONIC-BENTHONIC RATIO	0	.017	.17	2.6	.013	3.3	1.2	1.5	4.0	8.4	.20
SIMPSON'S DIVERSITY INDEX	3.12	6.90	6.11	5.61	7.05	11.32	15.68	15.61	25.32	8.11	24.90
PERCENTAGE CALCAREOUS FORAMINIFERA	1	86	96	99	88	95	61	73	64	96	8
LAGENA ASPERA								X		X	
STAINFORTHIA COMPLANATA								X	X	1	
GLABRATELLA MINUTISSIMA									X	X	
GYROIDINA ORBICULARIS									1		1
NODOSARIA DOLIOLARIS									X		
ORIDORSALIS TENERA									1	1	
O. SP. A									1	X	
SEABROOKIA CF. S. EARLANDI									X		
SPHAEROIDINA BULLOIDES									2		
EHRENBERGINA TRIGONA										1	
FISSURINA SP. A										X	
F. SP. B										X	
ISLANDIELLA ISLANDICA										X	
PULLENIA OSLOENSIS										X	
MELONIS POMPILIOIDES										1	
NUTTALIDES UMBONIFERA										1	1
ORIDORSALIS MARCIDA										X	
HERONALLENIA WILSONI										X	
DENTALINA COMMUNIS LARVA											
FISSURINA ANNECTENS											
NONIONELLA BRADII											
RUPERTINA STABILIS											
CIBICIDES BRADII											
C. LOBATULUS											
PATELLINA ANTARCTICA											
MELONIS AFFINIS											
CEROBERTINA ARCTICA											
ROBERTINA WIESNERI											
MELONIS UMBILICATULUS											
UVIGERINA ASPERULA											
PARAFISSURINA VENTRICOSA											
ANGULOGERINA EARLANDI F. PAUPERATA											
CASSIDULINOIDES PORRECTUS											
MISC. LAGENOIDS											

SLOPES — S. ORKNEY

STATION NUMBER	497	498	500	539	503	502	504	506	537	544	1087	1035	533	1060
DEPTH IN METERS	256	366	490	560	993	1279	1589	2159	2189	2627	2644	2790	2753	3642
PLANKTONIC-BENTHONIC RATIO	0	.029	.050	.014	.035	.037	.009	.087	.001	.005	.007	0	0	0
SIMPSON'S DIVERSITY INDEX	1.54	4.94	19.15	15.13	18.05	7.35	9.35	19.99	5.78	19.32	8.64	20.64	6.69	
PERCENTAGE CALCAREOUS FORAMINIFERA	0	53	36	16	35	44	20	4	3	3	0	X	0	
LAGENA ASPERA								X	X					
STAINFORTHIA COMPLANATA		3	X				1							
GLABRATELLA MINUTISSIMA														
GYROIDINA ORBICULARIS						X								
NODOSARIA DOLIOLARIS														
ORIDORSALIS TENERA														
O. SP. A														
SEABROOKIA CF. S. EARLANDI														
SPHAEROIDINA BULLOIDES														
EHRENBERGINA TRIGONA														
FISSURINA SP. A							X		X	X				
F. SP. B														
ISLANDIELLA ISLANDICA														
PULLENIA OSLOENSIS														
MELONIS POMPILIOIDES														
NUTTALIDES UMBONIFERA								1						
ORIDORSALIS MARCIDA														
HERONALLENIA WILSONI					X									
DENTALINA COMMUNIS LARVA		X												
FISSURINA ANNECTENS			X							X				
NONIONELLA BRADII			1		X	2	2		X	X				
RUPERTINA STABILIS			X											
CIBICIDES BRADII				X										
C. LOBATULUS				1										
PATELLINA ANTARCTICA								X		X				
MELONIS AFFINIS									1	1				
CEROBERTINA ARCTICA														
ROBERTINA WIESNERI														
MELONIS UMBILICATULUS														
UVIGERINA ASPERULA														
PARAFISSURINA VENTRICOSA														
ANGULOGERINA EARLANDI F. PAUPERATA														
CASSIDULINOIDES PORRECTUS														
MISC. LAGENOIDS														

SLOPES — S. SANDWICH

STATION NUMBER	652	658	657	651	569	654	657	630	650	649	624	648	1040	647
DEPTH IN METERS	558	659	805	851	1043	1058	1199	1244	1244	1841	2345	2976	3206	4493
PLANKTONIC-BENTHONIC RATIO	0	.041	.013	.014	.59	.009	.024	.44	0	.002	.93	.003	.009	.007
SIMPSON'S DIVERSITY INDEX	7.53	12.44	9.31	7.37	8.05	10.10	2.54	15.10	10.82	13.67	21.08	18.68	9.97	20.60
PERCENTAGE CALCAREOUS FORAMINIFERA	23	42	0	17	39	9	1	34	1	X	22	1	1	3
LAGENA ASPERA														
STAINFORTHIA COMPLANATA	X			1	X									
GLABRATELLA MINUTISSIMA														
GYROIDINA ORBICULARIS														
NODOSARIA DOLIOLARIS														
ORIDORSALIS TENERA														
O. SP. A									X					
SEABROOKIA CF. S. EARLANDI				X		X	X							
SPHAEROIDINA BULLOIDES														
EHRENBERGINA TRIGONA														
FISSURINA SP. A									1					
F. SP. B						X			X					
ISLANDIELLA ISLANDICA														
PULLENIA OSLOENSIS										X				1
MELONIS POMPILIOIDES														
NUTTALIDES UMBONIFERA				1										
ORIDORSALIS MARCIDA														
HERONALLENIA WILSONI														
DENTALINA COMMUNIS LARVA														
FISSURINA ANNECTENS	X				X			X						
NONIONELLA BRADII														
RUPERTINA STABILIS														
CIBICIDES BRADII							X							
C. LOBATULUS														
PATELLINA ANTARCTICA														
MELONIS AFFINIS														
CEROBERTINA ARCTICA			X		X									
ROBERTINA WIESNERI					X									
MELONIS UMBILICATULUS				1										
UVIGERINA ASPERULA														
PARAFISSURINA VENTRICOSA														
ANGULOGERINA EARLANDI F. PAUPERATA														
CASSIDULINOIDES PORRECTUS														
MISC. LAGENOIDS														

SLOPES — TRENCH, RIM

	TRENCH			RIM		
STATION NUMBER	638	646	645	574	604	607
DEPTH IN METERS	5545	6076	6167	3993	4644	4130
PLANKTONIC-BENTHONIC RATIO	.002	0	0	0	0	0
SIMPSON'S DIVERSITY INDEX	3.96	3.13	4.91	11.70	13.37	14.49
PERCENTAGE CALCAREOUS FORAMINIFERA	0	6	1	0	X	0
PULLENIA OSLOENSIS		6	1			

BASINS — SCOTIA SEA

STATION NUMBER	460	467	473	476	481	548	689	693	700	705	708	1067	1068	712	716	725	728	736	1031	1028	486	562
DEPTH IN METERS	2105	3472	3678	3382	2800	3854	3468	3138	3212	2937	2823	2485	3400	3157	3171	2722	2864	3084	3508	3880	5289	5587
PLANKTONIC-BENTHONIC RATIO	5.3	2.0	2.2	.040	.020	.011	.29	2.1	.46	.13	.017	0	0	0	.031	.18	.006	.039	0	0	.012	0
SIMPSON'S DIVERSITY INDEX	4.88	6.50	20.55	23.85	7.56	15.79	17.00	23.90	17.18	9.22	9.33	12.98	16.93	26.32	16.23	14.54	8.82	10.43			9.05	6.06
PERCENTAGE CALCAREOUS FORAMINIFERA	98	88	35	4	0	0	4	21	5	6	X	0	0	0	1	14	2	4			0	0
LAGENA ASPERA																						
STAINFORTHIA COMPLANATA	13	1							X													
GLABRATELLA MINUTISSIMA																						
GYROIDINA ORBICULARIS	X	1																				
NODOSARIA DOLIOLARIS																						
ORIDORSALIS TENERA	X	X	4	4																		
O. SP. A		X	1																			
SEABROOKIA CF. S. EARLANDI		2														X						
SPHAEROIDINA BULLOIDES		2	X																			
EHRENBERGINA TRIGONA																						
FISSURINA SP. A			X																			
F. SP. B																						
ISLANDIELLA ISLANDICA																						
PULLENIA OSLOENSIS		2	X																			
MELONIS POMPILIOIDES		1																				
NUTTALIDES UMBONIFERA	14	1	1	2																		
ORIDORSALIS MARCIDA			X																			
HERONALLENIA WILSONI																						
DENTALINA COMMUNIS LARVA				1																		
FISSURINA ANNECTENS																						
NONIONELLA BRADII																						
RUPERTINA STABILIS																						
CIBICIDES BRADII		1	X																			
C. LOBATULUS																						
PATELLINA ANTARCTICA																						
MELONIS AFFINIS	X																					
CEROBERTINA ARCTICA																						
ROBERTINA WIESNERI																						
MELONIS UMBILICATULUS																						
UVIGERINA ASPERULA	3	4	X																			
PARAFISSURINA VENTRICOSA	X		X																			
ANGULOGERINA EARLANDI F. PAUPERATA																						
CASSIDULINOIDES PORRECTUS																						
MISC. LAGENOIDS	X	X	X													X						

BASINS — WEDDELL SEA

STATION NUMBER	618	622	1045	1017	1016	1046	1062	1024	1021	1012	524	520	517	516T	516B	614	617	1074	513	528
DEPTH IN METERS	4558	3737	4787	4542	4513	3806	3644	3484	4110	4182	3422	3722	4196	4196		3770	3199	2796	3784	2968
PLANKTONIC-BENTHONIC RATIO	0	.31	0	0	.051	.010	.25	.13	0	0	.019	.017	.013	.10	.36	8.8	75	88	24	2.2
SIMPSON'S DIVERSITY INDEX	3.36	8.65			3.76	12.48	2.71			7.53		2.36	6.55	4.28	6.49		7.23	8.21	2.85	15.32
PERCENTAGE CALCAREOUS FORAMINIFERA	0	3			5	0	2			0		15	1	3	100	85	98	97	85	53
LAGENA ASPERA																				X
STAINFORTHIA COMPLANATA															X		X	1		X
GLABRATELLA MINUTISSIMA																	1			X
GYROIDINA ORBICULARIS																				
NODOSARIA DOLIOLARIS																				
ORIDORSALIS TENERA							X								33		3	4	1	1
O. SP. A																		1		X
SEABROOKIA CF. S. EARLANDI																				
SPHAEROIDINA BULLOIDES																	X			
EHRENBERGINA TRIGONA																X	5	X		X
FISSURINA SP. A																		1		
F. SP. B																				
ISLANDIELLA ISLANDICA																				
PULLENIA OSLOENSIS							X								1	X				
MELONIS POMPILIOIDES																X				
NUTTALIDES UMBONIFERA												12	X	1	20	25	7	15	58	13
ORIDORSALIS MARCIDA																				
HERONALLENIA WILSONI																				
DENTALINA COMMUNIS LARVA																X	X			
FISSURINA ANNECTENS																				
NONIONELLA BRADII																				
RUPERTINA STABILIS																				
CIBICIDES BRADII																X		X	2	
C. LOBATULUS					3													3	5	1
PATELLINA ANTARCTICA																				
MELONIS AFFINIS																				
CEROBERTINA ARCTICA																				
ROBERTINA WIESNERI																				
MELONIS UMBILICATULUS																				
UVIGERINA ASPERULA																				
PARAFISSURINA VENTRICOSA												X								X
ANGULOGERINA EARLANDI F. PAUPERATA																				X
CASSIDULINOIDES PORRECTUS																	6			X
MISC. LAGENOIDS												X			14	13	9	7	3	3

TABLE 2. (continued)

SLOPES — S. GEORGIA

STATION NUMBER	673	675	674	685	676	679	680	681	686	682	672
DEPTH IN METERS	201	329	531	636	750	1032	1500	1900	2288	2924	3697
PLANKTONIC - BENTHONIC RATIO	0	.017	.17	2.6	.013	3.3	1.2	15	4.0	8.4	.20
SIMPSON'S DIVERSITY INDEX	3.12	6.90	6.11	5.61	7.05	11.32	15.68	15.61	25.32	8.11	24.90
PERCENTAGE CALCAREOUS FORAMINIFERA	1	86	96	99	88	95	61	73	64	96	8
PORCELANEOUS											
CYCLOGYRA INVOLVENS											
KERAMOSPHAERA MURRAYI											
MILIOLINELLA SUBROTUNDA											
PYRGA MURRHINA											
QUINQUELOCULINA SEMINULUM				X							
TRILOCULINA TRICARINATA										X	
UNIDENTIFIED MILIOLIDS		X							1		
CALCAREOUS AGGLUTINATED											
DOROTHIA SP. A									X		
EGGERELLA NITENS											
E. PARKERAE VAR. A							1	3	7	1	
KARRERIELLA BRADYI											
K. CATENATA											
K. DEFORMIS									2		
K. NOVANGLIAE								2			
MARTINOTTIELLA MILLETTI										X	
RUDLGAUDRYINA INEPTA									8		
NON-CALCAREOUS BATHYAL											
AMMODISCUS CATINUS				X	1	X	2	X	X		
AMMOFLINTINA ARGENTEA											
CRIBROSTOMOIDES ARENACEA	X										
C. JEFFREYSI	3	X									
HAPLOPHRAGMOIDES CANARIENSIS						X	3	1			
MILIAMMINA ARENACEA	46	1	X		1				1		
M. LATA			X			X	X				
PORTATROCHAMMINA ANTARCTICA	32	1									
P. WIESNERI			X			X			1		
PSEUDOBOLIVINA ANTARCTICA	3	1	X		2	1	5	2	X		

SLOPES — S. ORKNEY

STATION NUMBER	497	498	500	539	503	502	504	506	537	544	1087	1035	533	1060
DEPTH IN METERS	256	366	490	560	993	1279	1589	2159	2189	2627	2644	2790	2753	3642
PLANKTONIC - BENTHONIC RATIO	0	.029	.050	.014	.035	.037	.009	.087	.001	.005	.007	0	0	0
SIMPSON'S DIVERSITY INDEX	1.54	4.94	19.15	15.13	18.05	7.35	9.35	19.99	5.78	19.32	8.64	20.64	6.69	
PERCENTAGE CALCAREOUS FORAMINIFERA	0	53	36	16	35	44	20	4	3	3	0	X	0	
PORCELANEOUS														
CYCLOGYRA INVOLVENS									X					
KERAMOSPHAERA MURRAYI														
MILIOLINELLA SUBROTUNDA							X							
PYRGA MURRHINA														
QUINQUELOCULINA SEMINULUM														
TRILOCULINA TRICARINATA			X											
UNIDENTIFIED MILIOLIDS														
CALCAREOUS AGGLUTINATED														
DOROTHIA SP. A														
EGGERELLA NITENS														
E. PARKERAE VAR. A														
KARRERIELLA BRADYI														
K. CATENATA														
K. DEFORMIS														
K. NOVANGLIAE														
MARTINOTTIELLA MILLETTI														
RUDLGAUDRYINA INEPTA														
NON-CALCAREOUS BATHYAL														
AMMODISCUS CATINUS					1		X	1						
AMMOFLINTINA ARGENTEA				7		1	X			1	1			
CRIBROSTOMOIDES ARENACEA			5	2	8	5	12	5	2			X		
C. JEFFREYSI					3									
HAPLOPHRAGMOIDES CANARIENSIS	1		2	8	1	2	1	1	2	X				
MILIAMMINA ARENACEA	80	34	1	2	3	29	5	X	3					
M. LATA		5	X											
PORTATROCHAMMINA ANTARCTICA														
P. WIESNERI		1	6	8	11	5	9	X	X	2	1	X	4	
PSEUDOBOLIVINA ANTARCTICA	5	1	7	2	6	1	8	1	37	13	2	X	2	

SLOPES — S. SANDWICH

STATION NUMBER	652	658	657	651	569	654	657	630	650	649	624	648	1040	647
DEPTH IN METERS	558	659	805	851	1043	1058	1199	1244	1244	1841	2345	2976	4206	4493
PLANKTONIC - BENTHONIC RATIO	0	.041	.013	.014	.59	.009	.024	.44	0	.002	.93	.003	[illegible]	.007
SIMPSON'S DIVERSITY INDEX	7.53	12.44	9.31	7.37	8.05	10.10	2.54	15.10	10.82	13.67	21.08	18.68	9.91	20.60
PERCENTAGE CALCAREOUS FORAMINIFERA	23	42	0	17	39	9	1	34	1	X	22	1	1	3
PORCELANEOUS														
CYCLOGYRA INVOLVENS														
KERAMOSPHAERA MURRAYI														X
MILIOLINELLA SUBROTUNDA														
PYRGA MURRHINA														
QUINQUELOCULINA SEMINULUM														
TRILOCULINA TRICARINATA														
UNIDENTIFIED MILIOLIDS														
CALCAREOUS AGGLUTINATED														
DOROTHIA SP. A														
EGGERELLA NITENS														
E. PARKERAE VAR. A								X						
KARRERIELLA BRADYI														
K. CATENATA														
K. DEFORMIS														
K. NOVANGLIAE														
MARTINOTTIELLA MILLETTI														
RUDLGAUDRYINA INEPTA														
NON-CALCAREOUS BATHYAL														
AMMODISCUS CATINUS														
AMMOFLINTINA ARGENTEA	6	5	18	1	2	2	2	X	3	1				
CRIBROSTOMOIDES ARENACEA	X			X		2	1	3		2				
C. JEFFREYSI	1	1	X					X						
HAPLOPHRAGMOIDES CANARIENSIS				1	5	10	1	3	4	7				
MILIAMMINA ARENACEA	7	7	8	6	22	2	61	2	4	1				
M. LATA	6	4	3	X	14		1		X	X				
PORTATROCHAMMINA ANTARCTICA	3	X	12					14	X					
P. WIESNERI		3		1		X	1		2	1	2			
PSEUDOBOLIVINA ANTARCTICA	30	8	14	31	1	16		1	14	12				

TRENCH / RIM

STATION NUMBER	638 (Trench)	646 (Trench)	645 (Trench)	574 (Rim)	604 (Rim)	607 (Rim)
DEPTH IN METERS	5545	6076	6167	3993	4644	4130
PLANKTONIC - BENTHONIC RATIO	.002	0	0	0	0	0
SIMPSON'S DIVERSITY INDEX	3.96	3.13	4.91	11.70	13.37	14.49
PERCENTAGE CALCAREOUS FORAMINIFERA	0	6	1	0	X	0
HAPLOPHRAGMOIDES CANARIENSIS		X	2			

BASINS — SCOTIA SEA

STATION NUMBER	460	467	473	476	481	548	689	693	700	705	708	1067	1068	712	716	725	728	736	1031	1028	486	562
DEPTH IN METERS	2105	3472	3678	3382	2800	3854	3468	3138	3212	2937	2823	2485	3400	3157	3171	2722	2864	3084	3508	3880	5289	5587
PLANKTONIC - BENTHONIC RATIO	5.3	2.0	2.2	.040	.020	.011	.29	2.1	.46	.13	.017	0	0	0	.031	.18	.006	.039	0	0	.012	0
SIMPSON'S DIVERSITY INDEX	4.88	6.50	20.55	23.85	7.56	15.79	17.00	23.90	17.18	9.22	9.33	12.98	16.93	26.32	16.23	14.54	8.82	10.43			9.05	6.06
PERCENTAGE CALCAREOUS FORAMINIFERA	98	88	35	4	0	0	4	21	5	6	X	0	0	0	1	14	2	4			0	0
TRILOCULINA TRICARINATA	2																					
E. PARKERAE VAR. A	1	2	X																			
HAPLOPHRAGMOIDES CANARIENSIS				X	X	X	X	1	X		1		1	X	2	X	1					1
PSEUDOBOLIVINA ANTARCTICA	1									X								1				

BASINS — WEDDELL SEA

STATION NUMBER	618	622	1045	1017	1016	1046	1062	1024	1021	1012	524	520	517	516T	516B	614	617	1074	513	528
DEPTH IN METERS	4558	3737	4787	4542	4513	3806	3644	3484	4110	4182	3422	3722	4196	4196		3770	3199	2798	3784	2968
PLANKTONIC - BENTHONIC RATIO	0	.31	0	0	.051	.010	.25	.13	0	0	.019	.017	.013	.10	.36	8.8	75	88	24	2.2
SIMPSON'S DIVERSITY INDEX	3.36	8.65			3.76	12.48	2.71			7.53		2.36	6.55	4.28	6.49		7.23	8.21	2.85	15.32
PERCENTAGE CALCAREOUS FORAMINIFERA	0	3			5	0	2			0		15	1	3	100	85	98	97	85	53
PYRGA MURRHINA															X		X	X		
TRILOCULINA TRICARINATA																		1		
UNIDENTIFIED MILIOLIDS															1		X			X
DOROTHIA SP. A																				X
EGGERELLA NITENS															X			X		
E. PARKERAE VAR. A																	2			
K. CATENATA															3					
K. DEFORMIS																			X	
K. NOVANGLIAE																				X
CRIBROSTOMOIDES ARENACEA																		X		X
P. WIESNERI																				2
PSEUDOBOLIVINA ANTARCTICA																				1

TABLE 2. (continued)

	SLOPES					BASINS	
	S. GEORGIA	S. ORKNEY	S. SANDWICH	TRENCH	RIM	SCOTIA SEA	WEDDELL SEA
STATION NUMBER	673 675 674 685 676 679 680 681 686 682 672	497 498 500 539 503 502 504 506 537 544 1087 1035 533 1060	652 658 657 651 569 654 657 630 650 649 624 648 1040 647	638 646 645	574 604 607	460 467 473 476 481 548 689 693 700 705 708 1067 1068 712 716 725 728 736 1031 1028 486 562	618 622 1045 1017 1016 1046 1062 1024 1021 1012 524 520 517 516T 516B 614 617 1074 513 528
DEPTH IN METERS	201 329 531 636 750 1032 1500 1900 2288 2924 3697	256 366 490 560 993 1279 1589 2159 2189 2627 2644 2790 2753 3642	558 659 805 851 1043 1058 1199 1244 1244 1841 2345 2976 3206 4493	5545 6076 6167	3993 4644 4130	2105 3472 3678 3382 2800 3854 3468 3138 3212 2937 2823 2485 3400 3157 3171 2722 2864 3084 3508 3880 5289 5587	4558 3737 4787 4542 4513 3806 3644 3484 4110 4182 3422 3722 4196 4196 3770 3199 2798 3784 2968
PLANKTONIC - BENTHONIC RATIO	0 .017 .17 2.6 .013 3.3 1.2 1.5 4.0 8.4 .20	0 .029 .050 .014 .035 .037 .009 .087 .001 .005 .007 0 0 0	0 .041 .013 .014 .59 .009 .024 .44 0 .002 .93 .003 .009 .007	.002 0 0	0 0 0	5.3 2.0 2.2 .040 .020 .011 .29 2.1 .46 .13 .017 0 0 0 .031 .18 .006 .039 0 0 .012 0	0 .31 0 0 .051 .010 .25 .13 0 0 .019 .017 .013 .10 .36 8.8 75 88 24 2.2
SIMPSON'S DIVERSITY INDEX	3.12 6.90 6.11 5.61 7.05 11.32 15.68 15.61 25.32 8.11 24.90	1.54 4.94 19.15 15.13 18.05 7.35 9.35 19.99 5.78 19.32 8.64 20.64 6.69	7.53 12.44 9.31 7.37 8.05 10.10 2.54 15.10 10.82 13.67 21.08 18.68 9.97 20.6C	3.96 3.13 4.91	11.70 13.37 14.49	4.88 6.50 20.55 23.85 7.56 15.79 17.00 23.90 17.18 9.22 9.33 12.98 16.93 26.32 16.23 14.54 8.82 10.43 9.05 6.06	3.36 8.65 3.76 12.48 2.71 7.53 2.36 6.55 4.28 6.49 7.23 8.21 2.85 15.32
PERCENTAGE CALCAREOUS FORAMINIFERA	1 86 96 99 88 95 61 73 64 96 8	0 53 36 16 35 44 20 4 3 3 0 X 0	23 42 0 17 39 9 1 34 1 X 22 1 1 3	0 6 1	0 X 0	98 88 35 4 0 0 4 21 5 6 X 0 0 0 1 14 2 4 0 0	0 3 5 0 2 0 15 1 3 100 85 98 97 85 53
REOPHAX SUBFUSIFORMIS	1 X X 1 1	2 X X 1 1	X 1 1 1 1				
SPIROPLECTAMMINA BIFORMIS	10 X	2					
TEXTULARIA EARLANDI	1		X 12 5 3 X 8				
TROCHAMMINA MALOVENSIS	1 X X 1	2 10 1 X 1	1 X X			X	
T. INTERMEDIA			3 2 7 1 1 1 1 1 1				
T. MULTICAMERATA	1 1 X X X	X X 1 8 13 1 15				2 1	X 1
VERNEUILINA EUROPEUM	3	1					
V. MINUTA	1 1 1 1 1 X	1 X 1 X 1 1 5 3 1 2	5 5 7 7 1 7 X 5 5 X X X			X 1 X X 1 1 1 1 2 2 1	1
ABYSSAL							
AMMOBACULITES AGGLUTINANS	X X X	2 2 X	1 X 7		X	4 X 22	1 P X 1 X 1 X
A. FOLIACEOUS	6 2 2	1 X X 2 1 1 X 2	X		1	1 2 1 X 1 4	X 1 3
A. FOLIACEOUS F. RECURVA	X X	1	2 1	1	1 X	1 X 2 2 3 3 3	3 3 1 1 X 2 P X 2 4 3 1
AMMOLAGENA CLAVATA	X X	X	X X		3	1 3 X 1 X 2	1 X X X X
AMMOMARGINULINA ENSIS	X	1 1 3	1 X 1 X 1 2	X	X	2 1 X X X 4 1 3 X 4 5 X X	7 2 2 3 2 2 X 4
BATHYSIPHON DISCRETA	X X	X 1 X	X X			X X X X X	
B. GRANULOSA	X X X		X X 4			X X X X X 1	1
B. RUSTICUM		X	X X		X X	X 1 1 X X 1	
B. SP. B	X	X X 1 X X			1	X 1 X 1 1	X
BIGENERINA MINUTISSIMA	X	1		4	4 X		1 X
CONOTROCHAMMINA KENNETTI		1 P	6	24 4 24	1 2	1 3 3 X	1 9 P 1 X X 4 6 4
C. RUGOSA		X	1 5 3		X	2 2 X 3 X 1	2 1 1 3 6 1
C. SP. 'A.	X						3 2 X 2 X
CRIBROSTOMOIDES SPHAERILOCULUS MEGALOSPH.		2	3 2			2 3	X
C. SPHAERILOCULUS MICROSPH.	10	2 1	3 9 2 6	29 3 10	2 7 3	4 4 2 17 2 1 X 6 3 11 4	2 2 P 1 3 2 X 1 2 1 X
C. SUBGLOBOSUS	X 4	1 10 1 2 X P	X 2 1 5 9 9 26 2	1		2 12 3 4 2 4 3 4 10 10 4 5 2 P 12 31	52 26 P P 50 11 5 P 14 P 10 5 15 1 X 1 1
C. UMBILICATULUS SOLDANII	X X 4	1 2 1 2 6	3			7 6 17 13 7 12 7 3 2 2 10 3 6 7	X 2
CYCLAMMINA PUSILLA		5				P	4 13 52 24 64 64 30 45 1 5 1
C. TRULLISSATA							1 P 6 1 1 2 1 2 X
CYSTAMMINA ARGENTEA	X X	X X	1 X 2 X			X X X 2 1	
C. PAUCILOCULATA	X		2 X 4 X		1 1	2 X X X	
EGGERRELLA PARKERAE VAR. B	1	X 1 1 3 P	3 1 7 7			2 8 6 8 11 22 27 17 15 8 6 10 28 6	
GLOMOSPIRA CHAROIDES	1 X	X X X 5 1 2 1 4	2 1 2 2 X 14 11 8 5	X	25 23 21	X 10 7 1 3 1 2 1 1 4 3 5 4 X	1 5 20 23 21 3 6 1 6 1 X 5
G. GORDIALIS	X 1 1 2	1 X 1 X X 1	3 X 1 1		1	X 1 X 1 X X 1	3 1 X P 3 X 1
GAUDRYINA PAUPERATA	X 1	X X 1 2 1 2	5	X		X X X 1 X X 2 1 2 X 2 2	1

TABLE 2. (continued)

	SLOPES: S. GEORGIA	SLOPES: S. ORKNEY	SLOPES: S. SANDWICH	TRENCH	RIM	BASINS: SCOTIA SEA	BASINS: WEDDELL SEA
STATION NUMBER	673 675 674 685 676 679 680 681 686 682 672	497 498 500 539 503 502 504 506 537 544 1087 1035 533 1060	652 658 657 651 569 654 657 630 650 649 624 640 1040 647	638 646 646	574 604 607	460 467 473 476 481 548 689 693 700 705 708 1067 1068 712 716 725 728 736 1031 1028 486 562	618 622 1045 1017 1016 1046 1062 1024 1021 1012 524 520 517 5167 5168 614 617 1074 513 528
DEPTH IN METERS	201 329 531 636 750 1032 1500 1900 2288 2924 3697	256 366 490 560 993 1279 1589 2159 2189 2627 2644 2790 2753 3642	558 659 805 851 1043 1058 1199 1244 1244 1841 2345 2476 3206 4493	5545 6076 6167	3993 4644 4130	2105 3472 3678 3382 2800 3854 3468 3138 3212 2937 2823 2485 3400 3157 3171 2722 2864 3084 3508 3880 5289 5587	4558 3737 4787 4542 4513 3806 3644 3484 4110 4182 3422 3722 4196 4196 3770 3199 2798 3784 2968
PLANKTONIC - BENTHONIC RATIO	0 .017 .17 2.6 .013 3.3 1.2 1.5 4.0 8.4 .20	0 .029 .050 .014 .035 .037 .009 .087 .001 .005 .007 0 0 0	0 .041 .013 .014 .59 .009 .024 .44 0 .002 .93 .003 .009 .007	.002 0 0	0 0 0	5.3 2.0 2.2 .040 .020 .011 .29 2.1 .46 .13 .017 0 0 0 .031 .18 .006 .039 0 0 .012 0	0 .31 0 0 .051 .010 .25 .13 0 0 .019 .017 .013 .10 .36 8.8 75 88 24 2.2
SIMPSON'S DIVERSITY INDEX	3.12 6.90 6.11 5.61 7.05 11.32 15.68 15.61 25.32 8.11 24.90	1.54 4.94 19.15 15.13 18.05 7.35 9.35 19.99 5.78 19.32 8.64 20.64 6.69	7.53 12.44 9.31 7.37 8.05 10.10 2.54 15.10 10.82 13.67 21.08 10.00 9.97 20.60	3.96 3.13 4.91	11.70 13.37 14.49	4.88 6.50 20.55 23.85 7.56 15.79 17.00 23.90 17.18 9.22 9.33 12.98 16.93 26.32 16.23 14.54 8.82 10.43 9.05 6.06	3.36 8.65 3.76 12.48 2.71 7.53 2.36 6.55 4.28 6.49 7.23 8.21 2.85 15.32
PERCENTAGE CALCAREOUS FORAMINIFERA	1 86 96 99 88 95 61 73 64 96 8	0 53 36 16 35 44 20 4 3 3 0 X 0	23 42 0 17 39 9 1 34 1 X 22 1 1 3	0 6 1	0 X 0	98 88 35 4 0 0 4 21 5 6 X 0 0 0 1 14 2 4 0 0	0 3 5 0 2 0 15 1 3 100 85 98 97 85 53
HORMOSINA DAVISI		3 1 X	1				P X 1 1 P 4 3 X
H. GLOBULIFERA	X	X 1 P	1 X X 1 2 1		X	X 1 X X X 1 X X 2 2 2 X X 1 1 P	1 1 1 X
HYPERAMMINA SP. A			1 1	X 2 1	1		
KARRERIELLA APPICULARIS			X		1 X	1 2 X X 1 2 X 1	
MARTINOTTIELLA ANTARCTICA	X 3	3 1 2 2 P	2 1 1	X 1 2		X 1 6 29 9 14 9 7 18 8 5 X 8 16 10 4 14 P P X	X X
MILIOLINELLA SP.	X	X X P	X X X		X	X X 1 1 1 2 P P	
NODELLUM MEMBRANACEA	X X	X	X 1 1 X 1	X	2 1 3	X X X 1 X	
PLACOPSILINELLA AURANTIACA	3	X	5 X X	X	2 1 X	1 3 1 2 X 1 1 1 1 2 X 1 5	5 3 2 X 1 1 X 1
PSAMMOSPHAERA FUSCA	1 3	1 X 13 X 1	1 1 1	2	X 1	1 8 1 3 X X X 1 X 1 2	3 2 3 2 1 2 6 3 2 3 1 X 1 4 1
REOPHAX NODULOSA		X	X 1		X	X X X	2 X X X X X
R. SP. A	10 1 X 3	2 2 16 6 18 P	2 1 X 4	1 15 4	2 1 X	X X 1 2 4 3 8 7 7 5 8 5 4 2 2 5 14 18 P 3 1	1 P 1 3 1 P 2 2
R. SP. B	X 1	1	X 4 X X X		3 X X	2 1 2 2 X	2
SACCAMMINA TUBULATA	1	1 1 1	X X 2 1 X 6	X	X X 1	2 3 2 2 1 3 2 2 X 1 1 1 X 2	1 3 1
SPIROLOCAMMINA TENUIS		1 P	X		X	X X X X 1 1 1 P P	1
SPIROPLECTAMMINA FILIFORMIS		X 2 1 4	2	3	1	1	2 1 X X X 2
S. AFF. S. FILIFORMIS	X X	X	1	X	2 2	1 X X 2	X 1
TEXTULARIA WIESNERI	7 1	1 3 2 4 2 1 X 10 14 3 22	X 6 7 X X			6 4 8 1 1 2 X 1 1 1 3 X 16 2 10 3	1 7 X X X 2
TRITAXIS INHAERENS	1 9	2 X 5 P	8 8 10 9		18 13 8	1 9 5 4 6 4 1 6 X 2 2 9 9 1 1 6 2	5 P 5 3 3 P X X 1 1
T. SQUAMATA	X	X X X	2 1 1 1		X	3 X	2 X X X X
TROCHAMMINA AFF. T. COMPACTA	X X	X 1 X	X 2		X	X X	1 X
T. CONICA	1 4	2 X X	X 3 X 2	X	1 1 4	X X 1 X 2 1 1 1 X X	X 1 X 1
T. DISCORBIS	2	2 X	4 X X 2		X X	X X 1 2 X X	
T. INCONSPICUA	X 1 X	1 1 5	1 2 1 6 X X 4		2 3	X X 2 X 7 7 7 2 1 X 4 4 8	P 1 1
T. LABIATA	4	1 1 1 X 1 1	1 X X X		1 3 3	2 1 1 1 4 1 1 X 1 X	1 1
T. QUADRILOBA	X 1 6	X X 1 1	1 3 7	1 X	1 7 3	1 2 1 6 1 X X X 2 1 5	
T. SOROSA	1 X 3	X X 1 1 2	6 2 2 2 1		1 3 2	X 1 3 1 4 1 2 X	
T. SUBCONICA	X	X 1 2	X			1 1 1 1	X
NON-DEFINITIVE							
ADEROCOTRYMA GLOMERATUM	2 X X X X 7	1 1 8 10 2 X X 9 6 2 15 P	X X 2 16 2 3 3 1	X 1 1	9 8 8	X 1 4 5 2 7 7 4 10 12 9 15 7 4 3 1 2 3 19	17 17 8 7 3 6 P 4 2 16 10 1 X 2
AMMOBACULITES FILIFORMIS	X X	14 1 X 1 5	X X X X	2 X 8	1 2	1 3 3 X 1 X X 1 X 1 1 6 X	1 X X X 1
AMMOSCALARIA TENUIMARGO	X X					X X	X 2
CONOTROCHAMMINA ALTERNANS	X	1	X X X X 1		1	1 1 X X	X
C. BULLATA	2 3 1 2 X 1 1 X 3	4 2 7 3 2 3 3 4 4 11 3 4 P	7 6 10 8 8 11 6 3 2 2 X 1	4 6 6	2 1	3 3 2 X 6 1 1 2 1 2 7 1 X 4	10 6 X 3 P 6 1 X X

TABLE 2. (continued)

SLOPES: S. GEORGIA

STATION NUMBER	673	675	674	685	676	679	680	681	686	682	672
DEPTH IN METERS	201	329	531	636	750	1032	1500	1900	2288	2924	3697
PLANKTONIC-BENTHONIC RATIO	0	.017	.17	2.6	.013	3.3	1.2	1.5	4.0	8.4	.20
SIMPSON'S DIVERSITY INDEX	3.12	6.90	6.11	5.61	7.05	11.32	15.68	15.61	25.32	8.11	24.90
PERCENTAGE CALCAREOUS FORAMINIFERA	1	86	96	99	88	95	61	73	64	96	8
CRIBROSTOMOIDES CONTORTUS											2
C. UMBILICATULUS											
C. WIESNERI										X	1
CYCLAMMINA CANCELLATA		X			1		X				
C. ORBICULARIS							X	X			
HAPLOPHRAGMOIDES PARKERAE											4
H. QUADRATUS									X	X	3
TROCHAMMINA QUADRICAMERATA									X		
HORMOSINA LAPIDIGERA											
PORTATROCHAMMINA ELTANENSIS							4	7	2	X	7
REOPHAX ADUNCA											
R. DISTANS											X
R. LONGISCATISFORMIS											
R. OVICULA							X	X	X	X	X
R. CF. R. ROSTRATA											
R. SUBDENTALINIFORMIS											
SACCORHIZA HEDRIX									X	X	X
SPIROPLECTAMMINA TYPICA							X				
THURAMMINA EX. GR. T. ALBICANS									X		
T. PAPILLATA								X	5		1
TOLYPAMMINA FRIGIDA		1	X		1			2	2		
TROCHAMMINA GLABRA		2	1		1	X	X	X		X	2
T. PYGMAEA											
T. TRICAMERATA											
VERNEUILINA MINUTA VAR. A											

SLOPES: S. ORKNEY

STATION NUMBER	497	498	500	539	503	502	504	506	537	544	1087	1035	533	1060
DEPTH IN METERS	256	366	490	560	993	1279	1589	2159	2189	2627	2644	2790	2753	3642
PLANKTONIC-BENTHONIC RATIO	0	.029	.050	.014	.035	.037	.009	.087	.001	.005	.007	0	0	0
SIMPSON'S DIVERSITY INDEX	1.54	4.94	19.15	15.13	18.05	7.35	9.35	19.99	5.78	19.32	8.64	20.64	6.69	
PERCENTAGE CALCAREOUS FORAMINIFERA	0	53	36	16	35	44	20	4	3	3	0	X	0	
CRIBROSTOMOIDES CONTORTUS			2	X	3		3	6	X	X		X		P
C. UMBILICATULUS				X	1		1	1						
C. WIESNERI			X		X	X		1	X	X		X		P
CYCLAMMINA CANCELLATA									X					
C. ORBICULARIS					X		1		X					
HAPLOPHRAGMOIDES PARKERAE			X	1		X	X	1	3	3	4	3		P
H. QUADRATUS			1	1	1	X	X	X		2				
TROCHAMMINA QUADRICAMERATA			9		3									
HORMOSINA LAPIDIGERA		X							X					
PORTATROCHAMMINA ELTANENSIS			8	5	11	6	25	10	16	10	20	9	24	P
REOPHAX ADUNCA														
R. DISTANS			X					X						
R. LONGISCATISFORMIS			X						X	X				
R. OVICULA					X		X	X	X	1	1	X		
R. CF. R. ROSTRATA		1	1											
R. SUBDENTALINIFORMIS	5			1								2		
SACCORHIZA HEDRIX			X							X				
SPIROPLECTAMMINA TYPICA														
THURAMMINA EX. GR. T. ALBICANS				1	1			X						P
T. PAPILLATA				X				X	X	X				
TOLYPAMMINA FRIGIDA			1	3	1			X	1	4		3		
TROCHAMMINA GLABRA			1	1	X				X	1	4	2	2	P
T. PYGMAEA									X	X				
T. TRICAMERATA			X		1		X	2	X					
VERNEUILINA MINUTA VAR. A				1			1					1		

SLOPES: S. SANDWICH

STATION NUMBER	652	658	657	651	569	654	657	630	650	649	624	648	1040	1647
DEPTH IN METERS	558	659	805	851	1043	1058	1199	1244	1244	1841	2345	2976	3206	4493
PLANKTONIC-BENTHONIC RATIO	0	.041	.013	.014	.59	.009	.024	.44	0	.002	.93	.003	.009	.007
SIMPSON'S DIVERSITY INDEX	7.53	12.44	9.31	7.37	8.05	10.10	2.54	15.10	10.82	13.67	21.08	18.68	9.97	20.60
PERCENTAGE CALCAREOUS FORAMINIFERA	23	42	0	17	39	9	1	34	1	X	22	1	1	3
CRIBROSTOMOIDES CONTORTUS	X	X	X	1		1	4	X	1	1	2	3	X	X
C. UMBILICATULUS								X			1	X		
C. WIESNERI												X	X	1
CYCLAMMINA CANCELLATA												1		1
C. ORBICULARIS						X		X				X		
HAPLOPHRAGMOIDES PARKERAE		1	1	1		3		1	19	6	3	3	5	2
H. QUADRATUS				3	2	5		X	3	1	2			
TROCHAMMINA QUADRICAMERATA													X	1
HORMOSINA LAPIDIGERA														
PORTATROCHAMMINA ELTANENSIS	6	4	11	13		21	11	11	12	10	4	6	2	8
REOPHAX ADUNCA														
R. DISTANS											X	X	X	
R. LONGISCATISFORMIS				X									X	
R. OVICULA	X			X		X		1	X	X	X	X	X	1
R. CF. R. ROSTRATA						1			1				X	
R. SUBDENTALINIFORMIS		1	X	1		2			X	X				
SACCORHIZA HEDRIX				X		X			X	X	X		X	X
SPIROPLECTAMMINA TYPICA			X			X			X					
THURAMMINA EX. GR. T. ALBICANS											X			X
T. PAPILLATA						X								
TOLYPAMMINA FRIGIDA	1		X			1		X	1	X		X	X	2
TROCHAMMINA GLABRA	1	2	3	3	5	2		2	5	X		2		3
T. PYGMAEA									X			1		2
T. TRICAMERATA												X		
VERNEUILINA MINUTA VAR. A								X		X				

BASINS: TRENCH and RIM

STATION NUMBER	638	646	645	574	604	607
	TRENCH			RIM		
DEPTH IN METERS	5545	6076	6167	3993	4644	4130
PLANKTONIC-BENTHONIC RATIO	.002	0	0	0	0	0
SIMPSON'S DIVERSITY INDEX	3.96	3.13	4.91	11.70	13.37	14.49
PERCENTAGE CALCAREOUS FORAMINIFERA	0	6	1	0	X	0
CRIBROSTOMOIDES CONTORTUS		1	1	3		X
C. UMBILICATULUS						
C. WIESNERI				X		
CYCLAMMINA CANCELLATA				6	1	2
C. ORBICULARIS						
HAPLOPHRAGMOIDES PARKERAE				3	2	1
H. QUADRATUS					1	
TROCHAMMINA QUADRICAMERATA				1		3
HORMOSINA LAPIDIGERA				X		
PORTATROCHAMMINA ELTANENSIS	34	54	36	X	5	6
REOPHAX ADUNCA						
R. DISTANS				X	X	X
R. LONGISCATISFORMIS	X		X	X	1	
R. OVICULA				X	1	1
R. CF. R. ROSTRATA						
R. SUBDENTALINIFORMIS		1	2			
SACCORHIZA HEDRIX	X			X		X
SPIROPLECTAMMINA TYPICA						
THURAMMINA EX. GR. T. ALBICANS						
T. PAPILLATA			X			
TOLYPAMMINA FRIGIDA	2	1	1		1	3
TROCHAMMINA GLABRA				X	4	3
T. PYGMAEA						
T. TRICAMERATA						
VERNEUILINA MINUTA VAR. A						

BASINS: SCOTIA SEA

STATION NUMBER	460	467	473	476	481	548	689	693	700	705	708	1067	1068	712	716	725	728	736	1031	1028	486	562
DEPTH IN METERS	2105	3472	3678	3382	2800	3854	3468	3138	3212	2937	2823	2485	3400	3157	3171	2722	2864	3084	3508	3880	5289	5587
PLANKTONIC-BENTHONIC RATIO	5.3	2.0	2.2	.040	.020	.011	.29	2.1	.46	.13	.017	0	0	0	.031	.18	.006	.039	0	0	.012	0
SIMPSON'S DIVERSITY INDEX	4.88	6.50	20.55	23.85	7.56	15.79	17.00	23.90	17.18	9.22	9.33	12.98	16.93	26.32	16.23	14.54	8.82	10.43			9.05	6.06
PERCENTAGE CALCAREOUS FORAMINIFERA	98	88	35	4	0	0	4	21	5	6	X	0	0	0	1	14	2	4			0	0
CRIBROSTOMOIDES CONTORTUS			2	4	4	3	2	1	2	2	X		2	4	4	1		1				
C. UMBILICATULUS			1	X		3			X												X	X
C. WIESNERI			1	X		2			X	X				X	X							
CYCLAMMINA CANCELLATA																						
C. ORBICULARIS																						
HAPLOPHRAGMOIDES PARKERAE		1	1	1		1	2	1	3	X	2	3	4	3	1	1	1	1				
H. QUADRATUS				2		1	3	X	5	X	X		4	X	4	1	4	2			6	1
TROCHAMMINA QUADRICAMERATA								5														
HORMOSINA LAPIDIGERA			X	X				X														
PORTATROCHAMMINA ELTANENSIS	X		1	1	6	5	4	6	5	7	4	7	11	5	2	9	7	16			19	7
REOPHAX ADUNCA																						
R. DISTANS				X							X	1										
R. LONGISCATISFORMIS									X												X	
R. OVICULA		X	X	X	X	X	1	X	1	X	2	1	2	1	X	1	1	1			X	
R. CF. R. ROSTRATA				X																		
R. SUBDENTALINIFORMIS						X		1	1							X						
SACCORHIZA HEDRIX	X	X	X	X		X	X	X	X	X	1	X			X		1				X	X
SPIROPLECTAMMINA TYPICA					X	X				X												
THURAMMINA EX. GR. T. ALBICANS		X			1	X					X											
T. PAPILLATA					X		X	X						X		X						
TOLYPAMMINA FRIGIDA			X			1		X	X			1			1	X		1			X	X
TROCHAMMINA GLABRA			X		X		1	1	2	3	5	9	7	2	1		1	5				1
T. PYGMAEA																						
T. TRICAMERATA			X											1		X						
VERNEUILINA MINUTA VAR. A												1	1			X						

BASINS: WEDDELL SEA

STATION NUMBER	618	622	1045	1017	1016	1046	1062	1024	1021	1012	524	520	517	516T	516B	614	617	1074	513	528
DEPTH IN METERS	4558	3737	4787	4542	4513	3806	3644	3484	4110	4182	3422	3722	4196	4196		3770	3199	2796	3784	2968
PLANKTONIC-BENTHONIC RATIO	0	.31	0	0	.051	.010	.25	.13	0	0	.019	.017	.013	.10	.36	8.8	75	88	24	2.2
SIMPSON'S DIVERSITY INDEX	3.36	8.65			3.76	12.48	2.71			7.53		2.36	6.55	4.28	6.49		7.23	8.21	2.85	15.32
PERCENTAGE CALCAREOUS FORAMINIFERA	0	3			5	0	2			0		15	1	3	100	85	98	97	85	53
CRIBROSTOMOIDES CONTORTUS						2		P			3			10						X
C. UMBILICATULUS					9		1				1	X	1	X		X				
C. WIESNERI																			X	
CYCLAMMINA CANCELLATA	1					1														
C. ORBICULARIS																				
HAPLOPHRAGMOIDES PARKERAE						1	1		X								1			X
H. QUADRATUS						1														
TROCHAMMINA QUADRICAMERATA							X													
HORMOSINA LAPIDIGERA						1							X							
PORTATROCHAMMINA ELTANENSIS	1	9			1	1	1		1				X					X	1	3
REOPHAX ADUNCA																				
R. DISTANS							X													
R. LONGISCATISFORMIS									X			X							X	X
R. OVICULA		2					X									X				X
R. CF. R. ROSTRATA																				X
R. SUBDENTALINIFORMIS								P												
SACCORHIZA HEDRIX		X										X		X		X				X
SPIROPLECTAMMINA TYPICA																				
THURAMMINA EX. GR. T. ALBICANS																				
T. PAPILLATA						1			X											
TOLYPAMMINA FRIGIDA									1							X				2
TROCHAMMINA GLABRA																1				
T. PYGMAEA														X						
T. TRICAMERATA																				
VERNEUILINA MINUTA VAR. A														X						1

Table 3. Relative Abundances of Foraminifera in Living Benthonic Populations of the Scotia Sea Area

	SOUTH GEORGIA						SOUTH ORKNEY									SOUTH SANDWICH							TRENCH RIM		SCOTIA SEA			WEDDELL SEA					
STATION NUMBER	673	679	680	681	686	672	497	498	500	539	502	504	537	544	1035	652	658	651	654	649	624	647	646	607	712	700	1068	622	1016	618	1046	1074	528
DEPTH IN METERS	201	1032	1500	1900	2288	3697	256	366	490	560	1279	1589	2189	2621	2790	558	659	851	1058	1841	2345	4493	6076	4130	3157	3212	3400	3737	4513	4558	3806	2796	2968
STANDING CROP (PER 10 CM²)	27	71	43	37		36										148		298	150	80	100	82	56	32		400	16	1	2	7	9	20	
NUMBER COUNTED	27	71	43	37	99	36	2	6	241	67	138	195	100	207	76	74	120	149	45	40	50	41	28	16	14	29	16	1	2	7	9	5	92
PERCENTAGE CALCAREOUS	0	90	58	62	70	19	0	83	62	75	83	68	16	16	0	77	78	48	49	3	62	79	46	0	0	10	0	0	100	0	0	100	70
SIMPSON'S DIVERSITY INDEX		2.34			21.75				11.50	4.06	6.74	8.06	8.26	11.21	18.75	3.72	5.39	10.48			10.84												5.55
CALCAREOUS SPECIES																																	
ANGULOGERINA EARLANDI					1				1			6				3	4	1															1
ANOMALINA SP.			5	8																													
ASTRONONION ECHOLSI		1	2		2	3		17	5	4	1		1			5	2		2														
BOLIVINA PSEUDOPUNCTATA				3													8																
B. DECUSSATA				3																													
BULIMINA ACULEATA			2		1				3												2												
B. ROSTRATA				3																													
CASSIDULINA SUBGLOBOSA						3			7		1											2							50				1
CASSIDULINOIDES PARKERIANUS					1											3																	
CEROBERTINA ARCTICA																		1	2														
CIBICIDES GROSSEPUNCTATUS					2							3									2												
C. LOBATULUS									1	9	1																					20	
C. LOBATULUS IRREGULAR					1							1									2								50				
CYCLOGYRA INVOLVENS										1																							
DENTALINA ITTAI														X																			
DOROTHIA SP.					2																												
EGGERELLA NITENS				14																													
E. PARKERAE VAR. A			7		4																												
EILOHEDRA WEDDELLENSIS			9	5	12	8			17	1	3	31	3	2			1	18	31	3	26	2										60	41
EPISTOMINELLA EXIGUA					1			33	1	0	1	0	1			1	30	3			2											20	7
EPONIDES TUMIDULUS				3	8	3						1	1								10	12											7
E. SP. A					1																												
FISSURINA SP. A														1																			
F. SP. B																					2												
F. SPP.			2						1			1																					1
FURSENKOINA EARLANDI		65	2	3					1	48	26					49	29	19	4			2											
F. FUSIFORMIS		1		3				17																									
GLABRATELLA MINUTISSIMA					2																												1
GYROIDINA ORBICULARIS			2		3	3					1																						
G. SUBPLANULATA		7	14						1	3	10	3		X				1				2											
ISLANDIELLA ISLANDICA																																	2
KARRERIELLA DEFORMIS					3																												
LAGENA DISTOMA																		1															
MELONIS AFFINIS												1	9	5																			
MILIOLINELLA SUBROTUNDATA																					2												2
NONIONELLA BRADYI									5		4	9		3		16	2	4	7			2				10							2
N. IRIDEA		3		3	2																												
OOLINA APICULATA												1																					
O. SPP.												1		1																			
ORIDORSALIS SIDEBOTTOMSI																					6												
O. TENERA					1																												
O. SP. Å					1																												1
PARAFISSURINA CURTA			2														1																1
P. FUSULINIFORMIS					2				X																								
P. LATERALIS																																	1
PATELLINA ANTARCTICA												1																					
PULLENIA OSLOENSIS																					2	5	46										1
P. QUINQUELOBA														X																			
P. SIMPLEX		1		11	1						24	1	1	2				1															
P. SUBCARINATA									1																								
P. SUBSPHAERICA		4	2	3					10	1	12	1							2														
ROBERTINA ANTARCTICA																		1															
RUPERTINA STABILIS									X																								
RUDIGAUDRYINA INEPTA					13								1																				
TRILOCULINA TRICARINATA									X																								
SEABROOKIA EARLANDI					1																												
SPHAEROIDINA BULLOIDES					2																												
STAINFORTHIA COMPLANATA				3				17	X			2		2																			
VALVULINERIA LAEVIGATA		7	7																														
UNIDENTIFIABLE CALCAREOUS					1																4	2											
NON-CALCAREOUS SPECIES																																	
ADERCOTRYMA GLOMERATUM		1				8			5			1	10	12	11					18	12	17	11	19		24		100		14	55		4
AMMOBACULITES FILIFORMIS													1	X	11									19									1
A. FOLIACEOUS			5							1																							1
A. FOLIACEOUS F. RECURVA															5																		
AMMODISCUS CATINUS		3	2	5																													
AMMOFLINTINA ARGENTEA										1	1					1	6	1						6									
AMMOMARGINULINA ENSIS															7																		4
ASTRORHIZA TRIANGULARIS						3																											
BATHYSIPHON GRANULOSA																														14			
BATHYSIPHON SP. B									X																								

TABLE 3. (continued)

	SOUTH GEORGIA						SOUTH ORKNEY									SOUTH SANDWICH							TRENCH RIM		SCOTIA SEA			WEDDELL SEA					
STATION NUMBER	673	679	680	681	686	672	497	498	500	539	502	504	537	544	1035	652	658	651	654	649	624	647	646	607	712	700	1068	622	1016	618	1046	1074	528
DEPTH IN METERS	201	1032	1500	1900	2288	3697	256	366	490	560	1279	1589	2189	2621	2790	558	659	851	1058	1841	2345	4493	6076	4130	3157	3212	3400	3737	4513	4558	3806	2796	2968
STANDING CROP (PER 10 CM²)	27	71	43	37		36										148		298	150	80	100	82	56	32		400	16	1	2	7	9	20	
NUMBER COUNTED	27	71	43	37	99	36	2	6	241	67	138	195	100	207	76	74	120	149	45	40	50	41	28	16	14	29	16	1	2	7	9	5	92
PERCENTAGE CALCAREOUS	0	90	58	62	70	19	0	83	62	75	83	68	16	16	0	77	78	48	49	3	62	79	46	0	0	10	0	0	100	0	0	100	70
SIMPSON'S DIVERSITY INDEX		2.34			21.75				11.50	4.06	6.74	8.06	8.26	11.21	18.75	3.72	5.39	10.48			10.84												5.55
CONOTROCHAMMINA ALTERNANS					1									6																			
C. BULLATA		1			1				3		1	2	1			3	2	5	2	3		2	7				6				11		
C. KENNETTI															1								4				6						
C. SP. C					1																2												
CRIBROSTOMOIDES ARENACEA									4		1	4	6	1				1	2											29			
C. CONTORTUS									1			4							4			2			7	6							
C. JEFFREYSI										1	1																						
C. SPHAERILOCULUS						17								X							8	5			7	3				14			
C. SUBGLOBOSUS													1	X			1			13	2				21					29	11		
C. UMBILICATULUS SOLDANII															3											7							
C WIESNERI						3																											
CYSTAMMINA ARGENTEA																				5													
C. PAUCILOCULATA																					2												
EGGERELLA PARKERAE VAR. B						3								6						10	4				21	7	31						
GAUDRYINA MINUTA														X																			
G. PAUPERATA													1																				
GLOMOSPIRA CHAROIDES									X					1																			1
G. GORDIALIS			2										1	X																	11		
HAPLOPHRAGMOIDES CANARIENSIS			9	3					2	10	3	1	4			1		1	9	5													
H. PARKERAE						3				3	1		5	1	1			1				2			4	3							
H. QUADRATUS											1		1	25				5	7		2												
H. QUADRICAMERATA					1				11		1				1											6							
HORMOSINA GLOBULIFERA																				3													
H. LAPIDIGERA																						2											
HYPERAMMINA LAEVIGATA																																	1
H. LAEVIGATA VAR. A													1																				
H. SP. A																							4										
MARTINOTTIELLA ANTARCTICA													1	X																			
MILIAMMINA ARENACEA	11						100				1	1					3	2															
M. LATA		1																1															
"MILIOLINELLA" SP.					1																2				7								
PLACOPSILINELLA AURANTIACA						3									1											3					11		1
PORTATROCHAMMINA ANTARCTICA	89																		2	8													
P. ELTANENSIS		1	5	3	1	8			5		3	7	10	4	8	1	2	6			2	17	21	13			13						3
P. WIESNERI					1			17	5	3	1	5		X		3		1			2												
PSAMMOSPHAERA FUSCA				3																													
PSEUDOBOLIVINA ANTARCTICA		1	2	3					2		1	5	30	4		9	4	13	7	3													
REOPHAX DAVISI													1	X																			
R. DISTANS									1																								
R. LONGISCATIFORMIS														X																			
R. OVICULA				3	1				X				1	1				3	7	5	2					7							1
R. REGULARIS																																	1
R. SUBDENTALINIFORMIS										1					11	1	1	3	2	3													
R. SUBFUSIFORMIS									1	1	1		1	X	5	1		3		3		2				7	19						2
R SP. A			9											X	8										7								
R. SP. B					1										1																		
SACCAMMINA SPHAERICA			2		1	3																											
S. TUBULATA						3																2		6									1
SACCORHIZA HEDRIX				3		X																	4		X								
SPIROPLECTAMMINA BIFORMIS																																	
S. FILIFORMIS														1	1							1											
S. AFF. S. FILIFORMIS																								13									
S. SUBCYLINDRICA						3																											
TEXTULARIA WIESNERI					6				1			1	1	3	3			1		5						3	6						
T. PAUPERATA																			2														
THURAMMINA PAPILLATA													1																				
TOLYPAMMINA FRIGIDA					3					1			3	6	3		2	1					4	6									2
TRITAXIS INHAERENS						11								X	5							5				3							2
TROCHAMMINA AFF. T. COMPACTA					1																												
T. CONICA					2	3																											
T. INCONSPICUA				3	1										4					8				13		3							1
T. GRISEA				3										1			2	2	2			2			7	7							
T. INTERMEDIA																		1															
T. LABIOSA					6							2		1								2			7	7							
T. MULTICAMERATA														1	3												6						
T. QUADRILOBA														1								2											
T. SOROSA				5	1	6														3													
T. SUBCONICA															1									6		3							
T. TRICAMERATA				5															2														
VANHOFFIELLA																					2												
VERNEUILINA EUROPEUM																																	
V. MINUTA			5		1								2	X	1	1		2		3													
V. MINUTA VAR. A															1																		
UNIDENTIFIABLE NON-CALCAREOUS						6					1	1		1	4					5													

X = <0.6 PERCENT

A sample from 1030 meters appeared transitional from the upper slope faunal zone to the lower faunal zone (>1500 meters), where *Eilohedra weddellensis, G. subplanulata,* and *N. iridea* are dominant species. *Eponides tumidulus,* a cosmopolitan abyssal species, has its upper depth limit in this profile at 1500 meters. *Melonis pompilioides,* another cosmopolitan abyssal species, is present only at 2930 meters.

The upper slope faunal zone corresponds well to the upper part of the Warm Deep Layer characterized by high temperatures and low oxygen (Figure 17). Sediment texture appears to exert no control over the faunal zones.

South Georgia, Bruce, and South Sandwich Ridges

One faunal boundary at 1500 to 1600 meters is recognized in this area. From 370 or 490 meters to 1600 meters three species more persistent and abundant than all other calcareous forms in both total assemblages (Table 2) and particularly in living faunas (Table 3) are:

Eilohedra weddellensis
Epistominella exigua
Fursenkoina earlandi

Eilohedra weddellensis and *Epistominella exigua* are also significant species in abyssal assemblages. Other species are locally abundant, but are not sufficiently persistent to be of use in defining zonal assemblages.

Two species that have their upper depth limits at 1590 meters in this area and are prominent in deeper samples, more so in living faunas than in total assemblages, are:

Eponides tumidulus
Melonis cf. *M. affinis*

Important differences exist between this zonation and the one established for the slope south of South Georgia. Only the vestiges of the upper slope faunal zone characterized on the South Georgia slope by an overwhelming preponderance of five species can be recognized in this area. *Cassidulinoides parkerianus* occurs as single specimens in two samples, and *Fursenkoina fusiformis* occurs at only one station. On the other hand, *Eilohedra weddellensis* is important at much shallower depths than on the South Georgia slope.

Noncalcareous Depth Zonation

A significant faunal change occurs between depths of approximately 1500 and 2000 meters whereby a group of species dominant above 1500 meters is almost completely replaced by another group of species dominant below 2000 meters. To illustrate this, the noncalcareous species occurring in more than five samples were divided into three groups. Species in the bathyal group occur primarily above 2000 meters, whereas those in the abyssal group occur primarily below 2000 meters. The third, or nondefinitive, group is persistent or abundant both above and below 2000 meters. The relative frequencies of the three groups plotted against depth for four areas along the Scotia Ridge are shown in Figure 18. The species in each group and their occurrences are shown in Table 2.

The faunal change occurs at remarkably similar depths throughout the Scotia Ridge, except in the area west of the South Orkney Islands, where four samples from below 2000 meters have high frequencies of bathyal species. Three of these samples are from the south side of the ridge and one is from the north side. Two species, *Pseudobolivina antarctica* and *Trochammina multicamerata,* primarily account for the high frequencies of bathyal species that occur deeper than 2000 meters in this area, but other bathyal species are also present. Since the bathyal species *P. antarctica, T. multicamerata,* and *Cribrostomoides arenacea* were living in at least two of these stations (USC 537, 544) (Table 3), the depression of the bathyal faunal zone here is not caused by downslope displacement of tests.

Generalized characteristics of the depth distribution of the most abundant and persistently occurring bathyal and abyssal noncalcareous species and of five nondefinitive species are shown in Figure 19. Species pairs with similar morphology and depth distributions have been combined. These are the pairs *Miliammina arenacea–M. lata, Portatrochammina antarctica–P. wiesneri,* and *Trochammina multicamerata–T. intermedia.*

Concurrence of upper and lower depth limits and changes in relative abundance of several dominant and persistent species within two restricted depth intervals suggest that the change from bathyal to abyssal faunas is stepped rather than continuous. The first step, or depth boundary, is at 1200 to 1300 meters and the second, the most important, is at 2100 to 2300 meters. A shallower depth boundary at 260 to 560 meters corresponding to the physiographic boundary between shelf and slope is likely, as many species were observed to have their upper depth limits here, but it should be substantiated by a more detailed study of shelf faunas than is possible with available samples.

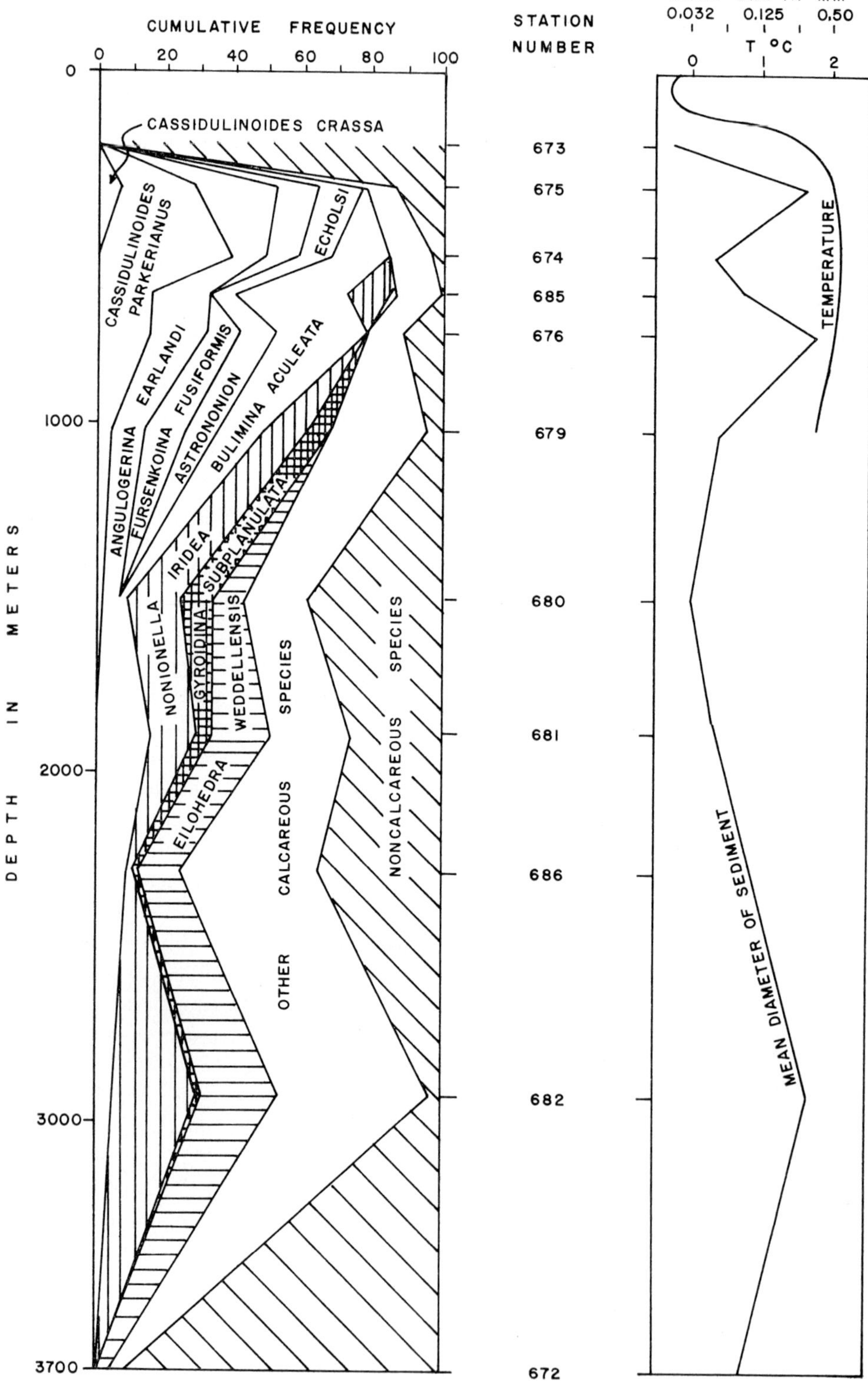

Fig. 17. Depth distribution of calcareous foraminifera on the slope south of South Georgia.

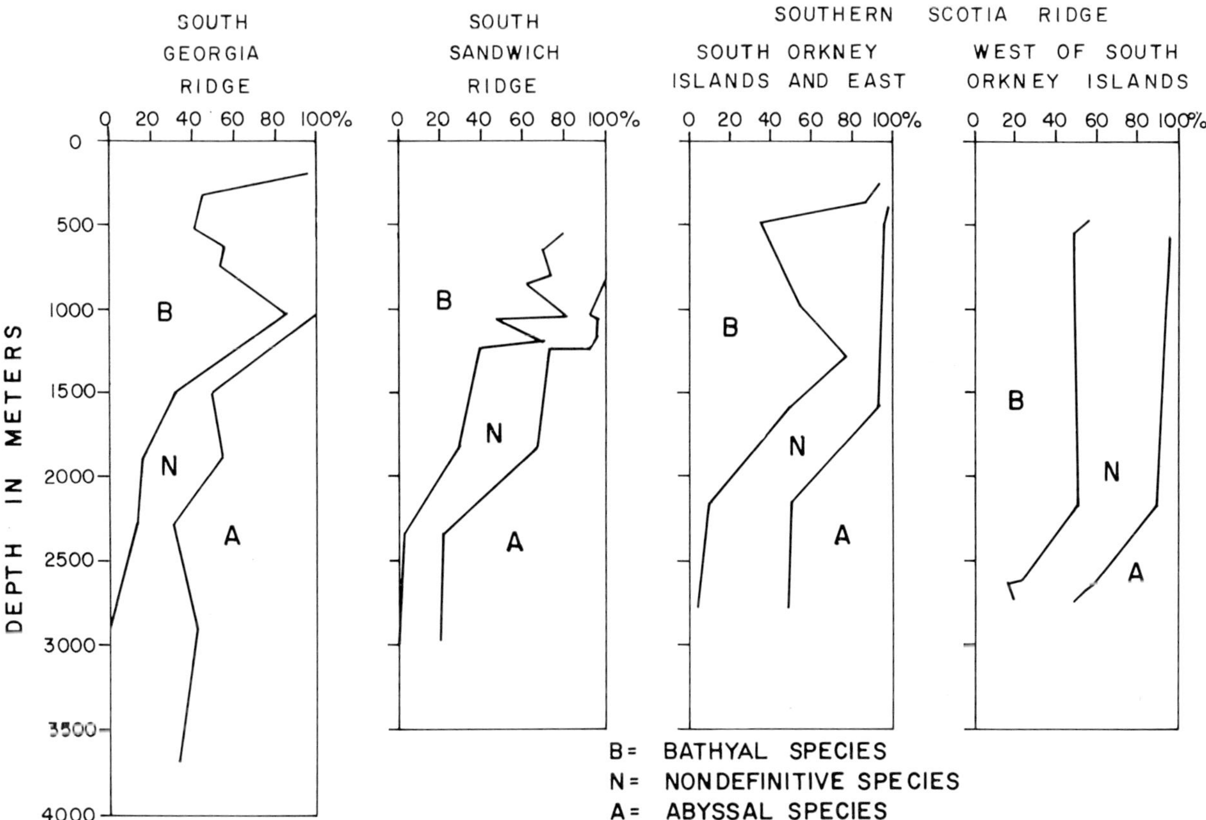

Fig. 18. Cumulative frequencies of noncalcareous, bathyal, abyssal, and nondefinitive species plotted against depth.

The boundary at 1200 to 1300 meters is marked by the highest or highest persistent occurrence of:

Cribrostomoides subglobosus
Gaudryina pauperata
Trochammina sorosa
Reophax sp. A

by the lower limit of:

Textularia earlandi

and by a downslope decrease in relative frequency of:

Ammoflintina argentea
Miliammina spp.

The boundary at 2100 to 2300 meters was recognized by the first occurrences of:

Cribrostomoides sphaeriloculus
C. umbilicatulus soldanii
Cyclammina pusilla
Martinottiella antarctica
Placopsilinella aurantiaca
Tritaxis inhaerens

by the highest persistent occurrences of:

Glomospira charoides
Psammosphaera fusca
Ammobaculites filiformis
Ammomarginulina ensis
Saccammina tubulata

by the deepest or deepest persistent occurrences of:

Miliammina arenacea
Ammoflintina argentea
Cribrostomoides arenacea
Reophax subfusiformis

Ammobaculites foliaceous undergoes a noteworthy depth-related morphologic change. This species, which has an upper depth limit in the Scotia Sea area of 490 meters, develops a concavo-convex planispire and a longitudinally folded uniserial portion (Plate 3, fig. 6) at depths below 2350 meters. This form, which has been counted separately as *A. foliaceous* f. *recurva*, was found at abyssal depths throughout the area in a wide variety of environments.

Abyssal and Trench Biofacies

Four biofacies are recognized on the abyssal basin floors, and a fifth one in the South Sandwich Trench, all of which are dominated by noncalcareous foraminif-

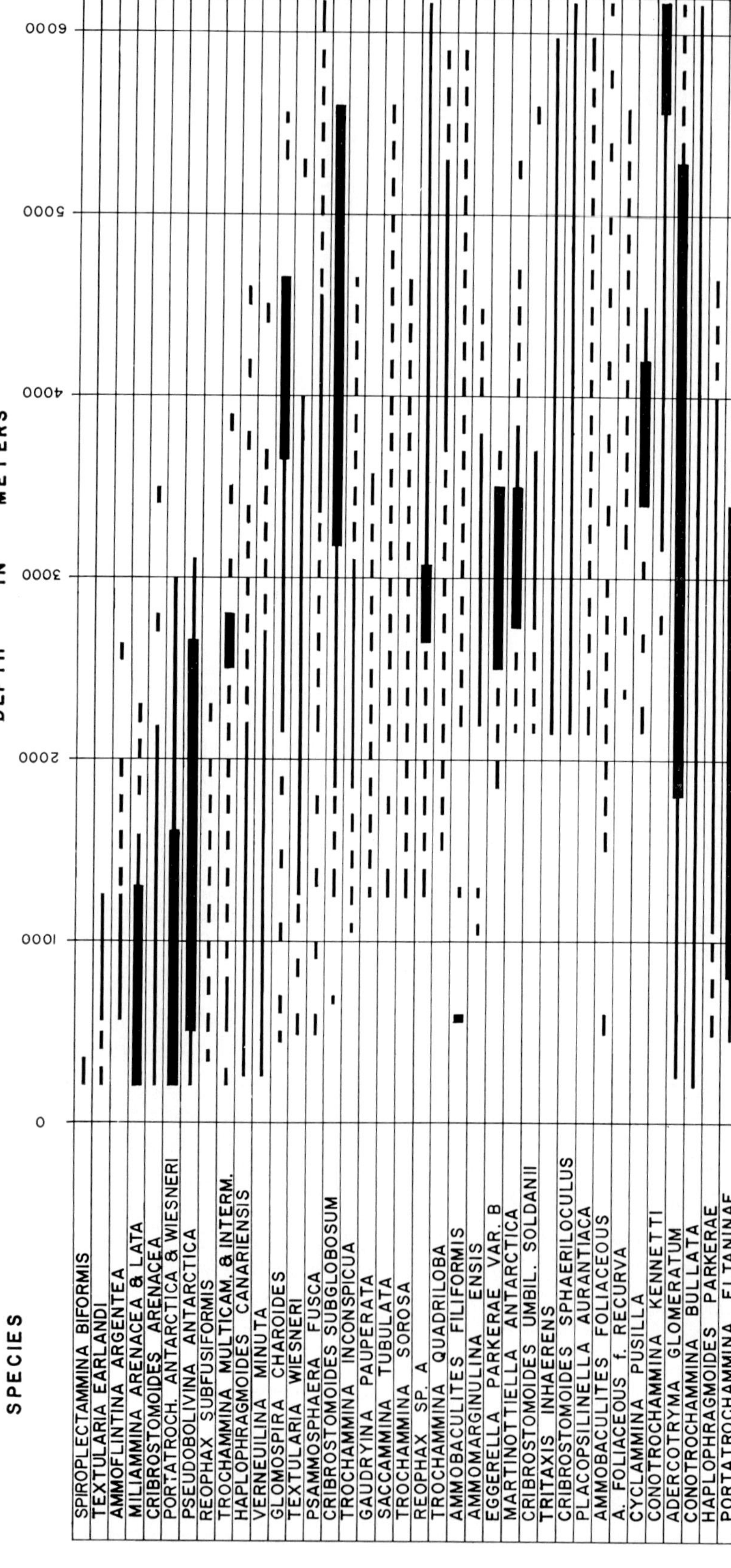

Fig. 19. Generalized depth distributions of important noncalcareous species.

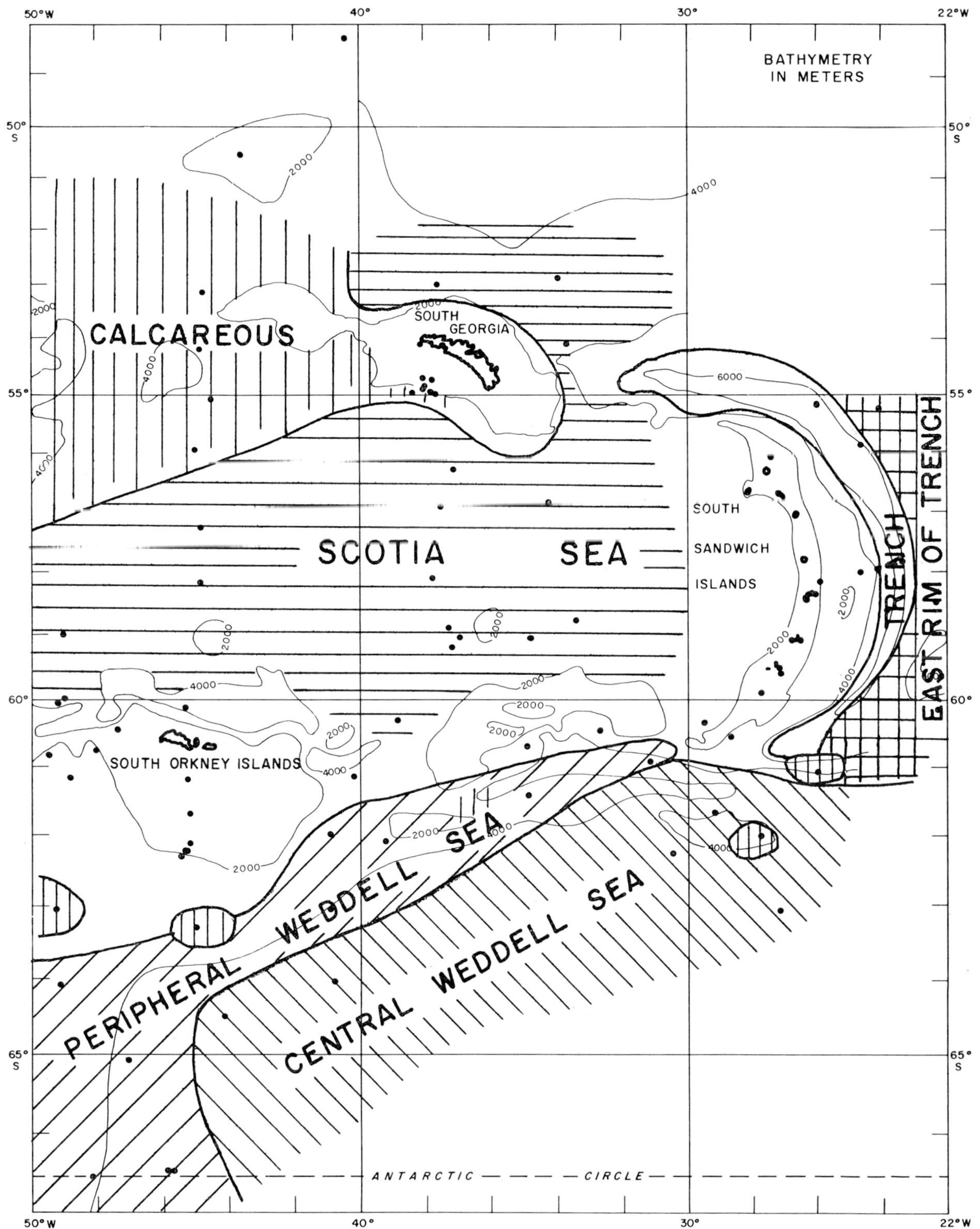

Fig. 20. Abyssal and trench biofacies.

TABLE 4. Summary of Trench and Abyssal Biotopes

	East Scotia Basin 2490–3470 meters	Peripheral Weddell Sea 3240–4200 meters	Central Weddell Sea 3740–4790 meters	Trench Rim 3980–4650 meters	Trench 5420–6170 meters 7000 meters
Dominant species	*Martinottiella antarctica* *Eggerella parkerae* var. B *Cribrostomoides umbilicatulus soldanii* *Reophax* sp. A	*Cyclammina pusilla*	*Cribrostomoides subglobosus*	*Glomospira charoides* *Adercotryma glomeratum* *Tritaxis inhaerens*	*Portatrochammina eltaninae* *Conotrochammina kennetti* *Cribrostomoides sphaeriloculus*
Rare or absent species	*Cyclammina pusilla*	*Martinottiella antarctica* *Eggerella parkerae* var. B *Cribrostomoides umbilicatulus soldanii*	*Martinottiella antarctica* *Eggerella parkerae* var. B *Cribrostomoides umbilicatulus soldanii* *Cyclammina pusilla*	*Eggerella parkerae* var. B *Cribrostomoides umbilicatulus soldanii* *Cyclammina pusilla*	Dominants of all other biotopes except *Reophax* sp. A
Benthonic foraminifera, no./g	10.3–166	3.07–29.3	less than 13	40.0–91.1	51–119 0
Simpson's diversity index	7.56–26.3	2.36–12.48	3.36–8.65	11.70–14.49	3.13–4.81
Diatoms	abundant	rare or absent	rare or absent	abundant	abundant
Sediment types	diatom ooze clayey silt sand silt clay	silty clay clay	clay	sand silt clay sand	silty clay sand silt clay

era (Figure 20). A sixth biofacies of calcareous foraminifera occurs in the northwestern Scotia Sea, the populations of which bear much in common with calcareous populations of the northern Weddell Sea that are probably relict, at least in part. The biofacies are defined by characteristic associations of abundant species which cumulatively total a large part of all the foraminifera found there. Special consideration was given those species which are restricted to certain biofacies. Table 4 lists significant faunal and environmental parameters for each of the biofacies dominated by noncalcareous foraminifera.

The faunas of the abyssal slopes of the Scotia Ridge have not been included in the above biofacies because to do so would require broadening the definitions to include either lower frequencies of diagnostic species or other associations of species. In general, the populations from the abyssal slopes are more similar to those on the adjacent basin floors than to one another; thus they do not themselves define a single biofacies. Undoubtedly additional samples in the areas of the abyssal slopes would result in the recognition of several geographic faunal units there.

East Scotia Basin Biofacies (14 Samples)

The East Scotia Basin Biofacies occurs at shallower depths (2490–3470 meters) than the other abyssal biofacies. Sediment types are diatom ooze: diatomaceous clayey silts and diatomaceous sand silt clays.

Martinottiella antarctica, *Eggerella parkerae* var. B, and *Cribrostomoides umbilicatulus soldanii* together comprise from 14 to 57 per cent of the foraminifera in all of the total populations. All three species occur with highest relative frequencies here, and *E. parkerae* var. B and *C. umbilicatulus soldanii* are restricted to this biofacies and adjacent slope populations. The relative uniformity of this biofacies is shown by the fact that of the 84 species recorded here, 17 occur in 12 or more samples. These 17 species include the three dominant species and *Adercotryma glomeratum*, *Cribrostomoides contortus*, *C. subglobosus*, *Haplophragmoides canariensis*, *H. parkerae*, *Hormosina globulifera*, *Portatrochammina eltaninae*, *Reophax* sp. A, *R. ovicula*, *Textularia wiesneri*, *Tritaxis inhaerens*, *Trochammina grisesa*, *T. inconspicua*, and *T. quadricamerata*.

TABLE 5. Occurrence of Rare Species

Agglutinated foraminifera occurring in five samples or less and calcareous foraminifera occurring in only one sample are excluded from Table 2 if they do not occur at relative frequencies greater than 2 per cent in any benthonic assemblage. These species and their occurrences are listed below.

Species	USC Station Numbers
Ammobaculoides cylindroides	712, 528
Ammoflintina trihedra	672, 604
Astrammina rara	658
Astrorhiza triangularis	672
Conotrochammina sp. A.	680, 569, 574, 1068, 503
C. sp. B.	647, 574, 604
Cribrostomoides scitulus	679
Dendrophrya erecta	652, 516
Gaudryina ferruginea	686, 506, 648, 544, 481
G. minuta	528, 649, 686
Haplophragmoides bradyi	617
H. cf. *H. kirki*	685, 676
Hemisphaerammina bradyi	500
Hippocrepina pusilla	658
Hippocrepinella crassa	712, 645
Hyperammina cylindrica	537, 647, 648, 604, 548
H. laevigata	648, 645, 604, 700, 1069
H. laevigata var. A	537, 736
H. subnodosa	460
H. tenuissima	650, 624
Jaculella cf. *J. obtusa*	648, 728, 646, 607
Marsipella cylindrica	528
Nodosinum gaussicum	574, 548, 476
Pelosina distoma	544
P. variabilis	544, 652, 638, 658
Pseudobolivina sp. A	537, 1035, 646, 544
Reophax curtus	685, 539, 676
R. regularis	682, 497, 675, 676, 504
R. turbo	652, 649, 648, 1040
Saccammina sphaerica	686, 650, 651
Spiroplectammina subcylindrica	473, 476, 693, 712, 716
Textularia paupercula	652, 651, 654, 657
Trochammina appressa	676, 504, 647
T. compacta	503
T. globigeriniformis	686
T. grisea	569
Angulogerina earlandi f. *pauperata*	528
Astrononion antarcticum	681
Buliminella tenuata	674
Dentalina cuvieri	630
D. frobisherensis	675
Discorbis translucens	1074
Ehrenbergina glabra	685
Hanzawaia complanata	1074
Heronallenia lingulata	617
H. parva	617
Keramosphaera murrayi	647
Melonis umbilicatulus	569
Quinqueloculina seminulum	685
Robertina wiesneri	654
Rupertina stabilis	500
Uvigerina bifurcata	544

Peripheral Weddell Sea Biofacies (9 Samples)

The Peripheral Weddell Sea Biofacies occurs south of the East Scotia Basin Biofacies beyond the Scotia Ridge. It is slightly deeper (3420–4200 meters) and sediments are finer, being silty clays and clays. Most significant, perhaps, diatoms are very rare in the sediments, possibly indicating lower productivity of the overlying waters and lower concentrations of dissolved silica in interstitial waters.

This biofacies is not uniform in detail, its principal unifying feature being the dominance of one species, *Cyclammina pusilla,* which comprises from 10 to 64 per cent of all assemblages and is found only in this biofacies and on slopes adjacent to this biofacies. Two other species, *Glomospira charoides* and *Cribrostomoides subglobosus,* shared dominance in some samples. Of a total of 60 species recorded from this biofacies, only six occurred in seven or more samples. These include the three above and *Adercotryma glomeratum, Ammobaculites foliaceous* f. *recurva,* and *Psammosphaera fusca.*

Central Weddell Sea Biofacies (4 Samples)

In four samples from the central Weddell Sea (and in one sample which lacked surface material), *C. pusilla* was very rare or absent. In three of these, sparse foraminiferal populations are dominated by *Cribrostomoides sphaeriloculus. Ammobaculites foliaceous* f. *recurva* and *Portatrochammina eltaninae* are also found in all three samples. Only a few foraminiferal specimens were found in the fourth sample and in the core without surface material.

The Central Weddell Sea Biofacies is related faunally and environmentally to the Peripheral Weddell Sea Biotope, the only important faunal difference being the absence of *Cyclammina pusilla* in the former. Its depth range (3740–4790 meters) overlaps that of the Peripheral Weddell Sea Biofacies, and in both the sediments are clays with very few diatoms.

Trench Rim Biofacies (3 Samples)

In three samples east of the South Sandwich Trench diatoms are abundant in the sediments, as they are in the East Scotia Basin Biofacies. There is, however, a 500-meter difference between the shallowest of these samples and the deepest of the East Scotia Basin Biofacies. Its depth range (3980–4650 meters) is more similar to that of the Central Weddell Sea Biofacies. Unlike the other three abyssal biofacies, much of the silt and sand consists of angular, vesicular volcanic debris, which could be unsuitable material for test construction of some agglutinated species. Sediments are sand silt clays.

TABLE 6. Station Locations and Sampling Data

Station	Position	Sampling Depth Range, meters	Sampling Gear*	Sample Interval,† cm	Preservative§
460	53°06'S, 44°48'W	2050	C/MT	0–5	alc
	53°06'S, 44°44'W	2159			
462	54°06'S, 45°04'W	3404	MT		fml
	54°09'S, 44°50'W	3404			
467	55°03'S, 44°38'W	3742	C/MT	0–5	alc
	55°02'S, 44°27'W	3596			
473	55°56'S, 45°07'W	3614	C/MT	0–5	alc
	55°56'S, 44°56'W	3614			
476	57°11'S, 44°53'W	3382	C/MT	0–5	alc
	57°14'S, 44°47'W				
481	58°05'S, 44°56'W	2800	C/MT	0–5	alc
	58°10'S, 44°47'W				
486	60°07'S, 45°14'W	5289	C/MT	0–5	alc
	60°06'S, 45°24'W				
497	61°10'S, 45°13'W	256	SC	0–2	alc
	61°10'S, 45°13'W				
498	61°40'S, 45°09'W	366	PG		alc
	61°42'S, 45°09'W				
500	62°06'S, 45°12'W	489	PG		alc
	62°07'S, 45°13'W	490			alc
502	62°14'S, 45°19'W	1250	PG		alc
	62°14'S, 45°20'W	1308			
503	62°14'S, 45°20'W	897	PG		alc
	62°14'S, 45°19'W	1089			
504	62°14'S, 45°20'W	1519	PG		alc
	62°14'S, 45°22'W	1556			
506	62°16'S, 45°25'W	2160	PG		alc
	62°17'S, 45°26'W				
513	63°15'S, 44°56'W	3784	C/MT	0–5	alc
	63°18'S, 44°53'W				
516	66°28'S, 45°42'W	4196	C/MT	0–5	alc
	66°26'S, 45°44'W			40–45	
517	66°26'S, 45°45'W	4196	PG		alc
	66°23'S, 45°49'W				
520	66°33'S, 48°11'W	3722	C/MT	0–5	alc
	66°29'S, 48°10'W				
524	64°05'S, 49°04'W	3404	C/MT	0–5	alc
	64°06'S, 49°13'W	3440			
528	63°03'S, 49°09'W	2998	PG		alc
	63°03'S, 49°10'W	2937			
533	61°09'S, 48°50'W	2754	C/MT	0–5	alc
	61°09'S, 48°46'W	2752			
537	60°47'S, 48°02'W	2187	PG		alc
	60°45'S, 47°58'W				
539	60°25'S, 47°23'W	551	PG		alc
	60°25'S, 47°22'W	569			
544	60°02'S, 40°10'W	2621	PG		alc
	60°02'S, 49°13'W				
548	59°01'S, 49°00'W	3847	C/MT	0–5	alc
	58°58'S, 49°04'W	3861			
562	48°13'S, 40°26'W	5587	DC	0–2	alc
	48°15'S, 40°24'W				
569	56°04'S, 27°28'W	1043	DC		alc
	56°04'S, 27°26'W				
574	55°11'S, 24°10'W	4008	C/MT	0–5	alc
	55°13'S, 24°05'W	3978			

TABLE 6. (continued)

Station	Position	Sampling Depth Range, meters	Sampling Gear*	Sample Interval,† cm	Preservative§
590	55°07'S, 26°01'W	ca.	C/MT	0–5	alc
	55°07'S, 25°59'W	7690			
595	55°52'S, 24°52'W	5847	C/MT	0–5	alc
	55°51'S, 24°48'W	5710			
604	58°27'S, 22°22'W	4645	C/MT	0–3	alc
	58°26'S, 22°20'W	4802			
607	60°05'S, 22°24'W	4187	C/MT	0–5	alc
	60°07'S, 22°17'W	4193			
614	61°05'S, 26°02'W	3770	C/MT	0–5	alc
	61°05'S, 26°03'W				
617	61°59'S, 27°40'W	3038	C/MT		alc
	62°00'S, 27°40'W	3349			
618	63°03'S, 27°10'W	4548	DC	0–2	alc
	63°02'S, 27°07'W	4557			
622	61°39'S, 29°15'W	3737	C/MT		alc
	61°42'S, 20°10'W				
624	60°21'S, 29°30'W	2330	C/MT	0–5	alc
	60°22'S, 29°30'W	2360			
630	59°53'S, 27°42'W	1244	C/MT	PB	alc
	59°52'S, 27°44'W				
638	58°35'S, 23°51'W	5417	C/MT	0–5	alc
	58°34'S, 23°55'W	5673			
645	57°54'S, 23°49'W	6167	DC	0–2	fml
	57°47'S, 23°47'W				
646	57°52'S, 24°00'W	6076	DC	0–2	fml
	57°52'S, 23°56'W				
647	57°55'S, 24°06'W	4493	DC	0–2	fml
	57°57'S, 24°18'W				
648	58°03'S, 24°46'W	2976	DC	0	fml
	58°04'S, 24°47'W				
649	58°17'S, 25°54'W	1841	DC	0–2	fml
	58°18'S, 26°02'W				
650	58°19'S, 26°06'W	1244	DC	0–2	fml
	58°20'S, 26°09'W				
651	58°20'S, 26°09'W	851	DC	0–2	fml
	58°20'S, 26°12'W				
652	58°20'S, 26°17'W	558	DC	0–2	fml
	58°20'S, 26°18'W				
654	57°56'S, 27°33'W	812	DC	0–2	fml
PC	57°51'S, 27°35'W				
657	59°33'S, 27°12'W	1171	C/MT	0–5	fml
	59°34'S, 27°11'W	1226			
658	59°05'S, 26°39'W	659	DC	0–2	fml
	59°05'S, 26°39'W				
659	59°05'S, 26°38'W	805	PG		alc
	59°05'S, 26°38'W				
662	50°32'S, 43°32'W	1272	C/MT	0–5	fml
	50°35'S, 43°35'W	1281			
672	54°57'S, 38°22'W	3697	DC	0–2	fml
	54°57'S, 38°21'W				
673	54°07'S, 38°09'W	201	DC	0–2	fml
	54°07'S, 38°09'W				
674	54°44'S, 38°04'W	531	DC	PB	alc
675	55°44'S, 38°04'W	329	DC	PB	alc
676	54°47'S, 38°01'W	ca. 750	DC	PB	alc
679	54°54'S, 37°06'W	ca.1032	DC	0–5	fml

TABLE 6. (continued)

Station	Position	Sampling Depth Range, meters	Sampling Gear*	Sample Interval,† cm	Preservative§
680	54°58′S, 37°59′W	1510	DC	0–2	fml
681	55°01′S, 38°00′W	1900	DC	0–5	fml
	55°03′S, 38°01′W				
682	55°03′S, 38°02′W	2924	DC	PB	alc
	55°03′S, 38°03′W				
685	54°55′S, 38°05′W	595	C/MT	0–5	fml
	54°55′S, 38°07′W	677			
686	54°59′S, 38°13′W	2196	M/T		fml
	55°04′S, 38°07′W	2379			
689	56°15′S, 37°03′W	3468	C/MT	0–5	fml
	56°17′S, 37°03′W				
693	56°53′S, 37°31′W	3138	C/MT	0–5	none
	56°54′S, 37°32′W				
700	58°04′S, 37°50′W	3166	C/MT	0–5	fml
	58°05′S, 37°44′W	3255			
705	58°51′S, 37°19′W	2928	C/MT	0–5	fml
	58°53′S, 37°17′W	2946			
708	59°11′S, 37°13′W	2818	C/MT	0–5	fml
	59°09′S, 37°04′W	2827			
712	58°43′S, 33°20′W	2983	C/MT	0–5	fml
	58°43′S, 33°23′W	3331			
716	56°51′S, 34°25′W	3144	C/MT	0–5	fml
	56°50′S, 34°09′W	3197			
725	54°05′S, 33°43′W	2714	C/MT	0–5	fml
	54°04′S, 33°37′W	2727			
728	52°53′S, 33°59′W	2855	C/MT	0–5	none
	52°53′S, 33°56′W	2873			
736	53°02′S, 37°40′W	3056	C/MT	0–5	fml
	53°02′S, 37°38′W	3102			
1012	65°03′S, 47°04′W	4182	HC	0–2	
1016	64°30′S, 44°06′W	4513	HC	PB	fml
1017	64°01′S, 40°44′W	4542	HC	0–2	fml
1021	63°02′S, 40°55′W	4110	HC	0–2	fml
1024	61°58′S, 40°54′W	3484	HC	0–2	fml
1028	61°08′S, 40°11′W	3880	HC	0–2	fml
1031	60°19′S, 38°50′W	3508	HC	0–2	fml
1035	60°42′S, 34°55′W	2679	C/MT	0–2	fml
	60°39′S, 34°53′W	2901			
1040	60°34′S, 28°37′W	3206	HC	0–2	fml
1045	62°15′S, 30°29′W	4787	HC	0–2	fml
1046	60°54′S, 31°08′W	3806	HC	0–2	fml
	60°52′S, 31°06′W				
1060	60°25′S, 32°46′W	3642	HC	0–2	fml
	60°26′S, 32°44′W				
1062	61°42′S, 34°58′W	3644	HC	0–2	fml
				33–35	
1068	59°01′S, 34°00′W	3400	HC	0–2	fml
1069	59°01′S, 37°09′W	2485	HC	0–2	fml
1074	62°05′S, 39°15′W	2796	HC	0–2	fml
1087	60°49′S, 49°25′W	2644	HC	0–2	fml
Samples Examined Only for Specimens Larger than 0.5 mm in Diameter					
459	53°06′S, 44°48′W	2050	MT		fml
	53°06′S, 44°44′W	2159			
462	54°06′S, 45°04′W	3404	MT		fml
	54°09′S, 44°50′W	3404			
472	55°56′S, 45°07′W	3742	MT		fml
	55°56′S, 44°56′W	3614			
475	57°11′S, 44°53′W	3382	MT		fml
	57°14′S, 44°47′W				
480	58°06′S, 44°56′W	2800	MT		fml
	58°10′S, 44°47′W				
488	60°60′S, 45°26′W	4721	PG		fml
	60°03′S, 45°25′W	5280			
505	62°14′S, 45°22′W	1656	PG		alc
	62°15′S, 45°23′W	1674			
543	60°01′S, 49°04′W	2906	C/MT		alc
	60°02′S, 49°09′W	2946			
573	55°11′S, 24°10′W	3978	MT		fml
	55°13′S, 24°05′W	4008			
603	58°27′S, 22°22′W	4643	MT		fml
	58°26′S, 22°20′W	4645			
606	60°05′S, 22°24′W	4118	MT		fml
	60°07′S, 22°17′W	4141			

* Sampling gear: DC, twin gravity cores suspended from spreader bar; C/MT, gravity core attached to Menzies trawl bridle; SC, gravity core; MT, mud sample retained in Menzies trawl; PG, Petersen grab; HC, core attached to end of line during hydrographic casts; BT, mud sample retained in Blake trawl.

† Sample interval: PB, sample in plastic bag; length of core segment uncertain.

§ Preservative: alc, alcohol; fml, buffered formalin.

Although these three samples are separated from one another by 5° of latitude, they have remarkably similar foraminiferal populations. The uniformity of this biofacies is shown by the fact that 23 species are common to all three samples. The dominant species, *Glomospira charoides, Tritaxis inhaerens,* and *Adercotryma glomeratum,* together comprise 37, 44, and 52 per cent of the forminifera in the three samples.

Trench Biofacies (4 Samples)

Three samples from the upper levels of the South Sandwich Trench (5420–6170 meters) contain unique foraminiferal populations. A number of species that occur persistently both on the west slope of the trench and on the eastern trench rim are absent within the trench; and a few species that occur elsewhere reach very high frequencies there. In upper trench samples, foraminiferal numbers are as high as those in the Trench Rim and Scotia Sea Biofacies; but the deepest trench sample (7690 meters) is barren of foraminifera

(Table 4). As previously noted, diversity is very low.

In Table 2, relative frequencies of species in the South Sandwich Trench Biofacies may be compared with those on the slope of the South Sandwich Ridge and with those of the Trench Rim Biofacies. *Portatrochammina eltaninae* comprises more than 30 per cent of the foraminifera in all three trench samples that contain foraminifera, and *Conotrochammina kennetti* comprises more than 20 per cent of the foraminifera in two of them. Except in the trench, these two species have very different distributions. *P. eltaninae* occurs in almost every sample below 490 meters, but *C. kennetti* occurs in waters no shallower than 2720 meters.

The uniqueness of the trench populations is shown just as clearly by the species that do not occur there. Two species which are abundant and persistent in the abyssal samples on both sides of the trench are *Glomospira charoides* (5 to 25 per cent) and *Tritaxis inhaerens* (8 to 18 per cent). Except for a single specimen of *G. charoides,* they are both absent from the trench. *Martinottiella antarctica* and *Haplophragmoides parkerae,* which are present in all abyssal samples immediately around the trench, though not as abundantly as the former two species, are also absent from the trench.

Another unusual feature is the absence from any of the trench samples of specimens large enough to be retained on a 0.5-mm screen. Moreover, no foraminifera are present in trench Menzies trawls (USC 589, USC 636, USC 637) taken with a 0.5-mm net. In contrast, three Menzies trawls (USC 573, USC 603, USC 606) from the eastern rim of the trench contained many foraminifera. Large foraminiferal specimens were specifically noted in the Peru-Chile Trench [*Bandy and Rodolfo,* 1964] and the Kuril Trench [*Shchedrina,* 1958].

The shallowest sample (5420 meters) of the Trench Biofacies is from below the sill depth, as shown by the fact that the 5000-meter contour closes around the trench, whereas the 4000-meter contour does not (Figure 2). Inspection of hydrographic data from four *Eltanin* stations from the trench reveals that the temperature rises adiabatically deeper than about 4500 meters, and at 6000 meters it is about 0.1°C higher than the minimum value recorded in the trench. Other hydrographic properties, including oxygen, do not differ significantly from their values at sill depth. Texturally, two of the samples are silty clays, but the other two are sand silt clays which are similar to textures on the slope of the South Sandwich Ridge and on the eastern rim of the trench. Both diatoms and radiolarians are abundant in trench sediments.

Abyssal Calcareous Biofacies

Including the calcareous populations from the South Georgia Ridge, the probable relict populations in the northern Weddell Sea, and the one subsurface calcareous population in core USC 516, there are only 12 abyssal samples (> 2000 meters) from the area in which calcareous foraminifera constituted more than 30 per cent of the total benthonics. Although species vary greatly in relative frequency from one calcareous assemblage to another, most of the populations have much in common. For example, *Eilohedra weddellensis* and *Epistominella exigua* were found in all of them. These two species are characteristic of abyssal calcareous populations from other parts of the Antarctic as well [*Uchio,* 1960*b; McKnight,* 1962; *Pflum,* 1966]. *Nuttallides umbonifera* occurs in all but two of them. This species was reported from the Scotia Sea area by *Earland* [1934] and has also been reported from the North Atlantic [*Phleger et al.,* 1953]; however, it has not been reported in previous quantitative studies in the Antarctic.

Dominant abyssal calcareous species, followed by the number of samples in which they constituted more than 10 per cent of the total, are:

Eilohedra weddellensis	9	*Cassidulina subglobosa*	1
Nuttallides umbonifera	7	*Epistominella ? arctica*	1
Epistominella exigua	5	*Oridorsalis tenera*	1
Nonionella iridea	3	*Stainforthia complanta*	1
Islandiella quadrata	2		

Assemblages dominated by *N. umbonifera* are found only at abyssal depths (below 2000 meters), whereas *E. weddellensis, E. exigua,* and *N. iridea* are important elements in the bathyal assemblages as well. Abundant specimens of *N. iridea* were noted in the northern calcareous province, but not in Weddell Sea samples.

DISCUSSION

Calcareous Test Distributions

The southward decrease in abundance of planktonic and calcareous benthonic tests to very low concentrations in the southern and eastern part of the Scotia Sea area is one of the most conspicuous aspects of foraminiferal distributions in the Scotia Sea area. Low concentrations of calcareous tests in the south and east are not caused by high detrital sedimentation rates, because noncalcareous tests are present in these same sediments in concentrations as high or higher than in those of the South Georgia Ridge.

South of the South Orkney Ridge and Bruce Ridge in the Weddell Sea and east of the South Sandwich

Ridge low concentrations of calcareous tests are expected as a result of test dissolution, because water depths in these areas exceed 4000 meters and thus approach the carbonate compensation depth of other areas. The carbonate compensation depth a short distance north of the Antarctic Convergence is more than 4000 meters [*Hough*, 1956], about the same as in the tropical and temperate Pacific Ocean, where it is between 4000 and 4500 meters [*Bramlette*, 1961]. It has been shown here, however, that test dissolution is probably also a contributing factor to low concentrations of calcareous benthonic tests at much lesser depths in the Scotia Sea and on the South Orkney, Bruce, and South Sandwich ridges, and, therefore, the carbonate compensation depth could occur at an exceptionally shallow depth in the southern and eastern Scotia Sea. In this regard the Scotia Sea area may be similar to the Ross Sea area, where virtually complete solution of calcareous tests occurs below 500 meters [*Kennett*, 1966] and apparently dissimilar to other areas around the Antarctic Continent, where dominantly calcareous populations persist to depths greater than 2000 meters [*Uchio*, 1960*b*; *Pflum*, 1966].

A recent field experiment in the tropical Pacific [*Peterson*, 1966] indicates that the carbonate compensation depth is approximately determined by a level below which the observed rate of solution of artificially suspended calcium carbonate samples increases markedly. This level, termed the lysocline [*Berger*, 1968], was postulated by *Berger* [1967] on the basis of *Kennett*'s [1966] observations in the Ross Sea to rise to very shallow levels in antarctic waters. A rise in the level of the lysocline to the south from greater than 3000 meters on the South Georgia Ridge to at least as shallow as 500 meters on the South Orkney, Bruce, and South Sandwich ridges could explain the higher proportions of calcareous benthonic and planktonic tests and the much lower apparent carbonate solution rates on the northern than the southern and eastern Scotia Ridge.

Another factor that could influence the distribution of concentrations of calcareous tests and of the evidence for solution of calcareous tests is their production rate. Semisaturation of bottom and interstitial waters with the products of solution of calcareous tests could stop or slow down further solution of calcareous tests. Benthonic calcareous tests may survive in sediments when their environment is semisaturated with the products of solution of abundant planktonic tests. Empty calcareous benthonic tests may undergo dissolution, resulting in high live-total ratios for calcareous benthonic populations when there are few planktonic tests in the same sediment because of low production rates. Semisaturated bottom layers protecting calcareous tests from solution have been postulated by *Phleger et al.* [1953] and by *Berger* [1967].

Planktonic tests, which are much more abundant than benthonic tests on the South Georgia Ridge, except in some areas of relatively shallow water, and which form a principal component of calcareous oozes near and north of the position of the Antarctic Convergence [*Blair*, 1965], are present in abundance in the southern and eastern parts of the Scotia Sea area only as possibly relict accumulations. Data are inadequate to speculate on their relative rate of production in the Scotia Sea area. Kennett, studying planktonic foraminifera in sediments southeast of New Zealand, postulates that low production south of the Antarctic Convergence is a principal factor causing low concentrations of planktonic tests in the underlying bottom sediments.

Comparison with Other Depth Zonations

Comparison of the depth zonations proposed here with those proposed by previous workers indicates considerable agreement as well as some differences. *Uchio* [1960*b*] and *Saidova* [1961] described bathyal faunas that were dominantly calcareous, and thus their zonations can be compared with those recognized on the southern slope of South Georgia. The faunal boundary transitional over the interval >750 to <1500 meters on the South Georgia slope appears comparable to one at 850 meters recognized by Uchio and one transitional over the interval 500 to 1000 meters identified by Saidova. Among the species considered typical of the upper zone by Saidova were *Cassidulinoides parkerianus*, *Angulogerina angulosa* (=*A. earlandi*), and *Astrononion* sp. (=*Astrononion echolsi?*), three of the dominant species in assemblages from above 750 meters around South Georgia. Uchio also considered *A. earlandi* characteristic of upper bathyal assemblages. In addition, Uchio considered *Eponides weddellensis* (=*Eilohedra weddellensis*) characteristic of assemblages deeper than 850 meters, whereas it is characteristic of samples below 1500 meters on the South Georgia slope. Both Uchio and Saidova found *Bulimina aculeata* more characteristic of depths greater than 850 or 1000 meters, and thus deeper than the greatest frequencies of this species recorded here.

The zonation of noncalcareous foraminifera proposed here is very similar to that proposed by *Kennett* [1968] for the Ross Sea. Because of a shallow depth of carbonate compensation in the Ross Sea—only 500 meters—the deeper faunal boundaries in Kennett's zonation are based on noncalcareous foraminifera also. Kennett recognized boundaries at 1300 and 2200 meters that correspond to boundaries in the Scotia and Weddell seas at 1200 to 1300 meters and 2100 to 2300 meters. Furthermore, *Cribrostomoides subglobosus, Ammomarginulina ensis, Miliammina arenacea,* and *Reophax subfusiformis* typify the same depth zones in the Ross Sea as in the Scotia and Weddell seas.

Water Masses and Benthonic Foraminifera Assemblages

Uchio [1960*b*] associated benthonic foraminiferal assemblages with the stratified antarctic water masses in the following manner:

Assemblage	Depth, m	Water Masses
1	350–850	surface water and circumpolar water
2	850–2000	lower circumpolar water
3	>2000	bottom water

Circumpolar water is synonymous with the Warm Deep Layer. The contrasting zonations of calcareous foraminifera on the South Georgia slopes and on the slopes of the South Orkney, Bruce, and South Sandwich ridges are associated with contrasting water masses in a way that may support Uchio's hypothesis.

Water masses are recognized by characteristic temperatures and salinities as established by *T-S* curves [cf. *Sverdrup et al.*, 1942]. Comparison of potential temperature and salinity relationships of water immediately south of the Antarctic Convergence to water in the northern Weddell Sea (Figure 21) emphasizes the differences between the two areas. The Warm Deep Layer on the upper slope south of South Georgia has properties similar to those found in this water mass just south of the Antarctic Convergence. Along the southern and eastern Scotia Ridge, the water at similar levels is far different, having been modified by mixing with Antarctic Bottom Water and Weddell Sea shelf water. A temperature maximum in the upper part of the layer and a salinity maximum in the lower part may be identified in both areas. However, the maximum temperature is about 1.6°C warmer south of South Georgia than along the southern Scotia Ridge, and the salinity maximum south of South Georgia lies at 1400 to 1500 meters, whereas it is at only 600 meters in the northern Weddell Sea. By extrapolation from the nearest complete deep hydrographic station, the water at 2000 meters south of South Georgia has salinity and potential temperature characteristics similar to water at 1000 meters in the Weddell Sea (Figure 21).

If water mass is an important factor affecting the distribution of benthonic foraminifera, then assemblages south of South Georgia should differ from those along the southern and eastern Scotia Ridge, whereas those features of bathyal foraminiferal assemblages shared by the northern and southern limbs of the ridge should occur deeper in the north. Calcareous benthonic assemblages show exactly this relationship. The five species characteristic of the upper bathyal faunal zone of the South Georgia slope are not significant species on the southern and eastern slopes of the ridge. On the other hand, *Eilohedra weddellensis,* a characteristic upper bathyal species on the southern and eastern slopes, is abundant only in the lower bathyal and abyssal zones of South Georgia. The upper bathyal zone of South Georgia is associated with the temperature maximum stratum of the Warm Deep Layer, which is not well defined on the southern and eastern slopes of the ridge.

Environmentally Restricted Abyssal Species

Each noncalcareous abyssal biotope has a relatively uniform environment that differs from that of the other biotopes. Environmental factors that differ between biotopes are diatom content of the sediments, character of the sediment particles (volcanic or terrigenous), sediment texture, and depth. Undoubtedly there are other factors, not considered in this investigation, which are equally or more important in influencing the distributions of abyssal species. Nevertheless, these three factors, operating in one or more ways, appear to have an important role. Four of the eleven abundant abyssal species have restricted geographic ranges clearly illustrating the effect of these environmental factors.

Martinottiella antarctica occurs in every sample of diatomaceous sediment below 2000 meters, except for those from the South Sandwich Trench below 5000 meters, two stations from the northern part of the area dominated by calcareous foraminifera, and two others on the southern Scotia Ridge. Other than a few specimens at a single station (USC 1062), it did not occur in nondiatomaceous sediments.

Eggerella parkerae var. B is second only to *M. antarctica* in characterizing diatomaceous abyssal sediments. Although it was absent in all samples dominated by calcareous foraminifera, it occurs in all other samples of diatomaceous sediments between 2000 meters and 3500 meters, except one of those from the southern Scotia Ridge, which also lacks *M. antarctica.* It does not occur in nondiatomaceous sediments. This species does not appear to tolerate greater depths

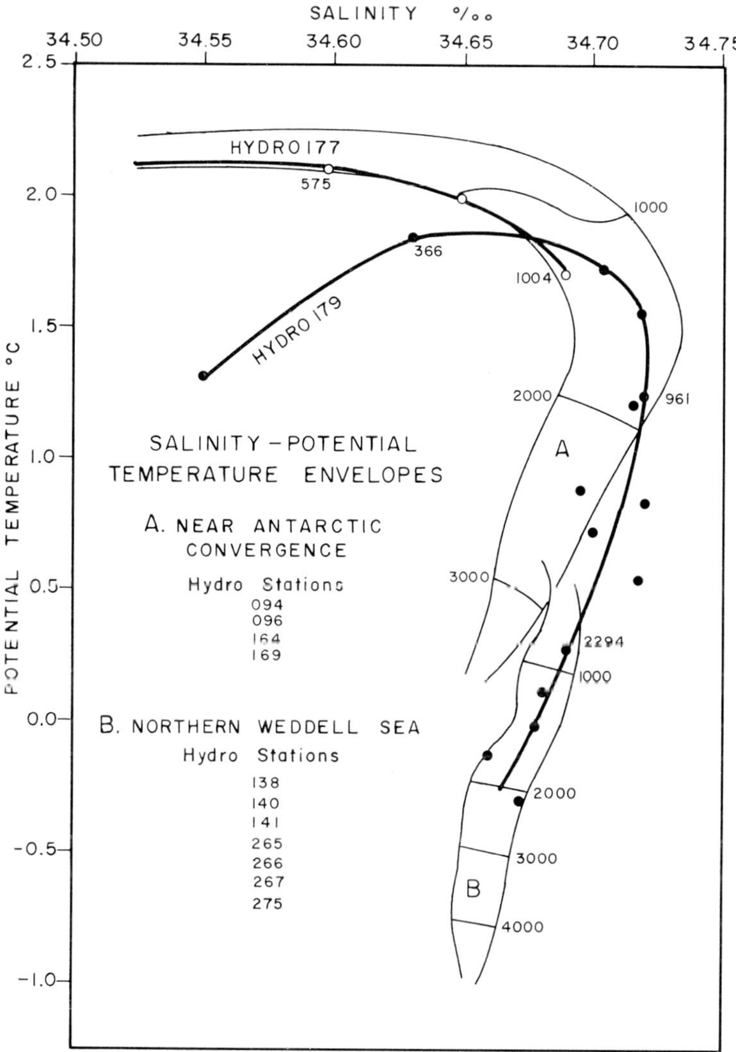

Fig. 21. Salinity-potential temperature curves south of South Georgia (hydro 177 and hydro 179) compared with curves near the Antarctic Convergence and in the Weddell Sea. Numbers are depths in meters.

(Figure 19), which may explain its absence from the Trench Rim Biotope.

Cribrostomoides umbilicatulus soldanii is restricted to diatomaceous sediments almost as completely as the former two. A second factor, however, seems to limit this species' distribution, as it was not found in sediments of volcanic composition, except for a few specimens at one station (USC 1040). Since this species constructs its test of mineral grains relatively large compared with its total size, the angular vesicular volcanic particles are possibly unacceptable building materials.

Cyclammina pusilla, in contrast to the above three species, is exceedingly abundant in some sediments with few or no diatoms, and totally absent in samples with abundant diatoms. It did not occur far from the slopes of the Antarctic Peninsula and the Scotia Ridge, however, being absent in those samples from the central and eastern Weddell Sea, although sediment type and depth appear favorable.

Earland [1933, 1934, 1936] recorded 40 occurrences of *M. antarctica* (as *Clavulina communis* d'Orbigny) and 23 occurrences of *Cyclammina pusilla* from 10°W to 90°W in antarctic waters. His records confirm the distributions of these species in the Scotia and northern Weddell seas as determined by the author and provide additional occurrences of the species south, east, and west of the borders of this study (Figure 22). He noted the abundance of diatoms in samples from which he obtained foraminifera, and, in addition, the sediments of the same samples studied by *Earland* [1936] were described by *Pirie* [1913] who estimated the abundance of diatoms in each sample. As Earland did not describe *Trochammina soldani* (=*Cribrostomoides umbilicatulus soldanii*) until his last report, nor recognize *E. parkerae* var. B as distinct from *Eggerella bradyi,* his records cannot be used to study further the distributions of these two species.

Figure 22 shows that *M. antarctica* and *C. pusilla* are associated around the perimeter of the Antarctic Continent but occur separately in the greater part of the Scotia and Weddell seas. *C. pusilla* occurs along the southern, western, and northern margins, but not in the interior of the Weddell Sea. Those samples containing both species appear to have at least two factors in common: proximity to land and a moderate quantity of diatoms. For example, diatoms are 1 and 2 per cent of the total sediment [*Pirie,* 1913] in those samples from the southeastern Weddell Sea (WS 406, 417, 418) in which both species occur. These percentages of diatoms are higher than for most other Wed-

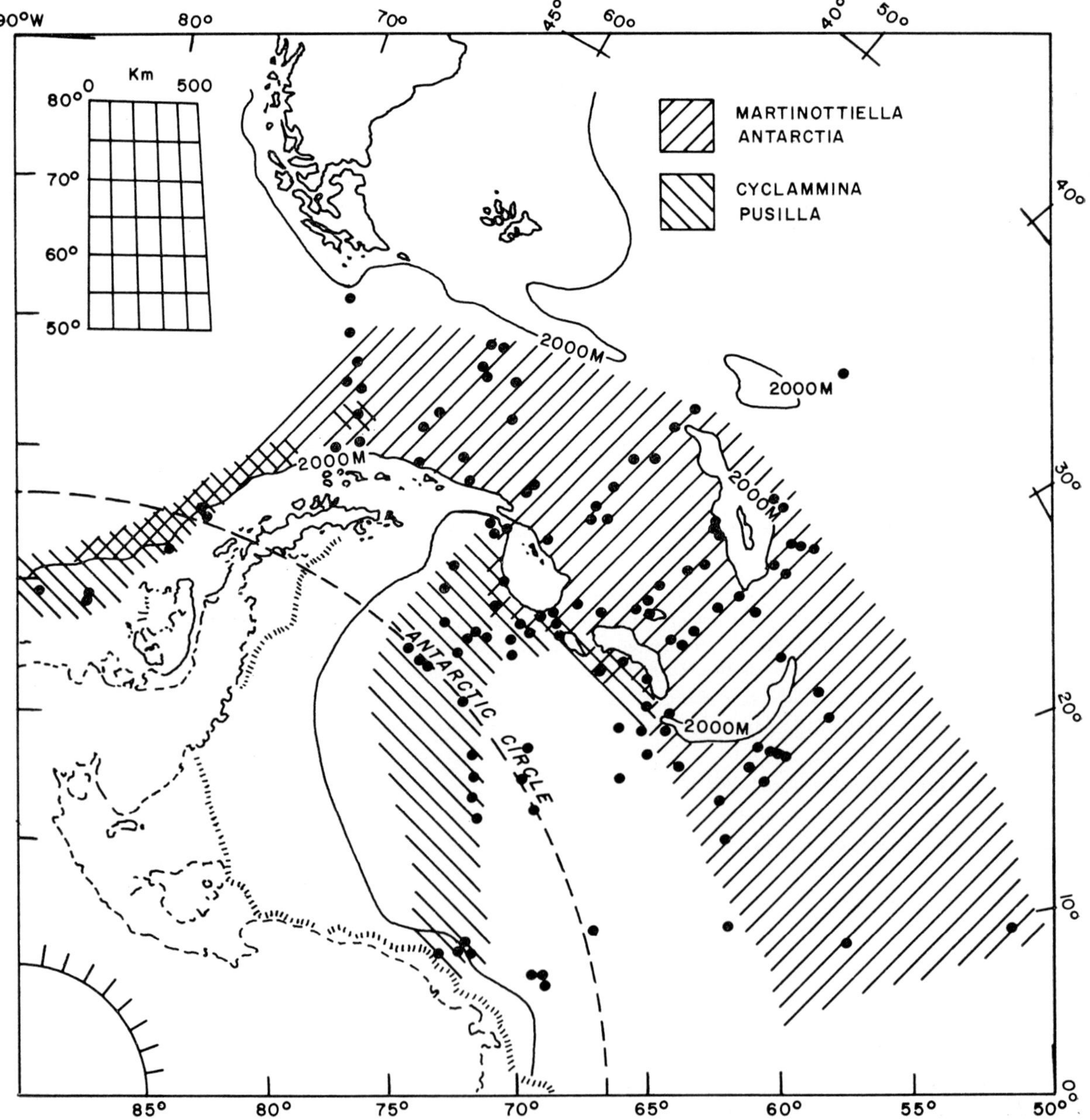

Fig. 22. Distributions of *Martinottiella antarctica* and *Cyclammina pusilla* from 10°W to 90°W in antarctic waters.

dell Sea sediments. Further, Earland notes diatoms in one of the three samples west of the Antarctic Peninsula, which also contained both species (WS 495, 502, 517).

If the distinctive wall type of *M. antarctica*, as well as of *Eggerella parkerae* var. B and *Spirolocammina tenuis* which are also confined to diatomaceous sediments, is symptomatic of a siliceous cement, as previously postulated, and if these species are unable to use dissolved silica in very low concentrations to form their walls, then the distribution of diatoms in bottom sediments may control their distributions. *Siever et al.* [1965] have shown that concentrations of dissolved silica are higher in interstitial waters than in sea water and that the dominant control on dissolved silica is the abundance and rate of dissolution of diatom frustules in sediment. Although the minimum amount of solid silica, in the form of diatoms, required to saturate the solution is very small, measured concentrations of dissolved silica in interstitial waters are nevertheless often below saturation, suggesting involved controls on the rate of dissolution. These authors, however, do report examples of low concentrations of dissolved silica in cores from northwest of Bermuda that may be explained by a paucity of diatoms. Because diatoms are very rare in Weddell Sea sediments, low concentrations of dissolved silica in interstitial waters are likely, and this may limit species that use dissolved silica to form their tests.

SUMMARY AND CONCLUSIONS

1. Total (live plus dead) foraminiferal populations on the South Georgia Ridge from 330 to more than 3000 meters are predominantly planktonics and calcareous benthonics. At similar and greater depths on the South Orkney, Bruce, and South Sandwich ridges and on the abyssal floors of the Scotia and northern Weddell seas, total foraminiferal populations are predominantly agglutinated benthonics. In some of the populations from 260 to 2350 meters on the South Orkney, Bruce, and South Sandwich ridges, the living populations are dominated by calcareous foraminifera. At greater depths, however, the living populations are usually dominated by agglutinated foraminifera.

2. In part, post-mortem dissolution causes the rarity of empty calcareous foraminiferal skeletons in the southern and deep regions of the area. The fact of solution is demonstrated by severely corroded calcareous specimens which occur in samples from throughout the area. The rate of solution has been qualitatively estimated from the ratio of living to total calcareous specimens, using the same ratio for agglutinated specimens as a standard. A very high ratio for calcareous specimens from a population in which the ratio for agglutinated specimens is low indicates a high rate of solution of calcium carbonate. Such a discrepancy between live-total ratios for calcareous and noncalcareous specimens exists in samples from the southern and deeper parts of the area where, in many cases, more than half of the calcareous specimens contain protoplasm. Live-total ratios in four samples from the South Georgia Ridge, however, do not suggest differential destruction of calcareous benthonics in that area, although planktonic specimens in the same samples are deeply corroded.

3. The foregoing suggests that the carbonate compensation depth which is deeper than 4000 meters in areas just north of the Antarctic Convergence [*Hough*, 1956] rises with increasing latitude south of the convergence to 3400 meters in the area of the South Georgia Ridge and to a very shallow depth in the area of the South Orkney, Bruce, and South Sandwich ridges. The carbonate compensation depth in the area of the South Orkney, Bruce, and South Sandwich ridges is probably no deeper than 500 meters, but there are too few shallow samples from that area to define it adequately. Conditions along the South Orkney, Bruce, and South Sandwich ridges, therefore, are like those in the Ross Sea, where the carbonate compensation depth is also very shallow [*Kennett*, 1966], and unlike those in some other areas of the Antarctic from which calcareous foraminiferal assemblages have been described from depths of 2000 meters and more [*Uchio*, 1960*b*; *Pflum*, 1966].

4. Distributions of calcareous and agglutinated foraminifera were studied separately. Calcareous foraminiferal faunas on the South Georgia Ridge south of South Georgia differ from those on the South Orkney, Bruce, and South Sandwich ridges. Two faunas, one occurring deeper than the other, are found in both areas. The faunas and the dominant species in each are:

SOUTH GEORGIA SLOPE

Upper Bathyal Fauna (300–750 meters)

Angulogerina earlandi
Astrononion echolsi
Bulimina aculeata
Cassidulinoides parkerianus
Fursenkoina fusiformis

Deep Fauna (deeper than 1500 meters)

Eilohedra weddellensis
Gyroidina subplanulata
Nonionella iridea

South Orkney, Bruce, and South Sandwich Ridges

Bathyal Fauna (370–1600 meters)

Eilohedra weddellensis
Epistominella exigua
Fursenkoina earlandi

Deep Fauna (deeper than 1600 meters)

Eponides tumidulus
Melonis cf. *M. affinis*

The five species of the upper bathyal fauna of the South Georgia slope are uncommon on the slopes of the South Orkney, Bruce, and South Sandwich ridges. *Eilohedra weddellensis*, common only below 1000 meters on the South Georgia slope, is common at 490 meters and deeper on the slopes of the South Orkney, Bruce, and South Sandwich ridges. These differences in calcareous assemblages appear related to differences between the water masses of the two areas. The upper slope faunal zone south of South Georgia is associated with the temperature maximum stratum of the Warm Deep Layer. Because of mixing with colder surface and bottom waters, this layer is much depleted along the South Orkney, Bruce, and South Sandwich ridges. The potential temperature and salinity characteristics of water at 600 meters on the slopes of the southern and eastern Scotia Ridge are similar to those of water below 1000 meters on the slope south of South Georgia.

5. The agglutinated species have been separated into a bathyal group, an abyssal group, and a nondefinitive group. The bathyal group of species is insignificant in most assemblages below 2200 meters and the abyssal group is insignificant in samples from above 1300 meters. In most samples the nondefinitive group comprises less than 50 per cent of the agglutinated foraminifera. The most abundant species in the bathyal and nondefinitive groups and selected dominants from the abyssal group are:

Bathyal Group

Ammoflintina argentea
Cribrostomoides arenacea
Miliammina arenacea
Miliammina lata
Portatrochammina antarctica
Portatrochammina wiesneri
Pseudobolivina antarctica

Abyssal Group

Ammomarginulina ensis
Cribrostomoides sphaeriloculus
Cribrostomoides subglobosus
Eggerella parkerae var. B
Glomospira charoides
Martinottiella antarctica
Saccammina tubulata
Tritaxis inhaerens

Nondefinitive Group

Adercotryma glomeratum
Conotrochammina bullata
Haplophragmoides parkerae
Portatrochammina eltaninae
Trochammina quadricamerata

6. From the upper and lower depth limits of abundant and persistent agglutinated species, two depth boundaries are suggested, occurring at 1200–1300 meters and 2100–2300 meters. The boundary at 2100–2300 meters is the most significant. It is defined by the first occurrences of six species and the first of the consistent occurrences of five other species.

7. Benthonic foraminifera biofacies occur on the abyssal floors of the Scotia and Weddell seas associated with distinctive environmental complexes. In the East Scotia Basin and Trench Rim Biofacies the diatom content of sediments is high. The sediments of the Trench Rim Biofacies are largely volcanic debris, and depths are greater than those of the East Scotia Basin Biofacies. In the Peripheral Weddell Sea Biofacies and the Central Weddell Sea Biofacies, diatoms are rare or very rare in clays and silty clays. The Central Weddel Sea Biofacies is more isolated from the possibly more productive marginal areas of the Weddell Sea. Dominant species in each biofacies are:

East Scotia Basin Biofacies

Cribrostomoides umbilicatulus soldanii
Eggerella parkerae var. B
Martinottiella antarctica
Reophax sp. A

Trench Rim Biofacies

Adercotryma glomeratum
Glomospira charoides
Tritaxis inhaerens

Peripheral Weddell Sea Biofacies

Cyclammina pusilla

Central Weddell Sea Biofacies

Cribrostomoides subglobosus

8. *Conotrochammina kennetti* and *Portatrochammina eltaninae* dominate benthonic foraminiferal assemblages of very low diversity in the upper levels of the South Sandwich Trench below sill level. No

foraminifera were found in the deepest sample (7690 meters). As in the Peru-Chile Trench [*Bandy and Rodolfo*, 1964] and in the upper levels of the Kuril Trench [*Shchedrina*, 1958], endemic species are rare if they exist at all. Unlike specimens from other trenches in which foraminifera have been studied, however, all foraminiferal specimens in the South Sandwich Trench were small.

9. Certain distinctive walls of agglutinated foraminifera have ecological significance. Nine species of the family Ataxophragmiidae having a calcareous cement occur consistently in assemblages dominated by calcareous benthonic foraminifera but rarely in assemblages dominated by other agglutinated foraminifera. Species of the families Ataxophragmiidae (*Martinottiella antarctica* and *Eggerella parkerae* var. B) and Rzehakinidae (*Spirolocammina tenuis*) that have white walls occur consistently in sediments having a high diatom content and rarely in sediments having few diatoms. These species with white walls possibly have a siliceous cement and thus may require large quantities of dissolved silica in interstitial waters which would be provided by a large diatom content.

SYSTEMATIC DESCRIPTIONS

One new genus is described and another genus is emended. Five new species are described and a sixth, of exceptional interest because it apparently secretes a test wall of opaline silica, is described but left unnamed pending further investigation of the wall. Since the purpose of this study is not primarily taxonomic, species that occur sporadically at frequencies of less than 3 per cent have not been named, although they appear to have no counterparts in the existing literature. To record their occurrence in the Scotia Sea area, most of these rare species are illustrated and the others are briefly described. As research on antarctic and deep-sea Foraminiferida continues, additional specimens of these species will undoubtedly be found, permitting a better understanding of them than the material of this study permits. The descriptions of rare species and references to the figures of all illustrated species appear in the list of species that follows.

Family Rzehakinidae Cushman, 1933

Genus *Ammoflintina* Earland, 1934

Ammoflintina argentea Echols, n. sp.

Plate 2, fig. 7

Diagnosis. Test free, small, irregularly planispiral, laterally compressed, subtriangular to subquadrate in outline, edge rounded; chambers few, crescent-shaped, three per whorl, located on either side of the medial plane of the test, but not regularly alternating; generally four to five chambers visible on one side of the test and three on the other side; sutures depressed, distinct; aperture an obscure, excentric interiomarginal slit; wall agglutinated, thin; surface uneven; color gray.

Holotype. USNM No. 687208; diameter 0.23 mm, thickness 0.11 mm; from USC 659.

Variation. *Ammoflintina argentea* is characterized by considerable irregularity in chamber arrangement. Although coiling is planispiral, the chambers are never located symmetrically to the plane of coiling, and successive chambers may be on the same or opposite sides of the test. Because septa are not clearly visible, even in specimens clarified with oil of anise, the internal chamber arrangement is uncertain, but most specimens appear to consist of no more than two whorls.

Occurrence. *Ammoflintina argentea* occurs at 15 stations from depths of 560 to 2640 meters. It is most abundant and persistent in the area of the South Sandwich Islands and did not occur in samples from the South Georgia slope.

Remarks. This species, which is unlike any previously described foraminiferan, is provisionally referred to the genus *Ammoflintina* because it has few crescent-shaped chambers arranged three in a whorl as does *A. trihedra* Earland, the type species of the genus. The aperture of *A. trihedra,* however, is a circular or semicircular opening of the distal end of the last chamber, whereas the aperture of *A. argentea* is a very small interiomarginal slit.

Genus *Cystammina* Neumayr, 1889, emended Echols

Plate 2, figs. 8, 9

Cystammina Neumayr, 1889, Die Stamme des Thierreiches; Wirbellose Thiere, v. 1, p. 167.

Ammochilostomella Eimer and Fickert, 1899, Zeitschr. Wiss. Zool., v. 65, 4, p. 692.

Type species. *Trochammina pauciloculata* Brady, 1879, subsequent designation, Galloway, 1933.

Emended diagnosis based on antarctic material. Test free; wall agglutinated; coiling milioline with apertures of each succeeding chamber alternating at either pole of a short axis of the test; chambers added nearly in a plane around this axis at more than 120 degrees, but less than 180 degrees from the preceding chamber; chambers globose and elongated perpendicular to the coiling axis, increasing rapidly in size as added; three chambers exposed around the perimeter

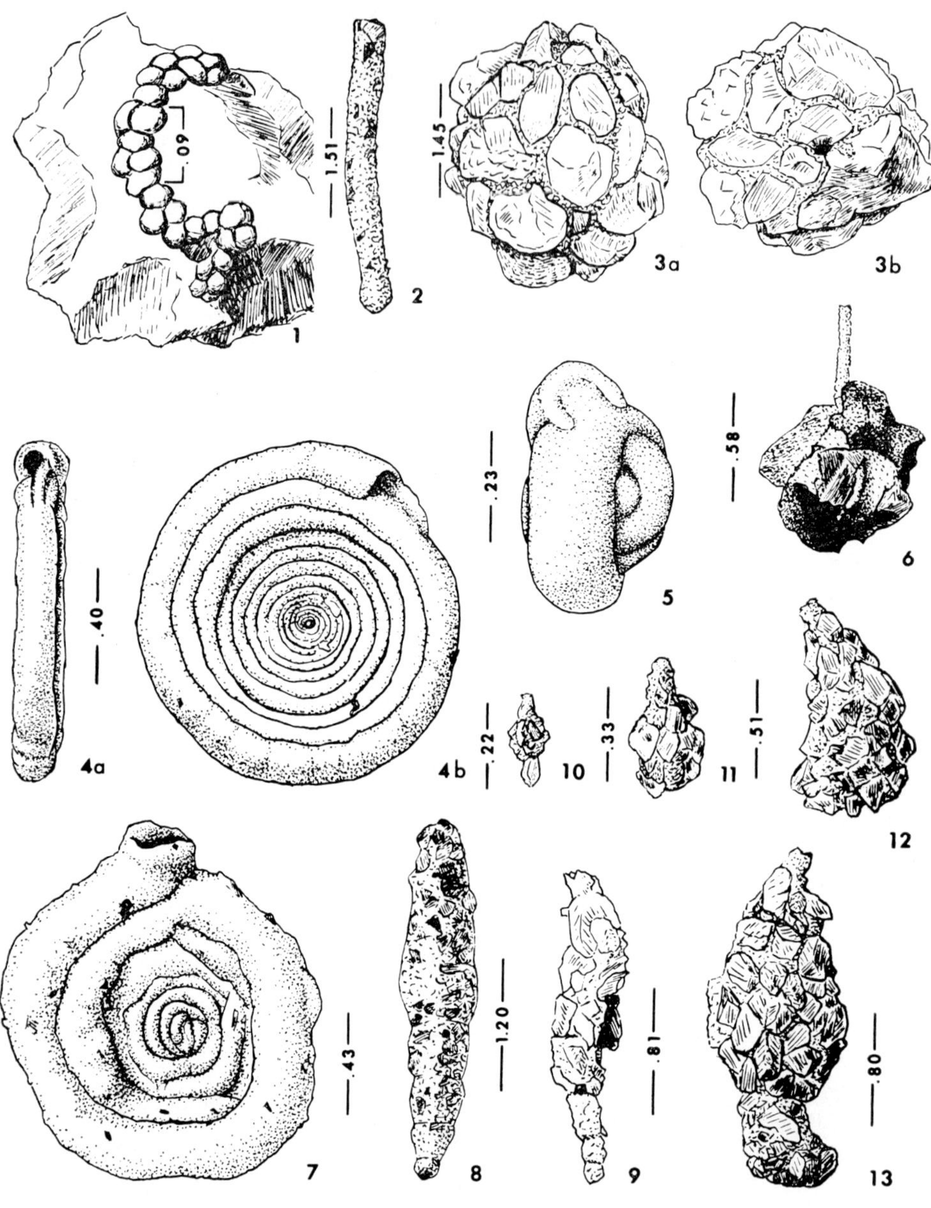

Plate 1

Maximum dimensions in millimeters of the specimens are shown beside the figures.

1. *Placopsilinella aurantiaca* Earland, ×119; USC 624; Hypotype, USC No. 1121.
2. *Hyperammina* sp. A, ×27; USC 646; Hypotype, USC No. 1122.
3. *Psammosphaera fusca* Schulze, ×26; *a*, side view; *b*, apertural view; USC 472; Hypotype, USC No. 1123.
4. *Ammodiscus catinus* Hoglund, ×119; *a*, edge view; *b*, side view; USC 503; Hypotype, USC No. 1124.
5. *Glomospira gordialis* (Jones and Parker), ×151; USC 647; Hypotype, USC No. 1125.
6. *Saccammina tubulata* Rhumbler, ×61; USC 648; Hypotype, USC No. 1126.
7. *Tolypammina frigida* (Cushman), ×119; USC 647; Hypotype, USC No. 1127.
8. *Reophax subdentaliniformis* Parr, ×42; USC 651; Hypotype, USC No. 1128.
9. *Reophax* sp. B, ×54; USC 654; Hypotype, USC No. 1129.
10. *Reophax* sp. A Earland, ×60; USC 700; Hypotype, USC No. 1130.
11. *Reophax* sp. A Earland, ×60; USC 700; Hypotype, USC No. 1131.
12. *Reophax* sp. A Earland, ×60; USC 700; Hypotype, USC No. 1132.
13. *Reophax* sp. A Earland, ×60; USC 700; Hypotype, USC No. 1133.

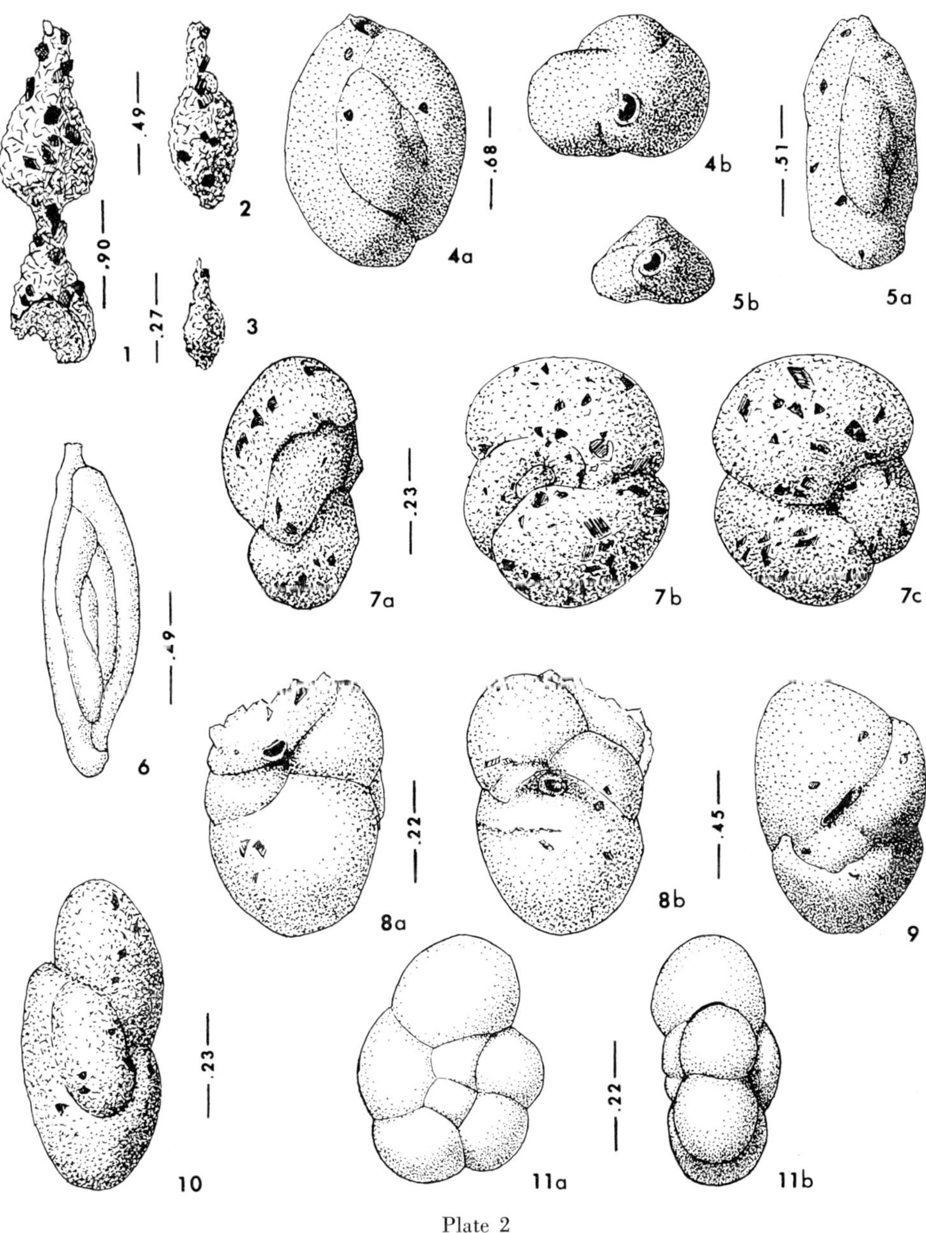

Plate 2

Maximum dimensions in millimeters of the specimens are shown beside the figures.

1. *Reophax ovicula* (Brady), ×56; USC 649; Hypotype, USC No. 1134.
2. *Reophax ovicula* (Brady), ×56; USC 649; Hypotype, USC No. 1135.
3. *Reophax ovicula* (Brady), ×56; USC 649; Hypotype, USC No. 1136.
4. *Miliammina lata* Heron-Allen and Earland, ×55; *a*, side view; *b*, apertural view; USC 652; Hypotype, USC No. 1137.
5. *Miliammina arenacea* (Chapman), ×74; *a*, side view; *b*, apertural view; USC 652; Hypotype, USC No. 1138.
6. *Spirolocammina tenuis* Earland, ×103; USC 1031; Hypotype, USC No. 1139.
7. *Ammoflintina argentea* Echols, n. sp., ×167; *a*, edge view; *b*, side view; *c*, opposite side; USC 659; Holotype, USNM No. 687208.
8. *Cystammina pauciloculata* (Brady), ×182; broken specimen showing apertures alternating on either side of test; *a*, oral view; *b*, aboral view; USC 648; Hypotype, USC No. 1140.
9. *Cystammina pauciloculata* (Brady), ×84; USC 648; Hypotype, USC No. 1141.
10. *Cystammina argentea* Earland, ×200; USC 649; Hypotype, USC No. 1142.
11. *Haplophragmoides parkerae* (Uchio), ×171; *a*, side view; *b*, edge view; USC 650; Hypotype, USC No. 1143.

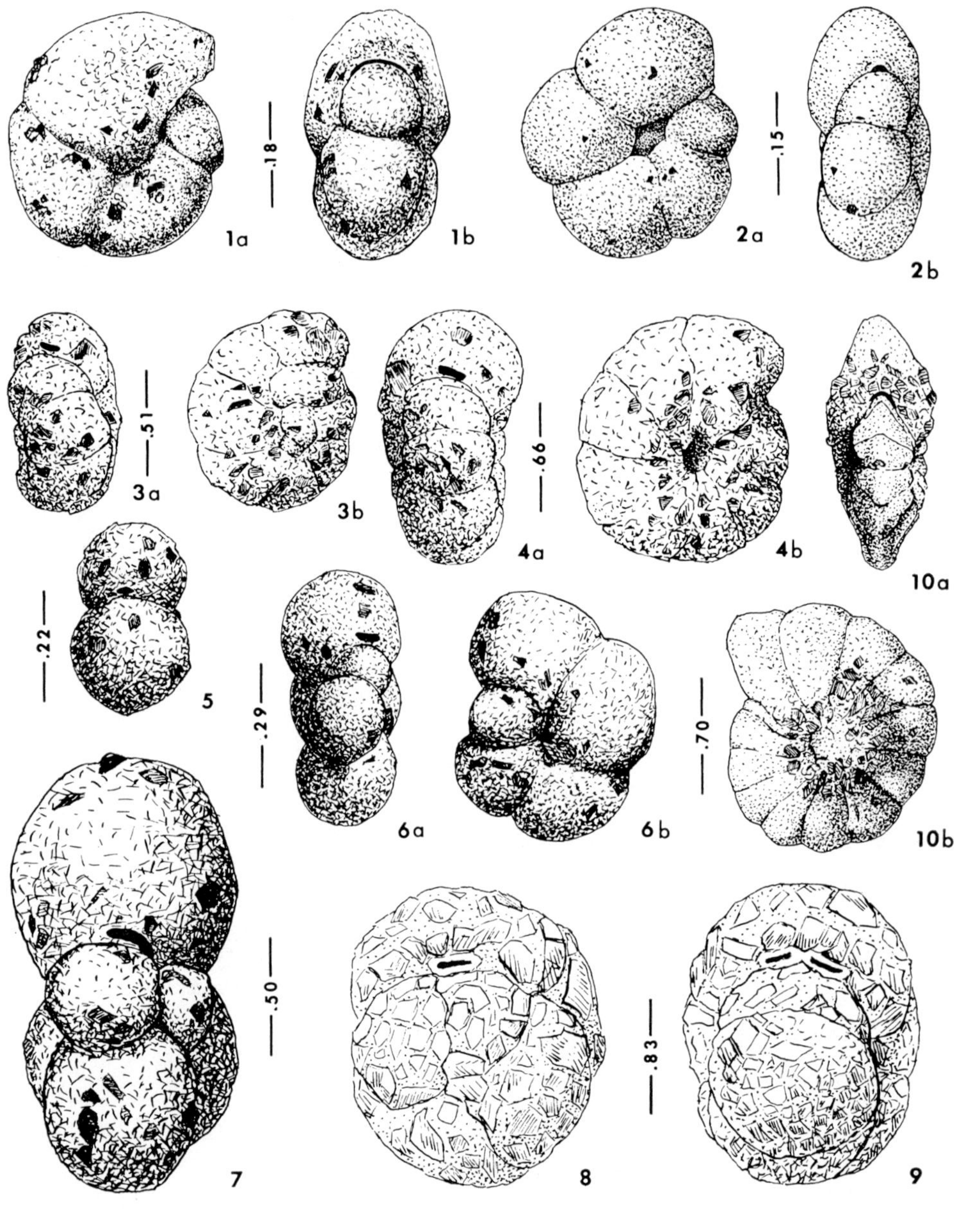

Plate 3

Maximum dimensions in millimeters of the specimens are shown beside the figures.

1. *Haplophragmoides quadratus* Earland, ×196; *a*, side view; *b*, edge view; USC 654; Hypotype, USC No. 1144.
2. *Haplophragmoides canariensis* d'Orbigny, ×247; *a*, side view; *b*, edge view; USC 649; Hypotype, USC No. 1145.
3. *Cribrostomoides contortus* (Earland), ×56; *a*, edge view; *b*, side view; USC 503, 505; Hypotype, USC No. 1146.
4. *Cribrostomoides contortus* (Earland), ×56; *a*, edge view; *b*, side view; USC 503, 505; Hypotype, USC No. 1147.
5. *Cribrostomoides sphaeriloculus* (Cushman), ×127; proloculus and first chamber of megalospheric form; USC 648; Hypotype, USC No. 1148.
6. *Cribrostomoides sphaeriloculus* (Cushman), ×127; microspheric form; *a*, edge view; *b*, side view; USC 648; Hypotype, USC No. 1149.
7. *Cribrostomoides sphaeriloculus* (Cushman), ×127; megalospheric form; USC 648; Hypotype, USC No. 1150.
8. *Cribrostomoides subglobosum* (Cushman), ×53; USC 475; Hypotype, USC No. 1151.
9. *Cribrostomoides subglobosum* (Cushman), ×53; USC 475; Hypotype, USC No. 1152.
10. *Cyclammina pusilla* Brady, ×52; *a*, edge view; *b*, side view; USC 520; Hypotype, USC No. 1153.

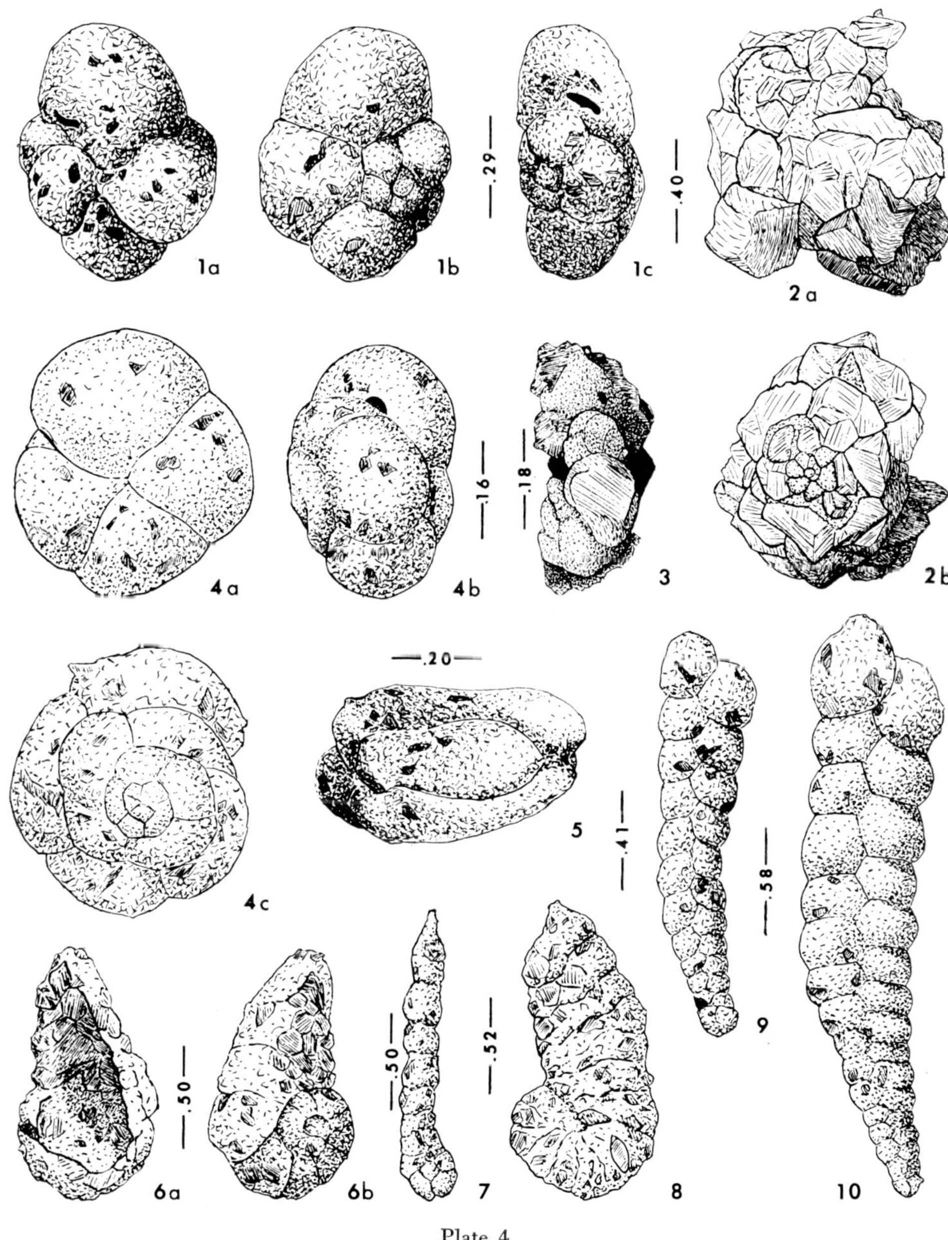

Plate 4

Maximum dimensions in millimeters of the specimens are shown beside the figures.

1. *Cribrostomoides arenacea* (Heron-Allen and Earland), ×128; *a*, involute side; *b*, evolute side; *c*, edge view; USC 500; Hypotype, USC No. 1154.
2. *Cribrostomoides umbilicatulum soldanii* (Earland), ×103; *a*, edge view; *b*, evolute side; USC 689; Hypotype, USC No. 1155.
3. *Cribrostomoides umbilicatulum soldanii* (Earland), ×207; edge view; USC 689; Hypotype, USC No. 1156.
4. *Trochammina quadricamerata* Echols, n. sp., ×221; *a*, ventral view; *b*, edge view; *c*, dorsal view; USC 500; Holotype, USNM No. 687212.
5. *Adercotryma glomerata* (Brady), ×198; USC 648; Hypotype, USC No. 1157.
6. *Ammobaculites foliaceous* (Brady) *f. recurva* Earland, ×74; *a*, side view; *b*, opposite side; USC 476; Hypotype, USC No. 1158.
7. *Ammobaculites filiformis* Earland, ×87; USC 1035; Hypotype, USC No. 1159.
8. *Ammomarginulina ensis* Wiesner, ×83; USC 528; Hypotype, USC No. 1160.
9. *Textularia wiesneri* Earland, ×145; USC 649; Hypotype, USC No. 1161.
10. *Textularia wiesneri* Earland, ×145; USC 649; Hypotype, USC No. 1162.

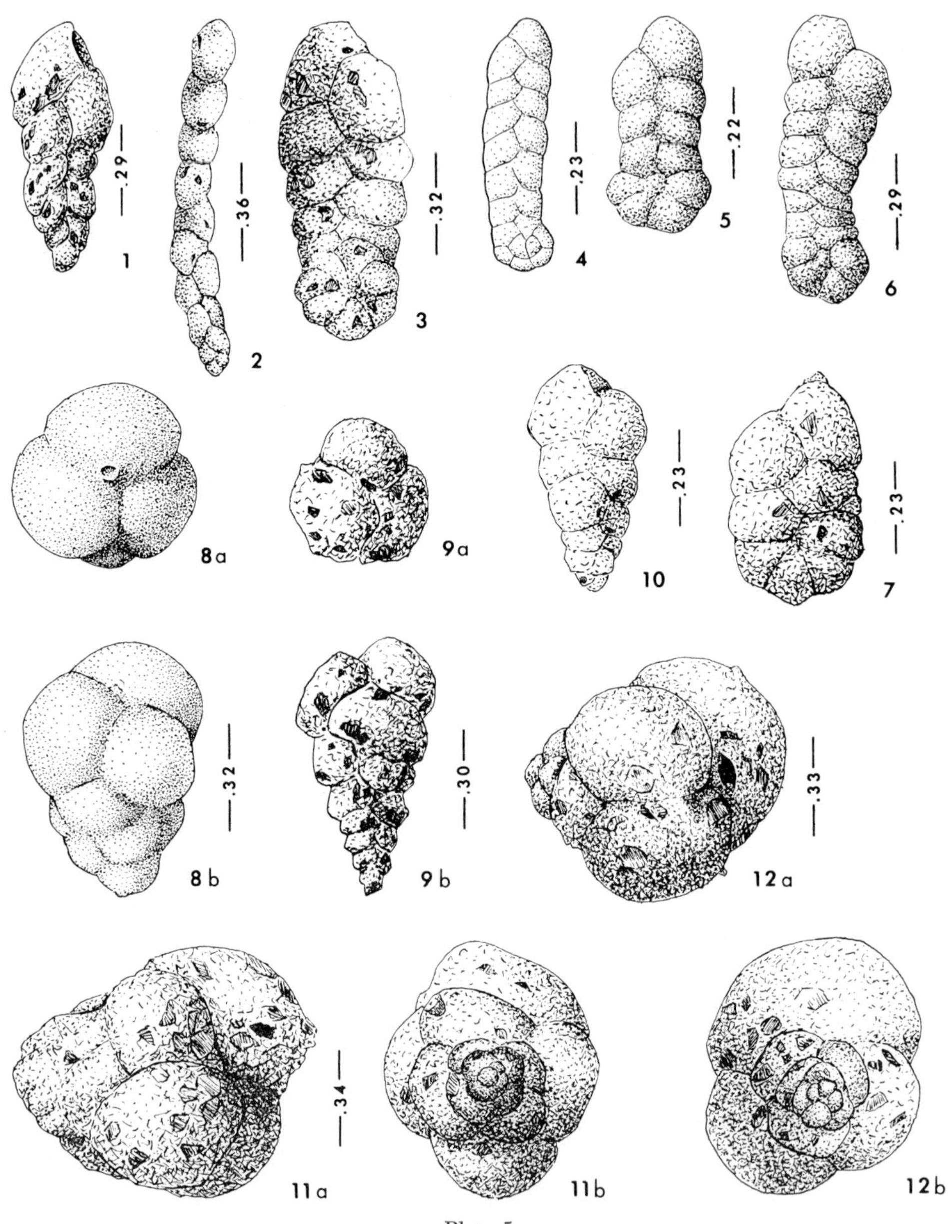

Plate 5

Maximum dimensions in millimeters of the specimens are shown beside the figures.

1. *Pseudobolivina antarctica* Wiesner, ×128; USC 658; Hypotype, USC No. 1163.
2. *Bigenerina minutissima* Earland, ×147; USC 645; Hypotype, USC No. 1164.
3. *Spiroplectammina biformis* (Parker and Jones), ×147; USC 497; Hypotype, USC No. 1165.
4. *Spiroplectammina filiformis* Earland, ×168; USC 645; Hypotype, USC No. 1166.
5. *Spiroplectammina* aff. *S. filiformis*, ×147; USC 647; Hypotype, USC No. 1167.
6. *Spiroplectammina* aff. *S. filiformis*, ×147; USC 647; Hypotype, USC No. 1168.
7. *Spiroplectammina subcylindrica* Earland, ×147; USC 473; Hypotype, USC No. 1169.
8. *Eggerella parkerae* (Uchio), ×118; *a*, apertural view; *b*, side view; USC 693; Hypotype, USC No. 1170.
9. *Verneuilina minuta* Wiesner, ×127; *a*, apertural view; *b*, side view; USC 649; Hypotype, USC No. 1171.
10. *Gaudryina pauperata* Earland, ×147; USC 708; Hypotype, USC No. 1172.
11. *Conotrochammina bullata* (Hoglund), ×108; *a*, edge view; *b*, dorsal view; USC 500; Hypotype, USC No. 1173.
12. *Conotrochammina bullata* (Hoglund), ×111; *a*, edge view; *b*, dorsal view; USC 647; Hypotype, USC No. 1174.

of the test; three exposed on the aboral side, but often four on the oral side; aperture areal, ovate in younger specimens, later slit-like, located near the suture.

Discussion. The emended diagnosis is based on antarctic material of *Cystammina pauciloculata*, the distinctive and cosmopolitan deep-water type of the genus. This species bears a superficial resemblance to the hyaline genus *Allomorphina*, which probably led Brady to assume that the coiling was trochospiral with later chambers encompassing much of the earlier test and concealing the spire, an interpretation accepted by later authors. As shown in Plate 2, figs. 8*a* and 8*b*, however, apertures alternate on either side of the test, and the chamber arrangement is milioline. The genus, therefore, is herein emended and transferred from the Trochamminidae to the Rzehakinidae.

Family TROCHAMMINIDAE Schwager, 1877

Genus *Conotrochammina* Finlay, 1940

Conotrochammina kennetti Echols, n. sp.

Plate 6, fig. 1

Diagnosis. Test free, small, trochospiral, subconical or globose; perimeter lobulate; up to three whorls exposed on the dorsal surface, which is domed or flat in the area of the early whorls such that the globose test appears truncated; four to six chambers in the earliest whorl; only the four highly inflated chambers of the last whorl visible on the ventral side; sutures depressed and somewhat curved on the dorsal side, deeply depressed on the ventral side; aperture a small areal slit facing the umbilicus; wall coarsely arenaceous, composed of a wide variety of particle sizes, roughly finished. Diameter of largest specimens about 0.27 mm.

Holotype. USNM No. 687209; diameter 0.16 mm, thickness 0.15 mm; from USC 638.

Variation. Conotrochammina kennetti shows a wide range of variation. Some immature specimens, composed of two whorls, are small and quadrate with a domed upper surface and a shallow umbilicus. Others of the same size have five or six chambers per whorl, a flat dorsal surface, and a narrow deep umbilicus. In the largest specimens, the last one or two chambers are usually added in an irregular manner across the umbilicus. Larger chambers are structurally weak and easily broken in handling; complete large specimens are therefore rare.

Occurrence. Conotrochammina kennetti occurs in 20 samples from the Scotia and northern Weddell Seas, all from below 2700 meters, but is abundant only in the South Sandwich Trench below 5500 meters, where it comprises 24 per cent of the foraminifera in each of two samples (USC 638, USC 646).

Comparison. Most specimens of *C. kennetti* are within the range of variation of *C. bullata* (Hoglund) in all characteristics except wall texture. The wall of *C. bullata* is smoother, composed of finer particles, and is usually almost polished. Occasional larger particles used by this species are set in the finer matrix and generally protrude little from the surface of the test. In contrast, the wall of *C. kennetti* is dominantly composed of larger particles, up to 0.04 mm in diameter; the surface is very rough and never polished. At the 14 stations where these two species occur together, they are easily distinguished by wall texture and do not intergrade.

Name. This species is named for Dr. J .P. Kennett.

Genus *Portatrochammina*, new genus

Type species: *Portatrochammina eltaninae* Echols, n. sp.

Diagnosis. Test free, trochospiral, expanding gradually; wall agglutinated; proloculus tectinous; dorsal side flat to moderately convex; ventral side convex; umbilicus covered by a series of overlapping flaps, one flap derived from each chamber; umbilical flap distinguished from the chamber by flatter contour and often by finer agglutination; flap of final chamber usually completely covering umbilicus concealing flap of penultimate chamber; aperture a low interio-marginal arch in the last septal face, continuing as a slit around the entire free edge of the flap.

Discussion. This genus most closely resembles *Siphotrochammina* Saunders, a form from the mangrove swamps of Trinidad. *Saunders* [1957, p. 9] describes the modified umbilical part of the chamber of *Siphotrochammina* as 'a ventral, siphonlike lobe extending partially across the umbilicus.' It was possible to examine the genoholotype and figured paratype of *Siphotrochammina lobata*, which are deposited in the U. S. National Museum. In these two specimens, the umbilical ends of the chambers are modified into triangular lobes that partially overlap in the umbilicus. Lobes of all chambers in the last whorl are visible; the trailing edge of the last lobe is attached to the lobe of the penultimate chamber, and the aperture is a semicircular opening beneath the leading edge of the lobe. *Portatrochammina* differs from *Siphotrochammina* in that the flaps consistently cover the umbilicus and conceal, or nearly conceal, the flaps of the preceding chambers. This produces a laminated struc-

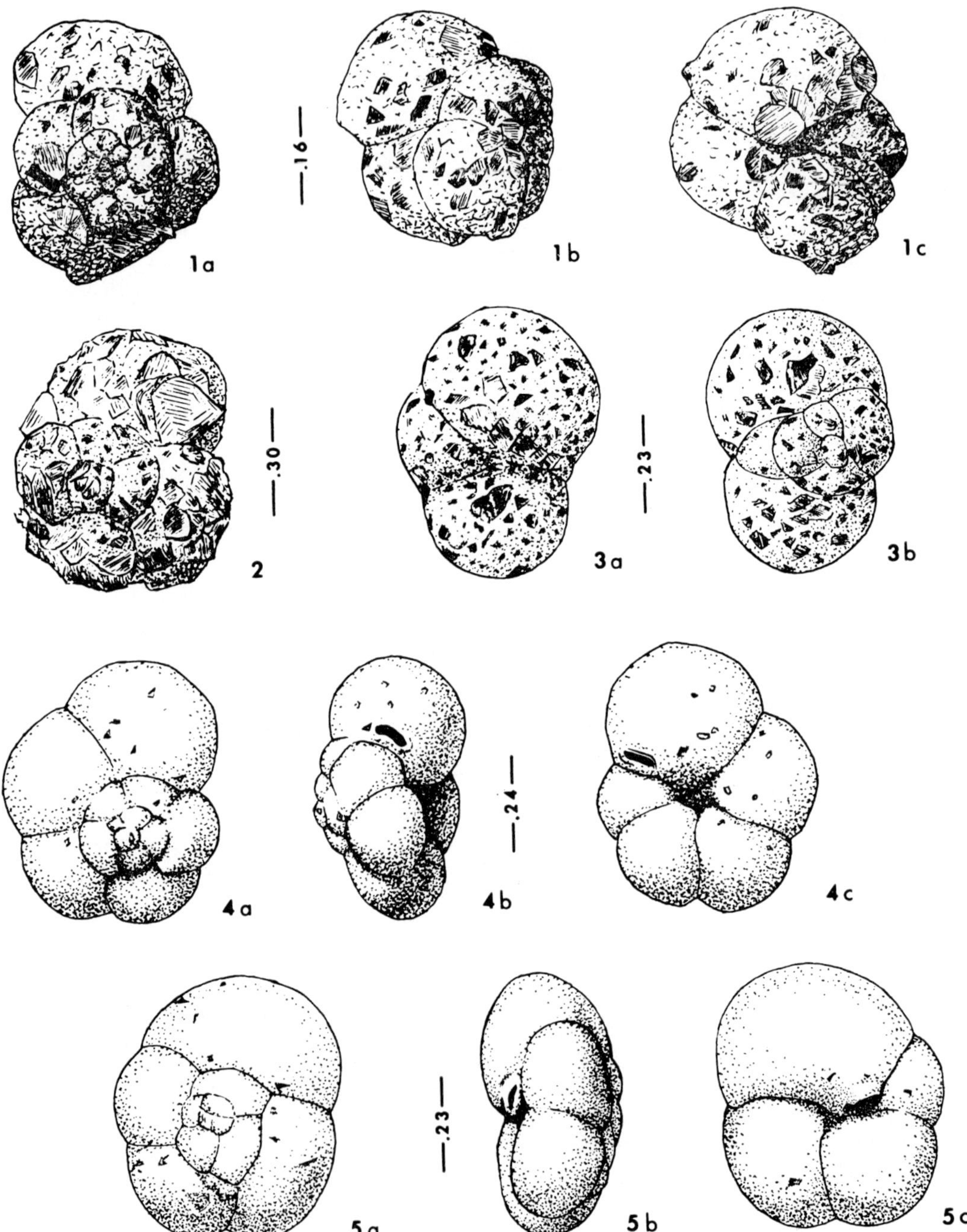

Plate 6

Maximum dimensions in millimeters of the specimens are shown beside the figures.

1. *Conotrochammina kennetti* Echols, n. sp., ×207; *a*, dorsal view; *b*, edge view; *c*, ventral view; USC 638; Holotype, USNM No. 687209.
2. *Conotrochammina rugosa* (Parr), ×125; dorsal view; USC 648; Hypotype, USC No. 1175.
3. *Conotrochammina alternans* Earland, ×159; *a*, ventral view; *b*, dorsal view; USC 544; Hypotype, USC No. 1176.
4. *Conotrochammina* sp. A, ×157; *a*, dorsal view; *b*, edge view; *c*, ventral view; USC 680; Hypotype, USC No. 1177.
5. *Conotrochammina* sp. B, ×159; *a*, dorsal view; *b*, edge view; *c*, ventral view; USC 604; Hypotype, USC No. 1178.

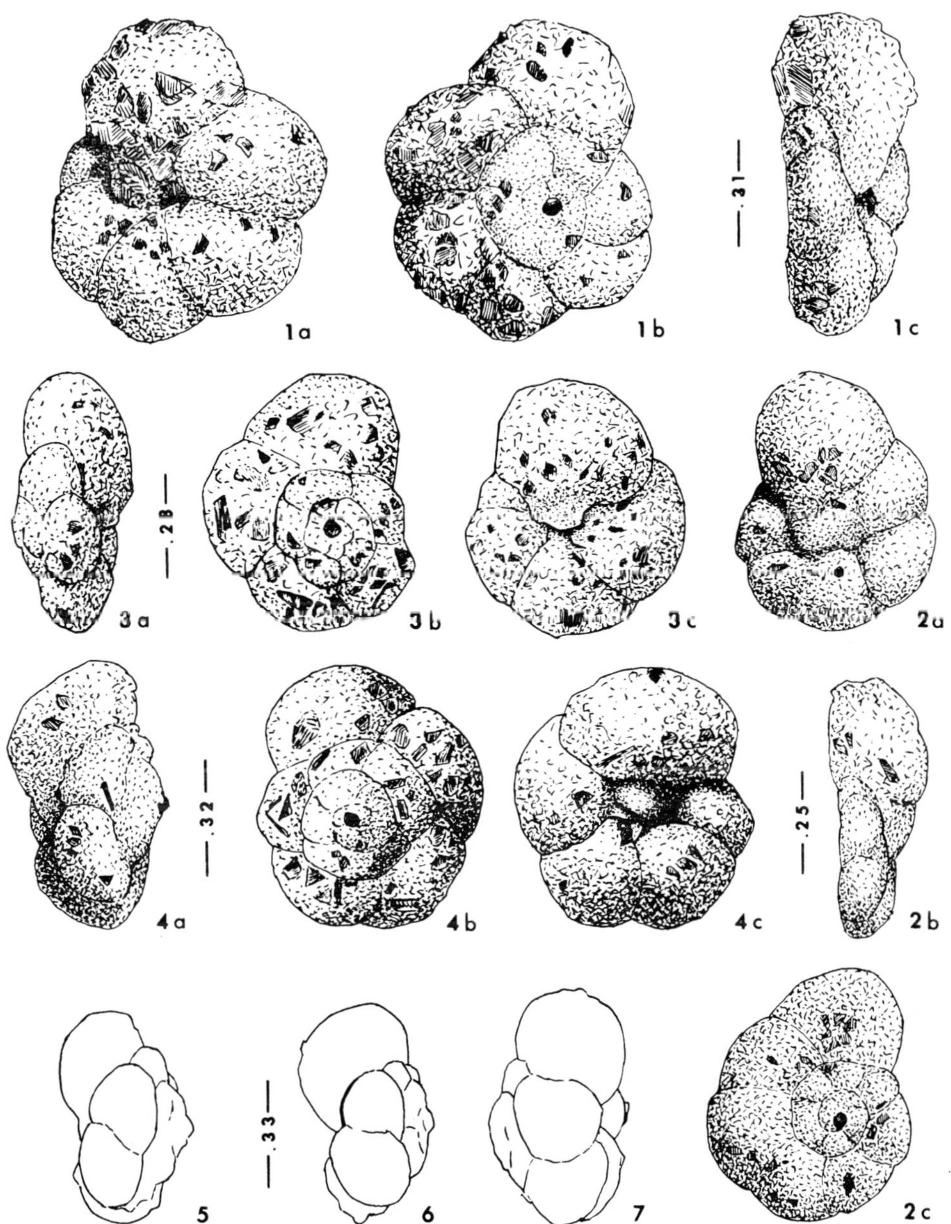

Plate 7

Maximum dimensions in millimeters of the specimens are shown beside the figures.

1. *Portatrochammina wiesneri* (Parr), ×168; *a*, ventral view; *b*, dorsal view; *c*, edge view; USC 500; Hypotype, USC No. 1179.
2. *Portatrochammina wiesneri* (Parr), ×168; *a*, ventral view; *b*, edge view; *c*, dorsal view; USC 500; Hypotype, USC No. 1180.
3. *Portatrochammina wiesneri* (Parr), ×149; *a*, edge view; *b*, dorsal view; *c*, ventral view; USC 503; Hypotype, USC No. 1181.
4. *Portatrochammina antarctica* (Parr), ×135; *a*, edge view; *b*, dorsal view; *c*, ventral view; USC 673; Hypotype, USC No. 1182.
5. *Portatrochammina antarctica* (Parr), ×106; edge view; Pennell Bank, Ross Sea, Antarctica (J. P. Kennett collection).
6. *Portatrochammina antarctica* (Parr), ×106; edge view; Pennell Bank, Ross Sea, Antarctica (J. P. Kennett collection).
7. *Portatrochammina antarctica* (Parr), ×106; edge view; Pennell Bank, Ross Sea, Antarctica (J. P. Kennett collection).

ture filling the umbilicus, the flap of each chamber adding one lamina. The umbilical flaps of *Portatrochammina* are therefore analogous to those of the hyaline genus *Valvulineria.* In contrast to the aperture of *Siphotrochammina,* the aperture of *Portatrochammina* extends completely around the free edge of the flap, occasionally being somewhat enlarged on the leading edge.

Trochamminula fissiperta Shchedrina, the genotype of *Trochamminula Shchedrina,* possesses chamber lobes which extend across the umbilicus, but its slit-like aperture extending into the apertural face distinguishes this genus from *Portatrochammina.*

Portatrochammina eltaninae Echols, n. sp.

Plate 8, figs. 1, 2

Trochammina inflata, Earland (not Montagu, 1808), 1934, Discovery Repts., v. 10, p. 99, pl. 3, figs. 41–43.

Diagnosis. Test free, small, trochospiral, compact; perimeter moderately lobulate; edge evenly rounded; dorsal side flat to moderately high-spired; ventral side convex, the umbilicus covered by a flap derived from the last septal face; test composed of two and a half or three whorls, four and a half to five chambers in each whorl; chambers closely appressed, subspherical, increasing gradually in size; sutures radial, depressed, and slightly curved on the dorsal side, deeply depressed and straight on the ventral side, usually distinct but details may be completely obscured in earlier whorls of more granular tests; umbilical end of each chamber modified into flap of gently convex curvature and finer agglutination than the remainder of the test, each flap covering umbilicus and concealing flaps of earlier chambers; aperture open around free edge of flap, supplemented by a small arched opening just inside or just outside the corner of the flap at the base of the last septal face in a few specimens; wall thin, granular to sublaevigate, composed of mineral grains up to 0.02 mm in diameter set smoothly in a finer groundmass; proloculus tectinous, lacking agglutinated particles; color light brown to medium brown. Larger specimens in assemblages range in diameter from 0.18 to 0.23 mm. Ratio of width of test to height of last chamber from 1.6 to 2.0.

Holotype. (Plate 8, fig. 1) USNM No. 687210; maximum diameter 0.28 mm, thickness 0.17 mm; from USC 503.

Figured paratype. (Plate 8, fig. 2) USNM No. 687211; maximum diameter 0.20 mm, thickness 0.12 mm; from USC 638.

Variation. The greatest variability of this species is in the height of the spire and the coarseness of agglutination; the range of variation commonly encountered is shown by the holotype and figured paratype. The holotype is flat on the dorsal side and relatively coarsely arenaceous; the paratype is high-spired and sublaevigate. Such variation in the height of spire is found in most samples. Coarseness of agglutination seems related to the quantity of medium silt available in the sample, but direct comparison with sediment texture data is not illuminating because of the preponderance of siliceous biogenic material in the silt fraction of many samples.

Occurrence. Portatrochammina eltaninae is one of the most common species in the samples of this study. Its occurrence in the most shallow waters is at 490 meters in samples from near the South Orkney Islands; it is present in all samples from near the South Sandwich Islands, the shallowest of which is 558 meters. In samples from the South Georgia insular slope, however, it is not found at depths shallower than 1500 meters. In the three samples from the upper levels of the South Sandwich Trench, it is 36, 41, and 54 per cent of the foraminiferal assemblages.

Comparison. Portatrochammina eltaninae is most similar to the two other species of the genus that occur in the Scotia and Weddell seas. It differs from *P. antarctica* (Parr) (Plate 7, figs. 4–7) in that the last septal face is evenly rounded in edge view rather than rhomboid, and in its smaller size. Specimens of *P. antarctica* in the Ross Sea, its type area, have chambers which are more rounded than those in specimens from the Scotia Sea, but even there a suggestion of a rhomboid profile can be seen in the last septal face (Plate 7, figs. 5–7). *Portatrochammina wiesneri* (Parr) differs in being more compressed (Plate 7, figs. 1–3). *Trochammina japonica* Ishiwada is remarkably similar in form, but differs in its larger size (0.38 mm), oblique sutures, and semicircular aperture.

Genus *Trochammina* Parker and Jones, 1859

Trochammina quadricamerata Echols, n. sp.

Plate 4, fig. 4

Diagnosis. Test free, small, trochospiral; dorsal spire low; ventral side slightly depressed or almost plane; perimeter slightly lobulate; edge rounded; chambers slightly inflated, increasing gradually in size; up to three and a half whorls visible on the dorsal side; only the last 4 or sometimes 5 chambers visible on the ventral side; proloculus depressed a little below the level of the first whorl in some specimens; sutures

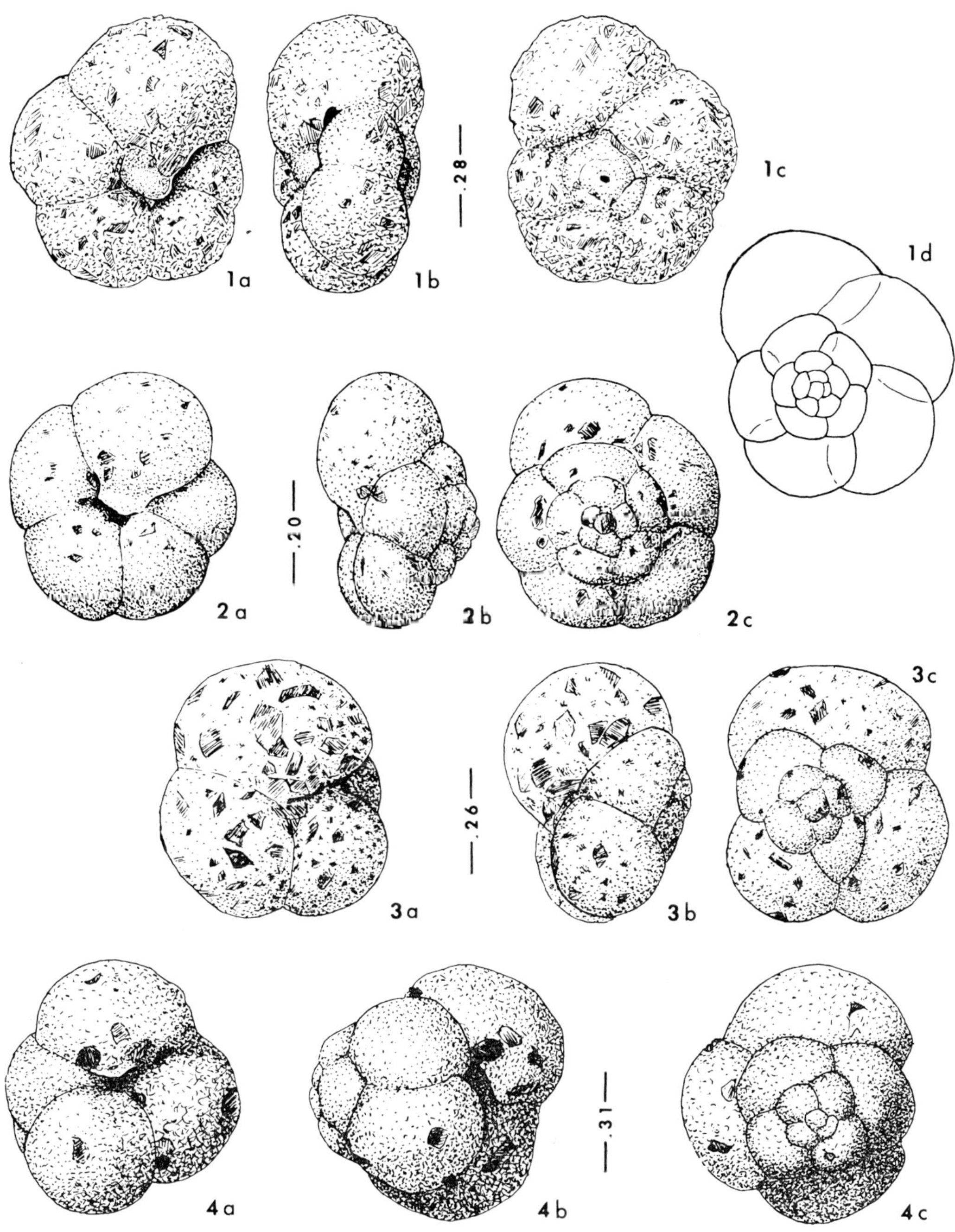

Plate 8

Maximum dimensions in millimeters of the specimens are shown beside the figures.

1. *Portatrochammina eltaninae* Echols, n. sp., ×154; *a*, ventral view; *b*, edge view; *c*, dorsal view; *d*, optical section (dorsal); USC 503; Holotype, USNM No. 687210.
2. *Portatrochammina eltaninae* Echols, n. sp., ×210; *a*, ventral view; *b*, edge view; *c*, dorsal view; USC 638; Paratype, USNM No. 687211.
3. *Trochammina tricamerata* Earland, ×159; *a*, ventral view; *b*, edge view; *c*, dorsal view; USC 500; Hypotype, USC No. 1183.
4. *Trochammina pygmaea* Hoglund, ×131; *a*, ventral view; *b*, edge view; *c*, dorsal view; USC 648; Hypotype, USC No. 1184.

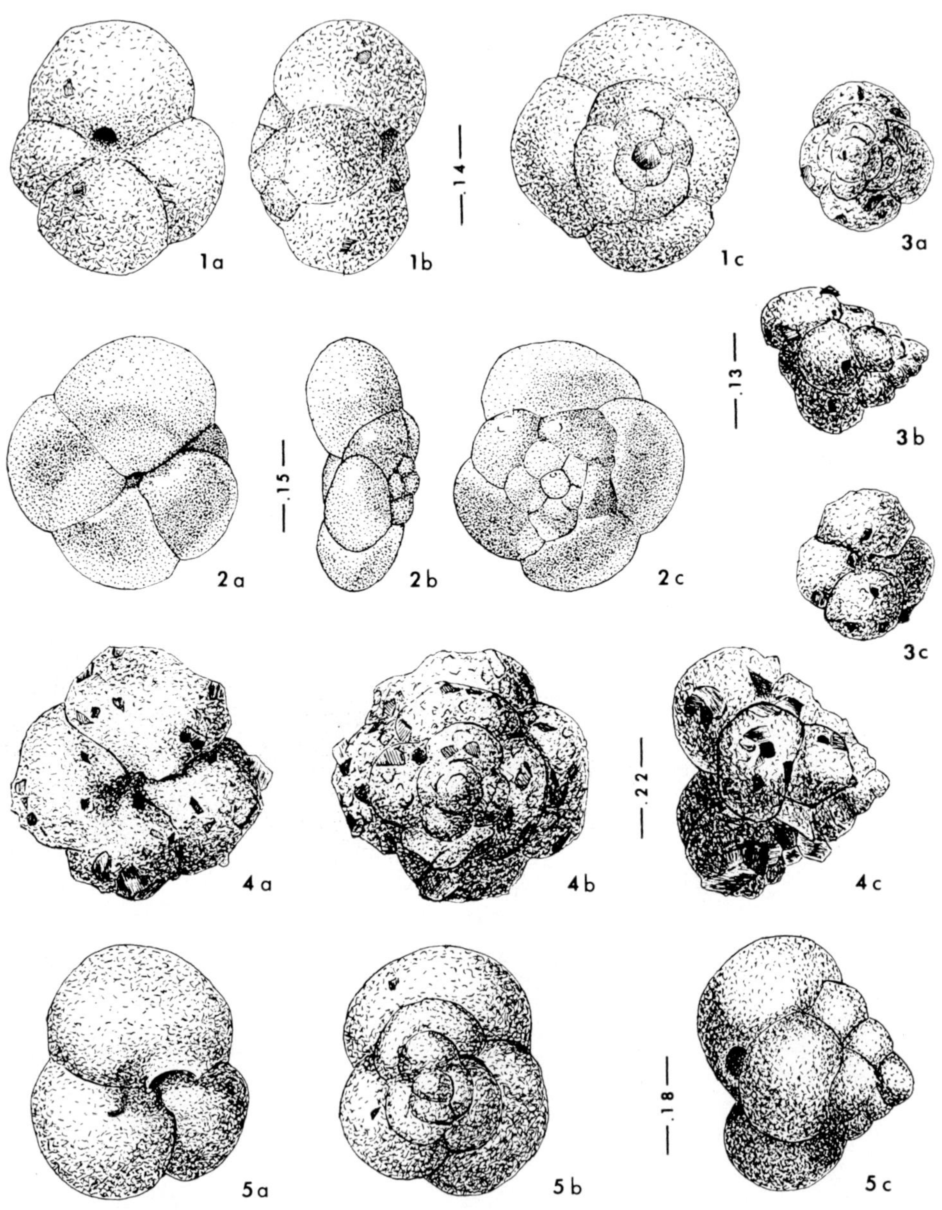

Plate 9

Maximum dimensions in millimeters of the specimens are shown beside the figures.

1. *Trochammina inconspicua* Earland, ×299; *a*, ventral view; *b*, edge view; *c*, dorsal view; USC 708; Hypotype, USC No. 1185.
2. *Trochammina labiata* Uchio, ×274; *a*, ventral view; *b*, edge view; *c*, dorsal view; USC 544; Hypotype, USC No. 1186.
3. *Trochammina subconica* Parr, ×183; *a*, dorsal view; *b*, edge view; *c*, ventral view; USC 647; Hypotype, USC No. 1187.
4. *Trochammina quadriloba* Hoglund, ×183; *a*, ventral view; *b*, dorsal view; *c*, edge view; USC 647; Hypotype, USC No. 1188.
5. *Trochammina conica* Earland, ×233; *a*, ventral view; *b*, dorsal view; *c*, edge view; USC 648; Hypotype, USC No. 1189.

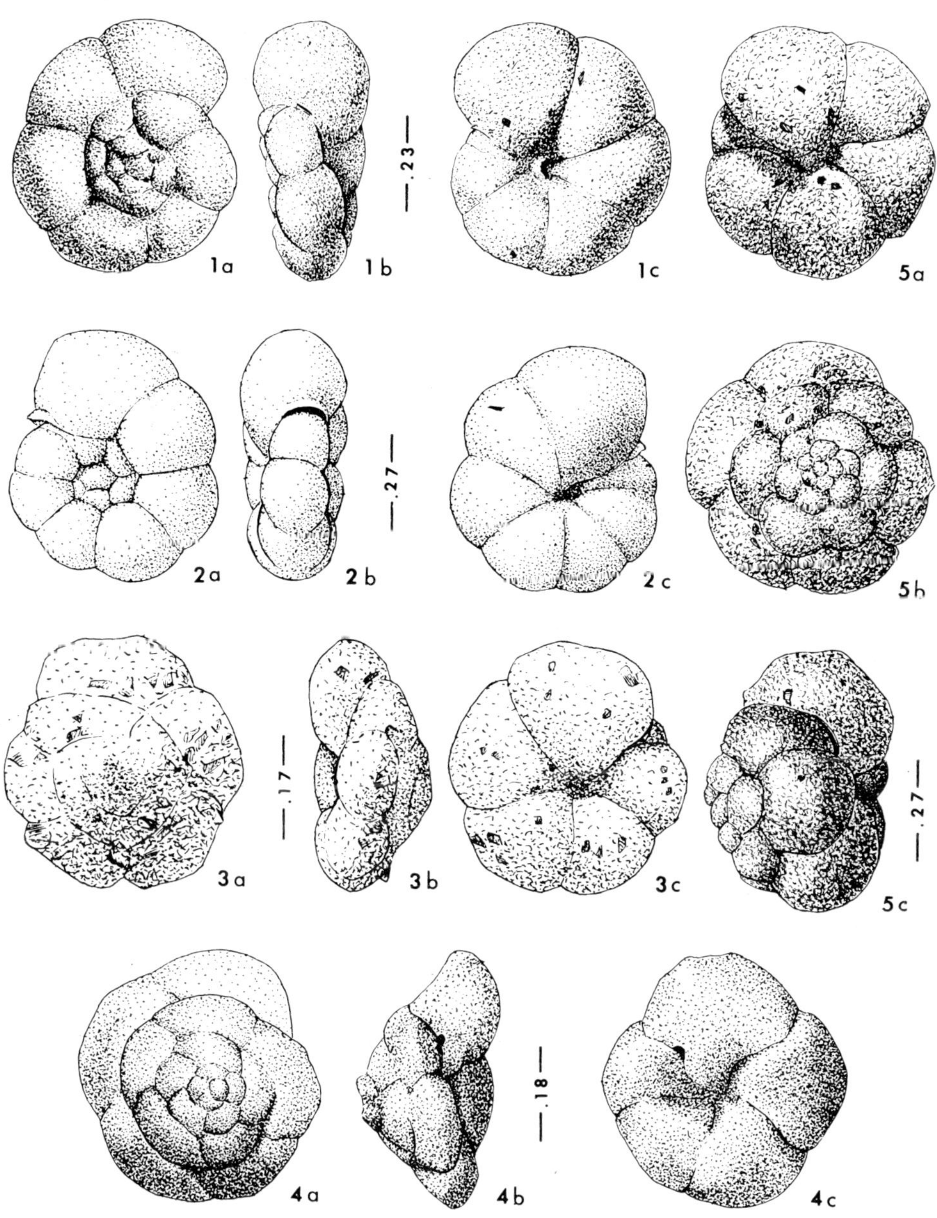

Plate 10

Maximum dimensions in millimeters of the specimens are shown beside the figures.

1. *Trochammina glabra* Heron-Allen and Earland, ×183; *a*, dorsal view; *b*, edge view; *c*, ventral view; USC 569; Hypotype, USC No. 1190.
2. *Trochammina glabra* Heron-Allen and Earland, ×156; *a*, dorsal view; *b*, edge view; *c*, ventral view; USC 630; Hypotype, USC No. 1191.
3. *Trochammina malovensis* Earland, ×247; *a*, dorsal view; *b*, edge view; *c*, ventral view; USC 675; Hypotype, USC No. 1192.
4. *Trochammina discorbis* Earland, ×234; *a*, dorsal view; *b*, edge view; *c*, ventral view; USC 648; Hypotype, USC No. 1193.
5. *Trochammina sorosa* Parr, ×162; *a*, ventral view; *b*, dorsal view; *c*, edge view; USC 604; Hypotype, USC No. 1194.

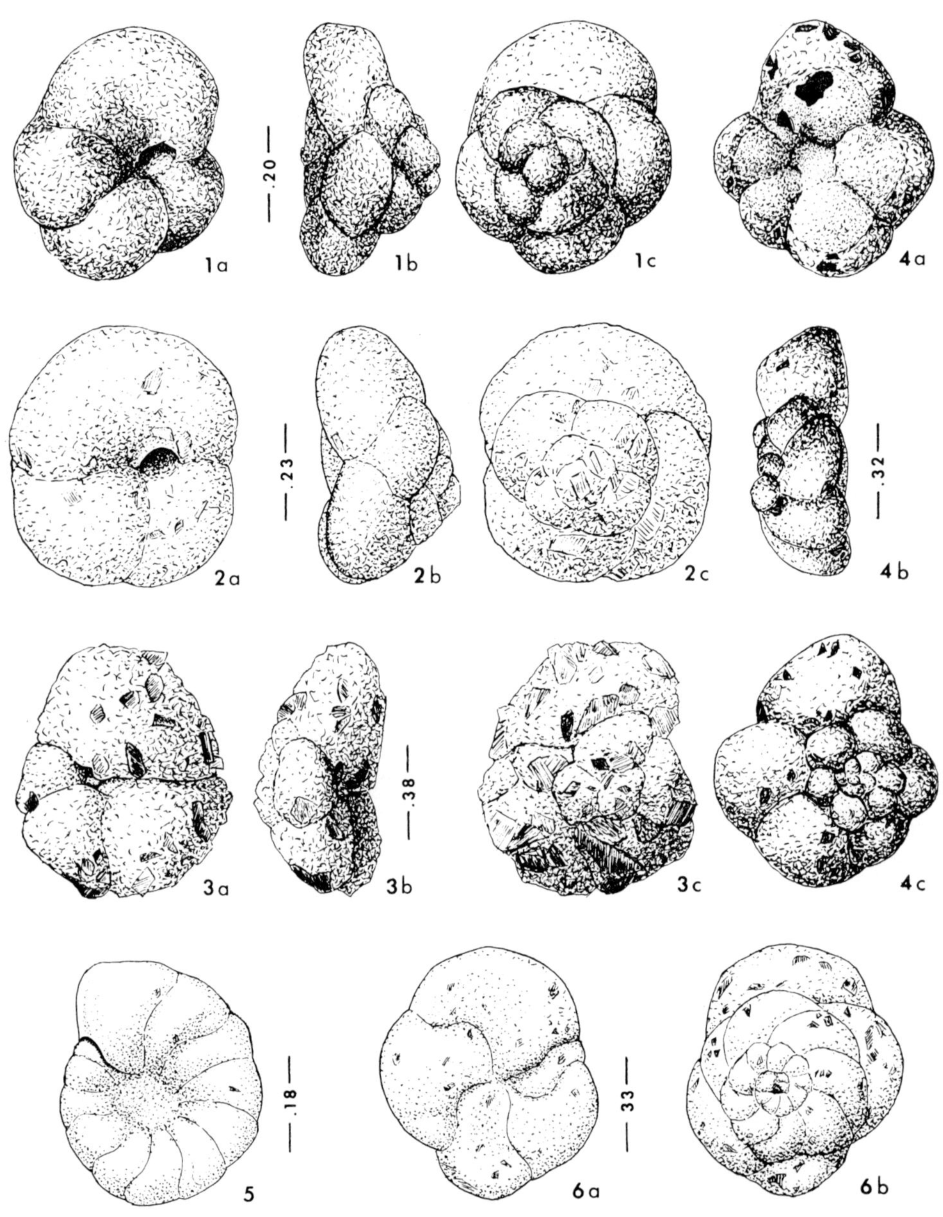

Plate 11

Maximum dimensions in millimeters of the specimens are shown beside the figures.

1. *Trochammina* aff. *T. compacta*, ×210; *a*, ventral view; *b*, edge view; *c*, dorsal view; USC 648; Hypotype, USC No. 1195.
2. *Trochammina compacta* Parker, ×184; *a*, ventral view; *b*, edge view; *c*, dorsal view; USC 503; Hypotype, USC No. 1196.
3. *Tritaxis squamata* Jones and Parker, ×110; *a*, ventral view; *b*, edge view; *c*, dorsal view; USC 624; Hypotype, USC No. 1197.
4. *Tritaxis inhaerens* (Wiesner), ×132; *a*, ventral view; *b*, edge view; *c*, dorsal view; USC 647; Hypotype, USC No. 1198.
5. *Trochammina multiloculata* Hoglund, ×228; ventral view; USC 544; Hypotype, USC No. 1199.
6. *Trochammina intermedia* Rhumbler, ×126; *a*, ventral view; *b*, dorsal view; USC 569; Hypotype, USC No. 1200.

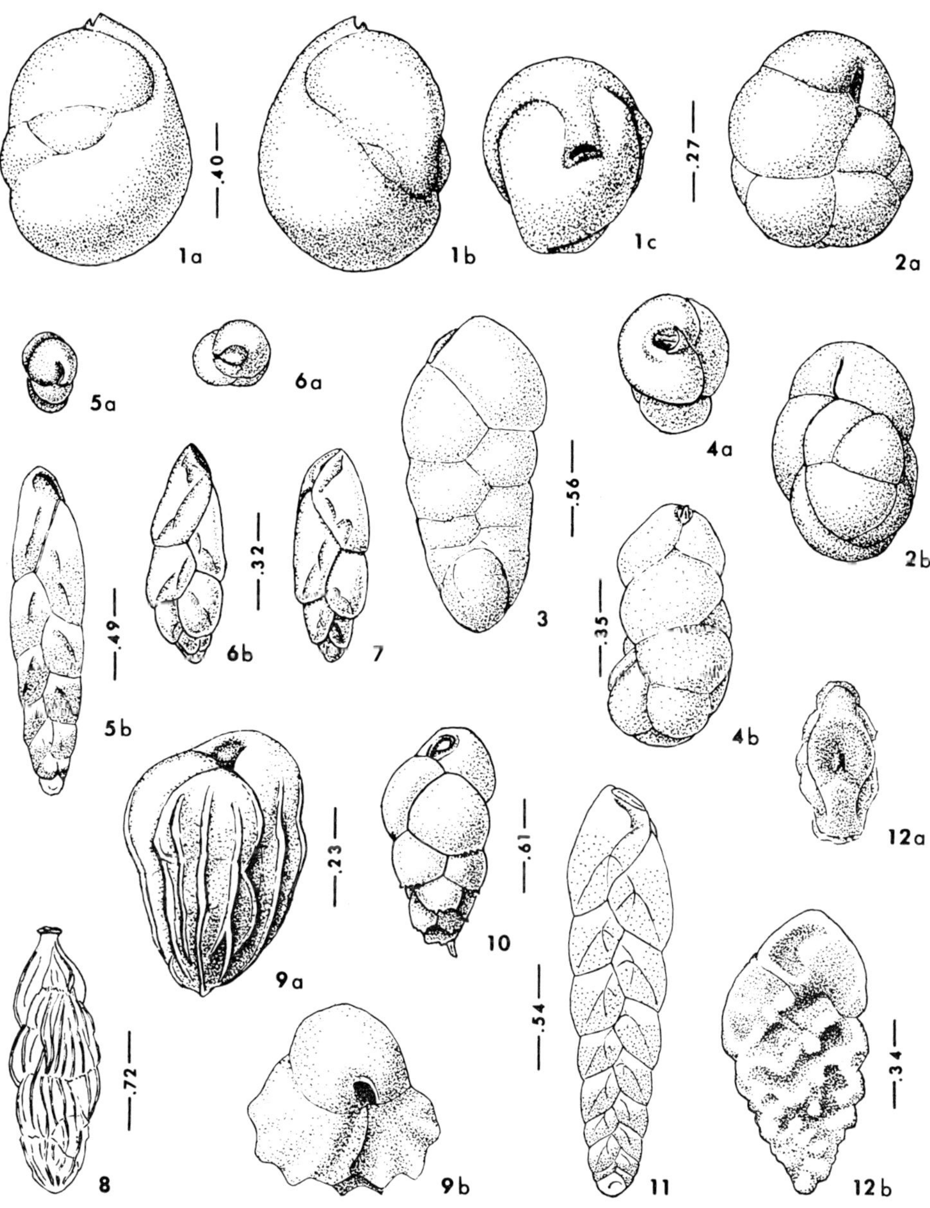

Plate 12

Maximum dimensions in millimeters of the specimens are shown beside the figures.

1. *'Miliolinella'* sp., ×93; *a,* side view; *b,* opposite view; *c,* top view; USC 503; Hypotype, USC No. 1201.
2. *Cassidulina subglobosa* Brady, ×120; *a,* side view; *b,* edge view; USC 500; Hypotype, USC No. 1202.
3. *Cassidulinoides crassa* (Earland), ×82; USC 675; Hypotype, USC No. 1203.
4. *Cassidulinoides parkeriana* (Brady), ×103; *a,* top view; *b,* side view; USC 658; Hypotype, USC No. 1204.
5. *Fursenkoina earlandi* (Parr), ×101; *a,* top view; *b,* side view; USC 500; Hypotype, USC No. 1205.
6. *Fursenkoina fusiformis* (Williamson), ×101; *a,* top view; *b,* side view; USC 679; Hypotype, USC No. 1206.
7. *Fursenkoina fusiformis* (Williamson), ×99; side view; USC 679; Hypotype, USC No. 1207.
8. *Angulogerina earlandi* Parr, ×55; USC 674; Hypotype, USC No. 1208.
9. *Bulimina rostrata* Brady, ×167; *a,* side view; *b,* top view; USC 680; Hypotype, USC No. 1209.
10. *Bulimina aculeata* d'Orbigny, ×55; USC 679; Hypotype, USC No. 1210.
11. *Bolivina pseudopunctata* Hoglund, ×113; USC 658; Hypotype, USC No. 1211.
12. *Bolivina decussata* Brady, ×125; *a,* top view; *b,* side view; USC 682; Hypotype, USC No. 1212.

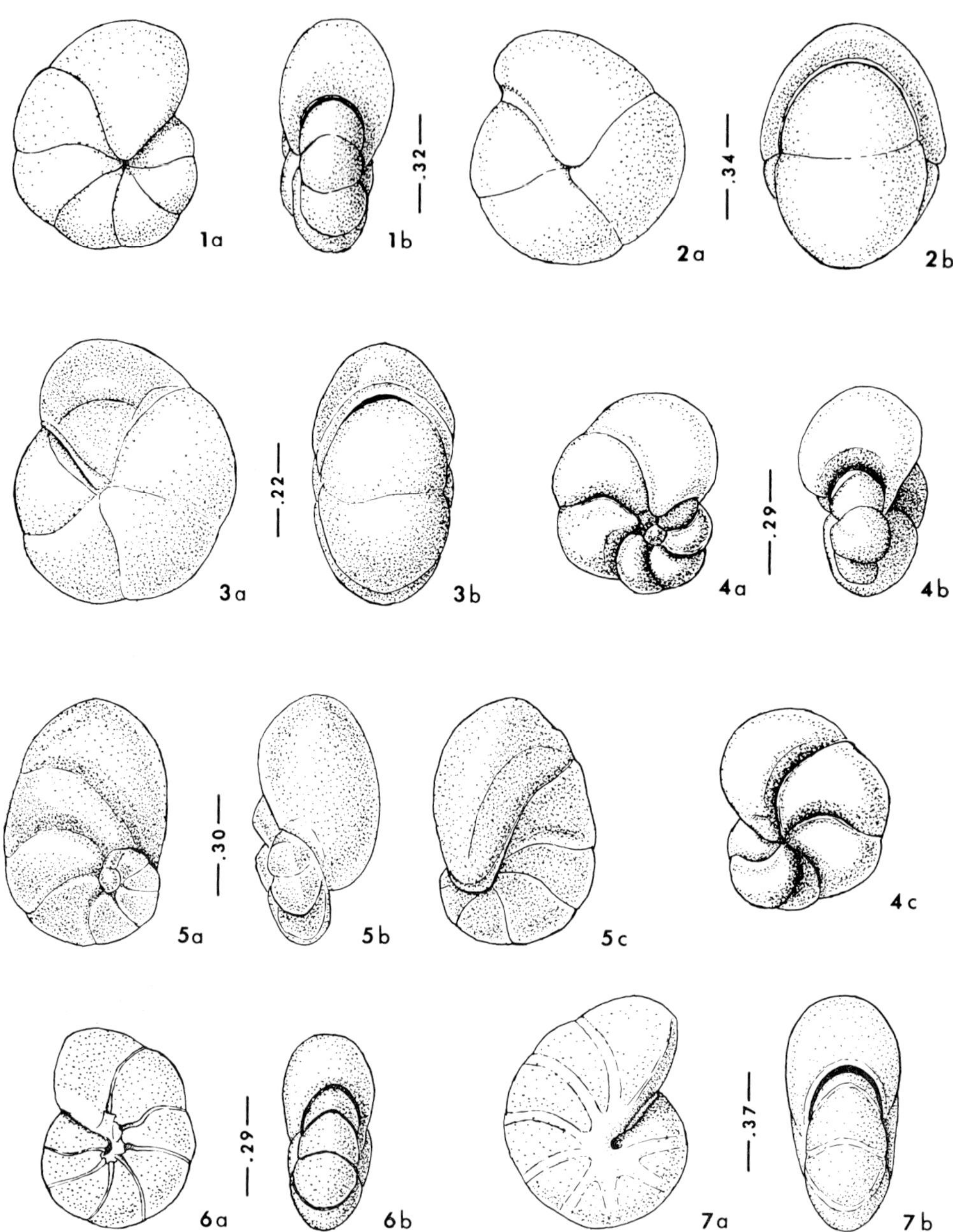

Plate 13

Maximum dimensions in millimeters of the specimens are shown beside the figures.

1. *Pullenia simplex* Rhumbler, ×105; *a*, side view; *b*, edge view; USC 502; Hypotype, USC No. 1213.
2. *Pullenia subsphaerica* Parr, ×100; *a*, side view; *b*, edge view; USC 685; Hypotype, USC No. 1214.
3. *Pullenia osloensis* Feyling-Hanssen, ×179; *a*, side view; *b*, edge view; USC 646; Hypotype, USC No. 1215.
4. *Nonionella iridea* Heron-Allen and Earland, ×102; *a*, side view; *b*, edge view; *c*, opposite side; USC 460; Hypotype, USC No. 1216.
5. *Nonionella bradii* (Chapman), ×124; *a*, side view; *b*, edge view; *c*, opposite side; USC 503; Hypotype, USC No. 1217.
6. *Astrononion echolsi* Kennett, ×104; *a*, side view; *b*, edge view; USC 500; Hypotype, USC No. 1218.
7. *Melonis* cf. *M. affinis* (Reuss), ×95; *a*, side view; *b*, edge view; USC 544; Hypotype, USC No. 1219.

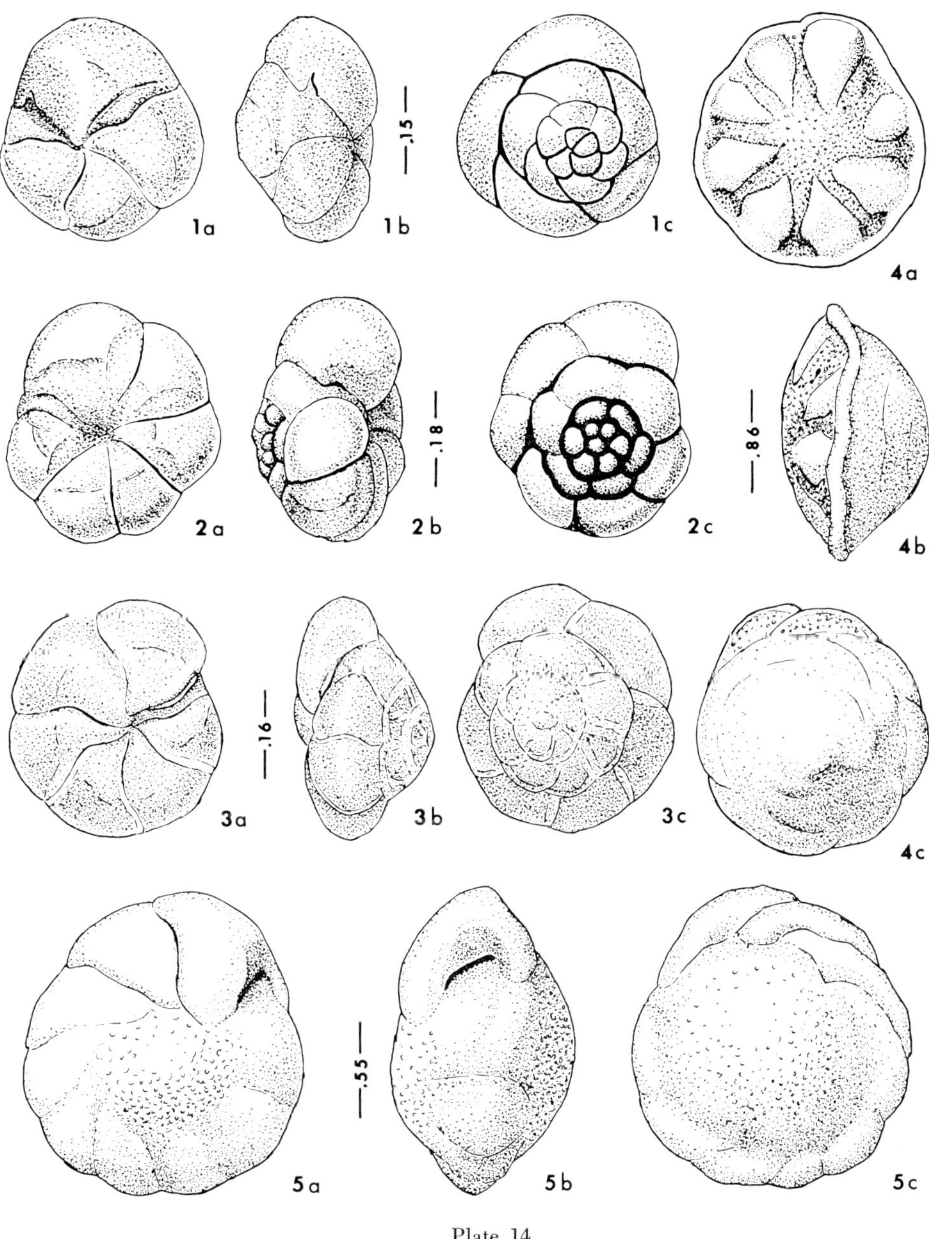

Plate 14

Maximum dimensions in millimeters of the specimens are shown beside the figures.

1. *Eilohedra weddellensis* (Earland), ×219; *a*, ventral view; *b*, edge view; *c*, dorsal view; USC 528; Hypotype, USC No. 1220.
2. *Eponides tumidulus* (Brady), ×196; *a*, ventral view; *b*, edge view; *c*, dorsal view; USC 528; Hypotype, USC No. 1221.
3. *Eponides* sp., ×230; *a*, ventral view; *b*, edge view; *c*, dorsal view; USC 630; Hypotype, USC No. 1222.
4. *Buccella tenerrima* (Bandy), ×43; *a*, ventral view; *b*, edge view; *c*, dorsal view; USC 685; Hypotype, USC No. 1223.
5. *Nuttallides umbonifera* (Cushman), ×84; *a*, ventral view; *b*, edge view; *c*, dorsal view; USC 513; Hypotype, USC No. 1224.

slightly depressed, a little curved and almost radial on the dorsal side and somewhat indistinct in the early part of the test, distinct, radial, and meeting at near right angles on the ventral side; aperture a restricted high interiomarginal arch near the perimeter on the ventral side; wall finely arenaceous, composed of grains of nearly equal size, not smooth, color light brown.

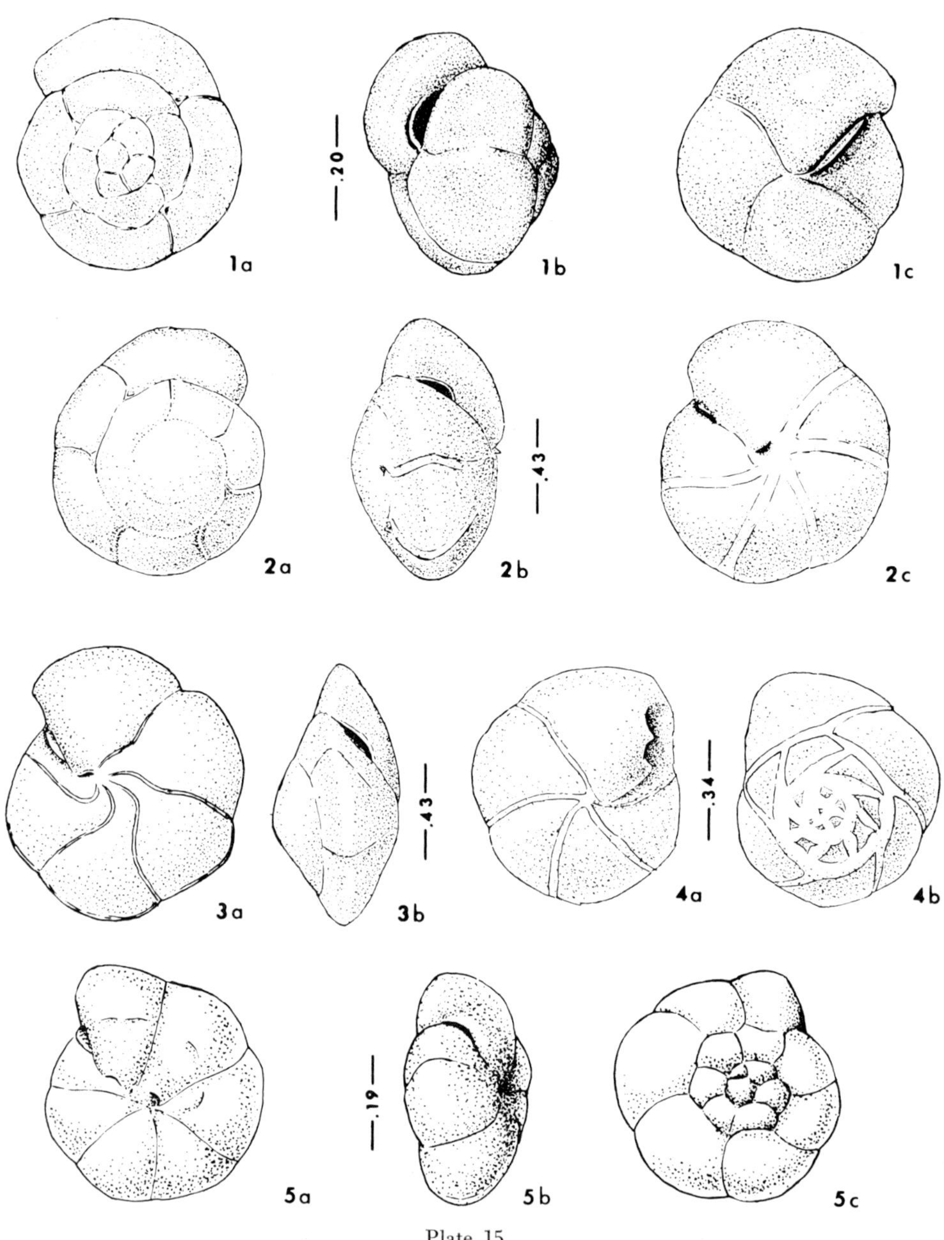

Plate 15

Maximum dimensions in millimeters of the specimens are shown beside the figures.

1. *Oridorsalis* sp., ×168; *a*, dorsal view; *b*, edge view; *c*, ventral view; USC 682; Hypotype, USC No. 1225.
2. *Oridorsalis sidebottomi* (Earland), ×91; *a*, dorsal view; *b*, edge view; *c*, ventral view; USC 462; Hypotype, USC No. 1226.
3. *Oridorsalis tenera* (Brady), ×91; *a*, ventral view; *b*, edge view; USC 1074; Hypotype, USC No. 1227.
4. *Epistominella exigua* (Brady), ×103; *a*, ventral view; *b*, dorsal view; USC 1074; Hypotype, USC No. 1228.
5. *Gyroidina subplanulata* Echols, n. sp., ×190; *a*, ventral view; *b*, edge view; *c*, dorsal view; USC 500; Holotype, USNM No. 687213.

Holotype. USNM No. 687212; maximum diameter 0.16 mm, thickness 0.11 mm; from USC 500.

Remarks. Some immature specimens of *Trochammina quadricamerata* are flat dorsally and ventrally and have an aperture located on the perimeter. This and the slightly depressed proloculus suggest relationship to the Lituolidae rather than to other species of *Trochammina.* A close resemblance exists between this species and some irregularly coiled specimens of *Haplophragmoides quadratus* Earland in size, gross morphology of the test and aperture, and wall texture. Early in this study, the two species were counted together, and thus they are undifferentiated for some stations in Table 2. *Haplophragmoides quadratus* differs from this species in being involute, at least in the early part of the test, in the proloculus which is surrounded by three relatively large chambers of the first whorl rather than four small chambers, and in the aperture which is less restricted.

Occurrence. *Trochammina quadricamerata* is an abundant and eurybathyal species (490 to 4490 meters) in the Scotia and Weddell Seas.

'*Miliolinella*' sp.

Plate 12, fig. 1

Miliolina labiosa, Earland (not *Triloculina labiosa* d'Orbigny, 1839), 1934, Discovery Repts., v. 10, p. 50, pl. 1, figs. 5–7.

Diagnosis. Test free, small, stout, ovate in side and apertural views; chambers lageniform, consisting of a hemispherical part followed by a tubular part leading to the aperture; coiling almost planispiral with each chamber added more than 180 degrees around the perimeter of the test from the preceding chamber; three chambers exposed around the perimeter of the test, a small part of a fourth chamber exposed on one side; successive chambers increasing rapidly in size such that the surface area of the last chamber composes about one-half of the surface area of the test; sutures almost flush, indistinct; aperture small, semicircular, partially closed by a broad flap; wall white and opaque when dry, transparent when wet, insoluble in dilute hydrochloric acid, lacking apparent agglutinated particles, possibly composed of opaline silica. Maximum length of figured specimen 0.40 mm; width 0.24 mm; thickness 0.22 mm.

Occurrence. Only 31 specimens of this species at 20 stations have been found. Depth of occurrence ranges from 990 to 4640 meters.

Wall composition. The wall composition of this species is being studied by R. L. Kolpack and the author. Only preliminary results based on the examination of fragments of the wall of one specimen are reported here. The fragments were mounted in Lakeside mounting medium on a glass slide and examined with a petrographic microscope. Under crossed nicols, extinction was complete and remained so when the microscope stage was rotated, indicating that the wall material is isotropic. The refractive index of the wall material is less than that of Lakeside (RI = 1.540). These are the properties of opaline silica [*Kerr*, 1959].

Two kinds of evidence indicate that the wall was not originally calcite that was subsequently replaced by silica. First, no specimens of calcareous species occurring with '*Miliolinella*' sp. are replaced by silica. Second, siliceous specimens of this species from station USC 712 contain material in the last and penultimate chambers which is stained by rose bengal, presumably indicating that the specimen was alive when collected.

Further discussion of this species is deferred pending completion of studies on the composition of the wall.

Family ALABAMINIDAE Hofker, 1951

Genus *Gyroidina* d'Orbigny, 1826

Gyroidina subplanulata Echols, n. sp.

Plate 15, fig. 5

Diagnosis. Test free, very small, trochospiral, biconvex, and compressed; perimeter very slightly lobulate; edge rounded; umbilicus shallow; two to two and a half whorls visible on the dorsal side; only the six to seven chambers of the last whorl visible on the ventral side; dorsal sutures gently curved and flush except for the distal part of the spiral suture which is slightly depressed; ventral sutures straight, radial, and slightly depressed; aperture a low restricted interiomarginal arch with a lip midway between the perimeter and the umbilicus; small supplementary umbilical aperture in the last chamber; wall calcareous, hyaline, finely perforate, transparent or translucent.

Holotype. USNM No. 687213; diameter 0.19 mm, thickness 0.10 mm; from USC 500. The holotype was the largest specimen found.

Variation. Typically, the margin is evenly rounded in edge view, but in some specimens, the ventral side is more highly convex than the dorsal side, resulting in slightly rhomboid chambers.

Occurrence. This species occurs at 24 stations in the Scotia and northern Weddell seas from 490 to 3770 meters.

Comparison. The small size, shallow umbilicus, and compressed biconvex test of *Gyroidina subplanulata* distinguishes it from other modern species of the genus. The middle Eocene species, *Gyroidina lottensis* Garrett, is similar, but has more chambers per whorl (8–9) and is less compressed.

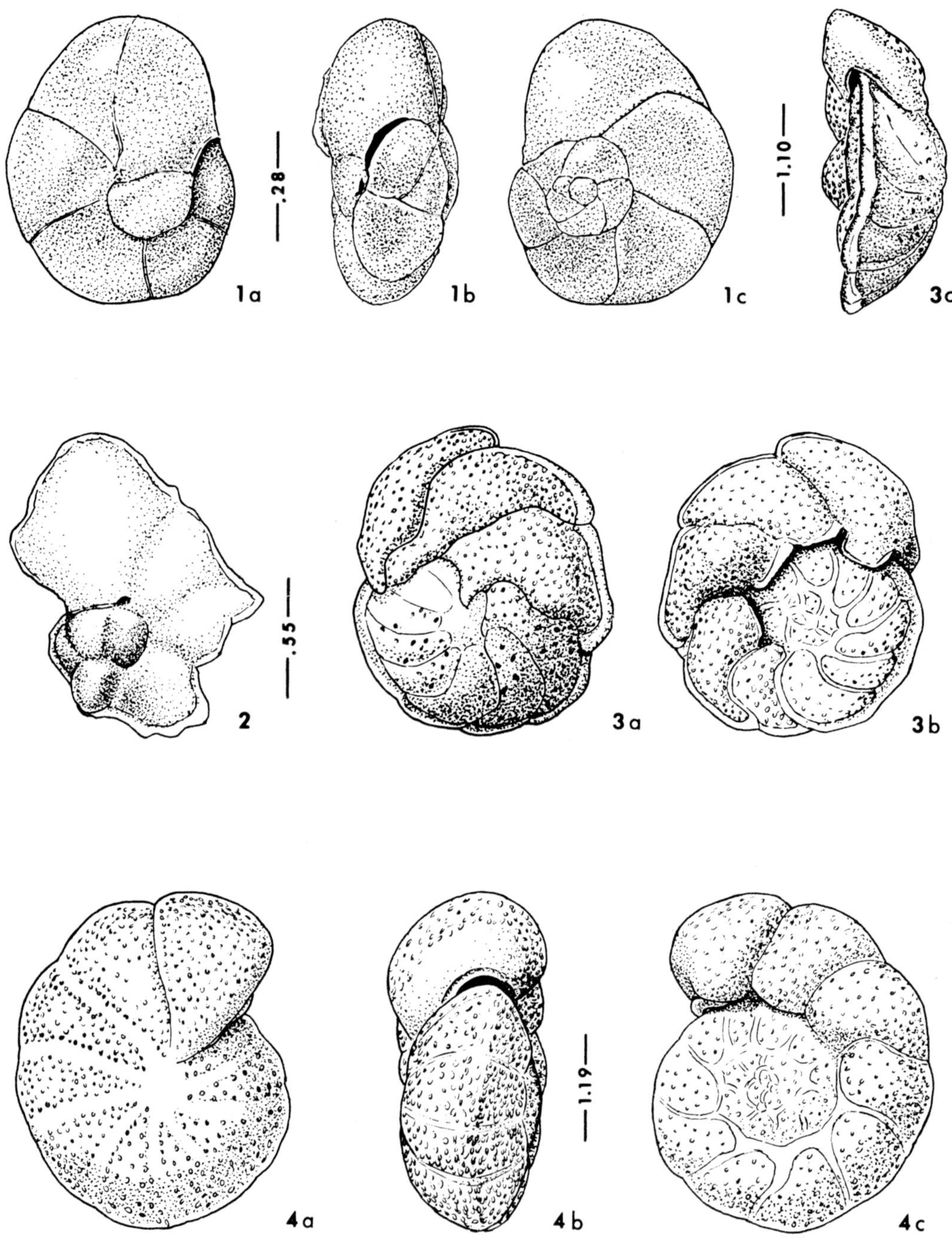

Plate 16

Maximum dimensions in millimeters of the specimens are shown beside the figures.

1. *Valvulineria laevigata* Phleger and Parker, ×149; *a*, ventral view; *b*, edge view; *c*, dorsal view; USC 685; Hypotype, USC No. 1229.
2. *Cibicides lobatulus* (Walker and Jacobs), irregular form, ×80; USC 1074; Hypotype, USC No. 1230.
3. *Cibicides bradii* (Tolmachoff), ×40; *a*, dorsal view; *b*, ventral view; *c*, edge view; USC 656; Hypotype, USC No. 1231.
4. *Cibicides grossepunctatus* Earland, ×41; *a*, ventral view; *b*, edge view; *c*, dorsal view; USC 656; Hypotype, USC No. 1232.

Acknowledgments. This study is part of a doctoral thesis completed at the University of Southern California.

The writer expresses sincere gratitude to Dr. Orville L. Bandy, who suggested the problem and whose guidance, criticism, and patience made the study possible. Special thanks are also directed to Dr. D. S. Gorsline and Dr. J. L. Mohr for critical reading of the thesis and for helpful suggestions. The writer benefited from discussions with Dr. J. P. Kennett, Dr. R. L. Kolpack, and members of the Micropaleontology Laboratory of the Allan Hancock Foundation.

Collection of the samples was facilitated by the wholehearted cooperation of the ship's personnel and scientific staff of the USNS *Eltanin.* Sediment textures were analyzed by Mr. Peter Barnes, Dr. R. L. Kolpack, Mr. David Cook, and Mr. Herman Zimmerman. Mr. R. K. Stauffer drafted the figures and Mr. M. T. Smith provided typing and editorial assistance. Illustrations of foraminiferal specimens are by the author's wife, Mary E. Wade Echols. Type specimens from the collections of the U. S. National Museum were examined through the courtesy of Dr. Richard Cifelli and the staff of the U. S. National Museum. Office and laboratory facilities were provided by the Allan Hancock Foundation of the University of Southern California. This study was supported by the Office of Antarctic Research of the National Science Foundation (grant GA 238).

REFERENCES

Anderson, J. J., Bedrock geology of Antarctica: A summary of exploration, 1831–1962, in *Geology and Paleontology of the Antarctic, Antarctic Res. Ser., 6,* edited by Jarvis B. Hadley, pp. 1–70, American Geophysical Union, Washington, D.C., 1965.

Avilov, I. K., and D. E. Gershanovich, Geomorphology of the Scotia Sea, *Second International Oceanographic Congress, Moscow, Abstracts of Papers,* pp. 12–13, 1966.

Bandy, O. L., and R. J. Echols, Antarctic foraminiferal zonation, in *Biology of the Antarctic Seas, Antarctic Res. Ser., 1,* edited by Milton O. Lee, pp. 73–91, American Geophysical Union, Washington, D.C., 1964.

Bandy, O. L., and K. S. Rodolfo, Distribution of foraminifera and sediments, Peru-Chile Trench area: *Deep-Sea Res., 11,* 817–837, 1964.

Bartlett, Grant A., Benthonic foraminifera ecology in St. Margareta Bay and Mahone Bay, Southeast Nova Scotia, *Bedford Inst. Oceanog. Rept. 64-8,* 1–162, 1964.

Bé, A. W. H., Planktonic foraminifera, in Distribution of Selected Groups of Marine Invertebrates in Waters South of 35°S Latitude, *Antarctic Map Folio Series, Folio 11,* pp. 9–12, American Geographical Society, New York, 1969.

Berger, W. H., Foraminiferal ooze: Solution at depths, *Science, 156,* 383–385, 1967.

Berger, W. H., Planktonic foraminifera: Selective solution and paleoclimatic interpretation, *Deep-Sea Res., 15*(1), 31–43, 1968.

Blair, D. G., The distribution of planktonic foraminifera in deep-sea cores from the Southern Ocean, Antarctica, 141 pp., *Contrib. 10,* Sedimentology Research Laboratory, Department of Geology, Florida State University, Tallahassee, 1965.

Blanc-Vernet, L., Note sur la repartition des foraminiferes au voisinage des Cotes de Terre Adelie (Antarctique), *Rec. Trav. Stat. Mar. End Scl. Fac. Marseille, 52,* 191–201, 1965.

Boltovskoy, E., Zonation en las latitudes atlas del Pacífico sur según los foraminíferos planctónicos vivos, *Rev. Inst. Nac. Invest. Cienc. Nat., Hidrobiol., 2*(1), 1–56, 1966*a*.

Boltovskoy, E., Depth at which foraminifera can survive in sediments, *Contrib. Cushman Found. Foram. Res., 17*(2), 43–45, 1966*b*.

Brady, H. B., Report on the foraminifera dredged by HMS *Challenger* during the years 1873–1876, xxi+ 814 pp., 115 pls. (in atlas), *Rept. Sci. Results Voyage HMS Challenger, 9,* 1884.

Bramlette, M. N., Pelagic sediments, in *Oceanography,* edited by M. Sears, pp. 345–366, American Association for the Advancement of Science, Washington, D.C., 1961.

Buzas, M. A., The distribution and abundance of foraminifera in Long Island Sound, *Smithsonian Misc. Collection, 149*(1), 1–89, 1965.

Chapman, Frederick, Report on the Foraminifera and Ostracoda out of marine muds from sounding in the Ross Sea, *Rept. Sci. Invest. Brit. Antarctic Exped., 1907–1909, Geol., 2*(3), 53–80, pls. i–vi, London, 1916*a*.

Chapman, Frederick, Report on the Foraminifera and Ostracoda from elevated deposits on the shores of the Ross Sea, *Rept. Sci. Invest. Brit. Antarctic Exped., 1907–1909, Geol., 2*(2), 25–52, pls. i–vi, London, 1916*b*.

Chapman, Frederick, and W. J. Parr, Foraminifera, *Australasian Antarctic Exped., 1911 1914, Ser. C, 1*(2), 1–190, 4 pls., 1937.

Chen, Chin, Calcareous zooplankton in the Scotia Sea and Drake Passage, *Nature, 212*(5063), 678–681, 1966.

Chen, C., and A. W. H. Bé, Zonation of calcareous zooplankton in the Scotia Sea and Drake Passage (abstract), *Program, Geol. Soc. Am. Ann. Meeting 1965,* p. 31, 1965.

Clowes, A. J., Phosphate and silicate in the Southern Ocean, *Discovery Rept., 19,* 1–120, 1938.

Cushman, J. A., Foraminifera of the United States Antarctic Service Expedition 1939–1941, *Proc. Am. Philos. Soc., 89*(1), 285–288, 1945.

Deacon, G. E. R., A general account of the hydrology of the South Atlantic Ocean, *Discovery Rept., 7,* 171–238, 1933.

Deacon, G. E. R., The hydrology of the Southern Ocean, *Discovery Rept., 15,* 1–124, 1937.

Deacon, G. E. R., The Southern Ocean, in *The Sea,* vol. 2, edited by M. N. Hill, pp. 281–296, Interscience, New York, 1963.

Earland, A., Foraminifera, 2, South Georgia, *Discovery Rept., 7,* 27–138, pls. 1–7, 1933.

Earland, A., Foraminifera, 3, The Falklands sector of the Antarctic (excluding South Georgia), *Discovery Rept., 10,* 1–208, pls. 1–10, 1934.

Earland, A., Foraminifera, 4, Additional records from the Weddell Sea sector from material obtained by the S.Y. *Scotia, Discovery Rept., 13,* 1–76, pls. 1, 2, 2A, 1936.

Echols, D. J., and A. E. Wegweiser, Naked foraminifera from shallow-water environments (abstract), *Am. Assoc. Petrol. Geol. Bull., 51*(3), 462, 1967.

Echols, R. J., Distribution of Foraminifera and Radiolaria in sediments of the Scotia Sea Area, Antarctic Ocean, 340 pp., Ph.D. dissertation, University of Southern California, Los Angeles, 1967.

Gibson, L. B., Some unifying characteristics of species diversity, *Contrib. Cushman Found. Foram. Res., 17*(4), 117–124, 1966.

Goodell, H. G., Marine geology of the Drake Passage, Scotia Sea, and South Sandwich Trench, USNS *Eltanin,* Marine Geology Cruises 1–8, text 13 pp., appendix 263 pp., *Sedimentol. Res. Lab. Rept.,* Department of Geology, Florida State University, Tallahassee, 1964.

Goodell, H. G., The marine geology of the Southern Ocean, 1, Pacific-Antarctic and Scotia basins, text 35 pp., appendix 196 pp., *Contrib. 2,* Sedimentology Research Laboratory, Department of Geology, Florida State University, Tallahassee, 1965.

Gordon, A. L., Potential temperature, oxygen and circulation of bottom water in the Southern Ocean, *Deep-Sea Res., 13*(6), 1125–1138, 1966.

Hedley, R. H., Cement and iron in the arenaceous foraminifera, *Micropaleontology, 9*(4), 433–441, 1963.

Heezen, B. C., and G. L. Johnson, Echo soundings, U. S. Antarctic Research Ship *Eltanin,* Cruise 7, February–March 1963, *Lamont Geol. Observ. Rept.,* 1965.

Heezen, B. C., and M. Tharp, *Physiographic Diagram of the South Atlantic Ocean,* Geological Society of America, New York, 1958.

Herdman, H. F. P., Report on soundings taken during the Discovery Investigations, 1926–32, *Discovery Rept.,* 6, 205–236, 1932.

Heron-Allen, E., and A. Earland, Protozoa, 2, Foraminifera, British Antarctic (*Terra Nova*) Expedition, 1910, *Nat. Hist. Rept., Zool., 6*(2), 25–268, 8 pls., 1922.

Heron-Allen, E., and A. Earland, Foraminifera, 1, The ice-free area of the Falkland Islands and adjacent seas, *Discovery Rept., 4,* 291–460, pls. 6–17, 1932.

Hough, J. L., Sediment distribution in the Southern Oceans around Antarctica, *J. Sediment. Petrol., 26*(4), 301–306, 1956.

Jacobs, Stanley S., Physical and chemical oceanographic observations in the Southern Oceans, *Tech. Rept. 1–CU–1–65,* Lamont Geological Observatory of Columbia University, Palisades, New York, 1965.

Jarke, J., Beobachtungen über Kalkauflösung an Schalen von Mikrofossilien in Sedimenten der Westlichen Ostee, *Deut. Hydrograph. Z., 14*(1), 6–11, 1961.

Kennett, J. P., Foraminiferal evidence of a shallow calcium carbonate solution boundary, Ross Sea, Antarctica, *Science, 153*(3732), 191–193, 1966.

Kennett, J. P., The fauna of the Ross Sea, part 6, Ecology and distribution of foraminifera, *New Zealand Dept. Sci. Ind. Res., Bull., 186,* 1–46, 1968.

Kennett, J. P., Distribution of planktonic foraminifera in surface sediments southeast of New Zealand, *Proceedings of the First International Planktonic Conference, Geneva, 1967,* vol. 2, 307–322, 1969.

Kerr, Paul F., *Optical Mineralogy,* 3rd ed., pp. 242–244, McGraw-Hill, New York, 1959.

Klepikov, V. V., Warm deep waters in the Weddell Sea, *Soviet Antarctic Exped. Inform. Bull.,* English Transl., *2,* 194–198, 1960.

Lisitzin, A. P., Bottom sediments of the eastern Antarctic and southern Indian Ocean, *Deep-Sea Res., 7,* 89–99, 1960.

Mackintosh, N. A., The Antarctic Convergence and the distribution of surface temperatures in Antarctic waters, *Discovery Rept., 23,* 177–212, 1946.

Mather, T. T., The deep-sea sediments of the Drake Passage and Scotia Sea, 100 pp., *Contrib. 15,* Sedimentology Research Laboratory, Department of Geology, Florida State University, Tallahassee, 1966.

McKnight, W. M., Jr., The distribution of foraminifera off parts of the Antarctic coast, *Bull. Am. Paleontol., 44*(201), 65–158, 1962.

Parker, F. L., and W. D. Athearn, Ecology of marsh foraminifera in Poponesset Bay, Massachusetts, *J. Paleontol., 33,* 333–343, 1959.

Parr, W. J., Foraminifera, *Rept. B.A.N.Z. Antarctic Res. Exped., 1929–1931, Ser. B, 5*(6), 235–392, pls. 3–15, 1950.

Pearcey, F. G., Foraminifera of the Scottish National Antarctic Expedition, *Trans. Roy. Soc. Edinburgh, 49,* 991–1044, pls. i, ii, 1914.

Peterson, M. N. A., Calcite: Rates of dissolution in a vertical profile in the Central Pacific, *Science, 154*(3756), 1542–1544, 1966.

Pflum, C. E., The distribution of foraminifera in the eastern Ross Sea, Antarctic, *Paleontol. Res. Inst., 50*(226), 1–65, 1966.

Phleger, F. B., Ecology of foraminifera, northwest Gulf of Mexico, part 1, Foraminifera distribution, *Geol. Soc. Am., Mem. 46,* 1–88, 1951.

Phleger, F. B., Foraminifera distribution in some sediment samples from the Canadian and Greenland Arctic, *Contrib. Cushman Found. Foram. Res., 3,* 80–89, 1952.

Phleger, F. B., Ecology of foraminifera in southeastern Mississippi Delta area, *Bull. Am. Assoc. Petrol. Geol., 39,* 712–752, 1955.

Phleger, F. B., *Ecology and Distribution of Recent Foraminifera,* 297 pp., Johns Hopkins Press, Baltimore, 1960.

Phleger, F. B., Patterns of living benthonic foraminifera, Gulf of California, in Marine Geology of the Gulf of California, *Am. Assoc. Petrol. Geol., Mem. 3,* 377–394, 1964.

Phleger, F. B., F. L. Parker, and J. F. Peirson, North Atlantic core foraminifera, *Rept. Swedish Deep-Sea Exped., 7*(1), 1–122, pls. 1–12, 1953.

Pirie, J. H. H., Deep-sea deposits, Scottish National Antarctic Expedition, 1902–1904, *Trans. Roy. Soc. Edinburgh, 49*(10), 645–686, 1913.

Saidova, Kh. M., The quantitative distribution of bottom foraminifera in Antarctica, *Dokl. Akad. Nauk SSSR, 139*(4), 967–969, 1961.

Saunders, J. B., Trochamminidae and certain Lituolidae (Foraminifera) from the Recent brackish-water sediments of Trinidad, British West Indies, *Smithsonian Misc. Collection, 134*(5), 1–16, 1957.

Shchedrina, Z. G., On the foraminifera fauna of the Kuril-Kamchatka Trench, *Tr. Inst. Okeanol. Akad. Nauk SSSR, 27,* 161–179, 1958.

Shchedrina, Z. G., The foraminiferan fauna of the eastern sector of the Antarctic, in *Soviet Antarctic Exped. Inform. Bull.,* English Transl., *1,* 125–127, 1964.

Shepard, F. P., Nomenclature based on sand-silt-clay ratios, *J. Sediment. Petrol., 24,* 151–158, 1954.

Shishkevish, L. J., The distribution of foraminifera in cores from the northern Scotia Arc, Scotia Sea, 128 pp., Ph.D. dissertation, New York University, New York, 1964.

Siever, R., K. C. Beck, and R. A. Berner, Composition of interstitial waters of modern sediments, *J. Geol., 73,* 39–73, 1965.

Simpson, E. H., Measurement of diversity, *Nature, 163,* 688, 1949.

Sverdrup, H. U., The influence of bottom topography on ocean currents, in *Applied Mechanics*, Theodore von Karman Anniversary Volume, 66–75, 1941.

Sverdrup, H. U., M. W. Johnson, and R. H. Fleming, *The Oceans*, 1087 pp., Prentice-Hall, Englewood Cliffs, New Jersey, 1942.

Uchio, T., Ecology of living benthonic foraminifera from the San Diego, California area, *Cushman Found. Foram. Res. Spec. Publ. 5*, 1–72, 1960*a*.

Uchio, T., Benthonic foraminifera of the Antarctic Ocean, *Seto Marine Biol. Lab. Spec. Publ. 12*, 3–20, 1960*b*.

Uchio, T., Planktonic foraminifera of the Antarctic Ocean, *Seto Marine Biol. Lab. Spec. Publ. 11*, 1–9, 1969*c*.

U. S. Navy, Oceanographic atlas of the polar seas, part 1, Antarctica, 70 pp., *Hydrograph. Off. Publ. 705*, 1957.

Walton, W. R., Techniques for recognition of living foraminifera, *Contrib. Cushman Found. Foram. Res., 3*, 56–60, 1952.

Warthin, A. S., Jr., Foraminifera of the Ross Sea, *Am. Museum Novitates, 721*, 1–4, 1934.

Wiesner, H., *Die Foraminiferen: Deutsche Südpolar Expedition 1901–1903, 20* (Zool., vol. 12), 53–165, 1931.

Wood, Alan, The structure of the wall of the test in the foraminifera; its value in classification, *Quart. J. Geol. Soc. London, 104*(414), 229–255, 1949.

FAUNAL REFERENCE LIST

Adercotryma glomeratum (Brady) = *Lituola glomerata* Brady, 1878, Ann. Mag. Nat. Hist., ser. 5, v. 1, p. 433, pl. 20, figs. 1a–1c.

Ammobaculites agglutinans (d'Orbigny) = *Spirolina agglutinans* d'Orbigny, 1846, Foram. Foss. Vienne, p. 137, pl. 7, figs. 10–12.

Ammobaculites filiformis Earland = *A. agglutinans* var. *filiformis* Earland, 1934, Discovery Repts., v. 10, p. 92, pl. 3, figs. 11–13.

Ammobaculites foliaceous (Brady) = *Haplophragmium foliaceum* Brady, 1881, Quart. Jour. Microscop. Sci., v. 21, p. 50.

Ammobaculites foliaceous (Brady) f. *recurva* Earland = *A. foliaceous* var. *recurva* Earland, 1934, Discovery Repts., v. 10, p. 98, pl. 3, figs. 14–17.

Ammobaculoides cylindroides (Earland) = *Spiroplectella cylindroides* Earland, 1934, Discovery Repts., v. 10, p. 114, pl. 4, figs. 36–38.

Ammodiscus catinus Hoglund, 1947, Uppsala Univ., Zool. Bidrag, v. 26, p. 122, pl. 8, figs. 1, 7, pl. 28, figs. 19–23, text-figs. 82–84, 105–109.

Ammoflintina argentea Echols, n. sp.

Ammoflintina trihedra Earland, 1934, Discovery Repts., v. 10, p. 98, pl. 3, figs. 20–23.

Ammolagena clavata (Jones and Parker) = *Trochammina irregularis clavata* Jones and Parker, 1860, Quart. Jour. Geol. Soc. London, v. 16, p. 304.

Ammomarginulina ensis Wiesner, 1931, Deutsche Südpolar Exped. 1901–1903, v. 20 (Zool., v. 12), p. 97, pl. 12, fig. 147.

Ammoscalaria tenuimargo (Brady) = *Haplophragmium tenuimargo* Brady, 1882, Proc. Roy. Soc. Edinburgh, v. 11 (1880–1882), no. 111, p. 715.

Angulogerina earlandi Parr, 1950, B.A.N.Z. Antarctic Res. Exped. 1929–1931, ser. B, v. 5, pt. 6, p. 341, pl. 12, fig. 21.

Angulogerina earlandi forma *pauperata* (Heron-Allen and Earland) = *Uvigerina angulosa* var. *pauperata* Heron-Allen and Earland, 1932, Discovery Rept., v. 4, p. 398, pl. 12, figs. 40–43.

Astrammina rara Rhumbler, in Wiesner, 1931, Deutsche Südpolar Exped. 1901–1903, v. 20 (Zool., v. 12), p. 78, pl. 2, fig. 19a, 19b.

Astrononion antarcticum Parr, 1950, B.A.N.Z. Antarctic Res. Exped. 1929–1931, ser. B, v. 5, pt. 6, p. 371, pl. 15, figs. 13, 14a, 14b.

Astrononion echolsi Kennett, 1967, Contrib. Cushman Found. Foram. Res., v. 18, pt. 3, p. 134, pl. 11, figs. 7, 8.

Astrorhiza triangularis Earland, 1933, Discovery Repts., v. 7, p. 52, pl. 1, figs. 8, 9.

Bathysiphon discreta (Brady) = *Rhabdammina discreta* Brady, 1881, Quart. Jour. Microscop. Sci., v. 21, p. 48.

Bathysiphon granulosa (Brady) = *Marsipella granulosa* Brady, 1879, Quart. Jour. Microscop. Sci., v. 19, p. 36, pl. 3, figs. 8, 9.

Bathysiphon rusticum de Folin, 1886, Actes Soc. Linn. Bordeaux, v. 40 (ser. 4, v. 10), p. 284, pl. 8, figs. 9a–9c.

Bathysiphon sp. A. Test a small tube of uniform diameter, open at both ends, with annular constrictions; wall coarsely arenaceous, but evenly finished; diameter of tube about 0.08 mm.

Bigenerina minutissima Earland, 1933, Discovery Repts., v. 7, p. 98, pl. 3, figs. 36–38.

Bolivina decussata Brady, 1881, Quart. Jour. Microscop. Sci., v. 21, p. 28.

Bolivina pseudopunctata Höglund, 1947, Uppsala Univ., Zool. Bidrag, v. 26, p. 273, pl. 24, figs. 5a, 5b.

Buccella tenerrima (Bandy) = *Rotalia tenerrima* Bandy, 1950, Jour. Paleontol., v. 24, p. 278, pl. 42, fig. 3.

Bulimina aculeata d'Orbigny, 1826, Ann. Sci. Nat., v. 7, p. 269.

Bulimina rostrata Brady, 1884, Rept. Voy. Challenger, v. 9 (Zool.), p. 408, pl. 51, figs. 14, 15.

Buliminella tenuata Cushman = *B. subfusiformis* var. *tenuata* Cushman, 1927, Bull. Scripps Inst. Oceanog., Tech. Ser., v. 1, p. 149, pl. 2, fig. 9.

Cassidulina laevigata d'Orbigny, 1826, Ann. Sci. Nat., ser. 1, v. 7, p. 282, pl. 15, figs. 4, 5.

Cassidulina lens Earland, 1934, Discovery Repts., v. 10, p. 135, pl. 6, figs. 17–20.

Cassidulina subglobosa Brady, 1881, Quart. Jour. Microscop. Sci., n.s., v. 21, p. 60.

Cassidulinoides crassa (Earland) = *Ehrenbergina crassa* Earland, 1929, Jour. Roy. Microscop. Soc., ser. 3, v. 49, pt. 4, p. 329, pl. 3, figs. 18–26.

Cassidulinoides parkerianus (Brady) = *Cassidulina parkeriana* Brady, 1881, Quart. Jour. Microscop. Sci., n.s., v. 21, p. 59.

Cassidulinoides porrectus Heron-Allen and Earland = *Cassidulina crassa* d'Orbigny var. *porrecta* Heron-Allen and Earland, 1932, Discovery Repts., v. 4, p. 358, pl. 9, figs. 34–37.

Cerobertina arctica (Green) = *Ceratobulimina arctica* Green, 1960, Micropaleontology, v. 6, p. 71, pl. 1, figs. 1a–1c.

Cibicides bradii (Talmachoff) = *Planulina bradii* Talmachoff, 1934, Ann. Carnegie Museum, Pittsburgh, v. 23, p. 333.

Cibicides grossepunctatus Earland, 1934, Discovery Repts., v. 10, p. 184, pl. 8, figs. 39–41.

Cibicides lobatulus (Walker and Jacobs) = *Nautilus lobatulus* Walker and Jacobs, 1798, in Adams Essays, Kanmacker's ed., p. 642, pl. 14, fig. 36.

Cibicides lobatulus, irregular form. Plate 16, fig. 2.

Conotrochammina alternans Earland, 1934, Discovery Repts., v. 10, p. 103, pl. 3, figs. 24–27.

Conotrochammina bullata (Hoglund), 1947, Uppsala Univ., Zool. Bidrag, v. 26, p. 213, pl. 17, fig. 5.

Conotrochammina kennetti Echols, n. sp.

Conotrochammina rugosa (Parr) = *Trochammina rugosa* Parr, 1950, B.A.N.Z. Antarctic Res. Exped. 1929–1931, ser. B, v. 5, pt. 6, p. 277, pl. 5, fig. 5.

Conotrochammina sp. A. Plate 6, fig. 4.

Conotrochammina sp. B. Plate 6, fig. 5.

Conotrochammina sp. C. Test a low trochoid spire of about two whorls with five or six chambers per whorl, periphery rounded; aperture areal, ovate, bordered by a thin lip. These rare forms could be aberrant individuals of *Conotrochammina bullata.*

Cribrostomoides arenacea (Heron-Allen and Earland) = *Truncatulina lobatula* (Walker and Jacob) var. *arenacea* Heron-Allen and Earland, 1922, Brit. Antarctic (Terra Nova) Exped. 1910, Nat. Hist. Rept. Zool., v. 6, no. 2, p. 208, pl. 7, figs. 32–35.

Cribrostomoides contortus (Earland) = *Recurvoides contortus* Earland, 1934, Discovery Repts., v. 10, p. 91, pl. 10, figs. 7–19. Reasons for not using the genus *Recurvoides* are discussed in the annotation for *Cribrostomoides subglobosus.*

Cribrostomoides jeffreysi (Williamson) = *Nonionina jeffreysii* Williamson, 1858, on the Recent foraminifera of Great Britain, Roy. Soc., London, p. 34, pl. 3, figs. 72, 73.

Cribrostomoides scitulus (Brady) = *Halplophragmium scitulum* Brady, 1881, Quart. Jour. Microscop. Sci., v. 21, p. 50.

Cribrostomoides sphaeriloculus (Cushman) = *Haplophragmoides sphaeriloculum* Cushman, 1910, U.S. Natl. Museum Bull., no. 71, p. 107, text-fig. 165.

Cribrostomoides subglobosus (Cushman) = *Haplophragmoides subglobosus* Cushman, 1910, U.S. Natl. Museum Bull., no. 71, p. 105, 106, text-figs. 162–164. Every test of this species from antarctic waters that appeared planispiral from the exterior (Plate 3, fig. 9) was found to be excentrically coiled to some degree if sectioned. Many tests have obvious changes in coiling direction (Plate 3, fig. 8). *Uchio* [1960*a*], noting the same coiling pattern in eastern Pacific material, referred the species to *Recurvoides* Earland. However, if the populations described by Uchio are, in fact, conspecific with *H. subglobosus* and *H. subglobosus* is conspecific with *Cribrostomoides bradyi* Cushman [*Earland,* 1934], then *Recurvoides* Earland, 1934, is a junior synonym of *Cribrostomoides* Cushman, 1910. Among the limited amount of eastern Pacific material of this form that the author has sectioned, both true planispiral and excentrically coiled populations have been noted. Because the author believes these two kinds of populations are conspecific with one another and with the Scotia Sea populations, the latter are referred to the genus *Cribrostomoides* as are other similar species whether planispirally or excentrically coiled.

Cribrostomoides umbilicatulus (Pearcey) = *Haplophragmoides umbilicatulum* Pearcey, 1914, Trans. Roy. Soc. Edinburgh, v. 49, pt. 4, no. 19, p. 1008, pl. 2, figs. 8–10.

Cribrostomoides umbilicatulus soldanii (Earland) = *Trochammina soldanii* Earland, 1936, Discovery Repts., v. 13, p. 38, pl. 1, figs. 32–34.

Cribrostomoides wiesneri (Parr) = *Labrospira wiesneri* Parr, 1950, B.A.N.Z. Antarctic Res. Exped. 1929–1931, ser. B, v. 5, pt. 6, p. 272, pl. 4, figs. 25, 26.

Cyclammina cancellata Brady, 1879, Quart. Jour. Microscop. Sci., n.s., v. 19, p. 62.

Cyclammina orbicularis Brady, 1884, Rept. Voy. Challenger, v. 9 (Zool.), p. 353, pl. 37, figs. 17–19.

Cyclammina pusilla Brady, 1884, Rept. Voy. Challenger, v. 9 (Zool.), p. 353, pl. 37, figs. 20–23.

Cyclammina trullissata (Brady) = *Trochammina trullissata* Brady, 1879, Quart. Jour. Microscop. Sci., n.s., v. 19, p. 56, pl. 5, figs. 10a, 10b, 11.

Cyclogyra involvens (Reuss) = *Operculina involvens* Reuss, 1850, Denkschr. Akad. Wiss. Wien, v. 1, p. 370, pl. 46, fig. 30.

Cystammina argentea Earland, 1934, Discovery Repts., v. 10, p. 105, pl. 4, figs. 17–19.

Cystammina pauciloculata (Brady) = *Trochammina pauciloculata* Brady, 1879, Quart. Jour. Microscop. Sci., n.s., v. 19, p. 58, pl. 5, figs. 13, 14.

Dendrophrya erecta Wright, 1861, Ann. Mag. Nat. Hist., ser. 3, v. 8, p. 122, pl. 4, figs. 4, 5.

Dentalina communis d'Orbigny f. *larva* Earland, 1934, Discovery Repts., v. 10, p. 167, pl. 7, figs. 40, 41.

Dentalina cuvieri (d'Orbigny) = *Nodosaria* (*Dentaline*) *cuvieri* d'Orbigny, 1826, Ann. Sci. Nat., ser. 1, v. 7, p. 255.

Dentalina frobisherensis Leoblich and Tappen, 1953, Smithsonian Inst. Misc. Collection, v. 121, no. 7, p. 55, pl. 10, figs. 1–9.

Dentalina ittai Leoblich and Tappen, 1953, Smithsonian Inst. Misc. Collection, v. 121, no. 7, p. 56, pl. 10, figs. 10–12.

Discorbis translucens Earland, 1934, Discovery Repts., v. 10, p. 181, pl. 8, figs. 20–22.

Dorothia sp. A. Test minute, triangular in outline with straight sides, about as wide as broad, only slightly compressed, periphery truncated, initial part a minute trochoid whorl of about four chambers, latter part biserial; chambers increasing rapidly in size as added, wider than high; sutures slightly depressed, almost straight, a little inclined, highest at the midline, apertural face flat; aperture an interiomarginal slit; wall finely arenaceous with calcareous cement, surface somewhat rough.

Eggerella nitens (Wiesner) = *Verneuilina bradyi* Cushman var. *nitens* Wiesner, 1931, Deutsche Südpolar Exped. 1901–1903, v. 20 (Zool., v. 12), p. 99, pl. 13, figs. 154a, 154b.

Eggerella parkerae (Uchio) = *Karreriella parkerae* Uchio, 1960, Cushman Found. Foram. Res. Spec. Publ., no. 5, p. 56, pl. 2, figs. 21–23.

Some individuals of *Karreriella parkerae* from the type area have a true, but short, biserial stage, whereas none of the hundreds of specimens identified as this species in the Scotia Sea area have reached that stage of development. Although the presence or absence of a biserial stage is the generally valid distinction between the genera *Karreriella* and *Eggerella*, the author questions whether, in this case, it is significant at the species level. Considering this uncertainty, it was decided not to describe the Scotia Sea form as a new species, but rather to assign it to the genus *Eggerella*, the definition of which is descriptive of its morphology.

Ehrenbergina glabra Heron-Allen and Earland = *Ehrenbergina hystrix glabra* Heron-Allen and Earland, 1922, Brit. Antarctic (Terra Nova) Exped., 1910, Nat. Hist. Rept. Zool., v. 6, no. 2, p. 140, pl. 5, figs. 1–6.

Ehrenbergina trigona Goës = *E. serrata* Reuss var. *trigona* Goës, 1896, Bull. Museum Comp. Zool., v. 29, p. 49, pl. 6, figs. 183, 184.

Eilohedra weddellensis (Earland) = *Eponides weddellensis* Earland, 1936, Discovery Repts., v. 13, p. 57, pl. 1, figs. 65–67.

Epistominella arctica Green, 1960, Micropaleontology, v. 6, p. 71, pl. 1, figs. 4a, 4b.

Epistominella exigua (Brady) = *Pulvinulina exigua* Brady, 1884, Rept. Voy. Challenger, v. 9 (Zool.), p. 696, pl. 103, figs. 13, 14.

Eponides tumidulus (Brady) = *Truncatulina tumidula* Brady, 1884, Rept. Voy. Challenger, v. 9 (Zool.), p. 666, pl. 95, fig. 8.

Eponides sp. A. Plate 14, fig. 3.

Fissurina annectens (Burrows and Holland) = *Lagena annectens* Burrows and Holland, in Jones, T. R., 1895, Palaeontog. Soc., London, p. 203, pl. 7, figs. 11a, 11b.

Fissurina fimbriata (Brady) = *Lagena fimbriata* Brady, 1881, Quart. Jour. Microscop. Sci., n.s., v. 21, p. 61.

Fissurina marginata (Montagu) = *Vermiculum marginatum* Montagu, 1803, Testacea Britannica, p. 524.

Fissurina semimarginata Reuss = *Lagena marginata* (Montagu) var. *semimarginata* Reuss, 1870, K. Akad. Wiss. Wien, Math. Naturwiss. Kl., Sitzungsber., v. 62, p. 468.

Fissurina sp. A. Test broadly fusiform in side view, only slightly compressed, margin rounded; surface smooth, without keel, but margin somewhat thickened, blunted pointed boss at adapertural end; aperture fissurine, large, funnel-shaped; wall hyaline, not clear, thick.

Fissurina sp. B. Test ovate in side view, slightly produced at apertural end, slightly compressed, margin rounded; surface smooth, without ornamentation of any kind; aperture fissurine, ovate, small.

Florilus japonicus (Asano) = *Pseudononion japonicum* Asano, 1936, Jour. Geol. Soc. Japan, v. 43, p. 347, text-figs. A–C.

Fursenkoina earlandi (Parr) = *Bolivina earlandi* Parr, 1950, B.A.N.Z. Antarctic Res. Exped. 1929–1931, ser. B, v. 5, pt. 6, p. 339, pl. 12, figs. 16a, 16b.

Fursenkoina fusiformis (Williamson) = *Bulimina pupoides* var. *fusiformis* Williamson, 1858, On the Recent foraminifera of Great Britain, Roy. Soc. London, p. 63, pl. 5, figs. 129, 130.

Gaudryina ferruginea Heron-Allen and Earland, 1922, Brit. Antarctic (Terra Nova) Exped., 1910, Nat. Hist. Rept. Zool., v. 6, no. 2, p. 123, pl. 4, figs. 13–15.

Gaudryina minuta Earland, 1934, Discovery Repts., v. 10, p. 121, pl. 5, figs. 45, 46.

Gaudryina pauperata Earland, 1934, Discovery Repts., v. 10, p. 121, pl. 5, figs. 47–49.

Glandulina antarctica Parr, 1950, B.A.N.Z. Antarctic Res. Exped. 1929–1931, ser. B, v. 5, pt. 6, p. 334, pl. 12, figs. 8, 9.

Glabratella minutissima (Chaster) = *Discorbina minutissima* Chaster, 1892, Southport Soc. Nat. Sci. Rept., 1st Rept. (1890–1891), append., p. 65, pl. 1, figs. 15a–15c.

Globigerina bulloides d'Orbigny, 1826, Ann. Sci. Nat., ser. 1, v. 7, p. 277, modèles no. 17.

Globigerina pachyderma (Ehrenberg) = *Aristerospira pachyderma* Ehrenberg, 1861, K. Preuss. Akad. Wiss. Berlin, Monatsber., pp. 276, 277, 303.

Globigerina quinqueloba Natland, 1938, Bull. Scripps Inst. Oceanog., Tech. Ser., v. 4, no. 5, p. 149, pl. 6, fig. 7.

Globigerinita glutinata (Egger) = *Globigerina glutinata* Egger, 1893, Abhandl. K. Bayer. Akad. Wiss. München, v. 18, p. 371, pl. 13, figs. 19–21.

Globigerinita uvula (Ehrenberg) = *Pylodexia uvula* Ehrenberg, 1861, K. Preuss. Akad. Wiss. Berlin, Monatsber., pp. 276, 277, 308.

Globorotalia inflata (d'Orbigny) = *Globigerina inflata* d'Orbigny, 1839, in Barker-Webb and Berthelot, Hist. Nat. Iles Canaries, Foraminiferes, v. 2, pt. 2, p. 134, pl. 2, figs. 7–9.

Globorotalia scitula (Brady) = *Pulvinulina scitula* Brady, 1882, Proc. Roy. Soc. Edinburgh, v. 11 (1880–82), no. 111, p. 716.

Globorotalia truncatulinoides (d'Orbigny) = *Rotalina truncatulinoides* d'Orbigny, 1839, in Barker-Webb and Berthelot, Hist. Nat. Iles Canaries, Foraminiferes, v. 2, pt. 2, p. 132, pl. 2, figs. 25–27.

Glomospira charoides (Jones and Parker) = *Trochammina squamata charoides* Jones and Parker, 1860, Quart. Jour. Geol. Soc. London, v. 16, p. 304.

Glomospira gordialis (Jones and Parker) = *Trochammina squamata gordialis* Jones and Parker, 1860, Quart. Jour. Geol. Soc. London, v. 16, p. 304.

Gyroidina orbicularis d'Orbigny, 1826, Ann. Sci. Nat., ser. 1, v. 7, p. 278.

Gyroidina soldanii d'Orbigny, 1826, Ann. Sci. Nat., ser. 1, v. 7, p. 278.

Gyroidina subplanulata Echols, n. sp.

Hanzawaia complanata (Sidebottom) = *Discorbina bertheloti* var. *complanata* Sidebottom, 1918, Jour. Roy. Microscop. Soc., p. 253, pl. 6, figs. 1–3.

Haplophragmoides bradyi (Robertson) = *Trochammina bradyi* Robertson, 1891, Ann. Mag. Nat. Hist., ser. 6, v. 7, p. 388.

Haplophragmoides canariensis d'Orbigny, 1938, in Barker-Webb and Berthelot, Hist. Nat. Iles Canaries, Foraminiferes, v. 2, pt. 2, p. 128, pl. 2, figs. 33, 34.

Haplophragmoides cf. *H. kirki* Wickenden, 1932, Trans. Roy. Soc. Canada, ser. 3, v. 26, sec. 4, p. 85, pl. 1, figs. 1a–1c.

Haplophragmoides parkerae (Uchio) = *Recurvoidella parkerae* Uchio, 1960, Cushman Found. Foram. Res. Spec. Publ., no. 5, p. 53, pl. 1, figs. 18, 19.

Haplophragmoides quadratus Earland, 1934, Discovery Repts., v. 10, p. 88, pl. 3, figs. 7–8.

Hemisphaerammina bradyi Leoblich and Tappen, 1957, U.S. Natl. Museum Bull., no. 215, p. 224, pl. 72, figs. 2a, 2b.

Heronallenia lingulata (Burrows and Holland) = *Discorbina lingulata* Burrows and Holland, in Jones, 1895, Monogr. Foram. Crag, pt. 2, pl. expl., pl. 7, figs. 33a–33c.

Heronallenia parva Parr, 1950, B.A.N.Z. Antarctic Res. Exped. 1929–1931, ser. B, v. 5, pt. 6, p. 358, pl. 14, fig. 10.

Heronallenia wilsoni (Heron-Allen and Earland) = *Discorbina wilsoni* Heron-Allen and Earland, 1922, Brit. Antarctic (Terra Nova) Exped., 1910, Nat. Hist. Rept. Zool., v. 6, no. 2, p. 206, pl. 7, figs. 17–19.

Hippocrepina pusilla Heron-Allen and Earland, 1930, Jour. Roy. Microscop. Soc., ser. 3, v. 50, p. 69, pl. 3, figs. 34, 35.

Hippocrepinella crassa Heron-Allen and Earland = *H. hirudinea* var. *crassa* Heron-Allen and Earland, 1932, Jour. Roy. Microscop. Soc., ser. 3, v. 52, pt. 3, p. 259, pl. 2, figs. 1–3.

Hormosina davisi (Parr) = *Reophax davisi* Parr, 1950, B.A.N.Z. Antarctic Res. Exped. 1929–1931, ser. B, v. 5, pt. 6, p. 265, pl. 4, fig. 11.

Hormosina globulifera Brady, 1879, Quart. Jour. Microscop. Sci., n.s., v. 19, p. 60, pl. 4, figs. 4, 5.

Hormosina lapidigera Rhumbler, 1905, Verhand. Deut. Zool. Ges., pp. 103, 104, text-fig. 8.

Hyperammina cylindrica Parr, 1950, B.A.N.Z. Antarctic Res. Exped. 1929–1931, ser. B, v. 5, pt. 6, p. 254, pl. 3, fig. 5.

Hyperammina leavigata J. Wright = *Hyperammina elongata* var. *laevigata* J. Wright, 1891, Proc. Roy. Irish Acad., ser. 3, v. 1 (1889–1891), no. 4, p. 466, pl. 20, fig. 1.

Hyperammina laevigata J. Wright var. A. Test consisting of a fusiform or tear-drop shaped proloculus followed by an elongate tubular second chamber initially of smaller diameter than the proloculus; tubular chamber straight, tapering slightly toward the proloculus, with diistinct annular constrictions; aperture the open end of the tube; wall coarsely arenaceous, but smoothly finished. The straight test and coarsely arenaceous wall disinguishes this variety from *H. laevigata*.

Hyperammina subnodosa Brady, 1884, Rept. Voy. Challenger, v. 9 (Zool.), p. 159, pl. 23, figs. 11–14.

Hyperammina tenuissima Heron-Allen and Earland = *H. elongata* Brady var. *tenuissima* Heron-Allen and Earland, 1922, Brit. Antarctic (Terra Nova) Exped., 1910, Nat. Hist. Rept. Zool., v. 6, no. 2, p. 88, pl. 1, fig. 17.

Hyperammina sp. A. Plate 1, fig. 2.

Islandiella islandica (Nörvang) = *Cassidulina islandica* Nörvang, 1945, The Zoology of Iceland, v. 2, pt. 2, p. 41, text-figs. 7, 8d 8f.

Islandiella quadrata (Cushman and Hughes) = *Cassidulina subglobosa* Brady var. *quadrata* Cushman and Hughes, 1925, Contrib. Cushman Lab. Foram. Res., v. 1, pt. 1, p. 15, pl. 2, figs. 7a–7c.

Jaculella cf. *J. obtusa* Brady, 1882, Proc. Roy. Soc. Edinburgh, v. 11 (1880–1882), p. 714.

Karreriella apicularis (Cushman) = *Gaudryina apicularis* Cushman, 1911, U.S. Natl. Museum Bull., no. 71, pt. 2, p. 69, text-fig. 110a, 110b.

Karreriella bradyi (Cushman) = *Gaudryina bradyi* Cushman, 1911, U.S. Natl. Museum Bull., no. 71, p. 67, text-figs. 107a–107c.

Karreriella catenata (Cushman) = *Textularia catenata* Cushman, 1911, U.S. Natl. Museum Bull., no. 71, p. 23, text-figs. 39, 40.

Karreriella deformis (Earland) = *Gaudryina deformis* Earland, 1934, Discovery Repts., v. 10, p. 120, pl. 5, fig. 37–40.

Karreriella novangliae (Cushman) = *Gaudryina baccata* Schwager var. *novangliae* Cushman, 1922, U. S. Natl. Museum Bull., no. 104, p. 76, pl. 13, fig. 4.

Keramosphaera murrayi Brady, 1882, Ann. Mag. Nat. Hist., ser. 5, v. 10, p. 243, pl. 13, figs. 1–4.

Lagena cf. *L. aspera* Reuss, 1862, K. Akad. Wiss. Wien, Math. Naturwiss. Kl., Sitzungsber., v. 44, pt. 1, p. 305, pl. 1, fig. 5.

Lagena distoma Parker and Jones, in Brady, 1864, Trans. Linn. Soc. London, v. 24, pt. 3, p. 467, pl. 48, fig. 6.

Lagena elongata (Ehrenberg) = *Miliola elongata* Ehrenberg, 1844, K. Preuss. Akad. Wiss. Berlin, p. 274.

Lagena meridionalis Wiesner = *L. gracilis* Williamson var. *meridionalis* Wiesner, 1931, Deutsche Südpolar Exped., v. 20 (Zool., v. 12), p. 117, pl. 18, fig. 211.

Lagena nebulosa Cushman = *L. laevis* (Montagu) var. *nebulosa* Cushman, 1923, U.S. Natl. Museum Bull., no. 104, p. 29, pl. 5, figs. 4, 5.

Lagena quadralata Brady, 1881, Quart. Jour. Microscop. Sci., n.s., v. 21, p. 62.

Lingulina translucida Heron-Allen and Earland, 1932, Discovery Repts., v. 4, p. 387, pl. 12, figs. 9–11.

Marsipella cylindrica Brady, 1882, Proc. Roy. Soc. Edinburgh, v. 11, p. 714.

Martinottiella antarctica (Parr) = *Schenckiella antarctica* Parr, 1950, B.A.N.Z. Antarctic Res. Exped., ser. B, v. 5, pt. 6, p. 284, pl. 5, fig. 27.

Martinottiella milletti (Cushman) = *Listerella milletti* Cushman, 1936, Cushman Lab. Foram. Res., Spec. Publ., no. 6, p. 41, pl. 6, fig. 10.

Melonis cf. *M. affinis* (Reuss) = *Nonionina affinis* Reuss, 1851, Deut. Geol. Ges. Zeitschr., v. 7, p. 339.

Melonis pompilioides (Fichtel and Moll) = *Nautilus pompilioides* Fichtel and Moll, 1798, Testacea Microscopica, p. 31, pl. 2, figs. a–c.

Melonis umbilicatulus (Heron-Allen and Earland) = *Anomalina umbilicatula* Heron-Allen and Earland, 1932, Discovery Repts., v. 4, p. 426, pl. 14, figs. 40–42.

Miliammina arenacea (Chapman) = *Miliolina oblonga* var. *arenacea* Chapman, 1916, Brit. Antarctic Exped. 1907–1909, Repts. Sci. Invest., Geol., v. 2, pt. 3, p. 59, pl. 1, fig. 7.

Miliammina lata Heron-Allen and Earland, 1930, Jour. Roy. Microscop. Soc., ser. 3, v. 50, p. 43, pl. 1, figs. 13–17.

Miliolinella subrotunda (Montagu) = *Vermiculum subrotundum* Montagu, 1803, Testacea Britannica, p. 521.

Miliolinella sp. Plate 12, fig. 1.

Nodellum membranacea (Brady) = *Reophax membranacea* Brady, 1879, Quart. Jour. Microscop. Sci., n.s., v. 19, p. 53, pl. 4, fig. 9.

Nodosaria doliolavis Parr, 1950, B.A.N.Z. Antarctic Res. Exped. 1929–1931, ser. B, v. 5, pt. 6, p. 330, pl. 12, fig. 2.

Nodosinum gaussicum (Rhumbler) = *Nodosinella gaussica* Rhumbler, 1913, Plankton Exped. Humboldt-Stiftung, Ergeb., v. 3, pp. 452, 459, 460, text-figs. 163, 169, 172.

Nonionella bradii (Chapman) = *Nonionina scapha* var. *bradii* Chapman, 1916, Brit. Antarctic Exped. 1907–1909, Repts. Sci. Invest., Geol., v. 2, pt. 3, p. 71, pl. 5, fig. 42.

Nonionella iridea Heron-Allen and Earland, 1932, Discovery Repts., v. 4, p. 438, pl. 16, figs. 14–16.

Nuttallides umbonifera (Cushman) = *Pulvinulinella umbonifera* Cushman, 1933, Contrib. Cushman Lab. Foram. Res., v. 9, pt. 4, p. 90, pl. 9, figs. 9a–9c.

Oolina apiculata Reuss, 1851, Naturwiss. Abhandl. Wien, v. 4, p. 22, pl. 2, fig. 1.

Oolina melo d'Orbigny, 1839, Voyage dans l'Amérique Méridionale, Foraminiferes, v. 5, pt. 5, p. 20, pl. 5, fig. 9.

Oridorsalis marcida (Emiliana) = *Eponides marcida* Emiliana, 1954, Palaeontol. Italica, v. 48 (n.s., v. 18), p. 124, pl. 22, figs. 24a–24c.

Oridorsalis sidebottomi (Earland) = *Eponides sidebottomi* Earland, 1934, Discovery Repts., v. 10, p. 188, pl. 7, figs. 33–35.

Oridorsalis tenera (Brady) = *Truncatulina tenera* Brady, 1884, Rept. Voy. Challenger, v. 9 (Zool.), p. 665, pl. 95, fig. 11.

Oridorsalis sp. Plate 15, fig. 1.

Parafissurina curta Parr, 1950, B.A.N.Z. Antarctic Res. Exped. 1929–1931, ser. B, v. 5, pt. 6, p. 318, pl. 10, figs. 6, 7.

Parafissurina dorbignyana (Wiesner) = *Ellipsolagena dorbignyana* Wiesner, 1931, Deutsche Südpolar Exped. 1901–1903, v. 20 (Zool., v. 12), p. 127, pl. 24.

Parafissurina fusuliniformis Leoblich and Tappen, 1953, Smithsonian Inst. Misc. Coll., v. 121, no. 7, p. 79, pl. 14, figs. 18, 19.

Parafissurina lateralis (Cushman) = *Lagena lateralis* Cushman, 1913, U.S. Natl. Museum Bull., no. 71, pt. 3, p. 9, pl. 1, fig. 1.

Parafissurina ventricosa (Silvestri) = *Lagena ventricosa* Silvestri, 1904, R. Accad. Sci. Torino, v. 39, p. 11, text-fig. 6.

Patellina antarctica Parr, 1950, B.A.N.Z. Antarctic Res. Exped. 1929–1931, ser. B, v. 5, pt. 6, p. 352, pl. 13, figs. 19–21.

Pelosina distoma Millet, 1904, Jour. Roy. Microscop. Soc., p. 608, pl. 11, figs. 5, 6.

Pelosina variabilis Brady, 1879, Quart. Jour. Microscop. Sci., v. 19, p. 30, pl. 3, figs. 1–3.

Placopsilinella aurantiaca Earland, 1934, Discovery Repts., p. 95, pl. 3, fig. 18.

Portatrochammina antarctica (Parr) = *Trochammina antarctica* Parr, 1950, B.A.N.Z. Antarctic Res. Exped. 1929–1931, ser. B, v. 5, pt. 6, p. 280, pl. 5, figs. 2–4.

Portatrochammina eltaninae Echols, n. sp.

Portatrochammina wiesneri (Parr) = *Trochammina wiesneri* Parr, 1950, B.A.N.Z. Antarctic Res. Exped. 1929–1931, ser. B, v. 5, pt. 6, p. 279, pl. 5, fig. 14.

Psammosphaera fusca Schulze, 1875, II Jahr. Comm. Wiss. Unt. Deut. Meer Kiel, p. 113, pl. 2, figs. 8a–8f.

Pseudobolivina antarctica Wiesner, 1931, Deutsche Südpolar Exped. 1901–1903, v. 20 (Zool., v. 12), p. 99, pl. 21, figs. 257, 258.

Pseudobolovina sp. A. Test minute, elongate, slender, somewhat compressed, tapering gradually, periphery rounded; chambers distinct, increasing regularly in size as added, about 12 in number; sutures slightly depressed, inclined, slightly convex toward the apertural end; aperture an elongate narrow slit extending from the suture into the apertural face; wall very fine grained, almost transparent.

Pullenia osloensis Feyling-Hanssen, 1954, Norsk Geol. Tidsskr., v. 33, no. 3, 4, p. 194.

Pullenia simplex Rhumbler, in Wiesner, 1931, Deutsche Südpolar Exped. 1901–1903, v. 20 (Zool., v. 12), p. 132, pl. 22, fig. 263.

Pullenia subcarinata (d'Orbigny) = *Nonionina subcarinata* d'Orbigny, 1839, Voyage dans l'Amérique Méridionale, Foraminiferes, v. 5, pt. 5, p. 28, pl. 5, figs. 23, 24.

Pullenia subsphaerica Parr, 1950, B.A.N.Z. Antarctic Res. Exped. 1929–1931, ser. B, v. 5, pt. 6, p. 346, pl. 13, fig. 6.

Pyrgo murrhina (Schwager) = *Biloculina murrhina* Schwager, 1866, Novara Exped. 1857–1859, Geol. Theil., v. 2, p. 203, pl. 4, figs. 15a–15c.

Quinqueloculina seminulum (Linné) = *Serpula seminulum* Linné, 1758, Syst. Nat., ed. 10, v. 1, p. 786.

Reophax adunca Brady, 1882, Proc. Roy. Soc. Edinburgh, v. 11 (1880–1882), no. 111, p. 715.

Reophax curtus Cushman, 1920, U.S. Natl. Museum Bull., no. 104, p. 8, pl. 2, figs. 2, 3.

Reophax distans Brady, 1884, Quart. Jour. Microscop. Sci., v. 21, n.s., p. 50.

Reophax longiscatiformis Chapman, 1916, Brit. Antarctic Exped. 1907–1909, Repts. Sci. Invest. Geol., v. 2, pt. 3, p. 63, pl. 3, fig. 18.

Reophax nodulosa, 1879, Quart. Jour. Microscop. Soc., n.s., v. 19, p. 52, pl. 4, figs. 7, 8.

Reophax ovicula (Brady) = *Hormosina ovicula* Brady, 1879, Quart. Jour. Microscop. Sci., n.s., v. 19, p. 61, pl. 4, fig. 6.

Reophax regularis Hoglund, 1947, Uppsala Univ., Zool. Bidrag, v. 26, p. 86, pl. 9, figs. 11, 12.

Reophax cf. *R. rostrata* Hoglund, 1947, Uppsala Univ., Zool. Bidrag, v. 26, p. 87, pl. 9, fig. 8.

Reophax subdentaliniformis Parr, 1950, B.A.N.Z. Antarctic Res. Exped. 1929–1931, ser. B, v. 5, pt. 6, p. 269, pl. 4, fig. 20.

Reophax subfusiformis Earland, 1933, Discovery Repts., v. 7, p. 74, pl. 2, figs. 16–19.

Reophax turbo Goës, 1896, Bull. Museum Comp. Zool., v. 29, p. 29, pl. 1, figs. 2, 3.

Reophax sp. A. Plate 1, figs. 10–13. Test composed of one, two, or less commonly, three chambers; chambers pyriform, widest in the lower part, tapering toward the very small aperture; in multilocular forms chambers loosely appressed, increasing rapidly in size as added; sutures deeply depressed and inclined; wall coarsely arenaceous; aperture at the end of a short neck of distinctly finer texture than the rest of the chamber.

Reophax sp. B. Plate 1, fig. 9.

Rhabdammina ? sp. A. Found only as broken tubes some of which have a diameter of 0.5 mm; flaring ends of some fragmented tubes suggest a large proloculus; wall coarsely arenaceous.

Robertina wiesneri Parr, 1950, B.A.N.Z. Antarctic Res. Exped. 1929–1931, ser. B, v. 5, pl. 6, p. 369, pl. 15, fig. 9.

Rudigaudryina inepta Cushman and McCulloch, 1939, Allan Hancock Pacific Exped., v. 6, no. 1, pp. 94, 95, pl. 9, figs. 3–10.

Rupertina stabilis (Wallich) = *Rupertia stabilis* Wallich, 1877, Ann. Mag. Nat. Hist., ser. 4, v. 19, p. 502, pl. 20, figs. 1–13.

Saccammina sphaerica Brady, 1871, Ann. Mag. Nat. Hist., ser. 4, v. 7, p. 183.

Saccammina tubulata Rhumbler, in Wiesner, 1931, Deutsche Südpolar Exped. 1901–1903, v. 20 (Zool., v. 12), p. 82, pl. 23, stereo-fig. a.

Saccorhiza ? hedrix (Rhumbler) = *Tolypammina hedrix* Rhumbler, in Wiesner, 1931, Deutsche Südpolar Exped. 1901–1903, v. 20 (Zool., v. 12), p. 94, pl. 11, fig. 130.

Seabrookia cf. *S. earlandi* Wright, 1891, Proc. Roy. Irish Acad., ser. 3, v. 1, no. 4, p. 477, pl. 20, figs. 6, 7.

Sphaeroidina bulloides d'Orbigny, 1826, Ann. Sci. Nat., ser. 1, v. 7, p. 267, modèles no. 65.

Spirolocammina tenuis Earland, 1934, Discovery Repts., v. 10, p. 109, pl. 4, figs. 13–16.

Spiroplectammina biformis (Parker and Jones) = *Textularia agglutinans* var. *biformis* Parker and Jones, 1865, Philos. Trans. Roy. Soc. London, v. 155, p. 370, pl. 15, figs. 23, 24.

Spiroplectammina filiformis Earland, 1934, Discovery Repts., v. 10, p. 112, pl. 4, figs. 30–32.

Spiroplectammina subcylindrica Earland, 1934, Discovery Repts., v. 10, p. 112, pl. 4, figs. 33–35.

Spiroplectammina typica Lacroix, 1931, Bull. Monaco Inst. Oceanog., no. 582, p. 14, text-fig. 9.

Spiroplectammina aff. *S. filiformis*. Plate 5, figs. 5, 6.

Stainforthia complanata (Egger) = *Virgulina schreibersiana* var. *complanata* Egger, 1895, Abhandl. K. Bayer. Akad. Wiss., Math. Physik. Kl., v. 18 (1893), p. 292, pl. 8, figs. 91, 92.

Textularia earlandi Parker, 1952, Bull. Museum Comp. Zool., v. 106 (1951–1952), no. 10, p. 458.

Textularia paupercula Earland, 1934, Discovery Repts., v. 10, p. 114, pl. 5, figs. 27–29.

Textularia wiesneri Earland, 1933, Discovery Repts., v. 7, p. 95, pl. 3, figs. 18–20.

Thurammina ex. gr. *T. albicans* Brady, 1879, Quart. Jour. Microscop. Sci., n.s., v. 19, p. 46.

Thurammina papillata Brady, 1879, Quart. Jour. Microscop. Sci., n.s., v. 19, p. 45, pl. 5, figs. 4–8.

Tolypammina frigida (Cushman) = *Girvanella frigida* Cushman, 1918, U.S. Natl. Museum Bull., no. 104, p. 93.

Triloculina tricarinata d'Orbigny, 1826, Ann. Sci. Nat., ser. 1, v. 7, p. 299, modèles no. 94.

Tritaxis inhaerens (Wiesner) = *Haplophragmoides canariensis* (d'Orbigny) var. *inhaerens* Wiesner, 1931, Deutsche Südpolar Exped. 1901–1903, v. 20 (Zool., v. 12), p. 95, pl. 12, fig. 137.

Tritaxis squamata Jones and Parker, 1860, Quart. Jour. Geol. Soc. London, v. 16, p. 304.

Trochammina appressa Parr, 1950, B.A.N.Z. Antarctic Res. Exped., ser. B, v. 5, pt. 6, p. 277, pl. 5, figs. 6, 7a, 7b.

Trochammina compacta Parker, 1952, Bull. Museum Comp. Zool., v. 106, no. 10, p. 458, pl. 2, figs. 13–15.

Trochammina conica Earland, 1934, Discovery Repts., v. 10, p. 104, pl. 3, figs. 47–49.

Trochammina discorbis Earland, 1934, Discovery Repts., v. 10, p. 104, pl. 3, figs. 28–31.

Trochammina glabra Heron-Allen and Earland, 1932, Discovery Repts., v. 4, p. 344, pl. 7, figs. 26–28.

Trochammina globigeriniformis (Parker and Jones) = *Lituola nautiloidea* var. *globigeriniformis* Parker and Jones, 1865, Philos. Trans. Roy. Soc. London, v. 155, p. 407.

Trochammina grisea Earland, 1934, Discovery Repts., v. 10, p. 100, pl. 3, figs. 35–37.

Trochammina inconspicua Earland, 1934, Discovery Repts., v. 10, p. 102, pl. 3, figs. 38–40.

Trochammina intermedia Rhumbler = *T. squamata intermedia* Rhumbler, 1938, Kiel. Meeresforsch, v. 2, no. 2, pp. 186, 187, text-fig. 27.

Trochammina labiata Uchio, 1960, Cushman Found. Foram. Res. Spec. Publ., no. 5, p. 59, pl. 3, figs. 15–17.

Trochammina malovensis Heron-Allen and Earland, 1929, Jour. Roy. Microscop. Soc., ser. 3, v. 49, pt. 4, p. 328, pl. 4, figs. 27–32.

Trochammina multiloculata Hoglund, 1947, Uppsala Univ., Zool. Bidrag, v. 26, p. 211, pl. 15, fig. 5, text-fig. 193.

Trochammina pygmaea Hoglund = *Trochammina globigeriniformis* var. *pygmaea* Hoglund, 1947, Uppsala Univ., Zool. Bidrag, v. 26, p. 200, pl. 17, fig. 3.

Trochammina quadricamerata Echols n. sp.

Trochammina quadriloba Hoglund, 1948, Contrib. Cushman Lab. Foram. Res., v. 24, p. 46.

Trochammina sorosa Parr, 1950, B.A.N.Z. Antarctic Res. Exped., ser. B, v. 5, pt. 6, p. 278, pl. 5, figs. 15–17.

Trochammina subconica Parr, 1950, B.A.N.Z. Antarctic Res. Exped., ser. B, v. 5, pt. 6, p. 281, pl. 5, fig. 22.

Trochammina tricamerata Earland, 1934, Discovery Repts., v. 10, p. 103, pl. 3, figs. 50–52.

Trochammina aff. *T. compacta*, Plate 11, fig. 1.

Uvigerina asperula Czjzek, 1848, Naturwiss. Abhandl., v. 2, pl. 1, p. 146, pl. 13, figs. 14, 15.

Uvigerina cf. *U. attenuata* Cushman and Renz = *U. auberiana* d'Orbigny var. *attenuata* Cushman and Renz, 1941, Contrib. Cushman Lab. Foram. Res., v. 17, p. 21, pl. 3, fig. 17.

Uvigerina bifurcata d'Orbigny, 1839, Voyage dans l'Amérique Méridionale, Foraminifères, v. 5, pt. 5, p. 53.

Valvulineria laevigata Phleger and Parker, 1951, Geol. Soc. Am., Mem. 46, pt. 2, p. 25, pl. 13, figs. 11a, 11b, 12a, 12b.

Verneuilina europeum Christiansen, 1958, Nytt Mag. Zool., v. 6, p. 66.

Verneuilina minuta Wiesner, 1931, Deutsche Südpolar Exped. 1901–1903, v. 20 (Zool., v. 12), p. 99, pl. 13, fig. 155, pl. 23, fig. d.

Verneuilina minuta Wiesner, var. A. Test minute, triserial, somewhat trihedral, about as wide as long, apertural end almost flat; chambers broad and low; about 12 in the adult test; sutures depressed, distinct on the apertural end, but obscure in the earlier part of the test; aperture a small interiomarginal arch near the umbilicus; wall coarsely arenaceous for the size of the test, color light brown. The short broad test flattened at the apertural end distinguishes this variety from typical *V. minuta*.

OCEANOGRAPHY OF ANTARCTIC WATERS

ARNOLD L. GORDON

Lamont-Doherty Geological Observatory of Columbia University, Palisades, New York 10964

Abstract. The physical oceanography for the southwest Atlantic and Pacific sectors of antarctic waters is investigated with particular reference to the water structure and meridional circulation. The cyclonic gyres of the Weddell Sea and area to the north and northeast of the Ross Sea are regions of intense deep water upwelling. Water at 400 meters within these gyres occurs at depths below 2000 meters before entering the gyral circulation. The northern boundary for the Weddell gyre is the Weddell-Scotia Confluence, and that for the gyre near the Ross Sea is the secondary polar front zone.

The major region for production of Antarctic Bottom Water is the Weddell Sea, whereas minor sources are found in the Ross Sea region and perhaps in the Indian Ocean sector in the vicinity of the Amery Ice Shelf. The Ross Sea Shelf Water contains, in part, water related to a freezing process at the base of the Ross Ice Shelf. The mechanism may be of local importance in bottom water production.

The salt balance within the Antarctic Surface Water indicates approximately 60×10^6 m^3/sec of deep water upwells into the surface layer during the summer. This value is also found from Ekman divergence calculation. In winter, only one half of this value remains with the surface water; the other half sinks in the production of bottom water. An equal part of deep water is entrained by the sinking water, making the total southward migration of deep water 10^8 m^3/sec during the winter. On averaging over a period of a year, it is found that the deep water meridional transport is approximately 77×10^6 m^3/sec. The ratio of zonal to meridional transport is, therefore, between 3:1 to 2:1.

The recirculation of water between the antarctic water masses and Circumpolar Deep Water is large. The volume of water introduced by the inflow of North Atlantic Deep Water is only a fraction of the recirculation transport but is essential in that its high salinity maintains the steady state salinity condition of antarctic waters.

INTRODUCTION

The three oceans are the Atlantic, Pacific, and Indian [*Fleurieu*, 1798–1800; *Krümmel*, 1879]. The north polar extremity of the Atlantic is occasionally considered to be a separate ocean, the Arctic Ocean, but more often it is recognized as a marginal sea of the Atlantic, in much the same manner as are the Caribbean and Mediterranean seas. The major oceans are bounded on the south by the shores of Antarctica. The zone between Antarctica and the southern coasts of Australia, South America, and Africa permits free interocean circulation. Such a zone allows processes that equalize the characteristics of the major oceans. Because of the importance of these processes and the obviously similar climatic conditions of this circumpolar zone, it is often given a separate name: the 'Antarctic Ocean,' 'Antarctic Seas,' or 'Southern Ocean (or Oceans).' However, this 'ocean' lacks a northern boundary in the classical sense, and so it is usually set at an arbitrary latitude or some oceanographic boundary as a convergence or divergence.

For the purpose of this study, it is sufficient simply to call the waters within this zone the antarctic waters. This general term is used to denote the waters from the coast of Antarctica northward to the Antarctic Convergence. The water within the zone between this convergence and the Subtropical Convergence is subantarctic water. This term is best applied only to the surface layers of this zone, since the intermediate, deep, and bottom layers are more or less continuous across the Antarctic Convergence.

REVIEW OF ANTARCTIC OCEANOGRAPHY

The basic structure and circulation of antarctic and subantarctic waters have been extensively studied by *Dean* [1937] and other members of the Discovery Expeditions. Table 1 lists the major general antarctic oceanographic references. The purpose of the present study is to: (1) elucidate the characteristics of water masses and transition zones making up antarctic waters; (2) further investigate bottom water formation and possible regions of formation; and (3) esti-

TABLE 1. General Antarctic Oceanographic Studies

Author	Date of Publication	Antarctic Area
Brennecke	1921	Atlantic
Drygalski	1926	Atlantic
Deacon	1933	Atlantic
Sverdrup	1933	Atlantic
Wüst	1933	Atlantic
Mosby	1934	Atlantic
Wüst	1935–1936	Atlantic
Deacon	1937	Circumpolar
Mackintosh	1946	Circumpolar
Midttun and Natvig	1957	Pacific
Model	1957–1958	Atlantic
Burling	1961	SW Pacific
Deacon	1963	Circumpolar
Ishino	1963	Circumpolar
Kort	1964	Circumpolar
Brodie	1965	Circumpolar
Tolstikov	1966	Circumpolar
Gordon	1967*a*	SW Atlantic; SE Pacific

mate the meridional water transport. The following is a very brief account of the oceanography of antarctic waters. The reader is referred to *Deacon* [1937, 1963], *Gordon* [1967*a*], and other authors shown in Table 1 for a more complete description.

Figure 1 is a schematic representation of the water mass structure, core layers, and meridional components of motion. The main flow is zonal, westward south of the Antarctic Divergence and eastward north of the divergence. The surface and bottom water masses are antarctic in origin, in that their characteristics are acquired south of the Antarctic Convergence. Their northward and downward component of motion is compensated by a southward and upward flowing deep water mass. The results of this important meridional exchange are that heat and nutrients are supplied to the surface of antarctic waters from lower latitudes, and the oxygen content of the deep water of the world is replenished. Such a process allows a steady heat flux from ocean to atmosphere and a high biological productivity rate in the photic zone, maintaining the proper environment for life in the deep water and the low temperatures of the deep ocean. The ratio of meridional zonal flow is discussed in a later section. The structure shown in Figure 1 is found around Antarctica. However, important variations with longitude occur within the water column. These variations can be correlated with the asymmetry of Antarctica and submarine ridges and basins.

Antarctic Convergence (Polar Front Zone)

The Antarctic Convergence, which can be considered as an oceanic polar front zone, is the region separating the antarctic and subantarctic water masses. It has characteristics that alternately suggest convergence, divergence, or a combination of both [*Wexler*, 1959]. The positions of the polar front found by the *Eltanin* and those determined by *Mackintosh* [1946] and *Houtman* [1964] are shown in *Gordon* [1967*a*, pl. 13]. Two expressions of the front are defined: the surface expression (large surface temperature gradients) and a subsurface frontal expression (the location where the temperature minimum begins to increase in depth toward the north at a relatively rapid rate). The polar front zone is found to be 2°–4° of latitude in width. The surface and subsurface expressions are many times separated by a number of kilometers; the more common case is a more southerly surface expression. In the western Southeast Pacific Basin, a double frontal system is found. In this region, the fairly stable T_{min} layer extends from Antarctica to the secondary frontal zone. Between the secondary and the more northern primary zone is a region of a weak and broken T_{min} layer and suggestions of divergences. Occasionally the T_{min} layer descends slightly at the secondary front, but the major descent occurs at the primary front. *Eltanin* BT data from cruises 25 and 27 (along longitudes 127° and 157°W) indicate that such a double structure also exists to the west of the Mid-Oceanic Ridge (see 'Antarctic Polar Front Zone,' this volume). *Houtman* [1967] shows a similar structure south of New Zealand. The occurrence of a double frontal system with combination of convergence and divergence may be fairly common.

Some of the Antarctic Surface Water sinking in the region of the frontal zone contributes to the formation of the low saline intermediate water of the world oceans. The rest mixes into the Subantarctic Surface Water contributing to the warm water sphere of the world ocean. The descent of the Antarctic Surface Water begins when the T_{min} layer is between 200 to 300 meters (see *Gordon* [1967*a*, pl. 3]). Although the T_{min} is quickly destroyed by mixing, the low salinity is maintained and is used as the identifying characteristic of the intermediate water masses of the world ocean. *Ostapoff* [1962] shows surface water cutting across the 200-meter level as a band of low salinity water. Figure 2 is the salinity at 200 meters constructed from *Eltanin* stations. The low salinity band shows some more detail than that of Ostapoff; it suggests that sinking is not uniform throughout the area.

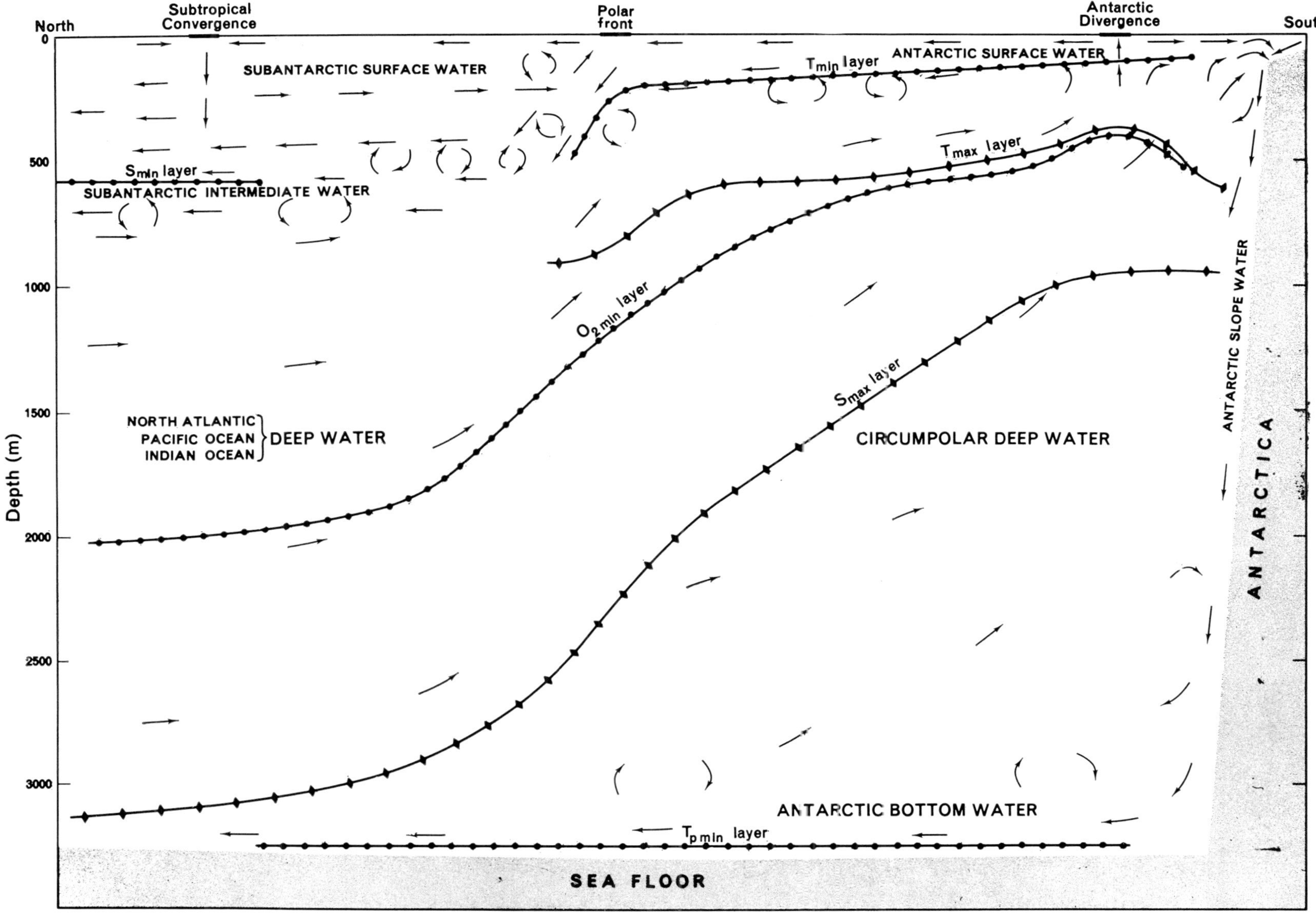

Fig. 1. Schematic representation of water masses and core layers in antarctic waters (from *Gordon* [1967*a*]).

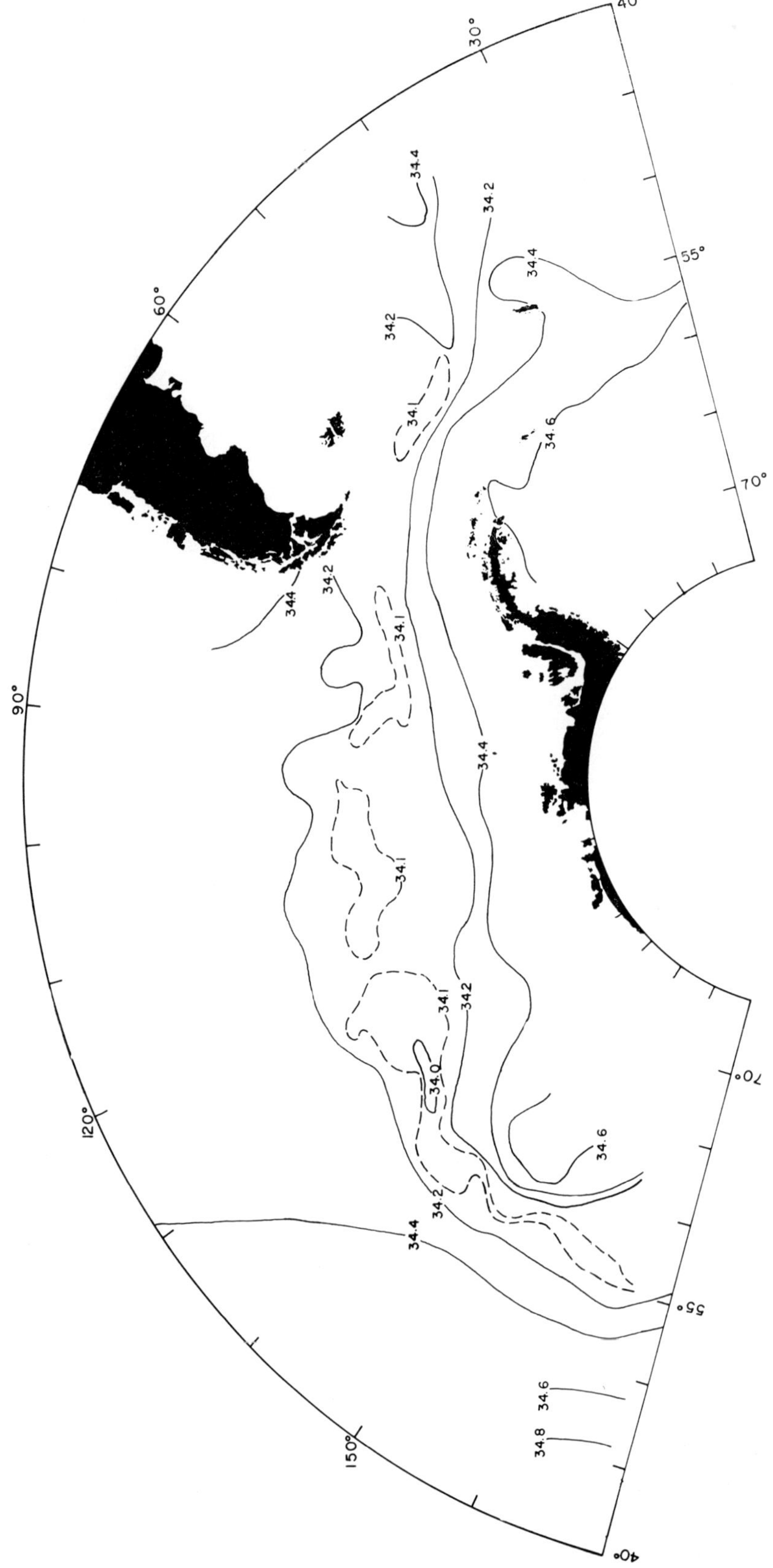

Fig. 2. Salinity distribution, 200 meters, *Eltanin* observations.

On comparing it with *Gordon* [1967*a*, pl. 14], it is found that the surface water descent compares well with the primary frontal zone. The temperature at 200 meters is shown in Figure 3. The isotherm distribution is extended to the continent by using the data in *Tolstikov* [1966]. The warmer band of water in the southern Southeast Pacific Basin and Weddell Sea shows the position of the Antarctic Divergence. The colder band just to its north is the Antarctic Surface Water. The convergence occurs in the large temperature gradient region. The mean position can be approximated by the 2° isotherm. *Botnikov* [1964] used the 2°C isotherm of the temperature minimum layer to define the summer position of the convergence.

Antarctic Divergence

The Antarctic Divergence (average latitude of 65°S) is essentially a wind-produced feature. The westerlies north of the divergence transport surface water eastward with a small component to the north, whereas the coastal easterlies cause a westerly flow with a southward component to the surface water. The resulting divergence and deep water upwelling, which may be of a diffusive nature or perhaps occur within limited regions over short time periods, are the most important oceanographic processes of antarctic waters. They allow the deep water contact with the antarctic atmosphere and the associated sea-air interaction. The upwelling necessitates a southward flow of the deep water. This flow on conserving its angular momentum may help create the zonal currents of antarctic waters and the small amount of attenuation of the current with depth.

Along the antarctic coasts, cold, relatively saline shelf water forms, owing to the intense cold and freezing of sea water. Shelf water on mixing with roughly equal proportions of deep water forms Antarctic Bottom Water, which flows northward. This northward motion initiates a westward component of motion along the continental rise of Antarctica and accumulation of bottom water to the east of the main submarine ridges.

Weddell-Scotia Confluence

The Weddell-Scotia Confluence [*Gordon*, 1967*a*] or Bellingshausen Front [*Model*, 1957, 1958] is the line separating the water derived from the Weddell Sea and that derived from the Pacific Ocean. It is a line extending from the Bransfield Strait through the central Scotia Sea and north of the South Sandwich Islands. It is most pronounced and stationary in the Circumpolar Deep Water. The small change in position and character from 400 to 4000 meters suggests only minor amounts of convergence at the Weddell-Scotia Confluence. In the surface layer, large horizontal variations are found. Here the boundary of the Weddell and Southeast Pacific surface water is much more turbulent than the deep water boundary. However, the separation is obvious on the *T/S* diagram of the area (Figure 4).

Water Masses

Temperature-Salinity Relation

Water masses can be conveniently defined by their particular relationship of temperature and salinity. For this purpose, a plot of temperature against salinity of all data points is made. Such a plot, the *T/S* diagram, was introduced to oceanography by *Helland-Hansen* [1916].

To construct a *T/S* diagram for the region investigated by *Eltanin*, the hydrographic data from most of cruises 7 to 27 were used. Figure 4 is the group *T/S* plot for *Eltanin* cruises 7, 8, 9, 12, and 22, which represent the Drake Passage, the Scotia and Weddell seas, and the areas immediately north and east of these seas.

The water masses were identified in the following manner: The Antarctic Surface Water includes the water within and above the temperature minimum layer (100–300 meters). The upper and lower deep water are identified by a temperature maximum and salinity maximum, respectively. The Weddell Deep Water (WDW) is that deep water south of the Weddell-Scotia Confluence. The deep water found in the Pacific sector and north of the Weddell-Scotia Confluence in the Scotia Sea is called the Southeast Pacific Deep Water (SPDW). The water between the Antarctic Surface Water and Circumpolar Deep Water and the water between the Circumpolar Deep Water and Antarctic Bottom Water constitute transitional zones. Within each of these zones, a layer of zero meridional motion exists. The bottom water boundary with the deep water is not well defined and is arbitrarily set at slightly below the 0°C isotherm in the Weddell Sea and +0.5°C in the Pacific sector. The Subantarctic Surface Water is the thick isohaline layer north of the polar front zone. At its base is the Antarctic or Subantarctic Intermediate Water, defined by a weak salinity minimum (it is much more obvious north of the Subtropical Convergence). A transitional zone between the Subantarctic Surface Water and the deep water is the relatively isothermal layer between these two water masses.

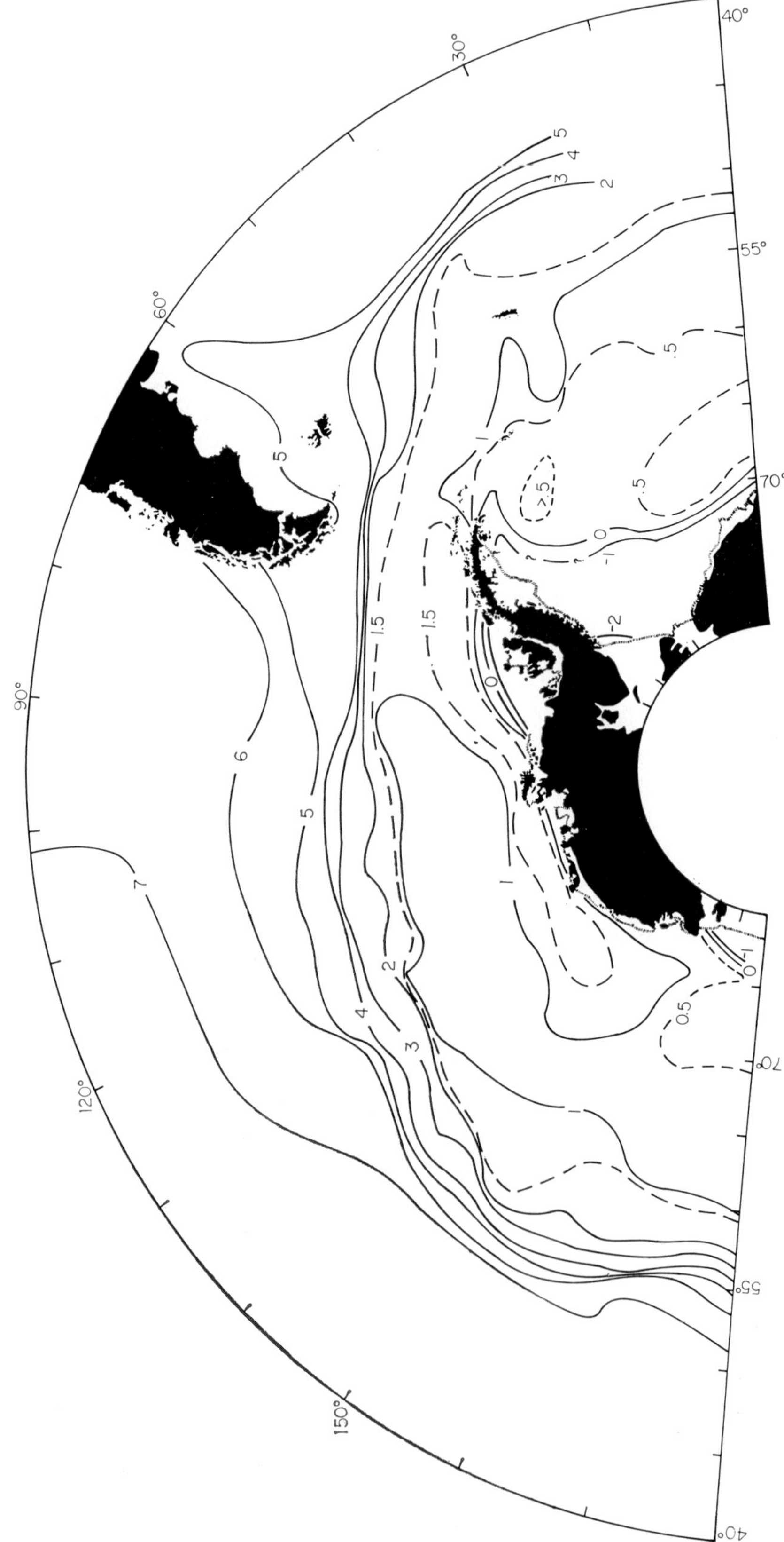

Fig. 3. Temperature distribution, 200 meters, *Eltanin* and IGY observations. Isotherms near Antarctica are taken from *Tolstikov* [1966].

Besides the general usefulness of such a diagram in identifying water masses and defining their T/S region, three important facts are found:

1. The deep water of the Weddell Sea is in the same T/S region as the bottom water of the Southeast Pacific Basin. Therefore, it is reasonable to conclude that the WDW at 400 meters is derived from that bottom water which occurs below 3000 meters in the northern Drake Passage. The Southeast Pacific Bottom Water leaves the sea floor in the northern Scotia Sea and the area to the northwest of South Georgia [*Gordon*, 1966, 1967*a*]. Therefore, great amounts of upwelling are associated with the transfer of water into the cyclonic Weddell gyre. The oxygen of the WDW is between 4.5–4.7 ml/l compared to the 4.7–4.9 ml/l range of the bottom water passing through the northern Drake Passage, indicating some oxygen consumption in transit from the Drake Passage to the Weddell Sea. It is interesting to point out that the bottom water formed in the Weddell Sea includes some of the warmer bottom water of the Southeast Pacific Basin, which may be derived from the area of the Ross Sea. The volume transport of the water below 3000 meters in the northern Drake Passage is 25 × 10^6 m^3/sec (calculated from *Gordon* [1967*b*, fig. 3]). The probable transfer is in the vicinity of 30°E [*Model*, 1957], where a broad southward penetration of warm water occurs.

The WDW is, in part, converted to surface water by sea-air exchange and, in part, entrained with the sinking shelf water in the production to AABW. In addition, some WDW may exit from the gyre directly. Therefore, it is not possible to arrive at a rate of AABW production; however, if all the WDW exits as a 50% component of the AABW, implying that the surface water of the Weddell gyre is derived from outside the Weddell Sea, an upper limit of 50 sv is placed on the AABW outflow. The actual value is probably much less than this value.

2. The warm water occasionally found to override the temperature minimum layer south of the subsurface expression of the polar front [*Gordon*, 1967*a*] is either Subantarctic Surface Water, as in the case of *Eltanin* cruise 8, or warmed (modified) Antarctic Surface Water, cruises 7 and 22, which represent January and February conditions. The warmed Antarctic Surface Water has salinities similar to the Antarctic Surface Water, that is, 0.2 to 0.3‰ lower than the Subantarctic Surface Water. The warming obscures the temperature surface expression of the polar front, and the surface boundaries of the Antarctic Surface and Subantarctic Surface Water, in these cases, are found only by a change in salinity. The water to the south is slightly less dense than the Subantarctic Water. In such a case, some Subantarctic Surface Water may sink at the front to join with water of the temperature minimum layer.

3. The Antarctic Surface Water can be subdivided into the surface water of the Weddell Sea and that of the Scotia Sea. The line of separation is the Weddell-Scotia Confluence. The surface water of the Weddell Sea is colder and spans a greater salinity range.

The T/S distribution of the *Eltanin* stations of the South Pacific sector of the antarctic waters is shown in Figure 5. The following cruises are included: 10, 11, 13, 14, 15, 17, 19, 20, 23, 27. The excluded cruises were either in the Tasman Sea, or mainly north of 50°S.

Basically, the same water masses shown in Figure 4 are found in Figure 5. It is possible to divide the Antarctic Surface Water and the underlying transition zone into two sections, as is done in the Weddell and Scotia seas. The division is the secondary polar front zone. Besides the sharp difference in the surface T/S points north and south of the secondary front, some difference is found in the deep water. The upper deep water south of the secondary front (that is, in the southwestern Southeast Pacific Basin and the area immediately northeast of the Ross Sea) is in the same T/S region as the lower SPDW and transition into the Southeast Pacific bottom water, indicating a return flow of the deep water to the southwest in the same manner as the flow into the Weddell Sea. From the core layer maps of *Gordon* [1967*a*] this return occurs between 130° to 140°W. Similar to the WDW, it represents an upwelling of deep water from between 2000 and 3000 meters to about 400 meters. The gradients across the secondary front zone in the deep water are not as intense as they are across the Weddell-Scotia Confluence.

The phenomenon suggested by the T/S diagrams of intense upwelling in the cyclonic gyres of the Weddell Sea and southwestern Southeast Pacific Basin may be the primary method in which deep water is carried upward. Similar conditions may exist near the Kerguelen Plateau.

The Subantarctic Intermediate Water is much more pronounced in the Pacific sector, covering a T/S region of slightly lower salinity, perhaps due to the lower salinity of the Antarctic or Subantarctic Surface Water. Warmed or modified Antarctic Surface Water is found on cruises 19 and 23, again indicating that the more

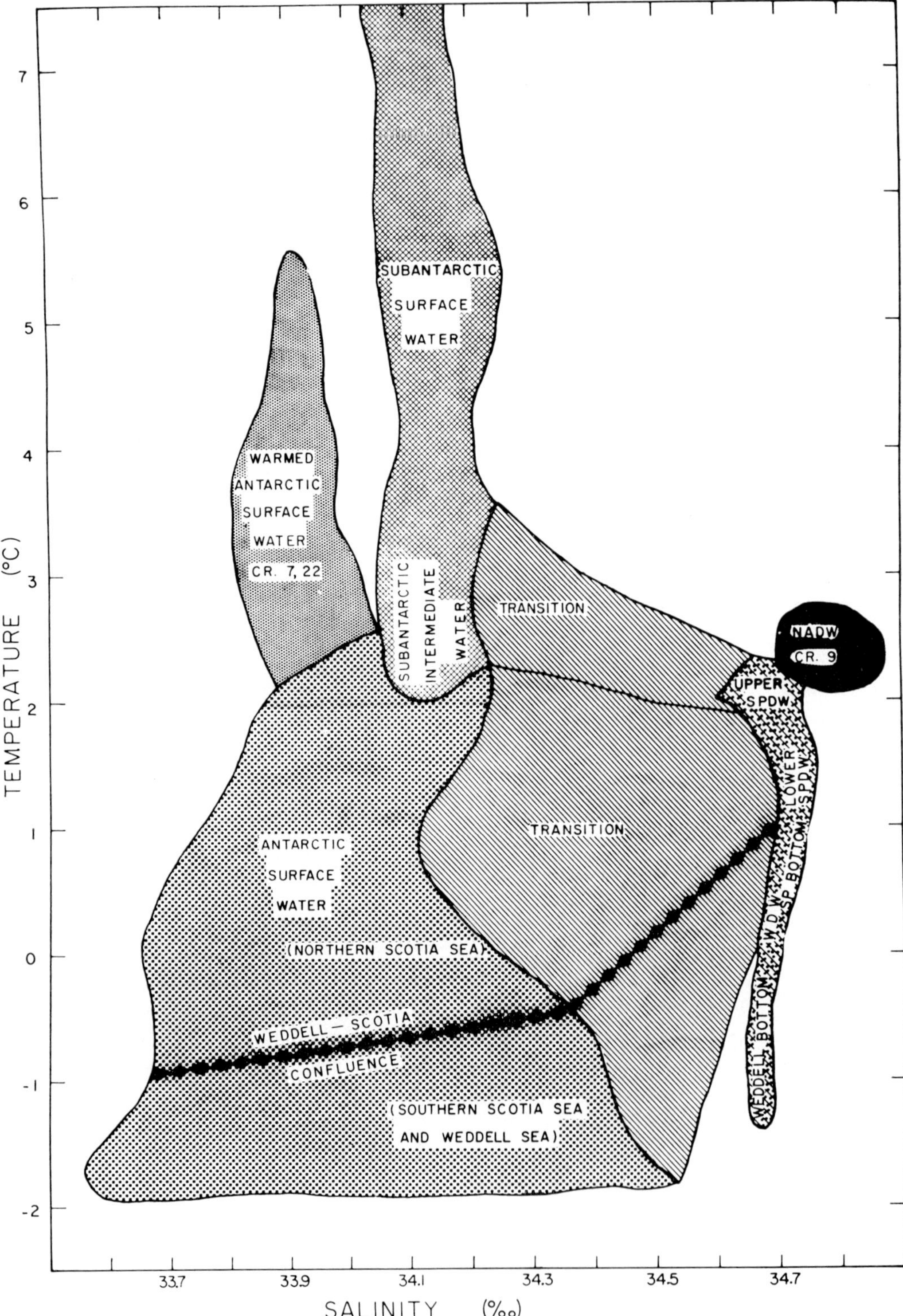

Fig. 4. Temperature-salinity diagram for Drake Passage, Scotia Sea, and Weddell Sea. SPDW = deep water of the Southeast Pacific Basin; SP Bottom = bottom water of the Southeast Pacific Basin; WDW = deep water of the Weddell Sea; NADW = North Atlantic Deep Water.

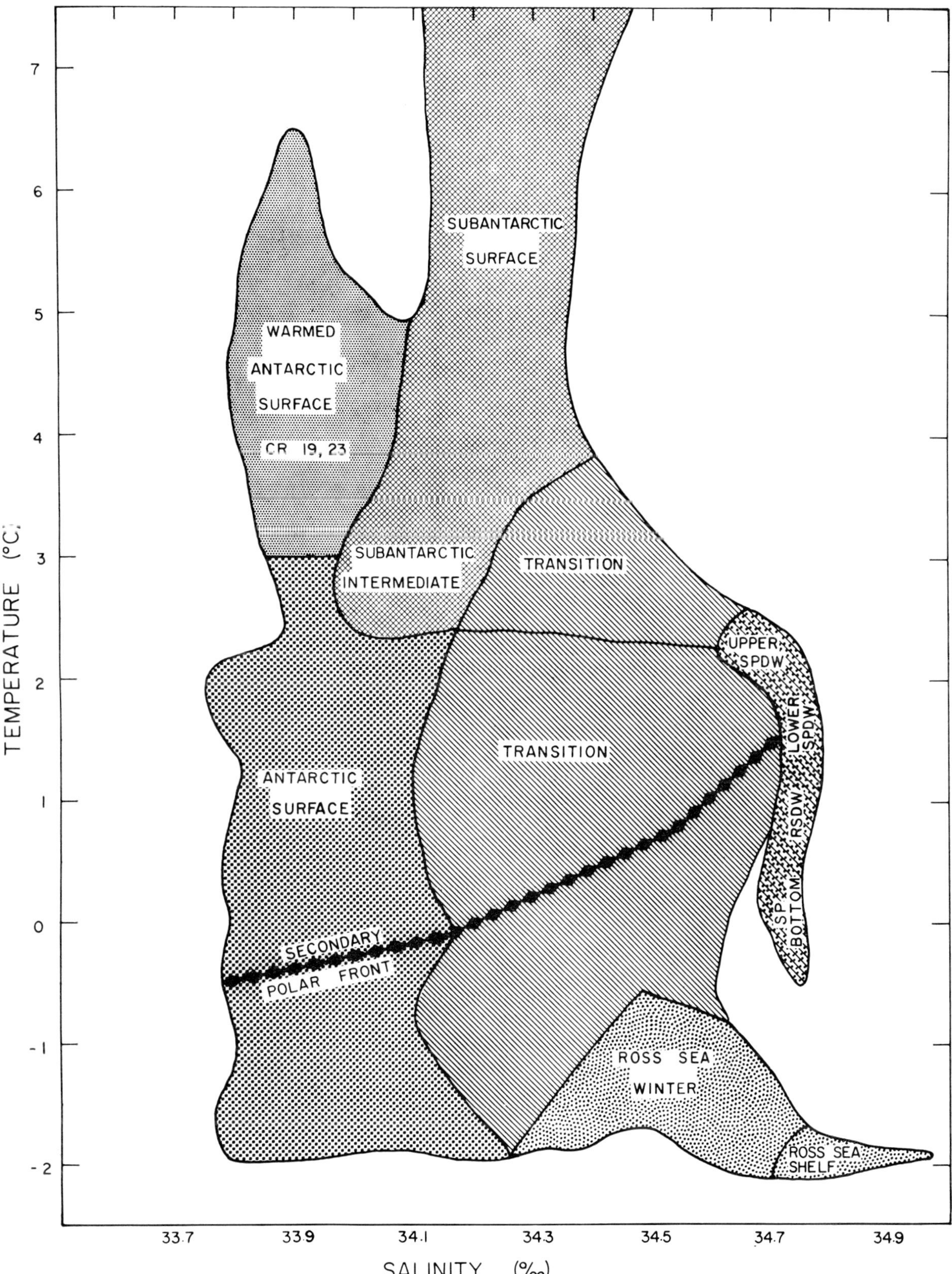

Fig. 5. Temperature-salinity diagram for Pacific Ocean sector of antarctic waters. Abbreviations as in Figure 4 caption; RSDW = deep water in the ocean region north and northeast of the Ross Sea, but south of the secondary polar front zone.

southern surface expression of the polar front zone relative to the subsurface expression is not always due to overriding of Subantarctic Surface Water.

Water masses associated with the Ross Sea are shown in Figure 5. These are the Ross Sea Winter Water and the dense Ross Sea Shelf Water, which is discussed below. Both of these water masses represent a protrusion on the T/S diagram to colder, more saline water and, therefore, must have an origin related to ice formation: either sea ice or freezing beneath the Ross Ice Shelf.

Oxygen Saturation of Antarctic Waters

The degree of saturation for all *Eltanin* oxygen data was calculated based on the solubility of oxygen in sea water given by *Green and Carritt* [1967]. The surface water has saturations between 95–100% with occasional observation of saturations above 100%. Surface values as high as 108% are found (station 522). Supersaturated values may be caused by rapid surface heating, observed to occur under calm summer conditions, which decreases the solubility of the surface water, causing the initial 100% saturation level to increase.

The vertical convection within the Antarctic Surface Water causes a high degree of oxygen saturation to the base of the surface water. The degree of saturation is fairly uniform from the surface to the 95% level; a sharp drop in saturation occurs below this. The 90% saturation level occurs only meters below the 95% level and can be taken as the base of free vertical convection. Figure 6 shows the depth of this surface. The depth of the convective layer south of the polar front zone rarely exceeds 200 meters. Depths of less than 100 meters are found in the stable surface water of the southern section of the Southeast Pacific Basin and the northern Weddell Sea.

The winter values tend to be slightly greater than those found in summer. In the polar front zone, large variations of depth of the 90% surface are found, owing, no doubt, to the fluctuating convergence and divergence within this zone. Within the Subantarctic Surface Water, the depths are greater than 300 meters, with values as high as 740 meters.

The lowest degree of saturation (between 50 and 60%) occurs in the vicinity of the temperature maximum and oxygen minimum. Below this oxygen saturation minimum, the saturation increases to values above 60%. Where a high percentage of Antarctic Bottom Water exists, the saturation reaches 80%. The high saturation of the bottom water, roughly intermediate between deep and surface water, indicates the recent contact with the sea surface of a substantial component. The ratio of shelf or surface water to deep water within the Antarctic Bottom Water cannot be far from unity for the bottom water leaving the Weddell Sea; this agrees with the conclusions of *Baranov* and *Botnikov* [1964] and other considerations discussed later in this study.

The upper boundary of the Antarctic Bottom Water can be seen by a rapid oxygen saturation increase close to the sea floor. Figure 7 shows the saturation versus depth of selected regions of antarctic water between 20°W and 170°W. Sections *a* to *d* are along the path of flow of the bottom water from the Weddell Sea [*Gordon*, 1966]. The rapid increase of oxygen saturation occurs approximately 1000 meters from the sea floor. Substantial amounts of bottom water are evident in sections *a*, *c*, and *d*, indicating that the main flow is east of the South Sandwich Trench. The bottom water of the trench first decreases in the degree of saturation by approximately 10% before an increase is observed to the bottom. Adiabatic warming would increase the bottom oxygen saturation level but not by the amount observed near the trench floor. Therefore some bottom water renewal occurs, but the trench floor appears not to be the major avenue of AABW flow.

Sections *e* to *g* are of stations located in the Scotia Sea. In the central Scotia Sea and northern Drake Passage where potential temperatures show little Antarctic Bottom Water, the saturation of the lower 1000 meters increases only slightly or decreases with depth. In the southern areas of the Scotia Sea which receive a fresh supply of bottom water from the passage between the Bruce and South Orkney ridges, the bottom saturation shows a marked increase. This increase begins about 800 meters above the bottom, which agrees well with the upper limits of the bottom water in the southern Drake Passage discussed by *Gordon* [1966] and used in geostrophic calculations [*Gordon*, 1967*b*].

Sections *h* to *j* in the Southeast Pacific Basin show only small increases in bottom oxygen saturation and, in the case of the southeastern region of the basin, a marked decrease. Such a decrease indicates that the bottom oxygen values are significantly influenced by organic decay and that renewal of highly oxygenated Antarctic Bottom Water is small. Section *j* in the northern Southeast Pacific Basin shows a steady increase in saturation from the minimum to the bottom. A higher percentage of Antarctic Bottom Water

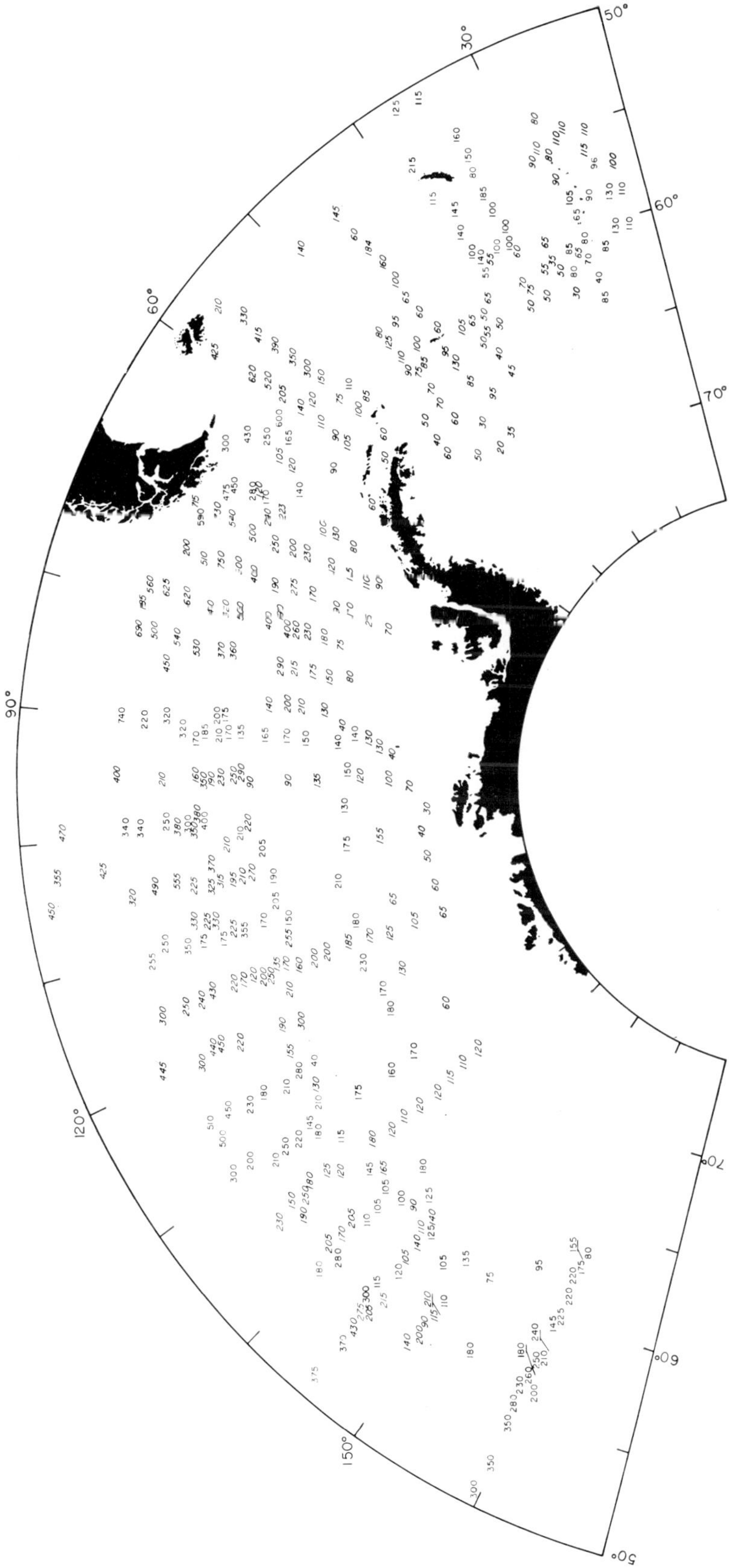

Fig. 6. Depth of 90% oxygen saturation level (values in slant letters represent summer conditions).

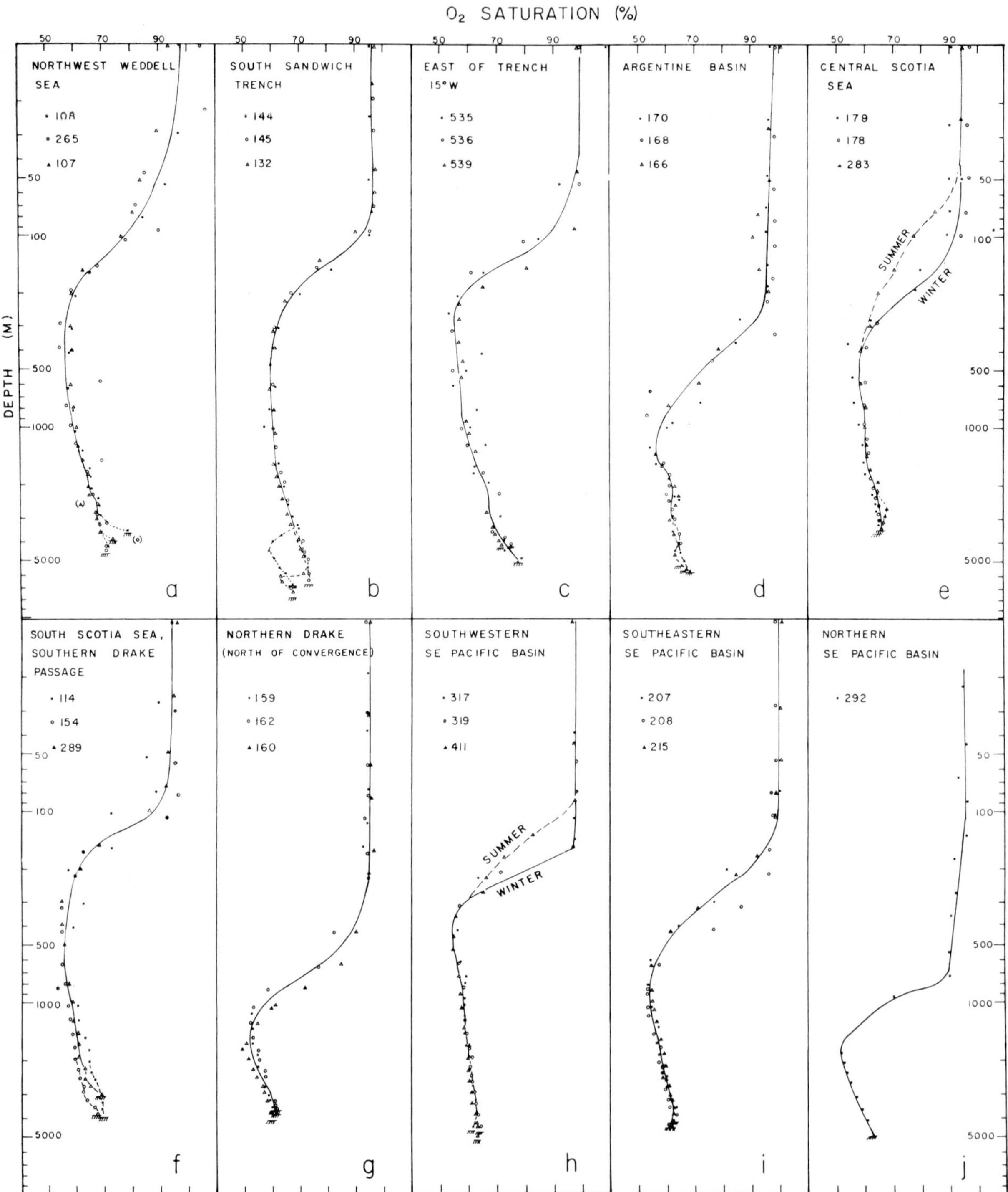

Fig. 7. Oxygen saturation versus depth for select areas of antarctic waters.

must reach this area than reaches the southeast regions of the basin. This is consistent with the bottom flow deduced by *Gordon* [1966].

Time Variation of Water Structure

Only in a general sense is the ocean in a steady state. Variability in the structure of antarctic waters must occur. It is likely that the polar front zone has periodic and nonperiodic fluctuations and may possess wavelike disturbances similar to the atmospheric polar front. Seasonal fluctuations of temperature, salinity, and circulation are also obvious. There are other variations: (1) tidal and inertia period fluctuations occur; (2) from temperature variations in the Antarctic Surface Water, it appears that a large horizontal translation of the Weddell-Scotia Confluence must exist in the surface layer; (3) it is generally accepted that the sinking of shelf water in bottom water production is a sporadic process [*Mosby*, 1968]; and (4) there are internal waves within the main pycnocline. The proper way to investigate such processes is through use of multiship operations and long-term recording sensors placed in numerous positions around Antarctica.

On September 30, 1965 (the same day as the *Eltanin* hydrographic station 473 of cruise 20), a series of bathythermograph observations was taken at approximately 15-minute intervals. The position of the observation and the times are shown in Figure 8. The ship was south of the Antarctic Convergence, which it crossed at 55°41′S and 144°32′W. The time plot of temperature versus depth is shown in Figure 9. (It is possible that the absolute temperatures are 0.3° too low.) The variations observed are no doubt a combination of time and space changes. In the first section, before the trawl, vertical migrations of isotherms, mostly just below the temperature minimum layer and at 250 meters, are evident. These may be associated with internal waves or turbulence. After the trawl, the characteristics of the structure change. The temperature minimum is not as extreme, and a fairly strong inverted thermocline occurs at 150 to 200 meters. The thermocline decreases in intensity during the last hour of observations. Between local time 1650 to 1730 and 1815 to 1845, a secondary temperature minimum layer exists above the main layer.

Repeated lowerings, such as the above experiment, would be more useful if they extended to deeper levels. This can be accomplished through the use of the continuously in situ salinity temperature-depth recorder (STD). The comparison of the up and down trace of the STD (a few hours separation) shows changes in the microstructure [*Gordon*, 1967*c*].

A study of standard level temperature, salinity, and oxygen data of relocated *Eltanin* stations at and below 2000 meters was carried out by *Jacobs* [1966]. On comparing 16 station pairs (see *Jacobs* [1966, table 2]), the stations of cruises 17–21 show a systematic difference from those of cruises 14 and 15. The average of these changes is slightly above the precision of the instruments, but the spread is too great to be significant.

A number of *Discovery* stations and *Eltanin* stations were taken along 79°W. The temperature and salinity above 1000 meters show large changes (Figure 10); below 1000 meters the variations are small and are about the equivalent to the error of the measurement. During the time of *Discovery* stations, the higher temperatures and salinities at 600 meters indicate that smaller amounts of sinking occurred at the polar front zone than at the time of the *Eltanin* stations. The 30-year spacing of the data is, of course, no indication of the periodicity of the process; however, it does show that such variations do occur.

Supercooled Water

The freezing point of water decreases with salinity; this has been shown experimentally by *Knudsen* [1903] and *Miyake* [1939]. The values found by Miyake's equation are approximately 0.08°C lower than those found using Knudsen's. The *Eltanin* data of cruises 7 to 27 were inspected for supercooled water (water below the freezing point) using both equations. There are 44 temperature observations below Knudsen's freezing point; their depths range from the surface to 890 meters, mostly between the surface and 200 meters. They are in the Ross Sea area and the waters south of the Weddell-Scotia Confluence. Using Miyake's equation, only three of these observations are below freezing. Because of the elimination of the majority of the Knudsen supercooled points using Miyake's equation, it is assumed that the latter equation is correct. At worst, it will indicate only the extreme case of supercooled water. Miyake's equation is as follows:

$$\Delta T = 0.056903\ (S - 0.030)$$

where ΔT is the freezing point depression and S is salinity in parts per thousand.

In addition to the *Eltanin* data, the hydrographic observations in the National Oceanographic Data Center marsden square files from 10°W westward to 180° and south of 50°S were inspected, as well as the Deep Freeze '63 and '64 data in the Ross Sea. The position of

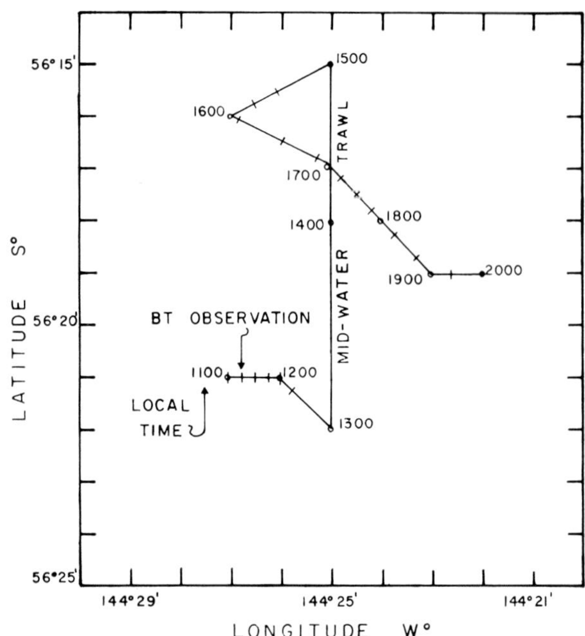

Fig. 8. Hourly *Eltanin* positions during repeated bathythermograph observations on September 30, 1965.

the stations showing supercooled water and the depths at which this water was found are shown in Figure 11. (The data of *Littlepage* [1965] in the McMurdo Sound are not included.) The data are clustered in the southern Weddell Sea and Ross Sea. Only the two *Eltanin* stations in the northern Weddell Sea are anomalous both in position and depth of the observation. They are assumed to be in error and are not included in the discussion below.

The T/S points of the supercooled temperature observations are shown in Figure 12. The salinities are fairly high, equivalent to that of the upper deep water. Therefore, if these temperatures were achieved at the sea surface where salinities are low, they must have been accompanied by freezing. In this case, it is difficult to imagine why supercooled water would occur, since it is probable that there would be sufficient nuclei and turbulent motion to produce freezing. It appears reasonable to assume that the water was not produced at the sea surface.

The depression of the freezing point of pure water with pressure is 0.075°C per 100 meters of water depth [*Lusquinos*, 1963]. Assuming that sea water also is affected in the same magnitude, it is found that none of the temperature observations shown in Figure 11 are supercooled. The temperature versus depth of the observations and depression of the freezing point with depth (34.65‰) is shown in Figure 13. It is reason-

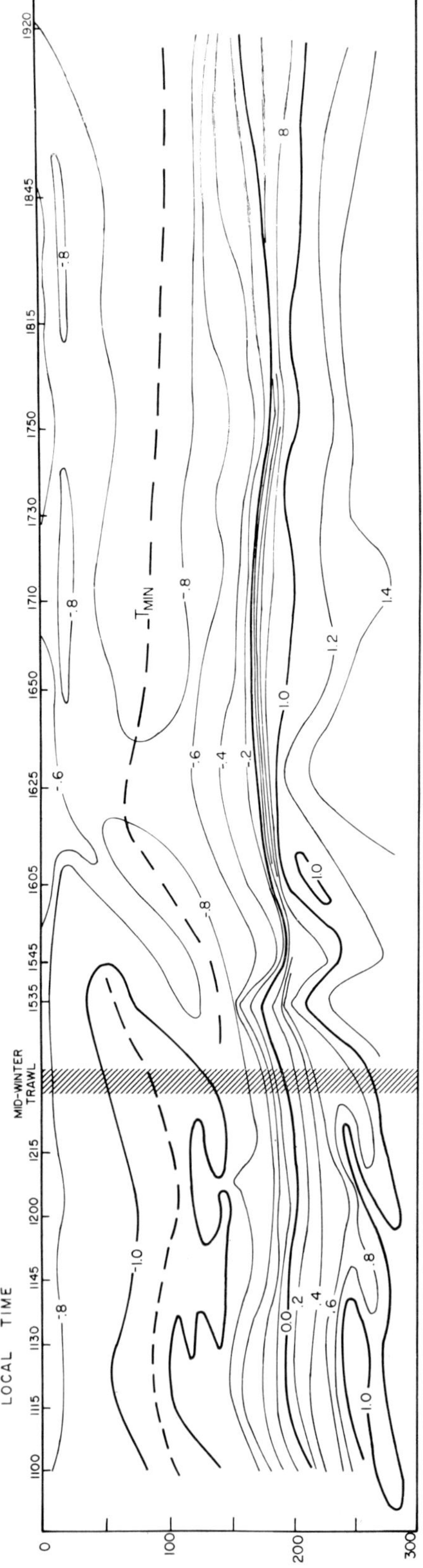

Fig. 9. Temperature versus depth of repeated bathythermograph observations along the ship's track shown in Figure 8.

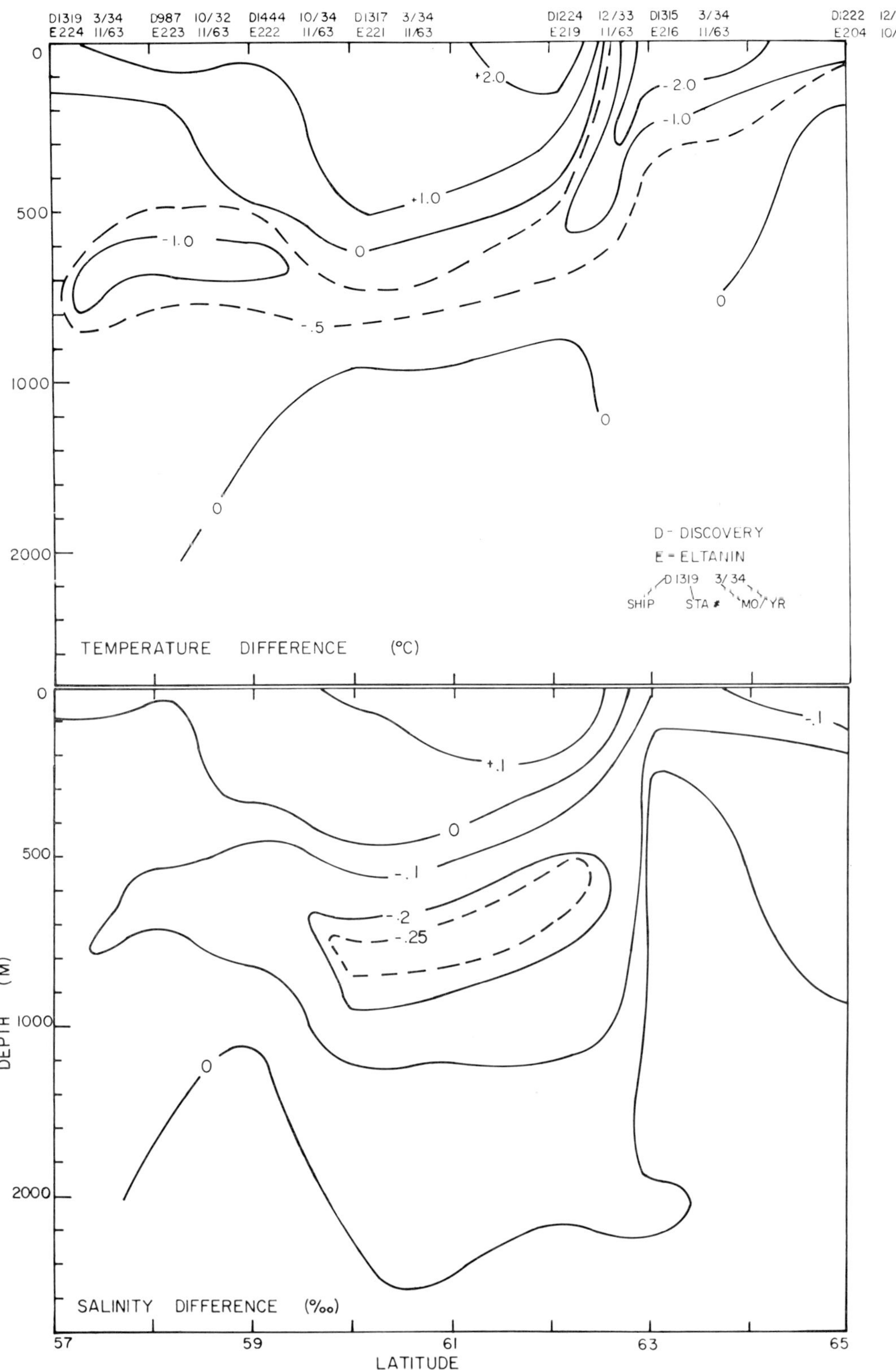

Fig. 10. Salinity and temperature differences of *Discovery* and *Eltanin* data in Southeast Pacific Basin (upper 1000 meters).

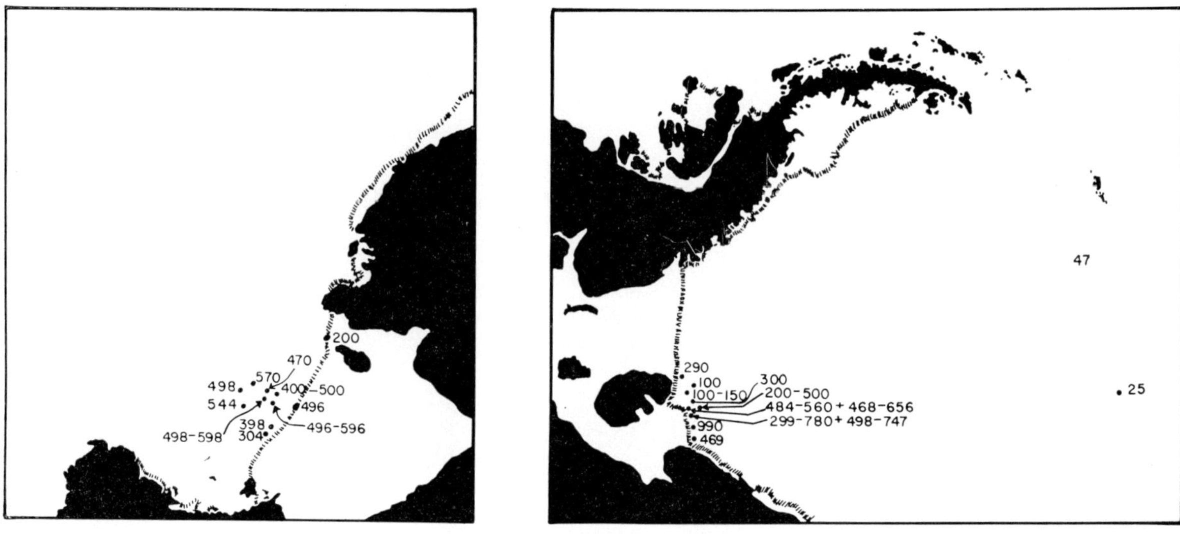

Fig. 11. Position and depth of supercooled sea water.

able to assume, as Lusquinos does, that the cold temperatures are produced below the sea surface and that no supercooling occurs. It has been suggested [*Littlepage*, 1965] that the salinity of the water is higher than that determined on the deck of the ship because of the suspension of small ice crystals that melt before the salinity of the sea water is determined. In this case, in situ measurements of salinity must be used. However, data of the STD aboard the *Eltanin* show that the in situ salinity of supercooled water is the same as the shipboard determined salinity. (See stations 648 and 649 of *Jacobs and Amos* [1967].) There is a pos-

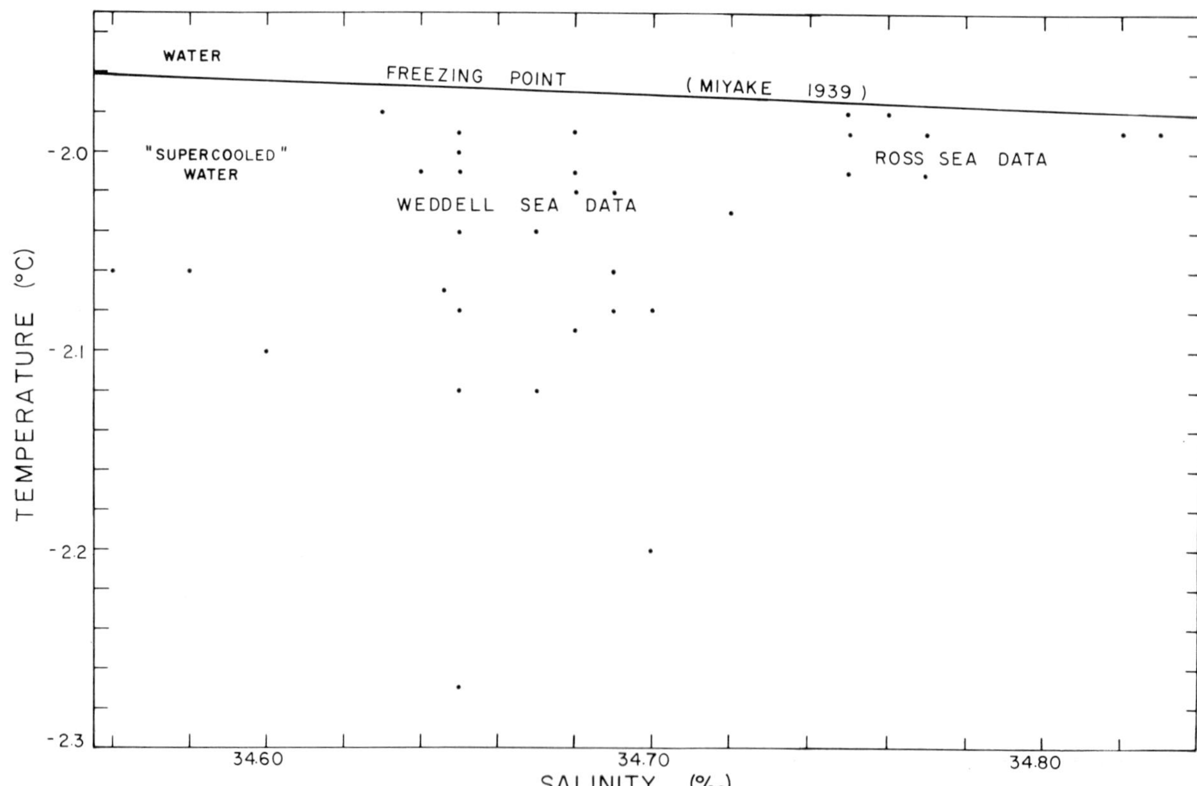

Fig. 12. Temperature-salinity diagram of supercooled water.

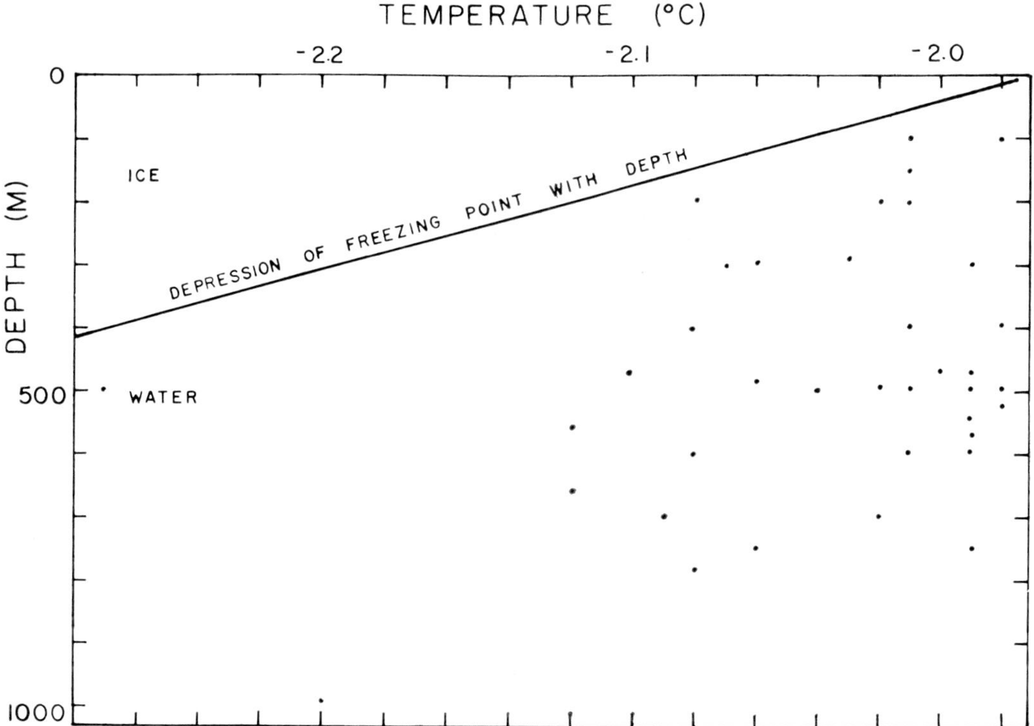

Fig. 13. Sea water freezing point versus depth and depth of observed supercooled water.

sibility that the STD is affected by the ice crystals in such a way as to give results similar to the shipboard value, but this is unlikely.

The striking similarity of the cold temperatures is their proximity to an ice shelf, and a minimum depth of 100 meters, with most of the observations at 400 to 600 meters. The undersides of the edge of the Ronne and Ross Ice Shelves are approximately 200 meters below sea level, increasing to over 500 meters before the ice contacts the sea floor [*Zumberge and Swithinbank*, 1965]. Both melting and freezing would yield water below the one atmosphere pressure freezing point of sea water. However, the salinity of the melted water would be lower than that salinity of the brine released in freezing. The salinity of the upper 200 meters of sea water along the ice front is only slightly above 34.0‰, which is below that of the supercooled water. Therefore, it is reasonable to conclude that the cold water is derived from freezing at the underside of the ice shelves. It is interesting to speculate that the melted water from the lower part of the ice shelf (15–20 g/cm^2/yr [*Shumsky and Zotikov*, 1963]) would rise to the sea surface (owing to its lower density), where because of the lower freezing point it would freeze. However, it is not known if there is upwelling or sinking along the ice front; *Thomas* [1966] believes that sinking occurs. Sinking would supply the water that freezes to the bottom of the shelf ice. The resulting higher saline water drops to the sea floor under the ice and flows northward, contributing to the Ross Sea Shelf Water.

Ross Sea Shelf Water

Of special interest, partly related to the above, is the saline water that fills the topographic depressions of the Ross Sea. (See the topographic map of Antarctica (1965) prepared by the American Geographical Society.) A dense network of hydrographic stations was tested during Deep Freeze '63 and '64 by the USS *Edisto* and USS *Atka* [*Countryman and Gsell*, 1966]. These data will be used in this discussion. In the *T/S* diagrams of the Ross Sea (see Figure 5) the shelf water is found in the *T/S* region from 34.75 to 35.00‰ and −1.8°C to slightly below −2.0°C [*Countryman and Gsell*, 1966]. The density (σ_t units) is above 28.0, which is greater than that of the bottom water of the open ocean. The interval from 34.75 to 34.80‰ is a transition with the shelf water; therefore, 34.80‰ will be taken as the upper boundary. The depth of this surface and the temperature on this surface are shown in Figure 14. The depths to the 34.80‰ isohaline surface are smallest in the extreme

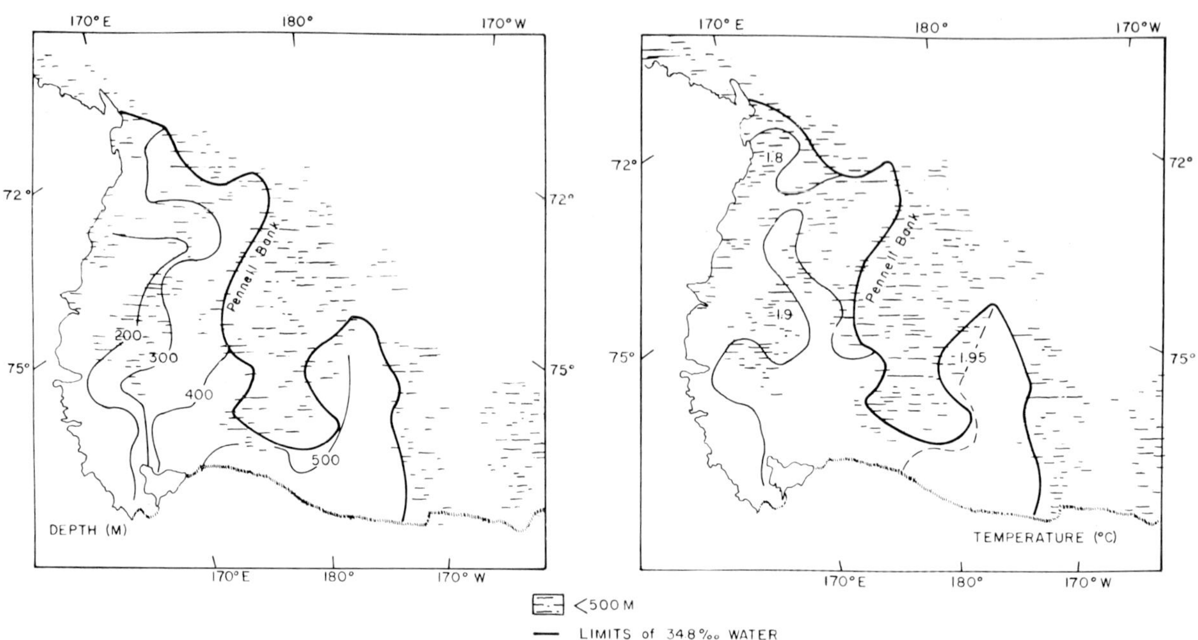

Fig. 14. Depth and temperature of upper boundary of the Ross Sea Shelf Water.

southwestern corner of the Ross Sea, coming to within 100 meters at the sea surface. The depth increases rapidly toward the east. The Pennell Bank protrudes through the shelf water. The thickest section of shelf water is over the three north-south oriented troughs of the southwestern Ross Sea. Since the 34.8‰ isohaline surface reaches bottom at the northern end of these troughs, it is probable that a blocking sill exists here. The slope in the shelf water may be in equilibrium with a northwest flowing geostrophic current.

The temperatures on the 34.8‰ surface are mostly near −1.9°C, although the coldest temperatures (near −2.0°C) are found at its southeastern limits. These temperatures are for the most part at or slightly below the *Miyake* [1939] freezing point values.

In the area shown in Figure 15 a temperature inversion is found in the lower hundred meters (average is 190 meters above the sea floor). The T/S diagram of four sample stations in this zone is shown in Figure 16. The in situ temperature is near −1.95°C (or in some stations −2.0°C) approximately 200 meters above the sea floor. Below this, the temperature increases by as much as 0.1°C, with an average increase of 0.05°C. The salinity also increases to the bottom in all cases. It is possible that the warmer bottom water represents a segment of the shelf water which is trapped in a topographic depression and is warmed by the geothermal heat flux. The volume of the shelf water below the temperature minimum layer is 7.7×10^{18} cm^3. Assuming normal continental shelf heat flow of 40 cal/cm^2/yr (M. Langseth, personal communication) and no water influx or discharge, this water must have been trapped in the depression for a period of ten years. Therefore, the lower part of the Ross Sea Shelf Water may be confined in the shelf depression for a number of years, while the upper part of the shelf water and the temperature minimum layer most likely have a much more active rate of renewal.

The formation of the highly saline shelf water is no doubt due to freezing, either at the sea surface or from below the Ross Ice Shelf. The presence of water with temperatures near −2.0°C indicates (as discussed above) an ice shelf origin. However, most of the shelf water is near or higher than the freezing point (the freezing point after Miyake for water of 34.85‰ is −1.98°C); therefore, a sea ice origin for at least part of the shelf water is not ruled out. A schematic of the possible origin for the bulk of the Ross Sea Shelf Water is shown in Figure 17.

Antarctic Bottom Water Production

The method of production of Antarctic Bottom Water is not exactly known, although it is generally accepted that the characteristics of the bottom water are attained by a mixture of surface water and deep water [*Brennecke*, 1921; *Mosby*, 1934; *Defant*, 1961]. It is not known if the surface component comes from the continental shelf regions, where owing to the shallow bottom, sufficiently dense surface water can form [*Brennecke*, 1921; *Mosby*, 1934, 1968] or it is de-

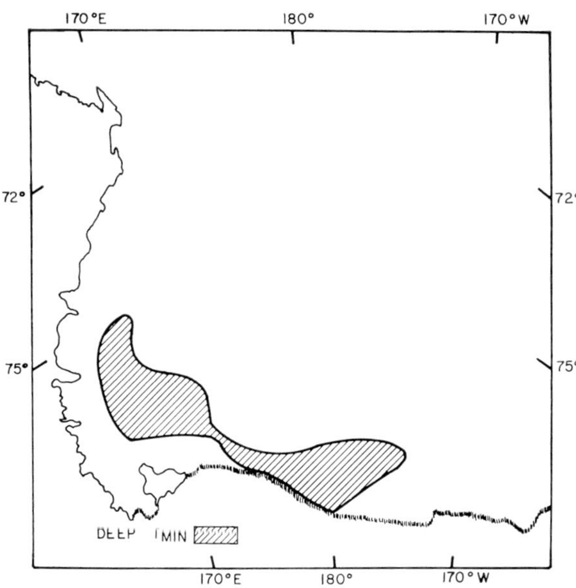

Fig. 15. Areal extent of deep T_{min} layer within Ross Sea Shelf Water.

rived directly from deeper oceanic areas (shown in schematic diagram by *Munk* [1966]). Either way the surface water temperature must decrease to near freezing and the salinity must increase, creating a surface density high enough to initiate sinking. Such conditions exist during ice formation periods. The period of most rapid formation is early winter (April to June) [*Neuman and Pierson,* 1966, fig. 4.10]. After June, the limit of the pack ice continues to advance slowly until September. As the ice thickens, the lower heat conduction of the ice slows the rate of thickening. However, breaks in the ice cover caused by icebergs flowing through the ice field or divergence in the wind or currents expose the water surface and ice forms rapidly. Such breaking of the ice field is fairly common in the Weddell Sea [*Heap,* 1964]. Therefore, the most rapid cooling and salinity increase of the surface water occurs in early to mid-winter, but the accumulating effect is to produce a late winter density maximum of the surface water; hence the bulk of bottom water production may occur in late winter [*Mosby,* 1934], when the critical salinity of 34.63‰ is attained on the shelf [*Fofonoff,* 1956].

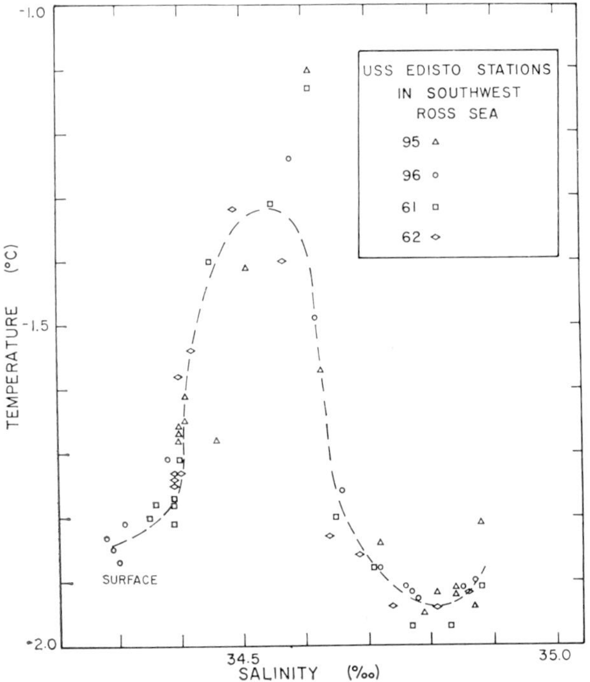

Fig. 16. Temperature-salinity diagram of Ross Sea Shelf Water.

Alternative methods for formation of bottom water involve evaporation of surface water, which leads to effects similar to ice formation [*Ledencv,* 1961] or freezing of sea water onto the bottom of the ice shelves. It is unlikely that either of these methods can account for the vast quantities of Antarctic Bottom Water observed through much of the world ocean (see below).

Fofonoff [1956] (also see *Mosby* [1968]) suggests that nonlinearity of the equation of state of sea water can result in the formation of water denser than either component and may explain Antarctic Bottom Water production from shelf water and deep water components. He shows that surface water of the Weddell Sea with salinities between 34.51 to 34.63‰ on mixing with the Weddell Deep Water will form water denser than either component and, therefore, surface water of these salinities is not present except where the surface water is not directly above the warmer deep water. On the continental shelf the water attains the high salinity necessary to produce the dense Antarctic Bottom Water. Other areas around Antarctica can be investigated by a similar technique.

For select areas around Antarctica (Figure 18) the observed T/S points within the temperature minimum layer and temperature maximum layer are plotted.

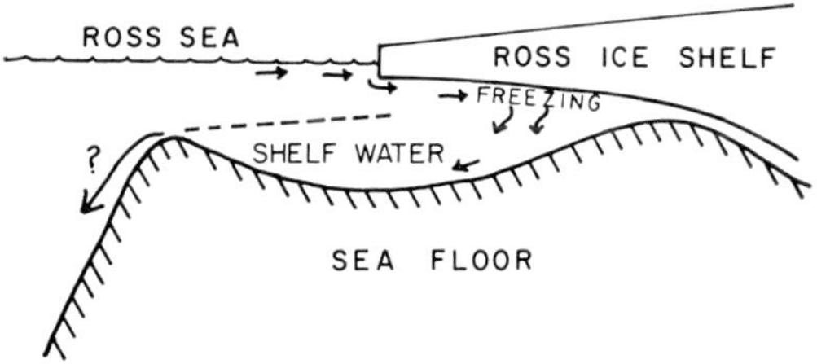

Fig. 17. Schematic of origin of Ross Sea Shelf Water.

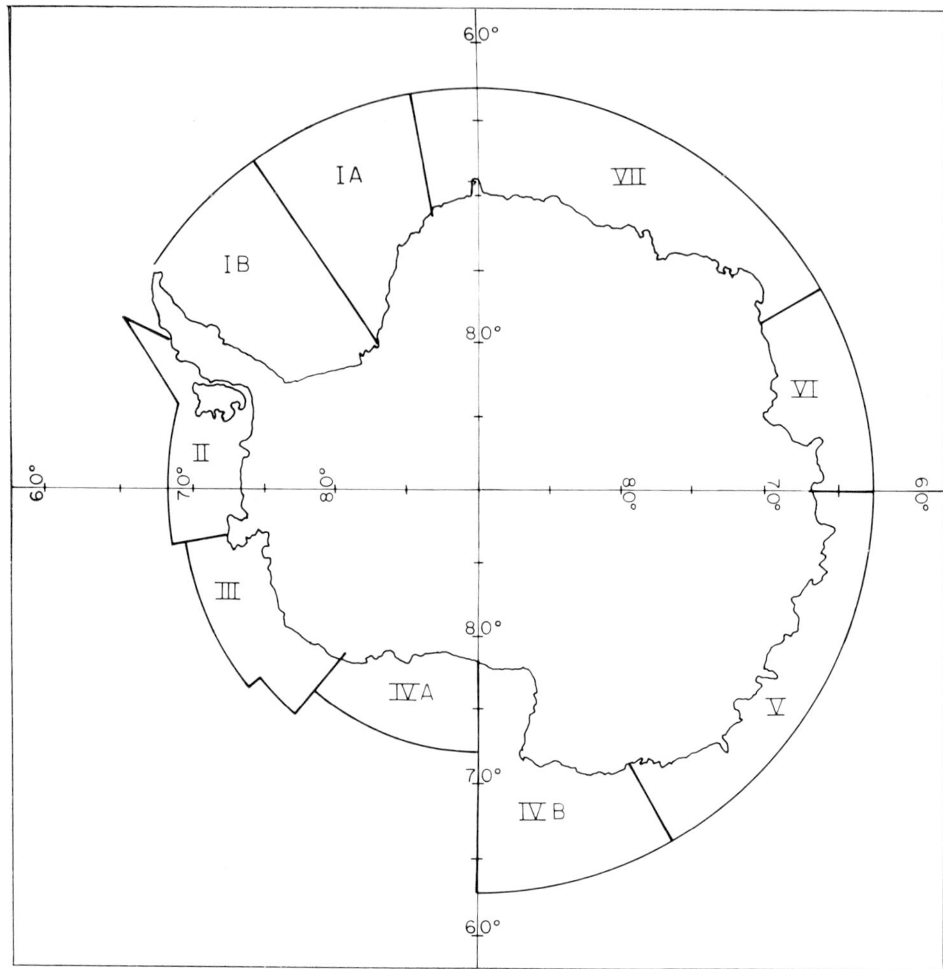

Fig. 18. Select areas for T_{max}/salinity and T_{min}/salinity diagrams.

The water in the temperature minimum layer is assumed to form the previous winter and so represents the densest surface water which has remained at the surface. Surface water which reached a higher density has dropped out of the surface layer and contributed in part to the Antarctic Bottom Water, and deeper transition zones. A tangent is drawn to the sigma-t at the mean T/S point of the T_{max} layer; in addition, a line connecting this point to a point on the freezing line with the same density is drawn. When salinities of the surface water are less than that at the intersection of the first line with the freezing point line, no mixture with the deep water can result in a denser water. Between this salinity and the salinity at the intersection of the second line with the freezing point, certain mixtures are denser than either component. As the salinity increases toward the second point, a smaller component of deep water is necessary to attain a denser solution. At salinities higher than the second point, sinking must occur. A decision can be made as to the probability of production of bottom water in the areas shown in Figure 18 by observing how closely the salinity of the temperature minimum layer comes to the first critical salinity.

Figure 19 shows the T/S plots and the two critical salinities for each area. Only areas I B (the western Weddell Sea) and IV B (the area northwest of the Ross Sea) show a high likelihood of bottom water production. Areas II and III (the Bellingshausen and Amundsen seas) show a very low likelihood of bottom water production. The other areas show fair possibilities.

When the salinity of the surface water at the freezing point increases above the first critical salinity value, only intense vertical mixing would cause conditions permitting production of water denser than either the surface or deep water. As the salinity increases further, the necessary vertical mixing decreases. There-

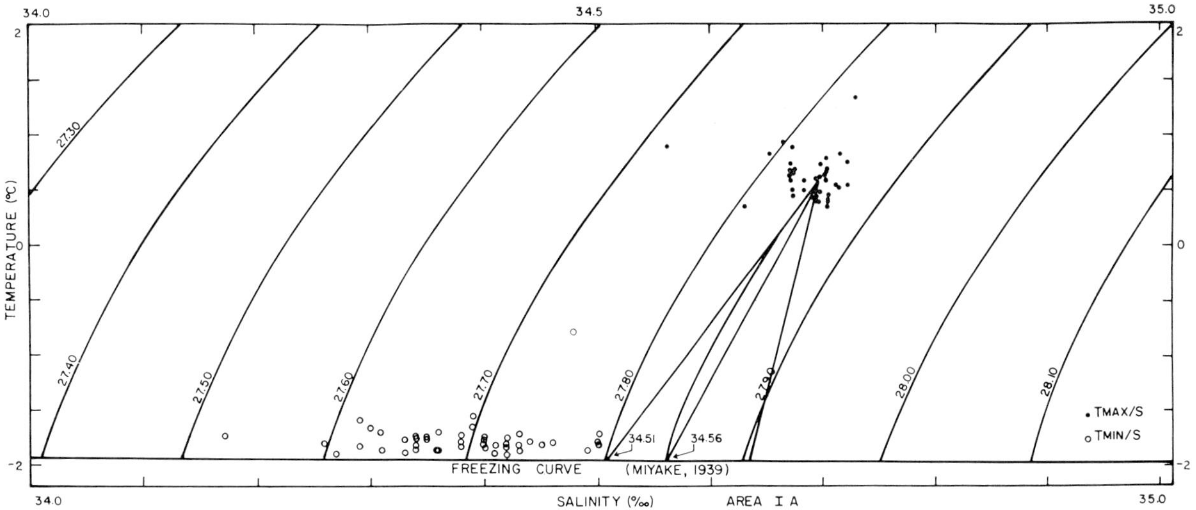

Fig. 19*a*. T_{max}/salinity and T_{min}/salinity diagrams.

fore, in the open sea where turbulence and vertical mixing in the surface layer are probably high owing to waves and wind, the surface water is quickly mixed, and high salinities in the T_{min} layer are not attained. However, where vertical mixing is small, the surface water can attain high salinities before sinking. For this reason, bottom water may be more likely to occur in areas somewhat sheltered from the open ocean turbulence, such as the Weddell Sea, the Ross Sea, and the indented bays around Antarctica.

Antarctic Bottom Water may have some contribution from shelf water produced by freezing at the bottom of the ice shelves, as discussed in the previous section. *Mellor* [1963] believes that 7.8×10^{17} g/yr of ice is discharged by the ice shelves of Antarctica. If the ice shelves are in equilibrium and the total volume is produced by bottom freezing, 1.2×10^6 m^3/sec of shelf water would be produced (−2.0°C and 34.9‰). This water would have to be diluted by at least 2 parts of the water found at the depth of the continental shelf break around Antarctica to produce water similar in temperature and salinity to Antarctic Bottom Water. Therefore, less than 4×10^6 m^3/sec of bottom water would be formed. This value would increase as it flows northward, owing to mixing with deep water. However, it is not probable that such a mechanism can explain the total amount of Antarctic Bottom Water, since 20×10^6 m^3/sec leaves the Weddell Sea [*Baronov and Botnikov*, 1964], and it is not reasonable to assume that all the ice shelves are produced by

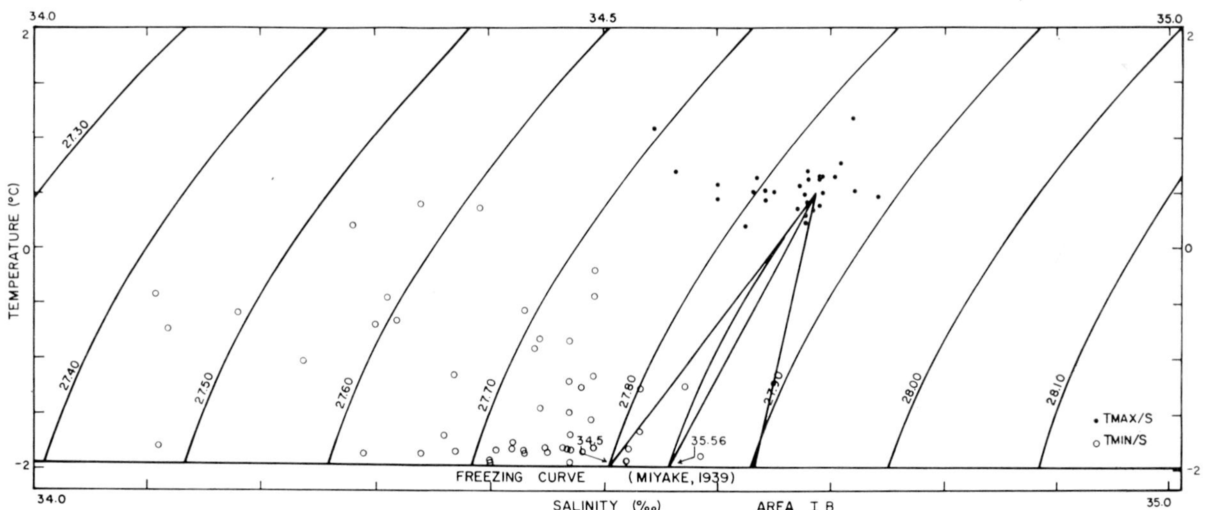

Fig. 19*b*. T_{max}/salinity and T_{min}/salinity diagrams.

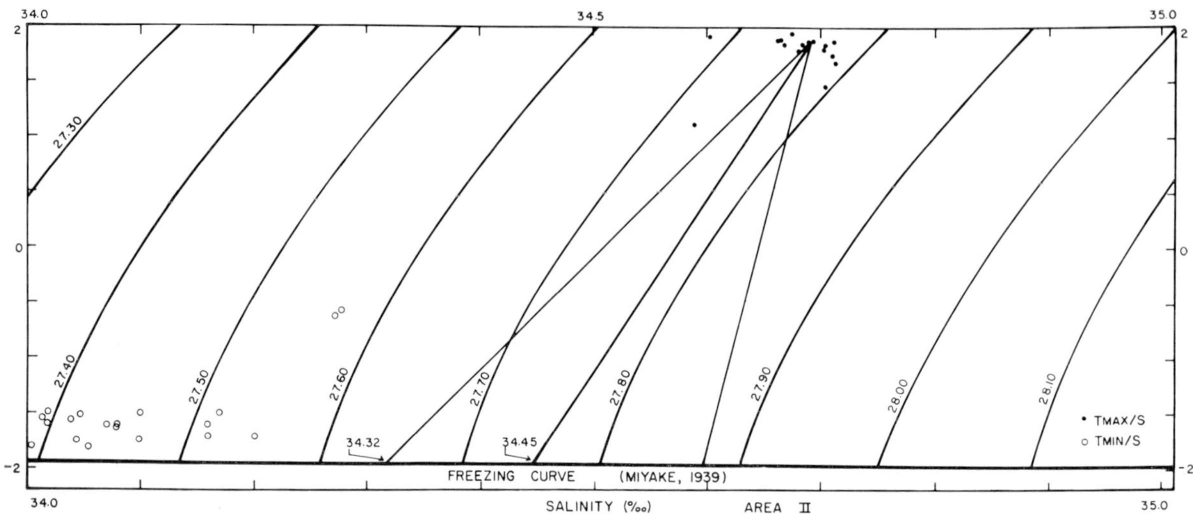

Fig. 19*c*. T_{max}/salinity and T_{min}/salinity diagrams.

freezing at the underneath side; however, such a mechanism may be of local importance, as in the Ross Sea.

Deacon [1937] has recognized the Ross Sea depression as a trap for catching the densest water produced at the sea surface; for this reason, the Ross Sea may be a poor source of Antarctic Bottom Water. *Mosby* [1968] suggests that the dense shelf water may act as an artificial sea floor, and the cold Ross Sea water may override it to reach the open ocean and contribute to bottom water.

It is conceivable that some of the dense shelf water does exist at the mouth of the troughs. This is expected during the winter when more shelf water may be formed or during periods when internal waves may cause 'blobs' of shelf water to escape in a manner similar to the formation of North Atlantic Deep Water [*Steele et al.*, 1962]. A likely place for this escape is the deep canyon cut into the continental slope near 178°E. However, no indication is found in the Deep Freeze '63 and '64 data. The non-steady-state character of such an overflow may be the reason. This canyon is a good location to place continuously recording bottom current meters.

There is evidence in the deep ocean that the high saline shelf water does escape and contributes to Antarctic Bottom Water. The bottom water of the southwest Pacific Ocean is a secondary salinity maximum, i.e., the salinity below the lower Circumpolar Deep Water first decreases, but on approaching the bottom

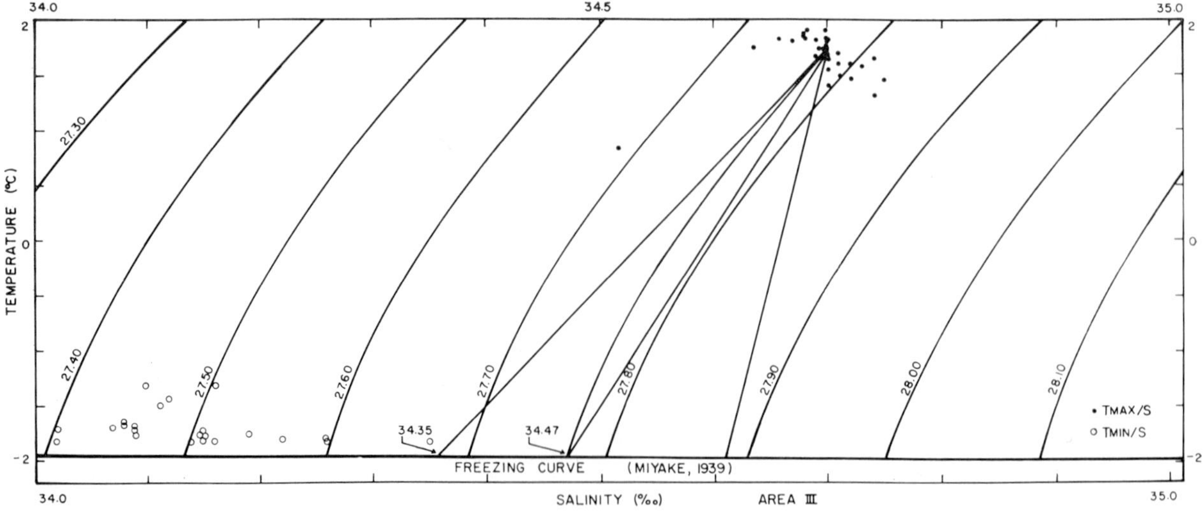

Fig. 19*d*. T_{max}/salinity and T_{min}/salinity diagrams.

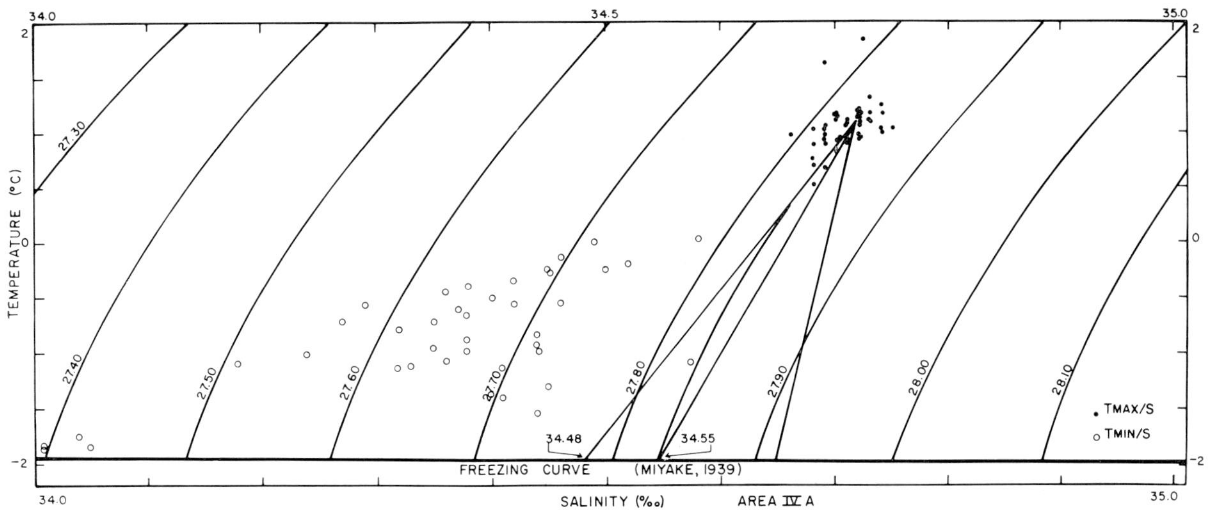

Fig. 19*e*. T_{max}/salinity and T_{min}/salinity diagrams.

increases. In the Weddell Sea, the salinity decreases slowly from the lower Circumpolar Deep Water to the sea floor. This difference is indicated on the curves of the deep water and bottom water shown in Figures 4 and 5. The curve of Figure 5 has an inflection point at temperatures about 0.3°C; this does not occur in Figure 4. The bottom salinity maximum and the Ross Sea Shelf Water intrusion to the high salinity part of Figure 5 suggest that the two water masses have a relationship. The USNS *Eltanin* cruise 37 (January–February, 1969) along the coastal area west of the Balleny Islands supports the view of a high salinity (> 34.72‰) Ross Sea outflow along the sea floor. This cruise will be discussed in future reports. The oceanography of the Ross Sea is discussed in a study by S. S. Jacobs and others (in preparation).

DEEP WATER MERIDIONAL TRANSPORT

Terms of Salt Balance Equation

The fresh water is introduced to Antarctic Surface Water from two sources: the excess of precipitation over evaporation and the continental runoff. To maintain the salt content of the surface water, it is necessary for deep water to upwell to the surface layer. Part of the fresh water input is seasonal in that the continental runoff is accomplished during the summer months. This, in addition to the alternating freezing and melting of the antarctic pack ice cover, causes seasonal surface salinity variation. If no deep water upwelled, the seasonal variations of surface salinity would fluctuate about a base line of decreasing salinity.

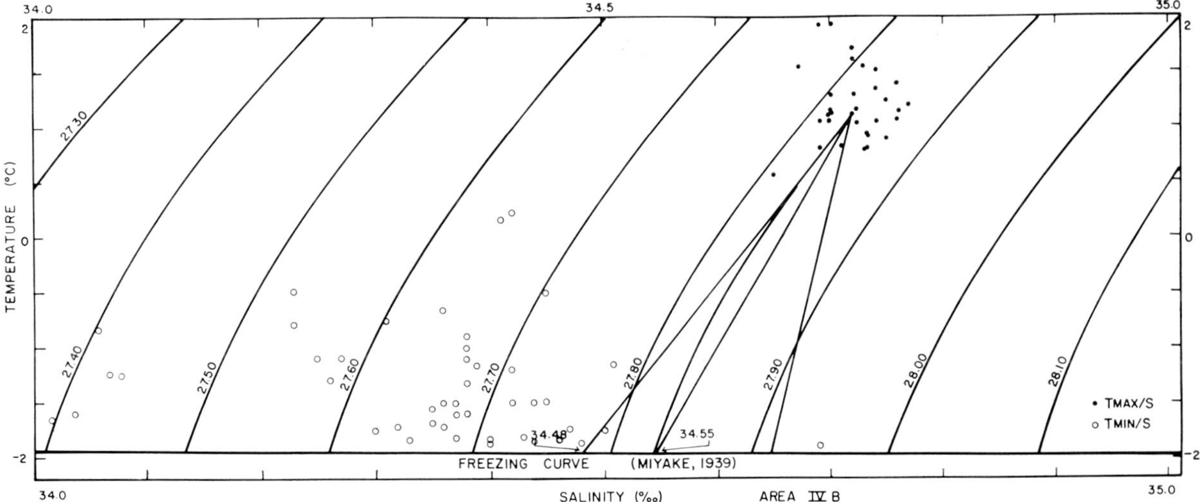

Fig. 19*f*. T_{max}/salinity and T_{min}/salinity diagrams.

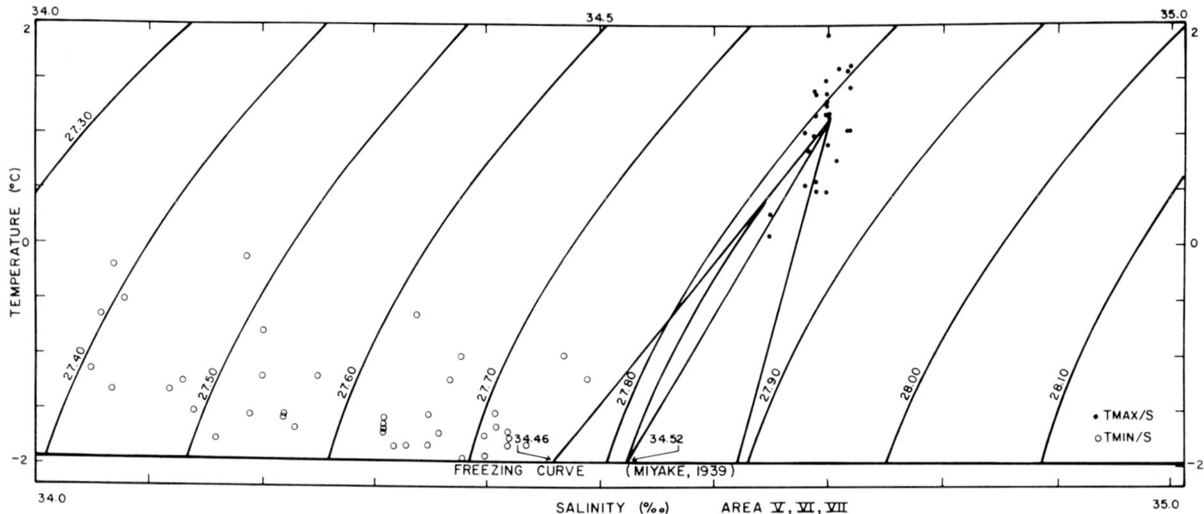

Fig. 19g. T_{max}/salinity and T_{min}/salinity diagrams.

The excess of precipitation over evaporation for all latitudinal belts has been estimated by *Wüst et al.* [1954]. From these data, the average value over antarctic waters is found to be approximately 40 cm for a period of one year. The area of the Antarctic Surface Water from the southern limits of the Antarctic Convergence near 56°S to the continent is 20×10^{16} cm^2; therefore, 8.0×10^{18} g of fresh water is introduced to the sea from the atmosphere each year.

The continental runoff includes ice calving, melting of ice shelves, blown snow, and fresh water runoff. An estimate can be made based on the annual precipitation minus evaporation and sublimation (net accumulation) and the assumption that the volume of the antarctic ice sheet remains constant. This appears to be a reasonable assumption [*Robin and Adie*, 1964; *Giovinetto*, 1964; *Gow*, 1965]. The net accumulation estimated by Giovinetto is $(2.1 \pm 0.4) \times 10^{18}$ g/yr. His calculations are based on measurement within ten drainage systems (including ice shelves), totaling 13.6×10^6 km^2, or 97% of the total areal extent of Antarctica. Therefore, approximately 2.1×10^{18} grams of water are transported directly from Antarctica to antarctic waters each year. *Mellor* [1963] estimates the iceberg discharge of ice shelves and continental ice as approximately 0.8×10^{18} g/yr (7.8×10^{17} from ice shelves and 0.37×10^{17} from unchanneled continental ice). *Shumsky et al.* [1964] use the value of $(1.63 \pm 0.1) \times 10^{18}$ g/yr, or twice that of Mellor. Various earlier estimates of the amount of calving [*Wexler*, 1961, table 1] range from 0.04×10^{18} to 1.21×10^{18} g/yr. A value of 1×10^{18} g/yr for iceberg discharge leaves 1.1×10^{18} g/yr to be discharged by melting at the ice-sea boundary, fresh water runoff, and blowing of snow off the continent. Most of the 10^{18} g/yr of ice that leaves Antarctica melts before reaching the Antarctic Convergence [*Tolstikov*, 1966, pl. 124]. For the purpose of these calculations, it is assumed that all the ice melts within the Antarctic Surface Water. In addition, all the ice-to-water phase change of the continental runoff is accomplished during the six summer months.

The amount of ice melting and freezing each year is estimated from variation in pack ice boundaries observed from ships and Nimbus 1 satellite views to be 2.3×10^{19} g [*Munk*, 1966]. Unlike the precipitation and runoff estimates, this value is fairly well agreed upon.

Summer Months

The water balance equation for the period October to March is as follows:

$$M_1S_1 + M_2S_2 + M_{ice}S_{ice} + M_{ASW}S_{AW} = [M_1 + M_2 + M_{ice} + M_{ASW}]\, S_{AS} \quad (1)$$

where

M_1, S_1 = mass and salinity of the fresh water input;

M_2, S_2 = mass and salinity of deep water entering the Antarctic Surface Water;

M_{ice}, S_{ice} = mass and salinity of melting water from pack ice;

M_{ASW} = mass of Antarctic Surface Water;

S_{AW} = salinity of Antarctic Surface Water at the end of September;

S_{AS} = salinity of Antarctic Surface Water at the end of March.

The value of M_{ASW} used for these calculations is based on a surface water areal extent south of the southern limits of the convergence of 20×10^{16} cm^2 and a depth of 100 meters, which is a reasonable average found from the depth of the 90% O_2 saturation surface. The S_{AW} and S_{AS} values are average values in the upper 100 meters of antarctic waters. During the summer months, it is expected that the entire annual continental runoff and seasonal melting of pack ice are accomplished. A further assumption is made: the precipitation over evaporation is constant throughout the year.

A further consideration is that during the initiation of pack ice melting in spring small pockets of brine drop out, enriching the salt content of the surface water. This process is counteracted by the accumulation on the pack ice of snow accumulated by precipitation and blown snow off Antarctica. The snow melts in spring when the pack ice becomes porous or 'rotten.' For the purpose of the salt budget approximation, it is assumed that these two processes cancel each other.

Solving equation 1 for M_2:

$$M_2 = \frac{M_{ASW}(S_{AS} - S_{AW}) + M_{ice}(S_{AS} - S_{ice}) + M_1 S_{AS}}{S_2 - S_{AS}} \quad (2)$$

Using $S_1 = 0$, $S_2 = 34.6‰$ (approximate salinity of the upper Circumpolar Deep Water) an ice salinity of 4.0‰ [*Serikov*, 1965; *Neumann and Pierson*, 1966], M_2 can be found as a function of ΔS, the seasonal variation of salinity of the upper 100 meters of the Antarctic Surface Water (Figure 20). Where S_{AS} or S_{AW} appear separately, the values 33.8 and 34.0 are used, respectively. Since ΔS is most sensitive in determining M_2, the relation shown in Figure 20 is a good approximation. Obviously, the value of ΔS is very critical to the outcome, in that the necessary upwelling of deep water into the surface layer varies from 34 to 80×10^6 m^3/sec, as the surface salinity difference decreases from 0.2‰ to 0.05‰.

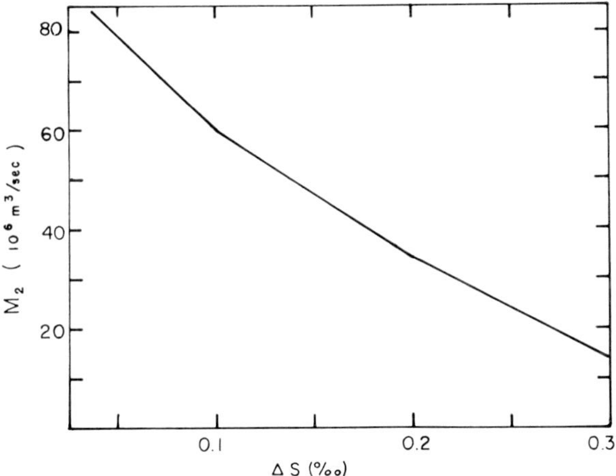

Fig. 20. Amount of necessary upwelling, M_2 versus salinity, seasonal variations of antarctic surrounding water, Δs.

The average salinity in the upper 100 meters of Antarctic Surface Water for all hydrographic stations in the western hemisphere south of the convergence is 33.9‰ for March and 34.0‰ for September. Therefore, ΔS is 0.1‰, and M_2 is 60×10^6 m^3/sec.

The average March and September salinities for the upper 100 meters show considerable regional variation. The Weddell Sea values are generally 0.2‰ to 0.3‰ higher than the Pacific values. However, the seasonal change at any particular geographic area can best be approximated by 0.1‰. The value calculated for M_2 is, of course, a rough approximation; estimate of the error based solely on the uncertainty in the ΔS value would be $\pm 20 \times 10^6$ m^3/sec. This, in addition to uncertainties in the value for precipitation minus evaporation, continental runoff, and pack ice fluctuations, indicates that 60×10^6 m^3/sec should be used with reservation. However, it does indicate that the upwelling of deep water into the surface layer is most probably between 40 to 80×10^6 m^3/sec.

The value of M_2 is not the entire southward transport of deep water. Additional quantities are needed to balance that which is entrained in the northward flowing bottom water, and that which mixes with antarctic shelf water in bottom water formation.

It is not expected that the deep water upwells into the surface layer around Antarctica. In certain regions, more intense upwelling would occur. Here surface waters would contain the highest percentage of deep water; hence, they would be relatively high in salinity and nutrients. Figure 21 shows the surface trace of the 34.0‰ isohaline [*Deacon*, 1937]. In general, the surface salinity is above 34.0‰ south of 65°S. In three regions, this isohaline penetrates northward: the Weddell Sea, Ross Sea, and Kerguelen Island regions. From the higher salinities, it is probable that upwelling is concentrated in these regions. (From the group T/S diagrams, it is found that upwelling is intense in the Weddell gyre and the area northeast of the Ross Sea.) It is interesting to point out that in these regions meridionally oriented ridges occur, vast ice shelves exist along the coast, and the first two are bottom water sources; the third is suspected as being a source area. Such an occurrence is

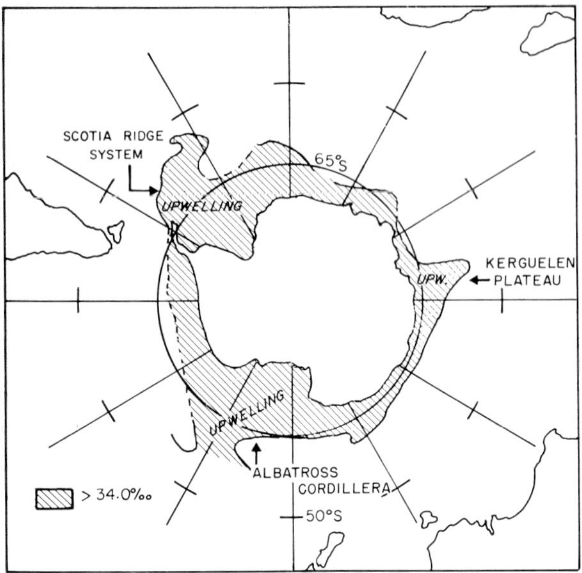

Fig. 21. Position of surface 34.0‰ isohaline (from *Deacon* [1937]).

no doubt due to the ridges that prohibit the warm circumpolar water from penetrating southward and permit extensive pack ice fields to form.

Upwelling in the vicinity of ridge crests would produce higher productivity of surface water within and downstream of these regions. Lower productivity is expected over the central and eastern portions of the basins.

Ekman Surface Divergence

It is generally accepted that the divergence of the Antarctic Surface Water and the associated deep water upwelling are mostly a result of the wind [*Sverdrup*, 1933]. Thermohaline effects no doubt play an important role, since the sinking shelf water must be replaced by deep water. However, in summer the wind is more important, since only minor sinking due to thermohaline alterations occurs. It is possible to calculate the wind-produced divergence by the following procedure.

In an unbounded homogeneous ocean, the stress of the wind on the sea surface would create a surface current system as derived by *Ekman* [1905]. The current vectors decrease in magnitude and rotate as the depth increases, forming the classical Ekman spiral. The surface current vector is directed at 45° to the left of the wind in the southern hemisphere. At a depth D, the current is directed in the opposite direction of the surface flow with a magnitude of $1/e$ of the surface value. The depth of D depends on the vertical eddy viscosity and the latitude. It usually occurs between 100 to 300 meters below the sea surface. The net total transport of the wind drift current is found to be directed at right angles to the wind, to the wind's left in the southern hemisphere, and given by the following expressions assuming that the wind is solely a zonal wind [*Sverdrup et al.*, 1942, 1946]:

$$T_\theta = + \tau_\lambda / \rho f \qquad (3)$$

where

T_θ = total meridional transport of the wind drift current across one centimeter of a parallel;
τ_λ = zonal wind stress, dynes/cm^2;
ρ = sea water density;
f = Coriolis parameter = $2\,\omega \sin\theta$;
ω = earth's angular momentum;
θ = latitude.

The total transport across a parallel T_θ' is found by multiplying equation 3 by the number of centimeters of that parallel given by $L = 2\,\pi r \cos\theta$, where r is the earth's radius. Therefore

$$T_\theta' = LT_\theta = \pi r \cos\theta\,(\tau_\lambda/\rho f) \qquad (4)$$

From the continuity equation, it is possible to calculate the amount of vertical motion between latitudes θ_1 and θ_2, $T_{vt(\theta 1\,-\,\theta 2)}$, at the base of the wind drift current, since

$$T_{vt(\theta 1\,-\,\theta 2)} = T'_{\theta 1} - T'_{\theta 2} \qquad (5)$$

Therefore

$$T_{vt(\theta 1\,-\,\theta 2)} = (\pi r/\omega\rho) \cdot [\tau_\lambda\,(\theta_1)\cot\theta_1 - \tau_\lambda\,(\theta_2)\cot\theta_2] \qquad (6)$$

The vertical transport can be calculated if the zonal stress, as a function of latitude, is known. To establish a realistic function, the following conditions must be met: (1) zero stress at the Antarctic Divergence at 65°S; (2) westward directed stress (negative) south of the divergence; and (3) the eastward stress, north of the divergence, must be at a maximum value in the vicinity of the central antarctic polar front zone, 53°S. For the purpose of calculation of the upward transport, a value of + 2 dynes/cm^2 is taken at 53°S, and a sinusoidal function is assumed. The expression for τ_λ (θ becomes

$$\tau_\lambda\,(\theta) = 2 \sin\,(-75\,(\theta) + 487.5) \qquad (7)$$

Since the stress increases toward the north, the vertical transport will be upward, i.e., a surface divergence with upwelling.

Table 2 shows the wind stress at each degree of latitude from 53°S to 70°S and the upward transport at the base of the wind drift current in 1° bands. The total upwelling is 54 × 10^6 m^3/sec. However, 20.2 ×

10^6 m^3/sec or 37% of the total value is accomplished in the 4° band between 58° and 62°S, and the maximum upward transport is found between 60° and 61°S or 4° north of the divergence. This is due to the increase in area of latitudinal bands as the latitude decreases.

The choice of +2 dynes/cm^2 at 53°S is open to debate.

The relation of stress (τ) to wind velocity (W) for neutral temperature profile of the air (neutral stability) just above the sea surface [*Malkus,* 1962] is

$$\tau = c\rho W^2 \tag{8}$$

where $c = 2 \times 10^{-3}$ and ρ = air density $= 1.27 \times 10^{-3}$. The zonal wind necessary to give 2 dynes/cm^2 stress is 20 knots.

The *Marine Climatic Atlas of the World* [*U.S. Navy,* 1965] charts on surface wind indicate that in the ocean region between 50°S and 60°S, the winds are most frequently from the northwest, west, or southwest in the range of Beaufort force 5 and 6 or 17 to 27 knots. Since the wind many times has a meridional component, a 20-knot value for the average zonal wind is reasonable, and the τ (θ) function used in the above calculation is satisfactory, at least to a first approximation.

The upwelling into the surface layer as found by the Ekman transport divergence agrees very well with that found by water budget considerations for the summer months. It is expected that owing to friction and other deviations from the original assumptions made in the calculations of the pure Ekman spiral, the wind-produced upwelling may deviate somewhat from that calculated above.

TABLE 2. Upwelling Transport in 1° Bands around Antarctica

Latitude θ	Dynes/cm^2	T_{vt} $(\theta_1 - \theta_2)$ m^3/sec
53	2.00	1.9×10^6
54	1.98	2.4
55	1.93	2.9
56	1.85	3.4
57	1.73	3.6
58	1.59	4.0
59	1.41	4.0
60	1.22	4.2
61	1.00	4.0
62	0.77	4.0
63	0.52	3.8
64	0.26	3.5
65	0	3.2
66	−0.26	2.9
67	−0.52	2.5
68	−0.77	2.0
69	−1.00	1.7
70	−1.22	
53–70		54.0

Winter Months

During the winter months, April to September, the continental runoff ceases and pack ice is forming. There is an additional loss of salt through the sinking of cold saline surface water, which eventually becomes part of the Antarctic Bottom Water. The water balance equation for the winter months is

$$M_1S_1 + M_2S_2 - M_{ice}S_{ice} - M_3S_3 + M_{ASW}S_{AS} = (M_1 + M_2 - M_{ice} - M_3 + M_{ASW})S_{AW} \tag{9}$$

where M_3, S_3 are the mass and salinity of the surface water which sinks to depths greater than 100 meters. Solving for M_3 with $S_1 = 0$ gives

$$M_3 = [M_1S_{AW} + M_2(S_{AW} - S_2) + M_{ice}(S_{ice} - S_{AW}) + M_{ASW}(S_{AW} - S_{AS})] / S_{AW} - S_3 \tag{10}$$

From the $(T_{min} - T_{max})/S$ diagrams (Figure 19), it is found that sinking of surface water occurs at salinities above 34.6‰. Using 34.6‰ for S_3, 33.9 and 34.0‰ for S_{AS}, S_{AW}, respectively, and other values as given in the previous section, then M_3 is calculated to be 35×10^6 m^3/sec, assuming M_2 as 60×10^6 m^3/sec. Therefore, during the winter months about one-half of the upwelling deep water contributes to water that sinks to depths greater than 100 meters. Only the densest of this water eventually becomes Antarctic Bottom Water. Part sinks to the transition zones between the surface and upper deep water and between the lower deep water and the bottom water. On sinking, this water entrains more deep water. This entrained deep water does not reach the surface and is not included in M_2. The amount of entrained water would be about the same magnitude as the sinking surface water, since bottom water temperatures and salinities are about midway between that of the surface water and the main mass of Circumpolar Deep Water. Thus, the total amount of southward transport of Circumpolar Deep Water during the winter months is about 10^8 m^3/sec, which is much less than the 8×10^8 m^3/sec estimated by *Kort* [1962, 1964]. Since the zonal transport of the circumpolar current is about 2×10^8 m^3/sec [*Gordon,* 1967*b*], during the winter months an approximate 2:1 ratio exists between zonal and meridional transport in antarctic waters. The Ekman Divergence of about 50×10^6 m^3/sec suggests that approximately one-half of the meridional transport is wind induced. The other half is initiated by the thermohaline effect of bottom water production.

During the summer, the meridional transport is 60 ×

10^6 m³/sec, all of which is M_2 and contributes to the Antarctic Surface Water. In winter, only half of this amount remains in the surface water. This assessment rests on the assumption made earlier that M_2 is constant throughout the year. A seasonal variation of divergence of the surface wind [*Tolstikov*, 1966, pl. 108], indicates that M_2 would vary somewhat. Variations in the value of M_2 and the southward migration of the deep water would be reflected in variations of the zonal transport. This is expected because of the relationship between zonal and meridional flow based on conservation of vorticity [*Kaplan*, 1967]: a southward transport initiates an easterly current. The Antarctic Circumpolar Current is largest during the months of March and April [*Yeskin*, 1962]. Therefore, it is probable that during these months M_2 is at a maximum. A large seasonal effect in the production of bottom water and renewal of surface water must occur.

World Ocean Meridional Transport

Owing to the strong stratification within the upper water column in the tropical and subtropical regions of the oceans, the deep ocean has only limited interaction with the surface layers, mainly through eddy diffusion. At high latitudes, the cold climate and lack of strong stratification permit deep vertical convection. The water masses below the main thermocline of the lower latitudes are derived from these polar and subpolar regions. Figure 22 depicts, in schematic form, the basic meridional ocean circulation. Sinking occurs at high northern latitudes, producing deep water; additional deep water is derived from the warm and salty subtropical marginal seas of the northern hemisphere. The loss of surface water is compensated by a flow from the warm to cold sphere by a northward current in the northeastern North Atlantic Ocean. The warm water sphere is, in turn, replenished by a transfer of water across the antarctic polar front zone and upwelling through the main thermocline. The upwelling is also necessary to compensate partially for the downward flux of heat by eddy diffusion [*Robinson and Stommel*, 1959]. The deep water flows south with increasing volume transport, owing to the addition of Antarctic Intermediate Water (with some Arctic or Subarctic Intermediate Water) and Antarctic Bottom Water. South of the polar front zone, the bottom water transport is increased by entrainment of deep water, but to the north the transfer is from bottom to deep water.

The water balance equation may be written as follows:

$$N_3 = N_1 + N_2 + A_3 + (A_2 - U) \qquad (11)$$

$$W = N_1 + N_2 + N_4 = A_1 + U + N_4 \qquad (12)$$

therefore

$$N_3 = A_1 + A_2 + A_3 \qquad (13)$$

where

N_3 = upwelling Circumpolar Deep Water;
N_2 = subtropical marginal sea produced deep water;
N_3 = upwelling Circumpolar Deep Water;
N_4 = intermediate water formed in the northern hemisphere (that part of northern hemisphere intermediate water which becomes incorporated into the deep water is included directly in the N_1 term);
A_1 = Antarctic Surface Water mixing across the polar front zone into the warm water sphere;
A_2 = intermediate water formation, southern hemisphere;
A_3 = bottom water;
U = water upwelling through main thermocline; all of this water is derived from the intermediate water, A_2 and N_4;
W = transfer from warm to cold water sphere.

The source region for the N_1 water is the North Atlantic. Some of the intermediate water of the North Pacific may become incorporated into the deep water and thus be included in N_1, but it is probably only a small amount. The N_2 water is derived mainly from the Mediterranean and Red seas and Persian Gulf. Intermediate water is formed in both hemispheres, but all of N_4 re-enters the warm water sphere before reaching the southern hemisphere (by definition of the N_4 term). The upwelling U water occurs throughout the tropical and subtropical regions of the world ocean with some variation with longitude [*Wyrtki*, 1961]. Since a portion of the W water is from the southern hemisphere, there must be a net northward transport across the equator. This transport would best develop in the Atlantic Ocean, where most of the deep water is produced. The northward transport prohibits a well-defined tropical or equatorial water mass from forming in the Atlantic unlike the other oceans [*Sverdrup et al.*, 1942].

It is possible to place values on some of the terms of equation 11. These values are considered to be only approximations. Of more importance is the relative magnitude of the terms.

The N_3 term from the salt budget considerations above is 100×10^6 m³/sec. Unknown is the amount

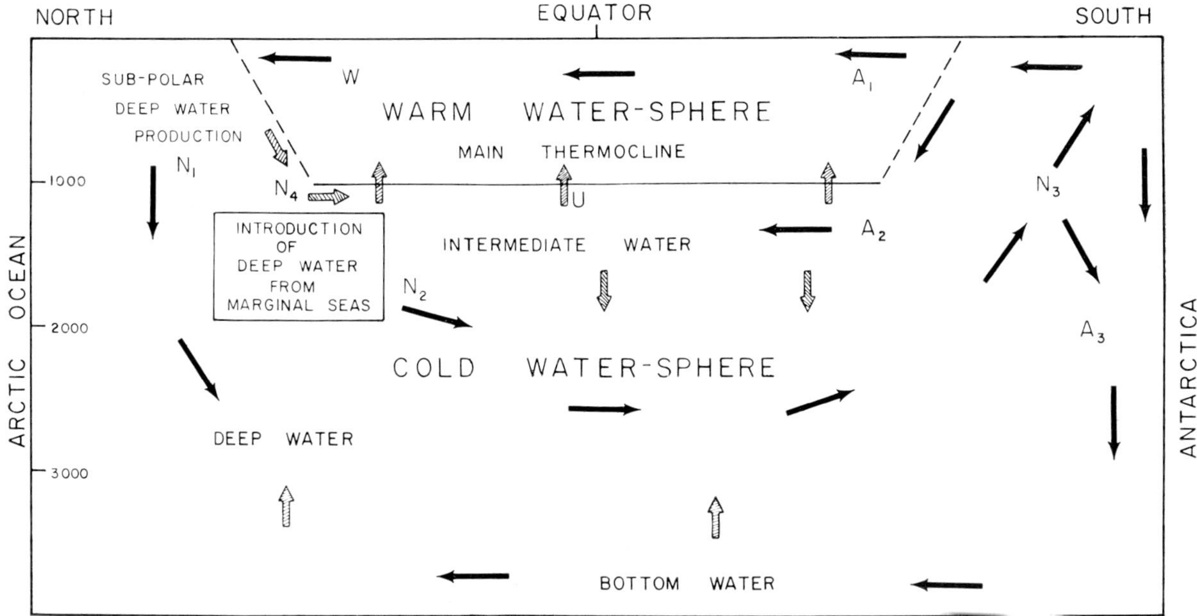

Fig. 22. Schematic of meridional transport of world ocean. See page 196 for key to abbreviations.

of water which is recirculated between A_2, A_3, and N_3, that is, the value of $A_2 - U$ and A_3. These may be calculated if, in addition to N_3, the terms U, N_1, N_2, and A_1 are known. The first three of these terms can be approximated. From heat budget consideration in the case of U, an average upward velocity of 1 to 5 $\times$ 10^{-5} cm/sec is expected in the main thermocline [*Robinson and Stommel*, 1959; *Wyrtki*, 1961]. The N_1 and N_2 terms can be approximated from recent measurements and calculations. The Atlantic-produced portion of N_1 from the Norwegian Sea overflow is most likely between 6 to 12 $\times$ 10^6 m^3/sec [*Worthington and Volkmann*, 1965], since 5 to 6 $\times$ 10^6 m^3/sec overflows to either side of Iceland on the ridge system from Greenland to the Faroes. However, it is not known how much of the flow to the west is entrained Iceland-Faroes overflow. The amount of deep water produced along the southern coast of Greenland [*Wüst*, 1935) is unknown, although it is expected to be less than the Norwegian Sea overflow. *Arons and Stommel* [1967] calculate a value of 6 $\times 10^6 \times$ m^3/sec for the Atlantic part of N_1, based on radiocarbon data in the North Atlantic. The values of N_2 for the Atlantic (outflow from Mediterranean) have been approximated as 1.5 $\times$ 10^6 m^3/sec by *Boyum* [1967]. *Ovchinnikov* [1966] states that the Atlantic inflow into the Mediterranean is between 0.84 to 1.05 $\times$ 10^6 m^3/sec. Since the outflow must equal this difference of river runoff and precipitation with the water lost by evaporation within the Mediterranean, N_2 is most likely less than 1 $\times$ 10^6 m^3/sec. The sum of N_1 and N_2 for the Atlantic Ocean, which must make up most of these components, is probably between 10 to 15 $\times$ 10^6 m^3/sec. Since N_3 is of order 10^8 m^3/sec, the values of A_3 and $A_2 - U$ are quite large, about 90 $\times$ 10^6 m^3/sec together. From the salt budget considerations, the ratio of these terms is most likely 1:1, with the possibility of A_3 being slightly larger. The recirculation of antarctic water masses into the deep water occurs all around Antarctica and is not restricted to the Atlantic Ocean; however, some longitudinal variation is natural. The deep water of Atlantic origin does not fit directly on the T/S curve of the Circumpolar Deep Water (see Figure 4). Therefore, the Circumpolar Deep Water is made of modified North Atlantic Deep Water and is to a large extent a closed system involving only southern hemisphere circulation. Perhaps only 10–20% of the transport of the Antarctic Circumpolar Current is due to additions from the northern hemisphere.

If the value of A_1 is known, it would be possible to calculate the above ratio. The A_1 term can be found using equation 12; however, the error in estimating N_1 and N_2 and especially the uncertainty of the value of U makes such a calculation impractical. It is best to arrive at A_1 directly from ocean observations. For

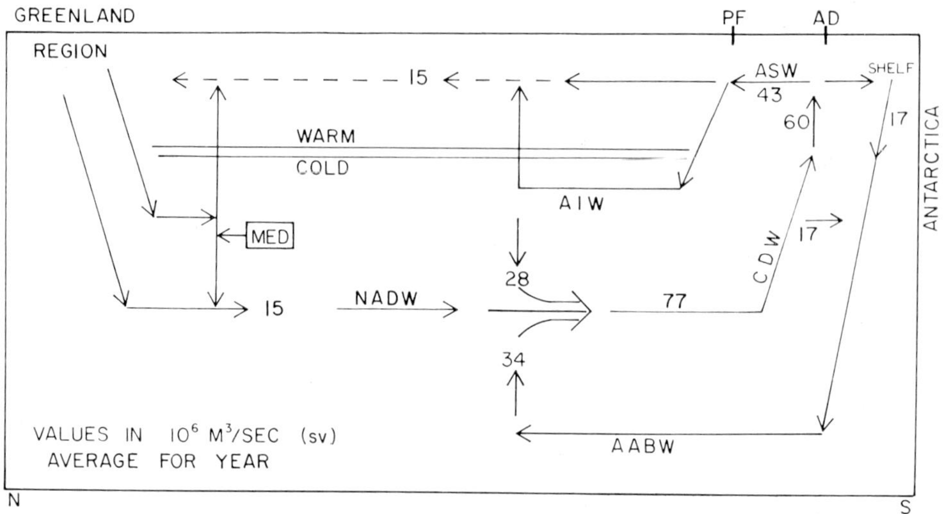

Fig. 23. Mean annual values of the meridional transport of the world ocean.

this purpose, radioisotope data are useful, as is, possibly, the ratio of antarctic to subantarctic fauna and flora in the surface water.

Figure 23 shows the magnitude of the net meridional transport at various levels for the world ocean. The values represent yearly averages from the salt budget considerations and estimates of the transport of the North Atlantic Deep Water. The relative values are of more significance than the absolute values, owing to the large uncertainties involved with such calculations. The annual average ratio of zonal to meridional transport in antarctic waters is between 3:1 to 2:1.

CONCLUDING REMARKS

The oceanographic processes that occur in antarctic waters are essential to: (1) maintenance of the intermediate, deep, and bottom water of the world ocean as an aerobic environment; (2) the removal of heat and addition of fresh water necessary for a steady-state character of the deep water; (3) renewal of the warm water sphere, which is depleted in the production of North Atlantic Deep Water; (4) the equalization of water characteristics of the three major oceans. The results of these processes lead to high biological productivity in antarctic waters and a net heat flux from the ocean to the atmosphere. The driving mechanism in antarctic circulation is the wind and the thermohaline effect along the coast of Antarctica. Both cause upwelling of deep water, which can only be replaced by a southward migration of the Circumpolar Deep Water.

The deep water that reaches the sea surface in the vicinity of the divergence is transformed into Antarctic Surface Water by sea-air interaction and vertical diffusion. Most of this water flows northward; part of it becomes incorporated into the Subantarctic Surface Water and the rest eventually sinks at the Antarctic Convergence, contributing to the formation of Antarctic or Subantarctic Intermediate Water. Some of the surface water flows southward to the shores of Antarctica, where intense climatic conditions produce a very cold, salty shelf water. This water sinks, mixing with equal proportions of deep water to produce Antarctic Bottom Water.

Within the Antarctic Circumpolar Current, an axis of flow can be found at the depth of the salinity maximum layer [*Goldberg*, 1967]. The axis occurs slightly south of the polar front zone. Such a situation is very similar to the atmospheric conditions of the midlatitudes, where a polar front separates the cold polar air masses from the tropical or subtropical air masses. Directly above or slightly poleward of the atmospheric polar front is the axis of flow of the westerlies. This axis is called the Jet Stream [*Hare*, 1963].

Perhaps the analogy can be drawn further: The mean flow within the axis of the Antarctic Circumpolar Current is maintained by a transfer of energy from large eddies in a fashion similar to the energy transfer by the high and low pressure systems of the midlatitudes into the Jet Stream [*Lorentz*, 1966]. Such speculation may be evaluated by the study of time variations within antarctic waters.

The above model depicts only the average conditions; there are strong variations with longitude, mainly due to the asymmetry of Antarctica and the submarine topography. The Antarctic Circumpolar Current is diverted northward and intensifies upon approaching a north-south oriented ridge. After passing the ridge, it turns southward and becomes more diffuse. On passing over the fracture zones through the ridges, the flow is constricted at all depths.

From the group T/S diagrams of the southwest Atlantic and Pacific sectors of antarctic waters, it is found that two cyclonic gyres exist in which water found at levels below 2000 meters to the northwest upwell to approximately 400 meters in the central parts of the gyre. These gyres bring higher salinities to the surface waters, as shown in Figure 22 and in Figure 2 (note the waters above 34.6‰ in the Weddell Sea and northeast of the Ross Sea).

The meridional transport is of the order of 10^8 m^3/sec or less. It is probable that the transport is not equally distributed about Antarctica, but that it is confined to the regions of the cyclonic gyres. It is expected that this transport has a seasonal variation because of such variations in the wind field and thermohaline alterations along the coast of Antarctica. That the zonal transport is greatest during the months of March and April indicates that meridional transport is greatest during these months. April begins the period of rapid ice production. Perhaps the maximum in meridional transport during April is due to a maximum in bottom water production.

Since the introduction of deep water from the north is most likely between 10 and 15 $\times$ 10^{+6} m^3/sec, most of the Antarctic Circumpolar Current is water which is recirculated between the antarctic water masses and the deep water. Such recirculation can occur in all three oceans. However, the introduction of deep water from more northern sources is confined mostly to the Atlantic Ocean.

The Antarctic Surface Water and the Antarctic Bottom Water both occur in the frictional boundaries of the ocean. The surface water receives vorticity from the wind. The Antarctic Bottom Water on flowing northward and conserving its vorticity tends to flow to the west along the continental margins of Antarctica. However, a circumpolar westward flow of bottom water is prevented by the presence of submarine ridges. The bottom water on reaching these ridges turns to the north.

SPECULATIONS OF PALEOCEANOGRAPHY

In the following speculations the ice cover of Antarctica is assumed to vary. Also, it is assumed that the continent has not moved relative to the South Pole. These assumptions may conflict with each other and should be noted when considering the following remarks.

If Antarctica were ice free, the air pressure over the continent would be expected to vary greatly with season, being low during the summer and high in winter, similar to seasonal variations over Siberia. In this case, the wind produced upwelling of deep water would be much reduced owing to the reduction in the offshore pressure gradient and associated winds. During the summer the monsoonlike antarctic winds would be westerly over the water and land areas with a slight onshore component. In winter, the atmospheric high over the land area would cause a zone of polar easterlies, but this zone would not extend seaward. The westerlies over the water areas would be more intense than in the summer but substantially less than at present. Therefore, the nonglaciated condition would initiate a strongly seasonal or monsoonal character in the wind and associated fluctuation in the divergence of surface water.

An additional effect would be the absence of the very cold dry katabatic winds that characterize ice-covered regions. These winds in the present condition of Antarctica can extend to the water, where they cause intense thermohaline alterations. In nonglaciated or partially glaciated conditions, offshore winds will occur during the winter; however, they will not be as cold as the present winds, since, in the absence of the very cold ice surface, some warming by the long wave ground radiation would occur. Therefore, thermohaline alterations of the shelf waters would be absent or minimal during nonglaciated or partly glaciated periods.

During periods of floating ice shelves, representing extensive glaciation, freezing and/or melting to the underside may produce additional thermohaline effects.

Both of these changes (decreased wind divergence and thermohaline alterations) would result in a marked decrease in the meridional transport of the deep water during summer and a lesser decrease during the winter months. Such a decrease would be reflected in a decreased Antarctic Circumpolar Current and a less vigorous vertical circulation. If deep water is still produced in the North Atlantic at times of an ice-free Antarctica, it is possible that the entire zonal transport of the Antarctic Circumpolar Current would not be greater than the transport of the North Atlantic Deep Water.

If Antarctica is only glaciated in the interior, the

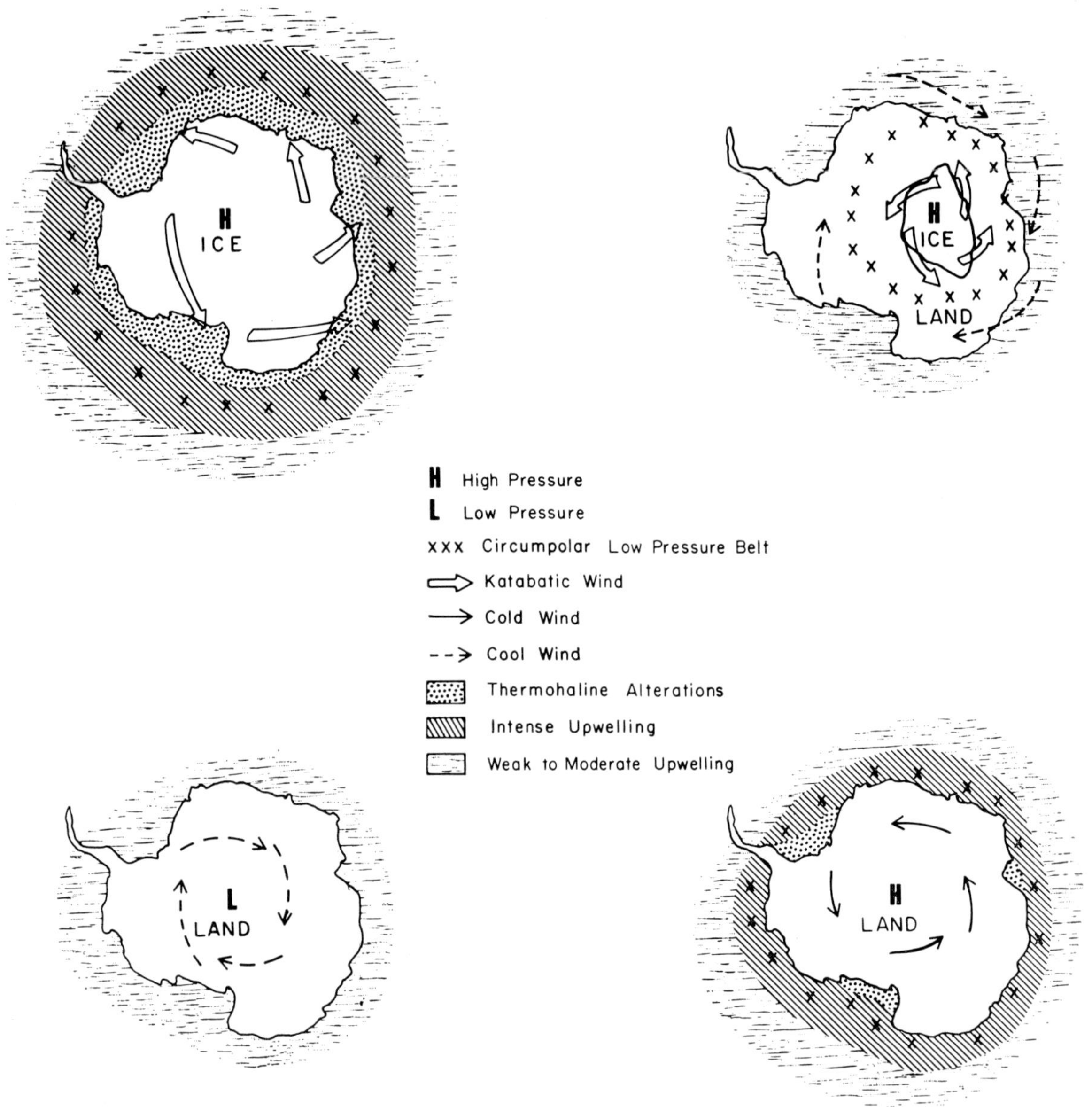

Fig. 24. Schematic representation of atmosphere sea level pressure and oceanographic conditions during times when Antarctica is (*a*) fully glaciated; (*b*) partially glaciated (summer); (*c*) ice free (summer); and (*d*) ice free or partially glaciated (winter).

pressure over the ice field would be high and the belt of low pressure surrounding the ice may not occur over the water area, but be entirely situated over land. In this case, the wind divergence over the sea would be small. In addition, the thermohaline effects at sea would not be as large owing to the absence of the katabatic winds and floating ice shelves. Therefore, the present antarctic circulation is not only dependent on the presence of a glaciated continent, but this glaciation must extend to the shores of the continent; that is, Antarctica must be fully glaciated. This condition has been mentioned by *Hays* [1967], based on a study of the sediment cores around Antarctica. Figure 24 shows in schematic form the three conditions: fully glaciated, partly glaciated, and ice free.

The results of the decreased circulation in Antarctica during periods of nonglaciation or partial glaciation would have certain major effects on the deep and bottom water of the world ocean and on the processes within antarctic waters: (1) reduction of the biological productivity of antarctic waters; (2) reduction in the renewal of oxygen of the cold water sphere; (3) decrease in the magnitude of bottom circulation, at least in the southern hemisphere; and (4) most likely an increase in the temperatures of the deep water.

In addition, changes would occur in the warm water sphere. The decrease of the volume transport of the Antarctic Circumpolar Current may cause surface conditions of the three oceans to differ more than they do at present. Now the oceans are equalized to a great extent by the large transport about Antarctica. On decreasing this transport, the larger rates of evaporation over the Atlantic may cause the Atlantic to be saltier, i.e., they may cause a growth in the size of the high saline 'Sargasso' gyres in the North and South Atlantic. An additional effect would be an increase in the depth of the main thermocline, due to an increase in the temperature of the deep water. This would deepen the oxygen minimum and nutrient rich layers that occur just below the thermocline. It is possible that such a deepening would decrease the amount of nutrients and associated high productivity in the surface waters of regions of subtropical upwelling, i.e., off the northwestern and southwestern coasts of Africa and off Peru and California.

Acknowledgments. The technical help of Robert C. Tsigonis and Bruce Weiner is greatly appreciated, as is the secretarial work of Mrs. Jeanne Stolz. The *Eltanin* data collection, data processing, and the analysis included in this report have been financed by grants from the U. S. National Science Foundation's Office of Antarctic Research (the grants for 1967 to 1970 are respectively GA-894, GA-1309, GA-10794, and GA-19032). Lamont-Doherty Geological Observatory contribution 1495.

REFERENCES

Arons, A. B., and H. Stommel, On the abyssal circulation of the world ocean, 3, *Deep-Sea Res., 14,* 441–457, 1967.

Baronov, G. I., and V. N. Botnikov, Surface of no motion and water masses in the Weddell Sea, *Soviet Antarctic Exped. Inform. Bull.,* English Transl., *5*(6), 385–388, 1964.

Botnikov, V. N., Geographic position of the Antarctic Convergence Zone in the Pacific Ocean, *Soviet Antarctic Exped. Inform. Bull.,* English Transl., *4*(6), 324–327, 1964.

Boyum, G., Hydrology and currents in the area west of Gibraltar, 19 pp., 25 figs., *Tech. Rept. 36,* Mediterranean Outflow Project, NATO Subcommittee on Oceanographic Research, Bergen, Norway, 1967.

Brennecke, W., Die ozeanographischen Arbeiten der Deutschen Antarktischen Expedition, 1911–1912, *Arch. Deutsche Seewarte, 39*(1), 1–216, 1921.

Brodie, J. W., Oceanography, Antarctica, in *New Zealand Antarctic Society Survey,* edited by T. Hatherton, pp. 101–127, Reed, Wellington, New Zealand, 1965.

Burling, R. W., Hydrology of circumpolar waters south of New Zealand, *New Zealand Dept. Sci. Ind. Res. Bull., 143, Mem. 10,* 9–61, 1961.

Countryman, K. A., and W. L. Gsell, Operations Deep Freeze '63 and '64 summer oceanographic features of the Ross Sea, *Tech. Rept. TR-190,* U. S. Navy Oceanographic Office, 1966.

Deacon, G. E. R., The hydrology of the Southern Ocean, *Discovery Rept., 15,* 1–24, 1937.

Deacon, G. E. R., A general account of the hydrology of the South Atlantic Ocean, *Discovery Rept., 7,* 171–238, 1933.

Deacon, G. E. R., The Southern Ocean, Ideas and observations on progress in the study of the seas, in *The Sea,* vol. 2, edited by M. N. Hill, pp. 281–296, Interscience, New York, 1963.

Defant, A., *Physical Oceanography,* vol. 1, 729 pp., Pergamon, New York, 1961.

Drygalski, E. V., Ozean und Antarktis, *Deutsche Sudpolar Exped., 1901–1903, 7,* 1926.

Ekman, V. W., On the influence of the earth's rotation on ocean currents, *Roy. Swed. Acad. Sci., 2*(11), 1905.

Fleurieu, C. P. Claret de, Observations sur la division hydrographique du globe, et changements proposes dans la nomenclature generale et particuliere de l'hydrographie, in Marchand, E., *Voyage Autour du Monde, 4,* 1–74, Paris, Imprimmerie de la Republique, VIII, 1798–1800.

Fofonoff, N. P., Some properties of sea water influencing the formation of Antarctic bottom water, *Deep-Sea Res., 4,* 32–35, 1956.

Giovinetto, M. B., Estimate of mass flux in Antarctica, *Geol. Soc. Am. Spec. Paper 76,* 309, 1964.

Goldberg, R., Mean oceanographic conditions within the Southeast Pacific Basin, 100 pp., Masters thesis, Columbia University, New York, 1967.

Gordon, A. L., Potential temperature, oxygen and circulation of bottom water in the Southern Ocean, *Deep-Sea Res., 13,* 1125–1138, 1966.

Gordon, A. L., Structure of Antarctic Waters between 20°W and 170°W, *Antarctic Map Folio Series, Folio 6,* edited by V. Bushnell, American Geographical Society, New York, 1967*a*.

Gordon, A. L., Geostrophic transport through the Drake Passage, *Science, 156*(3783), 1732–1734, 1967*b*.

Gordon, A. L., Physical oceanography aboard the *Eltanin, Antarctic J., 3*(5), 1967*c*.

Gow, A. J., The ice sheet, in *Antarctica,* edited by T. Hatherton, ch. 9, pp. 221–258, Praeger, New York, 1965.

Green, E. J., and D. E. Carritt, New tables for oxygen saturation of seawater, *J. Marine Res., 25*(2), 1967.

Hare, F. K., *The Restless Atmosphere, An Introduction to Chemistry,* p. 192, Harper Torchbooks, Harper and Row, New York, 1963.

Hays, J. D., Quaternary sediments of the Antarctic Ocean, *Progress in Oceanography,* vol. 4, pp. 117–131, Pergamon, New York, 1967.

Heap, J. A., Pack ice, in *Antarctic Research,* edited by R. Priestley, pp. 308–317, Butterworth, London, 1964.

Helland-Hansen, Bj., Nogen Hydrografisk Metoder., *Förh. Ved. Skand. Naturf., 16,* 357–359, Oslo, Juli 1916.

Houtman, T. J., Surface temperature gradients at the Antarctic Convergence, *New Zealand J. Geol. Geophys.*, 7, 245–270, 1964.

Houtman, T. J., Water masses and fronts in the Southern Ocean south of New Zealand, *New Zealand Dept. Sci. Ind. Res. Bull., 174, Mem. 36,* 1967.

Ishino, M., Studies on the oceanography of the Antarctic Circumpolar Waters, *J. Tokyo Univ. Fisheries, 49*(2), 73–181, 1963.

Jacobs, S. S., Physical and chemical oceanographic observations in the Southern Ocean, USNS *Eltanin* Cruises 16–21, 128 pp., *Tech. Rept. 1-CU-1-66,* Lamont-Doherty Geological Observatory of Columbia University, Palisades, New York, 1966.

Jacobs, S. S., and A. Amos, Physical and chemical oceanographic observations in the Southern Oceans, USNS *Eltanin* Cruises 22–27, 287 pp., *Tech. Rept. 1-CU-1-67,* Lamont-Doherty Geological Observatory of Columbia University, Palisades, New York, 1967.

Kaplan, S., A prolegomena to the dynamics of the Antarctic Circumpolar Current, 86 pp., Master's thesis, Columbia University, New York, 1967.

Knudsen, M., Gefrierpunkttabellen für Meerwasser, *Publ. Circ. 5,* Copenhagen, 1903.

Kort, V. G., The Antarctic Ocean, *Sci. Am., 207*(3), 113–128, 1962.

Kort, V. G., Antarctic Oceanography, in *Research in Geophysics,* edited by H. Odishaw, vol. 2, chap. 13, pp. 309–333, J. Engelhorn, Massachusetts Institute of Technology Press, Cambridge, 1964.

Krümmel, O., *Handbuch der Ozeanographie,* 1st ed., 2 vols., Stuttgart, 1897.

Ledenev, V. G., Contribution to the study of surface currents in the seas of the Pacific sector of the Antarctic, *Soviet Antarctic Exped. Inform. Bull.*, English Transl., *3,* 257–262, 1961.

Littlepage, J. L., Oceanographic investigations in McMurdo Sound, Antarctica, *Biology of the Antarctic Seas, II, Antarctic Res. Ser., 5,* edited by George A. Llano, pp. 1–37, American Geophysical Union, Washington, D.C., 1965.

Lorentz, E. N., The circulation of the atmosphere, *Am. Sci., 54*(4), 402–420, 1966.

Lusquinos, J. L., Extreme temperatures in the Weddell Sea, *Acta Univ. Bergen. Ser. Math. Rerumque Nat., 23,* 1963.

Mackintosh, N. A., The Antarctic Convergence and the distribution of surface temperatures in Antarctic Waters, *Discovery Rept., 23,* 177–180, 1946.

Malkus, J. S., Large-scale interaction, in *The Sea,* vol. 1, edited by M. N. Hill, pp. 88–294, Interscience, New York, 1962.

Mellor, M., Remarks concerning the Antarctic mass balance, *Polarforschung, Ser. 5, 33*(1/2), 179–180, 1963.

Midttun, L., and J. Natvig, Pacific Antarctic waters, 130 pp., *Sci. Res. Brategg Exped. 1947–1948, 3,* 1957.

Miyake, Y., Chemical studies of the western Pacific Ocean, 3, *J. Chem. Soc. Japan, 14*(3), 239–242, 1939.

Model, F., Ein Beitrag zur regionalen ozeanographic der Weddellsee, *Deutsche Antarctic Exped. 1938–1939 Wiss. Ergeb., 2*(2), 63–96, Georg Kartographers Anstalt 'Mundus' Helmut Striedieck, Hamburg, 1957–1958.

Mosby, H., The waters of the Atlantic Antarctic Ocean, *Sci. Res. Norwegian Antarctic Exped. 1927–1928, 11,* 1–131, 1934.

Mosby, H., Bottom water formation, in *Symposium on Antarctic Oceanography, September 13–16, 1966, Santiago, Chile,* Scott Polar Research Institute, Cambridge, England, 1968.

Munk, W. H., Abyssal recipes, *Deep-Sea Res., 13,* 707–730, 1966.

Neumann, G., and W. J. Pierson, Jr., *Principles of Physical Oceanography,* 545 pp., Prentice-Hall, Englewood Cliffs, New Jersey, 1966.

Ostapoff, F., The salinity distribution at 200 meters and the antarctic frontal zones, *Deut. Hydrograph. Z., 15,* 133–142, 1962.

Ovchinnikov, I. M., Circulation in the surface and intermediate layers of the Mediterranean, *Oceanology,* English Transl., *6*(1), 48–59, November 1966.

Robin, G. de Q., and R. J. Adie, The ice cover, *Antarctic Research,* edited by R. Priestley, pp. 100–117, Butterworth, London, 1964.

Robinson, A. R., and H. Stommel, The oceanic thermocline and associated thermohaline circulation, *Tellus, 11*(3), 295–308, 1959.

Serikov, M. I., Density and salinity of Antarctic sea ice, *Soviet Antarctic Exped. Inform. Bull.*, English Transl., *3,* 262–264, 1965.

Shumsky, P. and I. A. Zotikov, On bottom melting of the antarctic ice shelves, in *Snow and Ice Publication,* pp. 225–237, UGGI Association of Hydrologic Scientists, Berkeley, California, 1963.

Shumsky, P., A. N. Krenke, and I. A. Zotikov, Ice and its changes, in *Research in Geophysics,* vol. 2, *Solid Earth and Interface Phenomena,* edited by H. Odishaw, pp. 425–460, Massachusetts Institute of Technology Press, Cambridge, 1964.

Steele, J. H., L. V. Worthington, and J. R. Barrett, Deep currents south of Iceland, *Deep-Sea Res., 9,* 465–474, 1962.

Sverdrup, H. U., On vertical circulation in the ocean due to the action of wind with application to conditions within an Antarctic Circumpolar Current, *Discovery Rept., 7,* 139–170, 1933.

Sverdrup, H. U., M. W. Johnson, and R. H. Fleming, *The Oceans,* 1st ed., Prentice-Hall, Englewood Cliffs, New Jersey, 1942.

Thomas, C. W., Vertical circulation off the Ross Ice Shelf, *Pacific Sci., 20*(2), 239–245, 1966.

Tolstikov, E. I., Ed., *Atlas Antarktiki,* vol. 1, G.U.C.K., Moscow, 1966. (English Transl. in *Soviet Geography: Rev. Transl., 8*(5-6), American Geographical Society, New York, 1967.)

U. S. Navy, Oceanographic atlas of the Polar Seas, part 1, Antarctic, *Hydrograph. Off. Publ. 705,* 1957.

U. S. Navy, *Marine Climatic Atlas of the World,* vol. 7, NAVWEPS 50-1C-50, 1965.

Wexler, H., Ice budgets for Antarctica and changes in sea level, *J. Glaciol., 3*(29), 867–872, 1961.

Worthington, L. V., and G. H. Volkmann, The volume transport of the Norwegian Sea overflow water in the North Atlantic, *Deep-Sea Res., 12*(5), 667–676, 1965.

Wüst, G., Meteor Reports, *Wiss, Ergeb. Deut. Atlant. Exp. Meteor 1925–27,* Band *6,* Teil 1: Schichtung and Zirkulation des Atlantischen Ozeans. Lieferung: Das Bodenwasser und die Gliederung der Atlantischen Tiefsee, 1933. Lieferung: Die Stratosphäre, 1935. Band *6,* Atlas Schichtung und Zirkulation des Atlantischen Ozeans, Teil A and B: Stratosphäre, 1936.

Wüst, G., W. Brogmus, and E. Noodt, Die Zonale Verteilung von Salzgehalt, Niederschlag, Verdunstrung, Temperatur, und Dichte an der Oberfläche der Ozeane, *Kiel. Meersforsch.*, *10*, 137–161, 1954.

Wyrtki, K., The thermohaline circulation in relation to the general circulation in the oceans, *Deep-Sea Res.*, *8*, 39–64, 1961.

Yeskin, L. I., Water balance of the Drake Passage, *Tr. Sov. Antark. Exsp.*, *20*, 1962.

Zumberge, J. H., and C. Swithinbank, The ice shelves, in *Antarctica*, edited by T. Hatherton, chap. 8, pp. 199–220, Praeger, New York, 1965.

ANTARCTIC POLAR FRONT ZONE

ARNOLD L. GORDON

Lamont-Doherty Geological Observatory of Columbia University, Palisades, New York 10964

Abstract. The thermal structure across the antarctic polar front zone in the South Pacific is inspected. The structure is variable; however, it is often possible to identify some unifying pattern. A generalized thermal section can be constructed that contains all or most of the structural elements found by the particular bathythermograph sections. The basic components are as follows: The primary polar front zone is characterized by a cold water cell vertically elongated relative to other ocean features, which is isolated from the main mass of cold water further south. To the immediate south of the primary front is a warm water zone. The southern component of the polar front zone is the secondary polar front zone. Here the subsurface temperature minimum (T_{min}) that identifies the Antarctic Surface Water has a very variable structure. Occasional indications of vertical convection are found. South of the double polar front zone, the Antarctic Surface Water is found to lie uniformly over the upper Circumpolar Deep Water with little sign of instability.

The mechanism responsible for the formation of the double polar front zone is not known. Various possibilities are offered. The common occurrence of the double front suggests that the mean wind may be the cause. However, the mean wind field that could produce the double front is not consistent with the wind distribution thought to exist over antarctic waters. The wind variations may be more important, and the passing of an isolated storm system may produce the double front. Another possibility is the influence of bottom topography on the transport of the Antarctic Circumpolar Current. An additional possibility is the progression of internal waves from south to north between the Antarctic Surface Water and upper Circumpolar Deep Water. The pycnocline gradually weakens between these two water masses from the Antarctic Divergence to the polar front zone. This weakening distorts the internal waves near the northern limit of the T_{min} layer, causing a severance into two parts.

To study the antarctic double polar front zone properly, it would be necessary to conduct a multiship operation similar to those devoted to the Gulf Stream.

INTRODUCTION

The zone separating the antarctic and subantarctic surface water masses has been subject to much debate in oceanographic literature. This debate is not limited to the finer details of the boundary but involves its fundamental structure, and even the problem of the most suitable name to describe this feature. Much of the confusion is derived from the fact that the zone shows a great variability in both form and position and that the available data are too widely spaced for these variations to be understood properly. Many of the descriptions given are true relative to the specific data used, but are not valid in the general sense. Some data clearly show a convergence process with the Antarctic Surface Water slipping below and mixing with the Subantarctic Surface Water; hence the name Antarctic Convergence. Other data indicate more complicated processes that imply divergence, and so the name Antarctic Divergence has been proposed. Still other data show no evidence of either of these processes, or so complicated a structure that no simple circulation model is obvious. The term 'polar front' is preferred by many oceanographers, since it implies a situation analogous to an atmospheric polar front. This name implies only that along this boundary a fluid mass with polar characteristics abuts with one with subpolar properties.

The varying descriptions of the polar front naturally lead to varying methods used in its recognition. The most common is the presence of a relatively large drop in the surface temperature encountered on progressing from north to south. Although this method is acceptable in many crossings, it often leads to ambiguous results, since occasionally no sharp zone of temperature change is found. This condition occurs in summer when warming of the upper layers of the surface water obliterates the gradient, or when a thin layer of Subantarctic Surface Water overrides the Antarctic Surface Water. For this reason, a subsurface feature is often preferred in defining the polar front.

TABLE 1

Reference	Surface Expression	Subsurface Expression	Name
Meinardus [1923]	Grad T*		
Schott [1926]	Grad T		Meinardus Line (he uses term 'polar front' in 1944 ed.)
Deacon [1933] [1937]	Grad T	Northern limit of Antarctic Bottom Water	Antarctic Convergence
Mackintosh [1946]	Grad T	Position of temperature minimum at 200 meters	Antarctic Convergence
Garner [1958]	Grad T	Northern limit of the subsurface temperature inversion	Antarctic Convergence
Wexler [1959]	Grad T followed by a reversal in the north-south surface temperature gradient	Immediately north of an isolated core of cold water (> 50 miles wide)	Antarctic Divergence
Burling [1961]	Grad T	Northern extent of the 1°C isotherm in the T_{min} layer	Antarctic Convergence
Ostapoff [1962*b*]		The axis of the circumpolar salinity minimum belt at 200 meters	Polar Front
Botnikov [1963]	Surface position of the 2°C isotherm (winter only)	Northern limit of the 2°C isotherm within the T_{min} layer (summer only)	Antarctic Convergence Zone
Houtman [1964]	Mid-point of Grad T		Antarctic Convergence
Gordon [1967]	Grad T	Position at which the T_{min} layer ends or shows an abrupt change in depth	Polar Front Zone

* Grad T refers to a relatively large north-south surface temperature gradient with decreasing temperatures toward the south.

Table 1 lists the methods of identification of various authors and their choice for a name for what is called the polar front zone in this paper.

In 1946 Mackintosh constructed his much referenced chart of the mean position of the polar front based on crossings by the *Discovery II* and *William Scoresby*. This position must be used with reservation, since variations do occur; as Mackintosh points out: 'It forms twists and loops that may extend as much as 100 miles north and south, and it possibly even forms isolated rings.' Meanders and eddies or rings appear to be fairly common, a condition that prompts the often used comparison of the polar front with the 'cold wall' of the Gulf Stream and its meanders and eddies.

Some studies of the seasonal or longer time-dependent variations have been made. *Botnikov* [1963, 1964] concludes that the seasonal variations are usually 1° to 2° of latitude (60–120 miles) and that the long-term variations (from 1901 to 1960) are as much as 4° of latitude (180–240 miles). *Gordon* [1967] shows a polar front zone to be from 2° to 4° of latitude in width, whereas *Ostapoff* [1962*a*, 1962*b*] indicates an even broader 5° zone. Data from which indications of the short time variations (days or weeks) can be gained are not complete and only vaguely suggest that such fluctuations do occur.

From past work it can be said with some assurance that somewhere in a broad circumpolar belt there is a sharp or diffuse boundary separating the Antarctic and Subantarctic Surface Water masses, along which evidence of either convergence or divergence may be found. It is believed [*Gordon*, 1967] that the position of this wide belt or zone may be related to bottom topography, as is the northern limit of the Antarctic Bottom Water, but the position of the polar front within this zone is controlled by wind and/or thermohaline factors.

The terms 'primary' and 'secondary' were added to the polar front zone by *Gordon* [1967] to indicate the presence of a double frontal structure in the western section of the Southeast Pacific Basin. The basis in performing this separation deals with the detail structure of the subsurface temperature minimum (T_{min}). A similar structure was noted by *Wexler* [1959] along the 180° meridian and discussed further by *Burling* [1961], *Ostapoff* [1962*a*], and *Houtman* [1967]. In this paper the frontal structure is further investigated using primarily bathythermograph (BT) and expendable bathythermograph (XBT) data gathered by the USNS *Eltanin* cruises 25, 27, 32, and 33. The analysis is limited to the area east of the Macquarie Island. At present the USNS *Eltanin* is gathering data south of Australia. When this task is completed, a study of the polar front zone for that area will be published and related to this study.

The BT and XBT sections to be discussed are shown in Figure 1. Discussion of the other information shown in this figure is found below.

TEMPERATURE PROFILES ACROSS THE POLAR FRONT ZONE

In the course of studying the many bathythermograph profiles across the antarctic polar front zone, one is struck by the seemingly unlimited variations in the surface and subsurface temperature structure. On proceeding northward, the water temperatures increase; however, the rate of warming with latitude is highly varied with the presence of numerous reversals. The BT sections in the South Pacific do demonstrate some similarities, enabling an attempt at a generalized thermal section. This was first noticed in dealing with the sections of the western Southeast Pacific Basin, at which time the term double polar front zone was applied.

The generalized section is shown as Figure 2, and the following is a description of each component. The particular BT sections contain all or most of these elements. Certainly the daily weather conditions influence the surface temperature; however, since the double structure extends to depths as great as 800 meters and is found in numerous profiles, it is felt that it is of significance to the basic frontal structure and should be considered in any attempt to understand the polar front dynamics in the South Pacific sector of antarctic waters.

Proceeding from south to north, the sections encountered are as follows:

1. The stable zone is the area in which the cold Antarctic Surface Water mass lies uniformly above the upper Circumpolar Deep Water. The isotherms tend to be horizontal with a large gradient in temperature at the boundary of the surface and deep water. Toward the northern end, the T_{min} layer is variable in strength and depth.

2. The secondary polar front zone is separated from the stable zone by a drop in the depth of the T_{min} layer and an increase in the surface temperature. Within the secondary zone the T_{min} layer shows great variability but remains well defined. The isotherms tend to be vertically oriented, with occasional evidence of filaments or streams of T_{min} penetrating to fairly deep levels.

3. The warm water zone is the area in which the T_{min} weakens to become discontinuous or absent. This zone is relatively warm, with the surface layers demonstrating higher stability than that found in the zones to the immediate north and south.

4. The primary polar front zone is relatively narrow and shows much vertical stretching of the water properties. This feature is vertically elongated only relative to other ocean features and not in the absolute sense. In this zone, the cold water is cold and is marked by re-establishment of the T_{min} layer. The patch of cold water is generally isolated in a north-south plane from the main body of T_{min} water to the south. The influence of the water of this cell occasionally extends to the surface, where it lowers the surface temperature below that of the surface of the more southerly warm zone. At the surface of the northern boundary of the primary zone, there is a fairly rapid temperature change.

5. The Subantarctic Surface Water is the northernmost zone. This zone is warmer than the other zones; it is always above 3°C and usually above 5°C. The isotherms slope steeply toward the north. Occasional reversals of the slope of the isotherm surfaces are found.

Each of these components is a zone; that is, they are broad regions and not lines on the sea surface. The following is a display of BT and XBT sections in an area from 115°W westward to 160°E.

120°W

On *Eltanin* cruise 33 (March to May 1968) a temperature profile for the upper 800 meters along 120°W from 69°S to 55°S was obtained by the XBT system. This meridian traverses the double frontal zone shown on Plate 14 of *Gordon* [1967]. With the XBT probes, the finer details and change with depth of this apparently permanent feature could be studied. Figure 3 shows the thermal structure found along the ship's track.

The primary and secondary polar front zones were found in approximately the positions expected from the analysis of previous BT data: the primary zone at 57°30′ to 58°S and the secondary zone between 59°30′ to 63°S (see *Gordon* [1967, pl. 14]). The T_{min} layer, which represents the Antarctic Surface Water mass, shows a great variation within the secondary zone. Deep penetration of the cold surface water to 600 meters is found at various positions within this zone.

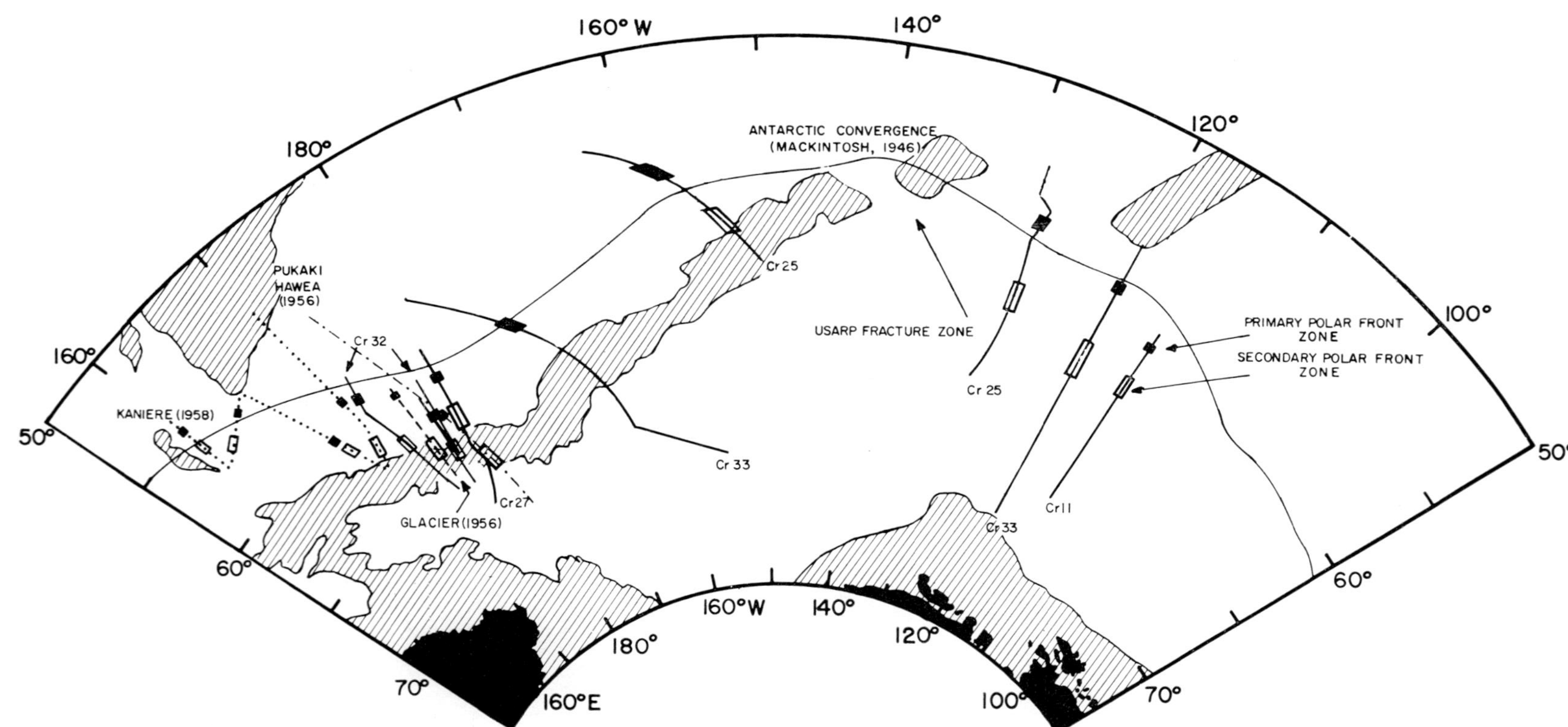

Fig. 1. Position of BT and XBT sections discussed in this paper. Hatched area has a depth of less than 3000 meters; the 3000-meter contour from 90°W to 170°W is taken from *Gordon* [1967] and west of 170°W from *Tolstikov* [1967].

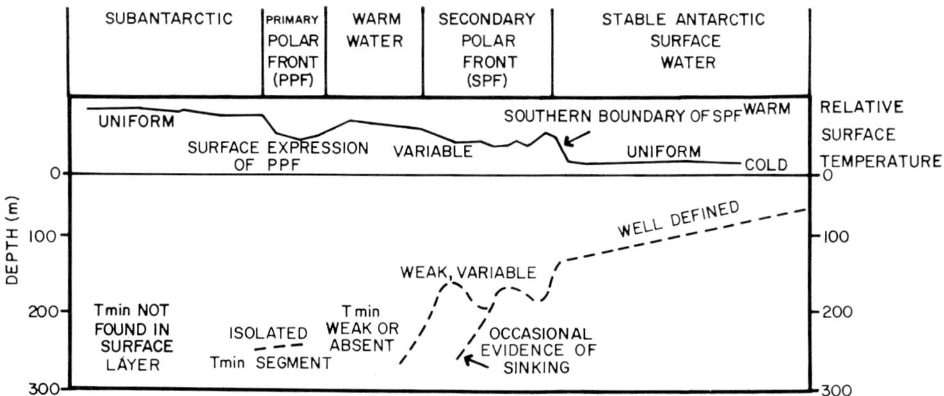

Fig. 2. Schematic diagram of the antarctic double polar front zone.

between which occur columns of warmer deep water. At 62°S (XBT 76) water of over 2°C ascends to within 180 meters of the surface. Within the secondary zone, the vertical trend of the isotherms suggests that the T_{min} forms many filaments or streamers, perhaps similar to the cellular convection discussed by *Turner* [1967] and *Foster* [1968]. However, in the above case, salinity is the stabilizing influence rather than temperature, as discussed by Turner. The arrows shown on Figure 2 indicate the possible vertical motion of the water with the secondary polar front zone.

South of the secondary polar front zone is the zone with a more stable water column. Here the isotherms tend to be horizontal, whereas in the secondary zone and to its north the isotherms are more vertical.

The primary polar front zone is characterized in a manner described by *Wexler* [1959]. Along the sea surface from north to south, the temperature first drops sharply, then reverses gradient, resulting in a temperature minimum immediately south of the high temperature gradient. Below the minimum is a vertically elongated cell of cold water isolated in a north-south plane from the main body of cold surface water further south.

Between the two polar front zones is a region of warmer water. In *Gordon* [1967], it is suggested that this warm water, occupying the region from 58° to 59°30′S for the section shown in Figure 3, results from upwelling, that is, a zone of divergence. In this case, the salinity of this zone should be above that of Antarctic Surface Water. However, the salinity of this zone for the upper 300 meters is shown in Figure 4 to be no higher than the Antarctic Surface Water mass, that is, less than 34.2‰, which is more characteristic of Subantarctic Surface Water and certainly less than that of the upper Circumpolar Deep Water (34.6‰). The higher temperatures, together with similar salinities, indicate that this water may be warmed Antarctic Surface Water.

115°W

Figure 5 shows the temperature profile for the upper 800 meters along 115°W constructed from cruise 11 data. The upper 275 meters are taken from the BT observations (see *Gordon* [1967, pl. 13]). Below this depth the hydrographic station data are used; since these observations are spaced much farther apart than the BT data, the section represents only general structure. The temperature distribution shown in Figure 5 is similar to that along 120°W (Fig. 3) in that the double polar front is present.

The T_{min} layer continues below BT depth, although it is not as extreme as it is at shallower levels. The level character of this layer is more probably the product of too widely spaced data than a reflection of reality. The deep penetration of the 2°C isotherm at 60°30′S and 61°30′S suggests a convective process similar to that found along the 120°W section. The elongated cold cell of the primary zone exists, but the northern extent of the cell is uncertain owing to a larger spacing of the hydrographic stations at these latitudes.

128°W

During cruise 25 another BT section was obtained in the region of the double frontal structure shown in Plate 14. The BT section is shown as Figure 6. In this section the primary polar front zone, although present, is not very well developed. The surface temperature drops suddenly from 6° to 5°C at 55°40′S, and a slight minimum of about 4°C occurs at 56°15′S, below which is the upper part of a cell of colder than 3.5°C. Although these values are a few degrees above those in the primary zone previously encountered, the

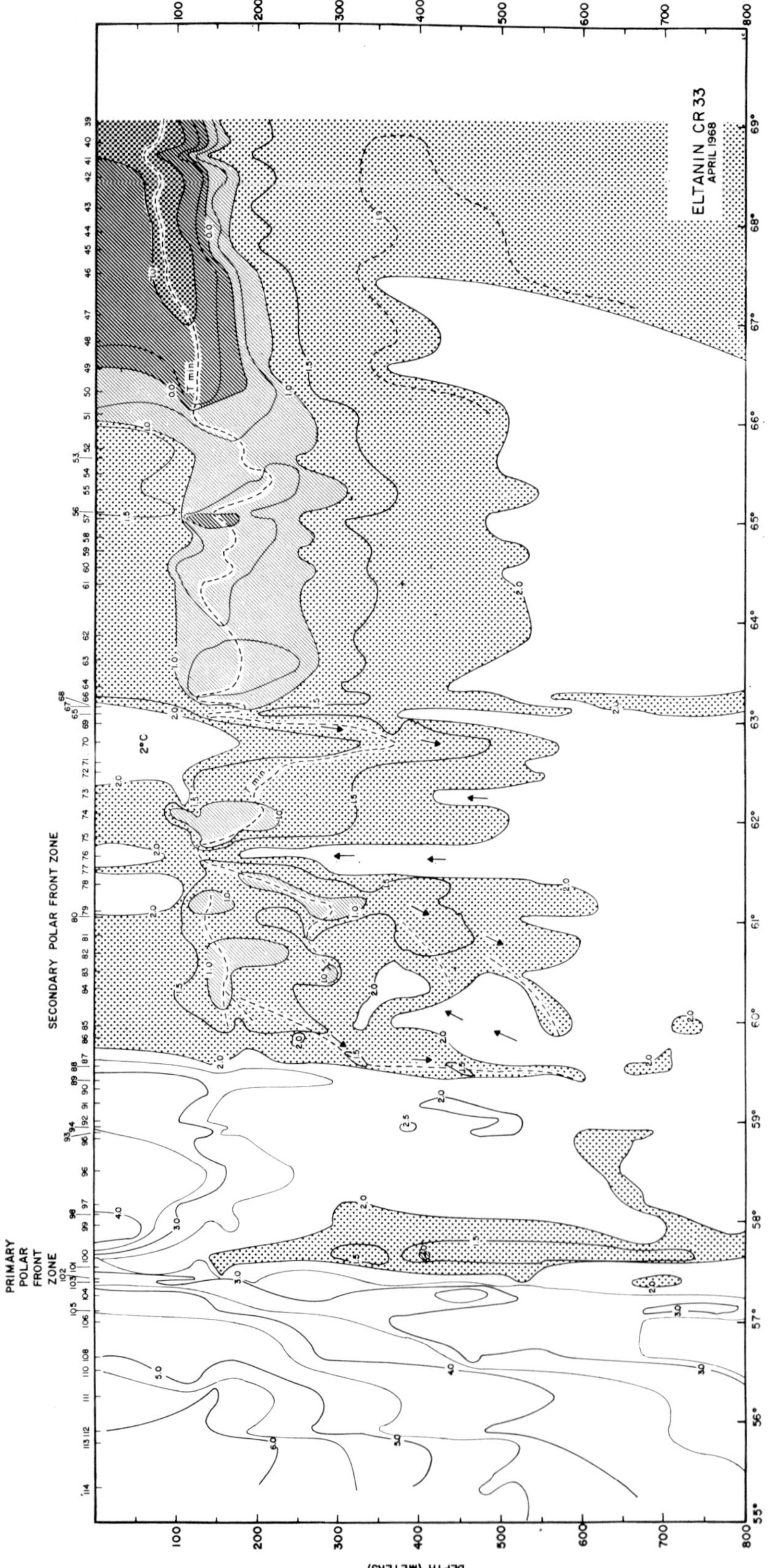

Fig. 3. Expendable bathythermograph section along 120°W, XBT observations 39 to 114, *Eltanin* cruise 33.

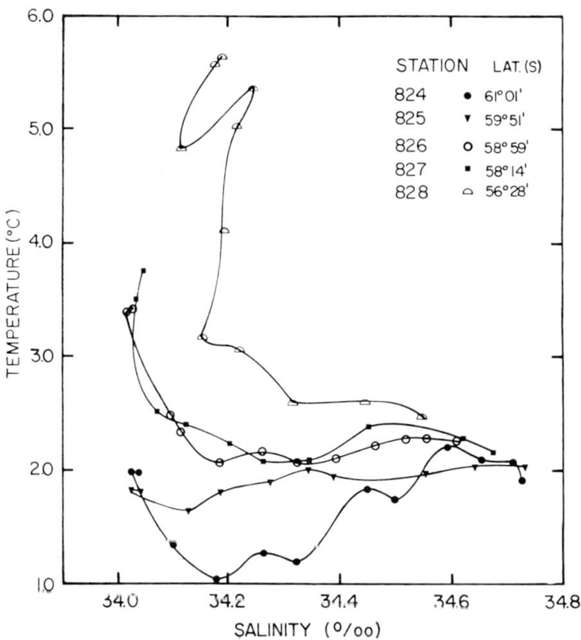

Fig. 4. Temperature/salinity diagram of hydrographic stations 824–828 along 120°W. The numbers next to symbols are observation depths in meters.

general form persists. The surface water salinity (found from hydrographic stations) south of the primary front is approximately 34.0‰ to 34.1‰, identifying the water as Antarctic Surface Water and the primary front as a genuine boundary of water masses.

The secondary zone is found between 59° to 60° 30′S. The structure is fairly typical in that the T_{min} layer undergoes a depth increase on entering the zone from the south accompanied by a relatively large surface temperature gradient. Within the secondary zone, the T_{min} is variable. Owing to the lack of closely spaced deeper data, it is not known if convection exists as found along 115° and 120°W.

The warm zone is fairly broad and is divided into two packets of warmer water: at 56°30′S and at 58°S. The two hydrographic stations in this zone (STD stations 603 and 604; see *Jacobs and Amos* [1967]) indicate no shallow T_{min} layer, but a weak T_{min} zone at 700 meters of approximately 0.5°C amplitude; this situation is similar to the warm zone along 120°W.

155°W (Average)

The return track of cruise 25 is the first section discussed which is west of the previously defined extent of the double frontal structure. The BT section is shown as Figure 7. It indicates a double zone similar to Figure 6 in that the form is present but the temperatures of the primary zone are higher than expected. The well-developed characteristics of a rapid change of surface temperature followed by a minimum above a cold cell occur between 55° to 55°30′S. A well-developed warm zone is found between 55°30′ and 56° 30′S. The secondary zone between 56°30′ and 59°S cannot be investigated in detail because of the lack of data below BT depth; however, two regions of sinking appear to be centered at 56°50′S and 58°S. The southern boundary of the secondary zone is again found by the change in the depth and continuity of the T_{min} layer and a high surface temperature gradient.

170°W (Average)

The next profile to the west was also obtained on cruise 33 with XBT and supplementary BT observations. This temperature section is shown as Figure 8.

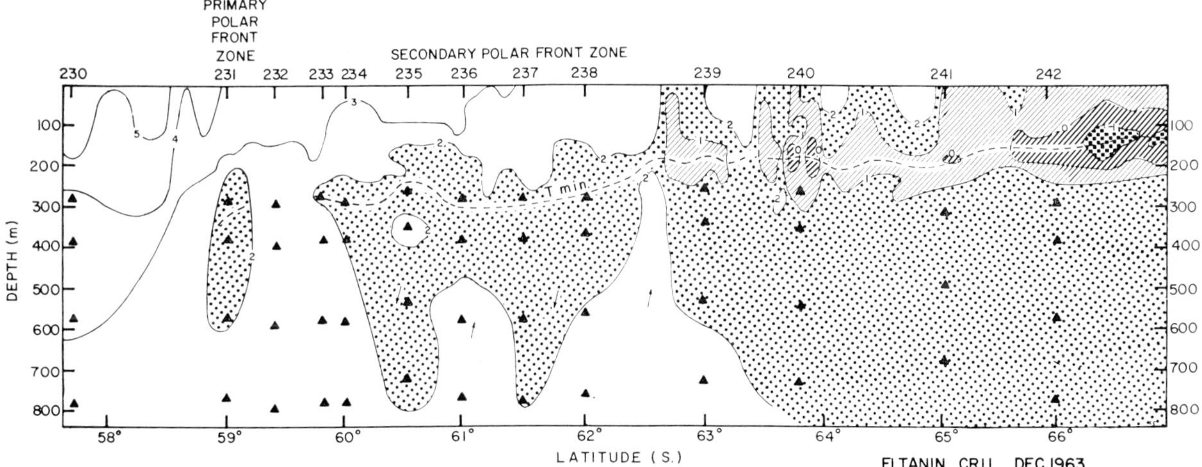

Fig. 5. Temperature profile along 115°W; upper 275 meters taken from *Gordon* [1967, pl. 13]; below these depths hydrographic stations 230 to 242 are used, *Eltanin* cruise 11.

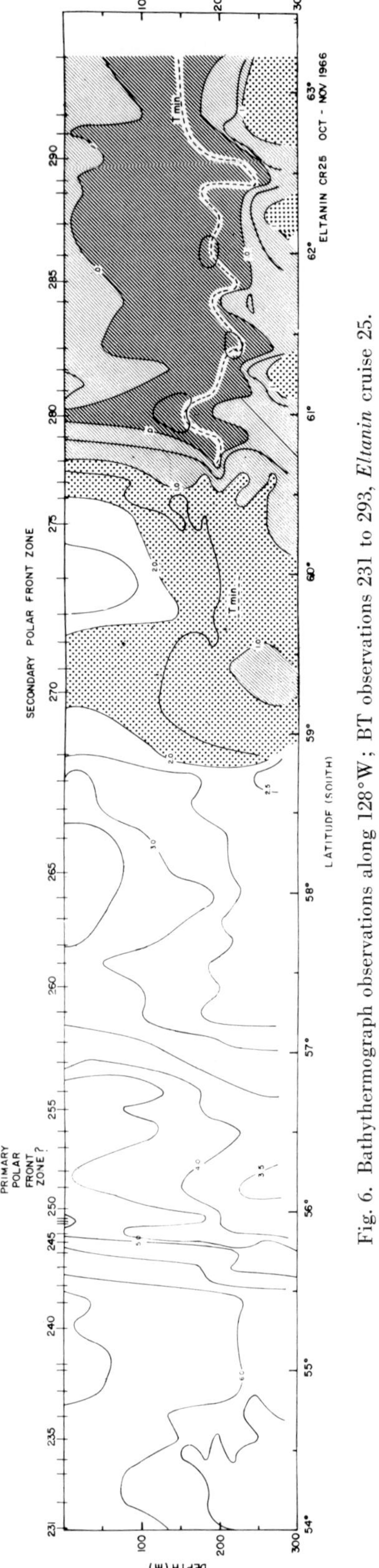

Fig. 6. Bathythermograph observations along 128°W; BT observations 231 to 293, *Eltanin* cruise 25.

No developed double frontal structure is found, although the T_{min} layer between 60° and 61°S does indicate vertical elongation similar to a primary zone; however, the isotherms are not isolated from the main body of T_{min} to the south, nor are there any large reversals of the north-south surface temperature gradient. Therefore, only a singular polar front zone is shown, as defined in Table 1.

178°E

The BT section obtained on cruise 27 is shown in Figure 9. No clear division into a double zone is found. However, the T_{min} does change in both temperature and depth immediately south of 63°S, and an increase in the surface temperature gradient is found. Therefore, the region between 62° and 63° is labeled as a secondary polar front zone, although the lack of a warm zone to the north does not permit definition of the northern boundary.

The region at 60°30′ is called the primary polar front zone, although again the lack of the warm zone and no observed isolation of a cold cell suggest a single polar front. Therefore, this section can be divided into a double zone only by the variation at 63°S. The other factors used in definition of this phenomena are absent.

176°E

During cruise 32 of the *Eltanin*, a series of BT's and XBT's (the probes used for this section extend to 500 meters) were taken along a track that recrossed approximately the same region three times in four days. During this time, variations were found in the frontal structure. These sections (A to C) are shown as Figure 10. Both sections B and C display strong double structure. Section A indicates only a poorly defined primary polar front zone, although it is possible that the large spacing between BT observations 223 to 227 may have missed the center of the cold cell.

The northern limit of the T_{min} layer in the secondary zone changes its form somewhat, although not dramatically. Most of the variation is found in the primary zone. Comparing the center of the cold cell shown in sections B and C, it is found that it moves toward the north at 17 cm/sec and elongates slightly. The 1.5°C isotherm moves upward from 100 to 60 meters with a vertical velocity of 4×10^{-2} cm/sec. The coldest water within the primary front is below −0.5°C. The northern limit of this isotherm with the T_{min} layer to the south is at 64°30′S or over 200 km to the south of the center of the primary front. The amount of water with a temperature below 0.0°C is

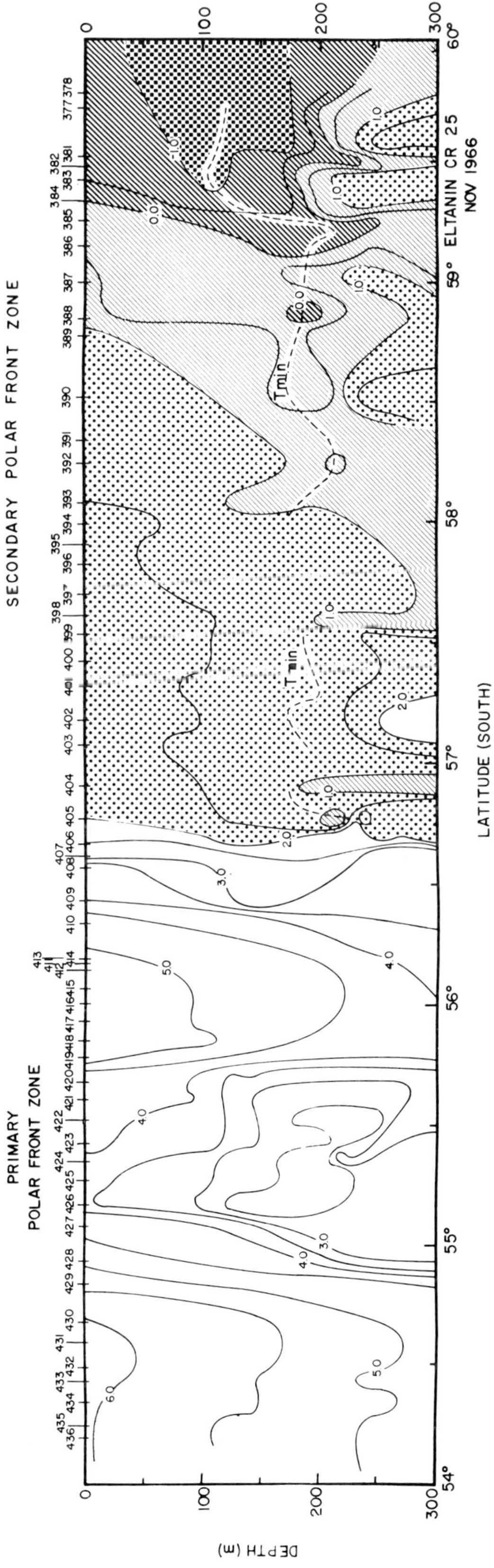

Fig. 7. Bathythermograph section along 155°W (average longitude), *Eltanin* cruise 25.

greater in section C. The variations in the primary front between sections A and B are in the same direction as are the variations between sections B and C, but they are more intensive.

The cold cell appears to be growing and becoming more intense from sections A to C. The decreasing temperature is also apparent at the surface, where the temperature drops from 4.5° to 3.5°C from sections A to C. The intensification is a product of transport perpendicular to the BT sections (zonal transport) rather than motion parallel (meridional transport), since the isolation and intensity of the cold cell indicate no way in which cold water can be added to the primary front except by zonal flow.

The three BT sections are positioned so that section B crosses the primary polar front zone 9 km east of the point that section A crosses this feature, and section C crosses it 55 km to the northeast of B. Since the satellite navigation system was not operative during these three BT sections, the accuracy of these distances is only fair. It is possible to visualize a number of circulation patterns that would be consistent with the observation and would be in steady state (no time variation). These are: (1) a westward flow along the core of the cold cell with diffusion; (2) no motion at all; (3) an eastward flow in the cold cell with renewal of cold water from the south at some point at the western end of the cold cell (between sections A and B). None of these conditions is realistic, since an eastward current is most probable for the Antarctic Circumpolar Current, and there is no evidence of a renewal of cold water from the main body of T_{min} water to the south, especially from the section colder than −0.5°C. Therefore, it is fairly certain that a time dependent component is important, although it is difficult to separate completely the space from the time variations without a number of simultaneous measurements of temperature at a great many points.

Assuming an eastward flowing current, its magnitude may be such that: (1) the ship would cross the primary front at the same relative point (this requires a current of 14 cm/sec between sections A and B and 48 cm/sec between sections B and C); (2) the ship may gradually approach (or 'overtake') the core of the cold cell from the west, i.e., the current is less than 14 and 48 cm/sec, respectively, between the two section pairs; or (3) the core of the cold cell is 'catching up' with the ship, i.e., a current of greater than 14 and 48 cm/sec, respectively. Certainly the first choice is not realistic, since the significant changes in the extent and temperature of the cold cell indicate zonal

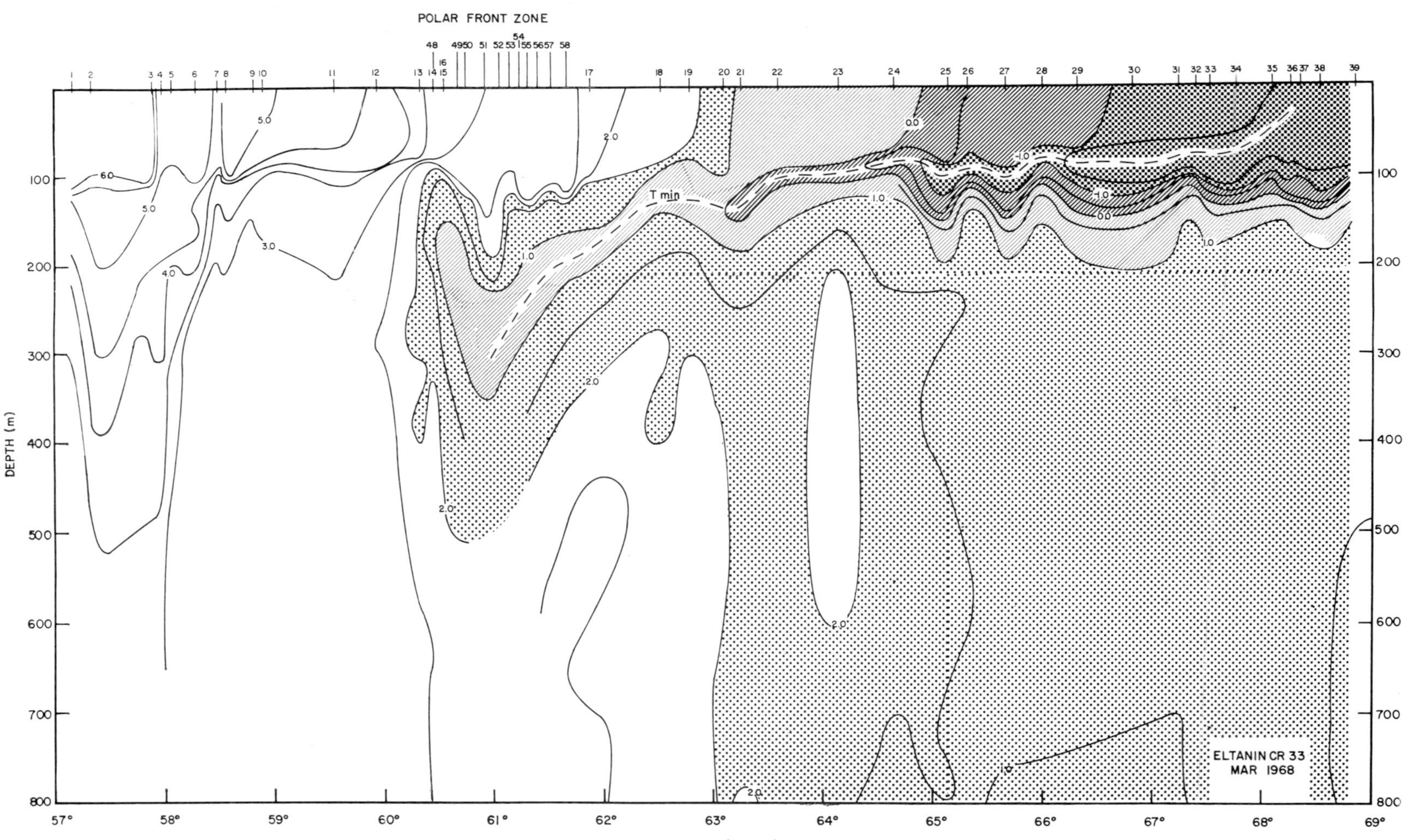

Fig. 8. Expendable bathythermograph section along 170°W (average longitude); XBT observations 1 to 39; BT observations 48 to 53 are used in the polar front zone, *Eltanin* cruise 33.

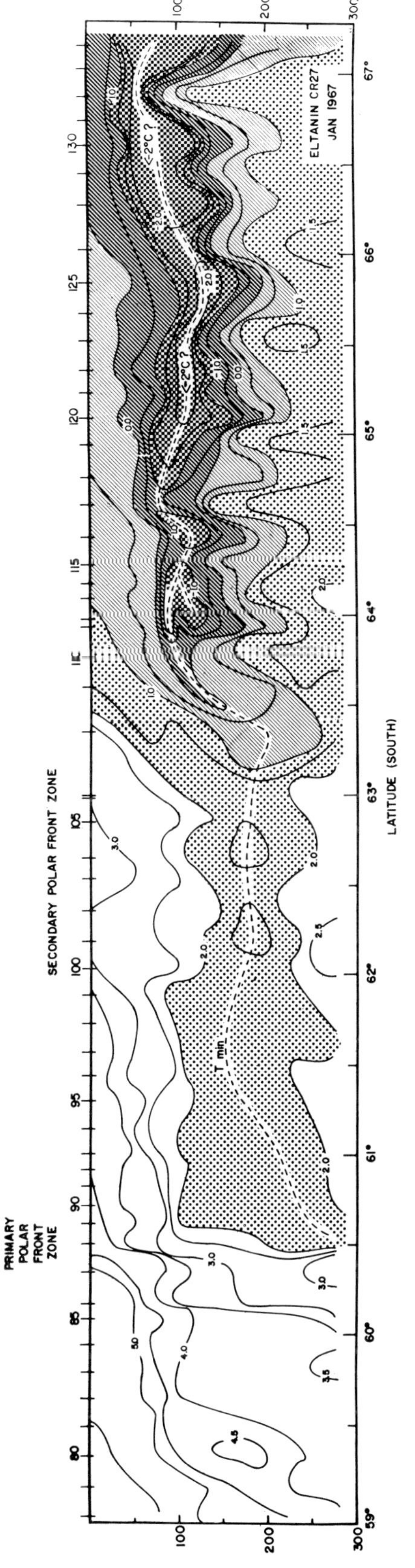

Fig. 9. Bathythermograph section along 178°E; BT observations 78 to 134, *Eltanin* cruise 27.

flow relative to the ship. However, the values 14 and 48 cm/sec are current magnitudes which are probably in the range of the actual velocity in this area; therefore, in addition to the motion of the cold cell relative to the ship, it is expected that the cold cell is undergoing deformation.

The vertical motion of the 1.5°C isotherm and the northward migration of the center of the cold cell referred to earlier are most likely both time and space dependent. From the wind data collected aboard the ship, it is found that strong Ekman divergence exists above the cold cell region. The increase in the vertical extent of the cold cell may be explained by this divergence. The Ekman meridional transport as a function of latitude is shown in Figure 11 for sections A, B, and C. These values were calculated from the equation based on the Ekman theory

$$T_\theta = \tau_\lambda / \rho f$$

where T_θ is the Ekman transport along a meridian; τ_λ is the zonal component of the wind stress, f is the Coriolis parameter, and ρ is the water density. In the regions where T_θ is increasing toward the north, divergence results, and the continuity equation requires either upwelling or variations in zonal transport, or both. The steeper the gradient of T_θ with latitude, the greater must be the upwelling and/or zonal transport variation. The maximum divergence is found directly above the primary polar front zone. Therefore, the divergence theory put forward by *Wexler* [1959] is supported by these data. However, problems still exist, since upwelling alone cannot explain the primary polar front zone. The remaining questions are: Where does the cold water within the primary front come from, since water cold enough to act as a source is found far to the south, and why does the double frontal structure extend to depths greater than the surface Ekman layer, which is expected to be 100–200 meters deep?

Although the three sections for cruise 32 do not lead to conclusive results, they do indicate that the primary polar front zone varies zonally and could easily be missed by hydrographic profiles because of its limited latitudinal extent as well as its apparent discontinuous zonal structure.

174°E

The BT profile obtained on cruise 32 is shown as Figure 12. Unfortunately, the depth penetration was less than the usual 275 meters, and it is unknown if the T_{min} layer continues north of 62°S in the near surface layers. The double frontal zone is poorly defined, although the characteristic dip in the T_{min} layer

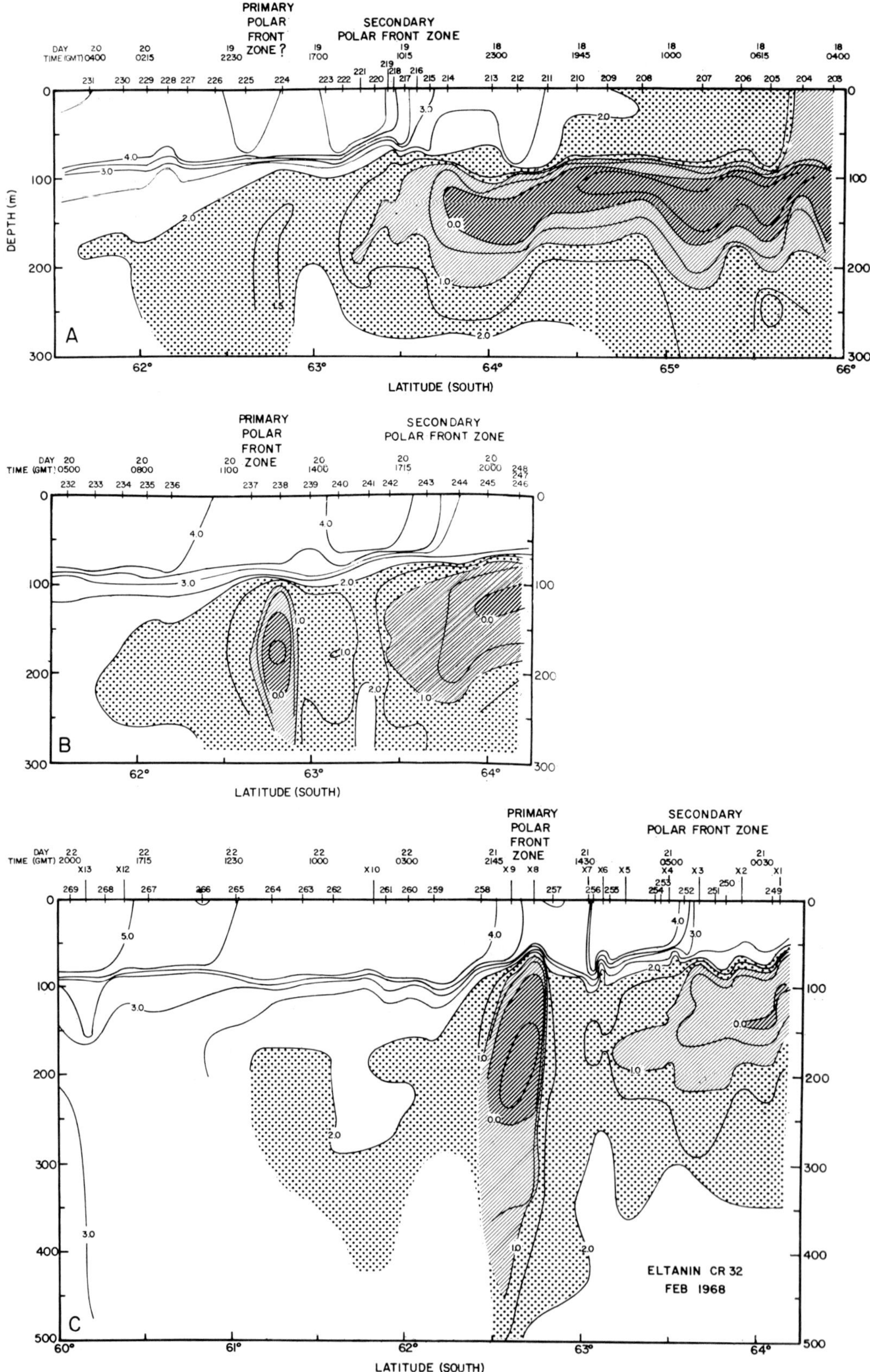

Fig. 10. Bathythermograph and expendable bathythermograph sections along 176°E; section C is partially composed of T4 XBT probes; BT observations 203 to 269; XBT observations 1 to 13, *Eltanin* cruise 32.

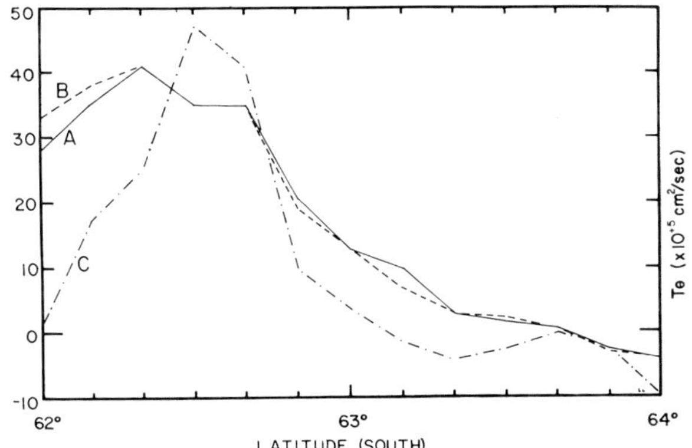

Fig. 11. Meridional transport within the Ekman layer for sections A, B, and C shown in Figure 10.

to the immediate south of the secondary polar front zone is present, as is the cold intrusion at 60°S similar to the cold cell of the primary front. The temperature structure is similar to that found on the two crossings of cruise 25, in that the primary front is present but is composed of water warmer than that found in other sections.

Other BT Sections South of New Zealand

In addition to the *Eltanin* BT sections, a number of sections obtained by other ships south of New Zealand also show a double frontal structure. The BT and hydrographic station data of the HMNZS *Kaniere* [*Houtman*, 1967], whose track is shown in Figure 1, show a clear double frontal structure, as do the BT data discussed by *Wexler* (1959—two sections of USS *Glacier* and one of HMNZS *Pukaki*). Since these last three sections all represent the same region, only the position of the second *Glacier* BT section is shown in Figure 1.

Two interesting BT sections are discussed by *Burling* [1961]. These are sections taken by HMNZS *Pukaki* and HMNZS *Hawea* only five miles apart at the same time. They are shown as one line on Figure 1. Burling's figures 4*b* and 4*c* are reproduced in Figure 13. Both show a strongly developed primary and secondary polar front zone, with only minor variation between the two sections. The BT sections taken during the northerly track of the two ships are far apart. The *Hawea* followed the 180° meridian and the *Pukaki* the 169° E meridian. The BT observation spacing on *Hawea* was too large to detect the narrow primary front. The *Pukaki* section shows a weak primary front (neither of these section positions are shown on Figure 1).

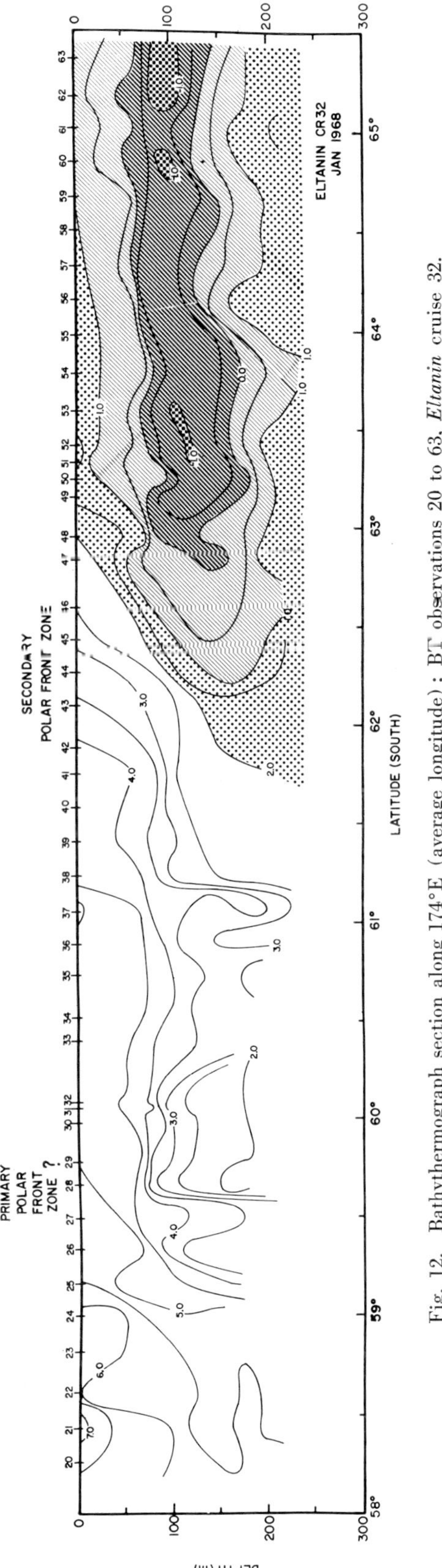

Fig. 12. Bathythermograph section along 174°E (average longitude); BT observations 20 to 63, *Eltanin* cruise 32.

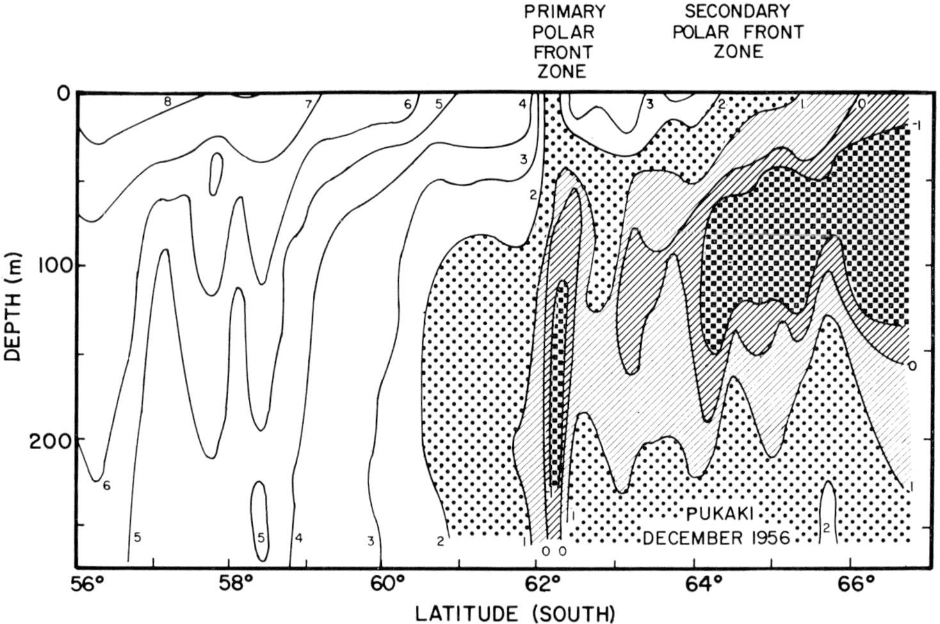

Fig. 13*a*. Bathythermograph section obtained by HMNZS *Pukaki* (modified from *Burling* [1961]).

DISCUSSION

The positions of the primary and secondary polar front zones of each of the BT and XBT sections discussed are shown in Figure 1, in addition to the mean position of the Antarctic Convergence determined by *Mackintosh* [1946]. The primary front is often in close proximity to the Mackintosh position, whereas the secondary front is 1 or 2 degrees of latitude further south. Between 170°E to 180° the primary front is found to be consistently south of the Mackintosh mean position. It is probable that the southernmost penetration of the Subantarctic Surface Water around Antarctica occurs between 170°E to 180°.

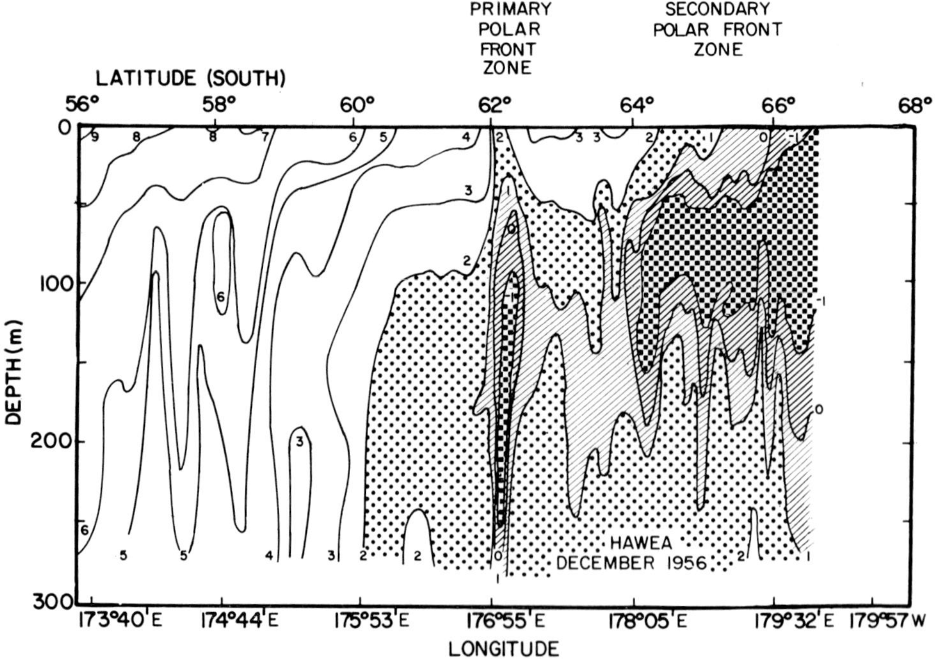

Fig. 13*b*. Bathythermograph section obtained by HMNZS *Hawea* (modified from *Burling* [1961]).

For cruise 32 sections A to C it was shown above that Ekman divergence of the surface water is found above the primary polar front zone and that the ensuing upwelling is consistent with the structure of this zone. The wind data collected simultaneously with the other *Eltanin* BT and XBT sections were also inspected for similar structure. It is found that divergent conditions occur over the primary zone for sections 5 and 7, but not for the other sections. Therefore, the double structure cannot be explained entirely by the local wind for this reason and for the following additional reasons: (1) the structure penetrates to depths far below the Ekman layer; and (2) the common occurrence of the double structure also suggests at least a semipermanent presence, since it would be fortuitous that most BT sections are obtained during the period that the double structure exists, unless this period is long. If it is the wind which is responsible for this phenomenon, it is more likely the mean wind or the mean effect of the passage of storm systems.

It is possible to envision a mean zonal wind field that would create an Ekman circulation within a meridional plane consistent with the suspected pattern in the double polar front zone. The latitudinal variation of the proposed mean wind would show: (1) a west wind maximum over the southern boundary of the secondary polar front zone; (2) a minimum or slightly negative value (east wind) over the warm zone; (3) a very rapid increase in the west wind over the primary polar front zone. A circumpolar belt of low pressure caused by the passage of storm systems over the primary front can produce such a wind pattern. However, storm tracks most likely pass south of this front [*Weyant*, 1967] with an average position in the region of the Antarctic Divergence, which divides the easterly directed Antarctic Circumpolar Current from the westerly directed coastal current [*Koopman*, 1953]. In this case, the zonal wind is expected to increase toward the north from the Antarctic Divergence and would not create the above circulation pattern. Perhaps the mean zonal wind and average storm tracks are not as important as the short period fluctuations in the wind field. Wind fluctuations may contribute to the mean ocean circulation [*Veronis*, 1966]. The occasional passage of a storm north of the average storm track may divide the T_{min} layer into the two components of the double front. The double structure is produced by the single storm and once produced is not destroyed by the return of the usual west wind profile. The cold cell flows eastward and slowly dissipates by diffusion, perhaps months after its creation by a storm.

It is possible to differentiate the relative 'age' of the double polar front zone. Cruise 25 sections with a weak primary frontal zone may represent the final stages, i.e., the cold cell is warmer than usual and almost dissipated. A young or active stage is represented by cruise 33, section 5, and cruise 32, section 7. In both cases, the local wind pattern would produce a strong Ekman divergence over the primary front. Section 5 displays a continuous T_{min} layer, but the distortion of this layer between 60° to 62°S suggests the beginning of a vertically oriented cold cell and subsequent primary front. The cruise 32 section taken along 173°E a few weeks before the 176°E sections shows dissipated conditions, indicating that during the intervening month a new double polar front was formed.

The sections along 115°W and 120°W represent 'middle-age' conditions, since the double frontal structure is well developed, but Ekman divergence does not occur over the primary front in either case. The dissipated condition is indicated by the cruise 27 section, in which the T_{min} of the secondary front moves northward to extend to the previous position of the primary front.

The speculation of *Wexler* [1959] on the formation of the cold cell by the wind leads to his suggestion that the entire polar front zone is a region of divergence. The cold cell results from strong winter winds north of the northern limit of the pack ice. The short summers do not allow sufficient time to destroy the cold cell. Wexler, by analogy with other upwelling areas, shows that the maximum upwelling is expected to occur 100 miles or so north of the maximum pack ice extent. His theory, while explaining the proposed upwelling within the primary polar frontal zone, does not explain the secondary front nor the problem of supplying cold water to the isolated cold cell.

Although a wind based theory is attractive, since the double polar front includes surface layer phenomena, the problems listed above are difficult to overcome. As pointed out by *Gordon* [1967], the primary and secondary polar frontal zones in the western part of the Southeast Pacific Basin converge to a point directly above the Usarp Fracture Zone. This zone contains a deep canyon cutting across the Mid-Oceanic Ridge. Therefore, it was suggested in this earlier study that a 'wake' phenomenon may occur and be in a quasi steady state.

The 3000-meter contour shown in Figure 1 indicates that both north and south of Macquarie Island (55°S, 160°E) are deep passages similar to the Usarp Fracture Zone. From inspection of the dynamic topography of the sea surface relative to 2500-db level, it is found that a steep gradient occurs over the northern passage. Such a constriction of the streamlines at the sea surface is similar to the pattern above the Usarp Fracture Zone [*Gordon,* 1967, pl. 11]. The northern passage was crossed on *Eltanin* cruise 16. A 5500-meter channel was found at 52°S, 161°30′E. In addition, the mean position of the Antarctic Convergence passes directly over the Usarp Fracture Zone and probably north of Macquarie Island, rather than intersecting the island as shown by Mackintosh. It appears that the structure of the water column has some similarities, and that propagation of a double polar frontal zone may occur over both regions. Perhaps its formation may be related to the theory of *Burling* [1961]: The northern extremity of a meander in the polar front breaks off, forming a cold eddy which, in conserving its vertical component of potential vorticity as the latitude decreases, must elongate into the observed cold cell. The deep channels may cause production of meanders that culminate in the form of cold eddies.

A third possible mechanism that may produce the double polar front zone is based on internal waves. The main pycnocline in antarctic waters occurs between the Antarctic Surface Water and upper Circumpolar Deep Water. On this pycnocline internal waves may occur. The wave patterns found in the isotherms below the T_{min} layer on all BT sections south of the secondary polar front zone are most likely due to such internal waves. Calculation of wave length is dubious, since the section is obtained over a period of days.

The density variation across the pycnocline decreases toward the north. The upper circumpolar deep water decreases from a σ_t of 27.8 near the Antarctic Divergence to 27.6 near the polar front zone. The σ_t of the T_{min} layer decreases from 27.4 to 27.3 across the same distance. The separation between the two layers is slightly greater near the polar front zone than in the Antarctic Divergence vicinity. Therefore, the strength of the pycnocline decreases slightly from south to north.

The internal waves are initiated at the Antarctic Divergence owing to the passage of storm systems. The waves travel northward. As the pycnocline weakens, the waves progress more slowly and the wave length decreases. Accompanying this shortening of the wave, the amplitude would increase. The increase in amplitude and decrease in wave length is due to the reduction of the restoring force as the pycnocline weakens. Smaller amounts of energy are needed to produce similar amplitude waves for a weak pycnocline than for a strong pycnocline. Therefore, the internal waves become large amplitude waves or relatively short-crested waves near the northern limit of the T_{min} layer. Such a situation is analogous to the flapping of a flag in the wind, where the tension on the cloth is less at the free end, so that it oscillates more violently than does the flag near the flagpole. The internal waves in the vicinity of the northern boundary of the T_{min} layer may become unstable with turbulence destroying the crests and troughs leaving only the sides of the wave. Such a process would produce the isolated cold water cell of the primary polar front zone and the cells of sinking within the secondary polar front zone.

CONCLUSION

The present paper deals only with the area east of Macquarie Island. The double polar front zone may exist further west. The future *Eltanin* cruises will investigate this possibility. If it is found west of Macquarie Island, either the bottom topography theory would be proven wrong or another deep channel further west may exist.

None of the above theories is conclusive. However, with these in mind field work can be planned to best obtain an understanding of the double polar front zone. Certainly time series data are needed, as is a rapid survey of an area of limited extent over the primary polar front zone.

Acknowledgment. Grateful acknowledgment is due to R. Tsgonis for preparing the figures, to L. Child for drafting them, and to J. Stolz for secretarial assistance. The manuscript was critically read by Stanley S. Jacobs, Kenneth Hunkins, and Neil Opdyke. The work is financially supported by the National Science Foundation grants GA-1309, GA-10794, and GA-19032. Lamont-Doherty Geological Observatory contribution 1499.

REFERENCES

Botnikov, V. N., Geographical position of the Antarctic Convergence Zone in the Antarctic Ocean, *Soviet Antarctic Exped. Inform. Bull.*, English Transl., *4*(6), 324–327, 1963.

Botnikov, V. N., Seasonal and long-term fluctuations of the Antarctic Convergence Zone, *Soviet Antarctic Exped. Inform. Bull.*, English Transl., *5*(2), 92–95, 1964.

Burling, R. W., Hydrology of circumpolar waters south of New Zealand, *New Zealand Dept. Sci. Ind. Res. Bull.*, *149*, 66 pp., 1961.

Deacon, G. E. R., A general account of the hydrology of the South Atlantic Ocean, *Discovery Rept.*, *7*, 171–238, Cambridge, 1933.

Deacon, G. E. R., The hydrology of the Southern Ocean, *Discovery Rept.*, *15*, 1–124, 1937.

Foster, T. D., Haline convection induced by the freezing of sea water, *J. Geophys. Res.*, *73(6)*, 1933–1938, 1968.

Garner, D. M., The Antarctic convergence south of New Zealand, *New Zealand J. Geol. Geophys.*, *1*(13), 577–594, 1958.

Gordon, A. L., Structure of Antarctic Waters between 20°W and 170°W, *Antarctic Map Folio Series, Folio 6*, edited by V. C. Bushnell, 10 pp. with maps, American Geographical Society, New York, 1967.

Houtman, T. J., Surface temperature gradients at the Antarctic convergence, *New Zealand J. Geol. Geophys.*, *7*(2), 245–270, 1964.

Houtman, T. J., Water masses and fronts in the Southern Ocean south of New Zealand, 40 pp., *New Zealand Dept. Sci. Ind. Res. Bull.*, *174*, 1967.

Jacobs, S. S., and A. F. Amos, Physical and chemical oceanographic observations in the Southern Oceans, USNS *Eltanin* cruises 22–27, 1966–1967, 287 pp., *Tech. Rept. 1-CU-1-67*, Lamont-Doherty Geological Observatory of Columbia University, Palisades, New York, 1967.

Koopman, G., Entstehung und Verbreitung von Divergenzen in der oberflächennahen Wasserbewegung der antarktischen Gewässer, *Deut. Hydrograph. Z.*, Ergan 2, 39 pp., 1953.

Mackintosh, N. A., The Antarctic convergence and the distribution of surface temperature in Antarctic waters, *Discovery Rept.*, *23*, 177–212, 1946.

Meinardus, W., Meteorologische Ergebnisse der Deutschen Südpolar Expedition 1901–1923, *Deut. Sudpolar Exped. III Meteor. I*(1) *Berlin*, 1923.

Ostapoff, F., On the frictionally induced transverse circulation of the Antarctic circumpolar current, *Deut. Hydrograph. Z.*, *15*(3), 103–113, 1962*a*.

Ostapoff, F., The salinity distribution at 200 meters and the Antarctic frontal zones, *Deut. Hydrograph Z.*, *15*(4), 133–142, 1962*b*.

Schott, G., *Geographie des Atlantischen Ozeans*, 1st ed., Hamburg, 1926; 2nd ed., 438 pp., Hamburg, 1944.

Tolstikov, E. I., Ed., *Atlas Antarktiki*, vol. 1, G.U.C.K., Moscow, 1966. (English Transl. in *Soviet Geography: Rev. Transl.*, *8*(5-6), American Geographical Society, New York, 1967.)

Turner, J. S., Salt fingers across a density interface, *Deep-Sea Res.*, *14*, 599–611, 1967.

Veronis, G., Generation of mean ocean circulation by fluctuating winds, *Tellus*, *18*(1), 67–76, 1966.

Wexler, H., The Antarctic convergence—or divergence?, *The Atmosphere and the Sea in Motion*, edited by B. Bolin, pp. 106–120, Rockefeller Institute Press, New York, 1959.

Weyant, W. S., The Antarctic atmosphere: Climatology of the surface environment, *Antarctic Map Folio Series, Folio 8*, edited by V. C. Bushnell, 4 pp. with maps, American Geographical Society, New York, 1967.

THE LOUISVILLE RIDGE—A POSSIBLE EXTENSION OF THE ELTANIN FRACTURE ZONE

Dennis E. Hayes and Maurice Ewing

Lamont-Doherty Geological Observatory of Columbia University, Palisades, New York 10964

Abstract. Evidence is given for existence of a continuous narrow aseismic ridge, probably a northwesterly extension of the Eltanin Fracture Zone to the Tonga-Kermadec Trench. Many of the traverses show the ridge crest to be flattened at a depth of about 800 fm.

The chart of the U. S. Navy Hydrographic Office [*U. S. Navy*, 1961] and the Russian chart of the Pacific [*Udintsev*, 1963] show many (about 40) seamounts that lie close to a great circle joining the Tonga and Kermadec trenches near 26°S, 175°W, with the western portion of the Eltanin Fracture Zone near 53°S, 135°W. Sounding tracks made subsequent to the publication of these charts show a prominent elevation within a short distance of the great circle on every one of 31 crossings examined. The fact that every sounding traverse across this line has shown an elevation on it is strong evidence that the feature is a continuous ridge rather than a series of isolated peaks. The name Louisville Ridge is adopted here for this 3500-km-long feature, which is an extension of the 350-km-long ridge that originally bore the same name. The name Louisville Ridge is not used in a generic sense and should not be confused with a mid-oceanic ridge.

The Louisville Ridge is of interest from several diverse points of view.

1. It is probably related to the northwesterly extension of the Eltanin Fracture Zone [*Gordon*, 1967; *Pitman et al.*, 1968; *Sykes*, 1963; *Heezen et al.*, 1968] and hence relevant to discussions of sea floor spreading [*Le Pichon*, 1968; *Morgan*, 1968]. The trace of the Louisville Ridge diverges considerably from the proposed westward extension of the Eltanin Fracture Zone of *van der Linden* [1967], which passes along the north edge of the New Zealand plateau and North Island, New Zealand.

2. This ridge is aseismic and at its intersection with the Tonga and Kermadec trenches it interrupts the belt of strong seismic activity [*Sykes*, 1966; *Barazangi and Dorman*, 1969] associated with the trenches. At this intersection, the maximum depth of the trench is reduced from more than 5000 fm to about 3500 fm.

3. The flow of the strong western boundary current of antarctic circumpolar deep water which is the source of all the deep water in the North and South Pacific [*Reid et al.*, 1968] must be strongly modified by the presence of this ridge, particularly so if the ridge proves to be continuous.

4. On many crossings of the ridge, the crest is flattened at approximately 800 fm below sea level, to an extent that suggests truncation. This aspect of the ridge and the short wavelength magnetic anomaly associated with the ridge are useful in discriminating between probable crossings of the ridge and those of isolated seamounts.

BATHYMETRIC DATA

Figure 1 is a bathymetric sketch of the area, which includes the Louisville Ridge, modified from *U. S. Navy* [1961] and *Udintsev* [1963]. All available new sounding tracks have been examined, and each confirms the presence of the ridge. Representative bathymetric and magnetic profiles are shown in the inset of Figure 1.

It is emphasized that very few isolated peaks and seamounts have been found in the immediate vicinity (within a few degrees) of the ridge. In the area between 145°W and 160° where we have the least control, *Udintsev* [1963] shows a continuous ridge, although sill depths are indicated at depths greater than 2400 fm. It is evident that the trend of the ridge approximates a small circle between ~ 26°S, 175°W, and 55.5°S, 120°W (see Figure 1, dashed line). The eastern segment of this small circle lies near the seismically active segment of the Eltanin Fracture Zone [*Sykes*, 1963]. The distribution of the mapped elevations strongly suggests that a change in the trend of the ridge occurs near 40°S and 166°W. The significance of this proposed change in trend will be dis-

TABLE 1. Minimum Depth along the Louisville Ridge

S. Lat.	W. Long.	Depth, fm	Source*
25°50′	174°50′	<2000	1
30°10′	173°20′	<2000	1
30°30′	172°40′	<2000	1
31°20′	172°20′	<1500	1
32°10′	171°50′	<2000	1
39°05′	168°15′	<1500	1
39°10′	167°20′	< 500	1
39°40′	164°50′	<2000	1
41°25′	164°10′	<1000	1
41°50′	163°45′	<1000	1
42°50′	161°50′	<2000	1
42°10′	162°45′	<1500	1
42°50′	162°15′	<1000	1
45°40′	159°10′	<2000	1
45°30′	157°45′	< 500	1
45°45′	155°50′	<2000	1
45°40′	155°10′	<2000	1
26°00′	175°00′	1038	2
26°20′	174°45′	1105	2
28°00′	173°50′	1298	2
30°20′	173°25′	1279	2
31°20′	172°15′	624	2
31°30′	170°25′	2230	2
31°50′	172°45′	1978	2
32°25′	171°50′	2186	2
32°45′	169°30′	1639	2
39°15′	167°30′	449	2
39°20′	165°30′	1919	2
41°40′	163°45′	430	2
41°30′	163°00′	1199	2
42°50′	162°00′	750	2
45°40′	157°45′	973	2
45°30′	156°10′	1718	2
50°50′	147°30′	2104	2
51°55′	144°30′	1875	2
53°10′	141°00′	1366	2
52°15′	139°30′	1836	2
54°40′	130°00′	480	2
55°20′	128°15′	400	2
37°03′	170°57′	1350	USNOO
36°54′	169°48′	650	USNOO
36°48′	169°42′	550	USNOO
33°52′	169°15′	2300	USNOO
38°12′	168°40′	990	USNOO
39°02′	168°17′	1310	USNOO
38°12′	168°04′	1340	USNOO
37°54′	167°24′	234	USNOO
25°50′	175°00′	1000	CO12
27°15′	174°20′	1092	HOCH
28°10′	173°45′	820	EL29
29°15′	173°25′	1366	HOCH
33°58′	171°14′	820	CO12
34°53′	170°41′	2140	CO12
35°07′	169°33′	2000	CO12
38°20′	168°00′	360	CO9
40°35′	165°30′	450	EL20
40°55′	164°40′	1950	CO9
43°37′	161°30′	350	EL17
43°12′	161°24′	2217	EL28
47°10′	155°00′	2000	CO8
52°10′	142°11′	1120	EL17
53°30′	140′00°	150	EL19
55°30′	139°30′	600	EL20
52°30′	138°30′	1450	EL17
53°40′	135°00′	1250	EL17
54°55′	129°06′	520	EL17
54°30′	127°30′	1150	EL25
55°00′	127°50′	1450	EL25

*1, *U. S. Navy* [1961]; 2, *Udintsev* [1963]; USNOO, U. S. Navy Oceanographic Office; HOCH, *Hochstein and Reilly* [1967]; EL, USNS *Eltanin;* CO, RV *Robert D. Conrad.*

cussed later. The sill depth of the ridge is variable, but with three exceptions has not been found to be greater than 2200 fm on any crossing (Table 1). The morphology of this ridge differs from many reported long fracture zones [*Heezen et al.,* 1968; *Menard,* 1967; *Heezen and Tharp,* 1965] in that it is not associated with an adjacent rift or depression or pronounced change in elevation on opposite sides of the feature. In this respect it resembles the Walvis Ridge of the South Atlantic. However, the sediment cover of the Louisville Ridge is very thin (< 50 meters) in contrast to the relatively thick sediments (> 300 meters) of the Walvis Ridge [*Ewing et al.,* 1966]. Profiles taken from seismic reflection profiler records suggesting truncation of the higher parts of the ridge are shown in Figure 2 (profiles D and E).

The available bathymetric data provide no convincing evidence that the ridge continues into the complicated topographic provinces of the South Fiji Basin, northwest of its intersection with the Tonga and Kermadec trenches. However, earthquakes deeper than 500 km, all of which lie west of the trenches [*Sykes,* 1966; *Barazangi and Dorman,* 1969], are confined to the area north of the intersection of the Louisville Ridge with the Tonga and Kermadec trenches and ridges. *Katsumata and Sykes* [1969] have also noted the correlation of seismic and morphologic boundaries along the Bonin-Mariana trench complex with the intersection of the Mid-Pacific Mountains (Marcus-Necker Ridge) and the trench system.

MAGNETIC ANOMALIES

Allowance for the effect of topography and depth must be made, but having considered it, the magnetic anomaly signature seems a valuable means of identi-

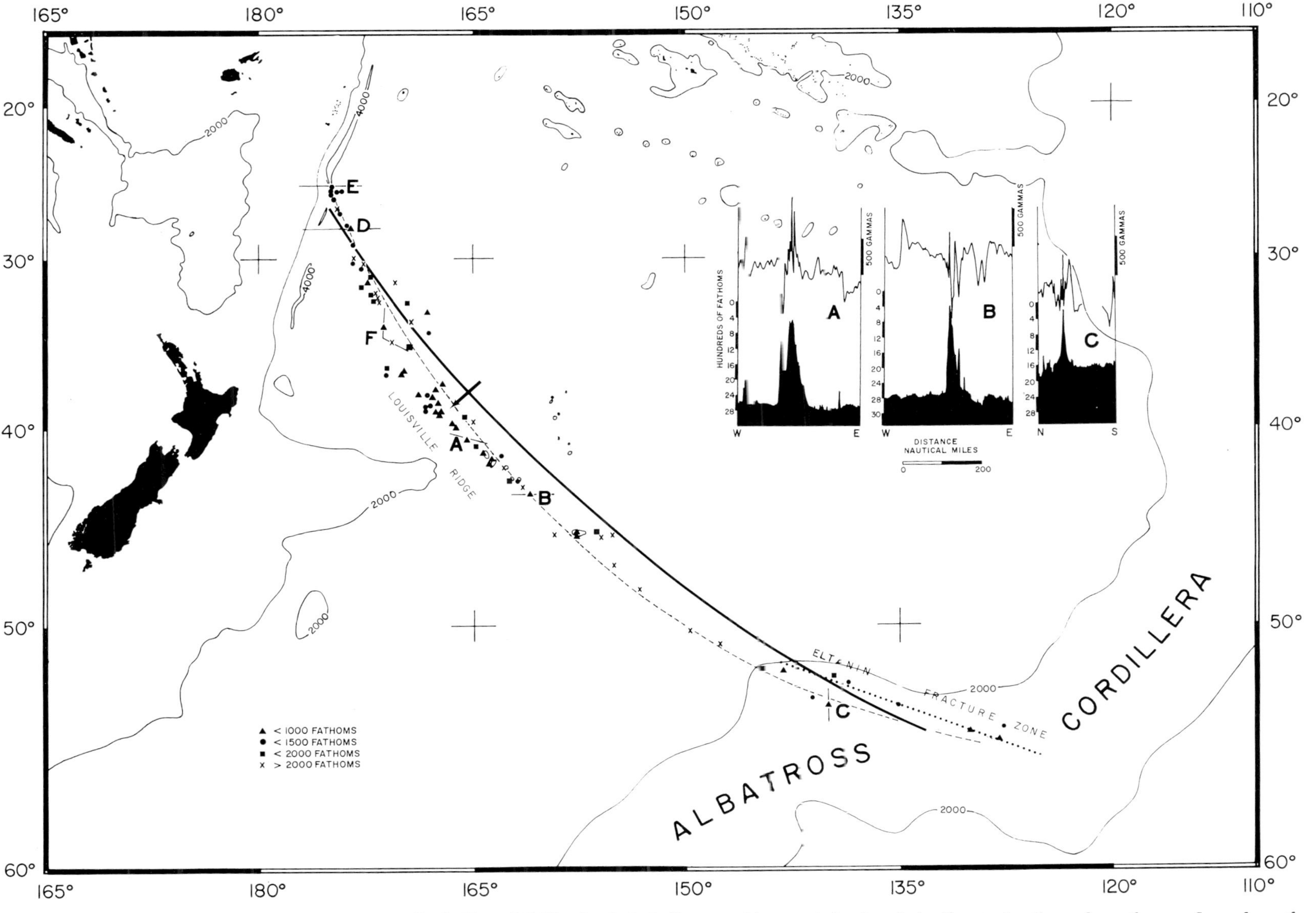

Fig. 1. Generalized regional bathymetry taken from *U. S. Navy* [1961]. Symbols indicate positions and depths of significant elevations above the sea floor along the extension of the Louisville Ridge. These data were compiled from several sources and are tabulated in Table 1. The bold black line indicates a great circle between 26°S, 175°W, and 55°S, 135°W for reference only. The dashed line represents an estimated best fit of the elevations to a single small circle (poles at 5°N, 120°W; 5°S, 60°E). The dotted line represents the approximate location of the seismically active portion of the Eltanin Fracture Zone as taken from *Heezen et al.* [1968] and *Sykes* [1963]. The arrow indicates the location where a break in the smooth trend of the Louisville Ridge is suggested. Locations of profiles A, B, and C as well as E, E, and F of Figure 2 are indicated.

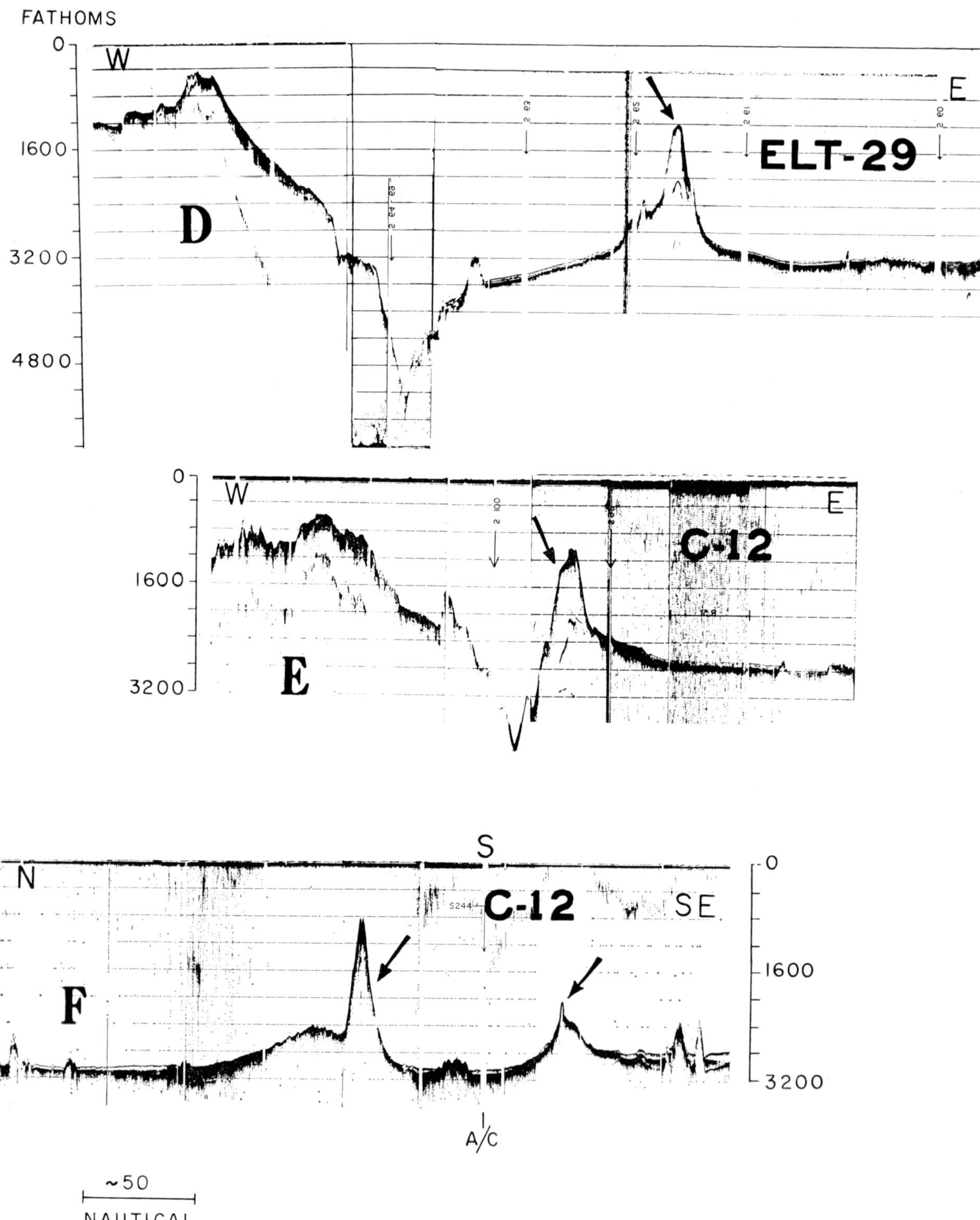

Fig. 2. Representative seismic profiler traverses of the Louisville Ridge. Locations of profiles are given in Figure 1. Arrows point to the Louisville Ridge. Depths are indicated in nominal fathoms (1/400 second reflection time). The vertical exaggeration is approximately 30:1.

fying the Louisville Ridge and if truly characteristic should eventually give important clues to its origin.

As shown in the inset of Figure 1, there are magnetic anomalies clearly associated with the ridge. The anomalies are high amplitude (> 500 γ), of short wavelength, and are not typical of the magnetic signature of many isolated seamounts in the region.

No magnetic data were available for most of the inferred ridge crossings indicated in Figure 1.

RELATION TO SEA FLOOR SPREADING

Based on the hypothesis that sea floor spreading occurs by the motion of large rigid plates, the fracture zone traces define the lines of relative motion [*Morgan*, 1968; *Le Pichon*, 1968]. The trend of the Louisville Ridge and Eltanin Fracture Zone would define uniquely a history of relative motion of major crustal plates. Under the related assumption that underthrusting of the lithosphere occurs at the trenches (particularly the Tonga and Kermadec trenches; see *Oliver and Isacks* [1968]), the shoaling of the trench might be attributed to the elevated topography of the ridge disappearing into the trench.

Inspection of the ridge sections shown by C-12 (E) and ELT-29 (D) (Figure 2) indicates that a ridge of this size could practically fill the trench, but the observed shoaling is far less. Alternatively, the shoaling might be related to formation of the ridge by uplift, which involved the trench as well as the crust to the east of it, without the necessity of underthrusting. The hypothesis that the Louisville Ridge marks the boundary of two crustal plates seems to be the favorable alternative in explaining the contrast in seismic activity north and south of Louisville Ridge. It is not clear that the topography along the boundary zone of two crustal plates should necessarily be moved along with either plate and still maintain its morphologic identity. Therefore, the relatively small shoaling of the trench near Louisville Ridge may not be a serious difficulty.

The pole of the small circle (dashed line of Figure 1) is at approximately 5°S and 60°E. This pole is quite different than that found to describe the motion between the antarctic and Pacific plates by *Le Pichon* [1968] and *Morgan* [1968] of roughly 70°S and 118°E. Their determinations are based on a relatively short and recent portion of the spreading history. The small circle shown in Figure 1 and its pole necessarily represent the average relative motion of two plates integrated over a much longer period of time (probably from mid-Mesozoic to present). The small circle only represents a 'best fit' by eye. By fitting two or more small circles to the data, better fits would be obtained, and the segment passing through the Eltanin Fracture Zone near the crest of the Albatross Cordillera (Pacific-Antarctic Ridge) would obviously agree with the solutions of *Le Pichon* [1968] and of *Morgan* [1968]. As mentioned earlier, a break in the smooth trend of the Louisville Ridge is suggested near 40°S and 166°W. This break lies northwest of the oldest mapped anomaly (#32) of *Pitman et al.* [1968], which is presumed to be of Late Cretaceous age. *Menard* [1967] and *Hayes and Pitman* [1970] have indicated a significant change in the trend of major fracture zones in the North Pacific at some time prior to the formation of anomaly 32. These changes in fracture zone orientation suggest that the spreading pattern may have undergone a major simultaneous change on a global scale. It is interesting, however, that the 'forced fit' of all the data points to one small circle gives an angular motion vector that is quite different from that derived for the Pliocene to present, but which, nonetheless, may be representative of the average relative angular motion of South Pacific crustal plates over a much longer period of time.

Confirmation of the Louisville Ridge as a long extension of the Eltanin Fracture Zone would lend strong support to the proposal that the motion of crustal plates of the South Pacific and perhaps those of global extent have changed significantly during the Late Mesozoic. Although the continuity of the Louisville Ridge and its relationship to the Eltanin Fracture Zone have not yet been firmly established, its presence as an important physiographic feature or zone is not in question. It is important that this feature be considered in studying the deep circulation and the tectonic evolution of the southwest Pacific.

Acknowledgments. We thank A. Gordon, W. Pitman, and L. Sykes for their critical review of the manuscript. This research was supported by the National Science Foundation and by the Office of Naval Research. Lamont-Doherty Geological Observatory contribution 1530.

REFERENCES

Barazangi, M., and J. Dorman, World seismicity maps compiled from ESSA, Coast and Geodetic Survey, epicenter data, 1961–1967, *Bull. Seismol. Soc. Am.*, *59*(1), 369–380, 1969.

Ewing, M., X. Le Pichon, and J. Ewing, Crustal structure of the mid-ocean ridges, 4, *J. Geophys. Res.*, *71*(6), 319–339, 1966.

Gordon, A., Structure of Antarctic Waters between 20°W and 170°W, *Antarctic Map Folio Series, Folio 6*, edited by V. Bushnell, American Geographical Society, New York, 1967.

Hayes, D. E., and W. C. Pitman III, Magnetic lineations in the North Pacific, *Geol. Soc. Am. Mem. 126*, edited by J. D. Hays, pp. 291–314, 1970.

Heezen, B. C., and M. Tharp, Tectonic fabric of the Atlantic and Indian oceans and continental drift, *Phil. Trans. Roy. Soc., 258*, 90–106, 1965.

Heezen, B. C., M. Tharp, and C. D. Hollister, Illustrations of the marine geology of the Southern Oceans, *Symposium on Antarctic Oceanography, September 13–16, 1966, Santiago, Chile*, pp. 101–109, Scott Polar Institute Scientific Committee on Antarctic Research, Heffer and Sons, Cambridge, England, 1968.

Hochstein, M. P., and W. I. Reilly, Magnetic measurements in the South-West Pacific Ocean, *New Zealand J. Geol. Geophys., 10*(6), 1527–1562, 1967.

Katsumata, M., and L. R. Sykes, Seismicity and tectonics of the Ryuku-Taiwan and Izu-Mariana-Caroline Regions (abstract), *EOS, Trans. Am. Geophys. Union 50*(4), 235, 1969.

Le Pichon, X., Sea-floor spreading and continental drift, *J. Geophys. Res., 73*(12), 3661–3697, 1968.

Menard, H. W., Extension of northeastern Pacific fracture zones, *Science, 155*, 72–74, 1967.

Morgan, W. J., Rise, trenches, great faults, and crustal blocks, *J. Geophys. Res., 73*(6), 1959–1982, 1968.

Oliver, J., and B. Isacks, Deep earthquake zones, anomalous structures in the upper mantle and the lithosphere, *J. Geophys. Res., 72*(16), 4257–4275, 1967.

Pitman III, W. C., E. M. Herron, and J. R. Heirtzler, Magnetic anomalies in the Pacific and sea floor spreading, *J. Geophys. Res., 73*(6), 2069–2085, 1968.

Reid, J. H., H. Stommel, E. D. Stroup, and B. A. Warren, Detection of a deep boundary current in the northern South Pacific, *Nature, 217*, 937, 1968.

Sykes, L., Seismicity of the South Pacific Ocean, *J. Geophys. Res., 68*(21), 5999–6006, 1963.

Sykes, L., The seismicity and deep structure of island arcs, *J. Geophys. Res., 71*(12), 2981–3006, 1966.

Udintsev, G. B., et al., A new bathymetric map of the Pacific Ocean, *Oceanological Researches: Articles*, no. 9, pp. 60–101, Academy of Sciences USSR, Soviet Geophysical Committee, Section 10 of the I.G.Y. Program, 1963.

U. S. Navy, Map of the world, *Hydrograph. Off. Misc. 15–254*, 1961.

van der Linden, W. J. M., Structural relationships in the Tasman Sea and South-West Pacific Ocean, *New Zealand J. Geol. Geophys., 10*(5), 1280–1301, 1967.

CRUSTAL PLATES AND SEA FLOOR SPREADING IN THE SOUTHEASTERN PACIFIC

ELLEN M. HERRON

Lamont-Doherty Geological Observatory of Columbia University, Palisades, New York 10964

Abstract. Within the past decade, abundant data have been collected in the South Pacific Ocean (Pacific-Antarctic Ocean), and analysis of the geophysical data has shown the southeastern Pacific to be extremely interesting geologically. Two active spreading ridges, the Albatross Cordillera (Pacific-Antarctic Ridge) and the Chile Rise (Chile Ridge) are present in this area, and no trench or evidence of an active compressional feature has been identified between these ridges. In addition, the trench flanking the west coast of South America is sediment filled opposite the Chile Rise. The Albatross Cordillera displays one of the best developed magnetic lineation patterns and can be easily traced across the Eltanin Fracture Zone, the largest fracture zone in the area.

Magnetic and topographic data collected by the USNS *Eltanin* in the Pacific south of 30°S and between 70°W and 150°W have been collated and plotted on Mercator projection. Combination of both topographic and magnetic data, together with seismicity data, allows a more detailed interpretation of the structure than is possible using only topographic or magnetic data in this area where no systematic surveys have been conducted. The present trend of the Eltanin Fracture Zone is quite different from the trend followed before 10 to 20 m.y.b.p., indicating that a change in the position of the rotational pole for the Albatross Cordillera crustal plate occurred during this interval. The present Chile Rise is a remnant of a once much larger northwest trending ridge system, which may have extended from the Eltanin Fracture Zone to the North Pacific during the Late Cretaceous. The well-developed Albatross Cordillera north of the Eltanin Fracture Zone is a comparatively young ridge, which has developed on the western flank of the older northwest trending system.

INTRODUCTION

Between 1963 and 1967, the USNS *Eltanin* operated in the South Pacific Ocean, collecting, as part of the scientific program, topographic and magnetic data in a previously unexplored area of the world's oceans. These data, although still sufficient for only a reconnaissance study of the area, have proved to be of major importance in our understanding of the history of the oceans. *Pitman and Heirtzler* [1966] demonstrated the remarkable symmetry of the magnetic anomalies about the axis of the Albatross Cordillera (Pacific-Antarctic Ridge) at 51°S as recorded on the *Eltanin* 19 crossing. They also showed that the pattern of the magnetic anomalies gave excellent correlation with the radiometrically dated pattern of reversals of the earth's magnetic field published by *Cox et al.* [1963]. These data provided excellent support for the hypothesis of sea floor spreading advanced by *Hess* [1962] and *Dietz* [1961] and led the way to intensive analysis of the magnetic anomalies recorded over the mid-ocean ridge system in all the major ocean basins.

This paper summarizes all the topographic and magnetic data collected by the *Eltanin* during cruises 11 through 28, together with several Lamont-Doherty cruises in the area south of 30°S and between 70°W and 150°W. Many of the magnetic data over the Albatross Cordillera have been described by *Pitman et al.* [1968] but more recent, previously unpublished data reveal additional detail in the magnetic pattern. In addition, topographic data in the area have not previously been presented and analyzed with the magnetic data. The combination of the two types of data, together with seismicity data, suggests a different interpretation to the trend of the Eltanin Fracture Zone from that obtained by analysis of either topographic or magnetic data [*Pitman et al.*, 1968; *Heezen et al.*, 1966]. Study of both types of data leads to a more complete understanding of the physical processes operative in the southeastern Pacific. The major topographic features and the cruises used in this study are outlined in Figure 1.

PREVIOUS STUDIES

In 1968, *Pitman et al.* presented all the *Eltanin* magnetic data then available south of 35°S between New

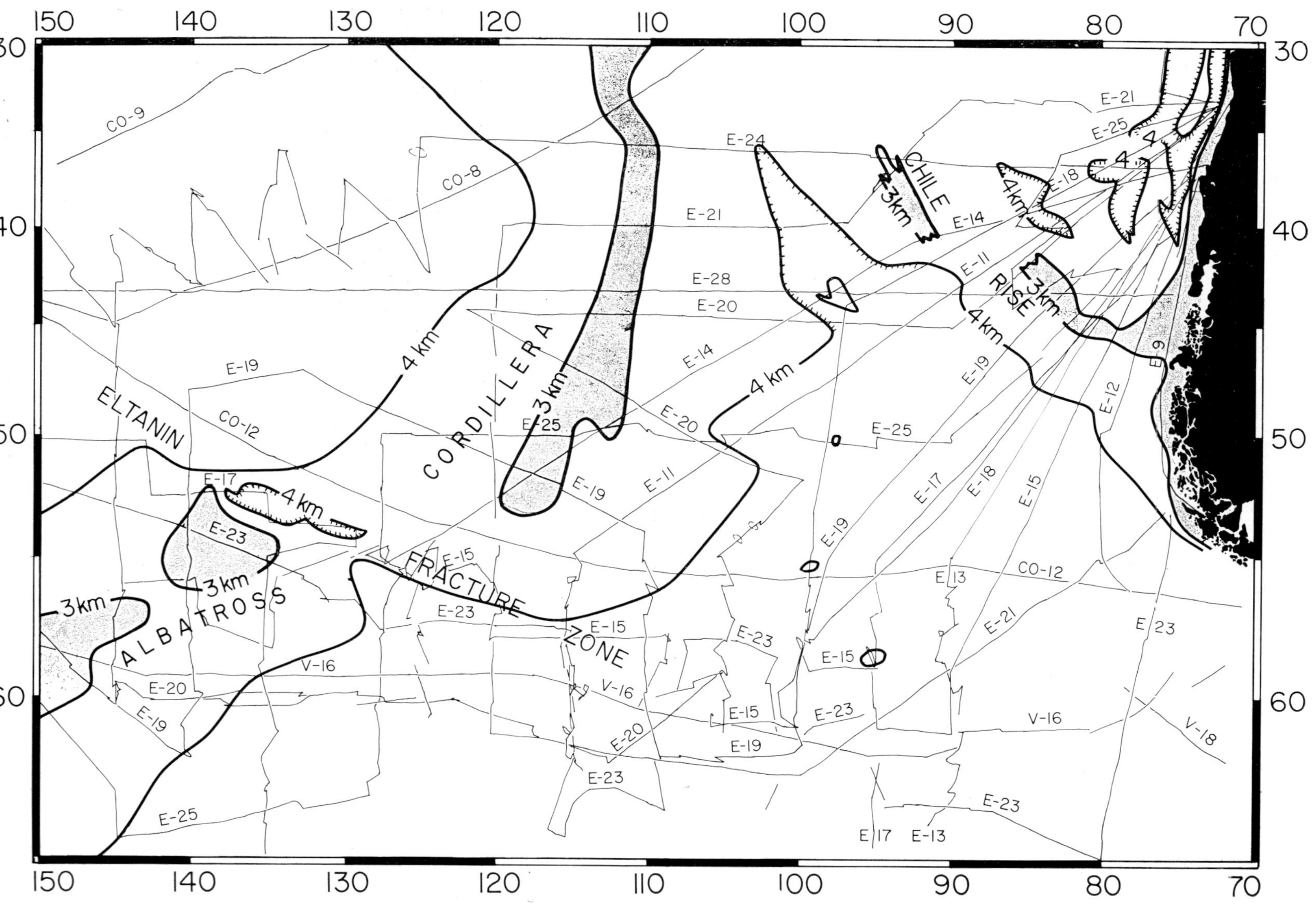

Fig. 1. Tracks used in this study are identified by a code letter (E for *Eltanin*, V for *Vema*, and CO for *Conrad*). The 3- and 4-km contours have been plotted and areas shoaler than 3 km have been shaded. Contours near the Eltanin Fracture Zone are highly generalized. Topographic data were collected on all cruises shown, but no magnetic data are available for *Eltanin* cruises 11 through 16.

Zealand and South America, together with data from Operation Deep Freeze during 1961–1962. The magnetic anomaly pattern, bilaterally symmetric about the Albatross Cordillera axis, was traced from the edge of the New Zealand plateau to 95°W and as far south as 67°S. Their paper describes the anomaly pattern in detail, and reference to their figures will be made in this paper.

The topography and magnetic pattern associated with the Chile Rise (Chile Ridge), which trends northwest from the coast of Chile at 45°S (Figure 1), have been described by *Herron and Hayes* [1969]. They showed that the ridge is presently a locus of sea floor spreading and suggested that this ridge is a relic of a once much larger, older ridge system. A similar pattern of magnetic anomalies in the area was identified by *Morgan et al.* [1969] on the basis of aeromagnetic flight lines across the northern and central sections of the Chile Rise.

DATA PRESENTATION

Topographic and magnetic data have been plotted by digital computer along the ship's track on a Mercator projection in Figures 2 and 3 (see foldouts at back of volume). The ship's track has been used as a base line, and values have been plotted perpendicular to this heading.

Figure 2 shows the topographic data in the southeastern Pacific. In plotting the data, the depths have been adjusted so that the position of the ship's track corresponds to 4-km depth, and depths shoaler than 4 km, plotted on the north side of the trackline, have been shaded. The dashed lines outline probable fracture zones inferred from the topography. Two major features, identified in Figure 1, can be traced on the map: the Albatross Cordillera, trending northeast from 60°S, 150°W, and the Chile Rise, trending northwest from 45°S, 80°W, to 36°S, 95°W. Several seamounts are also present, with summits often shallower than either ridge crest. The larger seamounts shown in Figure 2 appear to lie along fracture zones.

The two ridge crests exhibit quite different morphology. *Menard* [1964], using the *Vema* 16 topography data, described the Albatross Cordillera as forming a broad triangular bulge, with relatively small local relief on both the flanks and the axis. In contrast, the Chile Rise axis and upper flanks are extremely rough. In addition, these ridges differ in their relative seismicity. The existence of the Chile Rise was predicted on the basis of its seismicity [*Ewing and Heezen*, 1956]. Epicenters plotted in Figure 4, taken from *Barazangi and Dorman* [1969], show that whereas the Chile Rise is quite active along its entire length, no earthquakes were recorded during the interval 1961–1967 along the axis of the Albatross Cordillera between 36°S and 50°S. For an actively spreading ridge, the Albatross Cordillera shows anomalously low seismic activity. No explanation for this has yet been found.

The Albatross Cordillera and the Chile Rise are separated by a basin that trends and deepens to the southeast. Large seamounts are present within this basin at 43°S, 98°W, and at 59°S, 95°W, but there is no topographic or seismic evidence for any major contemporaneous compressional motion between these two ridges. Sediment accumulations in the southeastern Pacific are largely confined to the area south of 45°S [*Ewing et al.*, 1969]. In contrast to the more than 100 meters of sediment covering all but the axis of the Albatross Cordillera, sediment accumulations on the Chile Rise, both on the flanks and at the axis, are too thin to be resolved with the Lamont-Doherty profiling techniques [*Ewing et al.*, 1969]. At least part of the observed contrast in topographic roughness shown in Figure 2 results from the contrast in sediment accumulations on the two ridges.

Other major topographic features present in Figure 2 are the Peru-Chile Trench near 30°S and the fracture zones, especially the Eltanin Fracture Zone near 56°S. The Peru-Chile Trench is buried by sediment [*Hayes*, 1966; *Ewing et al.*, 1969] except near the northern map boundary, where it appears as a flat-bottomed feature with maximum depth of 5.5 km. Topography within the transform fault zone of the Eltanin Fracture Zone is extremely rugged with over 5-km relief in some areas. The axis of the Albatross Cordillera is offset in a dextral manner over 1000 km across this fault zone. The fracture zone complex has been traced southeast of the seismically active fault zone by using areas of anomalously rough topography. Other trends for the fracture zone can be chosen from the topography alone, and the choice of the trend outlined will be explained in the section describing the magnetic anomalies. The fracture zone topography shown in the area southeast of the transform fault is much less rugged than that within the transform fault region, and the fracture zone trace becomes increasingly more difficult to follow with distance from the axial zone. The southeastern extension of the fracture zone is almost entirely sediment covered. Another fracture zone at 50°S, 115°W, can be inferred by the abrupt change in depth at the axis of the Albatross Cordillera.

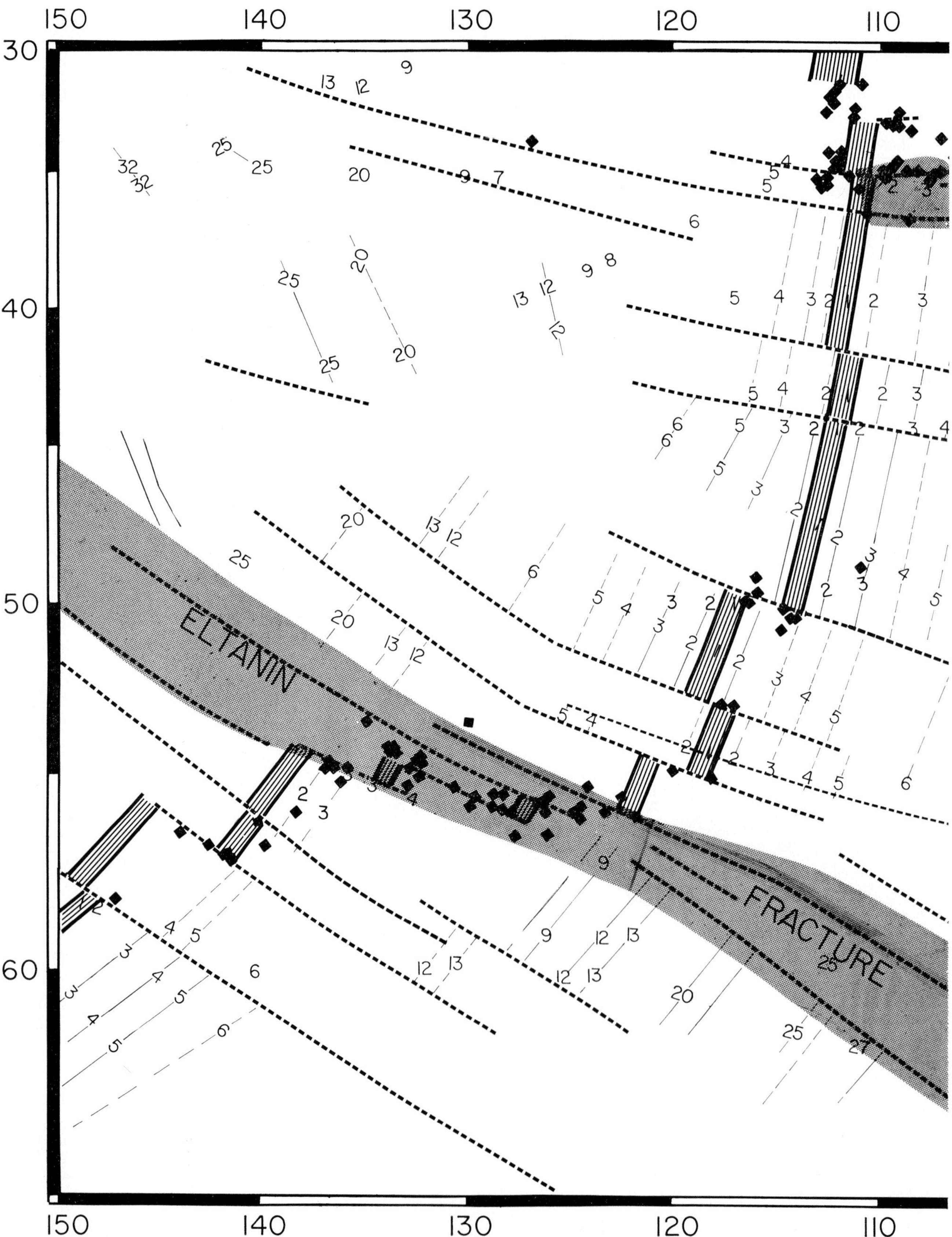

Fig. 4. Summary of the crustal features inferred from magnetic and topographic data. Earthquake epicenters taken from *Barazangi and Dorman* [1969] have been plotted as closed diamonds. Numbers indicate magnetic anomalies according to the *Pitman et al.* [1968] nomenclature. Heavy dashed lines indicate fracture zones inferred from topographic, magnetic, and seismicity data. Note that the axis of the Chile Rise lies oblique to the fracture zones crossing the rise axis. The dotted lines

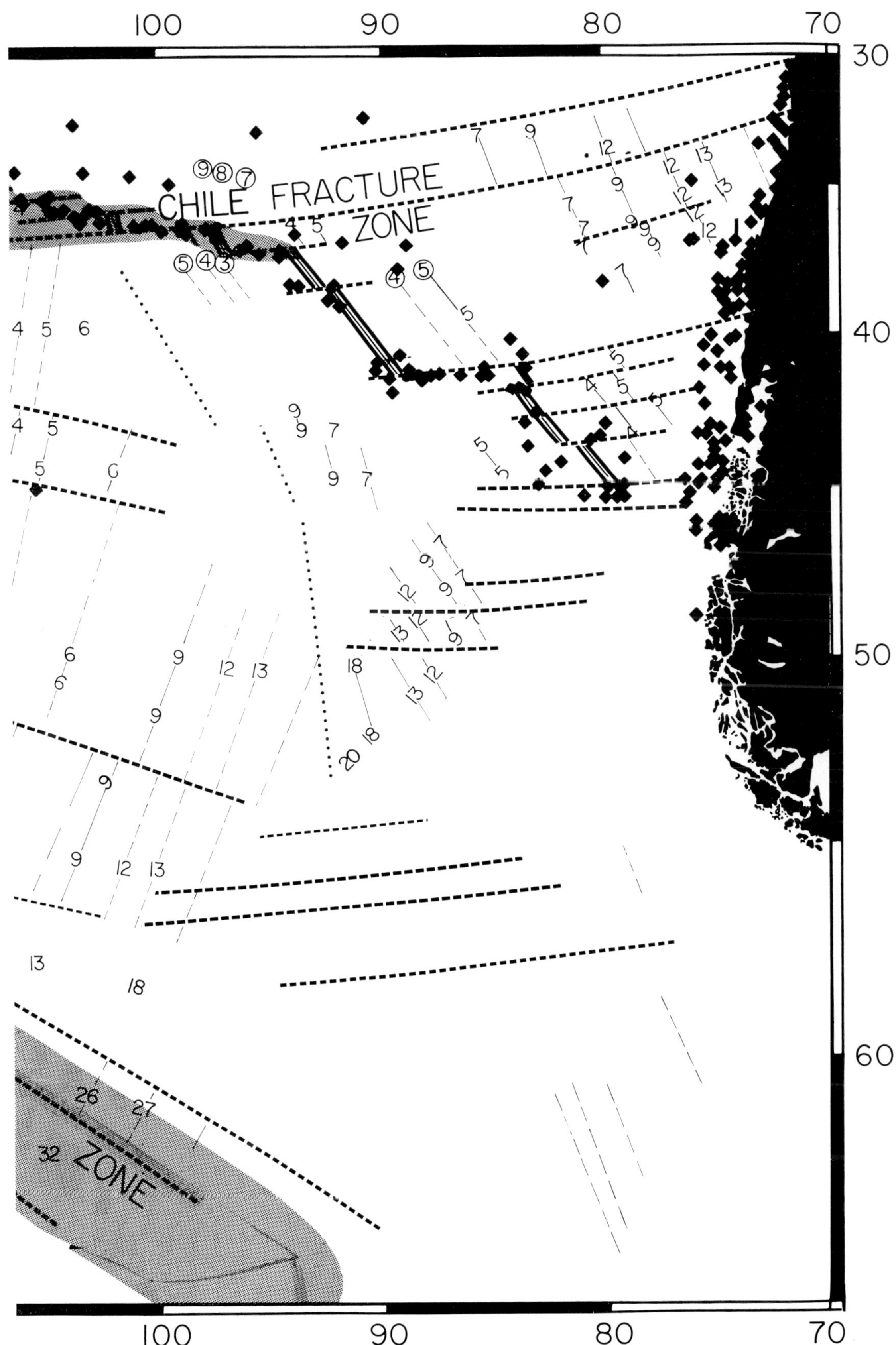

mark the approximate boundary between the Albatross Cordillera and the Chile Rise. Circled anomaly numbers are taken from *Morgan et al.* [1969]. Each anomaly number corresponds to an observation point. Solid connecting lines are drawn only where there are at least two points to define the lineation trend. Where the identification or correlation is tentative, light dashed lines have been used.

Residual magnetic data have been plotted in Figure 3 on a Mercator projection in a form analogous to that used for the topography in Figure 2. In this case, the ship's track has been set at the zero gamma contour, and positive anomalies have been shaded. The residual magnetic field has been computed using the reference field published by *Cain et al.* [1964] for epoch 1960. Dashed lines have been drawn to outline the position and trend of key anomalies, and dotted lines have been used to indicate the trend of fracture zones shown also in Figures 2 and 4.

Magnetic anomalies generated by spreading of the Albatross Cordillera have been identified and described in detail by *Pitman et al.* [1968]. Detailed correlations of many of the tracks shown in Figure 3 were presented as a series of magnetic profiles projected perpendicular to the strike of the ridge axis in their paper. Magnetic anomalies north and east of the area studied by *Pitman et al.* [1968] have been described by *Herron and Hayes* [1969]. Only the anomalies lying west of South America to 90°W and south of 55°S have not previously been described because of the paucity of data in the area.

Several key anomalies are prominent and have been correlated in Figure 3. The axial anomaly (#1 of *Pitman et al.* [1968] nomenclature), indicated by the striped pattern, appears as a broad positive anomaly on the northeast trending Albatross Cordillera crest. It is narrower on the northwest trending Chile Rise and is difficult to identify except near 43°S, 82°W. The broad positive anomaly present on the upper flanks on both sides of both ridges is number 5. A marked change in wavelength and amplitude occurs at this anomaly. Older anomalies are smaller and of shorter average wavelength. Anomalies 12 and 13, two positive spikes separated by a broad negative, lie within this generally small amplitude, short wavelength group and can be identified in the basins flanking the Chile Rise and on both sides of the Albatross Cordillera. Beyond anomaly 20, amplitudes and particularly wavelengths increase. Anomalies 25 and 26, two positive spikes separated from a group of three broad positive anomalies by a broad negative zone, can be identified only on the lower flanks of the Albatross Cordillera.

The magnetic anomalies shown in Figure 3 appear to follow two main trends: northeasterly following the Albatross Cordillera axis, and northwesterly subparallel to the Chile Rise axis. Northwest trending anomalies are found only to the north of the Eltanin Fracture Zone, and these are found on both east and west flanks of the Albatross Cordillera.

On the eastern flank of the Albatross Cordillera, the boundary between the two sets of magnetic lineations generated by the two spreading systems is distinct on several tracks in Figure 3. In the area bounded by 50°S to 55°S, 90°W to 100°W, three tracks bearing slightly east of north to northeast are present. The most westerly of these tracks contains only very long apparent wavelength anomalies, indicating that lineations here parallel the northeast trend of the Albatross Cordillera. An abrupt change in wavelength occurs at 51°S on the middle track. North of 51°S, anomalies cannot trend northeasterly parallel to the track because of their apparent short wavelengths, but must belong to the northwest set of anomalies. The most easterly of the three tracks lies entirely within the northwest trending set and contains only relatively short wavelength anomalies.

South of 55°S, between 70°W and 90°W, the paucity of magnetic data makes identification of individual anomalies extremely difficult. However, the wavelengths are too short, and the amplitudes are too large for the anomalies to fit in the Late Cretaceous group older than number 32, according to the data shown by *Raff* [1966] and *Pitman et al.* [1968]. Tentative correlation of these anomalies is shown in Figure 4, and the criteria used will be discussed in a later section.

INTERPRETATION OF THE DATA

The structural features in the southeastern Pacific are outlined in Figure 4. In constructing this figure, topographic, magnetic, and seismicity data have been used. Epicenters from *Barazangi and Dorman* [1969] have been plotted as open circles and outline the position of the major fracture zones and the Peru-Chile Trench. Data from these relatively small earthquakes are insufficient to determine the direction of motion along the fracture zones [*Sykes*, 1967]. Therefore, in tracing out the fracture zones, topographic, magnetic, and seismicity data have been used, together with the constraints demanded by the geometry of sea floor spreading.

Previous work [*Morgan*, 1968; *Le Pichon*, 1968] has shown that spreading ridges tend to orient themselves perpendicular to the fracture zones that form small circles about the pole of rotation of a crustal plate. The trend of the fracture zone gives the direction of relative motion between the bounding crustal plates or plate segments. Any change in the position of the rotational pole results in a change in the trend of the fracture zone, and the ridge axis also tends to reorient to the new system [*Menard and Atwater*, 1968]. If the clusters of epicenters marking the Challenger Fracture Zone (Figure 4), which extends from the Albatross Cordillera axis at 34°S, 110°W, to 36°S, 95°W, and the Eltanin Fracture Zone are interpreted as outlining single fracture zones, which follow curves giving the best fit to the epicenter groups, the trends of the fracture zones so obtained lie oblique to the topographic and magnetic lineations associated with the Chile Rise and Albatross Cordillera, respectively. However, if an en echelon series of fractures is assumed, not only do the epicenters follow the curves much more closely, but the trends defined under this assumption are much more nearly perpendicular to the topographic and magnetic lineations. In the case of the Challenger Fracture Zone, the difference in interpretation is particularly striking. If a single fracture is assumed, it trends east-southeast. *Herron and Hayes* [1969] have shown that the plate south of the Challenger Fracture Zone between the axes of the Albatross Cordillera and Chile Rise is stationary relative to the adjacent plates, whereas the plate east of the Chile Rise and the axis of this rise migrate east-northeast into the Peru-Chile Trench. If seismically active areas are used to define the boundaries of crustal plates, as *Isacks et al.* [1968] showed, the seismic data indicate that the plate east of the Chile Rise is continuous with the plate east of the Albatross Cordillera between the Challenger Fracture Zone and the equator. Fracture zones in this area should form small circles about a single rotational pole. If a single fracture zone is assumed for the Challenger Fracture, it does not agree with the trend of the fracture zones on the Chile Rise (Figure 4). However, with the en echelon pattern, the trend of these fractures agrees with those associated with the Chile Rise, and further, the trends defined with this assumption follow much more closely the epicenter locations (Figure 4).

Similarly, both the active Eltanin Transform Fault and the inactive Eltanin Fracture Zone can be interpreted as an en echelon series of fractures, and the trend obtained with this interpretation agrees with the topographic and magnetic data. South of the Eltanin Fracture Zone and east of the seismically active zone, the magnetic data have been used as the primary control in determining the trend of the fracture zone. The fractures have been drawn perpendicular to the relatively well controlled magnetic lineations, and the topographic data support this interpretation. The trend of the Eltanin Fracture Zone on the axis and on the flanks of the Albatross Cordillera cannot, however, be described by a single small circle, but suggests that a change in the position of the pole of rotation occurred between anomaly 5 and anomaly 7 time.

The trend of the Eltanin Fracture Zone shown in Figure 4 differs markedly from previously outlined trends east of the seismically active area and shows that the Albatross Cordillera crustal plate has rotated about at least two rotational poles since the Late Cretaceous. The pole as given by *Le Pichon* [1968] at 70°S, 118°E, is valid for the last 10 million years. For periods before this time, the trend of the Eltanin Fracture Zone outlined in this study suggests a pole near 62°S, 165°E.

Le Pichon [1968] and *Morgan* [1968] have shown that before 10 million years ago, the North Pacific rotated about a pole located at 79°N, 111°E. This pole represents an average of the four poles suggested by *Menard and Atwater* [1968] on the basis of changes in the trend of the fracture zones. Before 10 m.y.b.p., the rotational pole for the Albatross Cordillera plate west of the axis of the ridge was quite different from that of the North Pacific plate, indicating that these two crustal plates moved in different directions. Relative motion along the boundary between these plates should have produced an easily recognizable topographic lineation extending across the entire basin to the boundaries of the plates. This type of lineation contrasts with that of a fracture zone lying within a crustal plate system. The active transform fault extends only between the offset ridge axes, and the trace of the fracture zone, the fossil transform fault, cannot extend beyond the oldest crust generated by the cycle of sea floor spreading that produced the fracture zone [*Wilson*, 1965].

The Eltanin Fracture Zone appears as a major discontinuity in Figure 4. From Figure 10 of *Pitman et al.* [1968] and from Figure 4 of this study, it is obvious that the complete sequence of symmetrically disposed anomalies (1 through 32) following a northeasterly trend is present only south of the fracture zone. North of this boundary, northwest trending anomalies are encountered at increasingly younger areas on the flanks of the Albatross Cordillera until at 36°S, anomaly 5 is the oldest northeast trending anomaly that can be identified. These northwest trending anomalies obviously abut the east flank of the Albatross Cordillera discontinuously. On the west flank of this ridge, the discontinuity is not obvious, and the northwest trend of the lineations is poorly defined by the sparse data. However, although the age of the anomalies continues to increase to the west, the position of the anomalies requires either the presence of numerous large offsets not reflected in the magnetic lineations or topography closer to the Albatross Cordillera axis, or anomalous local changes in the spreading rates over small distances, if the anomalies are to conform to the northeast trending Albatross Cordillera system. A simpler explanation is the correlation of these anomalies with an old northwest trending system which has been interrupted by the development of the Albatross Cordillera on its western flank.

From the age sequences displayed by the two anomaly trends, the Albatross Cordillera north of the Eltanin Fracture Zone appears as a relatively recent feature that established itself on the western flank of an older northwest trending system. Possibly the area now comprising the eastern Pacific, from the Aleutian Trench to the Eltanin Fracture Zone, once rotated about a single rotational pole. Certainly there is no well-defined southern topographic boundary to the well-known anomaly set located west of North America [*Raff*, 1966]. *Herron and Talwani* [1969, and in preparation] have suggested that northwest trending lineations are found north of 30°S on both sides of the present Albatross Cordillera. The Eltanin Fracture Zone is the only major topographic feature in the South Pacific that could be the original boundary between these two old plate systems. It can possibly be traced west to the Tonga and Kermadec trenches north of New Zealand [*Hayes and Ewing*, this volume] and at least as far east as 95°W at 65°S.

The present Chile Rise is a relic of a once much larger northwest trending ridge system, and *Herron and Hayes* [1969] have indicated that northwest trending anomalies can be traced as far south as 52°S (Figure 4 of this paper). If the Eltanin Fracture Zone marks an old boundary between two crustal plates, then the anomalies south of 55°S, between 70°W and 90°W, may also be part of this northwest trending system. Several of the anomalies present in the area resemble the Late Cretaceous-early Tertiary anomalies 20 to 26, although the data are insufficient to make a definite identification. The absence of easily correlatable anomalies on adjacent tracks suggests further that this area may be highly fractured. The presence of the Scotia Ridge due east of this area also suggests that the area may be highly fractured. Geological data [*Hamilton*, 1967] indicate that the development of the ridge began during the Late Cretaceous because of relative movement between South America and West Antarctica. Detailed geophysical survey work in the eastern Pacific and in the Drake Passage may reveal the pattern of motion that generated the Scotia Ridge.

SUMMARY

The present data are quite adequate to outline the two ridge systems in the study area. However, if the history of the South Pacific is to be described in greater detail, systematic surveys of the major fracture zones and of the areas where the Albatross Cordillera and the old northwest trending ridges abut are required. In addition, study of Figure 4 shows that north of the Eltanin Fracture Zone the width of the zone containing anomalies 2 through 5 is consistently greater on the east flank of the Albatross Cordillera than on the west, and this difference increases to the north. This pattern may result because of the westward migration of the ridge axis over the past 10 m.y., or it may reflect a consistently unequal distribution of material generated by the sea floor spreading process. Until the mechanics of sea floor spreading are better understood, the origin of this asymmetry cannot be explained.

Present data over the Chile Rise suggest that the trend of the magnetic lineations generated within the past 10 m.y. is not perpendicular to that of the larger fracture zones outlined by the topography and seismicity. However, study of Figures 1 and 4 shows that no magnetic data have been collected in the seismically quiet axial zone between the Challenger Fracture Zone at 36°S and the fracture zone at 41°S. Data from this area could definitely show whether the Chile Rise strikes obliquely to the fracture zones.

Acknowledgments. The programs used in preparing Figures 2 and 3 were written at Lamont-Doherty and are outlined in a technical report by *Talwani* [1969]. All the *Eltanin* magnetic and bathymetric data for cruises 16 through 27 have been published in two technical reports edited by *Heirtzler et al.* [1969] and by *Hayes et al.* [1969]. I wish to thank A. L. Gordon, D. E. Hayes, N. D. Opdyke, and W. C. Pitman III for critically reviewing the manuscript. This research was supported by the National Science Foundation (grants GA-305, GA-175, GA-894, GA-1121, and GA-1523). Lamont-Doherty Geological Observatory contribution 1545.

REFERENCES

Barazangi, M., and J. Dorman, World seismicity maps compiled from ESSA, Coast and Geodetic Survey, epicenter data, 1961–1967, *J. Seis. Soc. Am.*, *59*, 369, 1969.

Cain, J. C., S. Hendricks, W. E. Daniels, and D. C. Jensen, Computation of the main geomagnetic field from spherical harmonic expansions, *Goddard Space Flight Center Publ. X-611-64-316*, 1964.

Cox, A., R. R. Doell, and G. B. Dalrymple, Geomagnetic polarity epochs, *Science*, *142*, 382, 1963.

Dietz, R. S., Continent and ocean basin evolution by spreading of the sea floor, *Nature*, *190*, 854, 1961.

Ewing, M., and B. C. Heezen, Some problems of Antarctic submarine geology, in *Antarctica in the International Geophysical Year, Geophys. Monograph 1*, edited by A. Crary, p. 75, American Geophysical Union, Washington, D.C., 1956.

Ewing, M., R. Houtz, and J. Ewing, South Pacific sediment distribution, *J. Geophys. Res., 74*, 2477, 1969.

Hamilton, W., Tectonics of Antarctica, *Tectonophysics, 4*, 555, 1967.

Hayes, D. E., A geophysical investigation of the Peru-Chile Trench, *Marine Geol., 4*, 309, 1966.

Hayes, D. E., J. R. Heirtzler, E. M. Herron, and W. C. Pitman III, Preliminary report of volume 21, USNS *Eltanin* cruises 22–27, January 1966–February 1967, *Tech. Rept. 2-CU-2-69*, Lamont-Doherty Geological Observatory of Columbia University, Palisades, New York, 1969.

Hayes, D. E., and M. Ewing, The Louisville Ridge—A possible extension of the Eltanin Fracture Zone, this volume.

Heezen, B. C., M. Tharp, and C. D. Hollister, Illustrations of the marine geology of the Southern Oceans, *Symposium on Antarctic Oceanography, September 13–16, 1966*, Scott Polar Research Institute, Cambridge, England, 1968.

Heirtzler, J. R., D. E. Hayes, E. M. Herron, and W. C. Pitman III, Preliminary report of volume 20, USNS *Eltanin* Cruises 16–21, January 1965–January 1966, *Tech. Rept. 3-CU-3-69*, Lamont-Doherty Geological Observatory of Columbia University, Palisades, New York, 1969.

Herron, E. M., and D. E. Hayes, A geophysical study of the Chile Ridge, *Earth Planet. Science Lett., 6*, 77, 1969.

Herron, E. M., and M. Talwani, Sea-floor spreading in the East, Central Pacific (abstract), *EOS, Trans. Amer. Geophys. Union, 50*(4), 185, 1969.

Hess, H. H., History of the ocean basins, in *Petrologic Studies, Buddington Volume*, p. 599, Geological Society of America, New York, 1962.

Isacks, B., J. Oliver, and L. R. Sykes, Seismology and the new global tectonics, *J. Geophys. Res., 73*, 5855, 1968.

Keller, G. H., and G. Peter, East-West profile from Kermadec Trench to Valparaiso, Chile, *J. Geophys. Res., 73*, 7154, 1968.

Le Pichon, X., Sea-floor spreading and continental drift, *J. Geophys. Res., 73*, 3661, 1968.

Matthews, D. J., Tables of the velocity of sound in pure water and sea water for use in echo-sounding and sound ranging, 2nd ed., 522 pp., H. M. Stationery Office, London, 1939.

Menard, H. W., *Marine Geology of the Pacific*, McGraw-Hill, New York, 1964.

Menard, H. W., and T. Atwater, Changes in the direction of sea floor spreading, *Nature, 219*, 463, 1968.

Morgan, J. W., Rises, trenches, great faults, and crustal blocks, *J. Geophys. Res., 73*, 1959, 1968.

Morgan, J. W., P. R. Vogt, and D. F. Falls, Magnetic anomalies and sea floor spreading on the Chile Rise, *Nature, 222*, 137, 1969.

Pitman, W. C., III, and J. R. Heirtzler, Magnetic anomalies over the Pacific-Antarctic Ridge, *Science, 154*, 1164, 1966.

Pitman, W. C., III, E. M. Herron, and J. R. Heirtzler, Magnetic anomalies in the Pacific and sea floor spreading, *J. Geophys. Res., 73*, 2069, 1968.

Raff, A. D., Boundaries of an area of very long magnetic anomalies in the northwest Pacific, *J. Geophys. Res., 71*, 2631, 1966.

Sykes, L. R., Mechanism of earthquakes and nature of faulting on the mid-Oceanic Ridges, *J. Geophys. Res., 72*, 2131, 1967.

Talwani, M., A computer system for the reduction, storage, and display of underwater data acquired at sea, *Tech. Rept. 1-CU-1-69*, Lamont-Doherty Geological Observatory of Columbia University, Palisades, New York, 1969.

Wilson, J. Tuzo, A new class of faults and their bearing on continental drift, *Nature, 207*, 343, 1965.

PROFILER DATA FROM THE MACQUARIE RIDGE AREA

R. Houtz, J. Ewing, and R. Embley

Lamont-Doherty Geological Observatory of Columbia University, Palisades, New York 10964

Abstract. Recently the Macquarie Ridge has come to be thought of as an island-arc system. Profiler data from the area show that, morphologically, the ridge is similar to a deep-ocean fracture zone. It also lies on the strike of the Alpine fault, a major right-lateral fault that extends the length of South Island, New Zealand. A sediment isopach map of the region shows that the mean depth to the basement surface is greater on the concave or eastern side of the ridge than it is in the Tasman Sea. East of the ridge, turbidites have filled north-south trending troughs and basins from the Solander Trough to about 60°S. Strong postdepositional faulting is recorded in the Solander Trough and at 60°S. Turbidites are not recorded in the Tasman Sea west of the Macquarie Ridge.

Introduction

The Macquarie Ridge is a complex arcuate structure that extends from South Island, New Zealand, to about 59°S where it ends on the northern flank of the Albatross Cordillera (Pacific-Antarctic Ridge). The most recent work on the ridge [*Hatherton,* 1969] concludes that it has, as far south as 51°S, 'the elements of an island-arc, or an active continental margin,' and is not a mid-ocean ridge, as judged much earlier by *Ewing and Heezen* [1956]. *Summerhayes* [1969] claims that the ridge is an island-arc system throughout its length.

The theory that the ridge is an island-arc has become possible during the past few years as a result of the publication of earthquake fault-plane solutions [*Sykes,* 1967; *Banghar and Sykes,* 1969], geomagnetic data [*Hatherton,* 1967], and seismicity studies [*Hamilton and Evison,* 1967].

Numerous profiler crossings of the ridge obtained by Lamont-Doherty personnel aboard USNS *Eltanin* and one crossing by RV *Conrad* provide enough data to draw representative sections across the ridge and to make a preliminary sediment isopach map of the region. This information is used to throw additional light on the tectonic nature of the ridge, emphasizing our results south of 51°S.

Bathymetry of the Ridge

The bathymetry used in Figure 1 has been modified after *Udintsev* [1963]. The chart in Figure 1 also shows the locations of profiler sections and the major trenches associated with the ridge. The profiler sections appear in Figures 2, 3, 4, and 5. The more detailed bathymetry of *Summerhayes* [1969] was not available when our charts were compiled.

The ridge system is characterized by at least five adjacent trenches, three of which are apparently in line to the west of the ridge. North of 56°S the western flank of the ridge falls away without interruption into the trenches. South of 56°S the ridge is separated from the western trench by a distance of about 150 km. One of the trenches at the base of the eastward flank of the ridge is partly filled with ponded sediments and has the same dimensions, in section, as the western trenches. The floors of the trenches to the west are not covered with ponded sediment. We have no profiler coverage between sections C and E in Figure 1, and the trenches to the east of the ridge are assumed to be separate. *Summerhayes* [1969] does not show a continuous trench in this area.

The central ridge is sharp and well defined to the north, diminishing to the south, and eventually disappearing near 59°S.

Seismicity of the Ridge

The work of *Hamilton and Gale* [1968] and *Dorman and Barazangi* [1969] shows that earthquake zones occur along the eastern edge of North Island and along the western edge of South Island. The zones are separated by a relatively inactive region throughout central South Island. Intermediate depth earthquakes occur east of North Island, and to a lesser extent along the western edge of southernmost South Island. The seismicity along the Macquarie Ridge is restricted to shallow-focus earthquakes. *Sykes* [1967] and *Banghar and Sykes* [1969] have inferred from fault-plane solutions that the Macquarie Ridge is characterized by

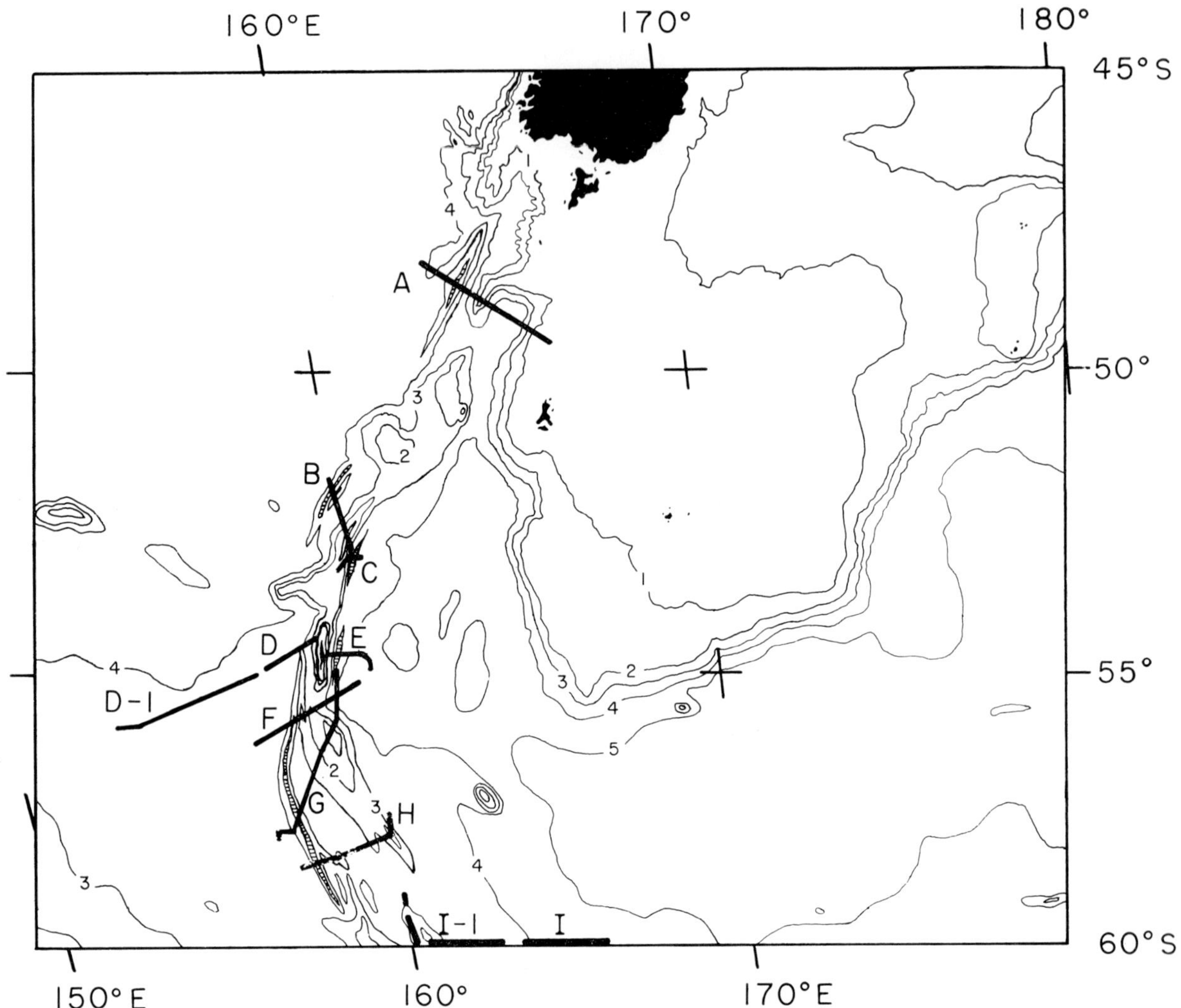

Fig. 1. Modified bathymetric chart (after *Udintsev* [1963]) showing locations of profiler sections and trenches (horizontally hatched) along the Macquarie Ridge. Contour interval is 1 km.

thrusting forces, but the compressional axes are not well determined. *Banghar and Sykes* point out that a large component of strike-slip motion cannot be ruled out. They emphasize (north of 55°S) that the ridge, unlike typical mid-ocean ridges, is under compression. The magnetic data of *Hatherton* [1967, 1969] fail to reveal the symmetric pattern of magnetic anomalies normally associated with mid-ocean ridges.

The incidence of earthquakes along the ridge is greatest in the region of 51°S, where the ridge may be offset; here there are no flanking trenches. Earthquakes are comparatively rare south of about 58°S, and it is likely that some of them are associated with the Albatross Cordillera rather than the Macquarie Ridge. To the extent that the earthquake epicenters define the location of the ridge, it is apparent from *Dorman and Barazangi*'s work that the ridge axis does not occur east of about 161°E at 60°S.

Sediment Distribution

The sediment isopach map of the region appears in Figure 6. Our profiler tracks are shown on the chart to indicate the control for contouring. The contours were extrapolated to nearby profiler crossings that pass outside the mapped area.

The thick sediments between the ridge and the Campbell Plateau are mostly land-derived turbidites and characteristically have a densely layered appearance in the profiler records. The band of thickest sediment defines an elongate basin that is roughly parallel to the Macquarie Ridge; at its northern end it is referred to as the Solander Trough. *Brodie*

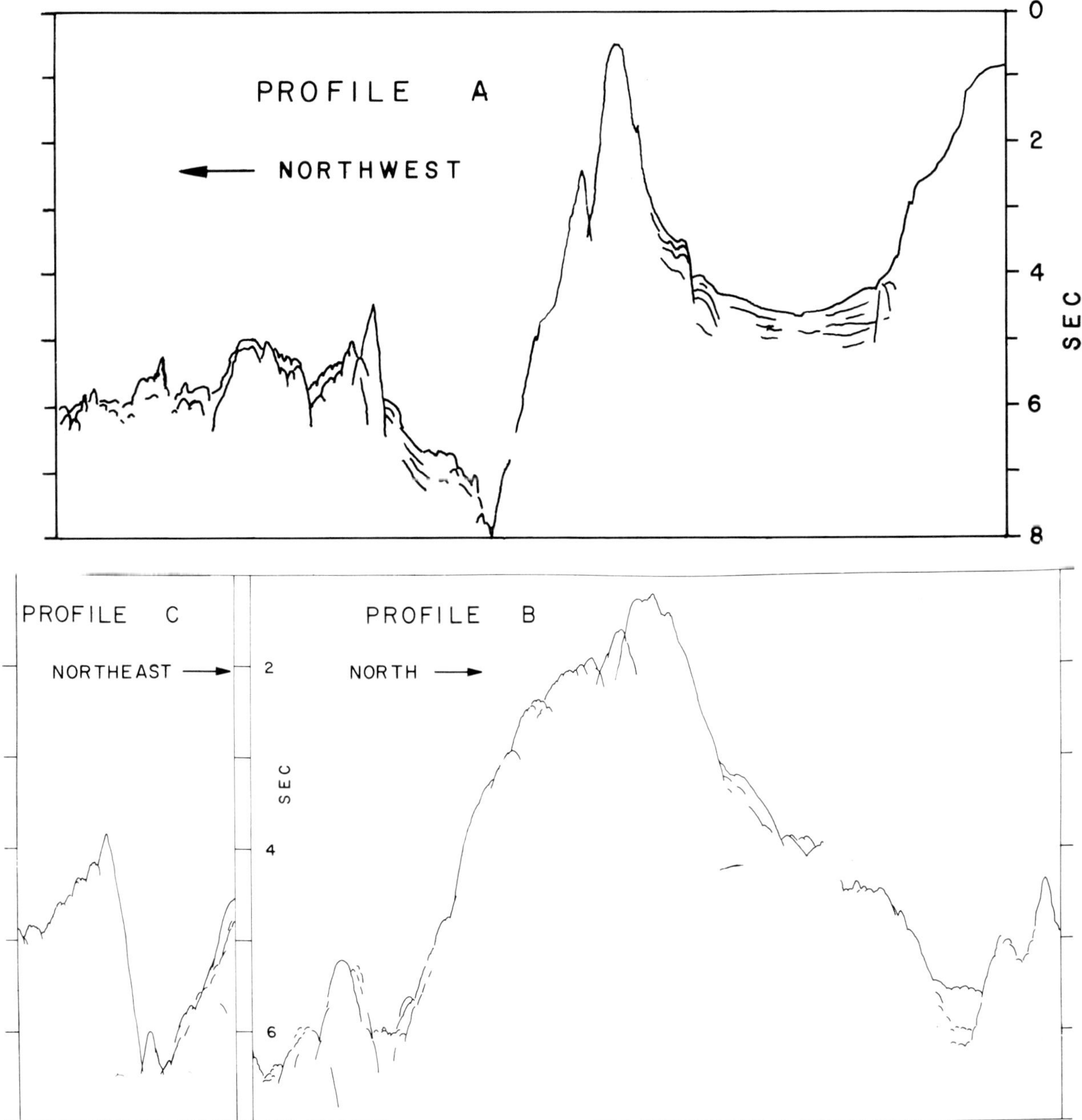

Fig. 2. Profiler sections of the Macquarie Ridge. Vertical exaggeration about 30:1.

[1958] considers the Solander Trough to be a continuation of the Waiau syncline, a mid-Tertiary fault depression. Section A (Figure 2) illustrates the faulted nature of the western edge of the trough. The basement surface in section A is masked by a thick cover of sediment in the Solander Trough; it is possible that the basement here is as deep as it is in the Tasman Sea. A Miocene core (FSU-16-4) at 55°36′S, 160°12′E, at the top of 600 meters of sediment, indicates a likely pre-Miocene age for the basin.

The Macquarie Ridge appears to separate comparatively densely layered turbidites in the east from nonlayered sediments, presumably pelagic in origin, in the west. To some extent the line drawings in sections A (Figure 2) and H (Figure 4) illustrate this difference. However, if the basin to the east of the ridge did not fill and overflow, it is not necessary to infer that the ridge existed and acted as a barrier before the turbidites were deposited. Section D-1 (Figure 3) shows a representative section of nonlayered sediments

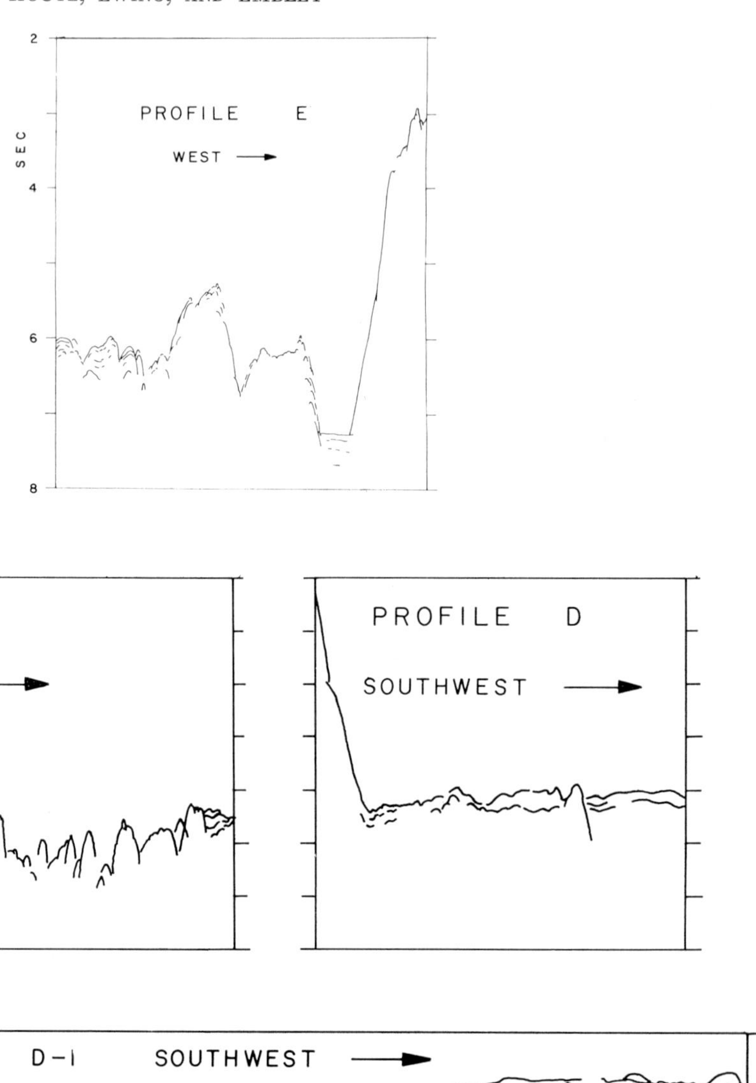

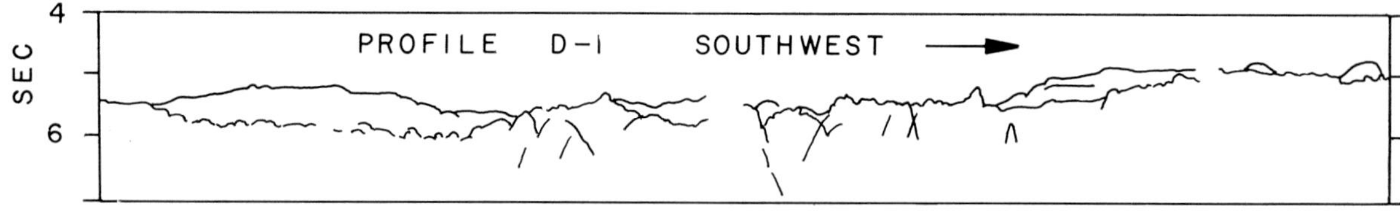

Fig. 3. Profiler sections of the Macquarie Ridge and south Tasman Sea. Vertical exaggeration about 30:1.

in the south Tasman Sea. The variable thickness can be attributed to bottom currents and possible variations in organic productivity. Note in the sections to the south that the basement surface of the Tasman Sea is actually at a shallower depth than it is to the east of the ridge.

Section I in Figure 5 shows comparatively rugged structures that are marked by deep, trench-like depressions filled with deformed, densely layered sediments. These sediments, presumably turbidites, are confined to the elevated trenches in section I and do not occur elsewhere at this latitude. Penetration to the basement surface was not achieved consistently to the north of section I, so that the trench-like features may extend to the north in an area where basement was not recorded. If they strike northeast, they are so diminished as to be undetected in the traverse that runs along the 170°E meridian. Both the epicentral and bathymetric data indicate that the trenches in section I are not associated with the main axis of the Macquarie Ridge. The ridge appears in none of our profiles south of section H.

Discussion

The band of thickest sediments to the east of the ridge in Figure 6 is composed largely of turbidites derived

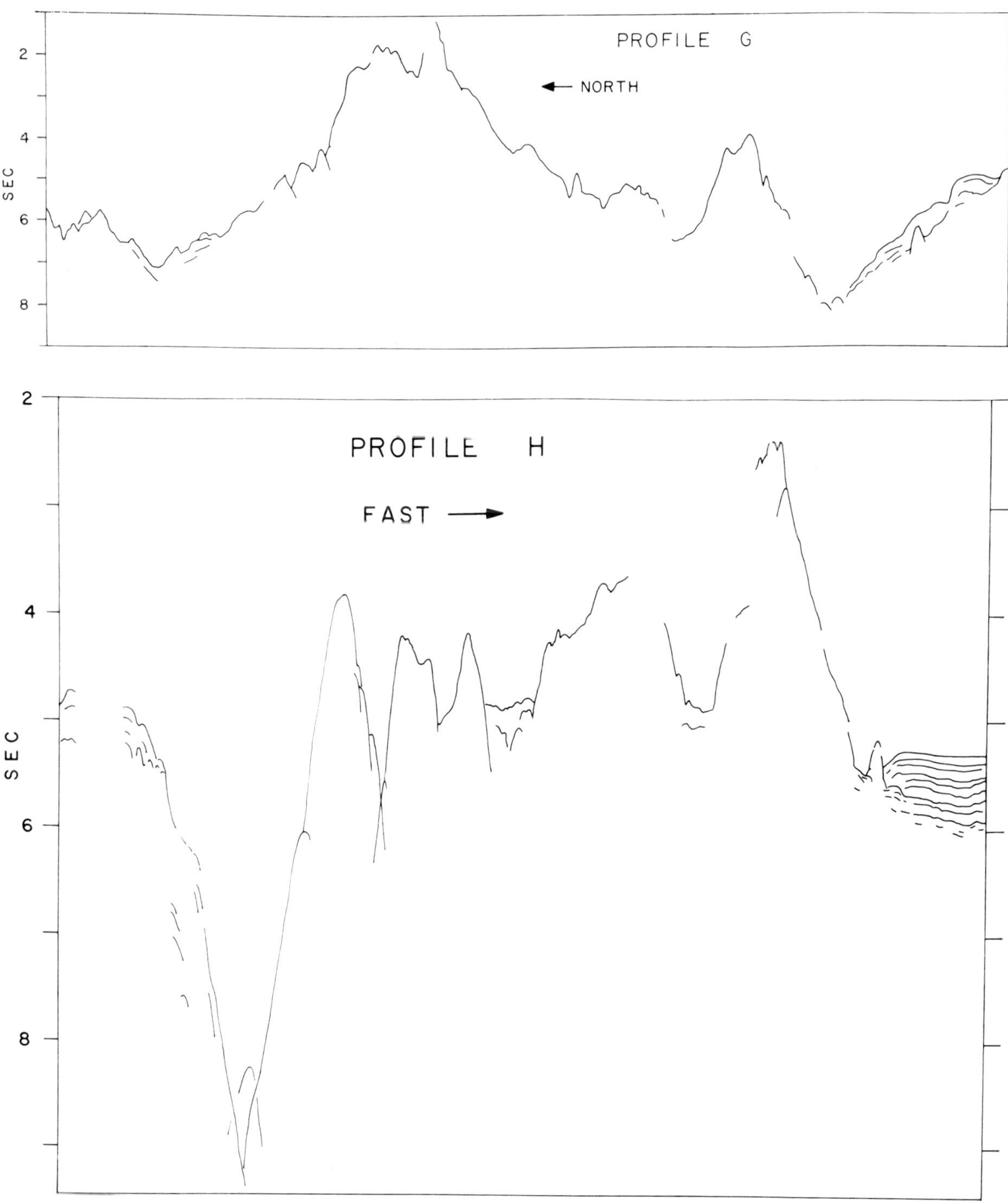

Fig. 4. Profiler sections of the Macquarie Ridge. Vertical exaggeration about 30:1.

from South Island and the Campbell Plateau. Further profiling may reveal that this feature is a continuous depression in the basement surface that extends from the Solander Trough in the north to about 59°S. The unique occurrence of turbidites in the deformed and elevated trenches in section I of Figure 5 implies that these trenches were formerly open toward the north, and may therefore be the southernmost continuation of the trough-basin system. Postdepositional faulting has clearly disturbed the west wall of the

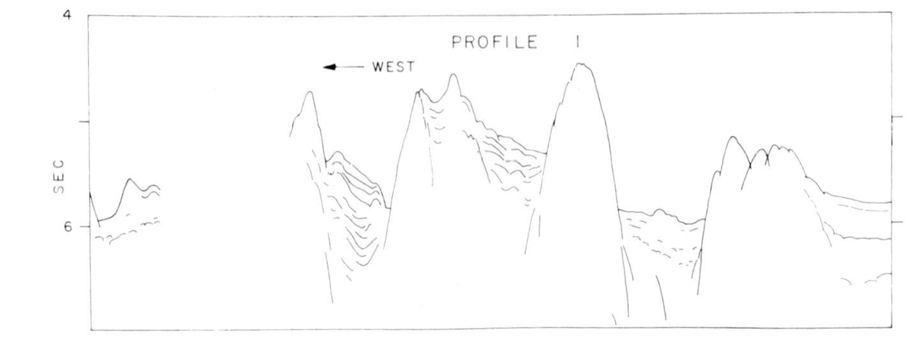

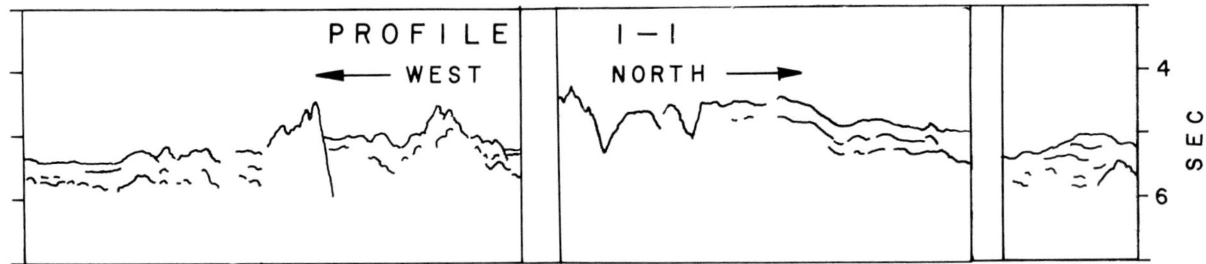

Fig. 5. Profiler sections south of the Macquarie Ridge. Vertical exaggeration about 30:1.

Solander Trough and the sediments in section I. In both sections the vertical displacement is about 750 meters.

North of 51°S, the geological and geophysical data cited by *Hatherton* [1969] led him to conclude that the Macquarie Ridge probably represents an active island-arc system. This system does not bear comparison with typical island arcs, which are on a much larger scale and define the boundary between the deep-sea and the shallower waters on the concave side of the arc. Although this relationship appears to exist in section A of Figure 2, it is at least partly accounted for by the thick cover of sediment to the east of the ridge.

South of 51°S, the sea floor east of the ridge, even with its thicker sediments, is at least as deep as the Tasman Sea. In sections F and H in Figures 3 and 4, the basement surface to the west is nearly one kilometer above the basement surface on the concave side. Our profiler data therefore show no convincing evidence that the Macquarie Ridge is an island-arc type of structure. If anything, the profiles of the ridge, especially those south of 55°S, are similar to asymmetric types of fracture zone [*Menard*, 1964]. Although the morphological evidence that the ridge is a shear zone is inconclusive, the ridge lies precisely on the strike of the Alpine fault, a major right-lateral fault that extends the length of South Island. Christoffel and Talwani (private communications) have judged that the floor of the Tasman Sea had a northern component of motion relative to the Macquarie Ridge. *Le Pichon* [1968] considers this area to be in the region of a pole of rotation, which suggests that the stress field will be variable and complex.

We suggest that the entire ridge was originally formed as a shear zone. If at some later time it experienced a change from shear to island-arc thrusting, that change probably occurred recently. If the ridge is considered to be a normal, fully developed island arc, the lack of intermediate depth earthquakes and the observation that the basement surface is lower on the concave side of the 'arc' are serious anomalies.

Acknowledgments. This work was supported by the National Science Foundation grants GA-375, GA-894, GA-1121, and GA-1523 for research aboard the USNS *Eltanin*. The RV *Conrad* was supported by the National Science Foundation GA-550, the U. S. Navy Office of Naval Research NONR 266 (48), and the Bureau of Ships NOBSR 64547. Lamont-Doherty Geological Observatory contribution 1522.

REFERENCES

Banghar, A., and L. Sykes, Focal mechanisms of earthquakes in the Indian Ocean and adjacent regions, *J. Geophys. Res., 74*(2), 632–694, 1969.

Brodie, J., The sea floor around the Solander Islands, *New Zealand J. Geol. Geophys., 1*, 419–431, 1958.

Dorman, J., and M. Barazangi, World seismicity maps compiled from ESSA, Coast and Geodetic Survey, epicenter data, 1961–1967, *Bull. Seismol. Soc. Am., 59*(1), 369–380, 1969.

Ewing, M., and B. Heezen, Some problems of antarctic submarine geology, *Antarctica in the International Geophysical Year, Geophys. Monograph 1*, edited by A. P. Crary, pp.

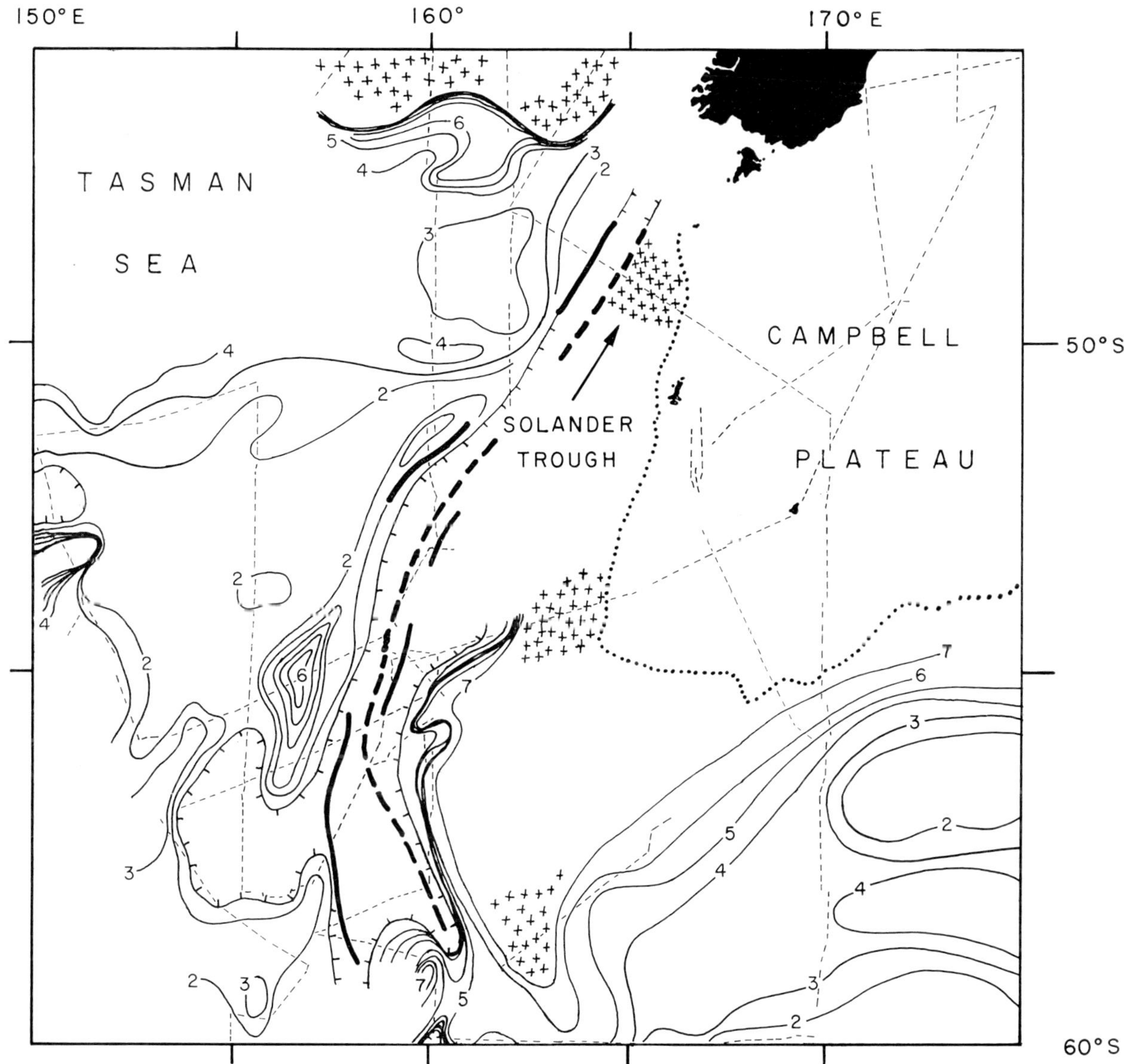

Fig. 6. Sediment isopach map of the Macquarie Ridge area. Contour interval is 0.1 sec of reflection time or about 100 meters. Heavy lines show locations of trenches, and the heavy dashed lines show the ridge crest. Profiler tracks are shown as thin dashed lines. Sediment thickness in excess of 1.0 sec are marked with small crosses.

75–81, American Geophysical Union, Washington, D.C., 1956.

Hamilton, R., and F. Evison, Earthquakes at intermediate depths in southwestern New Zealand, *New Zealand J. Geol. Geophys., 10,* 1319–1329, 1967.

Hamilton, R., and A. Gale, Seismicity and structure of the North Island, New Zealand, *J. Geophys. Res., 73*(12), 3859–3876, 1968.

Hatherton, T., Total magnetic force measurements over the north Macquarie ridge and Solander trough, *New Zealand J. Geol. Geophys., 10*(5), 1204–1211, 1967.

Hatherton, T., Geophysical anomalies over the eu- and miogeosynclinal systems of California and New Zealand, *Bull. Geol. Soc. Am., 80*(2), 213–229, 1969.

Le Pichon, X., Sea-floor spreading and continental drift, *J. Geophys. Res., 73*(12), 3661–3697, 1968.

Menard, H., *Marine Geology of the Pacific,* 271 pp., McGraw-Hill, New York, 1964.

Summerhayes, C., Marine Geology of the New Zealand sub-Antarctic seafloor, *New Zealand Oceanog. Inst. Mem. 50,* New Zealand Department of Scientific and Industrial Research, Wellington, 1969.

Sykes, L., Mechanism of earthquakes and nature of faulting on the mid-oceanic ridges, *J. Geophys. Res., 72*(8), 2131–2153, 1967.

Udintsev, G., Ed., *World Bathymetric Map, South-West Pacific Sheet,* Institute of Oceanology, Academy of Science, USSR, 1963.

LITHOLOGY AND CHEMISTRY OF SURFACE SEDIMENTS IN SUBANTARCTIC REGIONS OF THE PACIFIC OCEAN

Y. RAMMOHANROY NAYUDU

Institute of Marine Science, University of Alaska, Douglas, Alaska

Abstract. The area under investigation includes three major physiographic regions: the Southwest Pacific Basin, the Albatross Cordillera (Pacific-Antarctic Ridge), and a part of the Southeast Pacific Basin (Pacific-Antarctic Basin). Most of the Southwest Pacific Basin lies between 2500 and 3000 fm. The Albatross Cordillera and numerous scattered seamounts rise more than 1500 fm above the basin floor.

Five different sedimentary units have been defined for the area, based on the study of surface sediments from approximately 100 cores collected by the USNS *Eltanin* and others. These units are: (1) diatomaceous sediment; (2) carbonate (foraminifera-rich) sediment; (3) brown clay; (4) mixed diatom-carbonate sediment; and (5) diatomaceous clay. Surface sediments were analyzed for the major elements silicon, iron, aluminum, magnesium, calcium, sodium, potassium, titanium, manganese, phosphorus, and the trace elements cobalt, nickel, copper, and chromium. Second-degree trend surfaces of the areal distributions of these elements show broad correlation with sediment lithology. The variation in element association along two north-south lines of core stations (120°W and 145°W) also correlates with sediment lithology and suggests additional factors that control the sediment chemistry. The combined results of chemical analysis and petrographic examination suggest that biologic production, hydrography, and carbonate solution below 2500 fm were important in determining the sediment distribution. The chemical and mineralogical composition of the brown clay that covers most of the Southwest Pacific Basin indicates that submarine volcanism is also a major factor in determining the distribution of deep-sea sediments in subantarctic regions of the Pacific Ocean.

INTRODUCTION

The region under investigation lies between 120°W–180°W and 30°S–60°S. It is bounded on the east in part by the Albatross Cordillera, which trends diagonally through the area, and on the west by the Campbell Plateau. It includes most of the Southwest Pacific Basin. Two major oceanic west-east convergences transect the area: the Antarctic Convergence to the south and the Subtropical Convergence to the north. Most of the area lies between these convergences and has been referred to as the subantarctic region. It is influenced by the tropical regime to the north and the polar regime to the south.

The area is one of the least known in the South Pacific Ocean. *Murray and Renard* [1891], on the basis of a few samples collected on the Challenger Expedition, published a generalized map of the sediment distribution. *Bramlette* [1961], *Lisitzin* [1962], *Bonatti* [1963], *Goodell* [1965], and *Nayudu et al.* [1967*a*, *b*] have discussed some aspects of the sediment distribution. The distribution of clay minerals was presented by *Griffin et al.* [1968]. Most of the previous work covered limited portions or aspects of the area under discussion.

This report is based on study of the topmost sections of 119 piston and gravity core samples. Most of these cores were collected during cruises of the USNS *Eltanin* of the National Science Foundation Antarctic Programs. Additional samples were obtained through the cooperation of Scripps Institution of Oceanography. The source, location, and depth of these cores are listed in Table 1, and the geographic distribution of the cores is shown in Figure 3. This report deals with the surface sediment lithology and chemistry and discusses their relationship to the topography and oceanography. Study is in progress on significant changes at depth in these cores in order to evaluate the origin of the sediments, the paleoclimatic history, and the paleocurrent regime of this region.

BOTTOM TOPOGRAPHY

Generalized bathymetry of the area is shown in Figure 1. As there is no land above sea level within the area, base map limits extend to 115°W–165°E, 24°S–65°S, in order to provide geographic orientation and a better picture of the regional topography. On the basis of this bathymetric chart and additional data from

TABLE 1. Location and Depth of Cores

Core	Source	Latitude	Longitude	Depth, m
1	DW HG 20	19°36′ S	149°11′ W	4670
2	DW HG 23	24°19′ S	145°22′ W	4600
3	DW HG 26	28°34′ S	143°40′ W	4240
4	DW HG 34	44°13′ S	127°20′ W	4600
5	DW HG 36	45°30′ S	119°50′ W	3770
6	DW HG 37	46°03′ S	116°11′ W	3400
7	DW BG 36	26°19′ S	147°07′ W	3680
8	DW BG 38	29°43′ S	142°23′ W	4420
9	DW BG 41	32°08′ S	140°30′ W	4770
10	DW BG 46	36°23′ S	137°15′ W	4680
11	DW BG 47	36°33′ S	137°24′ W	4700
12	DW BG 56	42°16′ S	125°50′ W	4560
13	DW BG 58	43°07′ S	125°23′ W	4640
14	DW BG 59	44°23′ S	124°39′ W	4500
15	DW BG 60	45°27′ S	124°01′ W	4040
16	DW BG 61	46°44′ S	123°01′ W	4250
17	DW BG 62	47°37′ S	121°02′ W	3800
18	DW BG 63	47°50′ S	120°32′ W	3830
19	MSN 90 G	63°04′ S	178°29′ E	3583
20	MSN 91 G	64°11′ S	165°56′ W	2932
21	MSN 92 PG	63°17′ S	166°58′ W	2639
22	MSN 93 G	60°12′ S	171°32′ W	4060
23	MSN 97 G	55°39′ S	176°08′ W	5200
24	MSN 99 G	52°37′ S	178°57′ W	5200
25	MSN 100 G	51°06′ S	179°49′ E	4835
26	MSN 104 P	46°21′ S	175°14′ E	1865
27	MSN 109 PG	46°30′ S	176°46′ W	4637
28	MSN 111 G	40°37′ S	164°08′ W	5230
29	MSN 112 G	39°21′ S	163°21′ W	4840
30	MSN 113 G	38°25′ S	163°40′ W	5087
31	MSN 115 G	36°29′ S	163°09′ W	5410
32	MSN 117 G	34°09′ S	161°54′ W	5535
33	MSN 119 G	31°51′ S	161°13′ W	5250
34	MSN 121 G	29°35′ S	158°58′ W	5252
35	MSN 123 G	27°20′ S	157°31′ W	4957
36	ELT 13-20	62°01.0′S	129°47.1′W	4392
37	ELT 13-21	59°24.9′S	130°34.1′W	4132
38	ELT 13-22	58°04.9′S	130°21.3′W	4077
39	ELT 13-24	54°25.0′S	129°37.6′W	3521
40	ELT 14-1	50°01.6′S	159°42.8′W	5082
41	ELT 14-2	51°54.8′S	159°54.5′W	4738
42	ELT 14-3	53°53.8′S	159°58.8′W	4372
43	ELT 14-4	54°54.5′S	159°52.2′W	4463
44	ELT 14-5	56°12.0′S	160°32.3′W	4132
45	ELT 14-6	57°00.9′S	160°05.6′W	4612
46	ELT 14-7	58°03.1′S	160°09.0′W	4240
47	ELT 14-8	59°40.0′S	160°17.4′W	3938
48	ELT 14-9	60°47.1′S	160°12.8′W	3237
49	ELT 14-10	61°57.9′S	160°37.0′W	2300
50	ELT 14-11	62°51.9′S	159°55.2′W	2690
51	ELT 14-12	59°54.9′S	152°45.0′W	2694
52	ELT 14-13	60°01.9′S	145°16.9′W	3460
53	ELT 14-14	59°57.4′S	125°09.3′W	4747
54	ELT 14-16	58°59.3′S	125°02.0′W	4599
55	ELT 15-18	56°00.0′S	134°28.0′W	3268
56	ELT 15-19	57°06.0′S	134°41.0′W	3393
57	ELT 15-21	57°34.5′S	138°58.0′W	2952
58	ELT 15-22	56°53.0′S	139°39.0′W	2829

TABLE 1. (continued)

Core	Source	Latitude	Longitude	Depth, m
59	ELT 15-23	55°51.0′S	139°46.0′W	2890
60	ELT 15-24	56°05.0′S	144°49.0′W	2622
61	ELT 15-25	55°15.0′S	145°02.0′W	3193
62	ELT 15-26	54°02.0′S	145°18.0′W	3720
63	ELT 15-27	55°05.0′S	149°46.0′W	3450
64	ELT 15-28	56°01.0′S	149°49.0′W	3371
65	ELT 17-2	55°00.0′S	135°00.0′W	2937
66	ELT 17-3	56°01.0′S	135°01.0′W	3215
67	ELT 17-4	56°54.0′S	135°00.0′W	3331
68	ELT 17-5	58°59.0′S	135°30.0′W	3735
69	ELT 17-6	60°03.0′S	134°55.0′W	3869
70	ELT 19-15	57°08.0′S	132°36.0′W	4676
71	ELT 19-21	59°57.0′S	139°15.3′W	3934
72	ELT 19-22	61°07.0′S	140°28.2′W	3788
73	ELT 19-24	61°07.0′S	142°46.2′W	3568
74	ELT 19-26	59°01.0′S	147°36.6′W	2880
75	ELT 19-27	57°35.3′S	150°01.7′W	2862
76	ELT 20-1	47°02.0′S	144°54.0′W	4972
77	ELT 20-2	49°00.0′S	144°50.0′W	4635
78	ELT 20-3	51°06.0′S	145°03.0′W	4052
79	ELT 20-4	52°58.0′S	145°06.0′W	3766
80	ELT 20-6	58°05.0′S	144°57.0′W	3155
81	ELT 20-7	59°08.0′S	145°08.0′W	3190
82	ELT 20-8	60°10.0′S	142°33.0′W	3539
83	ELT 20-9	60°20.0′S	137°51.0′W	4342
84	ELT 20-10	60°12.0′S	127°03.0′W	4564
85	ELT 21-12	40°22.0′S	119°34.0′W	4196
86	ELT 21-13	43°59.0′S	120°03.0′W	4020
87	ELT 21-14	49°01.0′S	120°04.0′W	3382
88	ELT 21-15	52°01.0′S	120°03.0′W	3047
89	ELT 21-16	54°05.0′S	119°57.0′W	3190
90	ELT 21-17	55°29.0′S	119°56.0′W	2804
91	ELT 21-18	56°31.0′S	119°31.0′W	4676
92	ELT 21-19	56°27.0′S	119°39.0′W	4236
93	ELT 21-20	60°15.0′S	120°11.0′W	4844
94	ELT 21-21	61°09.0′S	120°17.0′W	5093
95	ELT 20-5	55°21.0′S	144°33.0′W	3440
96	ELT 24-2	39°57.0′S	150°01.0′W	5276
97	ELT 24-3	42°36.0′S	147°59.0′W	5389
98	ELT 24-4	45°01.0′S	145°17.0′W	5084
99	ELT 24-5	41°34.0′S	144°53.0′W	5530
100	ELT 24-6	40°10.0′S	144°46.0′W	5439
101	ELT 24-7	41°33.0′S	142°19.0′W	5267
102	ELT 24-8	42°53.0′S	134°38.0′W	5159
103	ELT 24-9	40°35.0′S	135°16.0′W	4979
104	ELT 24-10	37°58.0′S	134°59.0′W	4959
105	ELT 24-11	40°00.0′S	132°35.0′W	5010
106	ELT 24-12	41°59.0′S	130°00.0′W	5084
107	ELT 24-13	39°37.0′S	130°10.0′W	4893
108	ELT 24-14	39°32.0′S	127°26.0′W	4549
109	ELT 24-15	39°25.0′S	124°53.0′W	4491
110	ELT 24-16	35°13.0′S	124°59.0′W	3856
111	ELT 25-11	50°02.0′S	127°31.0′W	4057
112	ELT 25-12	60°34.0′S	127°45.0′W	4553
113	ELT 25-13	61°29.0′S	127°35.0′W	4333
114	ELT 25-14	63°00.0′S	128°13.0′W	4994
115	ELT 27-1	60°10.0′S	178°08.0′E	3404
116	ELT 33-1	60°34.6′S	171°46.8′W	3887

TABLE 1. (continued)

Core	Source	Latitude	Longitude	Depth, m
117	ELT 33-19	59°51.5′S	119°39.8′W	4476
118	ELT 33-20	59°01.6′S	119°49.0′W	4939
119	ELT 33-21	56°26.7′S	119°48.0′W	4180

DW, MSN, Scripps Institution of Oceanography; ELT, USNS *Eltanin*, National Science Foundation Antarctic Programs.

Depths adjusted according to *Matthews* [1939] tables of sounding velocities.

base map limits extend to 115°W–165°E, 24°S–65°S, *Zhivago* [1962], *Tolstikov* [1966], and bathymetric data from USNS *Eltanin* cruises, a physiographic diagram was constructed and is shown in Figure 2.

Figures 1 and 2 show that the Southwest Pacific Basin occupies the central part of the area below 2500 fm. The deeper parts of the basin are more than 3000 fm below sea level, and the total relief of the basin is more than 1500 fm. Numerous isolated seamounts are scattered throughout the area. Some of these rise more than 1500 fm above the ocean floor.

The Albatross Cordillera is a broad, subdued feature. It becomes more prominent to the east, with gentler slopes on the northern flank and steeper slopes on the southeast. There is a cluster of seamounts on the southwestern portion of the cordillera close to the intersection of another prominent structural element, the Macquarie Ridge (MacQuarrie-Balleny Ridge). In the vicinity of 60°S, 135°W, there is a change in the direction of the cordillera from almost east-west to north-south. Two prominent seamounts also occur at this locality. These seamounts seem to be a part of a major seamount chain which extends into the Southwest Pacific Basin. Projection of this trend to the southeast nearly coincides with a seamount located just east of 120°W. This northwest-trending line of

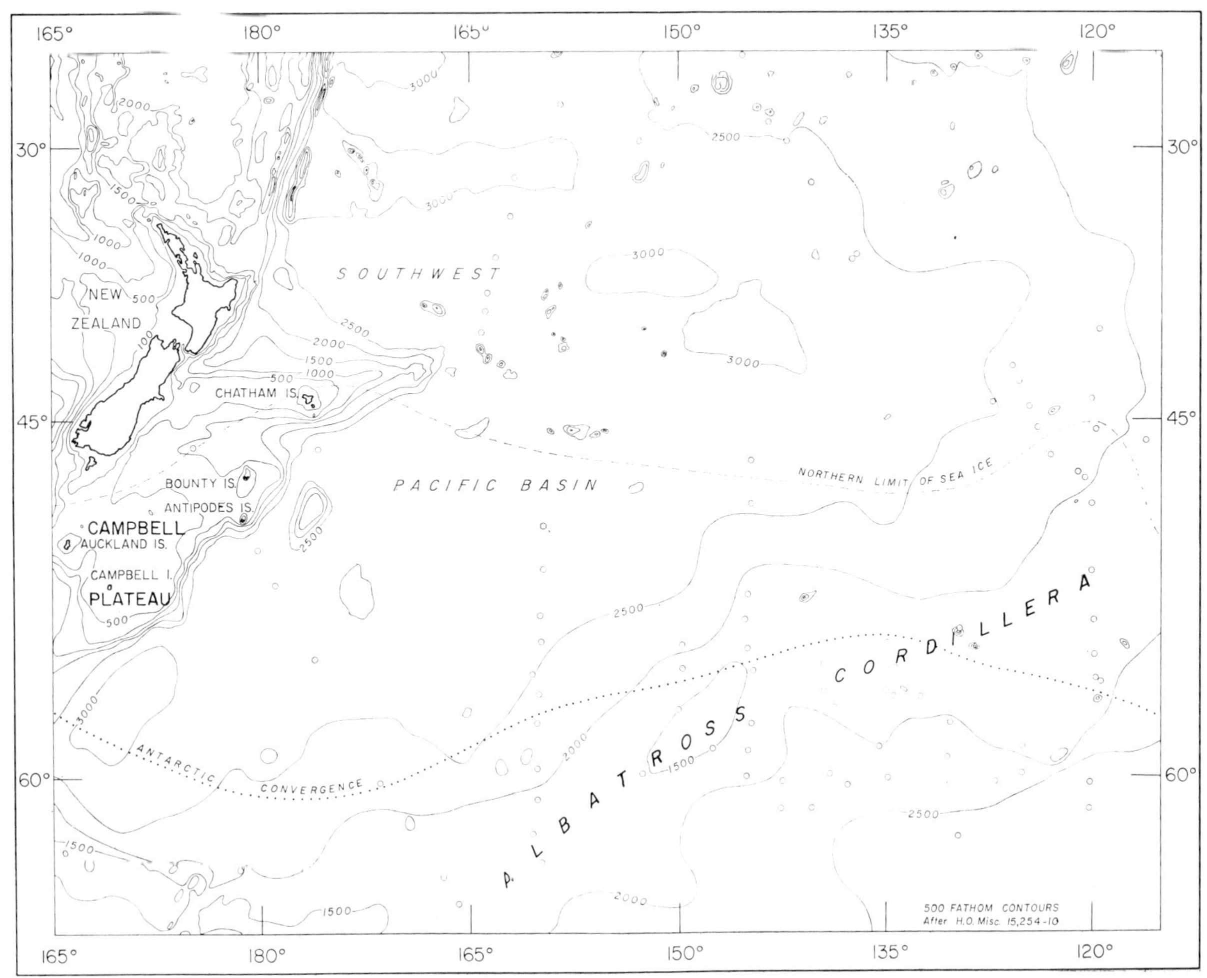

Fig. 1. Generalized bathymetric map of the subantarctic regions of the Pacific Ocean.

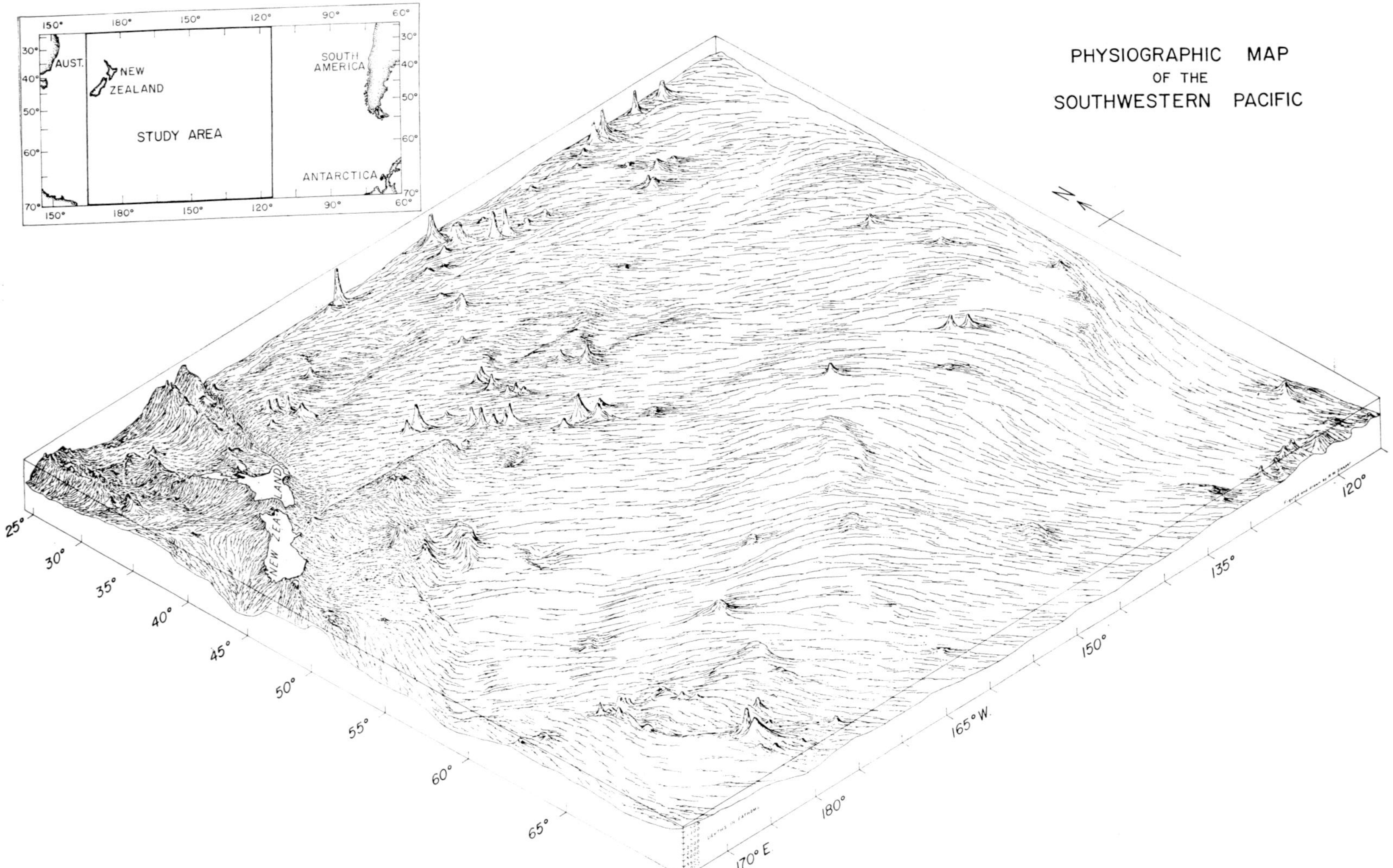

Fig. 2. Physiographic diagram of the subantarctic regions of the Pacific Ocean.

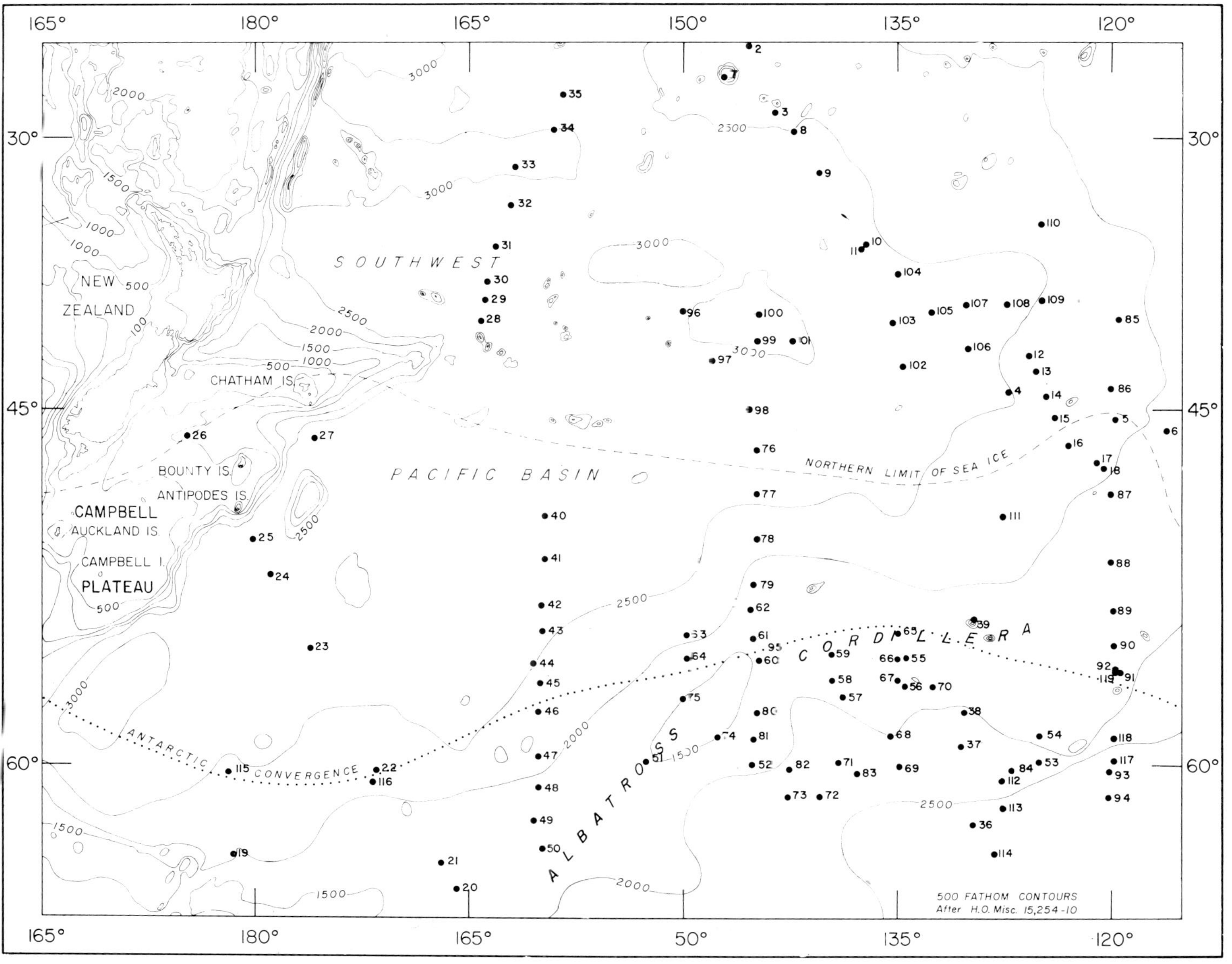

Fig. 3. Location of core samples.

seamounts may possibly represent a major transverse fracture zone.

Lithology of Surface Sediments

Samples of the top two centimeters of approximately 100 piston cores and gravity cores were studied by standard petrographic methods. On the basis of this study, five different sedimentary units have been delineated: (1) diatomaceous sediment; (2) carbonate (foraminifera-rich) sediment; (3) brown clay; (4) mixed diatom-carbonate sediment; and (5) diatomaceous clay. The areal distribution of these sediment types is shown in Figure 4. Following is a brief description of these units.

Diatomaceous Sediment

Sediment composed mostly of the remains of siliceous organisms, dominantly diatom frustules, covers the southern portion of the area as shown in Figure 4. Well-preserved and broken diatoms constitute at least 60% by volume of this sediment (Plate 1*a*). Other biogenic material includes radiolarians, silicoflagellates, sponge spicules, and up to 30% foraminifera tests. The remainder consists of brown clay and silt-size detrital minerals.

Carbonate (Foraminifera-Rich) Sediment

Carbonate sediment contains 60–70% by volume planktonic foraminifera, coccoliths, skeletal fragments of echinoderms, and unidentified carbonate fragments. This sediment covers the northern and western flank of the Albatross Cordillera and most of the Campbell Plateau (New Zealand Plateau). Brown clay, detrital minerals, and micromanganese nodules are present in increasing amounts toward the carbonate-brown clay contact.

Brown Clay

Brown clay is the second largest sedimentary unit and occupies most of the Southwest Pacific Basin. It is a complex and variable mixture of clay mineral aggregates, euhedral crystals of zeolites, relatively large proportions of detrital mineral grains, high concentrations of bone fragments, partly altered basaltic glass, and grains of palagonite (Plate 1*b*). The dominant zeolite is phillipsite (Plate 1*c*). In some samples, the zeolite content is as much as 50% of the sediment. Mineral fragments consist of pyroxene, plagioclase, and opaques. The opaques are dominantly micromanganese nodules, concentrates of which may exceed 50% of the volume of some samples (Plate 1*b*). Brown clay is transitional with other sediment types and may contain up to 30% biogenic silica and/or carbonate.

Mixed Diatom-Carbonate Sediment

This is the most extensive sedimentary unit in the area (Figure 4). It is dominantly composed of a mixture of diatoms and foraminifera in complementary proportions ranging from 30% to 70%. Southeast of the Campbell Plateau this mixed sediment includes nearly 40% by volume of mineral fragments smaller than 50 microns. These fragments are dominantly quartz and feldspar, with minor amounts of hornblende and pyroxene.

Diatomaceous Clay

East of New Zealand, between 50°S–35°S and 160°W–170°W, there is a tongue of mixed sediment containing a maximum of 40% diatoms and 60% or more brown clay (Figure 4). North of 40°S, the diatomaceous clay contains volcanic glass (cores 28–32). The refractive index of the glass is approximately 1.525. The glass content of this sediment reaches a maximum of 50% in core 29 and diminishes to the north. This sediment also contains high proportions of sodic plagioclase and altered mafic minerals.

Chemistry of Surface Sediment

Systematic study of the chemical composition of surface sediment was initiated in 1967. A portion of the topmost two centimeters of each core was selected for chemical analyses, with the exception of nine cores (10, 14, 20, 27, 30, 42, 45, 62, 67). For these cores, the highest available interval was taken. The absence of major lithologic changes in the upper 20–30 cm of cores from this region permitted substitution of a lower interval.

These samples were analyzed, using a Perkin-Elmer model 303 atomic absorption spectrometer for aluminum, iron, titanium, manganese, calcium, magnesium, sodium, potassium, and the trace elements cobalt, copper, nickel, chromium, and strontium. Silicon and phosphorus were determined by colorimetrically following the methods described by *Jackson* [1958], modified by an isobutanol separation to counteract the interference of iron in the phosphorus determination. The results of chemical analysis are given in Table 2.

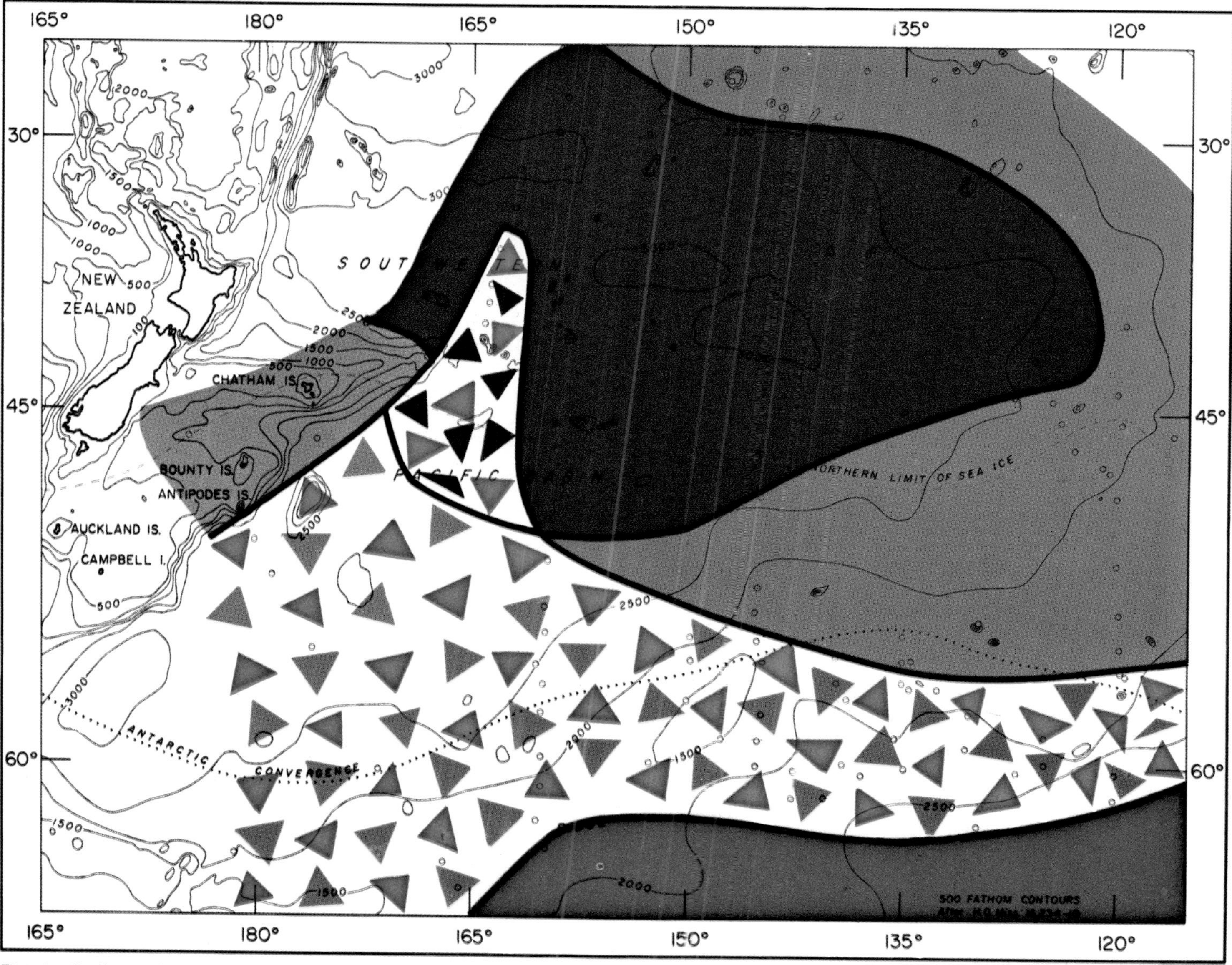

Fig. 4. Surface sediment distribution in the subantarctic regions of the Pacific Ocean. Diatomaceous sediment is shown in green, carbonate sediment (foraminifera-rich) is designated by orange, brown color denotes brown clay, and areas of mixed sediment are shown by combinations of these colors.

Trend-Surface Analysis

In order to evaluate better the regional distribution of element abundances, the data were subjected to trend surface analysis. A Fortran 4 program, written by *Heiner and Geller* [1967] for the IBM 360, model 40 computer, was used. This program was written to facilitate an understanding of various types of geologic, geochemical, geophysical and other data, through the use of trend surface analysis. Polynomial surfaces are fitted to data, which are expressed in x, y, z form; x and y represent map coordinates measured from some arbitrary origin; z, the dependent variable, represents the quantity of indicator element in each sample. The program is designed to calculate trend surfaces from the first through the sixth degree. The first-degree surface is a plane and contains only linear terms. The generalized second-degree surfaces contain both quadratic and linear terms and are either positive or negative bowl-shaped paraboloids. As the degree increases, all terms of the previous degree are included, as the program does not have the ability to exclude any of them. The least-squares method is used to fit a given surface, the objective being to make the sum of squared residual values the least possible. When a trend surface of given order is fitted in this manner, its shape and position are unique in that no other configuration will satisfy the least-squares criterion. A trend surface fitted by least squares passes below some data points and above others. The difference between the trend surface and actual surface is termed the residual and may be either positive or negative. Hence, regional trends of data with anomalous highs and lows eliminated may be contoured and mapped. The original data, along with contours of the second-degree trend surfaces, are shown in Figures 5–17.

The main objective of such analysis is to help to evaluate the correlation between element distribution and sediment type, which should lead to a better understanding of the processes responsible for the observed sediment distribution.

Comparison of the sediment distribution map (Figure 4) with elemental distributions shown in Figures 5–17 shows broad agreement. Biogenic calcium carbonate seems to control the main features of the calcium distribution, which shows higher values to the northeast and lower values to the northwest and south. Similarly, the silica distribution reflects the combined effects of diatomaceous sediment to the south and relatively high silicon content of brown clay to the northwest. The trends of aluminum, magnesium, and potassium (Figures 7, 8, 11) exhibit over-all decreases to the southeast. This is probably due to the lower clay content of sediment in the southeastern part of the area. Consideration of the composition of the main sedimentary components, calcium carbonate, opaline silica, and clay minerals, indicates that sodium would be expected to have a distribution similar to those of aluminum, magnesium, and potassium. However, comparison of Figures 6, 7, 8, and 9 reveals the influence of other factors. Inspection of the actual sodium values and examination of sediment lithology suggest that the sodium trend is probably affected by the presence of sodium-rich plagioclase and other minerals in sediment adjacent to New Zealand.

The manganese trend (Figure 13) shows a high in the Southwest Pacific Basin, as do the trends of chromium, cobalt, nickel, and copper (Figures 14, 15, 16, 17). Iron might be expected to have a similar regional trend, due to the common association of iron and manganese in micromanganese nodules. Instead, it shows a regional maximum approximately midway between the higher values of magnesium, potassium, aluminum, and those of manganese, cobalt, nickel, and chromium, which may be due to the partition of iron between brown clay and ferromanganese minerals.

Element Associations near 120°W and 145°W

In order to examine the variation of two or more elements simultaneously and to compare elemental abundances as a function of their geographic distri-

Plate 1

a. Photomicrograph of typical diatomaceous sediment, showing well-preserved diatoms, radiolarians, spines, and spicules. Polarized light ×360.

b. Photomicrograph of brown clay greater than 32 μ size, showing zeolite crystals, opaque ferromanganese oxide aggregates, and fish bone debris. Polarized light ×600.

c. Photomicrograph of typically twinned and euhedral zeolite crystals, showing concentration of ferromanganese oxides in the twinned crystals. Polarized light ×360.

d. Photomicrograph of zeolite showing specks of yellowish-brown palagonite and opaques within the crystal; opaque aggregates and zeolite crystals suggest genetic relationship to palagonite; also note fish tooth at the left. Polarized light ×1000.

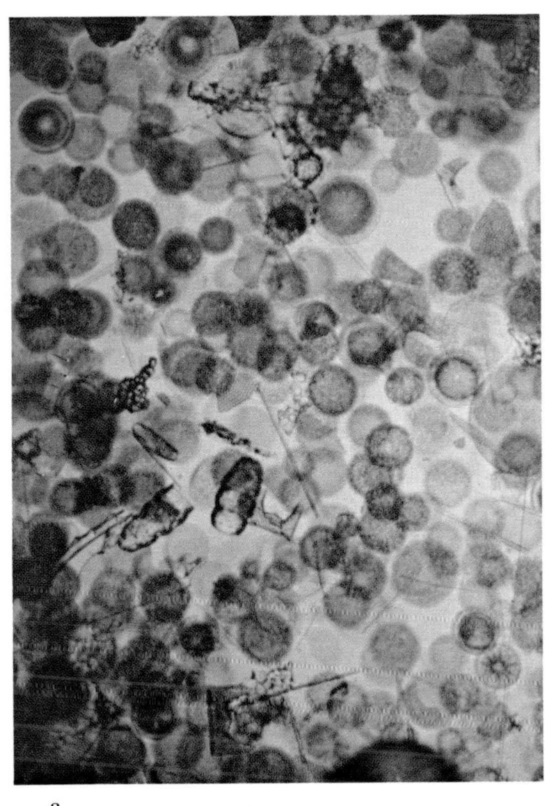
a

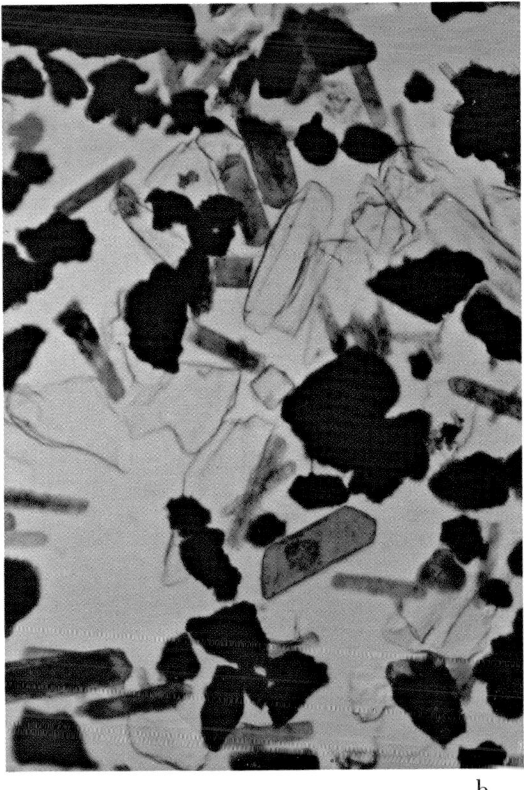
b

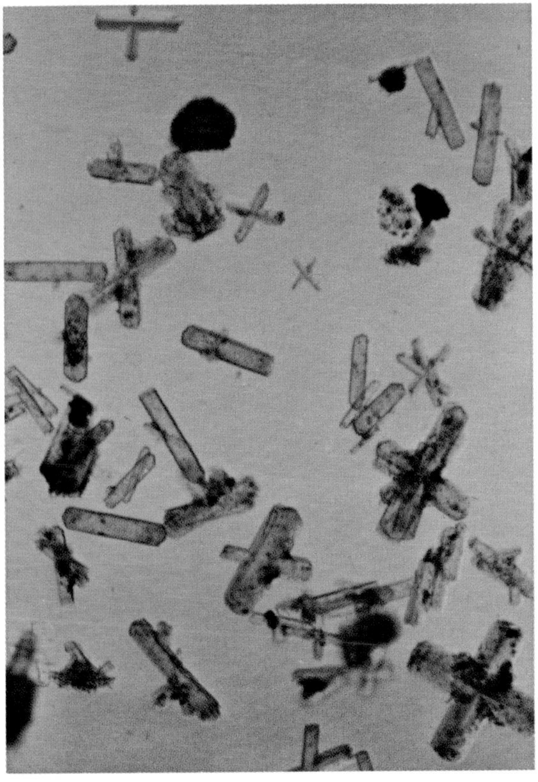
c

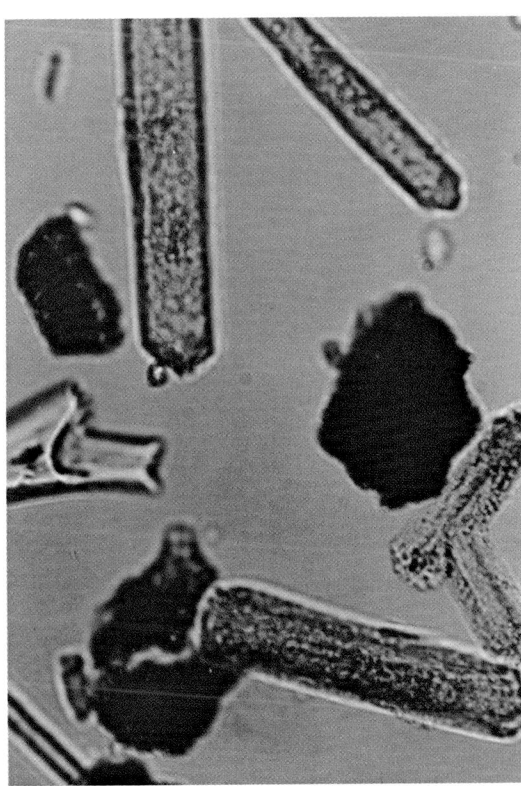
d

TABLE 2. Chemical Analyses of Surface Sediments

Intervals used for analyses appear beneath core numbers.

	Core 3 0–2 cm	Core 9 0–2 cm	Core 10 3–5 cm	Core 13 0–2 cm	Core 14 5–9 cm	Core 19 0–2 cm	Core 20 10–11 cm	Core 21 0–2 cm	Core 22 0–2 cm
Si, wt %	6.88	15.51	16.30	18.00	9.20	20.10	21.90	27.40	27.00
Fe, wt %	6.75	9.10	7.95	4.63	3.70	0.56	6.70	1.58	1.45
Al, wt %	3.58	5.06	6.21	4.34	2.81	1.18	4.76	0.80	1.41
Mg, wt %	1.15	1.38	0.97	1.22	0.83	0.74	1.81	0.70	0.90
Ca, wt %	19.13	3.01	11.90	12.55	22.10	14.21	6.10	6.05	11.30
Na, wt %	2.36	3.68	2.76	5.48	4.02	3.36	3.11	3.77	4.68
K, wt %	0.90	1.88	2.16	1.80	1.18	0.40	1.42	0.98	0.70
Ti, wt %	0.76	0.36	0.30	0.13	0.15	0.03	0.72	0.0002	0.002
P, wt %	0.32	1.02	0.22	0.22	0.42			0.02	0.02
Mn, wt %	0.60	3.06	1.50	0.92	2.88	0.07	4.28	0.14	0.16
Cr, ppm	475	20	0	225	185	24	78	4	4
Co, ppm	100	266	132	174	280	0	301	0	0
Ni, ppm	50	1126	455	605	1630	20	1720	28	68
Cu, ppm	390	768	470	524	846	70	808	150	118

	Core 23 0–2 cm	Core 24 0–2 cm	Core 25 0–2 cm	Core 26 0–1 cm	Core 27 8–10 cm	Core 28 0–2 cm	Core 29 0–2 cm	Core 30 8–10 cm	Core 31 0–2 cm
Si, wt %	26.00	24.70	18.80	8.45	23.00	29.10	26.30	23.70	23.70
Fe, wt %	7.05	6.00	5.45	0.80	4.78	6.72	5.05	5.82	6.48
Al, wt %	8.40	7.09	6.12	2.78	6.78	8.36	7.52	7.56	8.44
Mg, wt %	2.30	2.98	3.00	0.64	1.64	1.90	1.62	2.02	1.87
Ca, wt %	2.80	3.25	7.62	27.70	8.66	2.25	3.60	2.20	1.85
Na, wt %	3.82	3.50	3.52	1.90	3.47	3.50	3.43	4.05	4.11
K, wt %	2.35	1.52	1.30	0.70	1.85	3.25	2.48	2.58	3.18
Ti, wt %	0.28	0.66	0.51	0.12	0.43	0.40	0.44	0.44	0.48
P, wt %	0.05					0.05			0.05
Mn, wt %	0.48	0.28	0.24	0.03	0.06	0.48	0.27	0.25	0.47
Cr, ppm	26	124	148	32	90	46	56	69	50
Co, ppm	0	11	19	6	4	59	41	43	31
Ni, ppm	84	95	115	85	75	74	185	145	154
Cu, ppm	304	134	144	86	128	191	210	182	188

	Core 32 0–2 cm	Core 33 0–2 cm	Core 35 0–2 cm	Core 38 0–3 cm	Core 39 0–3 cm	Core 40 0–5 cm	Core 41 0–3 cm	Core 42 13–15 cm	Core 43 0–3 cm
Si, wt %	22.30	25.80	18.70	16.05	3.20	26.50	20.10	22.40	25.80
Fe, wt %	6.70	7.55	9.68	0.79	0.49	5.98	4.30	3.25	3.12
Al, wt %	7.67	8.90	7.05	1.03	1.20	7.65	5.65	4.20	4.57
Mg, wt %	2.38	1.93	2.26	0.46	0.43	1.06	1.32	1.14	1.22
Ca, wt %	2.08	2.30	5.38	19.94	34.25	0.80	8.70	7.80	7.40
Na, wt %	3.88	4.06	3.34	2.61	2.30	3.57	2.75	2.40	2.86
K, wt %	2.40	3.12	2.28	0.35	0.27	2.39	1.84	1.52	1.53
Ti, wt %	0.51	0.56	0.65	0.10	0.10	0.49	0.36	0.26	0.31
P, wt %	0.05	0.08		0.01	0.02	0.03	0.03	0.02	0.02
Mn, wt %	0.70	0.59	3.80	0.08	0.04	0.30	0.25	0.22	0.35
Cr, ppm	76	31	72	32	18	163	147	106	122
Co, ppm	80	102	563	19	10	100	80	100	75
Ni, ppm	215	150	1735	39	50	265	215	220	280
Cu, ppm	200	236	793	108	62	220	135	175	125

TABLE 2. (continued)

	Core 44 0–4 cm	Core 45 5–7 cm	Core 46 0–6 cm	Core 47 0–3 cm	Core 48 0–20 cm	Core 49 0–2 cm	Core 50 0–3 cm	Core 51 0–3 cm	Core 52 0–2 cm
Si, wt %	27.50	30.00	33.10	32.20	16.62	8.76	14.25	6.96	26.90
Fe, wt %	2.28	2.55	1.07	0.74	1.90	2.02	4.41	1.50	1.55
Al, wt %	2.88	1.70	1.43	0.88	2.53	1.78	2.62	1.02	0.97
Mg, wt %	1.08	0.75	0.74	0.54	0.78	0.76	0.68	0.55	0.34
Ca, wt %	5.30	7.30	6.80	5.50	16.94	25.94	17.06	29.06	11.45
Na, wt %	3.56	3.48	3.60	2.70	3.32	2.30	2.34	2.38	4.14
K, wt %	1.23	0.61	0.76	0.55	0.91	0.44	0.98	0.32	0.07
Ti, wt %	0.16	0.06	0.08	0.04	0.22	0.30	0.38	0.10	0.10
P, wt %	0.01	0.02	0.01	0.01	0.02	0.06	0.07	0.07	0.003
Mn, wt %	0.18	0.30	0.88	0.04	0.40	1.26	2.20	0.58	0.06
Cr, ppm	125	135	114	134	31	28	26	18	65
Co, ppm	75	245	60	70	51	105	255	35	250
Ni, ppm	210	220	230	245	118	573	385	263	190
Cu, ppm	215	290	145	270	201	349	302	264	465

	Core 54 0–10 cm	Core 58 0–3 cm	Core 60 0–2 cm	Core 62 12–16 cm	Core 64 0–3 cm	Core 65 0–10 cm	Core 66 10–12 cm	Core 67 0–4 cm	Core 68 0–3 cm
Si, wt %	29.70	8.44	19.10	12.94	26.62	9.70	15.31	7.78	34.60
Fe, wt %	1.09	0.95	4.35	3.06	0.50	16.00	0.90	2.82	0.65
Al, wt %	1.20	0.93	1.21	3.80	0.58	1.78	1.13	2.00	0.63
Mg, wt %	0.77	0.62	0.38	1.32	0.39	1.14	0.36	0.36	0.59
Ca, wt %	5.39	32.30	20.05	15.28	15.97	2.35	31.90	32.50	13.52
Na, wt %	4.18	0.15	2.60	3.11	2.90	2.03	1.36	1.54	3.36
K, wt %	0.56	0.37	0.22	1.36	0.24	0.57	0.64	0.42	0.57
Ti, wt %	0.12	0.06	0.07	0.32	0.06	0.50	0.09	0.01	0.00
P, wt %	0.01	0.01	0.003	0.09	0.01	0.10	0.01	0.005	0.02
Mn, wt %	0.12	0.10	0.11	1.58	0.08	19.50	0.07	0.06	0.16
Cr, ppm	4	115	245	26	2	450	141	88	224
Co, ppm	14	110	625	118	15	1915	90	70	80
Ni, ppm	41	250	325	1050	35	9210	230	160	400
Cu, ppm	109	75	395	1294	103	2140	120	70	170

	Core 69 0–2 cm	Core 71 0–3 cm	Core 73 0–3 cm	Core 76 0–10 cm	Core 77 15–18 cm	Core 78 0–7 cm	Core 79 0–5 cm	Core 80 0–5 cm	Core 81 0–2 cm
Si, wt %	23.08	32.50	34.30	24.60	7.60	7.20	25.00	27.50	18.50
Fe, wt %	0.78	0.88	1.88	6.55	1.83	2.92	13.28	5.22	15.08
Al, wt %	1.10	0.52	2.34	8.89	2.10	1.73	2.72	3.89	0.96
Mg, wt %	0.52	0.59	0.76	2.22	0.45	0.50	0.81	0.78	0.53
Ca, wt %	15.16	8.00	2.26	1.30	34.85	28.80	3.25	3.60	7.25
Na, wt %	3.10	3.02	3.03	2.63	2.34	1.52	2.65	2.40	2.76
K, wt %	0.45	0.56	0.90	0.40	0.55	0.14	0.28	0.26	0.14
Ti, wt %	0.10	0.02	0.19	0.40	0.10	0.04	0.26	0.17	0.50
P, wt %	0.02	0.01	0.03	0.03	0.01	0.01	0.05	0.003	0.07
Mn, wt %	0.06	0.10	0.12	2.22	0.09	0.12	20.68	0.14	6.58
Cr, ppm	6	352	21	85	70	170	90	185	125
Co, ppm	4	140	20	400	13	215	1545	185	1445
Ni, ppm	38	160	54	1145	52	315	9055	225	870
Cu, ppm	97	260	182	1290	194	145	5415	330	330

TABLE 2. (continued)

	Core 85 0–3 cm	Core 86 0–2 cm	Core 87 0–2 cm	Core 88 0–3 cm	Core 89 0–3 cm	Core 90 0–2 cm	Core 91 0–3 cm	Core 93 0–2 cm	Core 99 0–4 cm
Si, wt %	6.26	1.19	1.18	1.78	3.13	1.63	23.40	35.20	22.06
Fe, wt %	3.60	0.34	0.48	0.49	0.51	0.42	0.81	0.68	5.30
Al, wt %	2.46	0.72	0.56	0.64	0.56	0.55	1.66	0.68	7.84
Mg, wt %	0.78	0.26	0.22	0.23	0.38	0.30	0.59	0.50	1.82
Ca, wt %	24.25	34.84	36.20	35.78	33.70	34.50	13.10	0.30	0.89
Na, wt %	3.34	2.34	2.18	2.22	1.43	1.76	2.26	3.22	4.78
K, wt %	0.96	0.18	0.29	0.14	0.32	0.34	0.40	0.28	2.36
Ti, wt %	0.22	0.05	0.00	0.04	0.01	0.004	0.05	0.01	0.51
P, wt %	0.12	0.01	0.01	0.04	0.01	0.01	0.02	0.02	0.03
Mn, wt %	2.01	0.07	0.02	0.02	0.03	0.04	0.76	0.38	0.64
Cr, ppm	9	4	106	12	90	178	0	10	52
Co, ppm	161	20	90	5	80	70	24	0	118
Ni, ppm	1044	56	180	42	100	140	220	400	167
Cu, ppm	594	74	125	65	70	65	152	152	246
Sr, ppm	985	1358	1133	1184	1007	1040	180	0	

bution, graphs of the element content were constructed along 120°W and 145°W (Figure 18).

Cores taken near 120°W between 40°S and 60°S include nearly pure carbonate sediment, diatomaceous sediment, and mixed sediment. Toward the northern end of this line of cores, the sediment contains increasing amounts of brown clay. Graphs of element associations along this line are shown in Figures 19 to 23. Biogenic silica accounts for most of the silicon content (Figure 19) in the two southernmost cores, 93 and 91. In the two northernmost cores, 86 and 85, it is due to an increase in clay mineral content.

Calcium (Figure 19) is nearly constant along much of this traverse, primarily owing to high concentrations of planktonic foraminifera and coccoliths. South of 55°S, calcium decreases sharply, owing to replacement of biogenic carbonate as the major sediment component by diatoms and radiolarians. The strontium distribution in these sediments is probably a function of the proportion of biogenic calcium carbonate, as can be seen by comparison of calcium and strontium trends (Figures 19, 23).

Aluminum (Figure 19) ranges from approximately 0.5% to 2.5% in these cores. In general, this is a reflection of the increasing clay content toward the north. Minor fluctuations of aluminum are shared by iron, manganese, magnesium, and, to a lesser extent, potassium (Figures 20, 21). The over-all trend of sodium is generally similar to the variations between 45°S and 55°S, which are more or less paralleled by similar fluctuations in nickel and copper as far south as 56°S, where the association breaks down. Trace elements cobalt, nickel, and copper, which are usually associated with manganese minerals, here do not exhibit a close correlation with manganese. Iron, which may be associated with either clay minerals or manganese minerals, shows no clear association with either, but is grossly similar in variation and absolute amount to aluminum.

Titanium and phosphorus (Figure 21) show a strong correlation, and this similarity of trends is shared by iron and manganese, except in sample 88.

Samples taken along 145°W between 30°S and 60°S include diatomaceous sediment from the southernmost part of this region, mixed carbonate-diatomaceous sediment over the Albatross Cordillera, brown clay with zeolites in the central Southwest Pacific Basin, and carbonate-clay sediment in the northern part of the basin. Graphs of element association near 145°W are shown in Figures 24 to 29.

Calcium varies inversely with silicon and aluminum along this line of cores (Figure 24), owing to relative dilution of biogenic silica and brown clay with biogenic calcium carbonate. In general, no other element follows the calcium trend except chromium in some cores (Figure 29). Magnesium and potassium tend to follow aluminum (Figures 24, 25), all of which are probably controlled by the clay mineral content.

Sodium (Figure 25) would be expected to be related to the clay mineral content. However, it shows little relationship to the fluctuations of magnesium, potassium, and aluminum and, instead, maintains a relatively stable percentage in all these samples. This

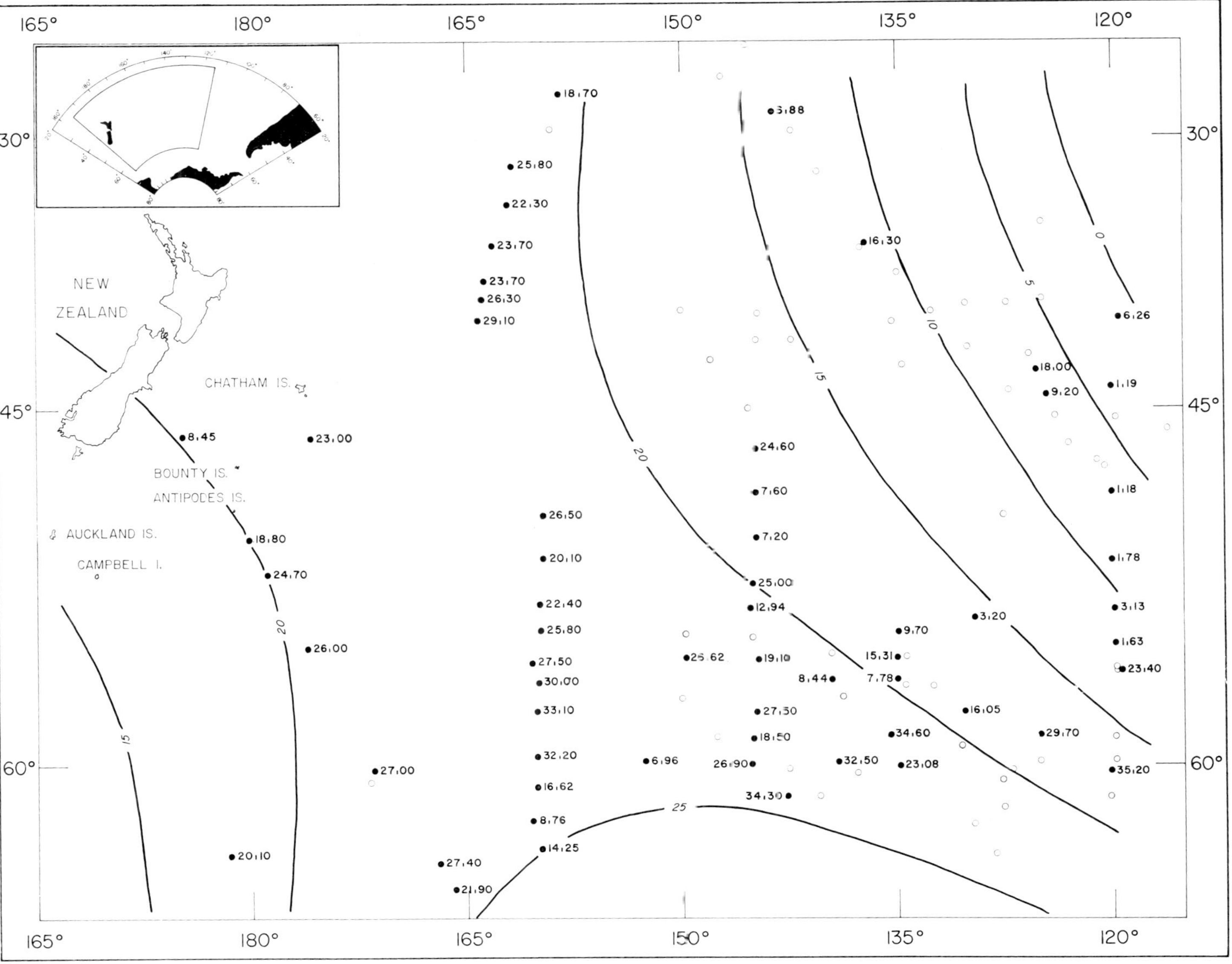

Fig. 5. Silicon in surface sediment of the subantarctic regions of the Pacific Ocean with contours of the second-degree trend surface. Silicon values are in weight per cent. Contour interval is 5.0%.

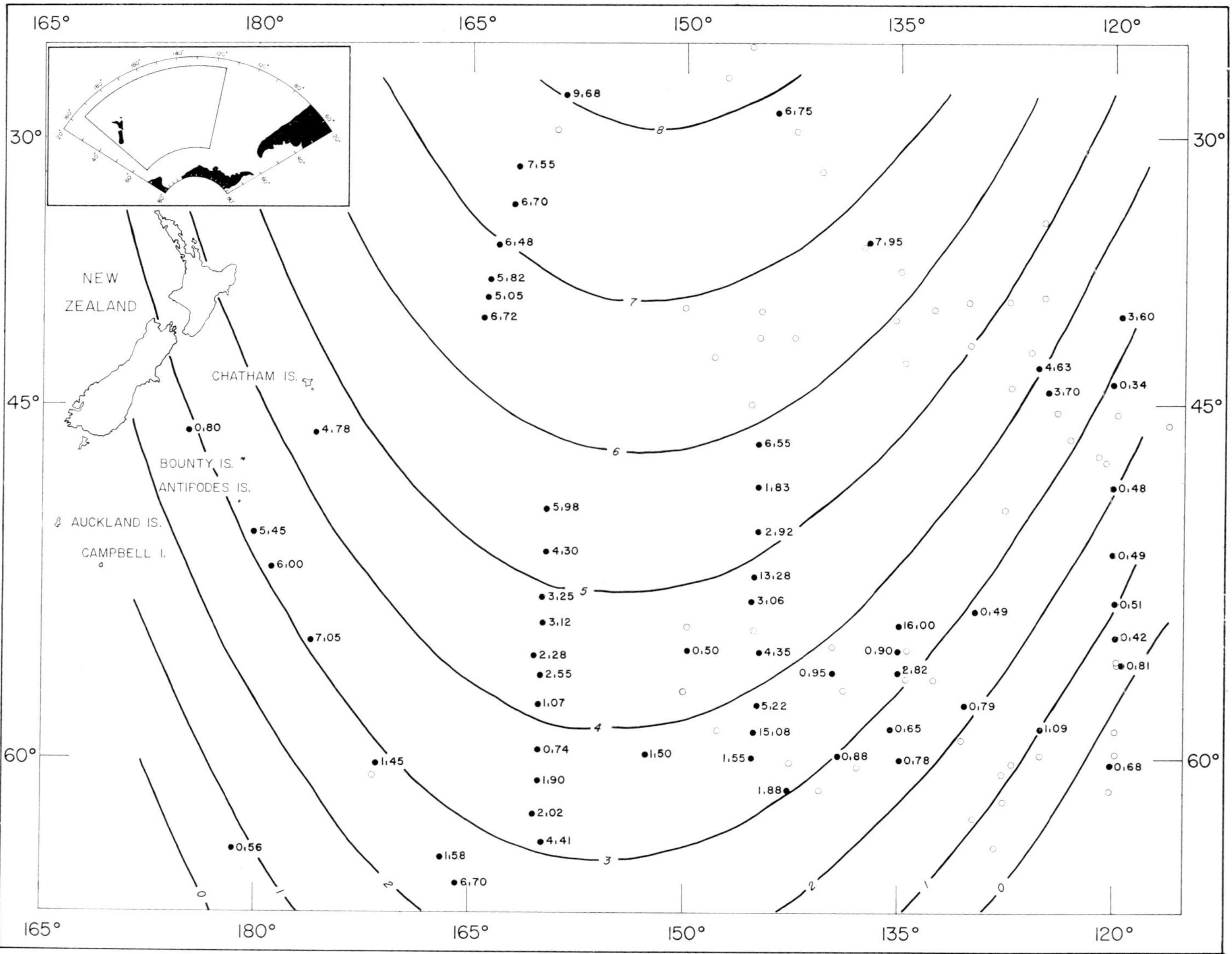

Fig. 6. Iron in surface sediment of the subantarctic regions of the Pacific Ocean with contours of the second-degree trend surface. Iron values are in weight per cent. Contour interval is 1.0%.

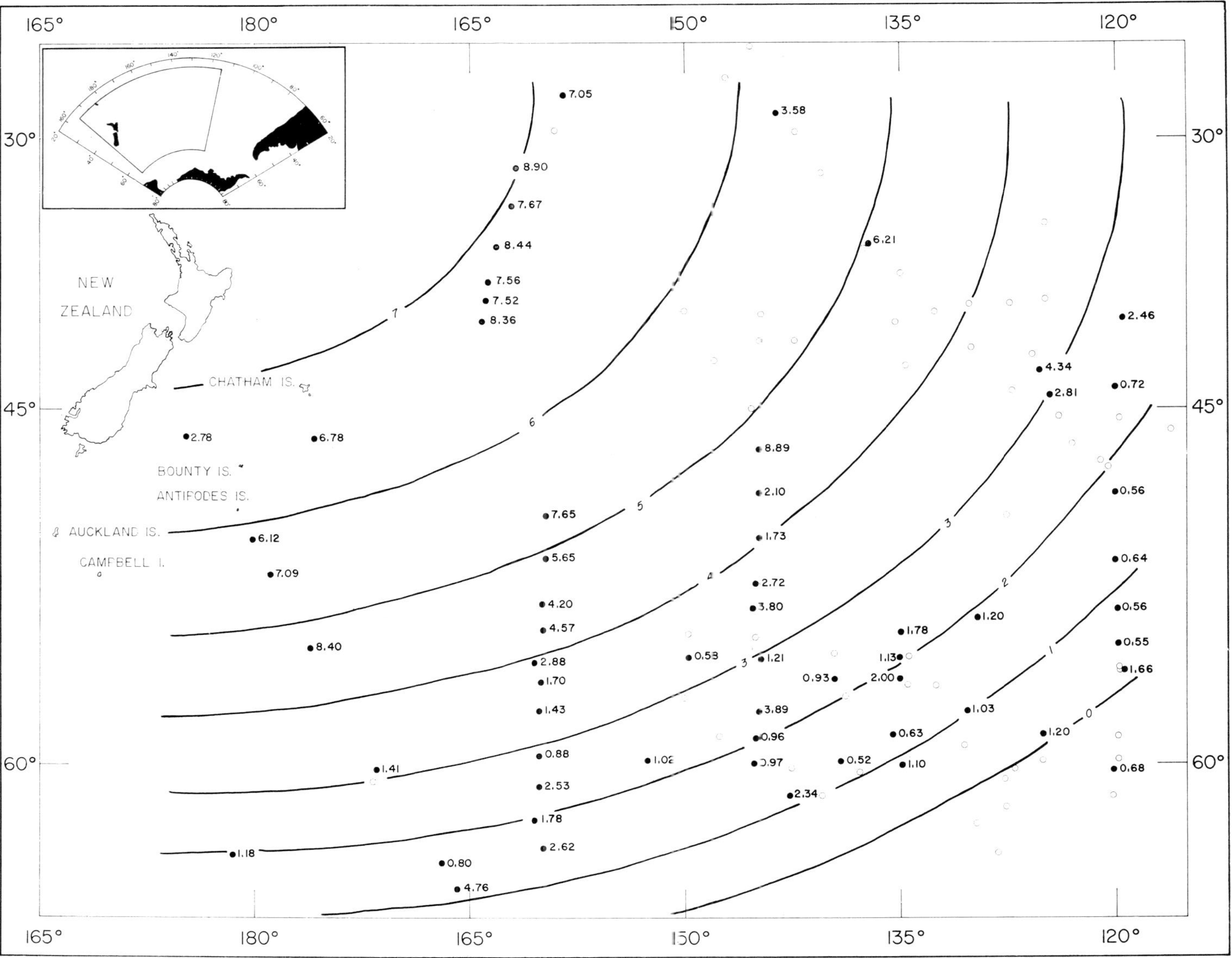

Fig. 7. Aluminum in surface sediment of the subantarctic regions of the Pacific Ocean with contours of the second-degree trend surface. Aluminum values are in weight per cent. Contour interval is 1.0%.

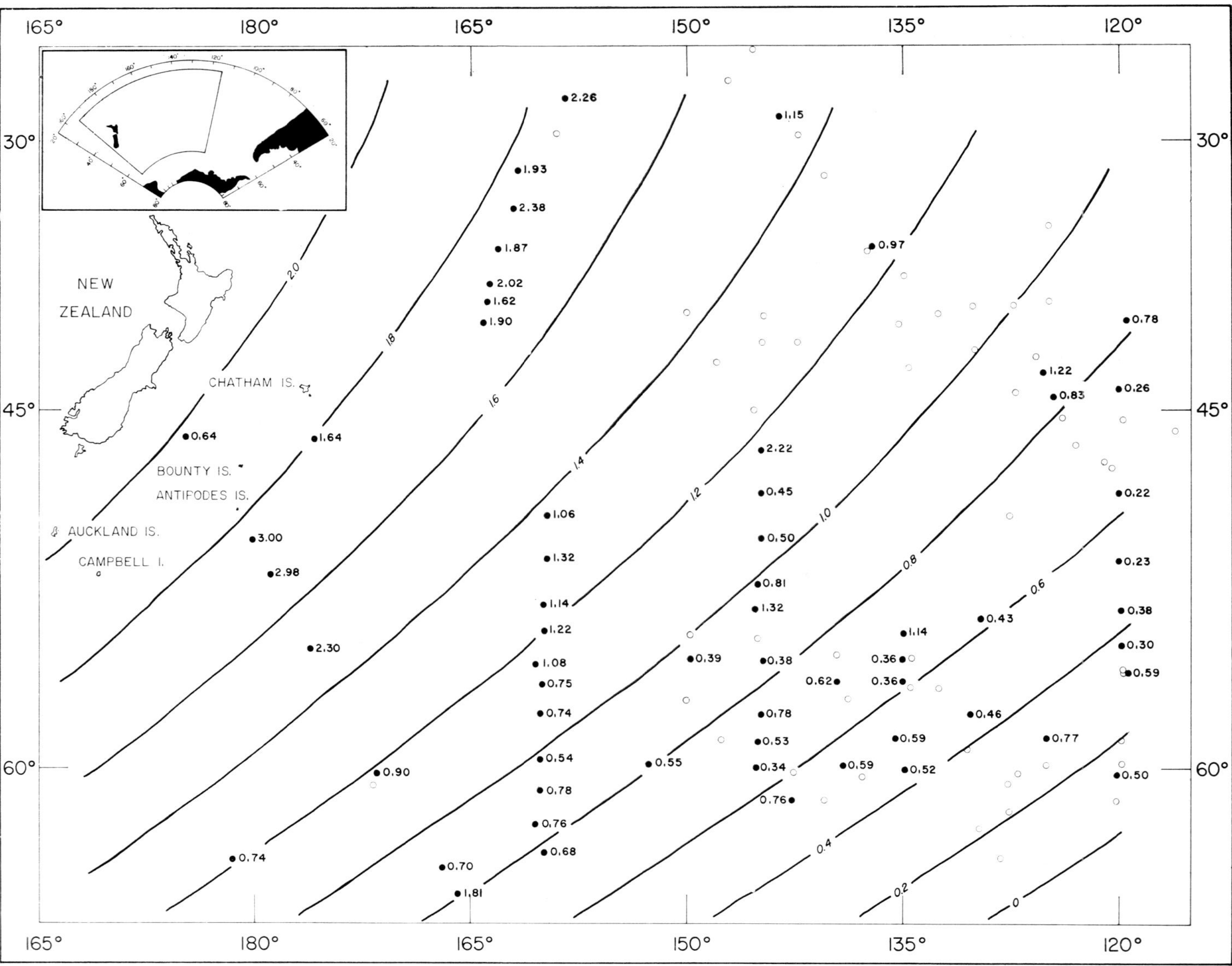

Fig. 8. Magnesium in surface sediment of the subantarctic regions of the Pacific Ocean with contours of the second-degree trend surface. Magnesium values are in weight per cent. Contour interval is 0.2%.

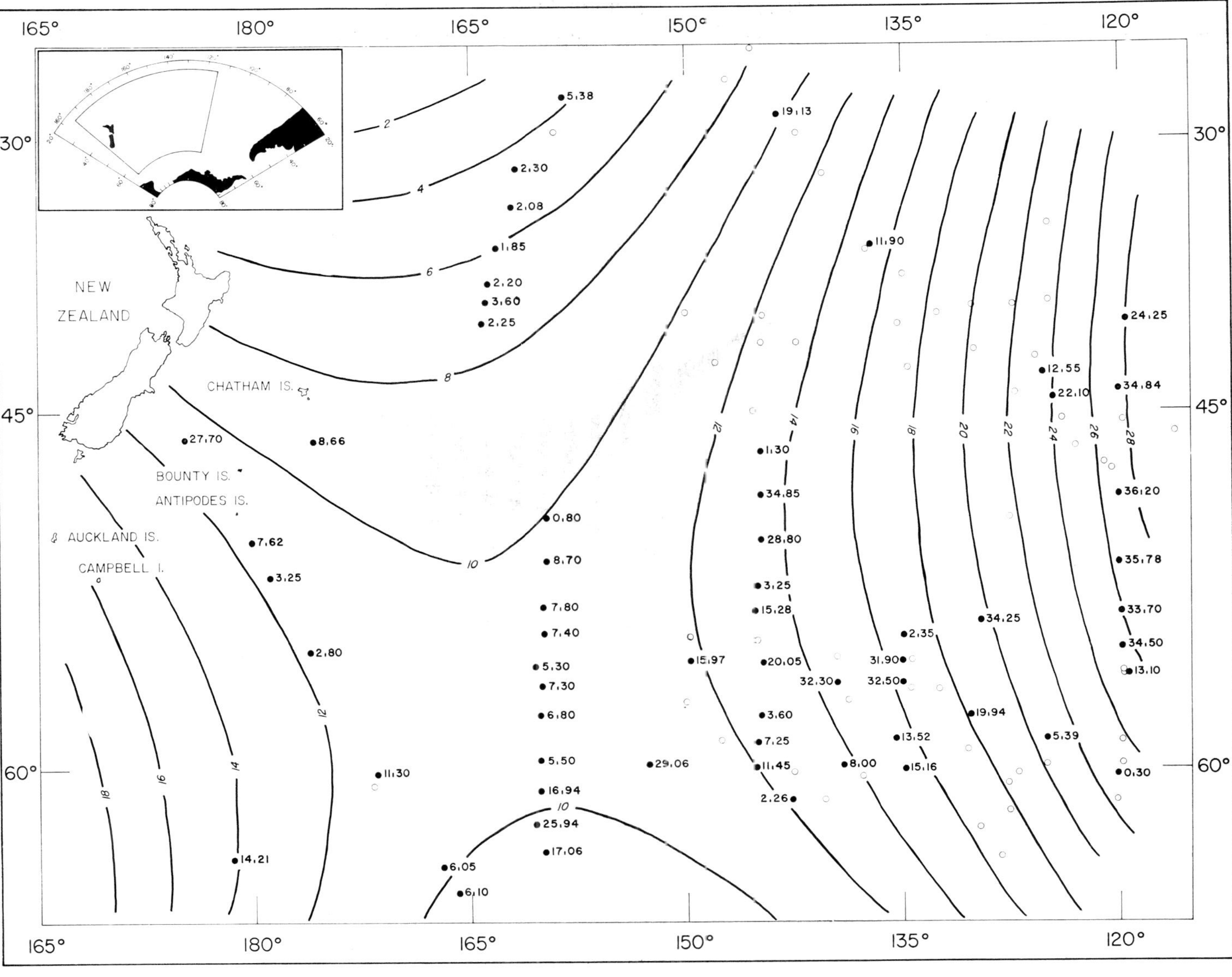

Fig. 9. Calcium in surface sediment of the subantarctic regions of the Pacific Ocean with contours of the second-degree trend surface. Calcium values are in weight per cent. Contour interval is 2.0%.

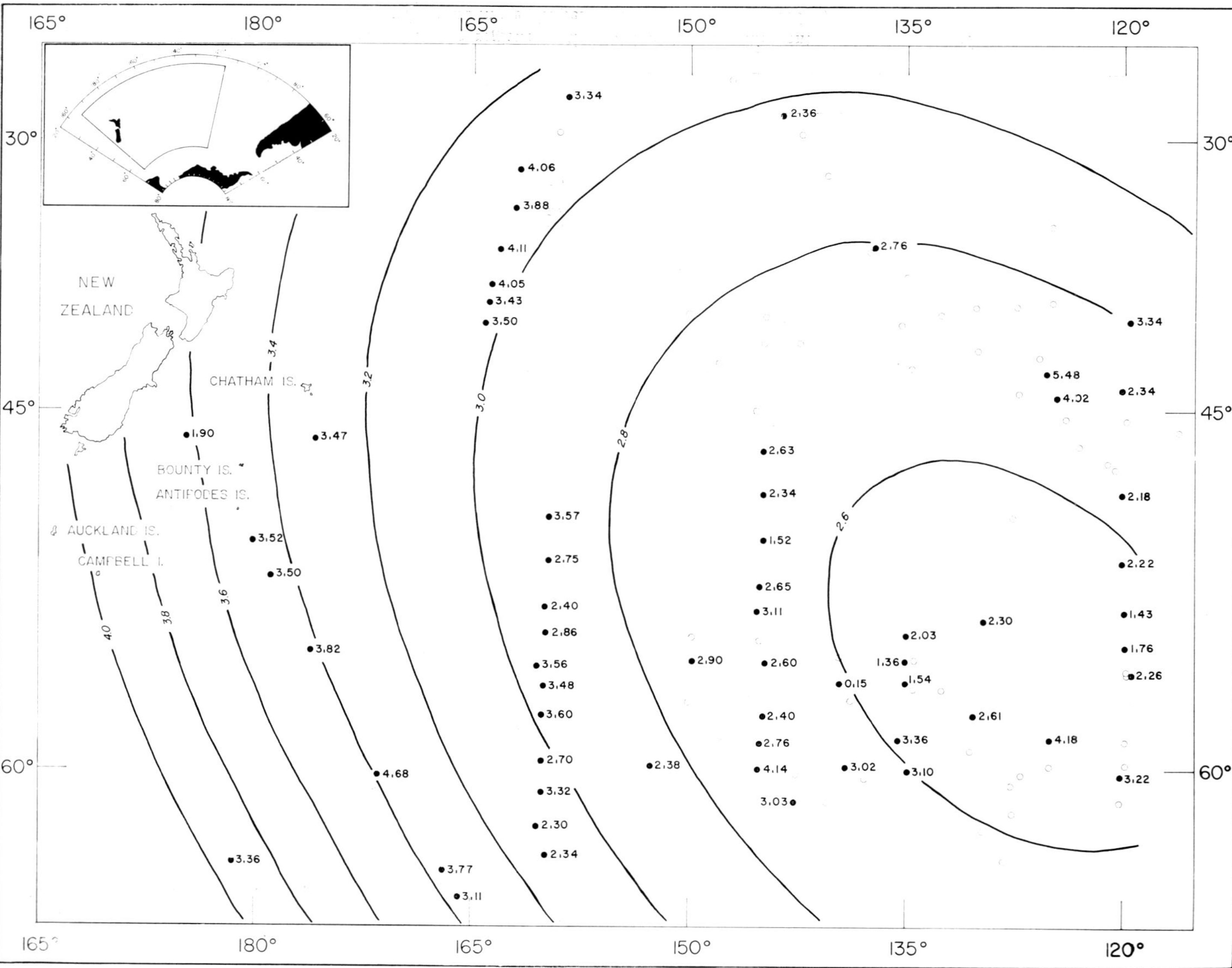

Fig. 10. Sodium in surface sediment of the subantarctic regions of the Pacific Ocean with contours of the second-degree trend surface. Sodium values are in weight per cent. Contour interval is 0.2%.

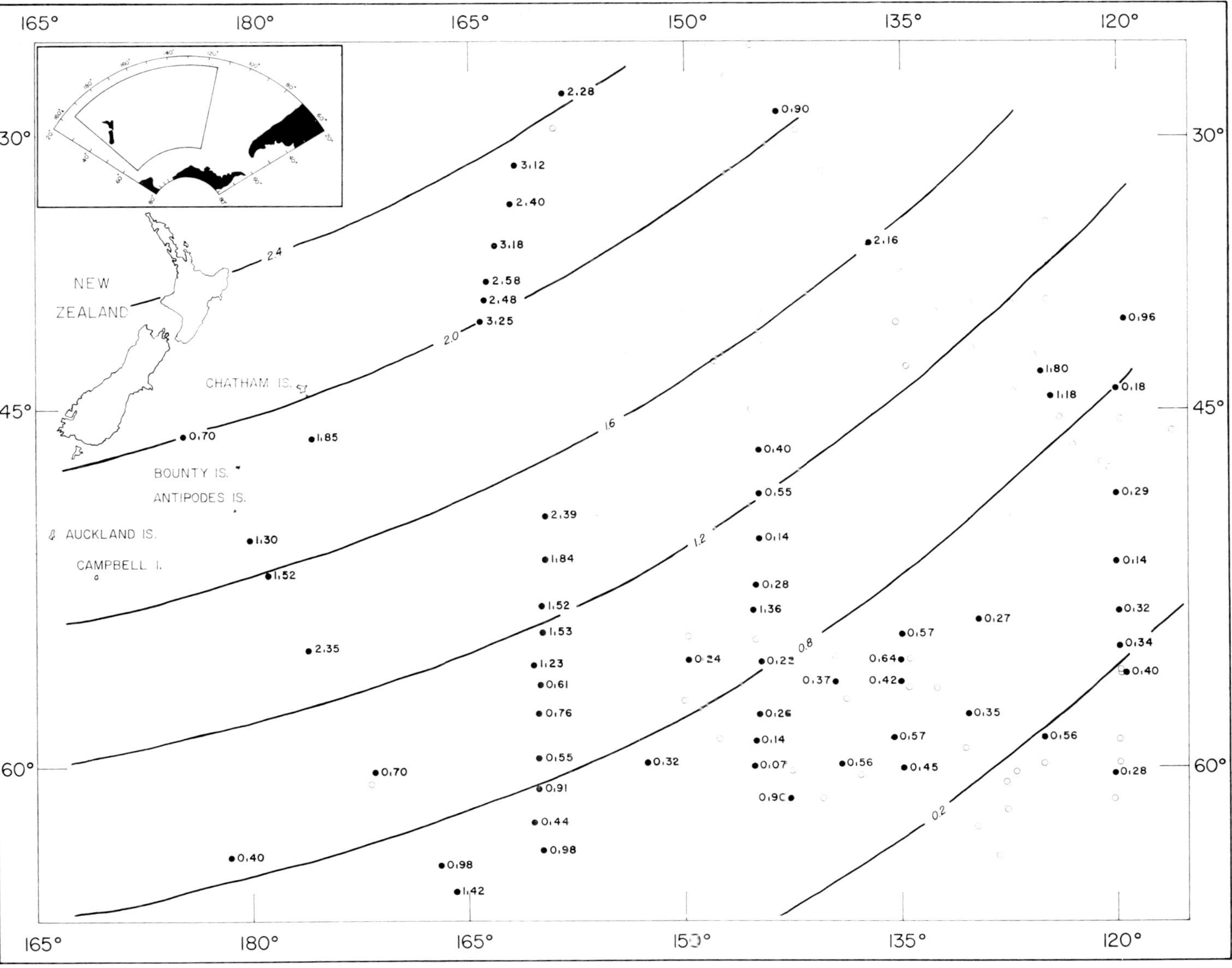

Fig. 11. Potassium in surface sediment of the subantarctic regions of the Pacific Ocean with contours of the second-degree trend surface. Potassium values are in weight per cent. Contour interval is 0.4%.

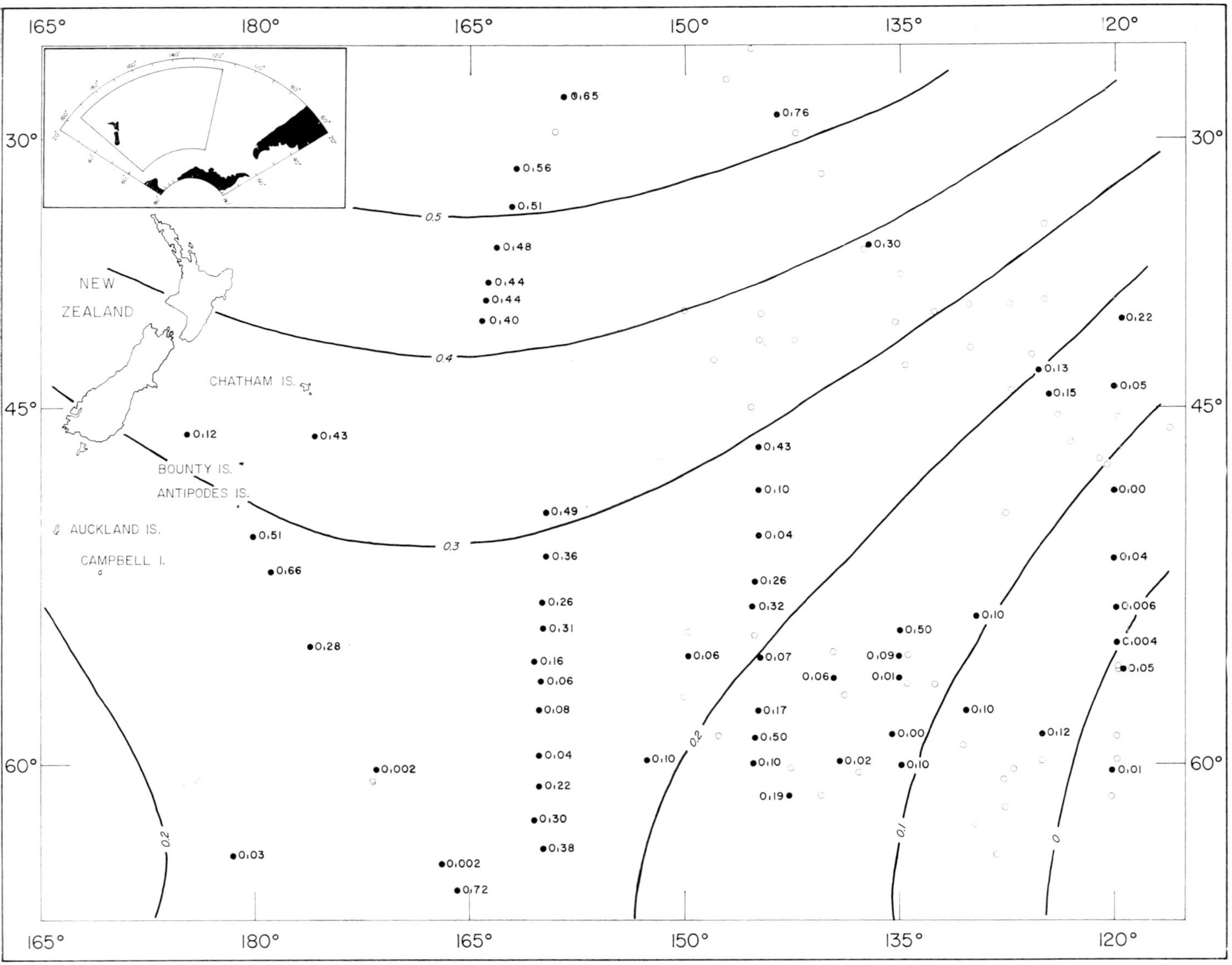

Fig. 12. Titanium in surface sediment of the subantarctic regions of the Pacific Ocean with contours of the second-degree trend surface. Titanium values are in weight per cent. Contour interval is 0.1%.

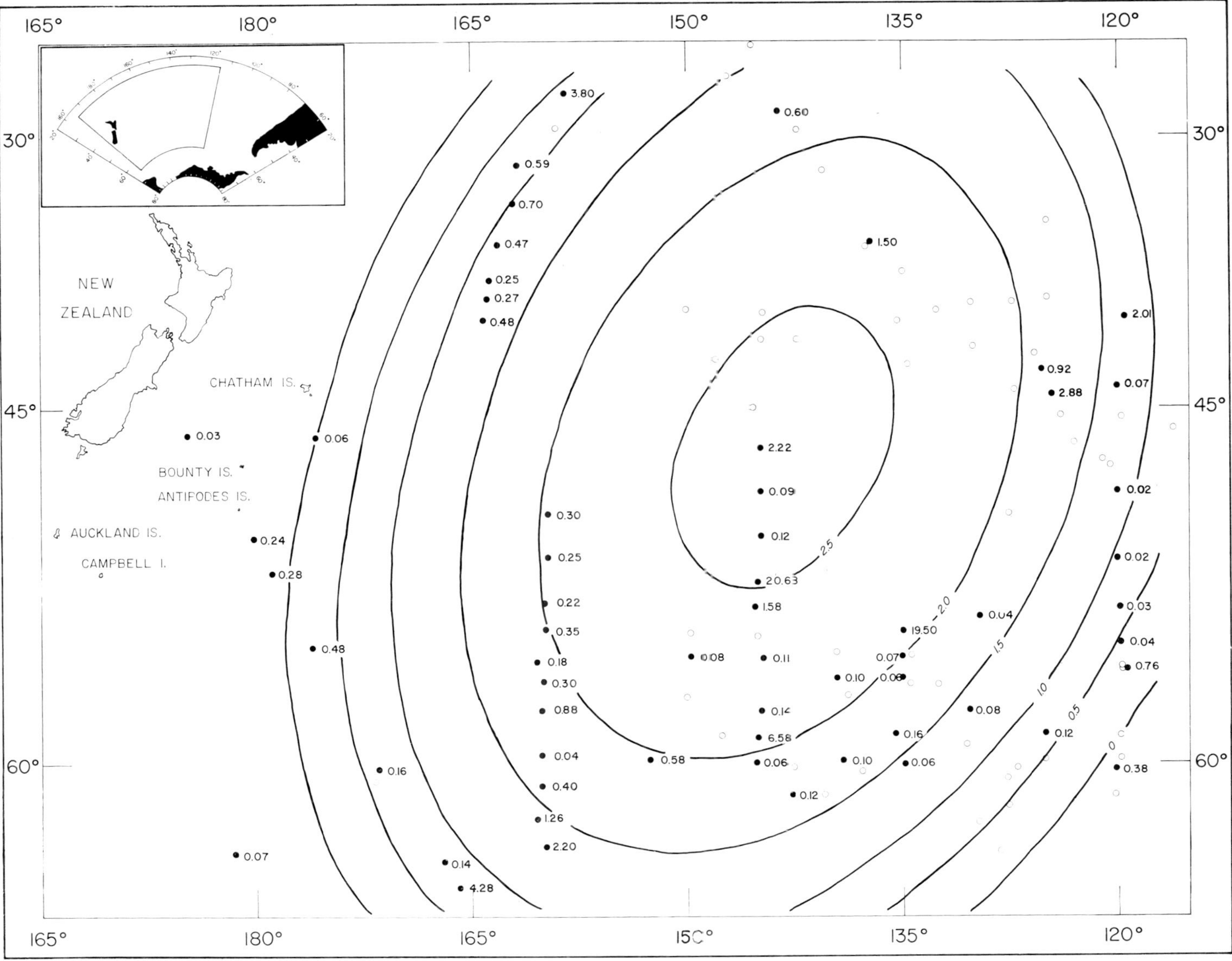

Fig. 13. Manganese in surface sediment of the subantarctic regions of the Pacific Ocean with contours of the second-degree trend surface. Manganese values are in weight per cent. Contour interval is 0.5%.

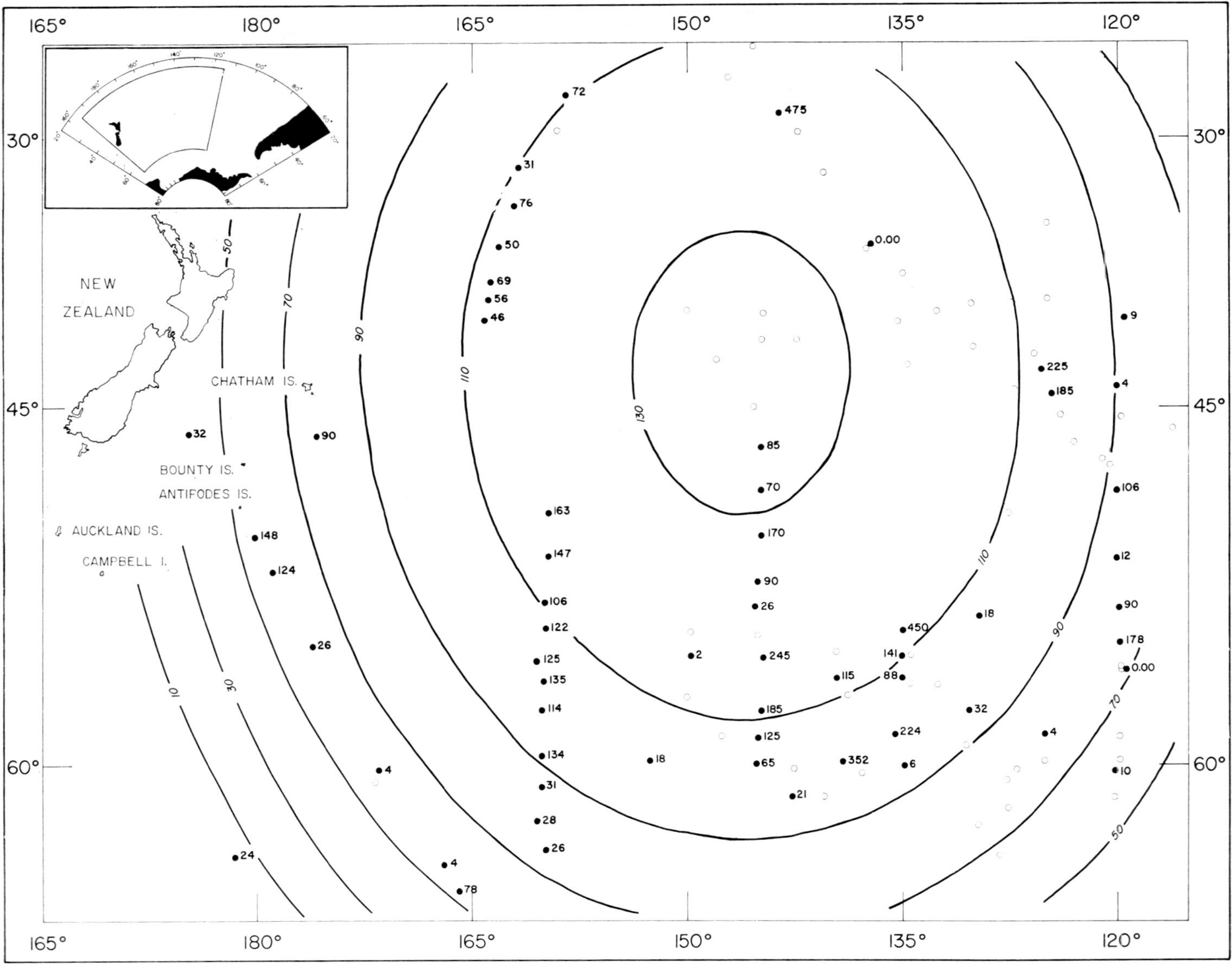

Fig. 14. Chromium in surface sediment of the subantarctic regions of the Pacific Ocean with contours of the second-degree trend surface. Chromium values are in ppm. Contour interval is 20 ppm.

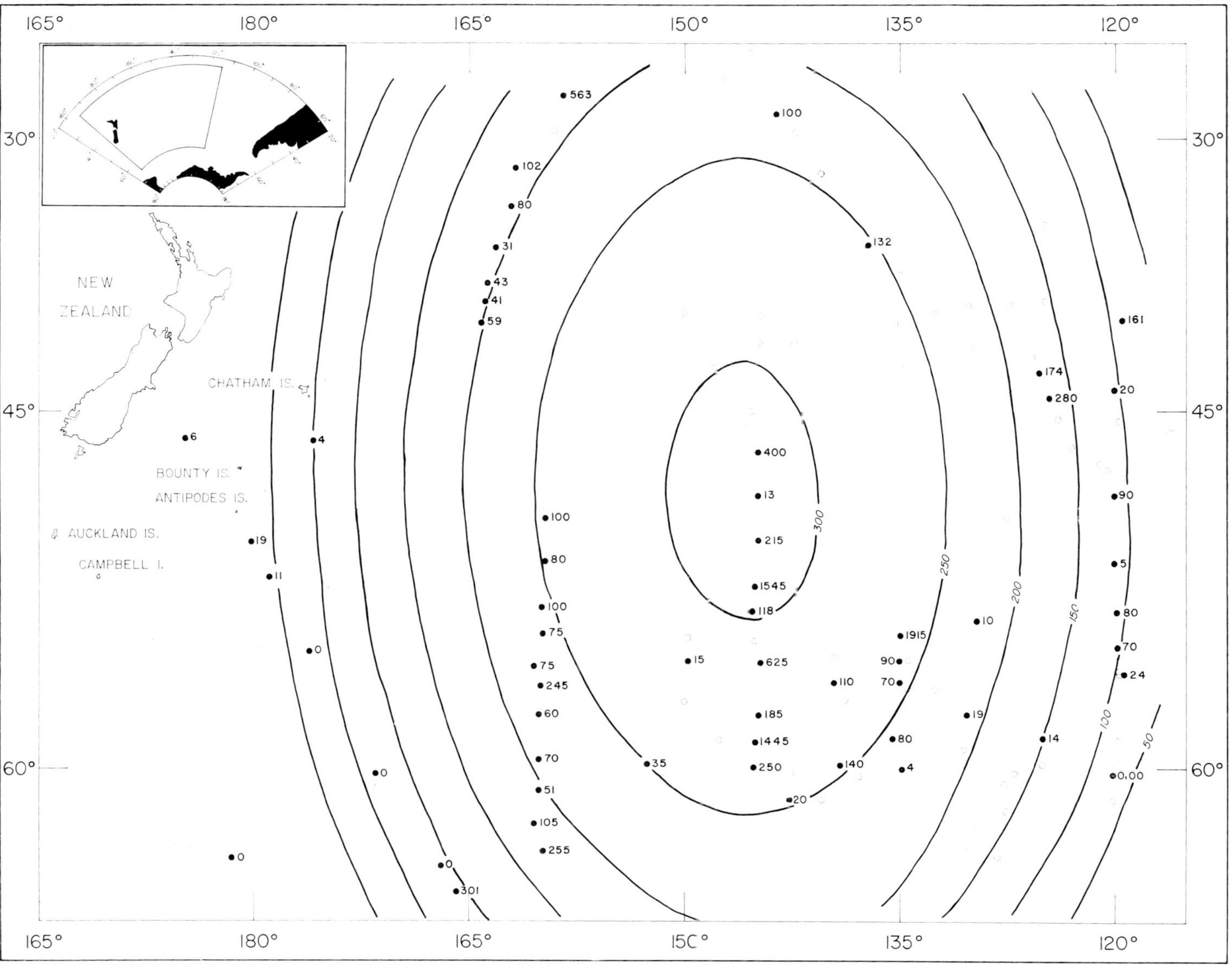

Fig. 15. Cobalt in surface sediment of the subantarctic regions of the Pacific Ocean with contours of the second-degree trend surface. Cobalt values are in ppm. Contour interval is 50 ppm.

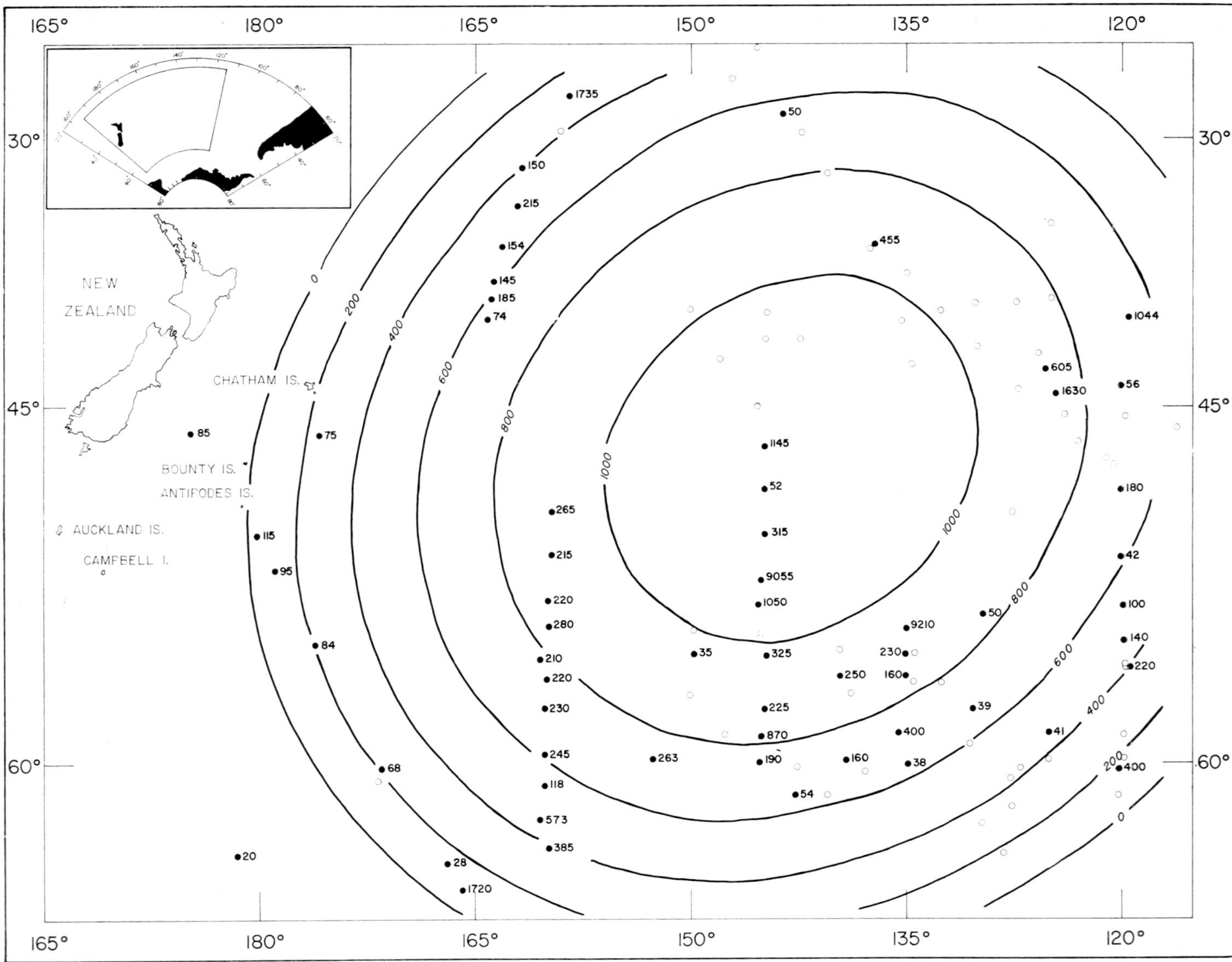

Fig. 16. Nickel in surface sediment of the subantarctic regions of the Pacific Ocean with contours of the second-degree trend surface. Nickel values are in ppm. Contour interval is 200 ppm.

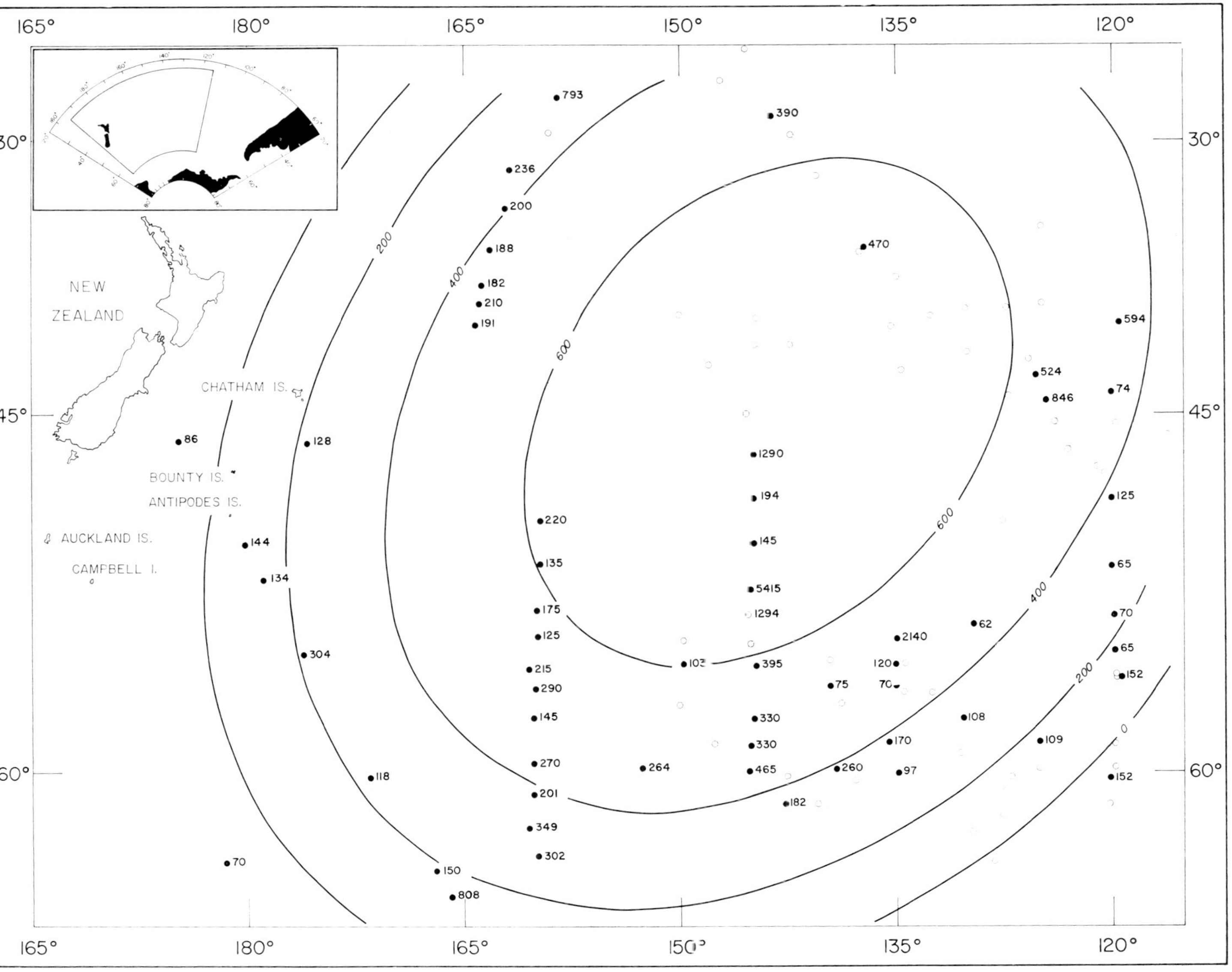

Fig. 17. Copper in surface sediment of the subantarctic regions of the Pacific Ocean with contours of the second-degree trend surface. Copper values are in ppm. Contour interval is 100 ppm.

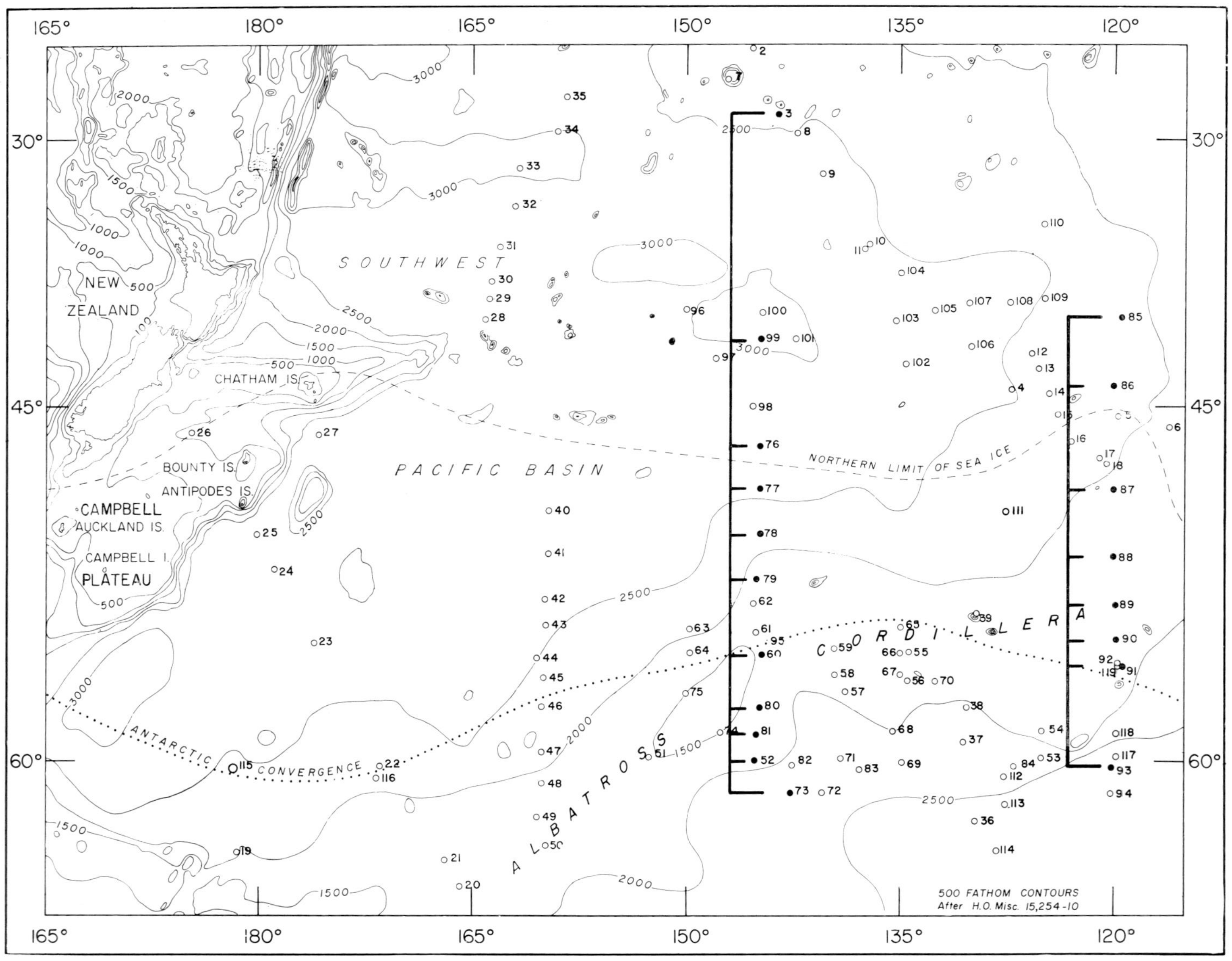

Fig. 18. Core locations near 120°W and 145°W for element association graphs.

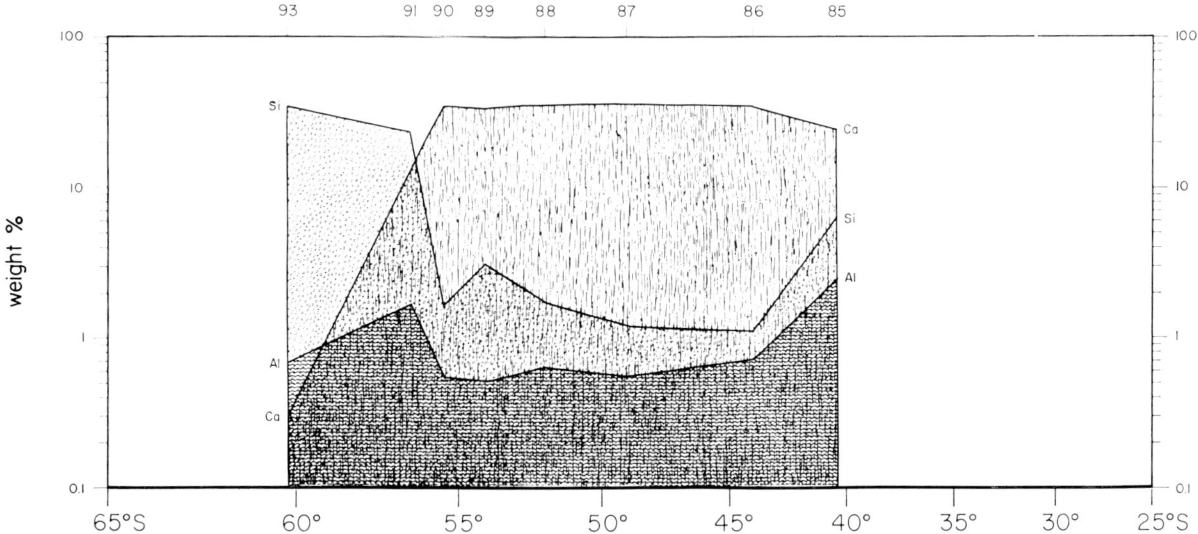

Fig. 19. Silicon, calcium, and aluminum in surface sediment near 120°W between 40°S and 60°S. Vertical axis is weight per cent.

is probably due to sodium content of the interstitial waters. Iron and manganese (Figure 26) vary sympathetically throughout this line of cores. Nickel, cobalt, and copper (Figures 28, 29) tend to follow iron and manganese, suggesting that the high concentration of these elements is a function of the micromanganese nodule content of the sediment.

Titanium and phosphorus (Figure 27) exhibit remarkably close relationship with manganese-rich sediment, as they did along 120°W (Figure 21). Chromium (Figure 29) also shows a strong correlation with titanium and phosphorus. In the southern half of this line of cores, titanium tends to vary directly with manganese; north of 45°S, there seems to be an inverse relationship.

HYDROGRAPHY

The region under investigation is in a broad sense a part of a circumpolar ocean comprising the South Atlantic, South Pacific, and the Indian oceans (South-

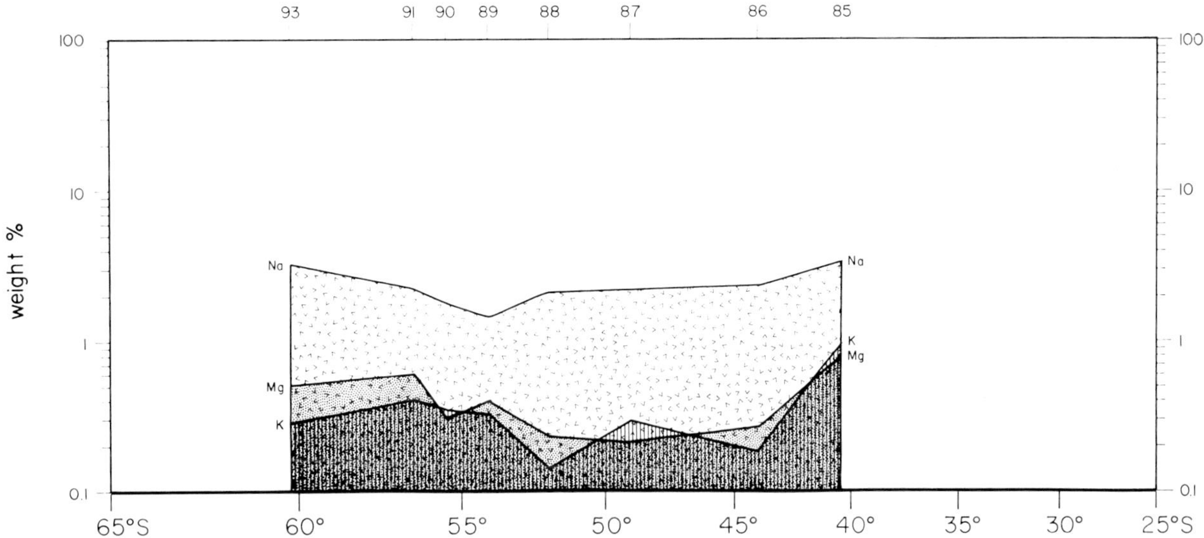

Fig. 20. Sodium, magnesium, and potassium in surface sediment near 120°W between 40°S and 60°S. Vertical axis is weight per cent.

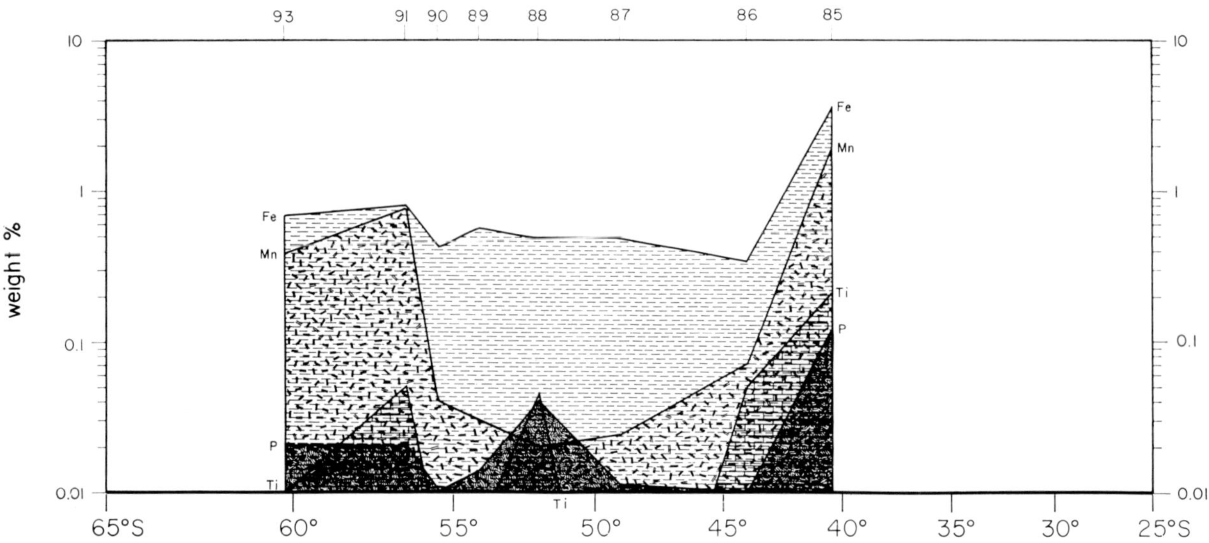

Fig. 21. Iron, manganese, titanium, and phosphorus in surface sediment near 120°W between 40°S and 60°S. Vertical axis is weight per cent

ern Ocean). *Deacon* [1937, 1963, 1964], *Mackintosh* [1946], *Stommel* [1957, 1958–1959], *Kort* [1959], *Stommel and Arons* [1960], *Wooster and Volkmann* [1960], and *Defant* [1961] have discussed various aspects of oceanography of this region. The distribution of potential temperature, oxygen, and the circulation of bottom water was treated by *Gordon* [1966]. *Lynn and Reid* [1968] presented additional information on the characteristics and circulation of abyssal waters. Most of these discussions cover only portions of the area under investigation and information is scanty, particularly north of 50°S.

Surface Currents

The main features of the surface currents are shown on the physiographic diagram in Figure 30. The dominant current of the region is the West Wind Drift. Two major oceanic west-east convergences transect the area under investigation.

Antarctic waters lie south of the Antarctic Convergence, and subtropical waters are to the north of the Subtropical Convergence. The area between the two convergences is considered the subantarctic waters.

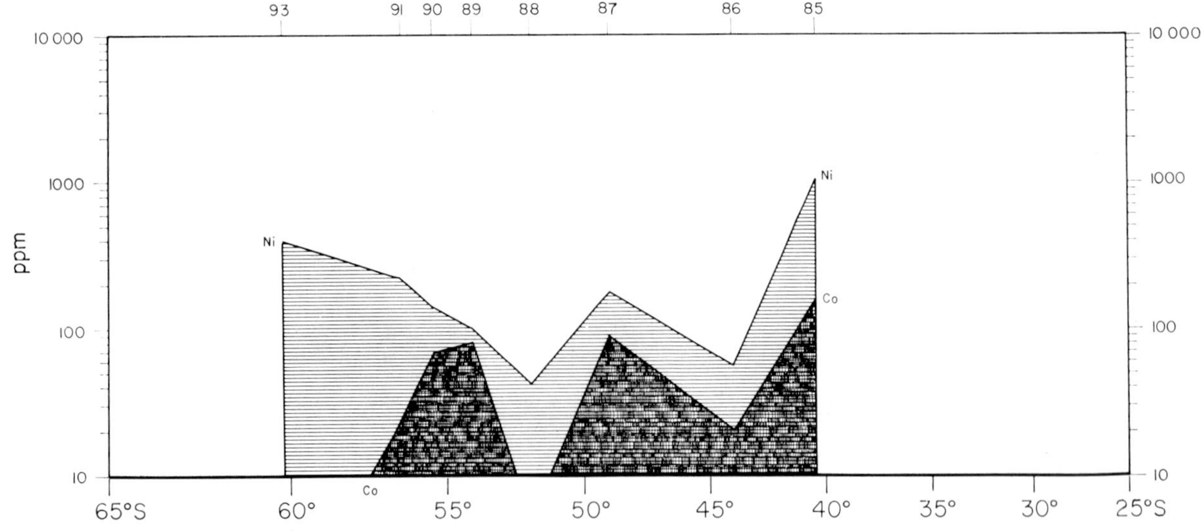

Fig. 22. Cobalt and nickel in surface sediment near 120°W between 40°S and 60°S. Vertical axis is ppm.

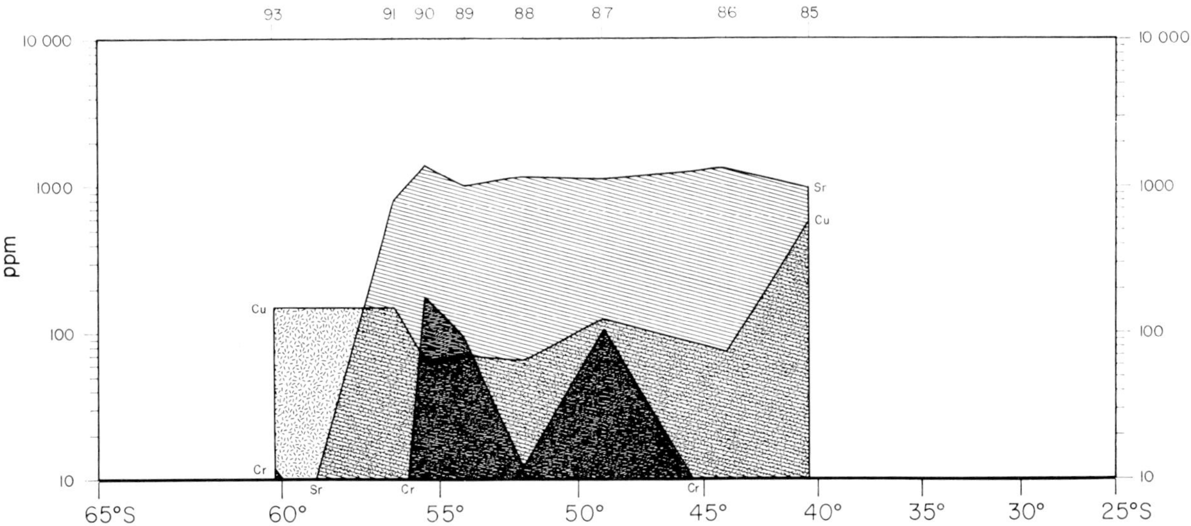

Fig. 23. Chromium, copper, and strontium in surface sediment near 120°W between 40°S and 60°S. Vertical axis is ppm.

The West Wind Drift is the major circumpolar current that flows to the east, north of the Antarctic Divergence. The East Wind Drift flows west around the Antarctic Continent, south of the Antarctic Divergence. The boundary between the two is in general along latitude 65°S, but between 90°W and 120°W it reaches south to 70°S. Within the region of the West Wind Drift there is a demarcation of great hydrographic importance, the Antarctic Convergence. The Antarctic Convergence forms the northern boundary of the antarctic surface water. At this convergence, the cold surface waters sink beneath the subantarctic waters and flow north, mixing with the warmer and more saline surface water to form the Antarctic Intermediate Current. North of the convergence, the West Wind Drift does not move directly east, but develops a northward component of flow. The Antarctic Convergence is characterized by a fairly abrupt change in temperature of approximately 2°C in the north-south direction. This convergence remains nearly stationary throughout its length. In general, the temperature of antarctic surface water during summer is 3.5° to 4.5°C; in winter, 1° to 2°C.

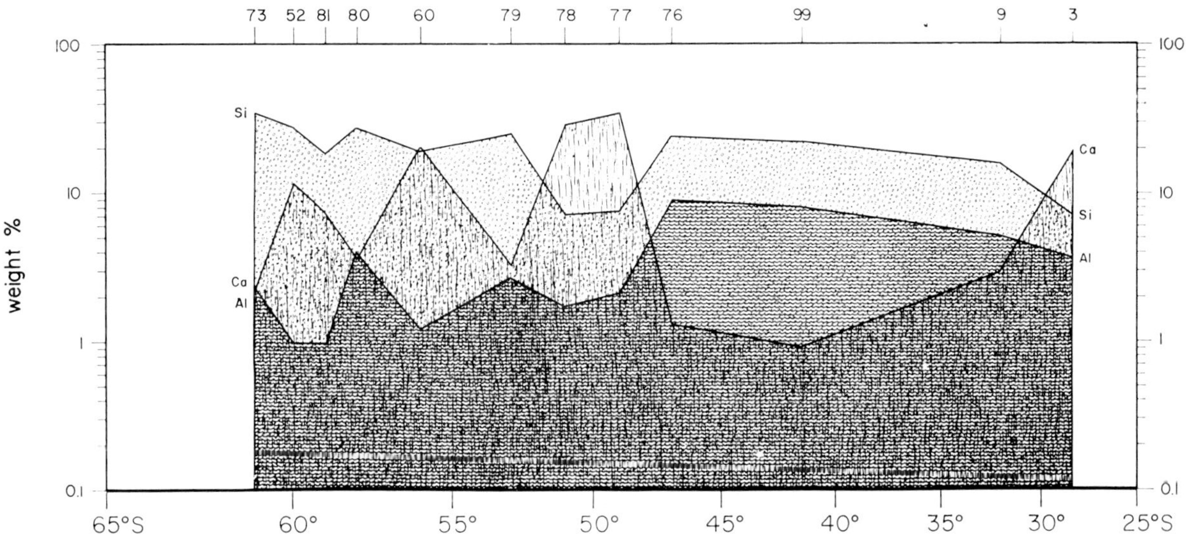

Fig. 24. Silicon, calcium, and aluminum in surface sediment near 145°W between 30°S and 60°S. Vertical axis is weight per cent.

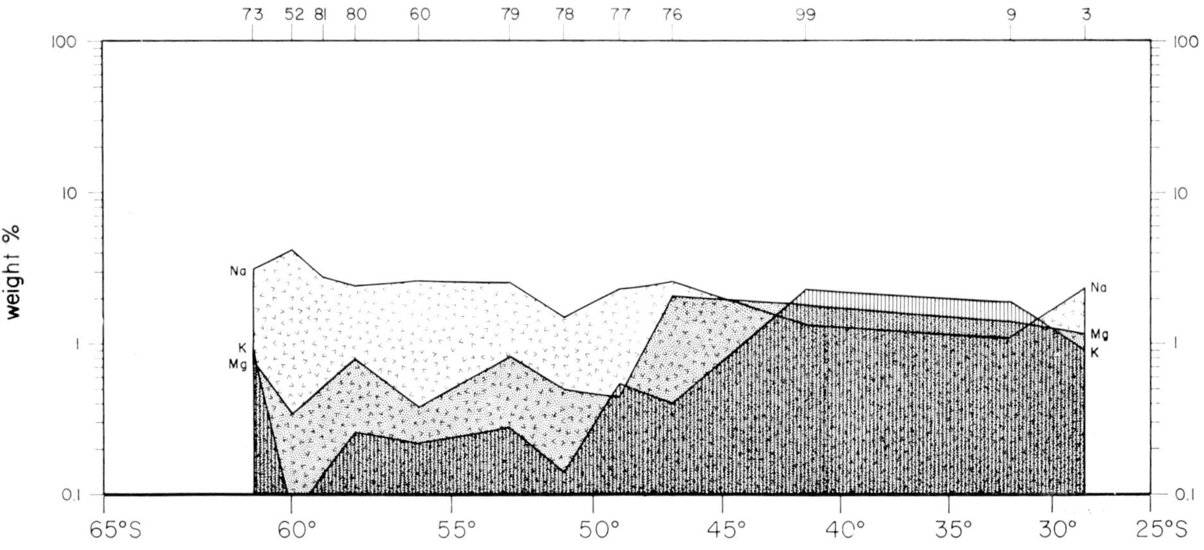

Fig. 25. Sodium, magnesium, and potassium in surface sediment near 145°W between 30°S and 60°S.

Farther north is another narrow zone in which the temperature changes rapidly over a relatively short distance. The temperature increases toward the north from 14° to 18°C during summer and from 10° to 14°C during winter. This is the Subtropical Convergence, which lies between 35°S and 45°S across most of the Pacific Ocean.

From south to north across the entire area there is an over-all increase in the salinity and temperature and decrease in oxygen and nutrients.

Vertical Circulation

The generalized vertical circulation along 150°W is shown in Figure 31. The major water masses are: antarctic surface water; cold, low salinity water which submerges along the Antarctic Convergence and flows north at a depth of 250 meters. Below the surface is (1) antarctic intermediate water; highly oxygenated, poorly saline water that flows north at about 1000 meters over the warmer, more saline deep

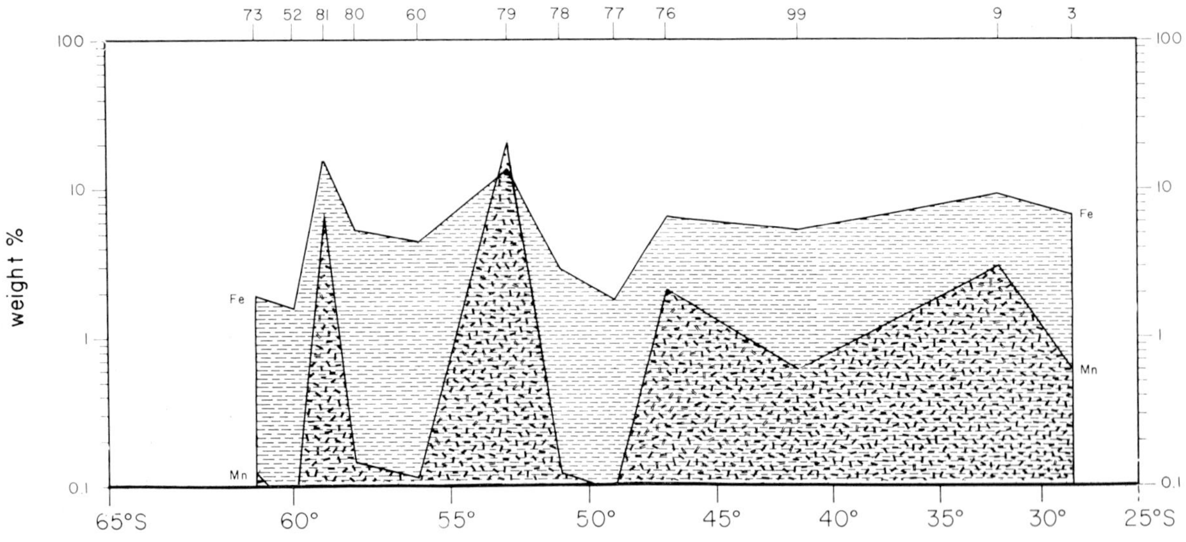

Fig. 26. Iron and manganese in surface sediment near 145°W between 30°S and 60°S. Vertical axis is weight per cent.

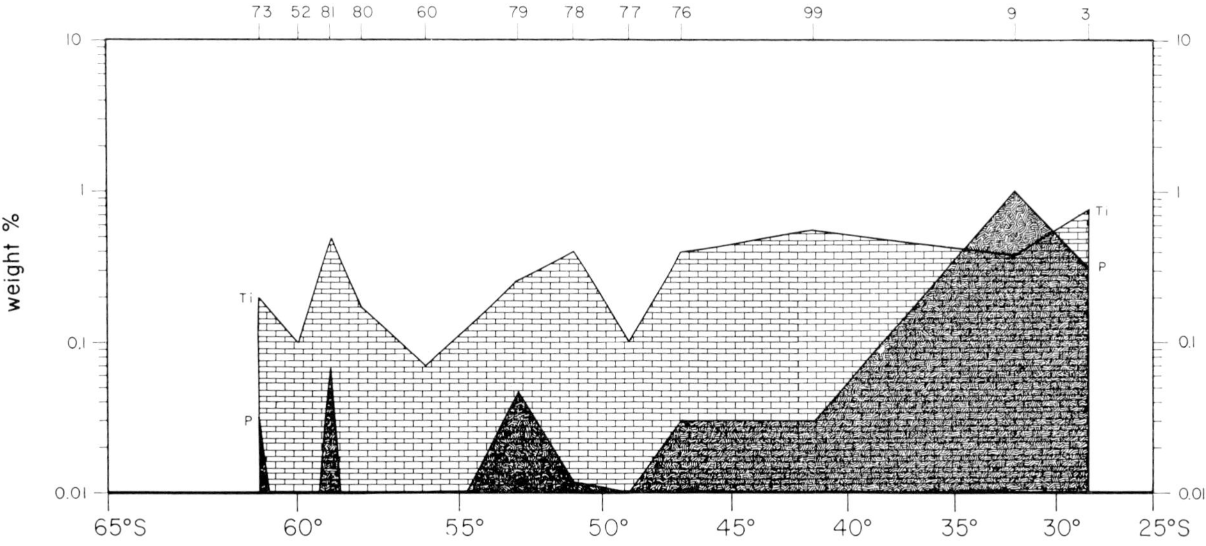

Fig. 27. Titanium and phosphorus in surface sediment near 145°W between 30°S and 60°S. Vertical axis is weight per cent.

warm water; (2) Deep warm water; highly saline water which moves south over antarctic bottom water and remains below the antarctic surface water south of the Antarctic Convergence; (3) antarctic bottom water; a northward-flowing cold water mass, 1° to 2°C cooler than deep warm water and slightly less saline than deep warm water.

DISCUSSION

The distribution of sediment types is fundamentally a function of the rates of organic and inorganic precipitation, solution, and transportation of the component mineral grains. These primary factors are affected by such things as biologic production, bottom topography, hydrography, and volcanism. Inadequate knowledge of these factors in the deep sea permits only tentative hypotheses as to the dominant processes that produced the sediment distribution in the subantarctic Pacific Ocean.

Comparison of the sediment distribution map (Figure 4), trend-surface analyses of the elements (Figures 5–17), and element associations along 120°W and 145°W, plus consideration of the oceanography and bathymetry, suggest some of the factors involved in the origin of the major sedimentary units.

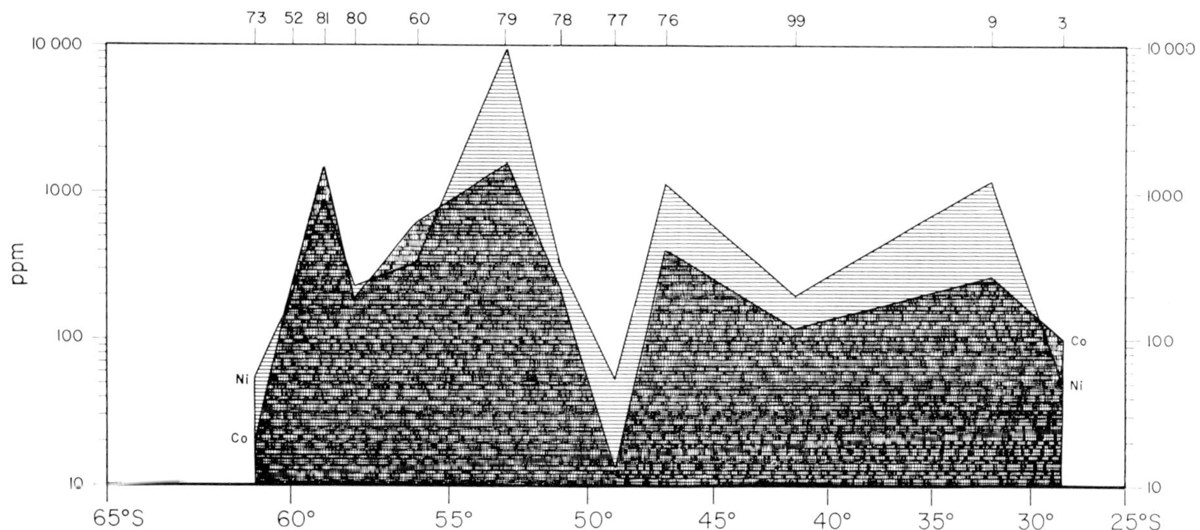

Fig. 28. Cobalt and nickel in surface sediment near 145°W between 30°S and 60°S. Vertical axis is ppm.

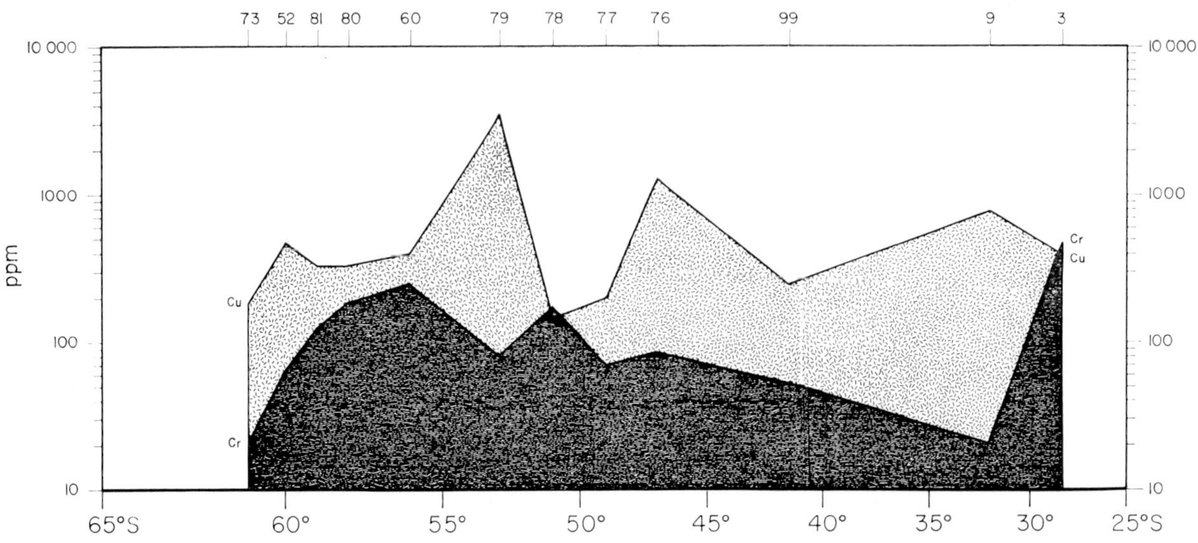

Fig. 29. Chromium and copper in surface sediment near 145°W between 30°S and 60°S. Vertical axis is ppm.

The diatomaceous sediment probably originated in the highly productive antarctic surface waters of the South Atlantic, South Pacific, and Indian oceans [*Fleming*, 1957]. The siliceous sediment distribution shown in Figure 4 suggests that the northern boundary of the diatomaceous sediment may in part be controlled by the Antarctic Convergence. Another indication of the possible influence of deep circulation patterns on the diatomaceous sediment distribution is suggested by the occurrence of diatomaceous clay at 40°S, 165°W, nearly 20° north of the main area of diatomaceous sediments. The diatoms in these sediments could have been transported north by the deep western boundary current described by *Stommel* [1958–1959] and reported by *Reid et al.* [1968]. There is a high content of volcanic glass in some of these diatomaceous clays (cores 28–32), which decreases abruptly in cores to the south and very gradually to the north. The glass probably originated from a volcanic eruption on North Island, New Zealand, was transported east by winds and settled quickly to the bottom by vertical density currents, as suggested by *Bradley* [1965]. It then could also have been transported north by the deep western boundary current depicted by *Stommel* [1958–1959] and reported by *Reid et al.* [1968].

Gordon [1966] stated that west of 120°W the main flow of bottom waters is northward into the Pacific. This suggests that the same deep current may also have transported the terrigenous sediments observed in cores 23 to 25, southeast of New Zealand. These sediments might have been transported by turbidity currents from the Campbell Plateau, but this is considered to be less likely because of the extensive areas of carbonate sediments rather than terrigenous sediments on the plateau.

Carbonate-rich sediments cover most of the area north of the Antarctic Convergence above 2500 fm Most workers in the South Atlantic, South Pacific, and Indian oceans attribute high planktonic foraminifera production to mixing of warmer subantarctic water with diatom-rich antarctic water along the zone of convergence. Foraminifera-rich sediment implies high primary productivity in the overlying waters, and this has been cited in the past [*Arrhenius*, 1963]. However, the carbonate distribution in the subantarctic Pacific Ocean shows no obvious relationship to a region of upwelling as do the equatorial carbonate sediments. Furthermore, *Fleming* [1957] estimates the productivity of the central South Pacific north of 45°S as less than 50 g carbon/m^2/yr, among the lowest in the world ocean.

Topography is probably a significant factor in the distribution of carbonate sediment (Figure 4). This could be due to pressure solution [*Murray and Renard*, 1891; *Owen and Brinkley*, 1941; *Peterson*, 1966] or it may be due to other factors [*Smith et al.*, 1968]. Additional information is needed on the ecological factors that control the production of biogenic calcium carbonate, as well as on the processes of deep-sea sediment transportation and dissolution.

The broad region of mixed diatomaceous-carbonate sediment may be due to migration of the Antarctic Convergence in time and space and subsequent blur-

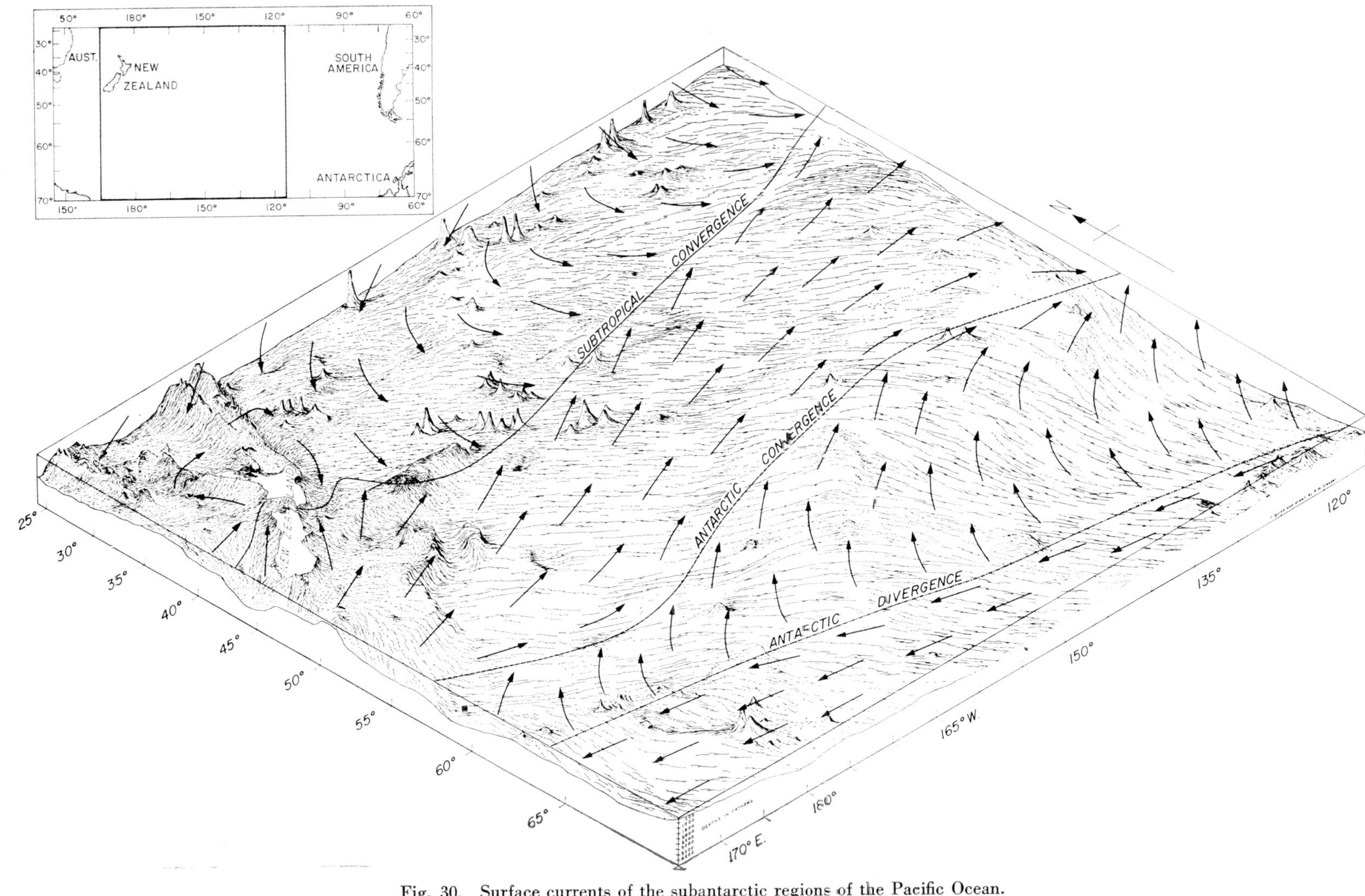

Fig. 30. Surface currents of the subantarctic regions of the Pacific Ocean.

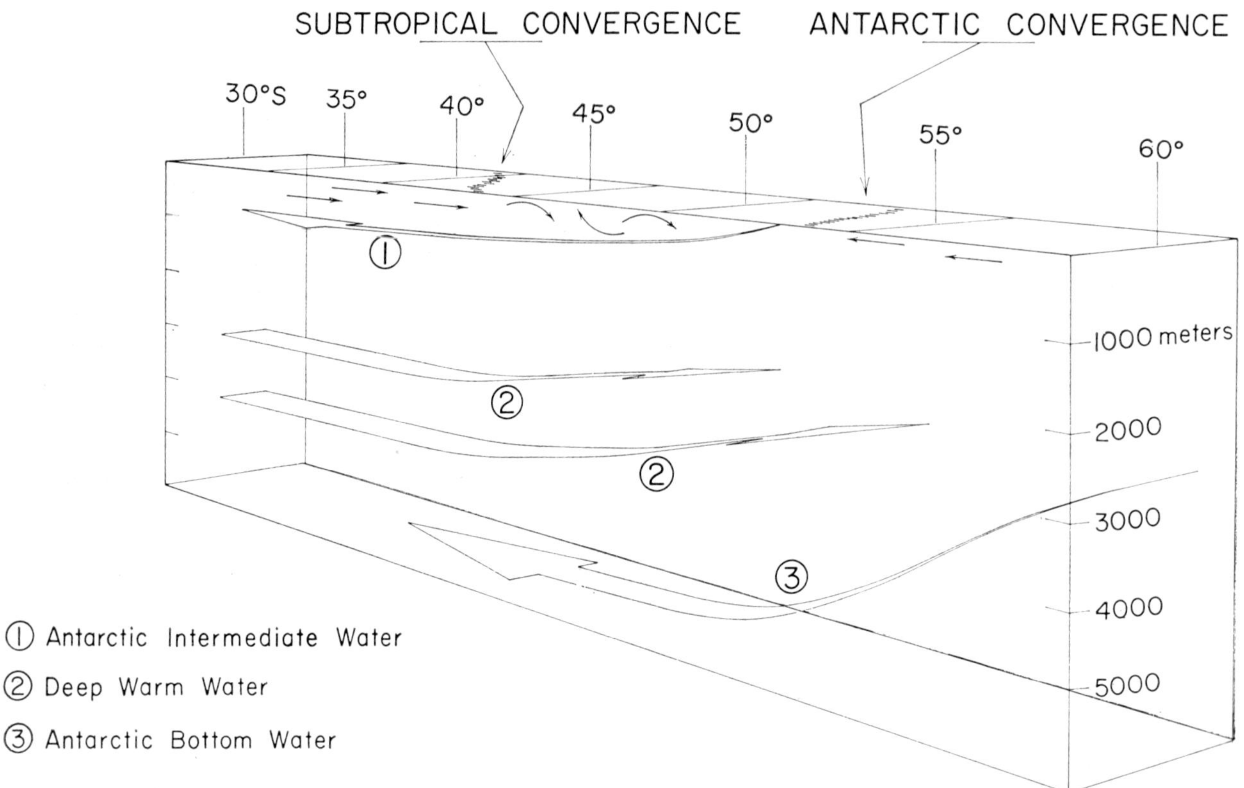

Fig. 31. Vertical circulation of the subantarctic regions of the Pacific Ocean along 150°W.

ring of the carbonate and diatomaceous horizons by biologic mixing.

Brown clay is almost exclusively confined to the Southwest Pacific Basin. Several factors probably contributed to this: (1) dissolution of carbonate at depth may prevent accumulation of carbonate sediments below 2500 fm; (2) the effect of the Albatross Cordillera as a barrier to northward circulation of deep and possibly diatom-bearing waters [*Gordon*, 1966]; (3) volcanism in and around the basin margin. Inasmuch as the first two have already been covered in the preceding discussion, the following discussion chiefly concerns the third factor.

Petrographic study of brown clay shows that it consists not only of clay minerals, but also of fresh and partly altered basaltic glass, palagonite, fragments of pyroxene and plagioclase, and a high content of fish bone. Brown clay also contains up to 50% ferromanganese oxide and zeolites (Plates 1*b*, 1*c*, and 1*d*). Zeolite, which is dominantly phillipsite, and opaque minerals show genetic relationships with basaltic glass and palagonite, as shown by earlier work [*Nayudu*, 1965*a*].

Nayudu [1962, 1964] discussed the problem of the alteration of submarine basaltic glass and palagonite, and suggested that montmorillonite, which is the dominant component of brown clay, zeolites, ferromanganese oxides, carbonate and/or chert are important products of these alterations in the deep-sea sediments. *Nayudu* [1965*b*] further showed that in the process of palagonitization, concentrations of iron, manganese, titanium, and phosphorus increase 2 or 3 times. In addition, it was also shown that the concentration of cobalt, nickel, strontium, and barium increases 2 or 3 times in palagonite and nearly 10 times in ferromanganese oxides. Study in progress also indicates high concentrations of potassium in palagonite.

There is a general paucity of data on the trace element geochemistry of deep-sea sediments. *Nicholls'* [1967] exhaustive review of the distribution of trace elements in the sediments included copper, cobalt, nickel, and chromium. He stated that there was no direct correlation of the distribution of these elements either with depth or temperature. He suggested that possibly cobalt greater than 40 ppm, copper greater than 90 ppm, and nickel greater than 150 ppm might be considered as being deposited in water deeper than

250 meters. He concluded that for a total evaluation of the problem, several elements, rather than one or a restricted number of elements, should be considered.

Examination of the trend-surface analyses (Figures 5 to 17) and element associations along 120°W and 145°W (Figures 19 to 29) show a close interrelationship of iron, manganese, cobalt, nickel, copper, and to a lesser extent, chromium. The iron concentration seems to increase toward the north and probably reflects the contribution of volcanic material from seamounts in the area (Figure 2). *Griffin et al.* [1968] discussed clay mineral distributions in the world ocean and pointed out that montmorillonite is the dominant clay, ranging from 50–70% with highest concentration north of 30°S in the central South Pacific. The iron distribution shown in Figure 6 corroborates the above observation.

The present study shows a strong affinity between titanium and phosphorus, which in turn show interrelationships with manganese and iron-rich sediments in the Southwest Pacific. *Goldberg and Arrhenius* [1958] and *Arrhenius* [1963] discussed the significance of titanium in deep-sea sediments and suggested that it may be contained in volcanic material of basaltic composition.

The data presented here and by *Nayudu* [1965*a*,*b*] substantiate this, emphasize the significant association of phosphorus and titanium, and strongly suggest their genetic relationship to pyroclastics of basaltic composition. This may explain *Nicholls'* [1967] evaluation of the lack of relationship between concentration of some of these elements with depth or temperature.

Boström and Peterson [1966] showed that sediment on the north part of the Albatross Cordillera was enriched in iron, manganese, copper, chromium, nickel, and lead, and suggested that it is due to volcanic exhalations. Analyses of sediments taken along transects farther south on the cordillera do not show such high concentrations of these elements. On the contrary, it appears that there are high concentrations of iron, manganese, and most trace elements in sediment from the Southwest Pacific Basin.

The fish bone content of brown clay (Plates 1*b*, 1*d*), especially in the northern part of the area, may be due to the relatively slower rate of accumulation of brown clay [*Arrhenius,* 1963]. Nevertheless, it is suggested that the concentration of fish debris could be due to the high mortality of fish and other animals during submarine eruptions.

From the petrologic and chemical studies, it is concluded that most of the brown clay is derived from volcanism in and around the basin margin, which generated turbidity currents, which in turn transported fine submarine volcanic material [*Nayudu,* 1969]. These turbidity currents would flow downslope and spread volcanic material over the basin floor. Mineral associations strongly suggest in situ alteration of the volcanic sediment.

Widely varying sinking rates have been implied in the above discussion. However, recent literature indicates that actual settling velocities of particulate matter in the ocean may depart significantly from standard settling velocities [*Bradley,* 1965], and little known processes of transportation may be important in oceanic sedimentation [*Heezen et al.,* 1966].

This discussion has assumed that the sediments are essentially contemporaneous. Different rates of accumulation for each sediment type argue against contemporaneity; however, biologic mixing would tend to make this assumption more nearly true.

Work is in progress on the vertical changes in the lithology and chemistry of these sediments. These data, together with further sampling in critical areas and additional oceanographic data, should refine the observations presented here.

Acknowledgments. Sincere thanks are due to Prof. C. A. Barnes and Prof. R. H. Fleming, Department of Oceanography, University of Washington, for helpful discussions and suggestions.

Thanks are due to Ray W. Sleeper for construction of physiographic diagrams and base maps and for his help in compiling the *Eltanin* data and in the laboratory. Thanks are also due to Charlette Chastain for valuable assistance in petrographic studies; to D. Y. Kode and Sally Wienke for chemical analyses; to Helen Latterell, Judy Potteiger, and Marieanna Lowe for their assistance in the laboratory; Lawrence E. Heiner, University of Alaska, for the trend-surface analyses; W. R. Riedel and Thomas J. Walsh, of Scripps Institution of Oceanography, for samples; and Julie Isaac for aid in the preparation of the manuscript.

This investigation was supported by the Antarctic Programs of the National Science Foundation grants GA-309, GA-1248, and GA-1463 to Y. R. Nayudu and in part by the Office of Naval Research contract to the University of Washington and the University of Alaska.

REFERENCES

Arrhenius, G., Pelagic sediments, in *The Sea,* vol. 3, edited by M. N. Hill, pp. 655–727, Interscience, New York, 1963.

Bonatti, E., Zeolites in Pacific pelagic sediments, *Trans. N.Y. Acad. Sci., II, 25,* 938–948, 1963.

Bostrom, K., and M. N. A. Peterson, Precipitates from hydrothermal exhalations on the East Pacific rise, *Econ. Geol., 61,* 1258–1265, 1966.

Bradley, W. H., Vertical density currents, *Science, 150,* 1423–1428, 1965.

Bramlette, M. N., Pelagic sediments, in *Oceanography*, edited by M. Sears, pp. 345–366, American Association for the Advancement of Science, Washington, D.C., 1961.

Deacon, G. E. R., The hydrology of the Southern Ocean, *Discovery Rept., 15,* 1–124, 1937.

Deacon, G. E. R., The Southern Ocean, in *The Sea*, vol. 2, edited by M. N. Hill, pp. 281–296, Interscience, New York, 1963.

Deacon, G. E. R., The Southern Ocean, in *Antarctic Research,* edited by R. Priestley, R. J. Adie, and G. de Q. Robin, pp. 292–307, Butterworth, London, 1964.

Defant, A., *Physical Oceanography,* vol. 1, pp. 669–682, Pergamon, New York, 1961.

Fleming, R. H., General features of the oceans, *Treatise on Marine Ecology and Paleoecology,* vol. 1, edited by J. W. Hedgpeth, chap. 5, pp. 87–108, Geological Society of America, New York, 1957.

Goldberg, E. D., and G. Arrhenius, Chemistry of Pacific pelagic sediments, *Geochimla. Cosmochim. Acta, 13,* 153–212, 1958.

Goodell, H. G., The marine geology of the Southern Ocean, USNS *Eltanin* Marine Geology Cruises 9–15 (offset), *Contrib. 11,* pp. 1–35, Sedimentology Research Laboratory, Department of Geology, Florida State University, Tallahassee, 1965.

Gordon, A. L., Potential temperature, oxygen and circulation of bottom water in the Southern Ocean, *Deep-Sea Res., 13,* 1125–1138, 1966.

Griffin, J. J., H. Windom, and E. D. Goldberg, The distribution of clay minerals in the World Ocean, *Deep-Sea Res., 15,* 433–459, 1968.

Heezen, B. C., C. D. Hollister, and W. F. Ruddiman, Shaping of the continental rise by deep geostrophic contour currents, *Science, 152,* 502–508, 1966.

Heiner, L. E., and S. P. Geller, Fortran IV trend-surface program for the IBM 360 model 40 computer, *Mineral Ind. Res. Lab. Rept. 9,* pp. 1–69, University of Alaska, 1967.

Jackson, M. L., *Soil Chemical Analysis,* pp. 141–144, 294–297, Prentice-Hall, Englewood Cliffs, New Jersey, 1958.

Kort, V. G., New results on the transport of Antarctic waters (in Russian), *Infm. Bull. Soviet Antark. Exped. 9,* 31–34, 1959.

Lisitzin, A. P., Bottom sediments of the Antarctic, in *Antarctic Research, Geophys. Monograph 7,* edited by H. Wexler, pp. 81–88, American Geophysical Union, Washington, D.C., 1962.

Lynn, R. J., and J. L. Reid, Characteristics and circulation of deep and abyssal waters, *Deep-Sea Res., 15,* 577–598, 1968.

Mackintosh, N. A., The Antarctic Convergence and the distribution of surface temperatures in antarctic waters, *Discovery Rept., 23,* 177–212, 1946.

Murray, J., and A. F. Renard, Report on deep-sea deposits based on specimens collected during the voyage of HMS *Challenger* in the years 1872–1876, *Challenger Report,* 525 pp., Neill, Edinburgh, 1891.

Nayudu, Y. R., Submarine eruption of basalts and the problems of palagonitization (abstract), *International Symposium on Volcanology, Japan,* 1962.

Nayudu, Y. R., Palagonite tuffs (hyaloclastites) and the products of post-eruptive processes, *Bull. Volcanol., 27,* 391–410, 1964.

Nayudu, Y. R., Petrology of submarine volcanics and sediments in the vicinity of the Mendocino fracture zone, *Progress in Oceanography,* vol. 3, edited by M. Sears, pp. 207–220, Pergamon, New York, 1965*a*.

Nayudu, Y. R., Petrologic and chemical studies of palagonites and manganese incrustations from the Atlantic and Pacific oceans (abstract), *International Symposium on Volcanology, New Zealand,* 123, 1965*b*.

Nayudu, Y. R., R. W. Sleeper, D. Y. Kode, and C. Chastain, Deep-sea sediments of the Southwest Pacific, 30°–60°S, 120°–180°W, paper presented at the 63rd annual meeting of the Geological Society of America, University of California, Santa Barbara, 1967*a*.

Nayudu, Y. R., R. W. Sleeper, D. Y. Kode, and C. Chastain, Physiography and petrology of deep-sea sediments of the Southwestern Pacific (abstract), *Trans. Am. Geophys. Union, 48*(1), 143–144, 1967*b*.

Nayudu, Y. R., Geologic implications of microfossils in submarine volcanics from the Northeast Pacific (abstract), *Eos, Trans. Am. Geophys. Union, 50*(4), 195, 1969.

Nicholls, G. D., Trace elements in sediments: an assessment of their possible utility as depth indicators, *Marine Geol., 5* (5/6), 539–555, 1967.

Owen, B. B., and S. R. Brinkley, Jr., Calculation of the effect of pressure upon ionic equilibria in pure water and in salt solutions, *Chem. Rev., 29,* 461–474, 1941.

Peterson, M. N. A., Calcite: Rates of dissolution in a vertical profile in the Central Pacific, *Science, 154,* 1542–1544, 1966.

Reid, J., Jr., H. Stommel, E. D. Stroup, and B. A. Warren, Detection of a deep boundary current in the Western South Pacific, *Nature, 217,* 937, 1968.

Smith, S. V., J. A. Dygas, and K. E. Chave, Distribution of calcium carbonate in pelagic sediments, *Marine Geol., 6,* 391–400, 1968.

Stommel, H., A survey of ocean current theory, *Deep-Sea Res., 4,* 149–184, 1957.

Stommel, H., The abyssal circulation, *Deep-Sea Res., 5,* 80–82, 1958.

Stommel, H., and A. B. Arons, On the abyssal circulation of the world ocean — An idealized model of the circulation pattern and amplitude in oceanic basins, *Deep-Sea Res., 6,* 217–233, 1960.

Tolstikov, E. I., Ed., *Atlas Antarktiki,* vol. 1, G.U.C.K., Moscow, 1966.

Wooster, W., and G. Volkmann, Indications of deep Pacific circulation from the distribiution of properties at five kilometers, *J. Geophys. Res., 65,* 1239–1249, 1960.

Zhivago, A. V., Outlines of Southern Ocean geomorphology, in *Antarctic Research, Geophys. Monograph 7,* edited by H. Wexler, pp. 74–80, American Geophysical Union, Washington, D.C., 1962.

PETROLOGIC VARIATIONS WITHIN SUBMARINE BASALT PILLOWS OF THE SOUTH PACIFIC OCEAN

THEODORE P. PASTER

Florida State University, Tallahassee, Florida 32306

Abstract. The chemistry of submarine basalts has been used in upper mantle petrogenesis models, but criteria for selecting fresh, representative samples and an understanding of within-specimen variations are vague. To define alteration criteria in the submarine environment, variations in the mineralogical and chemical compositions of one alkalic and eight tholeiitic basalt pillows from abyssal hills in eight widely scattered localities of the South Pacific Ocean and Drake Passage have been studied from glass rim to aphanitic interior. These variations are related to primary cooling (quenching and deuteric alteration) and secondary alteration (hydration and recrystallization).

Four texturally gradational zones are defined from glass rim inward: hydrated glass, unhydrated glass, 'variolitic' zone, and aphanitic zone. This transition occurs through a minimum thickness of 3 centimeters. Vesicularity in the eight tholeiites does not exceed 3% at depths greater than 3200 meters, which is consistent with physicochemical data.

Three types of alteration are common: (1) glass hydration (> 2.0% total H_2O) resulting in loss of magnesium and calcium and increase of total iron, ferric/ferrous ratio, and potassium; (2) serpentinization adjacent to joints and fractures; and (3) chloritization from higher temperature deuteric alteration in the aphanitic zone, causing depletion of magnesium and total iron as FeO (up to 2.0 wt % of rock). The iron migrates to joints, where it is either oxidized or escapes in significant quantities for redeposition in iron-rich sediments and ferromanganese concretions.

It is concluded that the unhydrated glass and variolitic zones are most representative of the pillows' chemical compositions, which are slightly undersaturated tholeiites. The chemical composition of one thoroughly hydrated tholeiite is significantly different from the other seven relatively unaltered tholeiites whose normative compositional ranges are: Ab, 22.5–24.1%; An, 23.5–30.0%; Di, 19.2–24.6%; Ol, 0.6–4.5%; Hy, 14.6–19.5%.

INTRODUCTION

The chemical characteristics of oceanic basalts have an important bearing on any possible sequence of differentiation among the various basalt types, because contamination from continental crust is minimal or absent in the ocean basins. Inasmuch as the chemistry of oceanic basalts is reported to be relatively uniform, surprisingly so in view of their areal extent, these basalts are believed to reflect the chemical characteristics of the earth's upper mantle [*Engel et al.*, 1965]. However, the extent of posteruptive chemical alterations in submarine basalts is little known, and interpretations concerning the composition of the parental mantle material based on altered basalts could be significantly in error. *Hart* [1969] has shown that one type of alteration produces an increase in the potassium content of the rock.

Further, the alteration of submarine basalt has been postulated to be an important source of the metal ions that comprise marine ferromanganese concentrations [*Bonatti and Nayudu*, 1965]. No definitive chemical or mineralogical data on the basalts themselves which could serve as direct evidence bearing on this hypothesis have as yet been presented.

Two modes of submarine volcanism have been reviewed by *Menard* [1964]: tranquil flow with the formation of pillow lavas and explosive emanations with the formation of ash. Both have been observed in shallow water, but their relative importance has not been established at abyssal depths. Pillow lavas can be recognized in bottom photographs, but explosion ash cannot be similarly distinguished from other sediments. *Bonatti* [1965, 1967] believed that explosive emanation with instantaneous hydration of hot basaltic glass is a major process on the deep ocean floor. This belief is based upon his observations of the abundance and characteristics of glass fragments in sediments.

Reports of voids or high vesicularity in some basalts dredged from abyssal depths conflict with the expected behavior of water vapor in basaltic melts under such pressure.

Nine pillows dredged by the USNS *Eltanin* from

eight widely separated South Pacific Ocean and Drake Passage localities were investigated texturally, mineralogically, and chemically for variations within single fragments that could be ascribed to the effects of water, both internal and external, on the final textural and chemical characteristics of the basalt. The variations in magnetic properties of these basalts are discussed elsewhere [*Watkins and Paster*, 1970].

Basalt E-5-4 is from a rise in the Drake Passage, as is E-5-5, the only sample obtained from a seamount. E-21-10-1 and E-21-10-2 are from the Chile Rise (Figure 1, Table 1). The rest of the pillows were dredged from abyssal hills. All of the basalts except E-5-5 are from depths ranging between 3200 and 4800 meters. With the exception of E-5-5, the basalts represent samples from localities that were dredged with no specific physiographic or geologic target in mind and therefore may be representative of submarine flows on the deep ocean floor.

The data presented herein should provide firmer criteria for establishing whether or not a particular major element analysis is representative of a particular submarine basalt fragment and so allow it to be used in general petrogenetic theory. In addition, the characterization of alteration in submarine basalts might be related to the source problem of elements in ferromanganese concretions.

PREVIOUS WORK

General Petrology

The petrographic classification used in this paper is that of *Macdonald and Katsura* [1964, pp. 88–89]. Accordingly, the most common basalts found in oceanic regions are tholeiites, olivine tholeiites, and alkalic basalts. Tholeiites are rocks saturated in silica in which magnesian olivine reacts with the melt to form calcium-poor pyroxene [*Kennedy*, 1933; *Tilley*, 1950; *Tilley and Muir*, 1967]. Olivine tholeiite contains more than 5% modal olivine, whereas tholeiite contains less than 5%. Alkalic basalts are generally similar in composition to tholeiites and olivine tholeiites, their principal difference being a relative enrichment in total alkalis, phosphorus, and titanium, with a relative depletion in silica.

Many petrologists have designated olivine tholeiite as the primitive magma from which tholeiite is derived through fractional crystallization and from which alkalic basalt is produced by either fractional crystallization, gaseous transfer, or assimilation [*Engel and Engel*, 1964]. It is now generally believed that alkalic

TABLE 1. Location, Depth, and Remarks on Sample Sites

Sample Number	Latitude	Longitude	Depth, meters	Remarks
E-5-4	59°02′S	67°15′W	3475	Tholeiite, Drake Passage, 180 meters relief.
E-5-5	59°45.5′S	68°50′W	1372	Alkali basalt, north slope of an unnamed seamount.
E-15-5	61°06′S	104°58′W	4828	Tholeiite, flat bottom.
E-15-15	56°02′S	149°40.9′W	3256	Tholeiite, abyssal hills, 390 meters relief.
E-21-8	32°58′S	87°59′W	3621	Tholeiite, rolling terrain, 55–70 meters relief.
E-21-10, 1 and 2	37°19′S	94°39′W	3292	Tholeiite, rugged hills on crest of Chile Rise, 550 meters relief.
E-24-15	35°58′S	134°50′W	4682	Tholeiite, undulating bottom, 20–90 meters relief.
E-25-5	49°57′S	89°59′W	4280	Tholeiite, undulating bottom, 550 meters relief.

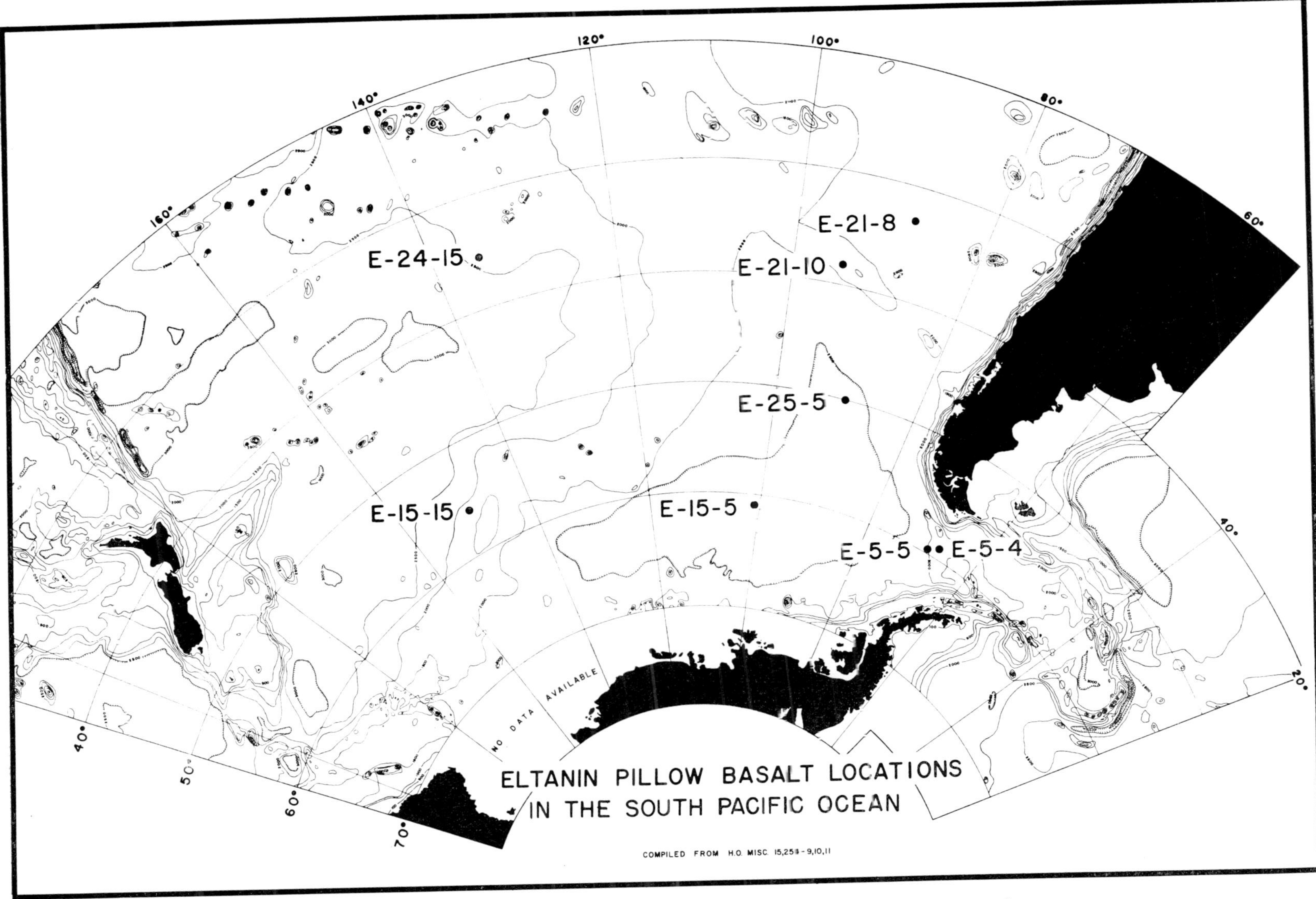

Fig. 1. Location map of *Eltanin* pillow basalts; 500-fathom bathymetric contour intervals.

basalt, tholeiite, and olivine tholeiite are products of partial melting at different depths in the mantle [*Yoder and Tilley*, 1962, p. 509; *Green and Ringwood*, 1967; *Kushiro*, 1968].

Photographs of submarine lava flows have been taken on the flanks of Hawaii [*Moor and Reed*, 1963], on the Albatross Cordillera (East Pacific Rise) [*Bonatti*, 1967; *Engel and Engel*, 1964], and on the Mid-Atlantic Ridge [*Muir et al.*, 1964]. Flows in many parts of the South Pacific Ocean have been photographed by the USNS *Eltanin* [*Goodell*, 1964, 1965, 1968]. The pillows are generally bulbous in shape with diameters ranging from 5 to 60 cm. Dredge hauls of pillows yield roughly wedge-shaped, angular slabs or blocks of basalt which are a product of columnar jointing perpendicular to the pillow surfaces. The distance between joints ranges from 2 to 15 cm. The blocks are composed of glass and aphanitic basalt; one end is usually convex or concave, being comprised of a dark rim of basaltic glass from 0.1 to 2.0 cm thick. The glass surfaces may be hydrated to a reddish-orange to buff layer of palagonite up to 2 mm in thickness. The glass surfaces of some pillows have been reported to show traces of pahoehoe ropy structure. The pillows may be vesicular or nonvesicular or may contain a concentration of vesicles beneath the glass rim. Vesicles beneath the glass rim have been reported to have coalesced into a nearly continuous cavity [*Moore*, 1965; *Bonatti*, 1967].

Evidence has been cited indicating that submarine lavas upon extrusion are in some cases more fluid than subaerial lavas. *Engel and Engel* [1964] reported that one thin edge of a pillow formed a cast of ripple-marked sediment over which it flowed; submarine flows of only 10 cm in thickness have been noted (Bonatti, personal communication). *Macdonald* [1968, p. 26] stated that the fluid interiors of some pillows have drained to leave cavities. He discussed the genetic relationship among pahoehoe toes (terminal tongue-shaped protrusions of solidified pahoehoe), pillows, and angular glass fragments (hyaloclasts) and demonstrated that all of these products could be produced from the pahoehoe flows of the tranquil type of submarine eruption. *Bailey et al.* [1964, p. 51] have reported hyaloclast concentrations of 50% intermixed with the smaller pillows of the Franciscan formation. This might be expected, as contraction of small pillows during cooling produces a greater differential stress in their glassy rims, thereby producing a greater volume of spallation hyaloclasts.

Vesicularity of Submarine Lavas

The role of water in the development of vesicles in basaltic lava at the temperatures and pressures involved at abyssal depths has been discussed in detail by *Menard* [1964], *Rittman* [1962], and *McBirney* [1963]. From the experimental data of *Kennedy* [1950], it can be shown that water vapor at pressures of 100 to 500 atmospheres (approximately 1000 to 5000 meters water depth) and a temperature of 1000°C rapidly rising from a depth of 3510 meters in a volcanic fissure to 3500 meters on the ocean floor will expand only about 2% with this sudden pressure decrease. Water vapor at the same temperature and rising at the same rate in a volcanic pipe from 10 meters below sea level to sea level with the same sudden pressure decrease will expand 1000%. As a result, a basaltic lava slightly oversaturated with as much as 2% total water will not vesiculate to more than a few per cent by volume upon eruption below 2000 meters water depth.

All other things being equal, the volume per cent of vesicles should be dependent upon water depth. Other gases, of course, are not considered, and if the lava is appreciably oversaturated in volatiles at the time of quenching a higher vesicle percentage may be expected. *Moore* [1965] substantiated the inverse relationship between saturated lava and pressure by plotting the volume per cent vesicles in pillows recovered near Hawaii versus water depth. Because the water in molten lava expands only slightly upon release of pressure at abyssal depths, 'pulverized' glass (hyaloclasts) is the dominant volcanic ash constituent at depth in contrast to ash formed under less confining pressure, which usually consists of shards formed by the fracturing of glass walls of gas bubbles.

Alteration

Textures in submarine basalts are as variable as in subaerial basalts with the exception of pillows, whose texture and mineralogy have been described in some detail by *Moore* [1966].

Alterations commonly reported in pillows include hydration (palagonitization) and zeolitization of basaltic glass and deuteric alteration of olivine and pyroxene to secondary minerals such as chlorite, serpentine, talc, goethite, and hematite.

The nature of some types of alteration reported earlier [*Matthews*, 1962] is suspect, since more recent comprehensive investigations indicate that alteration of crystalline basalt to clay minerals is restricted almost entirely to seamounts, banks, and guyots that may have been exposed to conditions approximating subaerial weathering [*Bonatti*, 1967; *Moore*, 1965, 1966; *Rex*, 1967].

Investigations of numerous samples of submarine basalt from all parts of the ocean floor suggest that spilitization of basalt on the ocean floor is rare [*Engel, Fischer, and Engel*, 1965; *Bonatti*, 1967] and is restricted to the oceanic ridge system, where processes of metasomatism appear to be significant [*Melson and Van Andel*, 1966]. There appears to be no evidence that calcic plagioclase is converted to sodium feldspar through direct contact of basalt with sea water, either when freshly erupted or when exposed for considerable periods of time at sea floor temperatures. Many submarine basalt descriptions, especially those of pillows, note the remarkably fresh appearance of the feldspars.

Moore [1966] presented evidence that the palagonitization of basaltic glass during initial cooling of the lava is relatively insignificant (~2 microns in thickness) and found a correlation between the thickness of the hydrated glass layer and the ages of the basalts. His results indicated a much higher rate of hydration for basaltic glass than for silica-rich glass. Experimental studies by *Hawkins and Roy* [1963] showed that the concentration of magnesium in both glass and the aqueous environment was a dominant factor in the rate of alteration. Where the magnesium content of the weathering solution is comparatively low, as in the case of sea water, the amount of silica and magnesium in the glass plays a greater role in alteration with the rate proceeding more rapidly in a glass of high magnesium and low silica content. The reduced rate of alteration in magnesium-deficient water might explain why Moore found lower rates of hydration of basaltic glass in a fresh-water lake as compared with those in sea water.

There are few available data suggesting what per cent water is necessary before a basaltic glass may be considered hydrated. Ten hydrated-nonhydrated silicic glass pairs studied by *Noble* [1967] include a water content of less than 0.5% for the nonhydrated glass. *Ross and Smith* [1955] give a value of 0.9% water content for unhydrated obsidian. The highest value for unhydrated glass of basaltic composition is reported by *Correns* [1930] to be 1.22%.

A number of analyses of hydrated glasses have been made to determine what chemical changes are attendant upon hydration. Most of these have been made on silicic glasses, and only a few on hydrated-nonhydrated basaltic glass pairs. The results, although tentative, indicate that chemical changes in the two types of glass are qualitatively the same.

Nicholls [1963] found a decrease in the percentage of calcium, magnesium, and sodium in hydrated basaltic glass and attributed the losses to leaching by sea water. *Noble* [1967] found an increase in potassium in hydrated silicic glass relative to unhydrated glass and interpreted the gain as an ion-exchange interaction between the glass and the hydrating water. An increase in total iron and ferric/ferrous ratio in hydrated basaltic glass relative to unhydrated glass has been reported by *Nicholls* [1965] and *Bonatti* [1965]. *Noble* [1967] suggested that aluminum is relatively immobile during hydration, whereas silicon may be lost.

The deuteric minerals reported to be in submarine basalts are: chlorite, calcite, iddingsite, serpentine, talc, chlorophaeite, quartz, zeolites, clay minerals, hematite, and iron oxides and hydroxides [*Quon and Ehlers*, 1963; *Engel and Engel*, 1963; *Shand*, 1949; *Poldervaart and Green*, 1965; *Muir et al.*, 1964]. These alteration products are commonly found in dolerites and diabases as well as in pillows.

PROCEDURES

Samples

Basaltic pillows have been chosen for this investigation for a number of reasons: (1) fragments of pillows are easily recognized megascopically and may therefore be selected from dredge hauls that may contain ice-rafted debris; (2) pillows contain glass which is believed to be the most representative material of the original basaltic melt; (3) these fragments are a common material from the deep ocean floor; and (4) direct interaction of hot lava with sea water would be optimum in pillows.

Petrography

Thin sections cut normal to the pillow surfaces and polished thin sections cut parallel to the glass surfaces at intervals from the surface to the interior of the pillows were prepared and examined under a polarizing and reflecting microscope by conventional techniques. Where mineral or vesicle percentages are reported, the values are based on a minimum of 2000 point counts on a grid pattern of 3.5 points per mm. The fine-grained texture of the material allowed such a closely spaced grid without two consecutive points falling on a single crystal with the exception of relatively large phenocrysts. The identification of minerals in joints and hydrated glass was supplemented by X-ray diffraction.

a

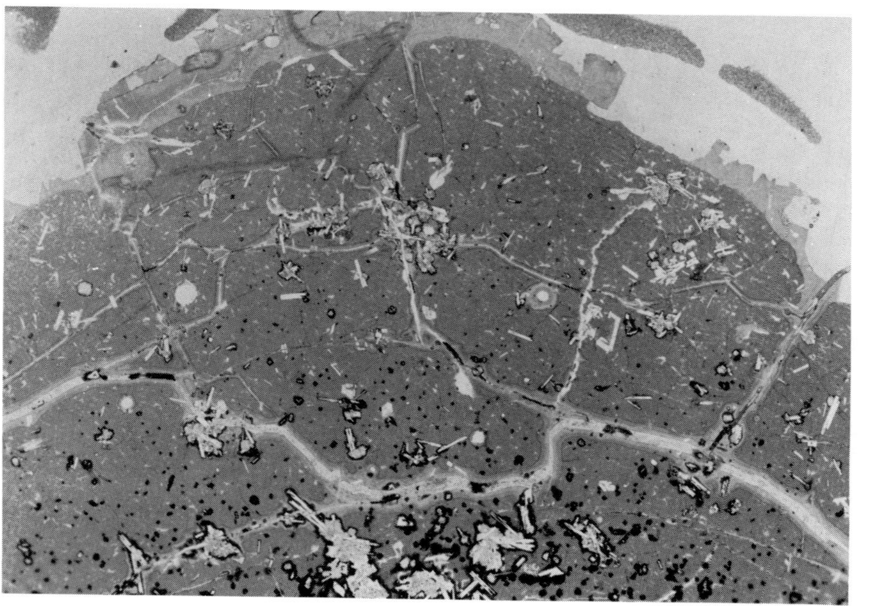

b

c

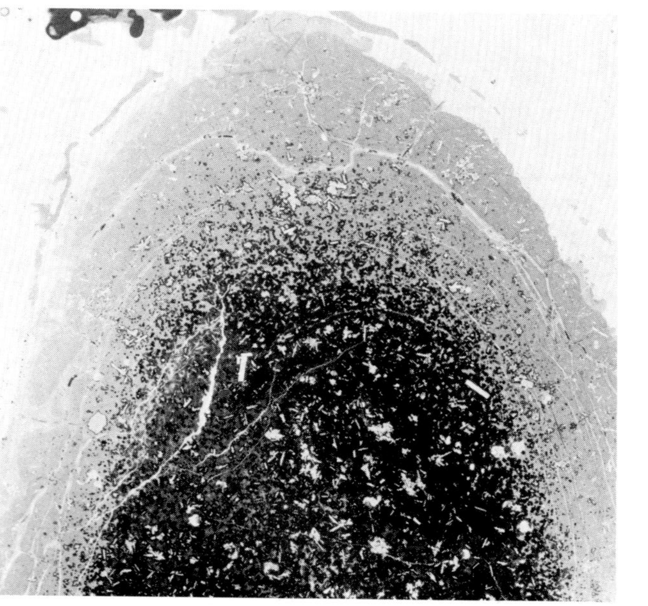

d

Chemistry

Each of the nine pillow fragments was sampled in at least two of the four pillow zones for major element chemical analysis. Twenty-five complete and two partial major element analyses were performed in duplicate with the exceptions of H_2O^+, H_2O^-, and FeO, which were performed only once on each sample. The method of analysis used for most elements has been outlined by *Shapiro* [1967]. SiO_2 and Al_2O_3 were determined by NaOH fusion in a nickel crucible as outlined by *Shapiro and Brannock* [1962]. FeO was determined by the method of *Reichen and Fahey* [1962], which consists of oxidizing the powdered samples with $K_2Cr_2O_7$ in the presence of HF and H_2SO_4, then titrating the excess dichromate. The water determinations were made using the method of *Shapiro and Brannock* [1962].

Where determinations in duplicate were made, they have been averaged. Standard basalt W-1 was used as a standard for all constituents except the alkalis, calcium, magnesium, and manganese, for which primary standards were used.

Results

Magascopic Description of Pillows

In contrast to most of the dredge hauls from the South Atlantic, South Pacific, and Indian oceans, the hauls containing these basalts contained little or no other rock types that could be attributed to ice rafting.

Most of the *Eltanin* basalts are angular blocks characteristic of jointed pillow fragments. They average 8 × 10 × 15 cm in size and are therefore much larger than the fragments described by *Moore* [1965]. Joint surfaces of the pillow blocks are commonly coated with α-goethite. The glass surfaces of the blocks do not display obvious pahoehoe structure.

Two basalt fragments of this study are in the shape of 'toes' approximately 30 cm in length, which taper to about 5 cm at their termini (Plate 1*a*).

The *Eltanin* pillows contain less than 3% vesicles and exhibit no concentration of vesicles within them, with the exception of toe E-5-4 (Plate 1*b*), which contains a large central cavity and E-5-5, which averages 37% vesicles in the 19 cm next to its glass surface and 13% vesicles below this zone (Figure 2).

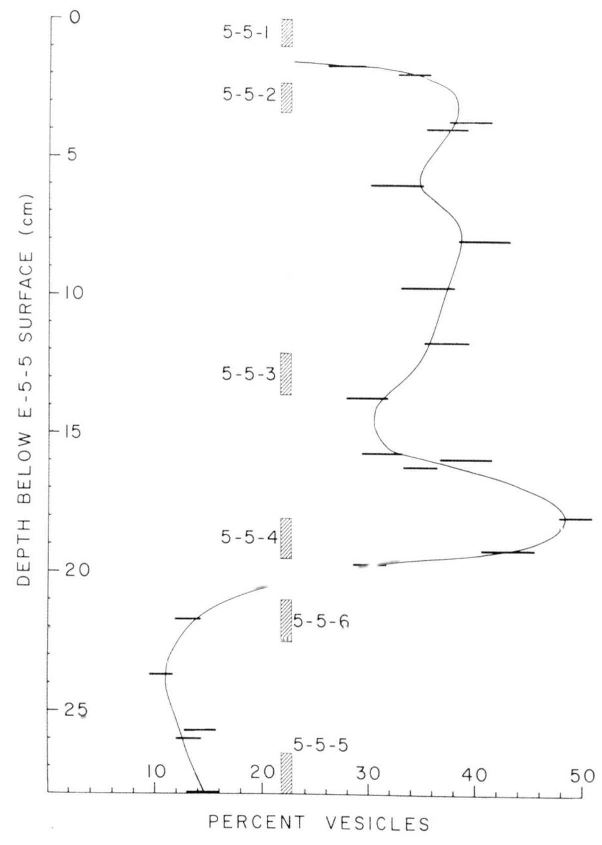

Fig. 2. Vesicularity versus depth in E-5-5. Chemically analyzed intervals are represented by diagonal lines with sample numbers.

Pahoehoe toes E-5-4 and E-24-15 contain many more concentric fractures in their glassy rims than do the rims of the larger pillows. These concentric fractures are unevenly spaced and are connected at irregular intervals by radial fractures (Plates 1*c*, 1*d*).

The vesicle percentage of the pillows is plotted in Figure 3, along with *Moore*'s [1965] data.

Plate 1

a. Pahoehoe toe E-24-15 with a ferromanganese crust from 1.0 to 1.4 cm thick. Scale: 22 cm × 12 cm.

b. Sections through toe E-5-4 showing central cavity and concentric fractures in glass rim filled with phillipsite. Scale: 8 cm section diameter.

c. Thin section through toe E-24-15 showing concentric fractures lined with palagonite and phillipsite. Note thick palagonite rim preserved at top and left edge of pillow, which is lighter in color than unhydrated glass. Scale: 5½ cm × 5½ cm.

d. Fractured rim of toe E-24-15 with a few scattered vesicles and agglomerates of olivine and plagioclase rimmed with incipient, variolitic pyroxene set in a clear light brown glass. Scale: 2.2 cm × 1.7 cm.

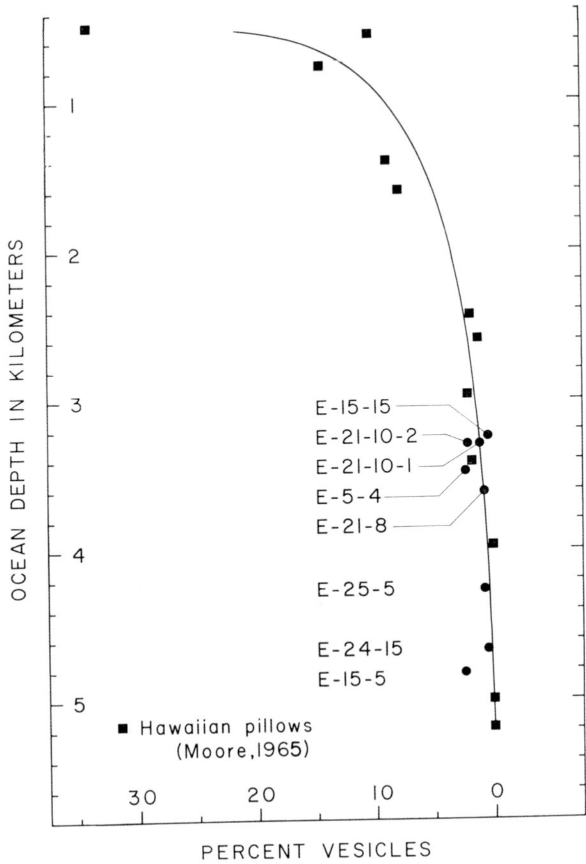

Fig. 3. Pillow vesicularity versus ocean depth.

Petrography of the Pillows

General Petrography

One of the most conspicuous features of the clear glass rim is the subparallel alignment of feldspar laths roughly parallel to the pillow zones. This alignment is less evident below the variolitic zone. All zones in the *Eltanin* pillows contain agglomerates of relatively large feldspar and olivine, or feldspar and augite phenocrysts. Modal olivine is less than 5% in all of the tholeiite samples and where present the domal-shaped, euhedral to skeletal phenocrysts are not discernibly zoned. Whereas four of the pillows contain large, zoned plagioclases, only E-21-10-2 contains plagioclase, which appears to have been resorbed. Measurements of combined albite-Carlsbad twins of only the unzoned plagioclase phenocrysts in the pillows reveal a range in composition between An_{62} and An_{80}. The plagioclase compositional range common to most of the pillows lies between An_{65} and An_{75} (Figure 5). This range is only slightly more sodic than the range of An_{70} to An_{76} for phenocrysts of basalts from the Mid-Atlantic Ridge reported by *Quon and Ehlers* [1963].

The purplish color and strong inclined dispersion of the pyroxene in E-5-5 indicate that it is high in titanium. Pigeonite was identified in the groundmass of all of the tholeiites by its small positive optic angle.

Palagonite Zone

The rims of these pillows are divided into four layers, discounting any manganese oxide crust, which is not considered a part of the rock itself (Figure 4).

The palagonite and clear glass layers may vary appreciably in thickness, depending upon the degree of hydration and preservation of the pillow rind. In general, the palagonite layer varies from 0.5 mm to 2 mm in thickness, is reddish- to yellowish-brown in color, and is in sharp contact with the clear glass below it. The only minerals definitely identified in the palagonite are phillipsite and montmorillonite.

Clear Glass Zone

Inward from the palagonite layer, there is a zone of pale yellowish-brown transparent glass normally from 5 to 17 mm in thickness and commonly containing phenocrysts of olivine and plagioclase. The inner portion of this clear glass is speckled owing to minute dark brown to black cryptocrystalline spherules (Plate 2*a*). Under high magnification these spherules are observed to be composed of fibrous or feathery, felted microlites dusted with very minute opaque minerals. The spherules commonly nucleate about phenocrysts of plagioclase and olivine.

Plate 2

a. Clear glass to variolitic transition showing nucleation of varioles around phenocrysts of olivine and plagioclase (E-21-10-2). Scale: 6.5 mm × 8.0 mm.

b. Variolitic texture at its fullest development in dark red-brown variolitic zone of E-15-15. Scale: 6.5 mm × 8.0 mm.

c. Variolitic zone with dusty opaques. The fine, fibrous pyroxene and incipient opaques give a fuzzy appearance to the groundmass and edges of the phenocrysts (E-21-10-2). Scale: 0.65 mm × 0.8 mm.

d. Variolitic zone with fine opaques. The groundmass pyroxene has formed fan-shaped and plumose aggregates with opaques in the intervariolitic spaces (E-21-10-2). Scale: 0.65 mm × 0.8 mm.

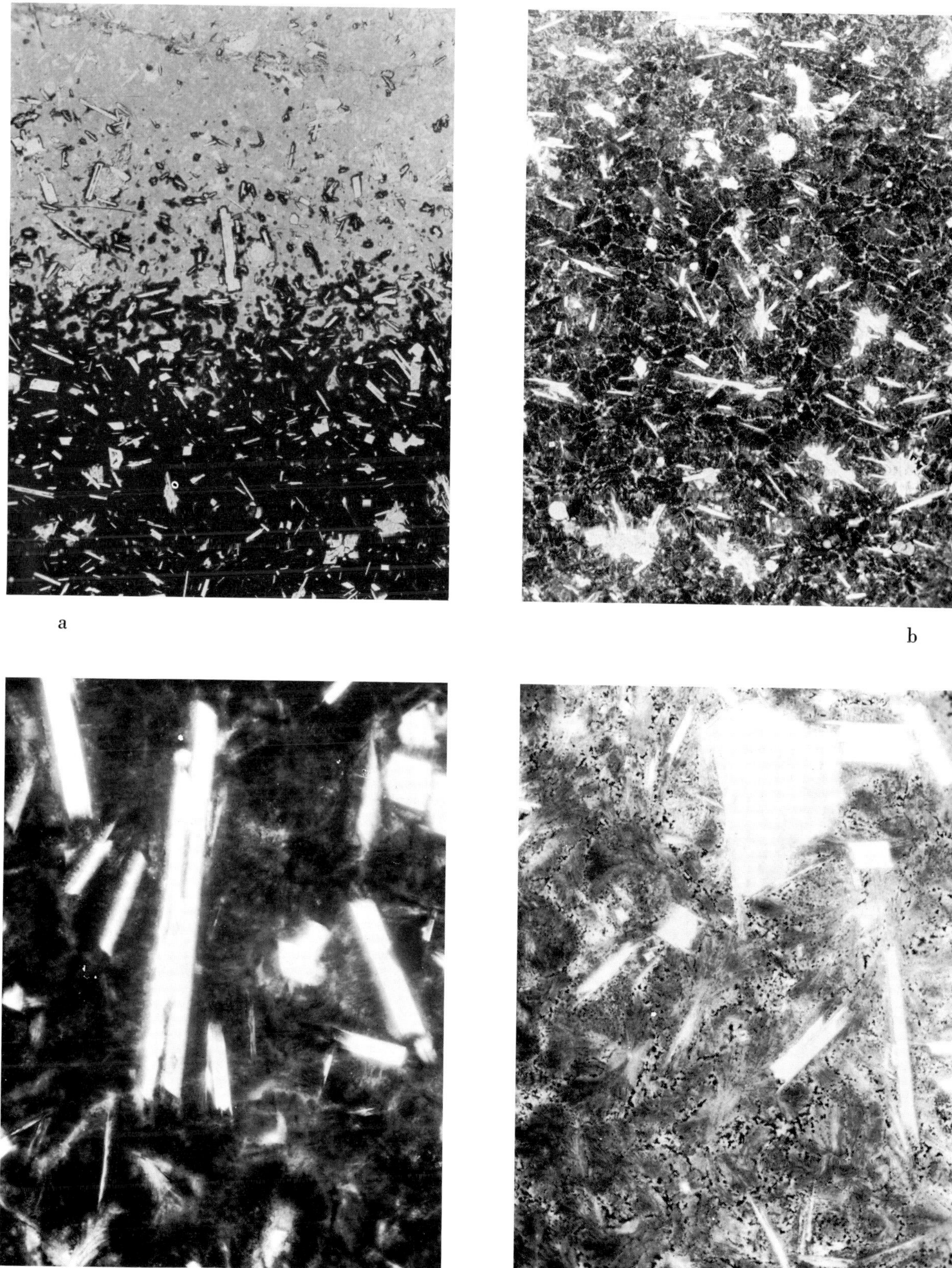
a
b
c
d

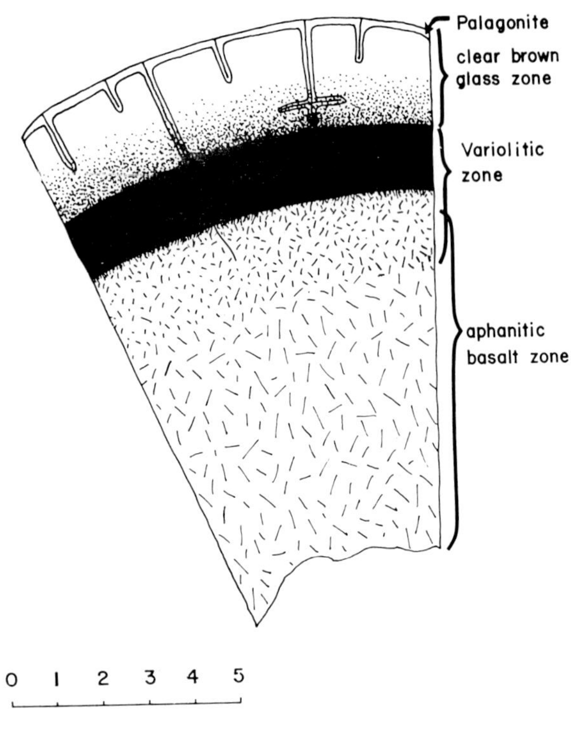

Fig. 4. Diagram of pillow zones.

Variolitic Zone

Below the transparent glass the spherules increase in density and size until they form a nearly opaque, dark brown or dark reddish-brown variolitic zone (Plate 2*b*). 'Variolitic' is used here to mean a texture comprised of subparallel fibers of clinopyroxene arranged in spherical or polygonal units. This dark variolitic zone varies from 5 to 12 mm in thickness and, where pillows are thick enough, grades inward to a lighter brown variolitic zone (Plate 3*a*) and then to a very fine-grained basalt toward the center of the pillows (Plate 3*b*). The pahoehoe toes do not exhibit the fine-grained stage of crystallization in their interiors.

The exceedingly fine size of the microlites comprising the varioles generally prohibits measurement of their optical properties. Where previous mineralogic identification of the varioles has been attempted, they have been considered to be incipient crystals of feldspar, or intergrowths of feldspar and clinopyroxene. By tracing the progressive growth of the varioles into the essentially holocrystalline, fine-grained interior of the pillows where optical measurements are possible, the varioles are identified as incipient clinopyroxene crystals, possibly laminated with plagioclase. The change in color from dark brown or dark reddish-brown to light brown from clear glass to crystalline interior, respectively, is accompanied by the development of titanomagnetite microlites. The opaque minerals exhibit a sequence of development from dispersed dust to discrete skeletal crystals that increase in size, decrease in number, and segregate at the peripheries of the varioles (Plates 2*c*, 2*d*, and 3*c*).

In some sections a subparallel arrangement of the clinopyroxene fibers in each of the varioles can be discerned. Individual varioles of the variolitic zone are polygonal at their largest development owing to mutual growth interference (Plate 2*b*). Within a relatively short interval the varioles reorganize into fans and plumes of coarser fibers that bear a strong resemblance to quench clinopyroxene, as illustrated by *Yoder and Tilley* [1962, plate 10 D]. Within a longer (~1.0 cm) interval these fans and plumes give way to discrete, smaller equant grains of clinopyroxene in the light-brown, fine-grained basalt. It is only in or below the variolitic-aphanitic basalt transition that minute laths of truly matrix plagioclase can be seen to appear where they are laminated with the clinopyroxene fibers. Measurement of these feldspars by the Michel-Levy method indicates a range in composition from An_{52} to An_{56}. The fine, optically interfering microlites comprising the varioles are undoubtedly intimately mixed with glass, although no glass can be distinguished. The presence of water in excess of

Plate 3

a. Variolitic to aphanitic transition. Varioles were breaking up into smaller, discrete, equigranular clinopyroxene crystals when crystallization was arrested (E-15-15). Scale: 6.5 mm × 8.0 mm.

b. Aphanitic texture. Groundmass is composed of plagioclase microlites and small, discrete clinopyroxene crystals, but turbid patches of variolitic groundmass remain. A large skeletal olivine phenocryst is near center of photograph (E-21-10-2). Scale: 6.5 mm × 8.0 mm.

c. Aphanitic zone with larger opaques. Groundmass granules of pyroxene have lost fibrous appearance (Plate 2*d*) and are more equigranular (E-21-10-2). Scale: 0.65 mm × 0.8 mm.

d. Hydrated aphanitic zone with sorbed iron and manganese hydroxides near joint surface. Turbid appearance of rock near hydroxide surface suggests hydrated glass in this zone. Scale: 6.5 mm × 8.0 mm.

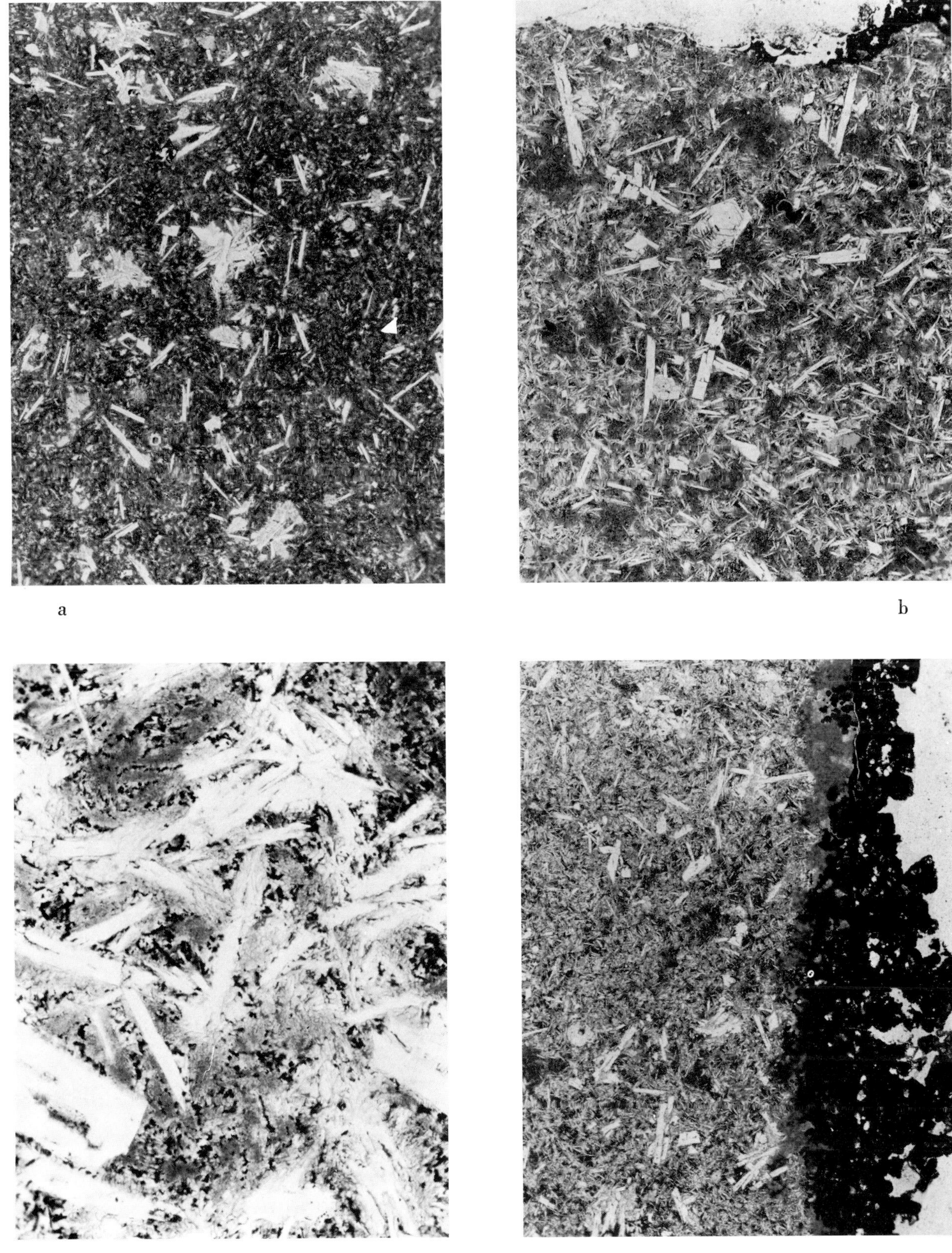
a
b
c
d

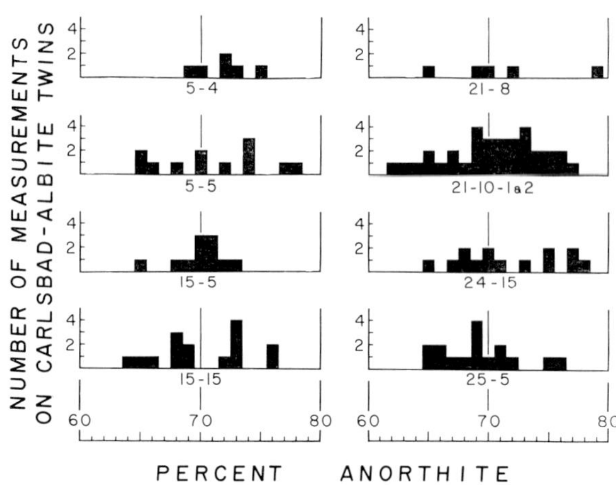

Fig. 5. Phenocryst plagioclase compositions in pillows.

2.0% in the variolitic zones of E-24-15 and E-25-5 may be interpreted as indirect evidence of glass in this zone. Hydration of the aphanitic zone of E-15-15 adjacent to a joint (Plate 3*d*) also indicates the presence of glass in this zone.

Alteration of the Pillows

Three types of alteration were found in the pillows: hydration and two types of deuteric alteration. Since *Moore* [1966] has sufficiently described hydration, the following discussion will deal with the deuteric types.

Chloritization

Chloritization is generally associated with the inner, aphanitic zone of the pillows and is characterized by the following minerals: reddish-brown chlorite (clinochlore?) and hematite in vesicles (E-5-5); chlorite and ferric iron staining after olivine (E-15-15); talc in vesicles and after olivine (E-21-8); magnesite after olivine (E-21-10-2); chlorite(?) (E-25-5); chlorite (?) after pyroxene (E-5 4). E-5-5 and E-25-5 have a higher concentration of alteration products (>7.0% by volume) in their interiors than do the other pillows, whose alteration products do not exceed 2.0% by volume.

In one instance pseudomorphs of chlorite after olivine are found in distorted forms, indicating alteration while plastic deformation was still in progress. Some of these pseudomorphs might even be classified as filled vesicles. The crystalline size of the alteration minerals is generally very fine-grained, and it is difficult to identify them and to determine their relative percentages precisely. These particular alteration products were not found in the glass layer of the pillows, however, and are less prominent or are absent in the variolitic zone.

Serpentinization

Serpentinization occurs invariably next to fractures and joints and in some cases is found in the variolitic zone. It involves the replacement of olivine by a material having the optical properties of α-serpentine [*Deer et al.*, 1962, p. 182]. In hand specimens the altered zone adjacent to joints is darker in color and is a surprisingly constant 6 mm in thickness among all the pillow fragments (Plates 4*a* and 4*b*). *Hart* [1969] has described some chemical alterations in this zone.

The fibrous serpentine is bright green farthest from fractures but becomes progressively more contaminated with ferric oxide and hydroxide stains toward fractures and joints. In all of the pillows but E-5-4, which contains no olivine, serpentine is found in vesicles, joints, and fractures as well as replacing olivine. In E-15-15 serpentine is found in the intervariole region at the base of the variolitic zone. Iron stains are prominent near joints and fractures where goethite, hematite, and serpentine are found as fracture fillings up to 0.3 mm thick (Plates 4*c*, 4*d*). Secondary magnetite is found within bright yellowish-green serpentine near joints of E-21-10-2, although the serpentine adjacent to the joints is stained reddish-brown and no secondary magnetite occurs.

In E-24-15 the minute opaque crystals, normally found in the intervariole region, are absent adjacent to fractures throughout the variolitic zone where, in addition, the color is an anomalously light tan. Within

---

Plate 4

a. Section normal to columnar jointing in fragment E-21-10-2 showing 6-mm-thick serpentinized rim of pillow fragment.

b. Section normal to pillow surface of E-21-8 showing darker serpentinized zones adjacent to fractures and lighter goethite stains in fractures. Black ferromanganese crust is on upper left corner of fragment. Note typical wedge-shaped outline of pillow fragment. Length from glass surface to inner apex is 11 cm.

c. Serpentine and iron stains in vesicles. Serpentine (gray areas) line vesicle walls and darker central areas are reddish-brown stained serpentine (E-21-10-2). Scale: 0.65 mm × 0.8 mm.

d. Serpentine and hematite in fracture of E-21-10-2. Scale: 0.65 mm × 0.8 mm.

a

b

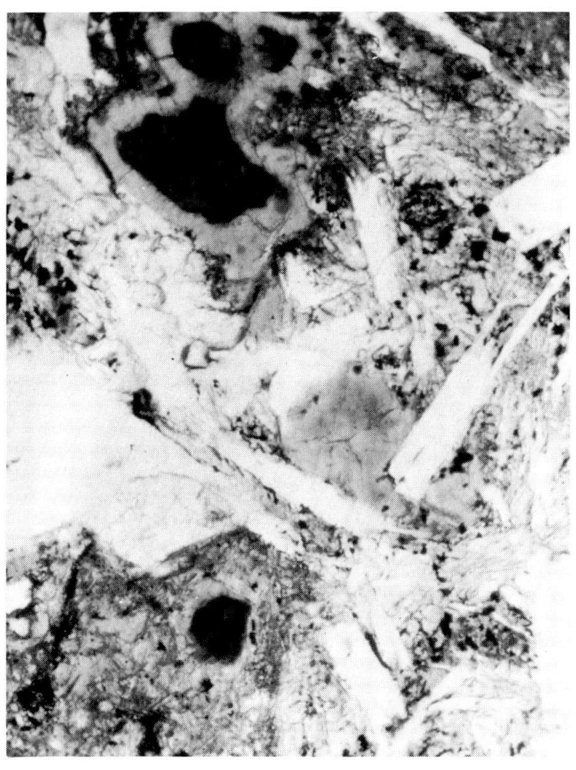

c

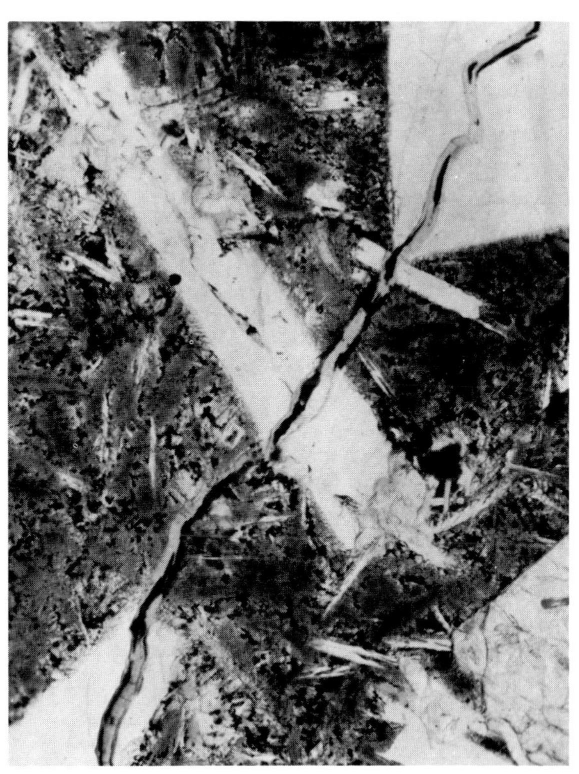

d

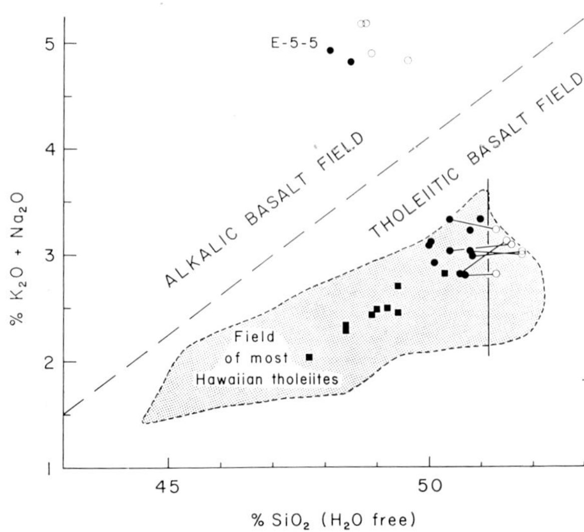

Fig. 6. Alkalis versus silica diagram (after *Macdonald and Katsura* [1964]. Solid circles are pillow glass and variolitic zones; open circles are aphanitic interiors of pillows. Lines connect two analyses from same pillow. Squares are olivine-enriched pillows from the flanks of Hawaii [*Moore*, 1965].

the variolitic zone, away from the fractures, the color is dark brown, and it again contains intervariolitic opaques. Olivine in the clear glass zone is completely free from both types of deuteric alteration.

Chemistry of the Pillows

The results of the chemical analyses are given in Table 2 with their C.I.P.W. norms calculated water-free in per cent by weight.

All of the summed percentages with the exceptions of E-5-4-1 and E-25-5-3 are low, which suggests a systematic error. This is probably owing in part to the recommended values for W-1, whose percentages sum to 99.71%. E-24-15-1 is exceptionally low, owing to a poor water determination. Petrographic work revealed a trace of sulfide in E-5-5 and a trace of carbonate in E-21-10-2, constituents not chemically determined.

The total alkalis are plotted against the silica percentage for the nine *Eltanin* pillows in Figure 6. The diagonal dashed line is an empirically determined line which separates the tholeiitic and alkalic fields for Hawaiian basalts [*Macdonald and Katsura*, 1964]. The unhydrated *Eltanin* samples plot in the upper right portion of the field for most Hawaiian tholeiites except for E-5-5, dredged from the flank of a seamount, which plots in the alkalic basalt field. Submarine tholeiites from the flank of Hawaii containing higher percentages of olivine [*Moore*, 1965] plot lower in the tholeiitic field.

The same analyses are displayed in the form of a Larsen plot in Figure 7. The per cent of each major oxide, adjusted to 100%, is plotted on the ordinate, whereas the abscissa is determined by the formula $\frac{1}{3}$ SiO_2 + K_2O − (MgO + FeO + CaO). Total iron is recalculated to FeO, and MnO is added to this value in the plot. Each line connects the oxide per cent from two portions of the same pillow. The serpentinized zones were not analyzed, but *Hart* [1969] reports that these zones are enriched in potassium.

Figure 8 is a Larsen plot of the alkalic basalt E-5-5, and Figure 9 illustrates the mineralogy of the zones

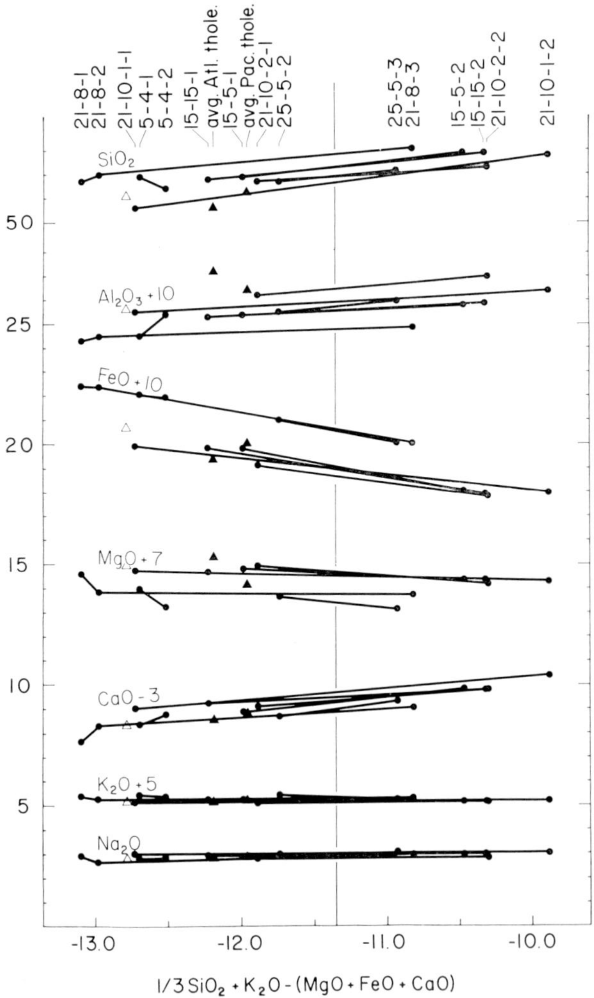

Fig. 7. Larsen plot of unhydrated tholeiites. Ordinate is per cent oxide. Each heavy line connects two analyses from the same pillow. Vertical line at −11.35 separates the aphanitic pillow zones on the right from the glass and variolitic zones on the left. Open triangles represent average of eight Mid-Atlantic Ridge tholeiites [*Muir and Tilley*, 1966]. Solid triangles are other tholeiite analyses [*Engel, Engel, and Havens*, 1965].

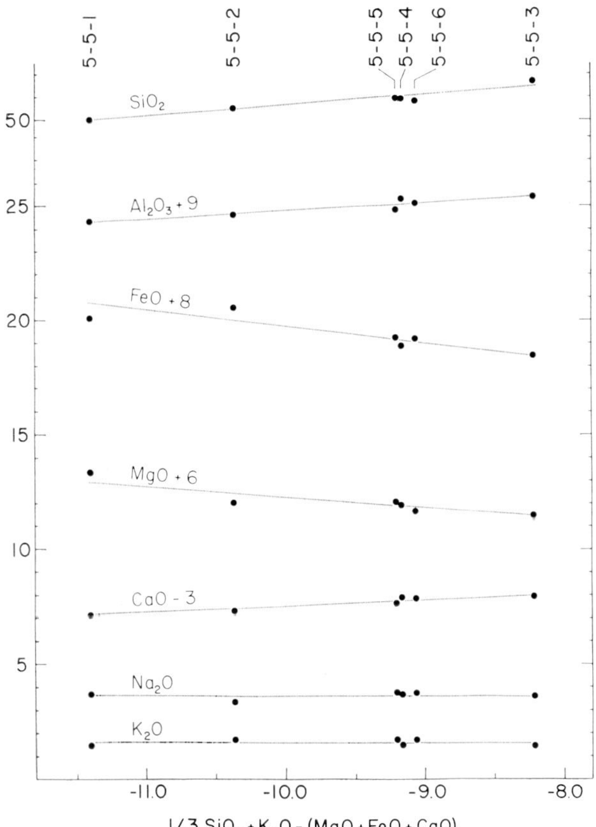

Fig. 8. Larsen plot of E-5-5.

from which the samples were taken for chemical analyses.

Figure 10 is an AFM diagram in which the *Eltanin* tholeiites are compared with the Hawaiian tholeiites. The seven analyses which yielded a total water percentage of greater than 2.0% are shown in Figure 11, which is a Larsen plot similar to that used for the nonhydrated zones.

DISCUSSION

Submarine Volcanism Products

The concentric fractures found in the pahoehoe toes (Plates 1*c* and 1*d*) probably exist because there are greater differential stresses in the chilled glassy crusts of these toes, owing to their smaller diameters. It is evident from the number and spacing of the fractures as well as from the poor coherency of the glass fragments in the rims of the toes that as hydration and zeolitization proceed along the fractures the fragments are loosened to yield a friable glass rim composed of a large number of angular glass fragments, which is preserved intact only by a thick ferromanganese crust.

It is conceivable that the disintegration of such a crust of a submarine flow, which consists of a large number of small pillows and toes, may provide an appreciable amount of angular glass fragments or a hyaloclastite, the association noted by *Bailey et al.* [1964].

Vesicularity of Pillows

The data shown in Figure 3 indicate that in these submarine pillows the theoretical pressure-versus-vesicularity relationship is supported and the lava was not appreciably oversaturated in volatiles at the time of cooling.

Toe E-5-4 (Plate 1*b*), which contains a central cavity, displays the normal sequence of crystallization from its rim to within about 20 mm from the cavity, where the most advanced texture of crystallization is the light-brown variolitic texture. At a distance of 10 mm from the cavity the light brown variolitic texture reverts to the red-brown variolitic texture characteristic of the earlier texture of crystallization which is normally found near the rim of the toe. This is interpreted as evidence of contamination by water which somehow entered the hot toe and subsequently expanded to form a central cavity and anomalous vesicles adjacent to the cavity. In view of the evidence for low viscosities in submarine lavas relative to subaerial flows discussed earlier, it appears that some cavities previously reported beneath glassy crusts of pillows from depth may be explained by either partial drainage of their molten interior, as Macdonald has suggested, or by vapor produced by contamination with sea water, or, most likely, by a combination of the two processes.

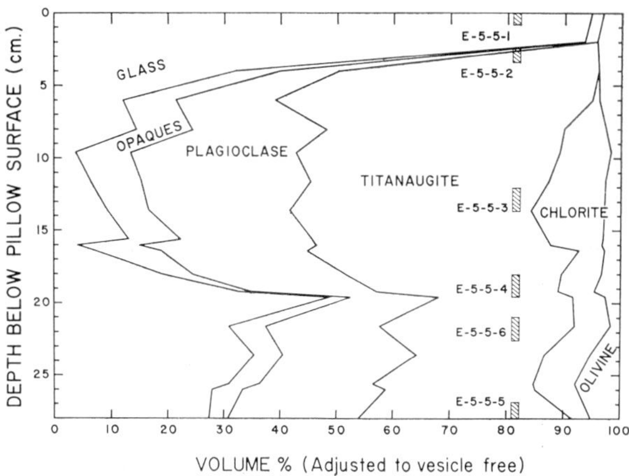

Fig. 9. Modal analysis of E-5-5. Chemically analyzed intervals are represented by diagonal lines.

TABLE 2. Chemical Analyses and C.I.P.W. Norms of *Eltanin* Pillow Zones

	W-1	5-4-1*a*	5-4-1	5-4-2	5-5-1	5-5-2	5-5-3	5-5-4	5-5-6	5-5-5	15-5-1	15-5-2	15-5-1	15-15-2
		G	G	V	G	V	B	B	B	B	V	B	V	B
			T	T	A	A	A	A	A	A	T	T	T	T
Chemical data (wt %)														
SiO_2	52.5	48.2	49.5	48.7	47.2	47.1	48.9	48.0	47.4	47.5	49.8	51.4	50.2	51.6
Al_2O_3	14.9	13.8	13.8	14.6	14.4	14.5	15.5	15.4	15.0	14.8	14.8	15.4	14.8	15.5
Fe_2O_3	.68	12.72	1.82	2.17	2.86	6.03	4.35	3.71	3.13	2.47	1.54	1.68	1.74	1.79
FeO	9.30		9.73	9.22	8.46	6.11	5.85	6.77	7.48	8.13	7.90	6.22	7.86	6.00
MgO	6.52	5.79	6.68	5.91	6.92	5.61	5.17	5.57	5.25	5.65	7.50	7.15	7.45	7.15
CaO	10.92	9.22	10.83	11.14	9.55	9.60	10.35	10.26	10.10	9.91	11.39	12.43	11.84	12.45
Na_2O	2.15	2.69	2.67	2.68	3.47	3.11	3.40	3.43	3.47	3.48	2.75	2.86	2.82	2.89
K_2O	.61	.80	.40	.32	1.38	1.58	1.38	1.40	1.58	1.58	.23	.13	.13	.13
H_2O+	.65	——	1.55	1.33	1.53	1.18	.80	1.28	1.64	1.40	1.15	.38	.44	.40
H_2O-	.07	——	.86	.39	.30	.58	.11	.09	.10	.09	.45	.06	.14	.02
TiO_2	1.10	2.12	2.06	2.04	2.17	2.46	2.71	2.62	2.73	2.76	1.43	1.42	1.42	1.42
P_2O_5	.14	.17	.18	.24	.52	.53	.57	.56	.56	.57	.14	.14	.14	.14
MnO	.17	.14	.14	.15	.36	.15	.12	.12	.13	.13	.15	.12	.13	.13
Total	99.71	95.65	100.22	98.89	99.66	98.54	99.21	99.21	98.57	98.47	99.23	99.39	99.11	99.62
Total Fe as Fe_2O_3	11.00	12.72	12.62	12.40	12.25	12.81	10.84	11.22	11.43	11.49	10.31	8.58	10.46	8.45
C.I.P.W. norms (wt %)														
Qz				.10								.60		.78
Or			2.40	1.94	7.48	9.54	8.21	8.02	8.98	8.84	1.36	.77	.76	.77
Ab			22.98	23.31	26.95	26.91	28.98	28.15	28.25	27.89	23.30	24.44	23.72	24.63
An			24.91	27.62	18.03	21.42	23.13	21.82	19.90	19.04	27.40	29.08	27.19	29.15
Di			23.42		18.14	18.79	19.75	19.29	20.09	19.54	23.00		24.64	
Hy			18.51	27.69	4.59		5.76	3.97	1.94	2.76	16.37	26.11	15.16	25.57
Wo				11.51								13.46		13.41
En						6.62								
Ol			.65		15.10	1.63	1.20	7.35	10.15	12.24	3.25		2.98	
Mt			2.71	3.26	3.84	9.02	6.41	5.27	4.41	3.42	2.26	2.48	2.53	2.64
Il			3.99	3.99	4.74	4.79	5.20	4.84	5.00	4.99	2.73	2.73	2.69	2.72
Ap			.43	.58	1.13	1.28	1.36	1.29	1.28	1.28	.33	.33	.33	.33
Norm. plag. composition (mole % An)			50	52							52	53	51	52

TABLE 2. (continued)

	21-8-1 G T	21-8-2 V T	21-8-3 B T	21-10-1-1 V T	21-10-1-2 B T	21-10-2-1 V T	21-10-2-2 B T	24-15-1 G	24-15-2 V T	24-15-3 V	25-5-1a G	25-5-1b G T	25-5-2 V T	25-5-3 B T
Chemical data (wt %)														
SiO_2	49.5	49.6	51.1	49.9	51.2	50.4	50.9	41.6	48.2	49.0	44.9	49.6	49.6	50.9
Al_2O_3	13.7	13.8	14.3	15.0	15.9	15.8	16.5	12.1	13.7	13.9	15.2	15.0	14.9	15.6
Fe_2O_3	1.39	1.60	2.53	1.66	1.63	.94	1.62	16.9	3.00	3.41	7.56	1.62	4.06	3.88
FeO	10.47	10.22	7.25	7.99	6.17	7.93	6.06	.00	9.25	8.66	3.81	8.21	6.77	5.21
MgO	7.30	6.55	6.47	7.49	7.09	7.75	7.00	3.23	5.96	6.26	4.44	6.92	6.42	6.01
CaO	10.19	10.77	11.57	11.65	12.02	11.81	12.42	1.92	9.27	10.89	5.69	10.29	11.20	12.00
Na_2O	2.79	2.52	2.84	2.89	2.92	2.72	2.72	1.34	2.55	2.54	2.72	2.79	2.88	3.01
K_2O	.37	.26	.27	.12	.17	.10	.11	3.22	.59	.32	1.83	.47	.41	.21
H_2O+	— —	1.19	.48	.47	.31	.48	.25	9.46	2.88	1.57	8.15	1.93	1.10	.67
H_2O-	.40	.34	.13	.11	.08	.12	.06	4.96	1.75	.53	2.75	.61	.29	.32
TiO_2	2.10	2.09	2.14	1.61	1.61	1.33	1.34	1.42	2.18	2.10	1.88	1.68	1.61	1.70
P_2O_5	.18	.18	.19	.16	.16	.13	.13	.11	.16	.19	.14	.15	.16	.17
MnO	.18	.14	.15	.14	.11	.12	.12	.59	.18	.16	.16	.14	.14	.14
Total	93.57	99.26	99.42	99.19	99.37	99.63	99.23	96.85	99.67	99.53	99.23	99.41	99.54	99.82
Total Fe as Fe_2O_3	13.01	12.94	10.58	10.53	8.48	9.74	8.35	16.9	13.27	13.02	11.79	10.73	11.57	9.66
C.I.P.W. norms (wt %)														
Qz		.81	2.58		.42		.46	15.51	2.17	2.19	4.97		1.10	3.08
Or	2.16	1.57	1.61	.70	1.01	.58	.66	22.94	3.66	1.94	12.22	2.84	2.47	1.25
Ab	23.38	21.79	24.29	24.08	24.94	22.54	23.25	13.68	22.66	22.03	26.00	24.11	24.79	25.74
An	23.53	26.14	25.75	27.18	30.06	29.99	32.82	10.62	25.42	26.22	26.96	27.60	26.98	28.74
Di	20.84			23.33		21.63						19.20		
Hy	19.53	31.41	24.51	14.64	25.54	16.65	25.61		27.52	26.32		18.74	23.21	19.12
Wo		11.38	12.94		12.14		11.92		9.10	11.63	1.63		11.89	12.65
En								9.67			12.46			
Ol	4.17			4.29		4.48						1.46		
Mt	2.01	2.39	3.74	2.39	2.41	1.35	2.39		4.61	5.11	8.78	2.42	6.05	5.74
Il	3.96	4.07	4.12	3.02	3.10	2.48	2.58	2.69	4.36	4.10	4.05	3.27	3.12	3.27
Ap	.42	.44	.46	.37	.38	.30	.31	.31	.40	.46	.38	.36	.39	.41
Hm								20.44			2.55			
C								3.84						
Rt								.30						
Norm. plag. composition (mole % An)	48	53	50	51	53	55	57	42	51	53	49	52	50	51

G, glass zone of pillow; V, variolitic zone; B, aphanitic basalt zone; C, corundum; Rt, rutile; T, tholeiite; A, alkalic basalt.

Alterations

Deuteric alteration of the *Eltanin* pillows is divided into two types that appear to be related to the amount of water and volatiles involved in the reactions and the temperatures at which the reactions occur. These types are superimposed in some cases.

Chloritization

The first type of alteration occurs under conditions of maximum magmatic volatile concentration. The water involved would be dissolved in the lava upon extrusion and is estimated to be about 2.0% or less for reasons to be discussed later. This type of alteration found in the interior of the pillow fragments is most likely high temperature in nature. Where an alteration mineral product is formed the mineral is commonly chlorite, although talc, magnesite, and hematite may be present in significant quantity.

Serpentinization

Because serpentine has a higher water content than any of the products of the first type of alteration, and because serpentinization is restricted to portions of the rock that were accessible to sea water, it is postulated that the serpentinization is due to reaction with sea water during cooling following jointing and is not due to a reaction between melt water and olivine.

In summary, the petrographic study of alteration in these pillows indicates that deuteric alteration destroys olivine, pyroxene, and, in one instance, intervariolitic opaques, produces chlorite and serpentine, and mobilizes iron and serpentine constituents to joints, vesicles, and fractures where the iron is oxidized to hematite and goethite.

Reports of deuteric alteration related to jointing in basalts are rare. *Smedes and Lang* [1955] reported alteration of a late Tertiary columnar basalt flow in which thin zones adjacent to joints contain chlorophaeite, a hydrous mineraloid produced by deuteric alteration of olivine and 'glassy base.' *Fuller* [1938] described a late Tertiary volcanic sequence of southeastern Oregon as being deuterically altered in the interiors of jointed columns, although the basalt adjacent to joints is unaltered. Neither of these investigators has considered the widths of the joints and their accessibility to possible water percolation during cooling. It is possible that Smedes and Lang were dealing with an alteration due to water in joints, whereas Fuller's volcanic joints were dry as he implied, and the higher temperature chloritic alteration occurred within the basalt columns.

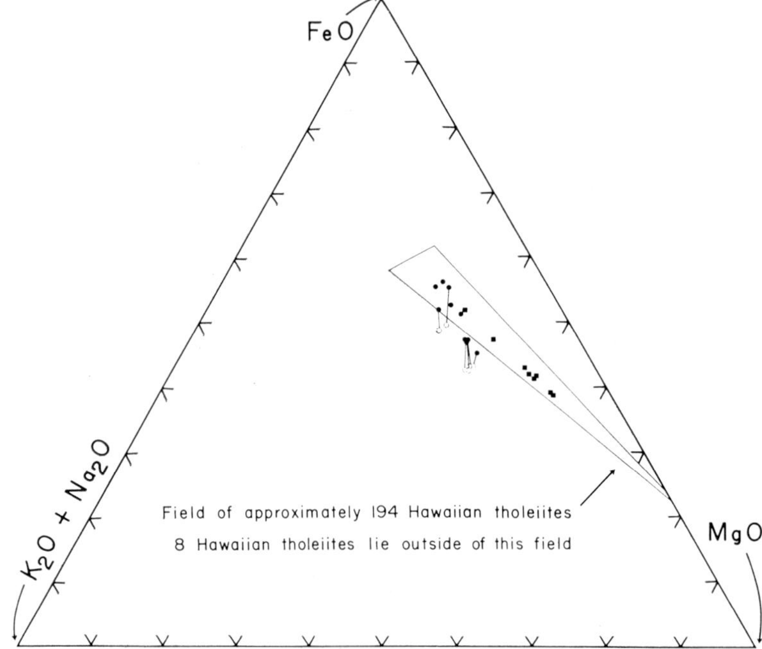

Fig. 10. AFM diagram. Total iron is computed as FeO. Solid circles represent analyses of glass and variolitic zones of pillows; open circles represent aphanitic zones. Each line connects two analyses from the same pillow. Squares represent pillows from the flanks of Hawaii [*Moore*, 1965].

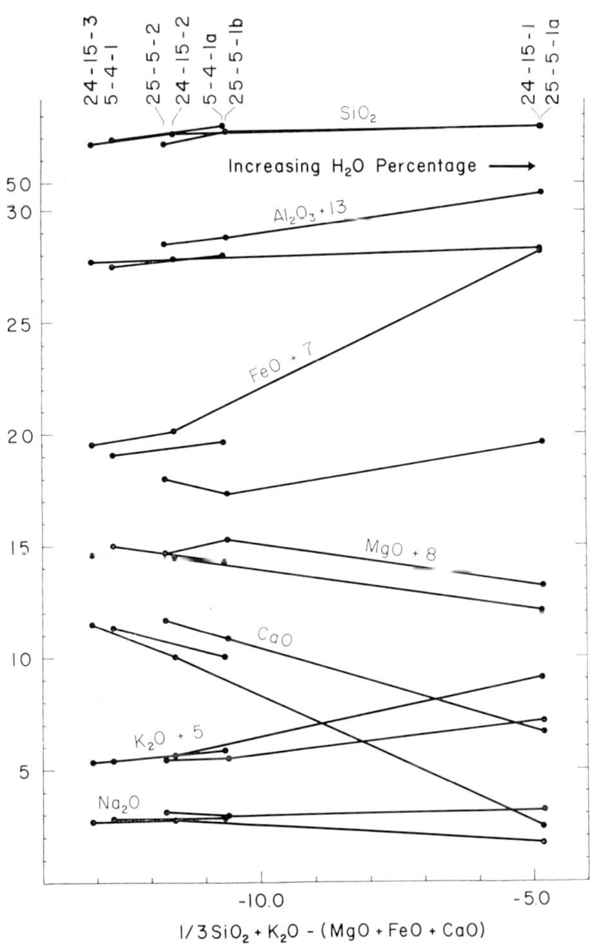

Fig. 11. Larsen plot of hydrated tholeiites. Ordinate is per cent oxide. Each line connects two analyses from the same pillow.

Forsterite with 10 mole % Fe_2SiO_4 is serpentinized at 340°C (water vapor pressure = 1000 atmospheres), whereas it is stable in the presence of water vapor above this temperature [*Bowen and Tuttle*, 1949], indicating that serpentinization occurs during later stages of cooling, long after the joints have formed. Indeed, the joints must have formed after the major silicate phases have crystallized, for there is no observed crystal size difference that can be associated with the joints.

Chemistry of the Pillows

One of the most interesting features of the *Eltanin* tholeiites (Figure 6) is that the silica percentages relative to total alkalis of the fine-grained interiors are apparently higher than the other pillow zones and plot toward the right margin of the tholeiitic field, being roughly separated from their variolitic equivalents by the vertical line at 51.1% silica.

The Larsen plot of Figure 7 illustrates the similarity in composition of the individual pillows, even though they were collected from widely scattered localities of the Drake Passage and South Pacific Ocean. Also plotted are an average of six Pacific tholeiites and an average of seven Atlantic tholeiites given by *Engel and Engel* [1964]. An average of eight Mid-Atlantic Ridge tholeiites reported by *Muir et al.* [1966] is plotted as open triangles. These basalt averages, especially that from the Mid-Atlantic Ridge suite, differ very little from the *Eltanin* tholeiites.

Of particular importance is the establishment of a small but definite change in chemical composition among the different zones of each pillow, advantageously illustrated by the Larsen plot. The vertical line at −11.35 on the abscissa in Figure 7 separates analyses of the unhydrated glass and variolitic layers on the left from the aphanitic interiors on the right. In these analyses 2.0% total water appears to be the approximate division value between hydrated and nonhydrated glass.

The chemical trend from glass and variolitic layers to the crystalline cores of the pillows is, essentially, a relative decrease in total iron content and a slight decrease in magnesium, with a corresponding increase in the other constituent oxides. The data indicate no consistent change in the alkali percentages for the zones studied.

The alkalic basalt pillow is much coarser textured in its interior, and therefore any alteration can be more readily recognized in thin section. No alteration rims exist around the olivine in this rock, and no obvious corrosion of the olivine is evident. The zone with maximum chloritization is represented on the Larsen plot (Figure 8) by analysis E-5-5-3. Analyses of three portions of this pillow (E-5-5-4,5,6) which are more or less equally spaced beneath E-5-5-3 (Figure 9) cluster on the diagram at a point between the analyses of the variolitic zone and the zone of highest chloritization. Because the lower portion of the pillow represented by the clustered points contains about 30% glass and a notable deficiency in vesicle content (Figure 2), the clustered points may represent the composition of a part of the alteration zone and chilled glass that became mixed during flowage of the basalt. In this zone circular patches of variolitic and glassy material are found in relic vesicles of the aphanitic basalt. Whatever the cause of the similarity in the chemistry of the lower portion of the pillow fragment, it is clear that a deficiency in iron and magnesium content similar to the deficiency in the tholeiitic pillows exists in the center of the alkalic basalt fragment. However, in this case the deficiency can be directly associated with deuteric alteration involving the formation of secondary chlorite.

To determine whether the variations in iron are due to enrichment in the glass and variolitic zones or depletion in the pillow interiors, a comparison of the iron, magnesium, and alkali composition was made with the tholeiites of Hawaii (Figure 10). Whereas most of the Pacific tholeiite glass and variolitic zones fall within the Hawaiian tholeiite field or slightly below it, the aphanitic zone in the *Eltanin* basalts in each case plots much lower than the tholeiite field, indicating an absolute drop in total iron percentage relative to most Hawaiian tholeiitic rocks. If these tholeiites can be compared with those of Hawaii, then the iron from the interiors has somehow been preferentially lost.

Hydration of the Pillows

Six analyses of the glass and variolite zones of E-5-4, E-24-15, and E-25-5 yielded a total water content of greater than 2.0%. E-5-4-1*a* is believed to have a high water content because of its low chemical total for all constituents except water and because the layer below it has a total H_2O content of 2.41%. These analyses, plotted in Figure 11, agree with previously published analyses of hydrated-nonhydrated glass pairs [*Noble*, 1967] in that, relative to silica and alumina, they show a deficiency in calcium and magnesium and an excess of total iron, ferric/ferrous ratio, and potassium. The trend of sodium in these samples is not definite. The *Eltanin* basalts show little change in silica and only a slight increase in alumina (Figure 11). However, the present study does not include examples of highly hydrated tholeiitic glass.

Because the chemical changes in the hydrated zones are only relative, some question arises as to which constituents are actually gained, or which are actually lost, if any. If the data are recalculated water-free as in Figure 11, it is found that, in general, there is little significant change in silica or alumina, in agreement with the results of *Noble* [1967]. If only a decrease in calcium and magnesium occurred, then there should be a proportionate increase in all other constituents, which is not the case. If only an increase in potassium and iron occurred, then there should be a proportionate decrease in all of the other constituents, which is not the case either. It seems safe to assume that silicon and aluminum are not as mobile as most of the other ions in the chemical reorganization upon hydration. Therefore, decreases in calcium and magnesium are offset by increases in potassium and iron, resulting in silica and alumina percentages which are close to the original unhydrated material.

The enrichment of glass in potassium with a leaching of magnesium and calcium leads to the growth of phillipsite and montmorillonite in the hydrated glass [*Hawkins and Roy*, 1963].

Iron enrichment in the glass can best be explained by the process of sorption [*Nicholls*, 1963]. The reddish lamellae in the outer palagonite layer of the pillows are most likely due to variations in iron percentage. In some cases iron and manganese hydroxides form dendritic growths from glass surfaces inward, presumably along fractures and grain boundaries (Plate 3*d*). In these cases it appears that the transporting agent to the sorption site is sea water.

Although the data are insufficient to make any definite statements concerning the original water content of the tholeiites, it is worth noting that the value found for saturated basalt at a pressure equivalent to 4000 meters water depth and a temperature of 1100°C by *Hamilton et al.* [1964] is 1.5%, which is very close to the maximum H_2O^+ content of what is taken to be unhydrated glass. The pillow zones below the unhydrated glass zones become more dehydrated, most likely because of the expulsion of most of the 1.5% water vapor during crystallization.

The Iron Enigma

The petrography of the pillows indicates that iron is mobile and is deposited within fractures and joints as hematite and goethite during cooling. The chemistry of the pillows indicates that the crystalline interiors of the pillows are depleted in iron relative to the unhydrated glass and variolitic zones by as much as 2.0% of the total rock weight, or roughly 20% of the total iron.

The chemical analyses show that the major part of the total iron discrepancy is in the ferrous iron. If iron is most mobile in its ferrous state, then low oxygen fugacities are required; otherwise magnetite would crystallize throughout the rock instead of near fractures as in E-21-10-2. Low oxygen fugacities are to be expected in the pillows, considering the relatively rapid rate of cooling the pillows must have undergone. *Hamilton et al.* [1964] showed that the highest oxygen fugacity at which magnetite is stable using a buffer of magnetite + wustite + water is 10^{-11} atmospheres at 1100°C and drops to 10^{-23} at 500°C.

An order of magnitude figure for the length of time required for the interior of a 30-cm-diameter pillow to cool from 1100°C to 500°C is 1.5 hours [*Jaeger*, 1968]. Because the effect of joints on the rate of cooling is not known, 1.5 hours is probably an upper limit. It is certain that jointing occurs after significant crystallization of the major mineral phases. The small amount of sea water entering a newly formed joint approximately 0.3 mm in width would have to by-pass effusing vapors. The exchange of heat at the pillow surface between 0.3-mm fractures and cold sea water would be only a small fraction of the heat dissipated from the joint surfaces were they directly exposed to freely circulating sea water.

It is assumed that the pillows did not pick up appreciable amounts of sea water for the following reasons:

1. The maximum solubility of water in the lava is about 1.5% H_2O or equal to the maximum value found in unhydrated glass.

2. The pillow zones below the glass contain less water than unhydrated glass, which is believed to be due to dehydration during cooling.

3. The deuteric serpentine zone which was formed in the presence of excess water is found within 6 mm of the joints and fractures and is rarely found deeper within the pillows.

The work of *Bernal et al.* [1959] indicates that at low temperatures and pressures ferrous hydroxide compounds are not sufficiently soluble to be transported by water in the concentrations required to deplete the pillows. The stability field relationships of the ferrous compounds at high temperatures and pressures may be favorable to high iron solubilities, but, at present, there is no available evidence to support any process involving excessive amounts of water as the transporting agent.

Krauskopf [1957] has presented thermodynamic arguments indicating that to account for a loss of 2% iron by vapor transport the amount of chloride-laden volatiles needed at 600°C and 1000 atmospheres would be on the order of 10,000 cm^3 volatiles per 1 cm^3 of pillow basalt. This figure does not seem at all practicable, and it seems highly unlikely that new thermodynamic information could make feasible a simple method of vapor transport by anion complexing.

That this problem is not confined to tholeiites is shown by the similar results for the analyses of the alkali basalt presented here and analyses of quartz monzonite bodies in the Iron Springs district of Utah reported by *Mackin* [1968]. Mackin found a depletion of iron in the interior of the jointed igneous intrusions relative to their 'fresh' peripheral shells, and he discussed the role of joints in mobilizing the iron. He ascribed the iron movement to deuteric alteration. Unfortunately, his data shed no light on the present problem, although a similar mechanism appears to operate in both types of rock.

Zelenov [1964] has described volcanic exhalations from an andesite-dacite submarine volcano in Indonesia. The last eruption ended in 1919, but in 1963, diving on the submerged summit disclosed continuous gaseous and hot water jets emanating from fissures in the rock outcrop. The rock showed no hydrothermal alteration in thin section and was too hot to handle 20 cm beneath the outcrop surface.

The most pertinent aspects of Zelenov's descriptions are the chemical constituents of the exhalations. Analyses of samples from the mouths of the hot water jets yielded 100 to 140 mg of iron and manganese per liter of water. The hot water issuing from fissures is initially colorless but becomes turbid about 1 meter above the bottom owing to the precipitation of iron and manganese hydroxides. Much of the hydroxides is swept away by currents, but some accumulates on the ocean floor around the fissures. Analyses of this dried precipitate yielded Fe_2O_3 + FeO up to 46%, MnO_2 + MnO_2 to 7%, P_2O_5 to 2.7%, TiO_2 to 0.25%, SiO_2 to 12%, Al_2O_3 to 4%, H_2O to 7%, and sea water salts about 25%. Analysis of the gas jets yielded 96.97% CO_2, 2.86% N, a trace of CH_4, He, and Ar. No oxygen or hydrogen was detected, which may indicate low oxygen fugacities.

Zelenov's report strengthens the case for high mobility of iron in volcanic rocks in the submarine environment, and it seems possible that the exhalations which he reports are products of the same type of deuteric alteration found in the pillow basalts.

Based on the foregoing discussion, the probable conditions under which iron migrates out of submarine pillows are as follows:

1. Temperature is between solidus of silicate phases (1100°C) and serpentinization (400°C).

2. Water content is about 1.5% by weight or less.

3. Oxygen fugacity is from 10^{-11} atmosphere at 1100°C to 10^{-28} atmosphere and lower at lower temperatures.

4. Iron is mobile in its ferrous state.

5. The mechanism is not dependent upon the bulk chemistry of the rock except, of course, for an initial iron content. The rate may be dependent upon many factors, however.

6. The time required can be as short as 1.5 hours

in the case of tholeiite pillows for the total temperature range from 1100°C to 400°C.

7. The system must be partially open (e.g., jointed) to provide an effective concentration gradient whereby iron may move.

An experimental study of the movement of iron in an aqueous vapor phase by *Martin and Piwinskii* [1969] indicates that iron fractionates significantly into the vapor phase within most of the above environmental limits. Depending upon the experimental conditions, however, it was found that hematite crystallized on or near the container walls in a temperature range of 470° to 950°C and only 6% by weight of the total iron (as Fe_2O_3) was leached from W-1 after 14 days at 10-kb water pressure. The ½-kb water pressure and shorter time of 'leaching' found in the submarine material might be attributed to lower oxygen fugacities, inasmuch as hematite was the iron mineral product in the experimental studies.

Whatever the ultimate cause of iron depletion in submarine pillows, the results are impressive. A conservative estimate of the quantity of iron released from the center of a spherical pillow 30 cm in diameter, of specific gravity 2.7, and 1.0% FeO depletion, would be on the order of 130 g Fe. Undoubtedly most of this iron remains in joints and fractures as oxidation products, but the potential source of iron is vast enough to account for its anomalously high accumulations in deep-sea sediments and ferromanganese concretions.

Representative Sampling

In the following discussion a normative percentage of 0.0% quartz and 0.0% olivine is termed 'saturated,' whereas quartz in the norm or olivine in the norm are termed 'oversaturated' or 'undersaturated,' respectively.

Nicholls et al. [1964] and *Yoder and Tilley* [1962, p. 375] have noted that alteration of basalt resulting in hydration and iron oxidation tends to produce silica oversaturated tholeiitic rocks from normative undersaturated rocks. It is not surprising, therefore, that the normative analyses of the *Eltanin* tholeiites show similar trends from undersaturation in the variolitic and unhydrated glass zones to silica saturation in the hydrated zones. What is apparent in these tholeiites is a definite reversal in trend from the undersaturated variolitic zones toward saturation in the interior of the pillows.

Seven of the eight tholeiitic pillows show this reversal in trend. The interior saturation is attributed to the loss of iron and magnesium and the oxidation of iron. The Larsen diagrams indicate this trend, inasmuch as the formula $\frac{1}{3}$ $SiO_2 + K_2O - (FeO + MgO + CaO)$ is a mafic (or salic) index. The higher (more positive) this index, the more salic is the rock. Thus, the hydrated glasses are on the right side of the diagram (Figure 11) owing to the loss of magnesium and calcium and the increase in potassium (saturated), the variolitic zones plot on the left side (undersaturated), and the aphanitic interiors are again on the right side of the diagram (Figure 7). The eighth tholeiitic rock, E-24-15, is slightly oversaturated and does not quite reach saturation in the variolitic zone. This may be due to the deep penetration of hydration in this sample. In view of these results, tholeiite analyses of glass and variolitic zones containing greater than 2.0% total water should be used with caution.

It appears that the most representative analyses of pillows are those of unhydrated glass and variolitic zones. Except for extreme hydration the alteration which has the greatest effect on the analyses is that involving the loss of iron, as can be seen in Table 2. Therefore as a 'best estimate' analyses involving slightly more than 2.0% water are included as 'most representative,' simply because iron has not escaped from these zones. The result is that the slightly hydrated samples may contain anomalously high potash values, but the much larger errors in the iron and magnesium are minimized. It is obvious that from a purely chemical standpoint very few of the analyses are ideal.

E-24-15 was thoroughly hydrated, but the remaining seven most representative analyses of the tholeiites were adjusted when slightly hydrated by substituting their potash percentages with the average potash of their analyses containing less than 2.00% total water. The analyses were then recalculated water-free and averaged (Table 3). The analyses used are those for which the norms are shown in Table 4.

The Primitive Basalt Problem

When the average of the *Eltanin* samples is compared with the average of eight tholeiites from the Mid-Atlantic Ridge reported by *Muir et al.* [1966] the similarity is evident (Table 3). The differences in silica and alumina may be due, in part, to analytical techniques, but the accuracy of the alumina is sufficient to show a lower alumina value than that reported by *Engel, Engel, and Havens* [1965], and therefore the present writer agrees with Muir and Tilley that the high alumina tholeiites implied by *Engel, Fischer, and Engel* [1965] may not be representative of the ocean

TABLE 3. Averages of Tholeiitic Rocks from Oceanic and Continental Provinces Recalculated Water-Free

	1	2	3	4	5
SiO_2	50.5	50.06	49.94	49.17	51.4
Al_2O_3	14.9	15.35	17.25	15.50	13.9
Fe_2O_3	1.55	2.19	2.01	2.90	3.9
FeO	8.70	8.48	6.90	8.59	9.3
MgO	7.39	7.80	7.28	8.64	5.3
CaO	11.28	11.14	11.86	10.68	9.9
Na_2O	2.80	2.78	2.76	1.87	2.8
K_2O	.20	.18	.16	.13	1.1
TiO_2	1.68	1.63	1.51	2.12	1.8
P_2O_5	.15	.13	.16	.22	.3
MnO	.15	.18	.17	.18	.3

1. Average of seven *Eltanin* tholeiites, this paper.
2. Average of eight Mid-Atlantic Ridge tholeiites [*Muir and Tilley*, 1966].
3. Average of ten oceanic tholeiites [*Engel, Engel, and Havens*, 1965].
4. Average of thirteen tholeiites, Pololu series, Kohala Mountains, Hawaii [*Macdonald and Katsura*, 1964, table 9, analysis 5].
5. Average of eight tholeiitic basalts from the Hebridean Province [*Turner and Verhoogen*, 1960, p. 226].

floor. The higher silica values for the *Eltanin* tholeiites, if real and not due to alteration, may reflect differences between the Mid-Atlantic Ridge and the deeper parts of the South Pacific Basin, but this is clearly only a tentative observation. The average of the Mid-Atlantic Ridge values, when plotted in Figure 7, lies in line with the *Eltanin* trend but toward the mafic side of the plot, suggesting that the Mid-Atlantic Ridge samples are even less altered than the *Eltanin* samples, i.e., contain more iron and magnesium. This possibility arises inasmuch as the boundaries of the alteration are not defined sharply, and the sampled variolitic zones may have been contaminated with altered zone below it. Indeed, Muir and Tilley state that their suite is 'beautifully fresh.' The low potash values previously reported for oceanic tholeiites are verified in the *Eltanin* tholeiites, although E-5-4 appears to be transitional in potash content. Averages of eight continental tholeiites from the Hebridean Province of Mull [*Turner and Verhoogen*, 1960, p. 226] are included in Table 3 for comparison. The higher potash percentage for these rocks is typical of the continental variety of tholeiitic rocks. The silica and alumina percentages for the *Eltanin* tholeiites fall between the values of other oceanic tholeiites and the Hebridean Province tholeiites. The lower ferric iron content of the *Eltanin* tholeiites is due to the lower oxidation state of the iron in the glass and variolitic layers of the pillows.

The only obvious similarity between the averages of 13 primitive tholeiites from the Pololu series of the Kohala Mountains, Hawaii, and the oceanic rocks is the low potash percentage. The Na_2O percentage is anomalously low for either type of tholeiite, and the titanium and phosphorus values are within a higher range common to oceanic island tholeiites.

When the best estimated analysis of each tholeiite in this study is selected for comparison in the norm, the tholeiites are found to have compositions that are very similar (Table 4).

It may be significant that these tholeiites are just undersaturated in the norm, containing a slight amount of olivine in contrast to many submarine basalts dredged from oceanic ridges or submarine escarpments that vary widely in olivine content. Table 1 shows that most of the *Eltanin* tholeiites were collected from areas of the deep-sea floor with 550 meters' relief or less. Olivine tholeiites produced by the gravity settling of olivine would commonly be dredged from regions of rugged bathymetry such as the Mid-Atlantic Ridge [*Muir et al.*, 1964], where they are brought to the sea floor surface through faulting or where magma reservoirs might be large enough to allow appreciable olivine cumulates to segregate. An alternative interpretation in the tholeiite-olivine tholeiite association would be that the tholeiites of the abyssal hills originate at a shallower depth than do the olivine tholeiites, although the parental material would be the same [*Yoder and Tilley*, 1962, p. 411]. One would then postulate that the magmatic source of oceanic regions of high relief lies, at least in part, at greater depths than that of abyssal hills.

The suggestion that alkalic basalts are generated at a greater depth in the mantle than tholeiites appears to be the best explanation, thus far, for the origin of the two basalt types. The observation that alkalic

TABLE 4. Norms of Most Representative Analyses of *Eltanin* Pillows

Sample	Or	Ab	An	Di	Hy	Ol	Mt	Il	Ap
5-4-1	2.40	22.98	24.91	23.42	18.51	.65	2.71	3.99	.43
15-5-1	1.36	23.30	27.40	23.00	16.37	3.25	2.26	2.73	.33
15-15-1	.76	23.72	27.19	24.64	15.16	2.98	2.53	2.69	.33
21-8-1	2.16	23.38	23.53	20.84	19.53	4.17	2.01	3.96	.42
21-10-1-1	.70	24.08	27.18	23.33	14.64	4.29	2.39	3.02	.37
21-10-2-1	.58	22.54	29.99	21.63	16.65	4.48	1.35	2.48	.30
25-5-1*b*	2.84	24.11	27.60	19.20	18.74	1.46	2.42	3.27	.36

basalts are associated with seamounts as opposed to the abyssal floor, if true, would then suggest either a greater volume of alkalic basalt extrusion to form seamounts or a more viscous lava, which builds a pedestal more rapidly. At present the evidence is meager that alkalic basalts are generated by some obscure process in the elevated conduits of seamounts as has been suggested [*Engel, Fischer, and Engel,* 1965]. The possibility that seamounts may be generated by alkalic basalt eruptions is just as likely.

CONCLUSIONS

Pahoehoe toes, pillows, and hyaloclastites found at abyssal depths can be explained as different products of an eruption similar to the pahoehoe type.

The vesicularity of the pillows from depths of 3200 meters to 4800 meters is less than 3%, indicating that the lavas were not greatly oversaturated in volatiles when they solidified. Their low vesicle content and H_2O contents of less than 2.0% are in agreement with the values predicted from considerations of temperature, pressure, and water solubility in basaltic melts. Higher vesicularities at these depths in the *Eltanin* samples are attributed to voids left from the deuteric alteration of olivine and contamination with sea water.

Three types of chemical alteration have been found in the submarine pillows:

1. Hydration (palagonitization) of the basaltic glass, found in analyzed zones to be greater than 2.0% total H_2O, results in a decrease in calcium and magnesium and an increase in total iron, ferric/ferrous ratio, and potassium. Hydrated glass commonly contains phillipsite and a subordinate amount of montmorillonite.

2. Serpentinization, a form of deuteric alteration, occurring below 400°C, is associated with an excess of water, resulting in the conversion of ferromagnesian minerals to serpentine in zones averaging 6 mm thick on each side of joints and fractures.

3. Chloritization, a higher temperature deuteric alteration (400°C–1100°C), is associated with the concentration of volatiles originating within the lava but is not necessarily apparent in all cases. This alteration produces trace amounts of chlorite, talc, hematite, and magnesite in the interior, aphanitic portion of the pillows. Olivine may be replaced in some instances, but this is not always apparent either. A major result of this alteration is a depletion of the interior of pillows by as much as 20.0% of the total FeO present with migration of the iron to joints, fractures, and vesicles, where it is oxidized to hematite and goethite.

From the chloritization type of alteration it is estimated that a spherical pillow 30 cm in diameter releases a minimum of 130 g of iron. If one considers the quantity of volcanics on the ocean floor, this process could release a prodigious amount of iron into the submarine environment. Such a process may account for the high iron content of 'red' clays and ferromanganese concretions.

Despite the chemical alterations, it is possible to select a chemically representative sample of basalt from the unhydrated glass or variolitic zones of the pillows. Remarkably similar major element chemistry is found in these zones for all but one of the eight tholeiites studied. Normative analyses of these zones are all slightly undersaturated, with a normative olivine content of less than 4.5% by weight. One tholeiite hydrated throughout contains 2.17% quartz in the norm. Some of the interiors approach high alumina tholeiites (21-10-1; 2; 25-5), but these compositions may be a result of iron loss. The association of the tholeiites with abyssal hills and rises of the South Pacific Ocean and their nearly identical composition suggest that they are representative of the deep ocean floor where bathymetric relief is not much more than 550 meters.

Acknowledgments. The author wishes to express his gratitude to H. Grant Goodell for giving freely of his inestimable support, suggestions, and constructive criticism during the course of this work. Thanks are also given to Norman D. Watkins, who supplied the facilities for the preparation of polished sections and continually encouraged the author in this study. The author is indebted to Detlef A. Warnke and Larry A. Haskin for reviewing the manuscript.

Special thanks are given to Mr. Dennis Cassidy for his invaluable assistance in many phases of the laboratory work and preparation of this publication and to Mr. Philip D. Dewitt, Jr., for the use of his computer program for the calculation of C.I.P.W. norms.

Grateful acknowledgment is given for support from the National Defense Education Association. Graduate Fellowship Program and National Science Foundation grants GA-523 and GA-1066 of the Antarctic Research Program, without which this work would not have been possible.

REFERENCES

Bailey, E. H., W. P. Irwin, and D. L. Jones, Franciscan and related rocks and their significance in the geology of western California, 177 pp., *Calif. Div. Mines Geol. Bull., 183,* 1964.

Bernal, J. D., D. R. Dasgupta, and A. L. Mackay, The oxides and hydroxides of iron and their structural inter-relationships, *Clay Minerals Bull., 4,* 15–30, 1959.

Bonatti, E., Palagonite, hyaloclastites and alteration of volcanic glass in the ocean, *Bull. Volcanol., 28,* 257–269, 1965.

Bonatti, E., Mechanisms of deep-sea volcanism in the South Pacific, in *Researches in Geochemistry,* vol. 2, edited by P. H. Abelson, pp. 453–491, John Wiley, New York, 1967.

Bonatti, E., and Y. R. Nayudu, The origin of manganese nodules on the ocean floor, *Am. J. Sci., 263*, 17–39, 1965.

Bowen, N. L., and O. F. Tuttle, The system MgO-SiO_2-H_2O, *Geol. Soc. Am. Bull., 60*, 439–460, 1949.

Correns, C. W., Über einen Basalt vom Boden des Atlantischen Ozeans und seine Zerstetzungsrinde, *Chem. Erde, 5*, 1930. (Analyses also in *Bonatti* [1965].)

Deer, W. A., R. A. Howie, and J. Zussman, *Rock-Forming Minerals*, vol. 3, *Sheet Silicates*, 270 pp., William Clowes, London, 1962.

Engel, A. E. J., and C. G. Engel, Igneous rocks of the East Pacific Rise, *Science, 146*, 477–485, 1964.

Engel, A. E. J., C. G. Engel, and R. G. Havens, Chemical characteristics of oceanic basalts and the upper mantle, *Geol. Soc. Am. Bull., 76*, 719–734, 1965.

Engel, C. G., and A. E. J. Engel, Basalts dredged from the Northeastern Pacific Ocean, *Science, 140*, 1321–1324, 1963.

Engel, C. G., R. L. Fischer, and A. E. J. Engel, Igneous rocks of the Indian Ocean floor, *Science, 150*, 605–610, 1965.

Fuller, R. E., Deuteric alteration controlled by the jointing of lavas, *Am. J. Sci., 235*, 161–171, 1938.

Goodell, H. G., The marine geology of the Drake Passage, Scotia Sea, and South Sandwich Trench, USNS *Eltanin*, Marine Geology Cruises 1–8 (mimeographed), 263 pp., Sedimentology Research Laboratory, Department of Geology, Florida State University, Tallahassee, 1964.

Goodell, H. G., The marine geology of the Southern Ocean, USNS *Eltanin*, Marine Geology Cruises 9–15 (offset), 196 pp., *Contrib. 11*, Sedimentology Research Laboratory, Department of Geology, Florida State University, Tallahassee, 1965.

Goodell, H. G., The marine geology of the Southern Ocean, USNS *Eltanin*, Marine Geology Cruises 16–28 (offset), 260 pp., *Contrib. 25*, Sedimentology Research Laboratory, Department of Geology, Florida State University, Tallahassee, 1968.

Green, D. H., and A. E. Ringwood, The genesis of basaltic magmas, *Contr. Mineral. Petrol., 15*, 103–190, 1967.

Hamilton, D. L., C. W. Burnham, and E. F. Osborn, The solubility of water and effects of oxygen fugacity and water content on crystallization in mafic magmas, *J. Petrol., 5*, 21–39, 1964.

Hart, S. R., K, Rb, Cs contents and K/Rb and K/Cs ratios in fresh and altered submarine basalts, 295 pp., *Earth Planet. Sci. Lett., 6*, 1969.

Hawkins, D. B., and R. Roy, Experimental hydrothermal studies on rock alteration and clay mineral formation, *Geochim. Cosmochim. Acta, 27*, 1047–1054, 1963.

Jaeger, J. C., Cooling and solidification of igneous rocks, in *Basalts: The Poldervaart Treatise on Rocks of Basaltic Composition*, vol. 2, edited by H. H. Hess, pp. 503–536, Interscience, New York, 1968.

Kennedy, G. C., Pressure-volume-temperature relations in water at elevated temperatures and pressures, *Am. J. Sci., 248*, 540–564, 1950.

Kennedy, W. Q., Trends of differentiation in basaltic magmas, *Am. J. Sci., 25*, 239–256, 1933.

Krauskopf, K. B., The heavy metal content of magmatic vapor at 600°C, *Econ. Geol., 52*, 786–807, 1957.

Kushiro, I., Compositions of magmas formed by partial melting of the earth's upper mantle, *J. Geophys. Res., 73*, 619–634, 1968.

McBirney, A. R., Factors governing the nature of submarine volcanism, *Bull. Volcanol., 26*, 455–469, 1963.

Macdonald, G. A., Forms and structures of extrusive basaltic rocks, in *Basalts: The Poldervaart Treatise on Rocks of Basaltic Composition*, vol. 1, edited by H. H. Hess, pp. 1–102, Interscience, New York, 1968.

Macdonald, G. A., and T. Katsura, Chemical composition of Hawaiian lavas, *J. Petrol., 5*, 82–133, 1964.

Mackin, J. H., Iron ore deposits of the Iron Springs district, Southwestern Utah, in *Ore Deposits of the United States 1933–1967*, Graton-Sales vol., edited by J. D. Ridge, pp. 992–1019, American Institute of Mining Engineers, New York, 1968.

Martin, R. F., and A. J. Piwinski, Experimental study of the movement of iron in an aqueous vapor phase, *Abstracts with Programs of the 1969 Annual Meetings, Atlantic City, New Jersey*, part 7, p. 143, Geological Society of America, 1969.

Matthews, D. H., Altered lavas from the floor of the Eastern North Atlantic, *Nature, 194*, 368–369, 1962.

Melson, W. G., and T. H. Van Andel, Metamorphism in the Mid-Atlantic Ridge, 22°N latitude, *Marine Geol., 4*, 165–186, 1966.

Menard, H. W., *Marine Geology of the Pacific*, 271 pp., McGraw-Hill, New York, 1964.

Moore, J. G., Petrology of deep-sea basalt near Hawaii, *Am. J. Sci., 263*, 40–52, 1965.

Moore, J. G., Rate of palagonitization of submarine basalt adjacent to Hawaii, *U.S. Geol. Surv. Prof. Paper 550-D*, D163–D171, 1966.

Moore, J. G., and R. K. Reed, Pillow structures of submarine basalts east of Hawaii, *U.S. Geol. Surv. Prof. Paper 475-B*, B153–B157, 1963.

Muir, I. D., C. E. Tilley, and J. H. Scoon, Basalts from the northern part of the rift zone of the Mid-Atlantic Ridge, *J. Petrol., 5*, 409–434, 1964.

Muir, I. D., D. C. E. Tilley, and J. H. Scoon, Basalts from the northern part of the Mid-Atlantic Ridge, 2, The Atlantis collections near 30°N, *J. Petrol., 7*, 193–201, 1966.

Nicholls, G. D., Environmental studies in sedimentary geochemistry, *Sci. Prog.*, 51, 12–31, 1963.

Nicholls, G. D., Basalts from the deep ocean floor, *Mineral. Mag., 34*, 373–388, 1965.

Nicholls, G. D., A. J. Nalwalk, and E. E. Hays, The nature and composition of rock samples dredged from the Mid-Atlantic Ridge between 22°N and 52°N, *Marine Geol., 1*, 333–343, 1964.

Noble, D. C., Sodium, potassium, and ferrous iron contents of some secondarily hydrated natural silicic glasses, *Am. Mineralogist, 52*, 280–286, 1967.

Poldervaart, A., and J. Green, Chemical analyses of submarine basalts, *Am. Mineralogist, 50*, 1723–1728, 1965.

Quon, S. H., and E. G. Ehlers, Rocks of northern part of Mid-Atlantic Ridge, *Geol. Soc. Am. Bull., 74*, 1–8, 1963.

Reichen, L. E., and J. J. Fahey, An improved method for the determination of FeO in rocks and minerals including garnet, 5 pp., *U.S. Geol. Surv. Bull. 1144-B*, 1962.

Rex, R. W., Authigenic silicates formed from basaltic glass by more than 60 million years' contact with sea water, Sylvania Guyot, Marshall Islands, in *Clays and Clay Minerals: Proceedings of the Fifteenth Conference, Clay Minerals Society*, edited by S. W. Bailey, pp. 195–203, Pergamon, New York, 1967.

Rittman, A., *Volcanoes and Their Activity,* 305 pp., Interscience, New York, 1962.

Ross, C. S., and R. L. Smith, Water and other volatiles in volcanic glasses, *Am. Mineralogist, 41,* 1071–1089, 1955.

Shand, S. J., Rocks of the Mid-Atlantic Ridge, *J. Geol., 57,* 89–92, 1949.

Shapiro, L., Rapid analysis of rocks and minerals by a single-solution method, *U.S. Geol. Surv. Prof. Paper 575-B,* B187–B191, 1967.

Shapiro, L., and W. W. Brannock, Rapid analysis of silicate rocks, 55 pp., *U.S. Geol. Surv. Bull. 1144-A,* 1962.

Smedes, H. W., and A. J. Lang, Jr., Basalt column rinds caused by deuteric alteration, *Am. J. Sci., 253,* 173–181, 1955.

Tilley, C. E., Some aspects of magmatic evolution, *Quart. J. Geol. Soc. London, 106,* 37–61, 1950.

Tilley, C. E., and I. D. Muir, Tholeiite and tholeiitic series, *Geol. Mag., 104,* 337–343, 1967.

Turner, F. J., and J. Verhoogen, *Igneous and Metamorphic Petrology,* 2nd ed., 694 pp., McGraw-Hill, New York, 1960.

Watkins, N. D., and T. P. Paster, The magnetic properties of igneous rocks from the ocean floor, *Proc. Roy. Soc. London,* November 1969 meeting, in preparation, 1970.

Yoder, H. S., Jr., and C. E. Tilley, Origin of basalt magmas: An experimental study of natural and synthetic rock systems, *J. Petrol., 3,* 342–532, 1962.

Zelenov, K. K., Iron and manganese in exhalations of the submarine Banu Wuhu volcano (Indonesia), *Dokl. Akad. Nauk SSSR,* English Transl., *155,* 94–96, 1964.

SIZE-DEPTH VARIATION IN *CYCLAMMINA CANCELLATA* BRADY, PERU-CHILE TRENCH AREA

Fritz Theyer

University of Southern California, Los Angeles, California 90007

Abstract. Ecophenotypes of *Cyclammina cancellata* Brady, living in different depth zones of the Peru-Chile Trench, are recognized by variations in mean diameter, mean width, and a ratio between both. Small and comparatively wide forms appear at about 500 meters; larger and proportionally narrower forms live at between 1000 and about 2500 meters; specimens living in deeper waters decrease slightly in diameter but widen considerably. Apparently, temperature is the principal factor affecting this trend, since it decreases markedly in the upper 2000 meters coinciding with the greatest size change. Oxygen may have an effect on width of specimens, since populations with relatively narrow individuals correlate with low oxygen levels.

INTRODUCTION

Correlation of morphology and environment exists in many plant and animal species. *Bandy* [1960] reviewed several such trends among foraminifera, including size variations in *Cyclammina cancellata* Brady occurring off southern California. This species is very important for paleoecological interpretations of the Tertiary [*Akers*, 1954]. Therefore, it seems desirable to establish a depth zonation based on its ecophenotypes.

Cruises 1 through 4 of the USNS *Eltanin* and cruise 17 of RV *Anton Bruun* recovered extensive material from a wide depth range in the Peru-Chile Trench area, with large numbers of *Cyclammina* in some samples (Figure 1, Table 1). Most samples had previously been treated with rose bengal and, whenever possible, only stained specimens were measured. To further minimize effects of reworking, badly eroded tests were not measured.

Measurements were taken with an ocular micrometer disc as indicated in Figure 2. Figure 3 shows the graphic representation of the statistical parameters used. A discussion of this graphic method and its advantages can be found in *Hubbs and Hubbs* [1953].

Sediments of the Peru-Chile Trench area are discussed by *Bandy and Rodolfo* [1964] and *Manera* [1969]. Oceanographic data are available in the reports of the RV *Anton Bruun* cruises in the Southeastern Pacific (Special Reports, Marine Laboratory, Texas A & M University, College Station, Texas).

PREVIOUS WORK

Although *Cyclammina cancellata* has been extensively cited in the literature since its description by *Brady* [1879], few studies have specifically dealt with it. *Akers* [1954] reviewed the ecology and stratigraphy of this species in an extensive compilation. Little can be added to this summary today, except in regard to morphologic trends.

Bandy [1960] first realized that different size groups of this species live in different environments off southern California. Subsequently, he showed that a relationship between hydrology and size groups exists [*Bandy*, 1963]. In a study of sediments and foraminifera of the Peru-Chile Trench area, *Bandy and Rodolfo* [1964] pointed out the possibility of size trends in *C. cancellata* of that area.

The upper depth limit of *C. cancellata* is a much discussed problem. Although *Akers* [1954] cites a few records in less than about 200 meters, these must be regarded as doubtful, since reworked specimens might have been involved, and sounding techniques were probably inaccurate. *Boltovskoy and Theyer* [1965] found abundant rose bengal stained specimens in depths of from 80 to 264 meters off southern Chile, presumably living and autochthonous. However, on a world-wide basis, it seems that the upper depth limit is about 500 meters. This agrees with the conclusions of *Bandy and Rodolfo* [1964] and is certainly the case in the area of this study.

It is interesting to note that *C. cancellata* does not occur in antarctic waters. According to *Bandy and Echols* [1964] it is replaced by *C. orbicularis* in the Antarctic. This was confirmed by *Herb* [1970], who found *C. orbicularis* and *C. pusilla* replacing *C. cancellata* south of about 52°S in the Drake Passage area. In the Southeast Pacific Basin area (Theyer, manuscript in preparation) *C. orbicularis* and *C. pusilla* are

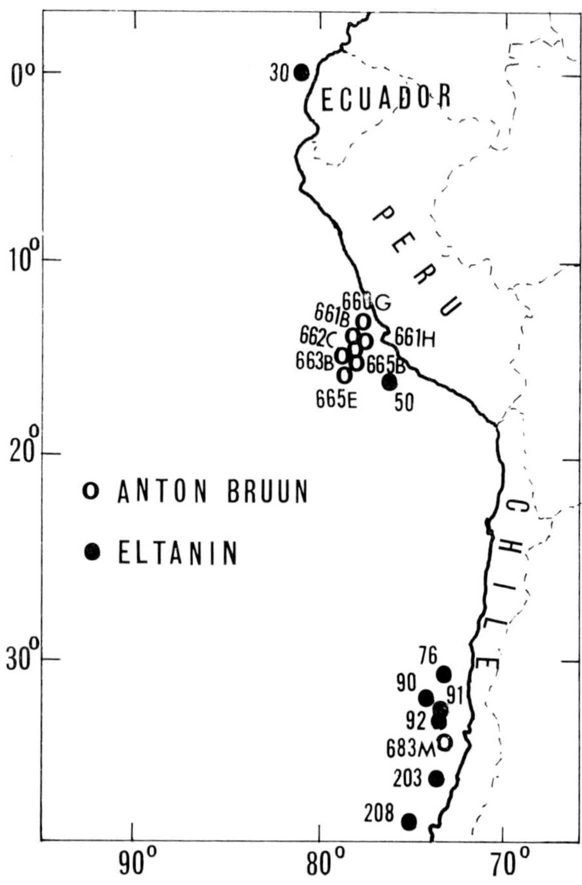

Fig. 1. Index map.

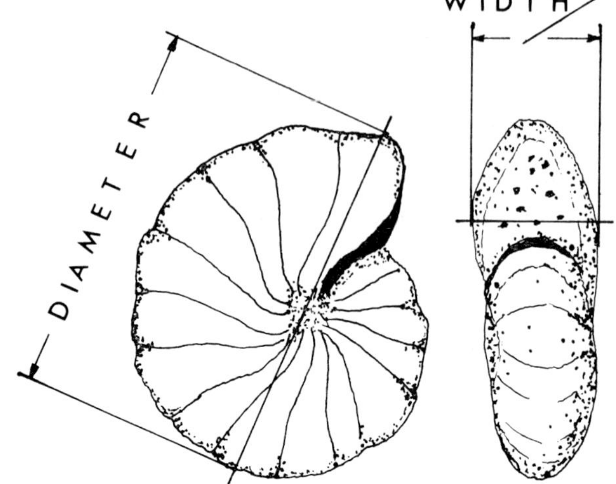

Fig. 2. *Cyclammina cancellata* Brady (modified after *Brady* [1884]) indicating sites of measurements.

usually the dominant foraminifera, and *C. cancellata* is virtually absent, although further north, along the Chilean coast, it is an abundant form.

With respect to its fossil range, *Akers* [1954] gives a complete summary of the literature. In general, the records cited range from Oligocene to Holocene. The inferred paleobathymetry seems to be mostly between about 500 and 2000 meters; paleotemperature estimates run from over 10° to 3°C in most cases; sediments, apparently, are judged of minor importance in determining the paleohabitat of the species [*Akers*, 1954].

TABLE 1. Station Data, USNS *Eltanin* and RV *Anton Bruun*

Station	Gear	Depth, meters	S Lat.	W Long.	No. of Specimens
EL 30	Menzies trawl	1180	0° 0′	81°45′	50
EL 50	Menzies trawl	2858	16°12′	74°40′	100
EL 76	Menzies trawl	3541	31°13′	72°21′	78
EL 90	Petersen grab	3371	32°18′	72°23′	12
EL 91	Petersen grab	1748	32°44′	72°56′	54
EL 92	Petersen grab	866	32°49′	71°51′	25
EL 203	Petersen grab	463	35°39′	73°08′	46
EL 208	Campbell grab	957	37°29′	73°55′	36
AB 660G	Campbell grab	1000	12°54′	77°16′	100
AB 661B	Campbell grab	1565	13°16′	77°30′	50
AB 661H	Menzies trawl	2120	13°23′	77°29′	44
AB 662C	Menzies trawl	3160	13°33′	77°26′	70
AB 663B	Campbell grab	4150	13°44′	77°31′	24
AB 665B	Agassiz trawl	3070	15°34′	77°36′	32
AB 665E	Menzies trawl	2780	15°36′	77°34′	35
AB 683M	Menzies trawl	585	33°08′	71°53′	29

RESULTS

The stations were arranged according to depth. Hydrographic conditions at the depth of the samples are essentially independent of latitude within the area of study, and the region can safely be treated as a unit in that respect.

Figure 4 shows the variation of the diameters. The

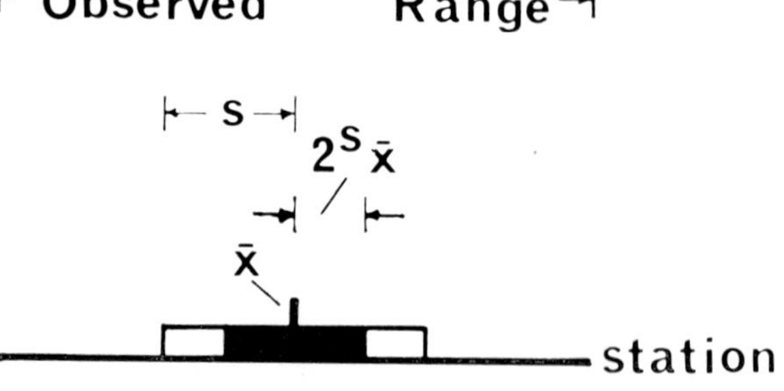

Fig. 3. Graphic representation of statisticial parameters s = standard variation; $^{S}\bar{x}$ = standard error of mean; $\bar{x}$ = mean; station = station numbers as indicated in Figure 1.

total observed range extends from less than 1 mm in the shallowest samples to over 6 mm at about 2000 meters. The mean diameter increases almost consistently from about 1.6 mm to close to 5 mm at just over 2000 meters. From 2000 to 4000 meters an irregular decreasing trend is seen. Unfortunately, the sample from station EL 90 is unreliable (12 specimens), and no information as to the consistency of this trend is available between the two deepest stations (EL 76 and AB 663B). This makes the deepest part of the trend somewhat questionable, and no strong emphasis will be placed on it here. However, one can generalize that the largest specimens occur in waters between 1000 and 3500 meters, whereas smaller forms live above and below this range.

Figure 5 shows the variation of the width. The total range goes from under 0.5 mm to nearly 2.5 mm. The mean width shows a similar trend, but in contrast to the diameter, the increase is continuous to over 3000 meters, followed by an indication of a decrease in still deeper samples. Thus, the widest forms do not coincide in depth with the largest ones.

These size variations become clearer if Figure 6 is considered. Using the mean diameter/mean width

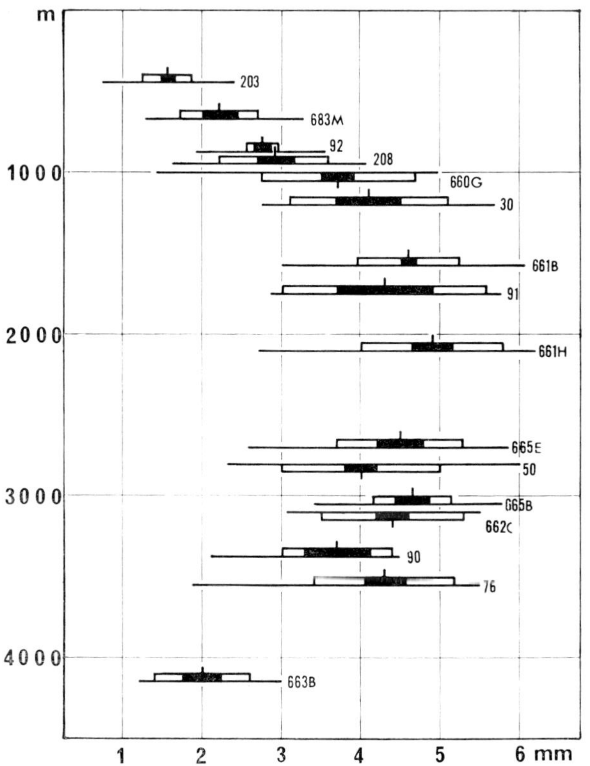

Fig. 4. Variation of the diameter. Arrangement of samples according to depth.

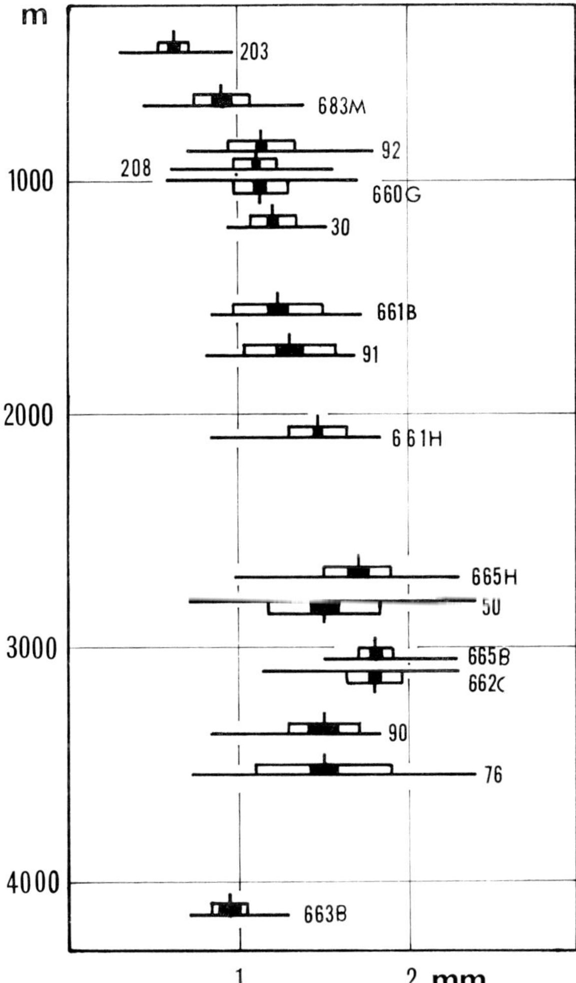

Fig. 5. Variation of width. Arrangement of samples according to depth.

ratio and the diameter plot as a reference, the populations of this study can be broadly subdivided into three depth groups: those living in less than about 1000 meters are small and relatively wide, as their high ratio indicates; those between 1000 and approximately 2000 meters are large but comparatively narrow, as shown by their lower ratio; conversely, populations in still deeper waters tend to become smaller in diameter but are wider in comparison. It should be noted here that if the questionable portion in this general size trend between 3500 and 4000 meters is real, then the populations living at both extremes of the depth range are essentially similar in structure, possibly indicating that these depths represent ecologically marginal environments for *C. cancellata*.

In a search for possible causes of the variations, neither organic carbon, organic nitrogen, nor salinity

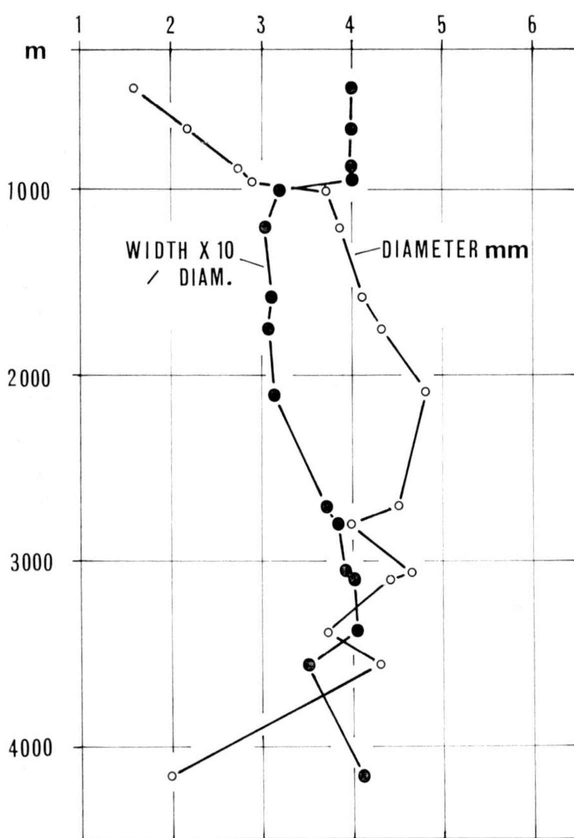

Fig. 6. Variation of mean diameter and mean diameter/mean width ratio.

data show correlative trends in the area. Sediment is variable and the available information [*Bandy and Rodolfo*, 1964; *Manera*, 1969] precludes a correlation between sedimentology and foraminiferal morphology in this particular case. This agrees with *Akers'* [1954] conclusions that sediments play a minor role in the distribution of lituolids. Depth, that is, pressure alone, could have some influence, and broadly similar size groups have been found by *Bandy* [1963] off southern California in depths comparable to those of the present work. Superficial analysis of a few samples from the Drake Passage-Scotia Sea area corroborates the existence of size variations in approximately the same depth zones. However, it is impossible to distinguish clearly between the pressure effect and temperature-oxygen effects. All these environments show similar variation patterns of major oceanographic conditions throughout most of the depth range of the samples.

Considering Figure 7, where the temperature-oxygen values at the sampling depths have been plotted, it becomes immediately apparent that the steady decrease in temperature in the upper 1000 to 2000 meters coincides remarkably well with the steady increase in diameter the populations undergo in about the same depth range. Whether oxygen has any influence is difficult to ascertain. It is tempting to assume that the depression of the width/diameter ratio between about 1000 and 2500 meters (Figure 6), which correlates approximately with the oxygen-minimum zone, is related to the role of oxygen in growth patterns. However, this is merely tentative, and the literature on the subject is controversial [*Boltovskoy*, 1965]. Among calcareous foraminifera (bolivinids) living in oxygen-depleted basins, some depressive action has been described [*Lutze*, 1964], perhaps supporting these ideas. It also seems appropriate to note here that experiments on marine invertebrates show [*Kinne*, 1963] that environmental factors (temperature, salinity, oxygen) regulate structure and physiology as a system by which variation of one factor may alter the action of the others. It is quite possible that some of these environmental factors have to be considered in relation to each other. *Lutze* [1965] has shown this to be the case in foraminiferal distribution in the Baltic Sea.

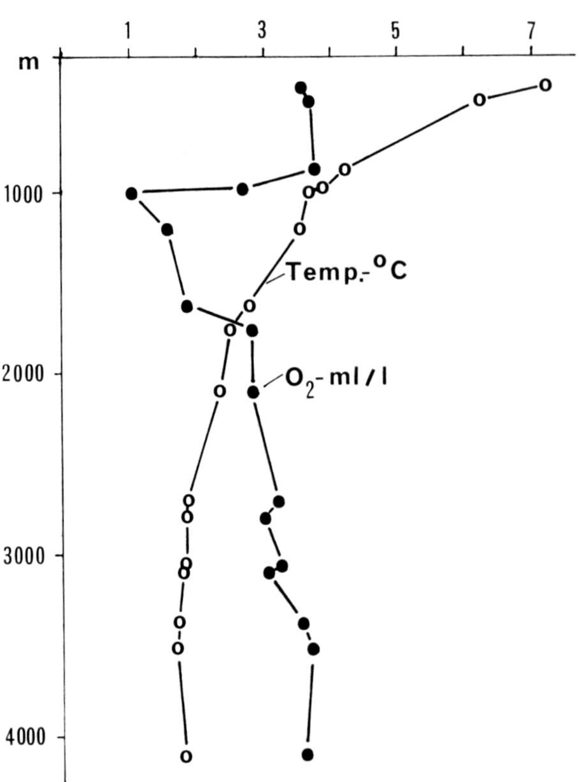

Fig. 7. Temperature and oxygen variation at sampling depths.

PALEOECOLOGICAL IMPLICATIONS

To summarize, the following paleoecological implications are possible: populations of *Cyclammina cancellata* with mainly small specimens and high width/diameter ratios can be correlated with depths of less than 1000 meters, temperatures above 3 to 4°C, and oxygen values exceeding 3 ml/l. Predominantly large specimens with lower width/diameter ratios indicate conditions below the permanent thermocline and oxygen contents below 3 ml/l. Finally, populations with similar diameters but higher ratios mark depths of 3000 meters or more, temperatures below 2°C, and oxygen values above 3 ml/l.

Acknowledgments. Grateful appreciation is extended to the National Science Foundation for partial support under grants GA-10204 and GB-8628 and for making the writer's participation on cruise 17 of RV *Anton Bruun* possible. Many thanks are due to Dr. Orville L. Bandy for encouragement and criticism. P. Lewis Steineck read the manuscript and furnished helpful suggestions.

REFERENCES

Akers, W. H., Ecologic aspects and stratigraphic significance of the foraminifer *Cyclammina cancellata* Brady, *J. Paleontol., 28*(2), 132–152, 1954.

Bandy, O. L., General correlation of foraminiferal structure with environment, *Intern. Geol. Congr., 21st, Copenhagen,* pp. 7–19, 1960.

Bandy, O. L., Larger living foraminifera of the continental borderland of southern California, *Contrib. Cushman Found. Foram. Res., 14*(4), 121–126, 1963.

Bandy, O. L., and R. J. Echols, Antarctic foraminiferal zonation, in *Biology of the Antarctic Seas, Antarctic Res. Ser., 1,* edited by Milton O. Lee, pp. 73–91, American Geophysical Union, Washington, D.C., 1964.

Bandy, O. L., and K. S. Rodolfo, Distribution of foraminifera and sediments, Peru-Chile Trench area, *Deep-Sea Res., 11,* 817–837, 1964.

Boltovskoy, E., Los foraminíferos recientes, *Eudeba,* pp. 1–510, Buenos Aires, 1965.

Boltovskoy, E., and F. Theyer, Neuere Daten über rezente Foraminiferen Zentralchiles, *Beitr. Neotrop. Fauna, 4*(3), 143–149, 1965.

Brady, H. B., Note on some of the reticularian Rhizopoda of the *Challenger* Expedition, *Quart. J. Microscop. Sci., New Ser., 19,* 62, 1879.

Brady, H. B., Report on the foraminifera dredged by HMS *Challenger* during the years 1873–1876, xxi+ 814 pp., 115 pls. (in atlas), *Rept. Sci. Results Voyage HMS Challenger, 9*(22), 1884.

Herb, R., Distribution of Recent benthonic foraminifera in the Drake Passage (Southern Seas), in *Biology of the Antarctic Seas IV, Antarctic Res. Ser., 16,* edited by George A. Llano, American Geophysical Union, Washington, D.C., in press.

Hubbs, C. L., and C. Hubbs, An improved graphical analysis and comparison of a series of samples, *Syst. Zool., 2*(2), 49–56, 1953.

Kinne, O., The effects of temperature and salinity on marine and brackish water animals, *Oceanog. Marine Biol. Ann. Rev., 1,* 301–340, 1963.

Lutze, F. G., Statistical investigations on the variability of *Bolivina argentea* Cushman, *Contrib. Cushman Found. Foram. Res., 15*(3), 105–116, 1964.

Lutze, F. G., Zur Foraminiferen-Fauna der Ostsee, *Meyniana, 15,* 75–142, 1965.

Manera, T. F., Sedimentology of Southeast Pacific deep-sea cores, M.S. thesis, pp. 1–142, University of Southern California, Los Angeles, 1969.

TRANSOCEANIC ALKALINITY PROFILES IN THE SOUTH PACIFIC

KARL K. TUREKIAN, PETER M. BOWER, AND J. WOODBURN

Yale University, New Haven, Connecticut 06520

Abstract. Alkalinity profiles in transoceanic sections at 43°S and 28°S based on samples collected on *Eltanin* cruises 28 and 29 are reported. A maximum in alkalinity is found at a depth of 2000 to 3500 meters. The western boundary is lower in alkalinity than the eastern part of the Pacific Basin. These patterns can be explained by a model of supply of low alkalinity water to the abyss via a western boundary current. As the initially low alkalinity water rises it dissolves sinking calcium carbonate tests, resulting in a maximum in alkalinity at intermediate depths.

INTRODUCTION

The use of alkalinity as a tracer in large-scale ocean circulation was suggested by *Koczy* [1956]. In the deep ocean, changes in alkalinity are due primarily to the extraction of calcium carbonate by organisms or the solution of calcium carbonate. Since surface waters are the zones of high productivity, alkalinity is lowered there. As a result of the resolution of the tests on sinking, alkalinity increases in deep water. A water type formed with a homogeneous alkalinity moving outward at depth will tend to increase in alkalinity monotonically in the direction of transport, and this property has the potential of being harnessed in the same way as phosphate and oxygen for the study of large-scale oceanographic processes. Its only common touchstone is the similar effect of productivity in the surface waters.

We have measured alkalinity profiles on water samples collected across the South Pacific at 28°S and 43°S as part of the study of the role of the waters adjacent to Antarctica on large-scale circulation in the Pacific Ocean.

METHODS

The samples used in this study were those obtained from hydrographic casts made during the *Eltanin* 28 and 29 cruises between March 10 and August 2, 1967. The measurements of salinity, temperature, and the other common chemical oceanographic parameters were performed aboard ship as part of the over-all program under the supervision of Joseph Reid, Henry Stommel, E. Dixon Stroup, and Bruce A. Warren. Peter M. Bower and Kathe K. Bertine, both of Yale, assisted in the shipboard chemistry and were responsible for the storage of the remaining water from each Nansen bottle for return to the laboratory.

Five hundred ml polyethylene bottles were filled to about half volume from each Nansen bottle and then sealed with tape. The samples were then transported to Yale and remained sealed until they were sampled for alkalinity measurements.

Alkalinity was determined by potentiometric titration of an accurately measured aliquot of sea water with dilute hydrochloric acid of a known normality by indicating the inflection in the titration curve. The procedure is as follows:

One hundred ml of sea water was pipetted into a clean 250-ml beaker. The precision of pipetting was ± 0.02 ml as determined by weighing multiple samples. With continuous stirring, using a magnetic stirrer, 18 ml of acid of 0.01 normality is added to the sea water and the *p*H recorded. Thereafter, exactly 1-ml aliquots of the standard acid are added and the *p*H recorded. About 12 titration points are obtained that describe the inflection of the titration curve. A smooth titration curve is drawn, and the inflection point is identified with a transparent straightedge. The precision of the titration and inflection point determination is 0.5% coefficient of variation. This is the major source of reproducibility error.

The acid is standardized by titration against dried, weighed aliquots of sodium carbonate. In all standardizations the same bottle of analytical grade sodium carbonate was used, thus minimizing systematic error between acids. An uncertainty remains about the absolute purity of the sodium carbonate.

One possible source of error is the chance that water was lost by evaporation from the bottles between the time of collection and the time of analysis (about 6 to 12 months). A record of the amount of water in each bottle indicated no systematic variation in alkalinity with quantity of water in the bottle. Since the samples were kept sealed and in the dark until analyzed, we think that the effect of evaporation on the alkalinity is small. We thus estimate that our over-all reproducibility error is 0.5% coefficient of variation. Only single determinations were commonly made.

RESULTS

Measurements of alkalinity were made primarily on water below 1000 meters, as the deep circulation of the Pacific was the prime interest. As there were no *p*H measurements made on a systematic basis on the cruise, exact corrections for the boron contribution could not be made to arrive at the carbonate alkalinity. If we assume a *p*H value, we can calculate the expected carbonate alkalinity from the titration alkalinity by subtracting the boron contribution according to the formula [Skirrow, 1965]

$$\text{carbonate alkalinity} = \text{alkalinity} - \frac{K'_B \times C_{\Sigma B}}{K'_B + a_H{}^+}$$

where K'_B is the apparent first ionization constant in sea water for boric acid ($H_3BO_3 = H^+ + H_2BO_3{}^-$), assumed $10^{-8.90}$ for a chlorinity of 19‰ and a temperature of 5°C; $C_{\Sigma B}$ is the titer concentration of boron in sea water, assumed 4.58×10^{-4} moles/liter; and $a_H{}^+$ is the hydrogen ion activity.

For example, a titration alkalinity of 2.40×10^{-3} equivalents/liter (approximately the value in sea water) will give the following carbonate alkalinities over a range of *p*H values:

*p*H	Calculated carbonate alkalinity, meq/l
7.8	2.37
8.0	2.35
8.2	2.32

The range of deep in situ *p*H values for the equatorial Pacific has been found to be between 7.8 and 8.0 [*Li et al.*, 1969]. The carbonate alkalinity thus will be about 1.6% lower systematically than the titration alkalinity. Major differences within the titration alkalinity values then may be ascribed to changes in carbonate alkalinity as the result of extraction or solution of calcium carbonate.

The titration alkalinity was converted to specific alkalinity (titration alkalinity × 10^3/chlorinity) using the shipboard salinity measurements. The results are shown graphically in Figures 1 and 2 for specific alkalinity and Figures 3 and 4 for titration alkalinity. The alkalinity, shipboard salinity, and temperature measurements are presented in the appendix.

DISCUSSION

The dominant features of the alkalinity distribution in the South Pacific are the following (Figures 1 through 4):

1. Along the 28°S traverse it is evident that the deepest parts west of the Albatross Cordillera (East Pacific Rise) have lower alkalinities and specific alkalinities than those east of the cordillera.

2. Along the 28°S traverse the highest alkalinities are generally not at the bottom of the section but are between 2000 and 3500 meters depth. The high values between these depths do not vary greatly across the Pacific Basin.

3. At about 145°W on the 28°S traverse a pocket of low alkalinity water is found at a depth of 4000 to 4800 meters similar to that reported at about 7°S, 150°W, by *Koczy* [1956].

4. Along the 43°S traverse the Pacific is divided into two basins, the Southwest Pacific Basin, which is continuous with the rest of Pacific, and the Southeast Pacific Basin (Bellingshausen Basin) which is circumscribed by the Albatross Cordillera and the Chile Rise with restricted contact with the major part of the Pacific Basin. The alkalinity is lower in the Southeast Pacific Basin than in the Southwest Pacific Basin.

5. The western section of the 43°S traverse is marked by a highly textured pattern with the lowest alkalinity values on the western boundary marked by the Chatham Rise.

These results will have to be fitted into self-consistent models of large-scale circulation but a preliminary model can be given to explain the observed patterns of alkalinity distribution.

Reid et al. [1968] analyzed the salinity-temperature data taken on *Eltanin* 28 and found confirmation of the existence of a deep boundary current along the Tonga-Kermadec Trench. Water from higher latitudes passes south of New Zealand and northward along their trench walls to supply the deep Pacific according to *Stommel and Arons* [1960]. At 28°S the core of the current is at about 175°W, occupies a width of 70 km from the Kermadec Ridge eastward, and is at a depth of 2500 to 4500 meters.

We believe that this current is represented by the low alkalinity values observed in this region (28°S traverse, Figures 1 and 3). The low alkalinity water extends eastward from the boundary along the bottom. This bottom water must rise to cool the major part of the deep Pacific with a tendency to fill the ocean

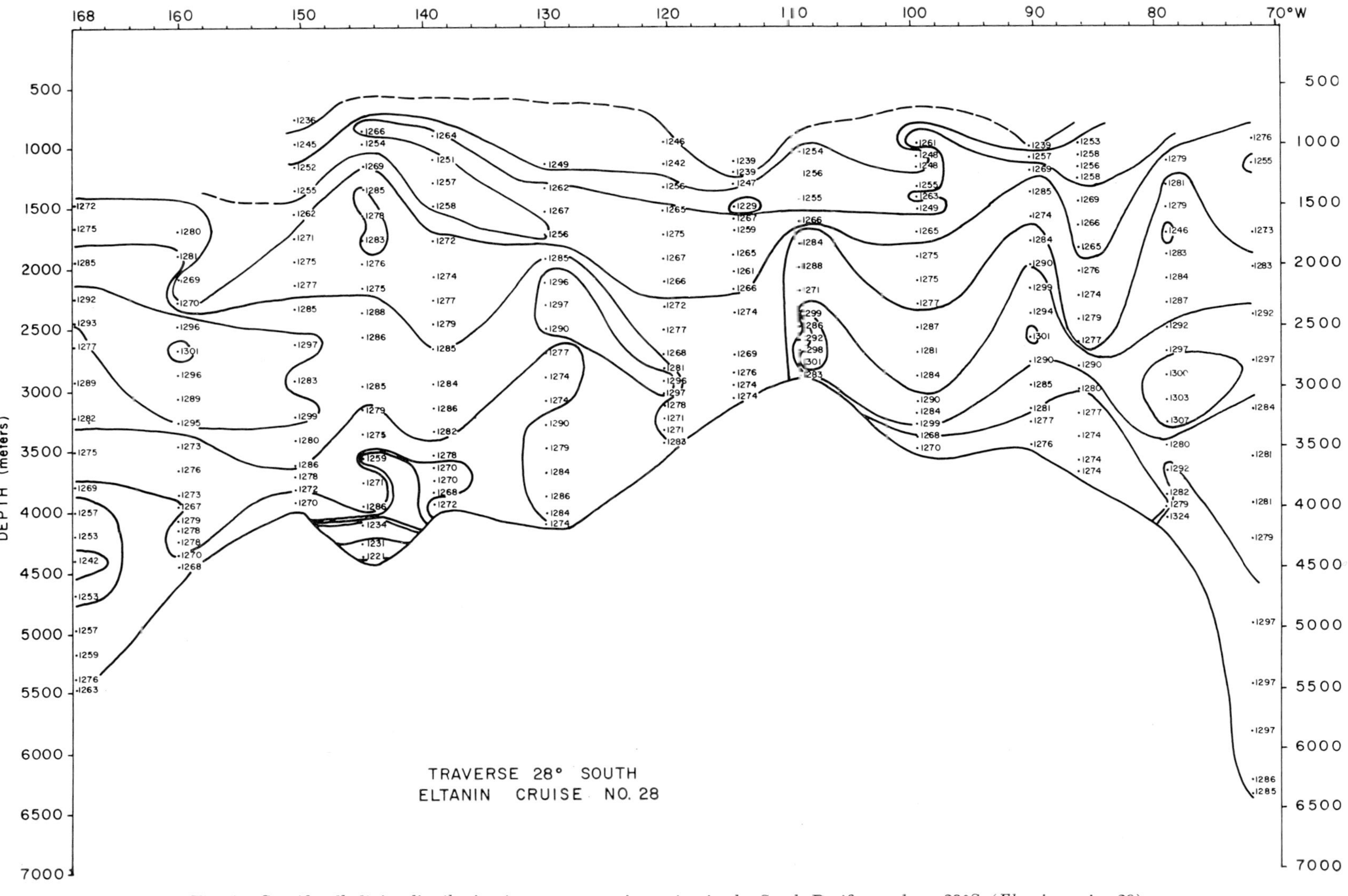

Fig. 1. Specific alkalinity distribution in a transoceanic section in the South Pacific at about 28°S (*Eltanin* cruise 29).

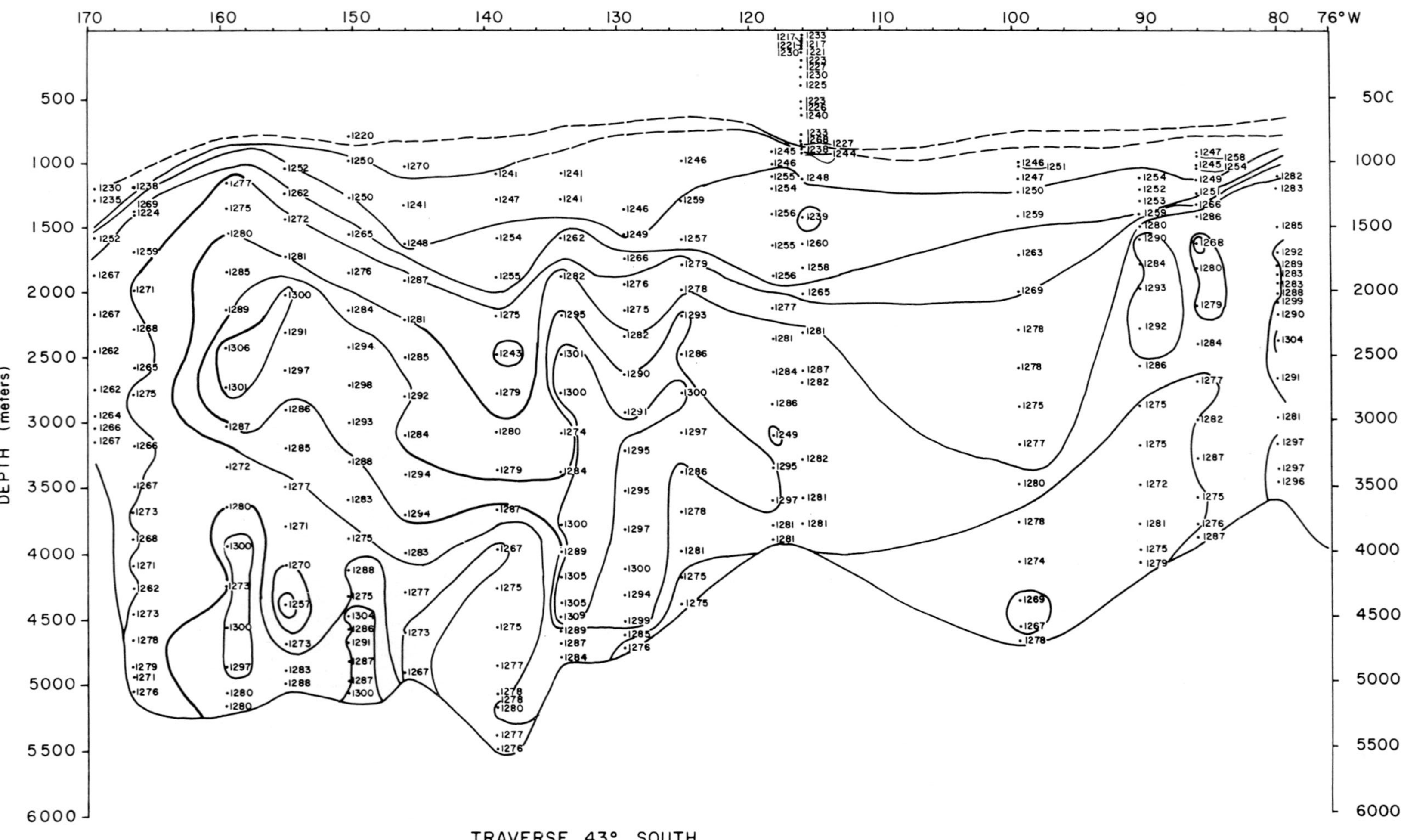

Fig. 2. Specific alkalinity distribution in a transoceanic section in the South Pacific at about 43°S (*Eltanin* cruise 28).

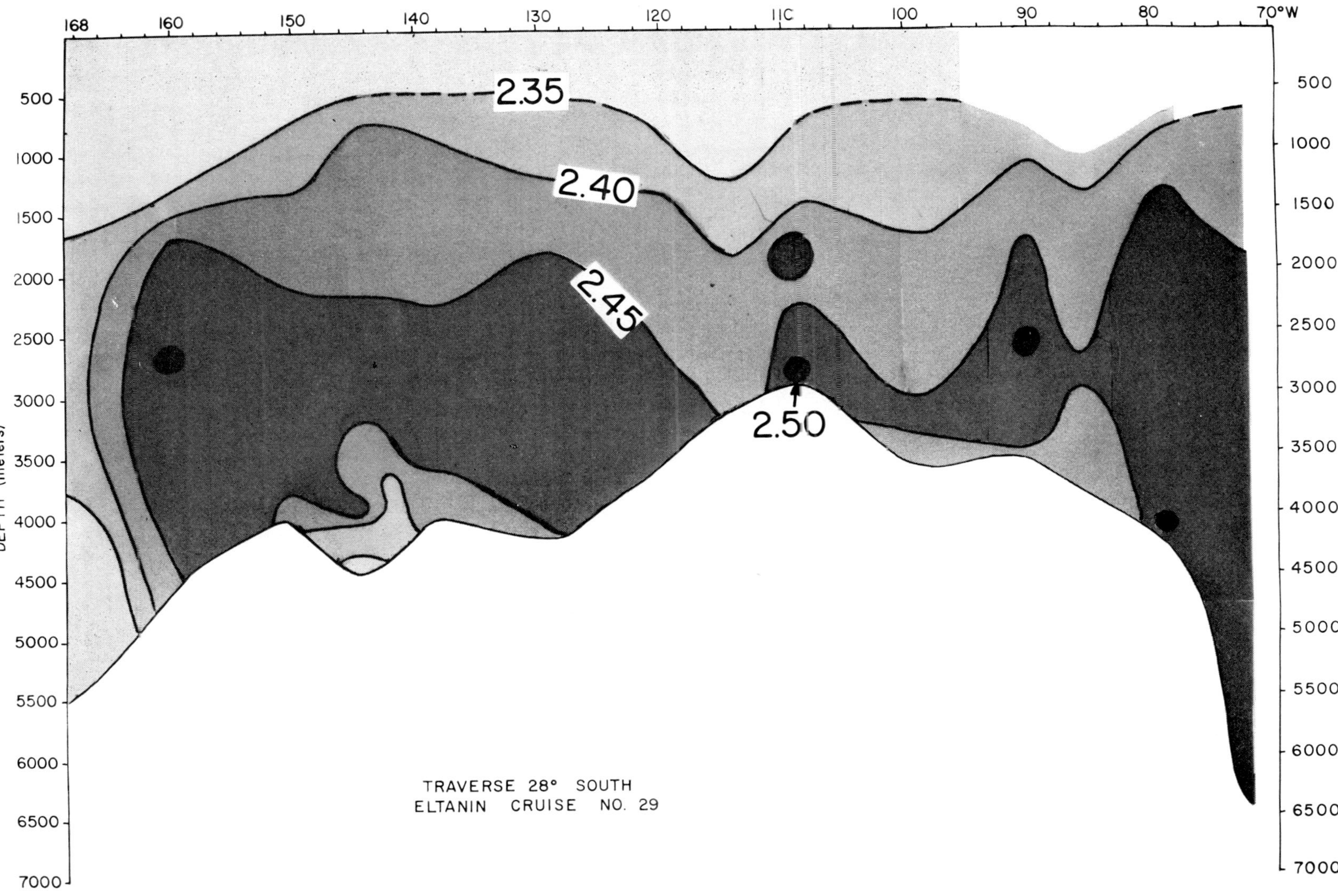

Fig. 3. Titration alkalinity distribution in a transoceanic section in the South Pacific at about 28°S (*Eltanin* cruise 29).

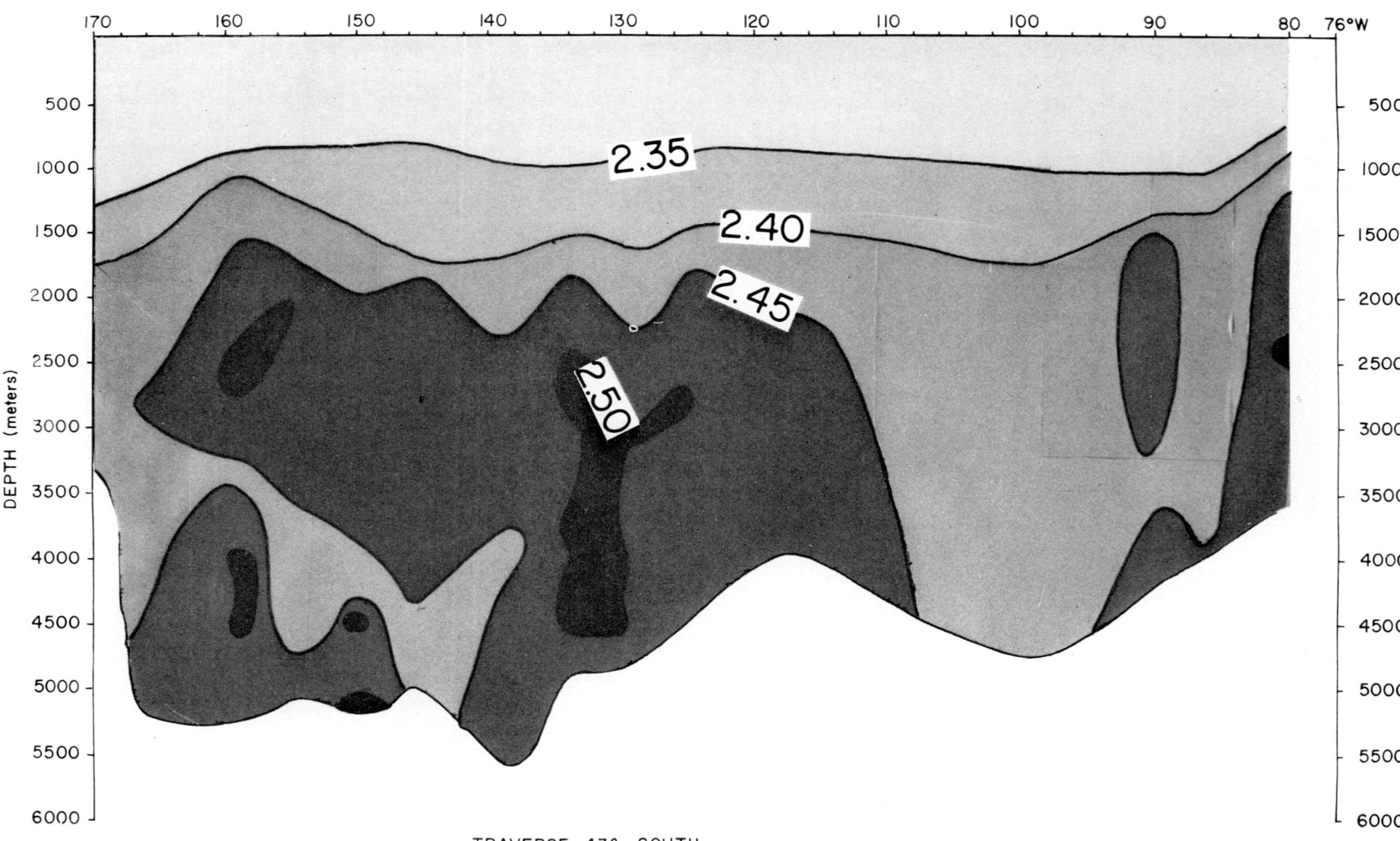

Fig. 4. Titration alkalinity distribution in a transoceanic section in the South Pacific at about 43°S (*Eltanin* cruise 28).

with water of low specific alkalinity typical of the source. Balancing this effect, calcium carbonate tests dropping from the surface seem to undergo maximum dissolution and alkalinity addition at depths between 2000 and 3500 meters. The actual depth of maximum dissolution is undoubtedly greater because of the transport of water from depth upward. This could correspond to the observation of *Peterson* [1966] and *Berger* [1967] on the depth of maximum dissolution of calcite spheres and calcitic tests of pelagic organisms.

Although *Koczy*'s [1956] concept of tracing a water mass in lateral transport is not testable with the range of alkalinities observed in our study, certainly the natural extension of this to general circulation problems seems useful.

Acknowledgment. This research was supported by the Antarctic Research Program of the National Science Foundation.

REFERENCES

Berger, W. H., Foraminiferal ooze: solution at depths, *Science, 156*, 383–385, 1967.

Koczy, F. F., The specific alkalinity, *Deep-Sea Res., 3*, 279–288, 1956.

Li, Y., T. Takahashi, and W. S. Broecker, Degree of saturation of $CaCO_3$ in the oceans, *J. Geophys. Res., 74*, 5507–5525, 1969.

Peterson, M. N. A., Calcite: Rates of dissolution in a vertical profile in the Central Pacific, *Science, 154*, 1542–1544, 1966.

Reid, J., Jr., H. Stommel, E. D. Stroup, B. A. Warren, Detection of a deep boundary current in the western South Pacific, *Nature, 217*, 937, 1968.

Skirrow, G., The dissolved gases—carbon dioxide, in *Chemical Oceanography*, vol. 1, edited by J. P. Riley and G. Skirrow, chap. 7, pp. 227–322, Academic, New York, 1965.

Stommel, H., and A. B. Arons, On the abyssal circulation of the world ocean, 2, An idealized model of the circulation pattern and amplitude in oceanic basins, *Deep-Sea Res., 6*, 217–233, 1960.

APPENDIX

Tables give alkalinity values for *Eltanin* cruise 28 and 29 samples. The titration alkalinities are in units of milliequivalents per liter. Salinities and temperatures are shipboard measurements. The various codes refer to the specific standardized acid used in the titration:

Code A	0.01010 *N* HCl
Code B	0.01015 *N* HCl
Code C	0.01038 *N* HCl

Eltanin 23

Sample	Depth	Temperature, °C	Salinity	Alkalinity	Specific Alkalinity
Series 29D, 43°15′S, 169°50′W, Code B					
1	1189	4.35	34.425	2.345	0.1230
2	1286	3.74	34.424	2.353	0.1235
3	1580	2.93	34.503	2.386	0.1252
4	1872	2.52	34.588	2.427	0.1267
5	2167	2.30	34.670	2.431	0.1267
6	2460	2.09	34.720	2.426	0.1262
7	2756	1.87	34.730	2.426	0.1262
8	2954	1.73	34.739	2.431	0.1264
9	3052	1.63	34.732	2.434	0.1266
10	3151	1.48	34.723	2.436	0.1267
Series 33D, 43°12.6′S, 166°47′W, Code B					
1	1391	3.52	34.446	2.334	0.1224
2	1687	2.93	34.545	2.407	0.1259
3	1985	2.56	34.609	2.436	0.1271
4	2235	2.29	34.665	2.434	0.1268
5	2585	2.14	34.710	2.430	0.1265
6	2885	1.91	34.737	2.451	0.1275
7	3186	1.66	34.739	2.435	0.1266
8	3486	1.42	34.730	2.436	0.1267
9	3687	1.30	34.729	2.446	0.1273
10	3890	1.16	34.722	2.438	0.1268
11	4092	1.05	34.714	2.441	0.1271
16	1181	4.42	34.378	2.356	0.1238
17	1380	3.76	34.445	2.420	0.1269
18	4263	1.00	34.711	2.424	0.1262
19	4463	0.96	34.713	2.446	0.1273
20	4663	0.95	34.709	2.454	0.1278
21	4864	0.95	34.713	2.456	0.1279
22	4965	0.96	34.708	2.441	0.1271
23	5063	0.97	34.707	2.452	0.1276
Series 36D, 43°12.5′S, 159°′W, Code B					
1	1150	4.05	34.363	2.428	0.1277
2	1349	3.33	34.432	2.430	0.1275
3	1549	3.02	34.519	2.446	0.1280
4	1846	2.62	34.596	2.461	0.1285
5	2145	2.36	34.629	2.471	0.1289
6	2442	2.20	34.658	2.507	0.1306
7	2742	2.04	34.692	2.497	0.1301
8	3043	1.90	34.720	2.474	0.1287
9	3346	1.68	34.732	2.444	0.1272
10	3649	1.46	34.732	2.460	0.1280
11	3955	1.27	34.724	2.498	0.1300
12	4259	1.16	34.719	2.446	0.1273
13	4566	1.12	34.718	2.497	0.1300
14	4872	1.09	34.713	2.492	0.1297
15	5074	1.09	34.715	2.460	0.1280
16	5176	1.09	34.716	2.460	0.1280
Series 38D, 43°13.8′S, 155°11.5′W, Code B					
1	1045	4.70	34.346	2.380	0.1252
2	1241	3.67	34.380	2.401	0.1262
3	1437	3.17	34.457	2.426	0.1272
4	1731	2.66	34.576	2.451	0.1281

Eltanin 28

Sample	Depth	Temperature, °C	Salinity	Alkalinity	Specific Alkalinity
Series 38D (continued)					
5	2024	2.41	34.625	2.492	0.1300
6	2320	2.21	34.652	2.476	0.1291
7	2615	2.07	34.680	2.490	0.1297
8	2910	1.92	34.705	2.470	0.1286
9	3208	1.75	34.719	2.469	0.1285
10	3504	1.58	34.729	2.454	0.1277
11	3802	1.37	34.721	2.443	0.1271
12	4099	1.24	34.720	2.441	0.1270
13	4397	1.18	34.721	2.416	0.1257
14	4695	1.17	34.717	2.446	0.1273
15	4895	1.19	34.717	2.466	0.1283
16	4994	1.20	34.719	2.476	0.1288
Series 40D, 43°16′S, 150°35′W, Code B					
1	797	6.00	34.355	2.320	0.1220
2	987	4.92	34.344	2.376	0.1250
3	1275	3.55	34.392	2.380	0.1250
4	1562	2.86	34.512	2.416	0.1265
5	1851	2.56	34.598	2.444	0.1276
6	2142	2.29	34.640	2.461	0.1284
7	2433	2.14	34.707	2.485	0.1294
8	2726	1.94	34.677	2.492	0.1298
9	3017	1.82	34.695	2.483	0.1293
10	3308	1.70	34.715	2.476	0.1288
11	3601	1.53	34.719	2.466	0.1283
12	3895	1.34	34.721	2.450	0.1275
13	4140	1.22	34.720	2.476	0.1288
14	4336	1.19	34.717	2.451	0.1275
15	4484	1.17	34.716	2.507	0.1304
16	4584	1.16	34.719	2.471	0.1286
17	4684	1.16	34.716	2.481	0.1291
18	4833	1.16	34.717	2.473	0.1287
19	4982	1.16	34.716	2.466	0.1283
20	5082	1.17	34.703	2.497	0.1300
Series 42D, 43°15.5′S, 146°03.3′W, Code B					
1	1129	4.01	34.364	2.416	0.1270
2	1328	3.25	34.424	2.365	0.1241
3	1624	2.72	34.540	2.387	0.1248
4	1921	2.40	34.623	2.465	0.1287
5	2219	2.16	34.652	2.456	0.1281
6	2518	1.98	34.669	2.466	0.1285
7	2814	1.85	34.684	2.481	0.1292
8	3110	1.72	34.698	2.466	0.1284
9	3408	1.59	34.711	2.485	0.1294
10	3707	1.44	34.717	2.487	0.1294
11	4007	1.28	34.717	2.466	0.1283
12	4307	1.19	34.716	2.454	0.1277
13	4611	1.15	34.716	2.446	0.1273
14	4918	1.14	34.715	2.436	0.1267
Series 45D, 43°13.8′S, 139°11.8′W, Code B					
1	1092	4.08	34.346	2.360	0.1241
2	1291	3.30	34.397	2.375	0.1247
3	1590	2.71	34.352	2.397	0.1254

Eltanin 28

Sample	Depth	Temperature, °C	Salinity	Alkalinity	Specific Alkalinity
Series 45D (continued)					
4	1888	2.39	34.621	2.404	0.1255
5	2187	2.14	34.656	2.446	0.1275
6	2485	1.98	34.670	2.386	0.1243
7	2785	1.82	34.685	2.456	0.1279
8	3084	1.72	34.698	2.458	0.1280
9	3382	1.58	34.709	2.456	0.1279
10	3679	1.42	34.716	2.474	0.1287
11	3979	1.26	34.715	2.436	0.1267
12	4277	1.18	34.716	2.451	0.1275
13	4576	1.17	34.716	2.451	0.1275
14	4874	1.18	34.714	2.454	0.1277
15	5070	1.19	34.716	2.456	0.1278
21SD	5092	1.19	34.717	2.456	0.1278
22SD	5193	1.19	34.714	2.460	0.1280
23SD	5398	1.20	34.715	2.454	0.1277
24SD	5500	1.21	34.716	2.452	0.1276
Series 47D, 43°13′S, 134°27.2′W, Code B					
1	1092	4.10	34.352	2.360	0.1241
2	1292	3.25	34.409	2.365	0.1241
3	1594	2.68	34.535	2.414	0.1262
4	1893	2.40	34.625	2.458	0.1282
5	2192	2.16	34.656	2.485	0.1295
6	2493	1.97	34.672	2.496	0.1301
7	2794	1.80	34.683	2.497	0.1300
8	3096	1.70	34.694	2.446	0.1274
9	3396	1.58	34.703	2.466	0.1284
10	3697	1.45	34.711	2.498	0.1300
11	3999	1.32	34.712	2.477	0.1289
19	4196	1.26	34.711	2.507	0.1305
20	4397	1.22	34.717	2.507	0.1305
21	4500	1.22	34.712	2.515	0.1309
22	4601	1.21	34.710	2.477	0.1289
23	4703	1.21	34.713	2.472	0.1287
24	4806	1.23	34.710	2.466	0.1284
Series 49D, 43°15.8′S, 129°53.6′W, Code B					
1	1365	3.10	34.425	2.375	0.1246
2	1562	2.72	34.516	2.386	0.1249
3	1757	2.52	34.593	2.424	0.1266
4	1955	2.29	34.636	2.446	0.1276
5	2152	2.14	34.657	2.446	0.1275
6	2349	1.98	34.671	2.461	0.1282
7	2644	1.82	34.676	2.477	0.1290
8	2942	1.71	34.685	2.478	0.1291
9	3239	1.61	34.696	2.487	0.1295
10	3537	1.52	34.701	2.487	0.1295
11	3834	1.43	34.708	2.491	0.1297
12	4133	1.31	34.714	2.497	0.1300
13	4331	1.27	34.716	2.487	0.1294
14	4530	1.25	34.719	2.496	0.1299
15	4629	1.25	34.717	2.469	0.1285
16	4728	1.26	34.713	2.451	0.1276
Series 51D, 43°15.3′S, 125°19.8′W, Code C					
1	997	4.30	34.324	2.368	0.1246

Eltanin 23

Sample	Depth	Temperature, °C	Salinity	Alkalinity	Specific Alkalinity
Series 51D (continued)					
2	1296	3.14	34.417	2.398	0.1259
3	1597	2.60	34.547	2.403	0.1257
4	1796	2.42	34.610	2.450	0.1279
5	1997	2.25	34.647	2.451	0.1278
6	2197	2.07	34.667	2.481	0.1293
7	2496	1.86	34.673	2.467	0.1286
8	2796	1.72	34.680	2.496	0.1300
9	3098	1.62	34.688	2.491	0.1297
10	3398	1.54	34.695	2.478	0.1286
11	3698	1.48	34.701	2.455	0.1278
12	3998	1.40	34.706	2.460	0.1281
13	4199	1.35	34.709	2.450	0.1275
14	4398	1.29	34.713	2.450	0.1275
Series 54D, 43°17.9′S, 118°23.8′W, Code C					
1	925	4.34	34.311	2.365	0.1245
2	1021	3.96	34.334	2.367	0.1246
3	1118	3.50	34.366	2.387	0.1255
4	1214	3.25	34.399	2.387	0.1254
5	1406	2.78	34.486	2.398	0.1256
6	1650	2.52	34.585	2.403	0.1255
7	1894	2.28	34.644	2.408	0.1256
8	2139	2.05	34.670	2.451	0.1277
9	2383	1.86	34.676	2.460	0.1281
10	2630	1.72	34.680	2.465	0.1284
11	2876	1.65	34.684	2.470	0.1286
12	3120	1.60	34.690	2.398	0.1249
13	3364	1.57	34.695	2.487	0.1295
14	3612	1.54	34.695	2.491	0.1297
15	3808	1.53	34.699	2.460	0.1281
16	3907	1.53	34.700	2.460	0.1281
Series 55S, 43°18.4′S, 116.5°5.1′W, Code A					
1	2	12.58	34.119	2.328	0.1233
2	61	12.60	34.116	2.299	0.1217
3	71	12.60	34.117	2.305	0.1221
4	81	11.56	34.128	2.309	0.1222
5	91	9.93	34.139	2.326	0.1231
6	101	9.02	34.187	2.340	0.1237
7	121	8.58	34.220	2.318	0.1224
8	150	8.22	34.284	2.334	0.1230
9	219	7.31	34.346	2.325	0.1223
10	272	6.90	34.370	2.335	0.1227
11	345	6.70	34.371	2.340	0.1230
12	418	6.48	34.358	2.330	0.1225
13	540	6.18	34.344	2.324	0.1223
14	589	6.02	34.328	2.330	0.1226
15	638	5.86	34.321	2.355	0.1240
16	785	5.20	34.291	2.340	0.1233
17	836	4.98	34.292	2.369	0.1248
18	935	4.57	34.300	2.362	0.1244
Series 55D, 43°18.4′S, 116°5.1′W, Code A					
1	865	4.89	34.293	2.330	0.1227
2	910	4.64	34.301	2.351	0.1238

Eltanin 28

Sample	Depth	Temperature, °C	Salinity	Alkalinity	Specific Alkalinity
Series 55D (continued)					
3	1132	3.66	34.348	2.372	0.1248
4	1430	2.86	34.473	2.365	0.1239
5	1628	2.58	34.560	2.411	0.1260
6	1827	2.36	34.623	2.410	0.1258
7	2024	2.17	34.656	2.427	0.1265
8	2322	1.90	34.673	2.465	0.1284
9	2620	1.78	34.680	2.470	0.1287
10	2918	1.68	34.686	2.462	0.1282
11	3117	1.64	34.688	2.462	0.1282
12	3317	1.62	34.693	2.460	0.1281
13	3417	1.60	34.699	2.460	0.1281
Series 62D, 43°15.4′S, 99°59′W, Code A					
1	1016	3.91	34.334	2.345	0.1246
2	1132	3.52	34.373	2.350	0.1247
3	1230	3.32	34.419	2.358	0.1250
4	1425	2.98	34.504	2.381	0.1259
5	1719	2.54	34.505	2.395	0.1263
6	2014	2.24	34.641	2.410	0.1269
7	2309	2.04	34.680	2.430	0.1278
8	2605	1.85	34.696	2.430	0.1278
9	2902	1.70	34.705	2.425	0.1275
10	3198	1.57	34.713	2.430	0.1277
11	3496	1.27	34.714	2.436	0.1280
12	3794	1.04	34.713	2.431	0.1278
13	4092	0.97	34.719	2.424	0.1274
14	4392	0.98	34.713	2.415	0.1269
15	4593	1.00	34.713	2.410	0.1267
16	4693	1.02	34.714	2.431	0.1278
Series 62S, 43°15.4′S, 99°59′W, Code A					
20	1035	3.86	34.334	2.355	0.1251
Series 66D, 43°16.5′S, 90°49.5′W, Code C					
1	1120	3.31	34.404	2.387	0.1254
2	1212	3.12	34.458	2.387	0.1252
3	1306	3.01	34.503	2.393	0.1253
4	1401	2.88	34.542	2.408	0.1259
5	1498	2.78	34.561	2.448	0.1280
6	1595	2.67	34.574	2.470	0.1290
7	1791	2.46	34.611	2.460	0.1284
8	1989	2.28	34.630	2.479	0.1293
9	2290	2.04	34.661	2.480	0.1292
10	2591	1.90	34.685	2.470	0.1286
11	2893	1.80	34.696	2.450	0.1275
12	3194	1.66	34.706	2.450	0.1275
13	3495	1.38	34.715	2.444	0.1272
14	3797	1.02	34.714	2.460	0.1281
15	3993	0.94	34.713	2.450	0.1275
16	4098	0.90	34.716	2.458	0.1279
Series 68D, 43°14′S, 86°11′W, Code A					
1	942A	3.80	34.309	2.345	0.1247
2	1040A	3.50	34.356	2.344	0.1245
3	1137A	3.26	34.412	2.355	0.1249
4	1236A	3.08	34.470	2.364	0.1251

Eltanin 28

Sample	Depth	Temperature, °C	Salinity	Alkalinity	Specific Alkalinity
Series 68D (continued)					
5	1333A	3.00	34.509	2.395	0.1266
6	1431A	2.85	34.541	2.435	0.1286
7	1623A	2.62	34.594	2.405	0.1268
8	1825A	2.42	34.615	2.429	0.1280
9	2119A	2.16	34.644	2.428	0.1279
10	2414A	1.98	34.674	2.440	0.1284
11	2709A	1.86	34.678	2.427	0.1277
12	3006A	1.80	34.691	2.437	0.1282
13	3301A	1.64	34.700	2.448	0.1287
14	3598A	1.48	34.710	2.425	0.1275
15	3798A	1.45	34.709	2.427	0.1276
16	3896A	1.45	34.713	2.450	0.1287
Series 68S, 43°14′S, 86°11′W, Code A					
19	948	3.79	34.305	2.365	0.1258
20	1044	3.49	34.358	2.361	0.1254
Series 71D, 43°14.7′S, 80°0.02.W, Code C					
1	1112	3.30	34.425	2.444	0.1282
2	1307	2.98	34.499	2.450	0.1283
3	1504	2.72	34.565	2.460	0.1285
4	1700	2.48	34.606	2.475	0.1292
5	1799	2.42	34.617	2.470	0.1289
6	1872	2.30	34.627	2.460	0.1283
7	1946	2.23	34.640	2.460	0.1233
8	2018	2.16	34.645	2.470	0.1288
9	2092	2.11	34.654	2.491	0.1299
10	2191	2.04	34.670	2.476	0.1290
11	2386	1.93	34.666	2.502	0.1304
12	2683	1.85	34.680	2.479	0.1291
13	2980	1.81	34.686	2.460	0.1231
14	3180	1.76	34.686	2.491	0.1297
15	3378	1.57	34.697	2.491	0.1297
16	3482	1.51	34.704	2.489	0.1296
Series 80D, 35°12.5′S, 76°41′W, Code A					
1	936A	3.82	34.418	2.385	0.1252
3	1132	3.32	34.501	2.420	0.1267
6	1819	2.36	34.622	2.428	0.1267
7	2113	2.12	34.650	2.458	0.1281
8	2406	1.94	34.664	2.463	0.1284
11	3300	1.74	34.688	2.455	0.1279
12	3601	1.68	34.693	2.485	0.1294
13	3801	1.58	34.699	2.457	0.1279
14	3903	1.56	34.699	2.471	0.1287
Series 80S, 35°12.5′S, 76°41′W, Code A					
1	1	14.93	33.806	2.300	0.1229
3	30	13.35	33.914	2.287	0.1218
6	73	10.23	34.055	2.306	0.1223
7	87	9.77	34.062	2.293	0.1216
8	107	9.66	34.263	2.304	0.1215
10	155	9.64	34.460	2.316	0.1214
11	194	9.12	34.476	2.315	0.1213
12	242	8.56	34.479	2.328	0.1220
13	315	7.60	34.426	2.348	0.1232

Eltanin 28

Sample	Depth	Temperature, °C	Salinity	Alkalinity	Specific Alkalinity
Series 80S (continued)					
16	583	5.03	34.246	2.320	0.1224
17	682	4.57	34.262	2.350	0.1239
18	781	4.20	34.303	2.355	0.1240
19	906	3.88	34.389	2.391	0.1256

Eltanin 29

Sample	Depth	Temperature, °C	Salinity	Alkalinity	Specific Alkalinity
Series 89D, 28°16.5′S, 72°04.9′W, Code C					
1	966	4.24	34.485	2.436	0.1276
2	1159	3.74	34.519	2.398	0.1255
3	1448	3.04	34.570		
4	1736	2.54	34.611	2.439	0.1273
5	2026	2.24	34.640	2.459	0.1233
6	2411	1.96	34.665	2.479	0.1292
7	2798	1.84	34.677	2.491	0.1297
8	3187	1.80	34.681	2.465	0.1284
9	3577	1.79	34.684	2.460	0.1281
10	3969	1.74	34.691	2.460	0.1281
11	4265	1.73	34.691	2.455	0.1279
12	4965	1.77	34.695	2.491	0.1297
13	5467	1.82	34.697	2.491	0.1297
14	5869	1.88	34.696	2.491	0.1297
15	6276	1.92	34.696	2.471	0.1286
16	6380	1.94	34.696	2.468	0.1285
Series 95D, 28°15.7′S, 79°07.3′W, Code C					
1	1134	3.58	34.516	2.444	0.1279
2	1333	3.14	34.546	2.450	0.1281
3	1532	2.78	34.590	2.450	0.1279
4	1730	2.51	34.616	2.387	0.1246
5	1917	2.30	34.633	2.460	0.1283
6	2114	2.12	34.649	2.462	0.1284
7	2311	1.99	34.666	2.470	0.1287
8	2509	1.90	34.680	2.480	0.1292
9	2707	1.84	34.679	2.491	0.1297
10	2905	1.78	34.680	2.496	0.1300
11	3104	1.75	34.687	2.502	0.1303
12	3294	1.72	34.689	2.510	0.1307
13	3494	1.70	34.690	2.458	0.1280
14	3694	1.69	34.690	2.480	0.1292
15	3885	1.70	34.692	2.462	0.1282
16	3986	1.70	34.694	2.455	0.1279
17	4086	1.70	34.695	2.543	0.1324
Series 99D, 28°15.1′S, 86°35.5′W, Code A					
1	991A	4.08	34.462	2.367	0.1253
2	1088A	3.82	34.495	2.378	0.1258
3	1184A	3.60	34.510	2.375	0.1256

Eltanin 29

Sample	Depth	Temperature, °C	Salinity	Alkalinity	Specific Alkalinity
Series 99D (continued)					
4	1281A	3.36	34.525	2.380	0.1258
5	1475A	2.95	34.565	2.405	0.1269
6	1669A	2.59	34.594	2.401	0.1266
7	1863A	2.30	34.615	2.400	0.1265
8	2057A	2.08	34.635	2.421	0.1276
9	2250A	1.94	34.651	2.420	0.1274
10	2445A	1.86	34.663	2.430	0.1279
11	2640A	1.81	34.673	2.426	0.1277
12	2834A	1.78	34.679	2.452	0.1290
13	3029A	1.74	34.690	2.435	0.1280
14	3225A	1.70	34.689	2.428	0.1277
15	3420A	1.68	34.690	2.422	0.1274
16	3615A	1.69	34.690	2.422	0.1274
17	3713A	1.69	34.690	2.422	0.1274
Series 101D, 28°15′S, 90°27′W, Code C					
1	1017	3.95	34.429	2.361	0.1239
2	1115	3.68	34.479	2.399	0.1257
3	1214	3.49	34.506	2.424	0.1269
4	1411	3.03	34.554	2.457	0.1285
5	1606	2.64	34.586	2.439	0.1274
6	1806	2.34	34.608	2.460	0.1284
7	2003	2.09	34.634	2.473	0.1290
8	2200	1.92	34.652	2.491	0.1299
9	2398	1.84	34.666	2.484	0.1294
10	2595	1.80	34.672	2.496	0.1301
11	2795	1.79	34.678	2.477	0.1290
12	2993	1.77	34.683	2.467	0.1285
13	3192	1.77	34.681	2.460	0.1281
14	3293	1.77	34.684	2.452	0.1277
15	3392	1.76	34.684	2.450	0.1276
Series 106D, 28°12.5′S, 99°54.8′W, Code A					
1	990	4.08	34.390	2.355	0.1261
2	1090	3.74	34.450	2.358	0.1248
3	1189	3.50	34.494	2.360	0.1248
4	1344	3.08	34.527	2.375	0.1255
5	1441	2.86	34.554	2.391	0.1263
6	1538	2.58	34.572	2.367	0.1249
7	1734	2.28	34.604	2.400	0.1265
8	1930	2.07	34.629	2.420	0.1275
9	2126	1.93	34.647	2.421	0.1275
10	2322	1.86	34.654	2.425	0.1277
11	2519	1.84	34.663	2.445	0.1287
12	2718	1.83	34.666	2.435	0.1281
13	2918	1.83	34.670	2.440	0.1284
14	3118	1.83	34.673	2.452	0.1290
15	3218	1.83	34.677	2.440	0.1284
16	3318	1.83	34.679	2.470	0.1299
17	3418	1.82	34.678	2.410	0.1268
18	3520	1.82	34.679	2.413	0.1270
Series 111D, 28°15.1′S, 109°16.6′W, Code C					
1	1058	4.00	34.404	2.387	0.1254
2	1247	3.31	34.474	2.396	0.1256

Eltanin 29

Sample	Depth	Temperature, °C	Salinity	Alkalinity	Specific Alkalinity
Series 111D (continued)					
3	1438	2.75	34.546	2.399	0.1255
4	1628	2.37	34.592	2.424	0.1266
5	1821	2.19	34.622	2.460	0.1284
6	2013	2.04	34.642	2.470	0.1288
7	2208	1.92	34.657	2.439	0.1271
8	2405	1.88	34.661	2.493	0.1299
9	2503	1.86	34.664	2.467	0.1286
10	2603	1.85	34.669	2.479	0.1292
11	2702	1.85	34.667	2.491	0.1298
12	2802	1.85	34.671	2.497	0.1301
13	2901	1.85	34.669	2.462	0.1283
Series 114D, 28°16′S, 114°56.4′W, Code A					
1	1133A	3.55	34.416	2.338	0.1239
2	1226A	3.24	34.463	2.342	0.1239
3	1320	2.92	34.509	2.360	0.1247
5	1511	2.58	34.570	2.329	0.1299
6	1607	2.44	34.589	2.378	0.1267
7	1704	2.32	34.606	2.388	0.1259
9	1900	2.14	34.627	2.400	0.1265
10	2045	2.01	34.627	2.394	0.1261
11	2190	1.94	34.650	2.403	0.1266
12	2384	1.82	34.659	2.420	0.1274
14	2729	1.76	34.669	2.411	0.1269
15	2880	1.74	34.672	2.424	0.1276
16	2980	1.76	34.676	2.420	0.1274
17	3080	1.75	34.676	2.420	0.1274
Series 117D, 28°13′S, 120°31.7′W, Code C					
1	967	4.56	34.332	2.367	0.1246
2	1156	3.68	34.502	2.372	0.1242
3	1346	3.02	34.503	2.399	0.1256
4	1542	2.62	34.570	2.422	0.1265
5	1739	2.38	34.604	2.441	0.1275
6	1937	2.16	34.626	2.429	0.1267
7	2133	2.01	34.647	2.429	0.1266
8	2329	1.88	34.657	2.441	0.1272
9	2524	1.80	34.663	2.450	0.1277
10	2717	1.74	34.672	2.433	0.1268
11	2845	1.70	34.673	2.458	0.1281
12	2945	1.68	34.679	2.489	0.1296
13	3045	1.66	34.680	2.491	0.1297
14	3147	1.64	34.681	2.453	0.1278
15	3247	1.64	34.683	2.440	0.1271
16	3349	1.64	34.684	2.441	0.1271
17	3450	1.63	34.685	2.464	0.1283
Series 122D, 28°16′S, 130°02.8′W, Code B					
1	1156	3.62	34.417	2.380	0.1249
2	1349	2.95	34.512	2.406	0.1262
3	1543	2.59	34.566	2.420	0.1267
4	1738	2.36	34.601	2.404	0.1256
5	1931	2.18	34.627	2.461	0.1285
6	2126	2.02	34.645	2.482	0.1296
7	2319	1.93	34.655	2.487	0.1297

Eltanin 29

Sample	Depth	Temperature, °C	Salinity	Alkalinity	Specific Alkalinity
Series 122D (continued)					
8	2512	1.80	34.664	2.475	0.1290
9	2709	1.74	34.672	2.451	0.1277
10	2905	1.67	34.677	2.446	0.1274
11	3101	1.63	34.681	2.446	0.1274
12	3299	1.59	34.685	2.476	0.1290
13	3497	1.56	34.688	2.456	0.1279
14	3696	1.55	34.691	2.466	0.1284
15	3896	1.55	34.692	2.470	0.1286
16	4038	1.57	34.694	2.466	0.1284
17	4120	1.57	34.692	2.446	0.1274
Series 127D, 28°13.6′S, 139°20.3′W, Code C					
1	914	4.87	34.333	2.401	0.1264
2	1107	3.82	34.396	2.382	0.1251
3	1302	3.13	34.479	2.400	0.1257
4	1496	2.70	34.548	2.406	0.1258
5	1790	2.30	34.611	2.437	0.1272
6	2081	2.03	34.644	2.443	0.1274
7	2276	1.91	34.658	2.450	0.1277
8	2471	1.79	34.664	2.455	0.1279
9	2667	1.70	34.671	2.465	0.1285
10	2960	1.62	34.681	2.465	0.1284
11	3158	1.57	34.685	2.470	0.1286
12	3354	1.52	34.690	2.461	0.1282
13	3551	1.46	34.695	2.455	0.1278
14	3652	1.45	34.695	2.439	0.1270
15	3752	1.44	34.696	2.439	0.1270
16	3852	1.44	34.699	2.436	0.1268
17	3952	1.44	34.698	2.444	0.1272
Series 130D, 28°15′S, 145°01.9′W, Code B					
1	868	5.21	34.334	2.406	0.1266
2	972	4.65	34.359	2.386	0.1254
3	1172	3.62	34.420	2.418	0.1269
4	1369	2.89	34.524	2.456	0.1285
5	1570	2.53	34.572	2.446	0.1278
6	1770	2.27	34.606	2.456	0.1283
7	1970	2.13	34.633	2.446	0.1276
8	2170	1.98	34.647	2.446	0.1275
9	2371	1.86	34.658	2.471	0.1288
10	2571	1.79	34.670	2.467	0.1286
11	contaminated				
12	2971	1.67	34.676	2.468	0.1285
13	3171	1.61	34.684	2.456	0.1279
14	3371	1.57	34.686	2.448	0.1275
15	3572	1.53	34.690	2.418	0.1259
16	3772	1.46	34.696	2.441	0.1271
17	3972	1.42	34.698	2.471	0.1286
14S	4122	1.39	34.701	2.370	0.1234
15S	4272	1.39	34.706	2.365	0.1231
16S	4372	1.38	34.705	2.345	0.1221
Series 133D, 28°14.6′S, 150°51′W, Code C					
1	776	5.82	34.340	2.350	0.1236
2	970	4.50	34.348	2.367	0.1245

Eltanin 29

Sample	Depth	Temperature, °C	Salinity	Alkalinity	Specific Alkalinity
Series 133D (continued)					
3	1164	3.70	34.415	2.384	0.1252
4	1359	2.97	34.509	2.398	0.1255
5	1555	2.62	34.563	2.415	0.1262
6	1749	2.32	34.614	2.434	0.1271
7	1945	2.10	34.642	2.443	0.1275
8	2139	1.98	34.650	2.450	0.1277
9	2335	1.88	34.659	2.465	0.1285
10	2627	1.79	34.666	2.479	0.1291
11	2921	1.68	34.677	2.465	0.1283
12	3218	1.57	34.685	2.491	0.1297
13	3418	1.49	34.693	2.458	0.1280
14	3620	1.41	34.694	2.470	0.1286
15	3722	1.35	34.701	2.455	0.1278
16	3824	1.32	34.702	2.442	0.1272
17	3927	1.33	34.701	2.439	0.1270
Series 138D, 28°16.1′S, 160°06.1′W, Code B					
1	1700	2.40	34.603	2.451	0.1280
2	1894	2.24	34.634	2.456	0.1281
3	2090	2.08	34.640	2.433	0.1269
4	2284	1.98	34.652	2.436	0.1270
5	2479	1.92	34.659	2.487	0.1296
6	2674	1.87	34.663	2.497	0.1301
7	2868	1.78	34.674	2.487	0.1296
8	3065	1.71	34.679	2.475	0.1289
9	3263	1.61	34.685	2.487	0.1295
10	3462	1.54	34.698	2.446	0.1273
11	3659	1.46	34.705	2.451	0.1276
12	3857	1.39	34.710	2.446	0.1273
13	3956	1.35	34.716	2.436	0.1267
14	4056	1.32	34.716	2.458	0.1279
15	4155	1.27	34.716	2.456	0.1278
16	4254	1.19	34.716	2.456	0.1278
17	4354	1.17	34.715	2.441	0.1270
18	4454	1.12	34.714	2.436	0.1268
Series 143D, 28°16.5′S, 168°49.5′W, Code C					
1	1470	2.91	34.523	2.340	0.1272
2	1663	2.56	34.583	2.350	0.1275
3	1952	2.24	34.630	2.374	0.1285
4	2244	2.09	34.651	2.388	0.1292
5	2438	1.98	34.654	2.390	0.1293
6	2633	1.91	34.662	2.360	0.1277
7	2926	1.80	34.673	2.385	0.1289
8	3220	1.69	34.688	2.373	0.1282
9	3514	1.56	34.713	2.360	0.1275
10	3807	1.42	34.725	2.350	0.1269
11	4004	1.28	34.723	2.328	0.1257
12	4198	1.16	34.720	2.320	0.1253
13	4394	1.08	34.719	2.300	0.1242
14	4687	1.04	34.714	2.320	0.1253
15	4983	1.05	34.713	2.327	0.1257
16	5181	1.07	34.713	2.320	0.1253
17	5379	1.10	34.713	2.361	0.1276
18	5477	1.11	34.711	2.338	0.1263

AN EXAMINATION OF THE *ELTANIN* DREDGED ROCKS FROM THE SCOTIA SEA

N. D. Watkins[1] and R. Self[2]

Florida State University, Tallahassee, Florida 32306

Abstract. As a preliminary to a detailed study, the contents of each of over one hundred rock-dredge hauls, taken during *Eltanin* cruises 5 to 9, 12, and 22 in the Scotia Sea, have been classified in a system involving division of each recovered haul into rock groups which we call granitic, felsitic, basaltic, metamorphic, sedimentary, and manganese nodules, but which are sufficiently broad so that in most cases diverse associated rock types are incorporated. Estimates of the size of the rounded fraction of each haul were also made. Second-order trend surfaces and corresponding residual maps have been constructed on the normalized rock groups and the 'roundness' parameter of each dredge haul. East-west elongations characterize the metamorphic and roundness fractions, whereas other surfaces trend either north-south or southeast-northwest. Inconsistencies in collection methods and diversity of sources inhibit confident interpretation of the geological meaning of these observations. Since roundness and all rock fractions except basalt increase southward, however, it is suggested that the Antarctic Continent south of the Weddell Sea and the southeast coast of the Antarctic Peninsula are the dominant sources of ice-rafted rocks in the Scotia Sea.

INTRODUCTION

The age and petrogenesis of deep-sea rocks have assumed much importance during the last half decade. This reflects the obvious relevance of such materials to the resolution of current hypotheses involving oceanic crustal genesis, as well as the increasing availability of such materials, which is resulting from the rise in geological oceanographic activities.

The critical significance of mid-oceanic rises in an understanding of oceanic crustal origins has, not surprisingly, resulted in a concentration of dredging and analyses in such areas, particularly in latitudes equatorward of 45°, where the problem of modern ice rafting of materials does not exist.

Methods of distinguishing in situ from ice-rafted materials are at present dangerously subjective: fragments of pillow basalt with chilled outer parts are thought to be strongly indicative of an in situ origin, although igneous extrusion into glacial lakes before glacial transport is a mechanism easily capable of producing material of very similar appearance. Similarly, it is well known that low potassium tholeiitic basalts are not uniquely identifiable as submarine materials. There is no particular reason as yet to be completely confident about rejecting the possibility that granite or any other known rock type can occur in situ in oceanic crusts, particularly in areas immediately adjacent to continents. We would, however, feel that it is virtually impossible to argue that a very well-rounded abraded rock sample above sand size is anything other than ice-rafted when recovered from deeper parts of the oceans.

In high latitudes, the problem of finding a rock specimen which is definitely in situ in origin becomes, therefore, extremely difficult, unless collection is simultaneously aided by detailed sea-bottom photography and seismic profiling. Generally, previous descriptions of rocks from high latitude dredge hauls do not have this control. In addition to simply describing the rock types in a set of antarctic dredge hauls, *Stewart* [1963] provides a comprehensive set of references to previous work on rocks from high latitude dredge hauls.

Watkins and Self [1969] have proposed a statistical means to determine whether a collection of sea-bottom samples is dominantly in situ or ice rafted: if a marked departure from a regional distribution of a given rock type is closely associated with a submerged physiographic feature, then it is very probable that the departure reflects the dominance of an in situ fraction, since icebergs would not selectively deposit their debris on a submerged feature. This method has been applied to the *Eltanin* dredged rocks from the South Pacific Ocean and a subsequent series of geochemical and

[1] Now at University of Rhode Island, Kingston, Rhode Island 02881.

[2] Now at Rice University, Houston, Texas 77001.

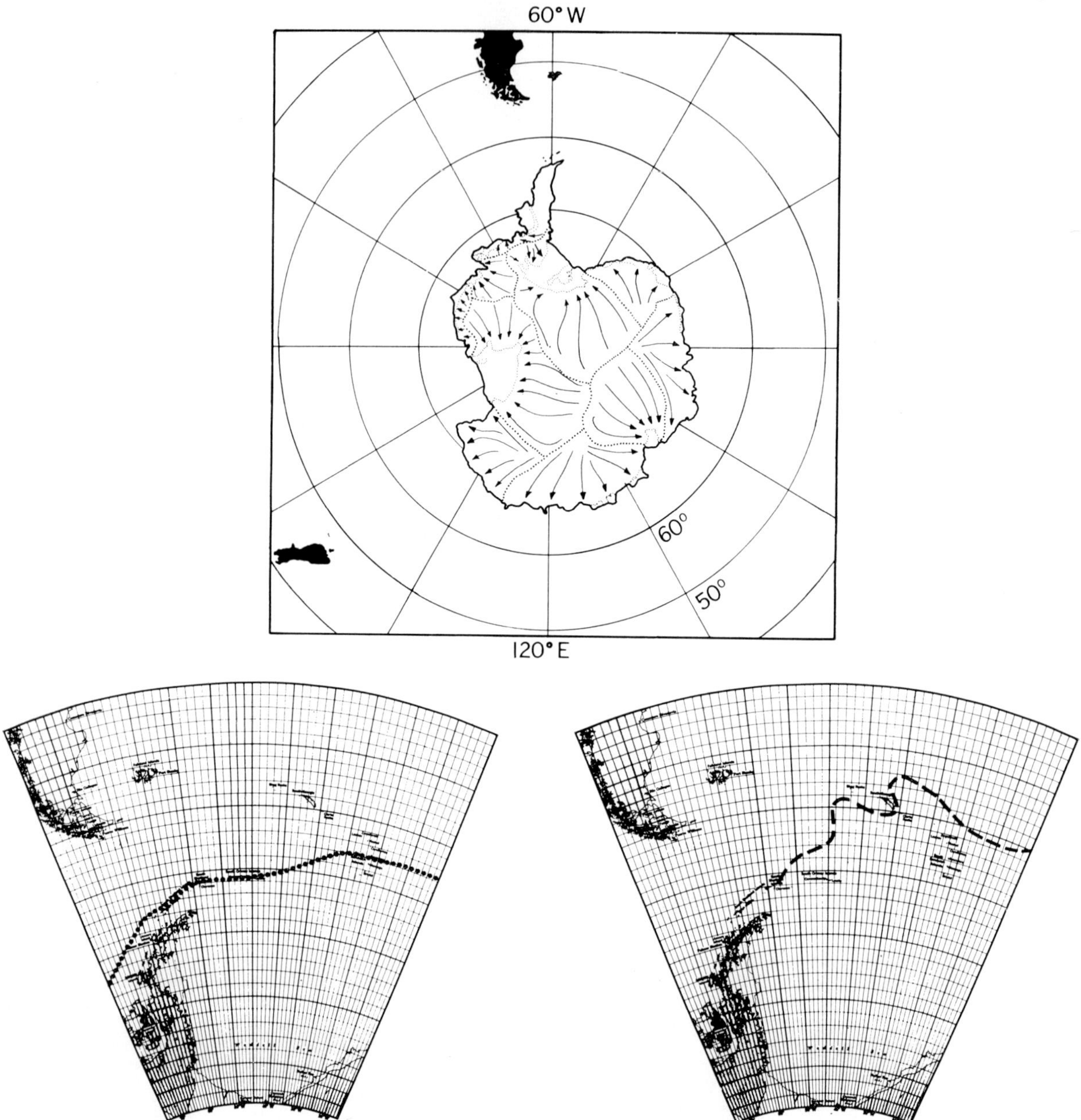

Fig. 1. Sketch maps showing the present sea ice limit in the Scotia Sea (lower left); the major directions of ice movement on the Antarctic Continent (upper center); and northern limit of present Weddell Sea current (lower right). (Sources of data: *U. S. Navy* [1957], *Priestley et al.* [1964, p. 302]).

magnetic property analyses have been made on in situ rocks from the Macquarie Ridge [*Watkins and Gunn*, 1970].

If no major physiographic features exist in a high latitude area, such as is the case in the Scotia Sea, then the regional distribution of dredged rocks can only be expected to be a function of preferred iceberg tracks and favored source areas, somewhat analogous to unroofing and redeposition of an igneous body by normal erosion processes in continental areas. This analogy must almost certainly be clearly unrealistically simple in practice in the South Atlantic, Pacific, and Indian oceans, however, if for no other reason than the very wide geographic sources of icebergs (Figure 1). In spite of this we nevertheless feel that the considerable efforts which have been involved in recover-

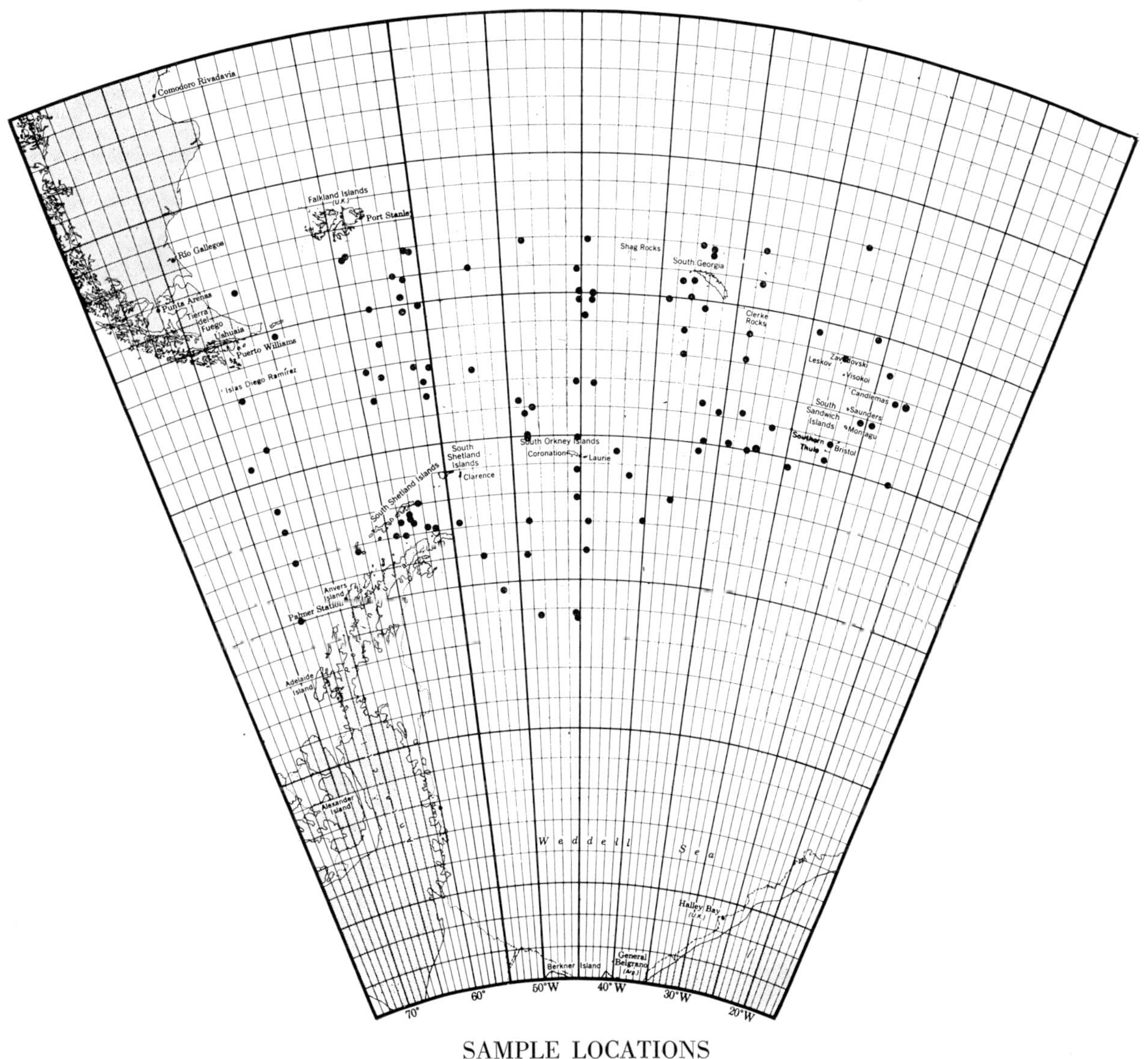

SAMPLE LOCATIONS

Fig. 2. Map showing the locations of the *Eltanin* rock dredge hauls. See Table 1 for latitude and longitude and water depth of each dredge haul.

ing the *Eltanin* dredged rock collection justify an attempt to detect an underlying natural controlling factor. We present here a description of the regional pattern of dredged rock type collected during *Eltanin* cruises of the Scotia Sea (Figure 2). We shall emphasize analytical difficulties resulting from the collection and on-board sorting operations, in order to make constructive suggestions for future work.

GEOLOGY OF SOURCE AREAS AROUND THE SCOTIA SEA

What is known about the geology of the area immediately around the Scotia Sea can obviously be relevant to the meaning of any trends in regional patterns of rocks dredged from the Scotia Sea. The geology of Antarctica in the Pacific would of course also be relevant, but would perhaps be less significant.

Baker [1968] has summarized the geology of the islands of the Scotia Arc or South Sandwich Islands. As far as is known, the islands are predominantly basaltic.

Trendall [1953, 1959] has described the geology of South Georgia. A wide range of sedimentary and igneous rock types, and some metasediments and spilites ranging back to Upper Paleozoic age are exposed. The South Orkney Islands and Antarctic Peninsula

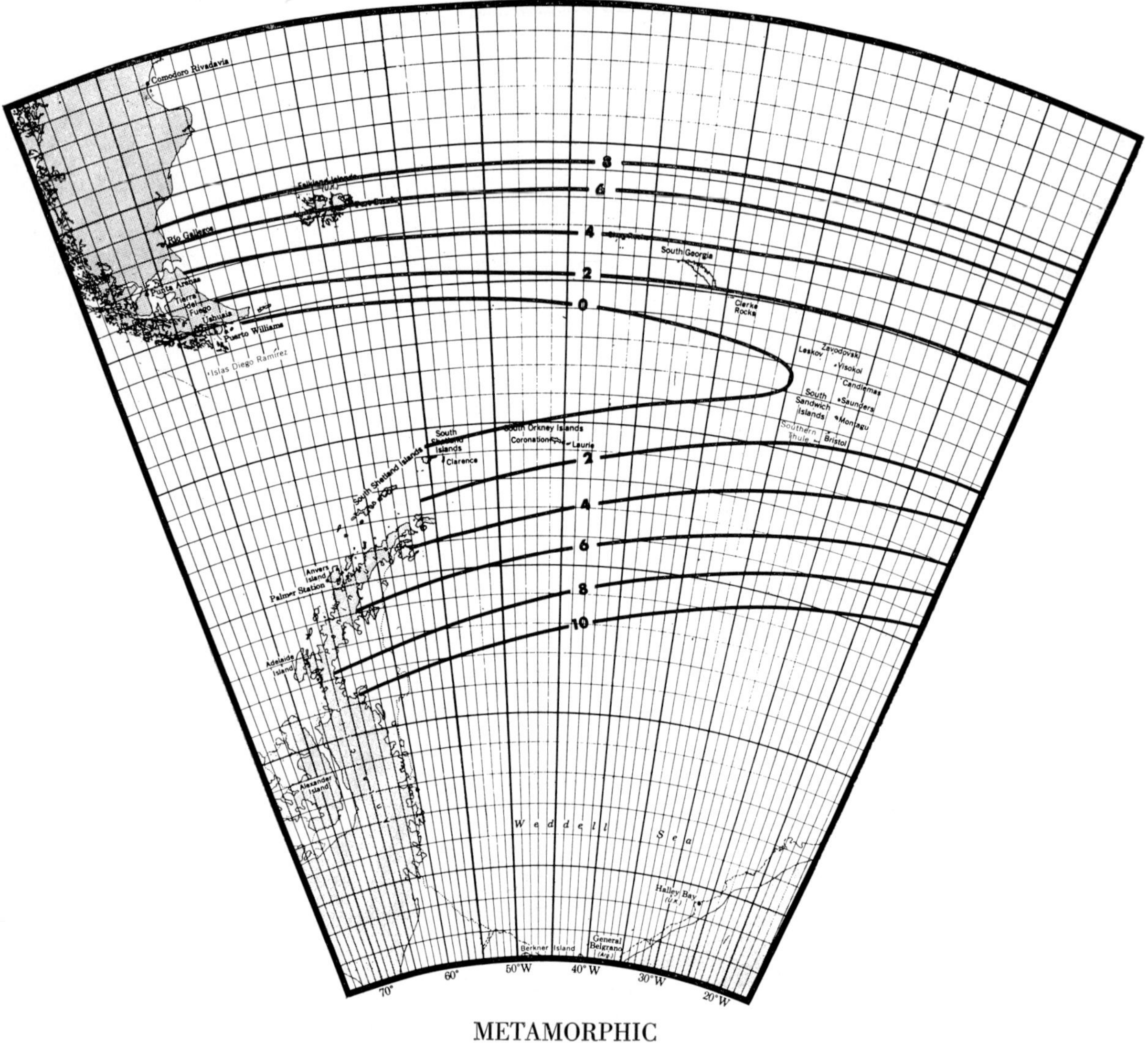

Fig. 3. Second-order trend surface maps of the metamorphic fraction of the *Eltanin* rock dredge hauls in the Scotia Sea. See text for definition of the fraction, computational methods, and discussion of limitations.

both include very diverse rocks as old as Precambrian (summary by *Adie* [1964]).

It is probable that various rock types are transported by ice great distances from part of Antarctica west of the Antarctic Peninsula. Except for icebergs originating from the South Sandwich Islands, then, there is no known natural limitation whatsoever for the range of rock types carried by icebergs that melt at least in part in the Scotia Sea. Therefore no model of preferred rock dredge content can be formulated, except very close to the South Sandwich Islands, where basalts should predominate. Nevertheless, it is perfectly reasonable to imagine that rock types incorporated into glaciers will, in some areas at least, be restricted in compositional range for long periods, since physiography and therefore local glacial transportation and depositional patterns are frequently a function of rock type, and therefore regional patterns may emerge.

Unfortunately, no unique or highly distinctive rock type has been described as outcropping in the vicinity of, or west of, the Scotia Sea, and so no natural 'tracers' can as yet be utilized.

COLLECTION AND ANALYTICAL METHODS

Collection. The methods used to dredge rock samples from the *Eltanin* are highly variable.

Five different dredge types have been used (Table

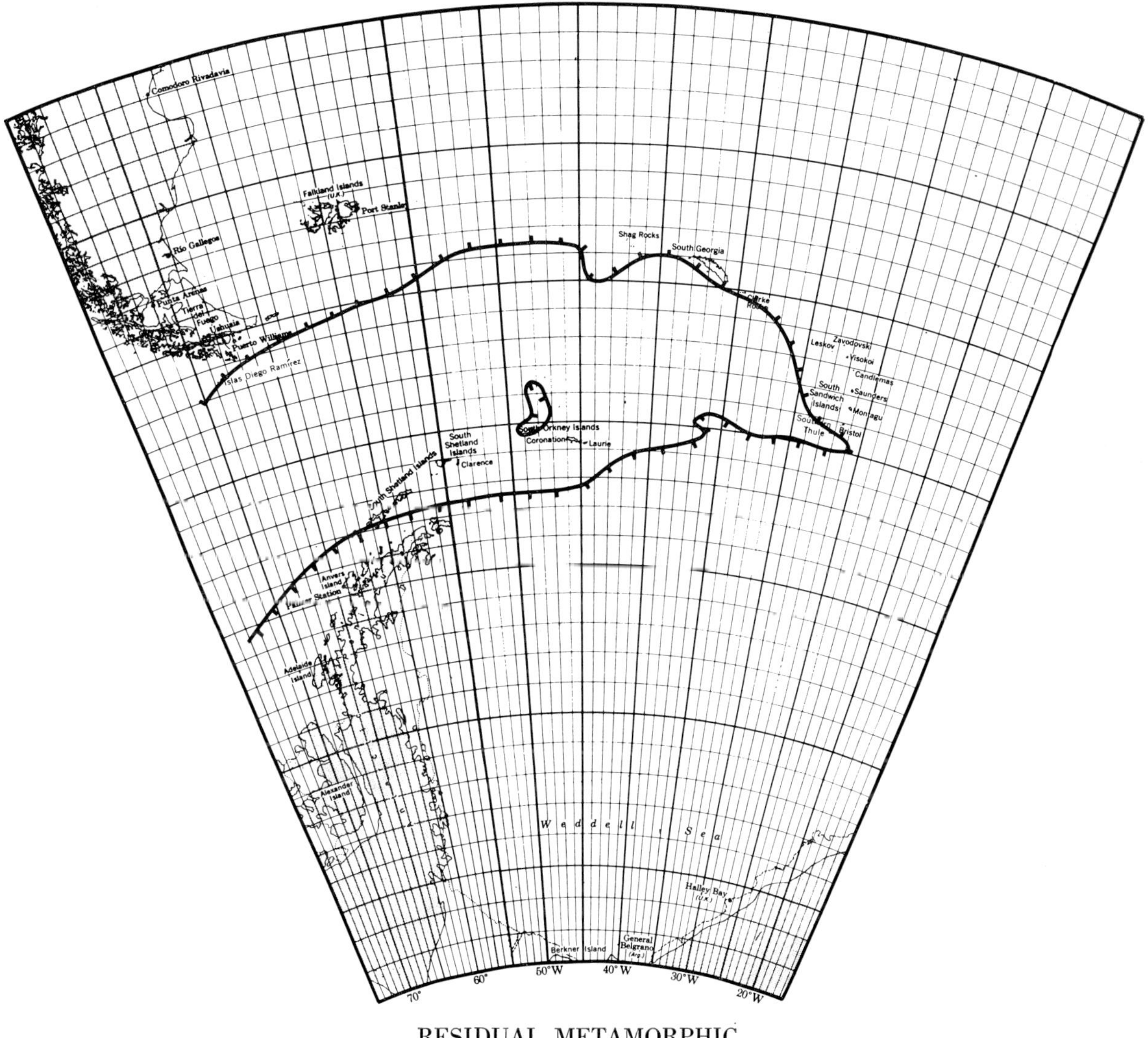

RESIDUAL METAMORPHIC

Fig. 4. Map of residuals resulting from subtraction of second-order trend surface values from observed metamorphic fraction. Contour line separates positive from negative residuals, with hashers on negative side of line.

1). Three of these are used for mainly biological purposes, the recovered rocks being simply a by-product of the operation. The rock dredge has been used for nearly half of the hauls. Recovered materials range in size from rocks of several tons to sand-size particles.

The dredges bite into only 10 to 20 cm of the surface sediments and/or rocks. Recovery of an in situ rock fraction depends, of course, on many variables: easy breaking off of all rock types can be envisaged under certain circumstances, but on the other hand, rocks that simply cannot be sampled by dredging methods must certainly exist. In the Scotia Sea, we believe that ice-rafted rocks are in any case likely to constitute virtually the entire recoverable fraction.

The dredge haul locations are shown in Figure 2. The hauls are not constant in either their absolute azimuth, or azimuth with respect to any coastal physiographic features. The duration in time and distance of the dredges are similarly not constant. No particular emphasis has been applied to sampling physiographic anomalies: the sites are more a function of attempts to obtain simple areal coverage (Figure 2). The dredge hauls are unloaded on deck and sorted by nonspecialist student investigators. Simple but variable logistic limitations prohibit retention of all recovered material. Methods of taking a 'representative' sample from the over-sized dredge hauls have been inconsistent, as far as we can determine, ranging from

TABLE 1. Number, Latitude, Longitude, and Depth of Each Dredge Haul

Sample numbering system as follows: letter refers to dredge haul type (*A*, Otter trawl; *B*, Rock Dredge; *C*, Menzies trawl; *D*, Blake trawl); first number or first two numbers refer to cruise; last two numbers refer to the specific dredge. Percentage

SAMPLE	LAT S	LONG W	PERCENTAGE							DEPTH FM
			GRANITE	BASALT	FELSITE	META	SED	MNN	ROUNDED	
A503	53.21	66.34	0	50	0	0	50	0	50	43
B503	57.08	67.58	6	30	0	0	64	0	45	1500
B505	59.45	68.50	0	60	0	0	40	0	0	65
B506	61.15	67.42	26	07	17	4	46	0	11	2055
B507	62.19	67.48	26	13	13	0	48	0	22	2080
B508	63.01	67.36	20	15	14	14	37	0	12	2006
B509	64.55	68.35	21	11	11	4	52	0	40	225
A602	53.06	59.27	6	04	0	0	91	0	37	300
A603	63.16	58.47	13	4	36	4	45	0	45	40
C603	57.25	58.35	75	0	25	0	0	0	75	2135
C605	53.01	55.51	60	10	15	0	15	0	50	1072
C607	57.40	55.56	23	12	29	2	35	0	31	2110
D602	53.56	55.55	0	0	0	0	0	100	0	
D604	58.20	55.52	25	8	4	17	46	0	33	2185
D605	62.07	56.01	14	14	11	29	31	0	20	628
D606	62.30	58.10	13	19	0	19	50	0	19	985
D607	62.08	57.57	25	14	4	18	39	0	11	440
D608	62.40	57.47	18	09	16	22	36	0	06	373
D610	62.53	59.20	0	0	100	0	0	0	0	591
D611	63.19	62.36	0	28	22	0	50	0	17	84
D613	61.13	58.51	17	11	14	25	33	0	22	0
B602	53.08	59.36	0	0	0	0	100	0	0	323
B604	55.00	58.48	0	0	0	0	100	0	0	1550
B605	56.15	58.15	1	2	4	4	3	88	6	2205
B606	57.07	59.33	20	20	18	20	27	0	40	1950
B607	58.08	59.33	33	7	4	16	19	0	25	2260
B608	53.01	55.54	50	50	0	0	0	0	0	1065
B609	54.03	56.04	2	0	29	17	51	0	26	947
B610	55.06	55.46	10	20	4	16	46	0	67	1575
B611	55.50	56.05	0	0	0	0	0	100	0	
B612	53.38	56.32	20	12	12	28	28	0	24	1695
B613	57.44	55.57	11	3	1	5	9	0	7	2227
B616	61.14	56.12	0	0	0	0	100	0	0	131
B618	62.41	56.11	5	2	8	6	79	0	7	238
B619	62.14	58.17	9	9	3	9	71	0	29	290
B622	62.33	57.52	0	22	22	22	33	0	0	852
B624	62.48	57.42	33	10	10	6	41	0	20	340
C702	58.04	58.29	0	20	20	10	50	0	30	1542
C703	63.13	44.58	25	0	25	0	50	0	75	2060
C701	55.50	45.00	4	8	6	16	65	0	4	2010
C704	66.28	45.39	18	6	6	35	35	0	41	2293
C705	66.33	48.10	11	11	11	39	28	0	6	2046
C706	60.00	49.05	9	9	9	45	27	0	18	1595
D701	55.02	44.23	20	9	17	15	39	0	26	1985
D702	55.30	44.45	8	15	19	15	42	0	39	1951
D703	58.00	44.30	31	8	11	25	45	0	3	1525
D704	60.03	45.25	31	7	29	43	0	0	7	2890
D706	64.04	49.20	21	13	8	46	25	0	4	1844
D707	58.59	49.02	8	10	11	21	49	0	21	2111
D709	60.02	49.11	8	0	0	0	100	0	0	1835
B701	53.06	44.56	0	14	0	29	57	0	43	1194
B702	54.05	45.11	0	2	0	56	24	0	40	1873
B703	55.05	44.52	18	2	2	22	51	0	49	1910
B704	55.46	44.52	12	7	12	20	41	0	21	1222
B705	60.09	45.00	20	3	10	74	10	0	29	2890
B706	60.42	42.40	3	0	1	20	65	0	29	665
B707	61.10	45.10	14	9	0	64	27	0	23	130

columns give the percentage of specimens (with at least one dimension greater than 2 cm) in each dredge haul in the appropriate classes (granitic, basaltic, felsitic, metamorphic, sedimentary, and manganese nodule) and the percentage of 'rounded' samples in each dredge haul. Latitude in degrees south; longitude in degrees west; depth in fathoms.

B708	62.06	45.09	0	6	0	31	39	0	27	266
B709	63.10	45.07	24	8	0	25	58	0	25	2000
B710	66.28	45.33	8	7	36	14	21	0	29	2296
B713	63.00	49.15	21	7	12	14	36	0	38	1553
B715	60.02	49.07	15	8	4	40	31	0	19	1920
B716	55.00	48.53	21	5	7	29	38	0	38	2105
B717	53.03	48.57	19	0	0	31	50	0	19	1769
D802	57.20	23.09	0	0	100	0	0	0	100	2515
D803	55.08	25.58	0	0	13	0	88	0	63	4100
D804	58.15	25.42	0	0	0	0	100	0	0	1360
D805	60.06	22.13	0	12	0	0	88	0	0	2038
D806	57.20	27.41	0	31	63	0	6	0	6	1685
B801	55.36	29.24	0	71	0	14	14	0	0	1785
B803	56.01	27.42	0	4	88	0	8	0	0	560
B807	57.03	22.50	10	30	20	20	20	0	15	2525
B809	58.14	24.50	0	50	0	0	50	0	11	1311
B815	60.59	27.56	14	7	0	0	79	0	21	2185
B816	59.58	27.36	11	11	0	33	44	0	11	645
B818	59.27	27.15	0	25	0	0	75	0	38	506
D903	54.38	37.57	11	14	7	14	54	0	75	425
D902	54.39	38.35	11	7	15	37	30	0	37	148
C904	54.55	38.06	0	10	0	65	25	0	47	347
D906	56.21	37.01	21	9	12	32	26	0	12	1873
C909	56.54	37.33	27	7	5	39	22	0	7	1732
D912	58.49	36.24	8	8	8	62	15	0	23	962
D913	58.45	35.23	14	7	0	32	46	0	7	1125
C914	58.43	33.27	22	0	11	67	0	0	22	1725
C915	56.52	34.13	0	18	0	45	36	0	27	1730
D916	56.02	33.58	11	8	2	27	52	0	15	1742
D917	54.02	33.41	2	6	33	20	39	0	39	1470
D918	52.52	33.55	0	14	0	27	59	0	14	1550
D919	53.30	36.53	0	25	0	5	70	0	32	132
D920	53.23	37.16	4	16	0	0	80	0	16	737
D921	53.02	37.38	10	15	0	5	70	0	30	1682
D1118	61.25	56.31	19	9	6	31	34	0	34	164
D1201	55.10	64.45	18	0	0	0	82	0	18	1116
D1204	62.40	54.44	8	0	21	13	58	0	63	145
D1205	64.02	52.58	0	13	7	7	73	0	47	1275
D1206	65.10	51.59	15	0	31	8	46	0	46	1540
D1208	64.08	44.50	22	0	0	56	22	0	0	2483
D1210	60.16	36.19	0	0	36	14	50	0	43	720
D1212	60.36	29.58	0	8	13	21	54	4	38	535
D1214	59.51	32.25	25	8	42	0	25	0	33	357
D1221	60.35	24.44	0	25	50	25	0	0	25	347
D1216	59.56	24.37	20	0	6	20	54	0	26	610
D1217	59.05	35.13	29	0	16	27	29	0	20	1538
D1218	60.22	36.56	26	0	13	26	33	0	17	652
D1220	61.24	41.54	17	7	33	0	43	0	27	325
D1223	60.48	52.29	21	3	21	26	31	0	8	321
D1224	60.47	53.30	0	4	8	46	42	0	31	350
B2201	57.52	56.51	0	0	0	0	0	100	0	
B2202	57.49	52.03	0	0	0	0	0	100	0	
B2203	54.07	52.04	0	11	0	44	44	0	33	760
B2205	55.06	39.50	17	25	8	25	25	0	50	1650
B2206	62.12	38.17	36	29	14	14	7	0	14	1868
B2207	60.02	32.58	45	10	10	10	25	0	0	498
B2209	54.55	14.50	13	25	13	38	13	0	0	2204
B2210	56.34	24.15	0	20	80	0	0	0	0	1109
B2211	56.15	38.34	38	0	0	38	25	0	0	1569
B2212	54.43	56.37	0	0	0	0	100	0	0	190

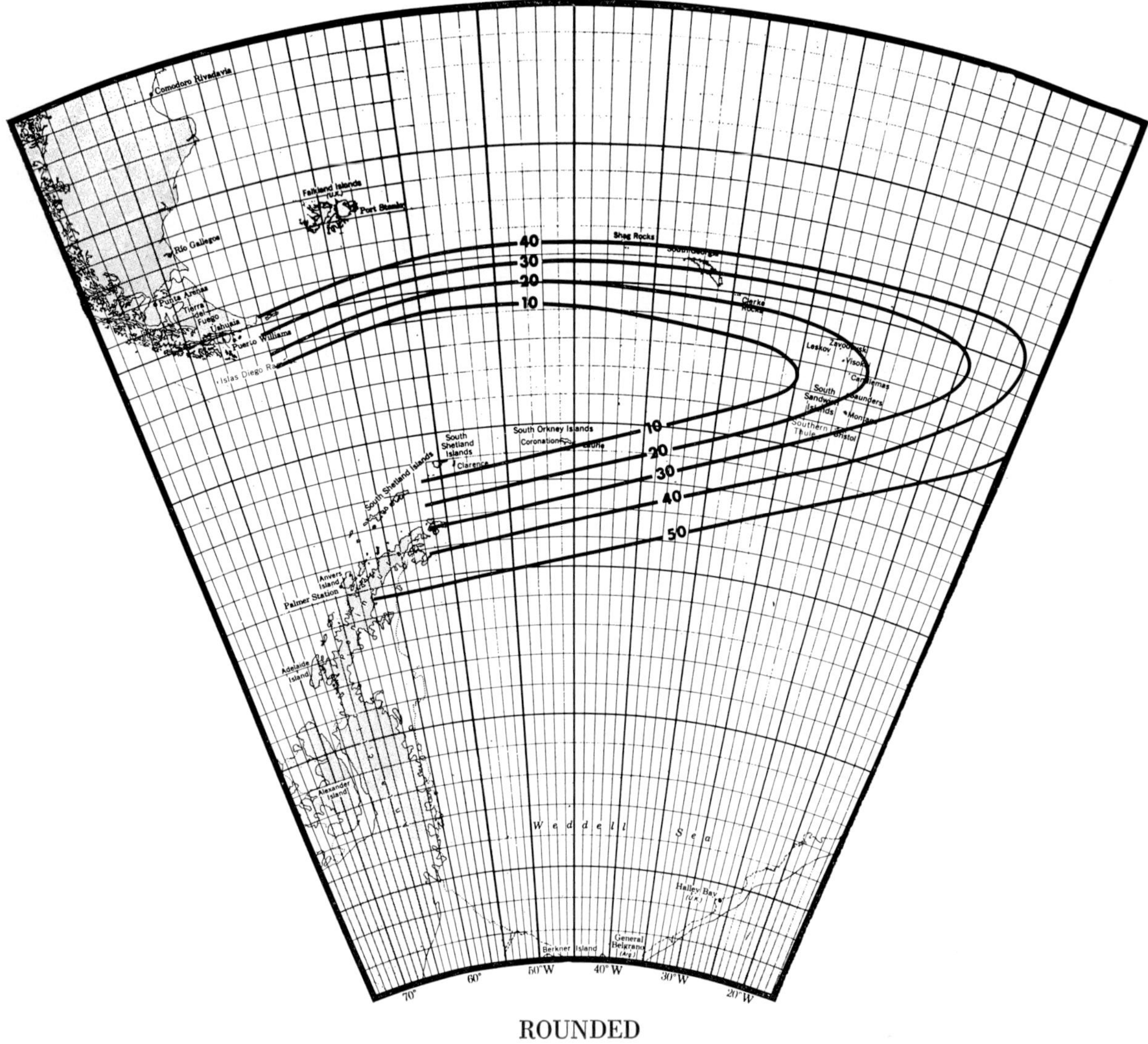

Fig. 5. Second-order trend surface maps of the 'roundness factor' fraction of the *Eltanin* rock dredge hauls in the Scotia Sea. See text for definition of the fraction, computational methods, and discussion of limitations.

hand sorting (with a probable overemphasis on 'interesting' rocks) which is made extremely difficult by the common high degree of manganese staining, to simple stirring and an attempt at effective random sampling with a metal bucket. It must be emphasized that this apparently simple task frequently took place at night in rough seas. Another human factor determining the nature of the collection is that as many as ten different personnel have been involved in the deck sorting.

These diverse factors make a consistent recovery of either a specified rock assemblage or a completely random sample virtually an impossible task.

Following this 'sorting', the materials are packed in sacks and freighted to Florida State University. As far as we know, only a few rock samples have been removed from the collection but the manganese nodules have been in part systematically removed. As we shall show, however, neither of these two activities will affect our analyses.

Observations. It can be confidently stated that there is no way in which the *Eltanin* dredged rock samples delivered to our laboratory can be categorized as clearly representative or not representative of either the original hauls recovered, or, in turn, the true submarine rock distribution at the dredge locations. This difficulty is probably characteristic of large-scale high latitude rock-dredging programs. We suggest, how-

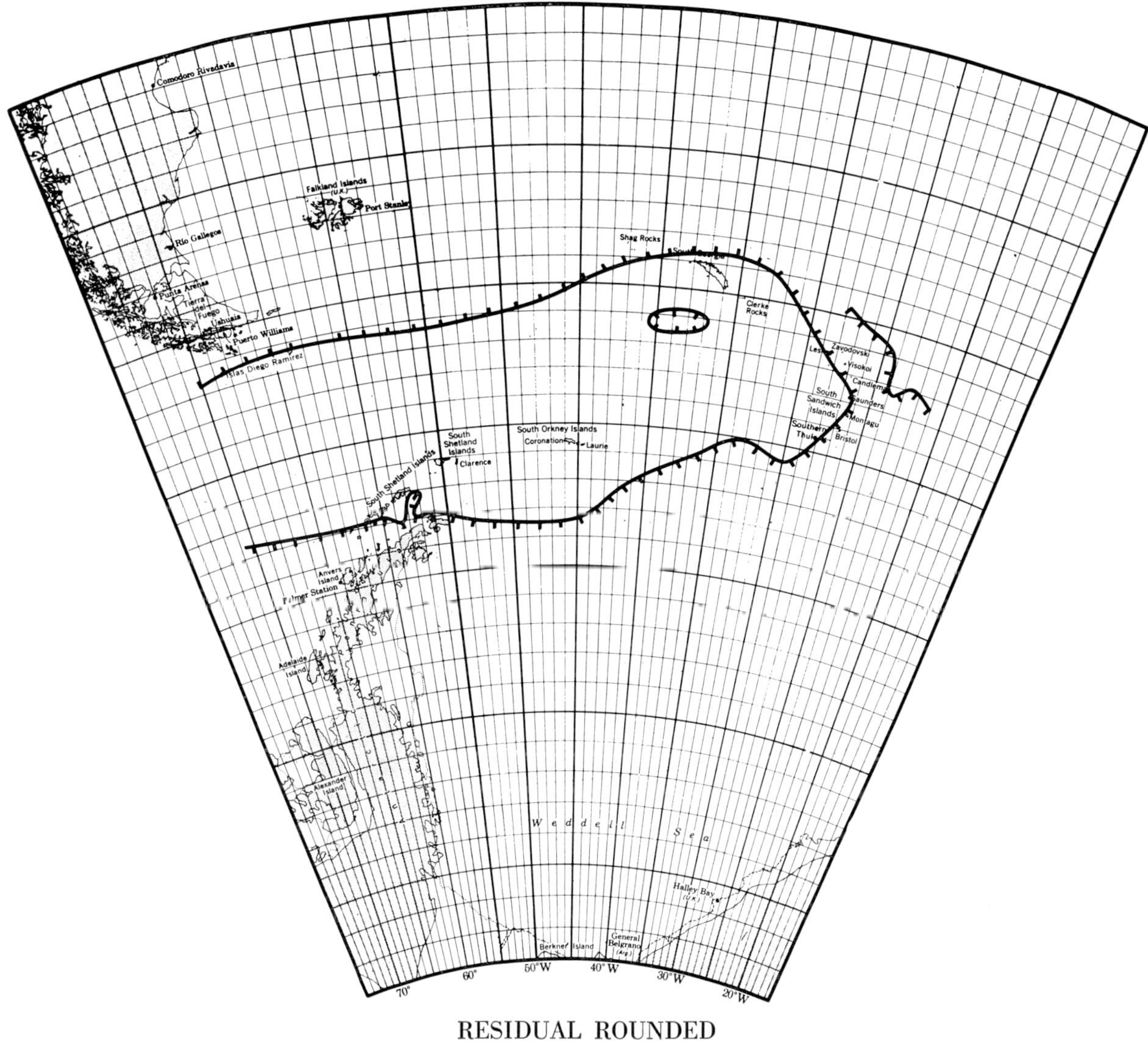

RESIDUAL ROUNDED

Fig. 6. Map of residuals resulting from subtraction of second-order trend surface values from observed 'roundness factor' fraction. Contour line separates positive from negative residuals, with hashers on negative side of line.

ever, that given the numerous variables involved, then with a large number of dredge recoveries over a long period in a large area, it would be impossible for any regional pattern to be the result of systematically varying biases, the effect of which surely must become essentially random given sufficient repetition.

We therefore feel that computation of regional patterns of rock type distribution would be likely to provide the best possibility of reflecting the major geological factors involved. As discussed above, these would be dominantly the preferred iceberg tracks and source areas.

In trying to determine a regional pattern of dredged rock character, and in common with the initial stage of any classification system, a wide set of rock categories is appropriate, because detailed petrological descriptions would inevitably create a very large number of categories which, being far more susceptible to local sampling biases, would therefore not be amenable to regional analyses.

The categories are:

1. Granitic (includes coarse to medium grained light to medium colored igneous rocks: granites, granodiorites, syenites, monzonites, and other varieties of sialic rocks).

2. Felsitic (includes fine to medium grained light to medium colored igneous rocks: felsites, rhyolites, trachytes, and trachy-andesites).

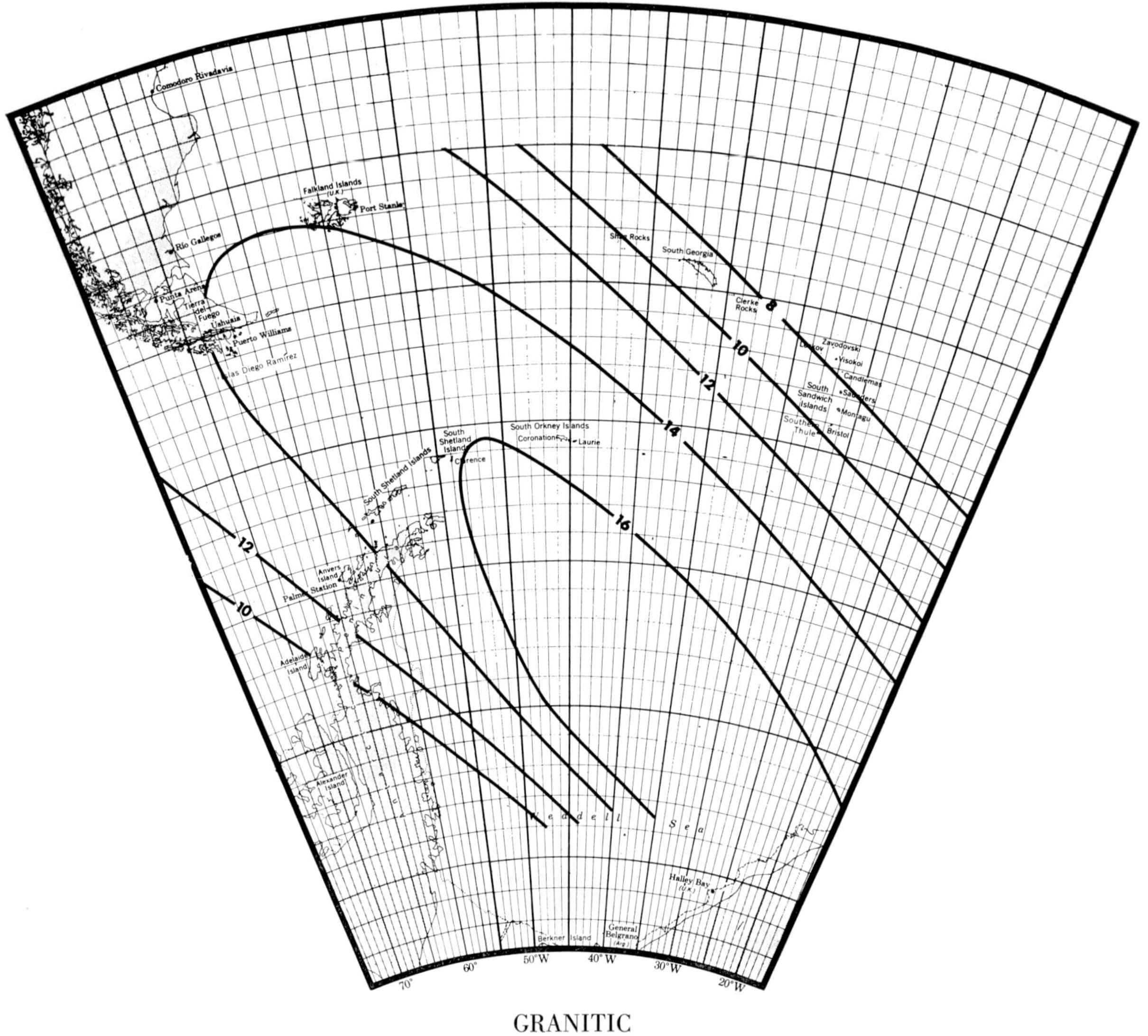

Fig. 7. Second-order trend surface maps of the granitic fraction of the *Eltanin* rock dredge hauls in the Scotia Sea. See text for definition of the fraction, computational methods, and discussion of limitations.

3. Basaltic (includes fine to medium grained dark to medium colored igneous rocks: basalts, basaltic andesites, dolerites, and also fine to medium grained ultrabasic rocks and spilites).

4. Metamorphic (high grade metamorphic rocks only, such as gneisses and schists).

5. Sedimentary (includes materials which are possibly low grade metamorphic sediments and volcanic agglomerates).

6. Manganese nodules (refers to true nodules, and not simply to encrustations).

Additional rock categories were not found to be necessary: surprisingly, no gabbroic rocks were identified. We have included, however, an additional parameter to describe the igneous fraction of each dredge haul which is well rounded. We simply categorize each sample as 'rounded' or 'not rounded'. This then, is our seventh category (Table 1).

Each specimen with one dimension of at least 2 cm from each of over 100 hauls (Figure 2) has been categorized using this simple system. It was found necessary to chip the surface of many samples because of the high degree of manganese staining. Using conventional field identification methods (involving an eye lens, hardness tester, etc.) and a binocular microscope, relatively little difficulty was encountered in placing samples in categories 1 to 3. Where any doubt existed about a sample's being metamorphic, it was either

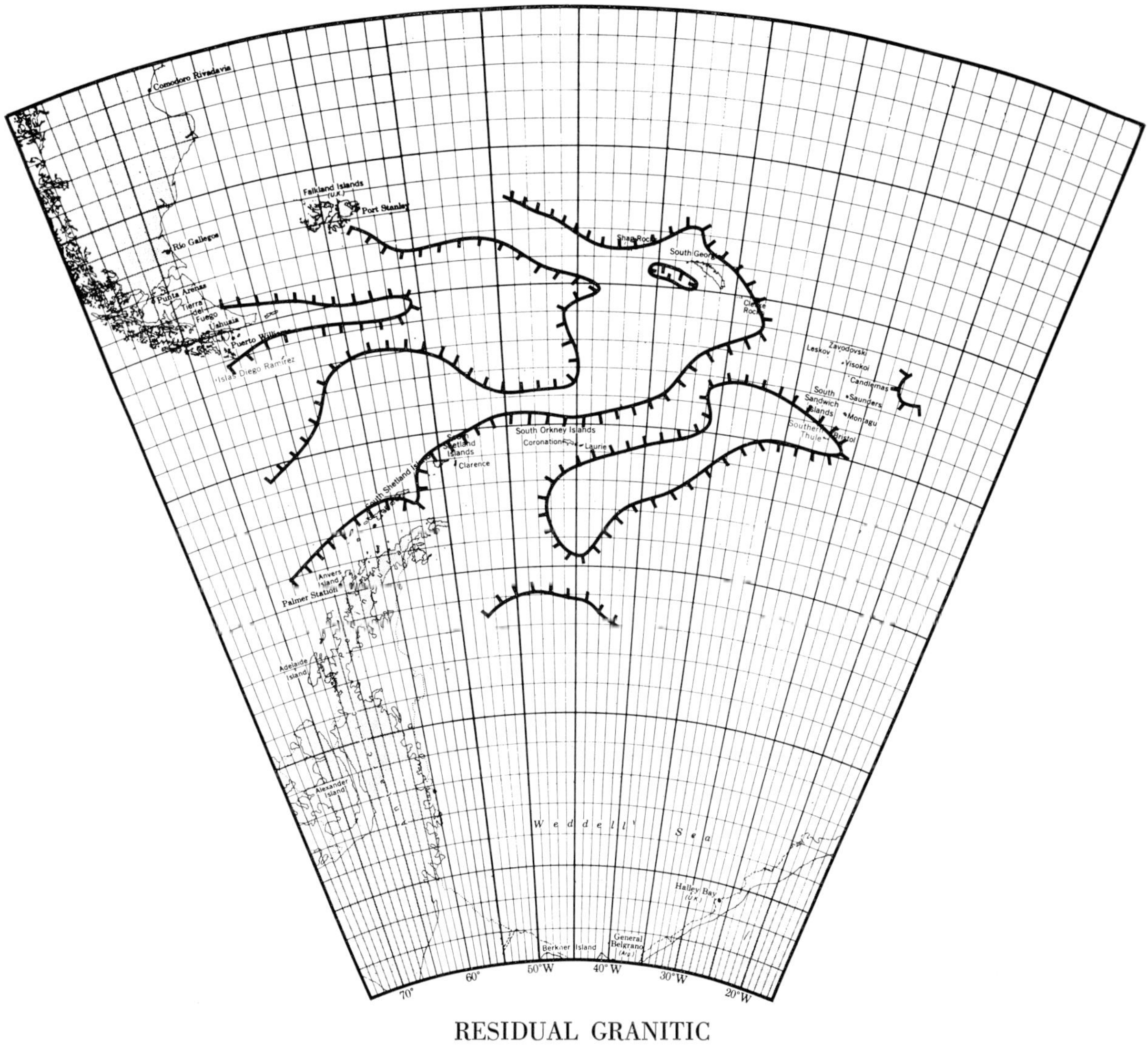

Fig. 8. Map of residuals resulting from subtraction of second-order trend surface values from observed granitic fraction. Contour line separates positive from negative residual, with hashers on negative side of line.

assigned to the appropriate igneous or sedimentary category. Repeated categorizing of many hauls indicates a ± 5 to 10% precision.

Category 5 (sedimentary) includes a wide range of coarse and fine sediments with various degrees of lithification. Considerable difficulties exist in determining the real fraction of this category in each dredge haul, because the less lithified samples have frequently crumbled into much smaller fragments which are sometimes nonsedimentary. We have tried to estimate the sedimentary fractional content of each dredge haul by counting the specimens, as with the other categories, but have found it necessary in some cases to estimate subjectively the crumbled sedimentary fractions as an equivalent number of whole samples of small dimension. This category is by far the most unsatisfactory of those used, since it undoubtedly includes materials with very widely differing origins, some of which if of larger size would not be in the sedimentary category. It constitutes essentially that fraction of each dredge haul which is not in the other five categories, and is therefore necessary for determining the fraction of the dredge haul content for each of the other rock categories, which is the basis of the regional analytical method, as discussed below.

Analyses. Since the number of samples recovered from

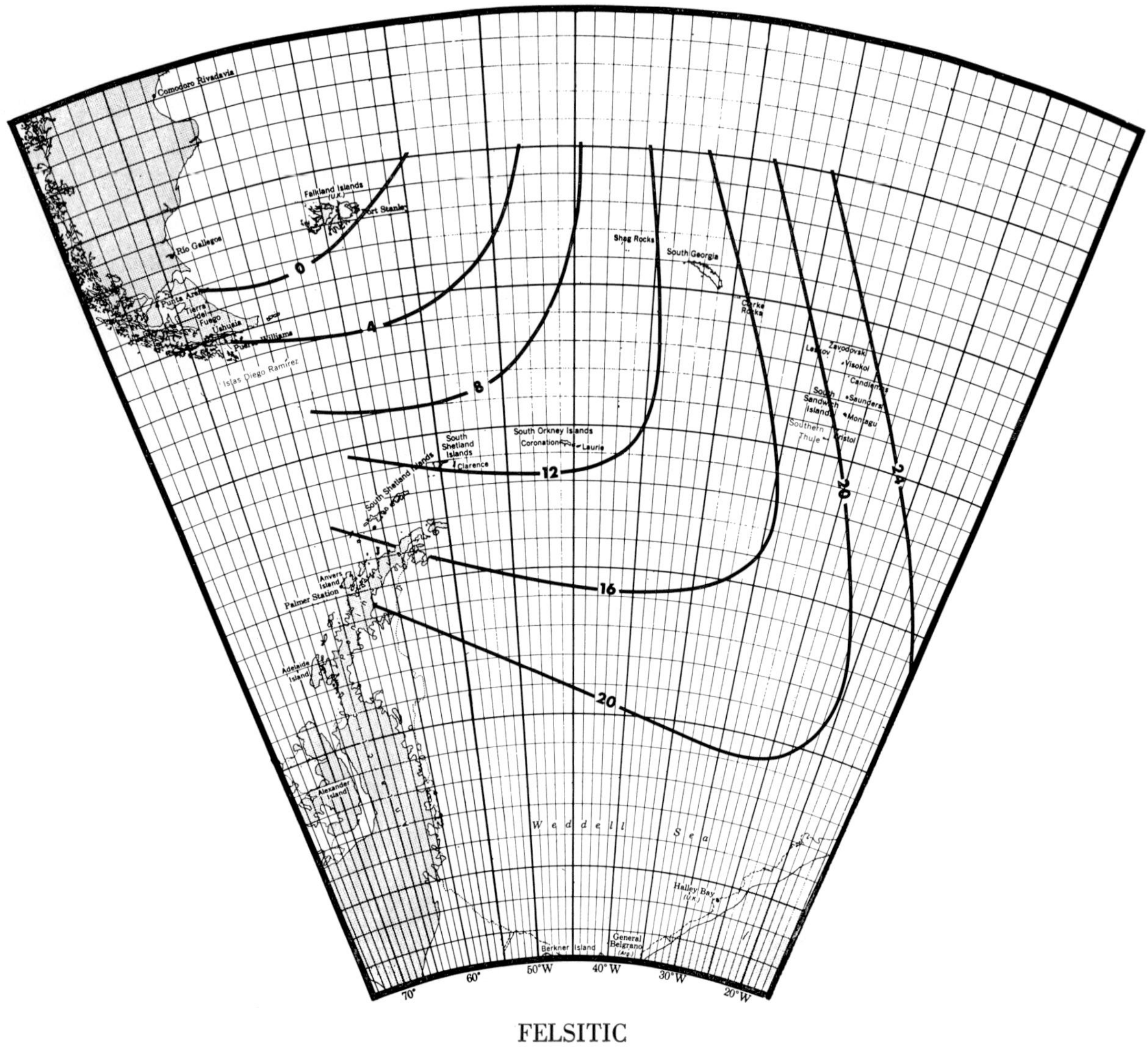

Fig. 9. Second-order trend surface maps of the felsitic fraction of the *Eltanin* rock dredge hauls in the Scotia Sea. See text for definition of the fraction, computational methods, and discussion of limitations.

each dredge varies greatly, it is clearly of no use to make regional analyses of the total number of recovered samples of each category.

We have normalized each dredge haul by expressing the rock category content as a percentage of the whole. The 'whole' however, does not include the manganese nodule content, which is clearly of different origin from the other dredged material. It is not included in our analyses. This, of course, also removed any difficulty resulting from removal of nodules from the collection. The results are given in Table 1.

These normalized data points have been subjected to conventional trend surface analyses. Considerable debate is possible about the validity of fitting high-order surfaces to data of the type obtained from the *Eltanin* dredge rock collection. This hinges simply on the reality of the defined surface: no matter what the quality of the data, a sufficiently high-order surface can be used to fit the data with misleading accuracy. As discussed above, the sampling procedure has a great many imperfections, which could conceivably be expressed as details in high-order trend surface maps. We therefore argue that the data can be subjected only to the broadest of analyses, if a realistic (however broad) picture of the dredge rock distribution is to become known. In other words, we feel that the sometimes conventional choosing of a surface reflecting a low significance reduction of root mean square resid-

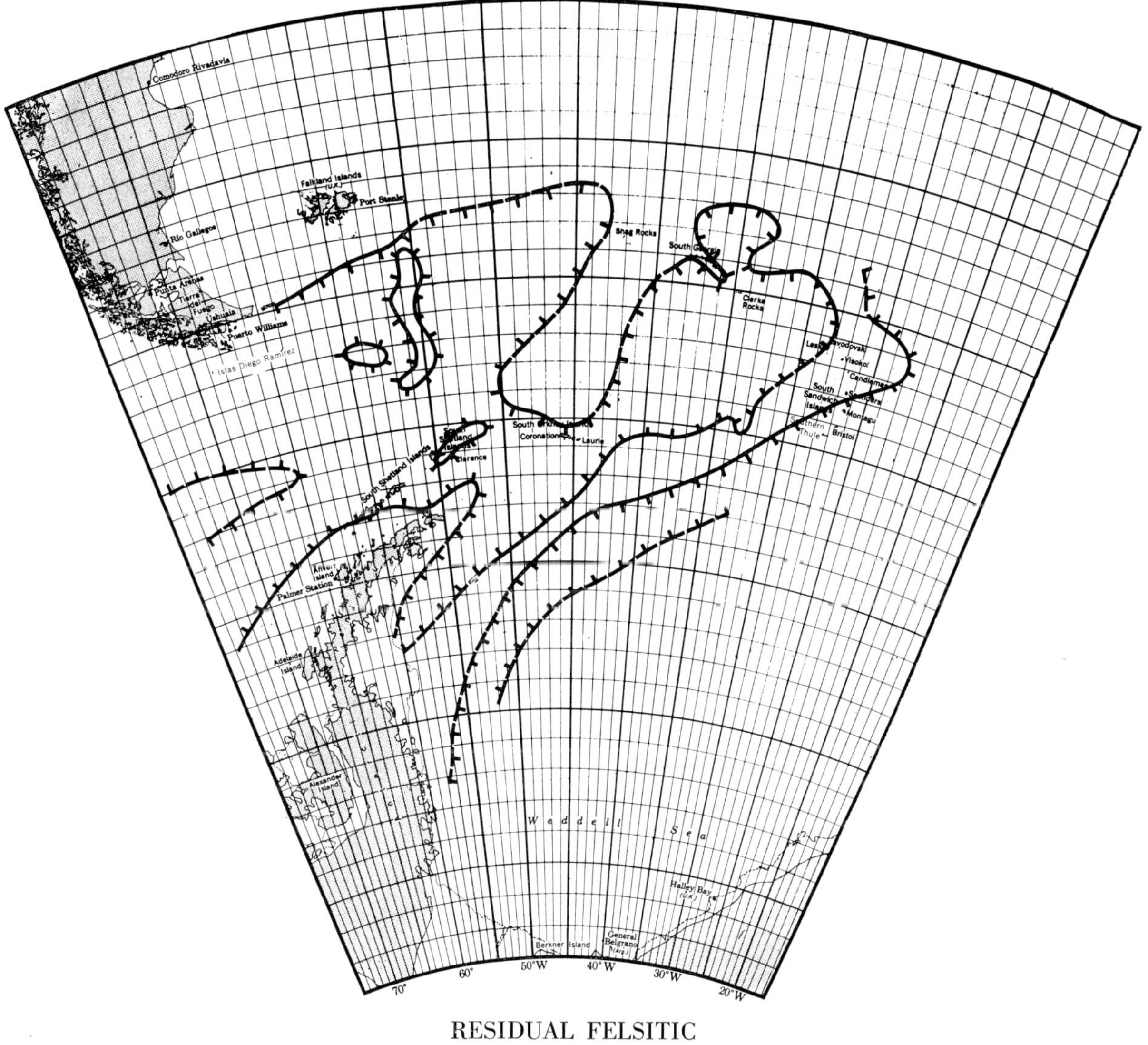

Fig. 10. Map of residuals resulting from subtraction of second-order trend surface values from observed felsitic fraction. Contour line separates positive from negative residuals, with hashers on negative side of line.

ual, relative to the next lowest order surface, although objective with idealized sampling procedures, cannot be meaningfully applied to our data. We therefore subjectively choose to limit our computation to production of the second-order trend surface and corresponding residual maps. We contend that while finite linear trend surfaces are unlikely to occur commonly in nature, third and higher-order finite surfaces will, as argued above, increasingly reflect sampling inadequacies rather than regional dredged rock distributions. The second-order and residual maps for the rock categories and the 'roundness' fraction are given in Figures 3 to 12. The available manganese nodule data are insufficient for map construction, mostly because of the fact that nodules have been removed from the sample bags. We have also not included maps of the sedimentary fraction; because of the highly variable sources in this category, we believe that while it is essential for computation of the whole collection, it cannot reflect the same geological agents that control the character of the rest of the rock collection, and is therefore justifiably excluded. If needed, the excluded maps can be compiled from Table 1.

The fit of the surfaces to the data is low: no more than 26% of the observed variations can be explained by any of the surfaces.

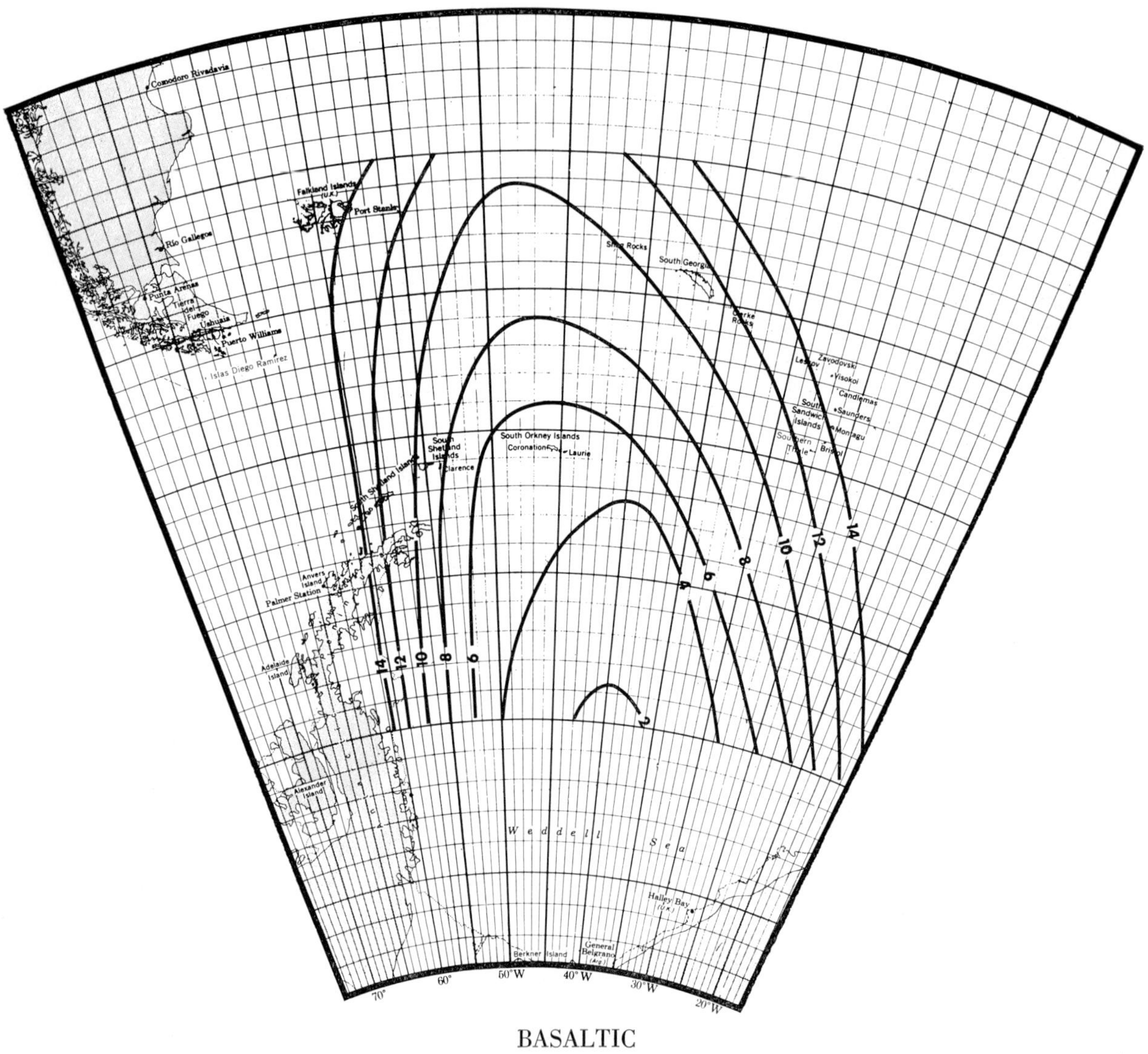

Fig. 11. Second-order trend surface maps of the basaltic fraction of the *Eltanin* rock dredge hauls in the Scotia Sea. See text for definition of the fraction, computational methods, and discussion of limitations.

DISCUSSION

It has already been argued that except for the basaltic islands of the Scotia Ridge, the rock types in probable source areas for antarctic icebergs are so diverse that no model involving a preferred source is possible. The roundness factor, however, although not completely independent of rock type, is nevertheless presumably a clear function of an ice-rafted origin.

We will therefore comment on the general configuration of the trend surfaces, and mention possible geological explanations, partly on the basis of the possible relationship between the residual maps and known features. Generally, of course, the residual maps resulting from any trend surface analysis can be of considerable qualitative value in assessing the significance of the trend surface, since it is clearly difficult to envisage residual maps being systematically related to known geographic features if the parent trend surface is not valid. We nevertheless stress the speculative nature of the possible explanations. This qualification is to be expected, of course, in any exploratory exercise of the type described in this paper.

The maps are best examined where possible in complementary groups:

1. Metamorphic and roundness fraction (Figures 3 and 5). Both maps have an east-west configuration closing at the eastern end with a minimum in the center of the Scotia Sea. The residuals (Figures 4 and 6)

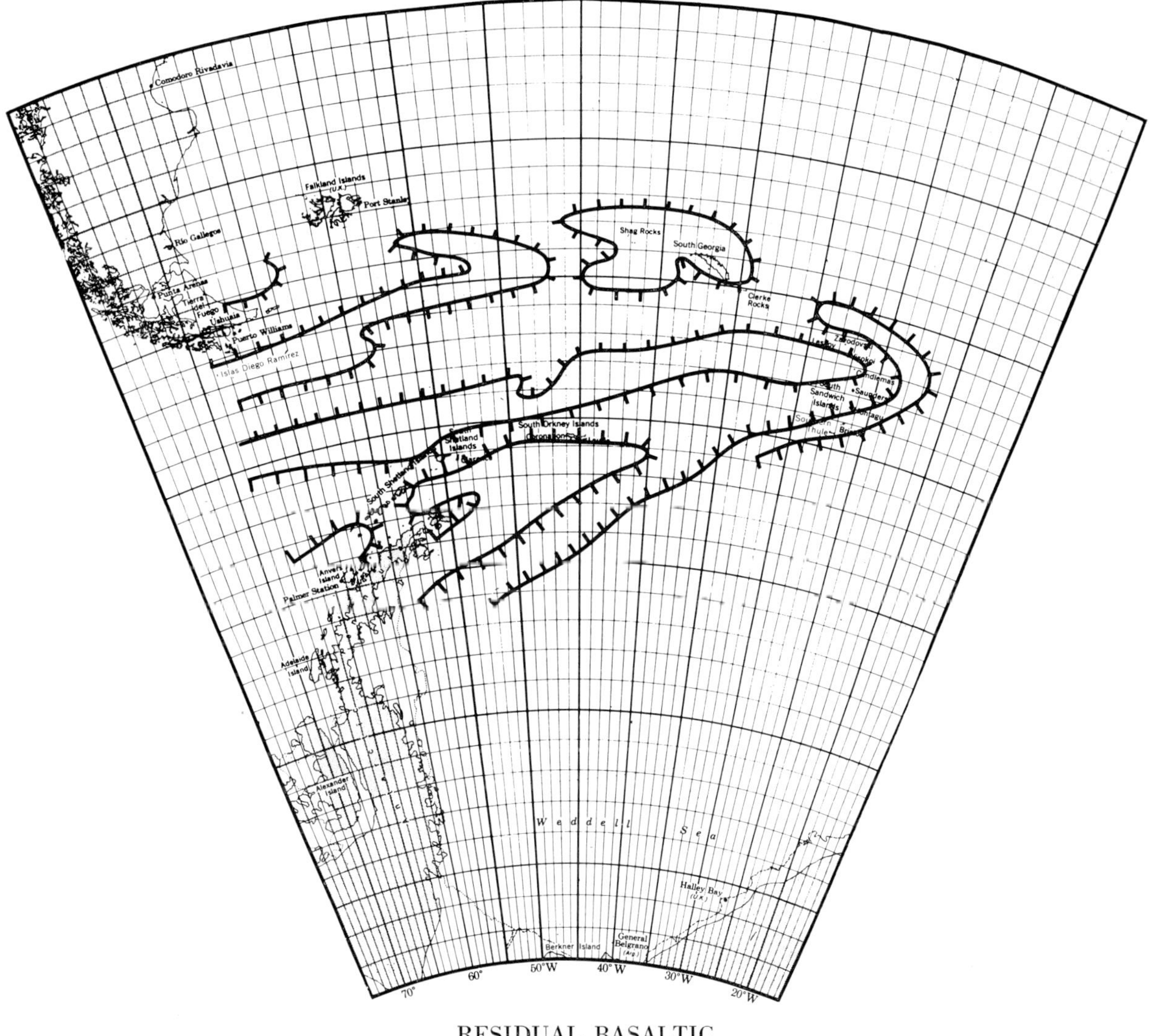

RESIDUAL BASALTIC

Fig. 12. Map of residuals resulting from subtraction of second-order trend surface values from observed basaltic fraction. Contour line separates positive from negative residuals, with hashers on negative side of line.

also reflect this distribution (not surprisingly) in their positive departures, the limits of which are those of the Scotia Sea. The implications in these maps are that the metamorphic fraction contributes significantly to the 'rounded' factor distribution, which in turn suggests that the metamorphic fraction is dominantly rounded and therefore, as assumed, ice rafted. The increase of the metamorphic surface south and north from the Scotia Sea may be due at least in part to the metamorphic sources being more common to the south and north, rather in the Pacific.

2. Granitic and felsitic fraction (Figures 7 and 9). Both surfaces trend roughly northwest-southeast. The granitic surface has only a small gradient in the Scotia Sea, however, compared to the felsitic surface, which increases greatly southeastward. The residual maps (Figures 8 and 10) show complementary relationships: there exists a positive felsitic residual around the Antarctic Peninsula, but the granitic residual is negative. The meaning of these observations cannot be determined. The gradient of the felsitic surface (Figure 9) suggests that a source area exists south of the Scotia Sea.

3. Basaltic fraction (Figure 11). The basaltic surface trends north-south, with a strong gradient increasing westward toward the Scotia Ridge (Scotia Arc). It is therefore difficult to believe that the several positive residual features around the Scotia Ridge

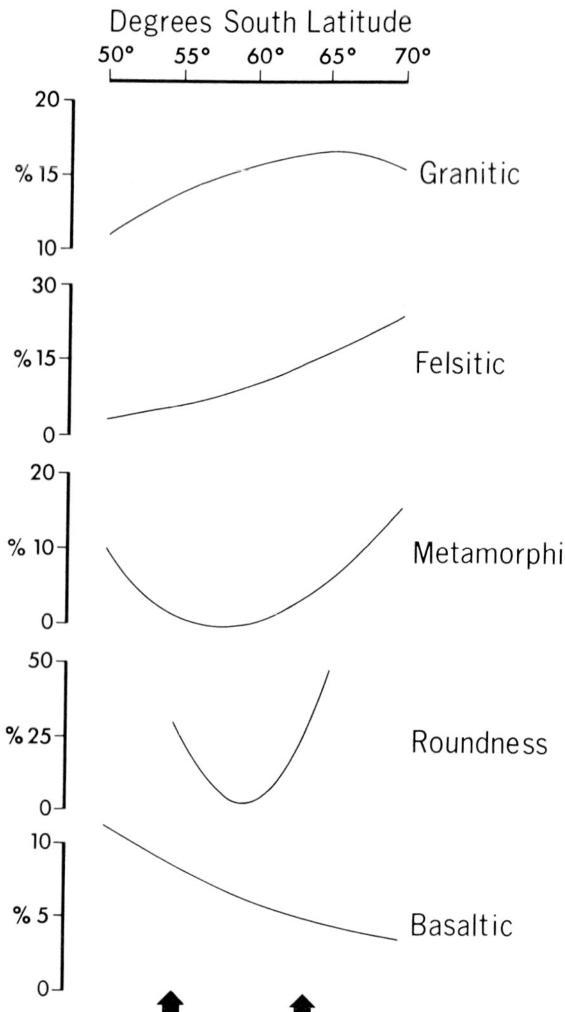

Fig. 13. Diagram showing north-south cross section along the 50° west longitude of the second-order trend surfaces shown in Figures 3, 5, 7, 9, and 11. See text for definition of the fractions, computational methods, and discussion of limitations. Arrows at bottom are north and south geographical limits, respectively, of the Scotia Sea.

(Figure 12) are not associated with local sources, particularly as some of them are normal to the trend surface configuration.

Comparison of the basaltic residual surface (Figure 12) with the granitic residual surface (Figure 8) reveals relationships that may be meaningful. The respective residuals tend to be curiously complementary: for example, southeast of the Falkland Islands a high in the granitic residual passes through a low in the basaltic residual; and west of the Scotia Ridge a basaltic residual high exists in a granitic residual low, as is also the case along a northwest-trending extension of the Antarctic Peninsula. Of course, several different interpretations of the meaning of those observations are possible.

In summary, the second-order trend surfaces show an increase in all rock fractions except basalt, and in the roundness factor, toward the Weddell Sea. This is emphasized in Figure 13, in which north-south sections of the trend surfaces from South Georgia to the Weddell Sea are shown. Whether or not the very simple geological implication in Figure 13, which is that the major source area for dredged rock found in the Scotia Sea is that part of continental Antarctica south of the Weddell Sea and the southeastern coast of the Antarctic Peninsula, is a reality can clearly be tested further. The northern boundary of the Weddell Sea current (Figure 1) is sufficiently far north to be entirely consistent with the observation.

COMMENTS ON THE COLLECTION METHOD

We have attempted to provide a regional description of the Scotia Sea dredged material, collected during *Eltanin* cruises. The difficulties in this preliminary study are common to any examination of a regional dredged rock collection. The question remains whether or not the effort required both to recover and to transport such a rock collection from high latitudes is justifiable, and if the effort is justifiable, then should the collection method be modified?

Our examination of the *Eltanin* dredged rock collection has yielded only very broad geological information. On this basis, we would argue that dredging rocks at high latitudes should occupy only a low priority in geological oceanographic activities. We are unable to be certain, however, that the rock specimens will not provide a source of important information when examined in a different context. (For example, it is conceivable that future antarctic geological mapping will lead to definition of a unique 'tracer' rock type.) Numerous examples exist in science of available specimens and/or data suddenly assuming great importance because of the emergence of new techniques and hypotheses.

It is our opinion, therefore, that it is not impossible for rock dredges of the type conducted during *Eltanin* cruises to become more obviously pertinent to meaningful geological problems. Specific hypotheses will undoubtedly lead to correspondingly specific collection programs, most probably over significant submerged physiographic features. In the meantime, it appears advisable to consider some modification of the collection procedures, so that they at least approach that required in an ideal collection: all the several pertinent on-board activities discussed in this paper should be standardized. Similarly, no unrecorded separation of any fraction of the dredge content should take place.

Acknowledgments. Thanks are due to Dennis Cassidy for his invaluable role in the systematic storing and cataloging of the *Eltanin* rock dredge hauls. We have benefited from discussions with several past and present Florida State University graduate students who took part in the rock dredging operations from the *Eltanin*. Mr. Norman Mark assisted with the rock categorizing. Dr. D. Meeter of the statistics department at Florida State University kindly advised on trend surface analyses and programming. This work represents part of a program supported by National Science Foundation grants GA-602, GA-1123, and GA-1620. The Florida State University computer center is gratefully acknowledged for the provision of computer time on its CDC 6400. Preparation of this manuscript was supported in part by the Office of Naval Research contract N00014-68-A-0159. Contribution 28, Geophysical Fluid Dynamics Institute, Florida State University.

REFERENCES

Adie, R. J., Geological history, in *Antarctic Research*, edited by R. Priestley, R. J. Adie, and G. de Q. Robin, pp. 118–162, Butterworth, London, 1964.

Baker, P. E., Comparative volcanology and petrology of the Atlantic island-arcs, *Bull. Volcanol.*, *32*(1), 189–206, 1968.

Stewart, D., Petrography of some dredgings collected by operation Deep Freeze IV, *Proc. Am. Philos. Soc.*, *107*(5), 431–442, 1963.

Trendall, A. F., The geology of South Georgia, 1, 26 pp., *Falkland Is. Dept. Surv. Sci. Rept.*, *7*, 1953.

Trendall, A. F., The geology of South Georgia, 2, 48 pp., *Falkland Is. Dept. Surv. Sci. Rept.*, *19*, 1959.

U. S. Navy, Oceanographic atlas of the Polar Seas, part 1, Antarctic, *Hydrograph. Off. Publ. 705*, 1957.

Watkins, N. D., and B. M. Gunn, Magnetic properties and geochemistry of some rocks dredged from the Macquarie Ridge, *New Zealand J. Geol. Geophys.*, in press.

Watkins, N. D., and R. Self, An examination of the 'Eltanin' dredged rocks from the South Pacific Ocean, in preparation, 1970.